LABOR–MANAGEMENT RELATIONS IN A CHANGING ENVIRONMENT

LABOR–MANAGEMENT RELATIONS IN A CHANGING ENVIRONMENT

Michael Ballot
University of the Pacific

with contributions from
Laurie Lichter–Heath
University of the Pacific
Thomas Kail
University of the Pacific
Ruth Wang
California State University, Sacramento

JOHN WILEY & SONS, INC.
New York • Chichester • Brisbane • Toronto • Singapore

Acquisitions Editor:	Timothy Kent
Production Manager:	Katy Rubin
Designer:	Laura Nicholls
Production Supervisor:	Nancy Prinz
Manufacturing Manager:	Lorraine Fumoso
Copy Editor:	Elizabeth Swain
Photo Researcher:	Jennifer Atkins
Photo Research Manager:	Stella Kupferberg

331.0973
B19L

Recognizing the importance of preserving what has been written, it is a policy of John Wiley & Sons, Inc. to have books of enduring value published in the United States printed on acid-free paper, and we exert our best efforts to that end.

Library of Congress Cataloging-in-Publication Data:

Ballot, Michael.
    Labor-management relations in a changing environment / Michael
Ballot.
        p.   cm.
    Includes bibliographical references and index.
    ISBN 0-471-62018-1 (cloth)
    1. Industrial relations–United States.   2. Collective bargaining-
-United States.   3. Trade-unions–United States.   I. Title.
HD8072.5.B35 1992
331' .0973–dc20   91-25544
                                                           CIP

Printed in the United States of America

TP 10 9 8 7 6 5 4 3 2 1

To
Nancy, Don, Ruth, and Chiang

PREFACE

In 1957, Wiley published a unique textbook, *Labor in a Growing Economy*, by Melvin Reder. It was designed for labor economics courses, but a substantial part was devoted to labor–management relations. Now, over 30 years later, Wiley is publishing another unique textbook in the labor field. This text is pointed at labor–management relations, or industrial relations, courses, but a substantial portion is devoted to economic issues and analysis in the labor field.

Like Reder's, this book is set in an environment of change. In the 1950s it was growth: of the economy, the labor force, and the union movement. In the 1980s and 1990s, it is not growth. True, the U.S. economy has just undergone its longest peacetime expansion, but that expansion had never been very robust. The labor force, and employment, had grown apace with the economy. However, this growth was concentrated in the service sector. Over three-quarters of the U.S. labor force is employed in the service sector, a great many of them in relatively low-paying jobs. Only in the last two to three years of the expansion of the 1980s did the unemployment rate drop below 6% and manufacturing employment increase; unemployment is now on its way back up. Finally, trade union membership has dropped from a high of about 33% of the labor force in the 1950s to about 15% at the start of the 1990s.

In the 1950s and 1960s, most students felt that studying union–management relations was important, given the extent of unionization of the labor force and the strength of those unions, especially following the AFL–CIO merger in 1955. In the 1980s and 1990s, unions have a much smaller presence on the economic scene. However, it is still very important to study unions and the union movement. Even though approximately 85% of workers are nonunion, the conditions they work under are greatly influenced by the conditions unions establish in business firms, other private organizations, and public agencies in which they represent the workforce.

To understand the work environment of a nonunion organization, you must understand the environment of a unionized one. The spillover effects of union-won gains to the nonunion workforce are substantial. Union-negotiated wages, fringe benefits, and worker protection measures have been adapted by many nonunion companies. To understand how an organization averts unionization, you must understand what unions do for workers. If a nonunion organization doesn't meet the needs of its work force, it will soon become a unionized one.

To understand the American labor movement, you must first look back to its beginnings and trace the history and relevant philosophies through the major periods of growth. It is also important to know something about the basic laws that form such an integral part of the environment of labor–management relations, and to have a feeling for union structure and government, especially of the dominant group of labor organizations in the U.S., the AFL–CIO and affiliates. And to better understand the context within which labor–management relations takes place, some background knowledge of labor relations systems in other countries is needed. We discuss these points in Part I of the text.

Part II covers the essential function of a trade union: to bargain collectively for all the workers it represents. The text begins with a general introduction to the process of collective bargaining and bargaining power and then moves through the major subjects of collective bargaining: (1) wages, (2) economic supplements or fringe benefits, (3) institutional concerns of both unions and management, and (4) administrative issues.

In the present environment, administrative issues focusing on work rules, broadly defined to include job classifications, work restrictions, and subcontracting rules as well as production standards, and their relationship to productivity and flexibility, might well be the most important area of interaction between unions and management for the foreseeable future. This issue of productivity and flexibility occupies a central point in the text.

In Part III, Labor Disputes and Their Resolution, the resolving of grievances, or shop floor disputes over rights guaranteed workers in the collective bargaining contract or the organization's personnel manual are addressed first; in Chapter 12, alternative dispute-resolution methods in labor–management relations are next examined, covering techniques of grievance resolution without arbitration, an approach commonly used in nonunion organizations. Contract impasse resolution is also highlighted, as is the union strike or management lockout, an action that usually occurs when labor and management can't resolve their contract disputes through negotiations and contract impasse resolution techniques of one type or another.

The strike is the major source of union power. Many labor relations people look at the strike as the last step in collective bargaining negotiations when those negotiations reach impasse. The inclusion of the strike or lockout in a separate section is motivated by the importance of emphasizing collective bargaining per se, as is done in Part II, coupled with the desire to focus separately on disputes and the growing use of alternative dispute-resolution techniques, as is done in Part III. The strike and grievance/arbitration are really bridges between the subject of collective bargaining and labor–management disputes and their resolution. Finally, the last chapter in Part III examines other forms of disputes and the exercise of union power and corporate responses.

The discussion of unionization in the public sector, the brightest spot in trade union growth over the past quarter century, is contained in Part IV. This part opens with an overview of the political and legal framework of labor relations in the public sector (Chapter 15). This is followed by separate chapters focusing on unions in the federal government and in state, county, and municipal governments. Throughout these chapters, the issue of dispute resolution short of the strike continually reappears. The nature of public service and the operation and goals of the public sector make alternative dispute resolution a major issue.

In Part V, The Future of Labor–Management Relations, three major issues are examined. The first is the impact of unions on the general price level, exploring the interrelationship of wages, productivity, and prices. Second is the growth in labor–management cooperation. The third and last issue is comparable worth, an issue with significant legal and social content. Indeed it is a major issue of the 1990s and will continue to be of primary importance into the 21st century because of the growth of female participation in the labor force and related trends. Part V concludes with a summary chapter that focuses on the future shape of labor–management relations. The trends discussed throughout the book, but especially those relating to union growth and decline, technological change and work rules/productivity/flexibility, and labor–management cooperation are integrated in this summary. This integration is the basis for several predictions, with appropriate caveats included, of course.

This book is a comprehensive treatment of the relationship between labor and management. It is not designed to turn the reader into a labor relations expert, either for management or for the union/workers. Nor is it designed to turn the reader into a labor lawyer or arbitrator. Rather, its main purpose is to instill in the reader some understanding as to how and why labor and management act in their unique relationship, and the effect of the action on the environment, primarily the organization, union and/or nonunion.

ACKNOWLEDGEMENTS

It is difficult to single out individuals to acknowledge for their inspiration and help in the development and completion of an undertaking like this. We would like to acknowledge the help and support of six individuals. First, chronologically and spiritually, is Melvin Reder. His inspiration has provided the underpinnings for a long teaching career in the labor area, and for this type of book. Two other acknowledgments for inspiration are due G. Allen Brunner and Alexander L. Stevas, who provided the guidance for embarking on teaching careers in business administration and law. A debt is also owed Sidney Turoff, who has worked with all four of us. And last, but certainly not least, we would like to thank Karen Hope and Barbara Garcia for their untiring effort helping us get this manuscript completed.

Finally, we would like to thank those who reviewed the manuscript, including Stephen Hills, University of Ohio-Columbus; Douglas M. McCabe, Georgetown University; Elizabeth C. Wesman, Syracuse University; Howard Harris, Pennsylvania State University; Denise Hoyer, Eastern Michigan University; Hugh M. Shane, Western Illinois University; Nancy Kauffman, University of North Carolina-Asheville; Rajib N. Samjal, Trenton State College; Aubrey Fowler, University of Central Arkansas; Gilbert J. Gall, Pennsylvania State University; Anthony V. Sinicropi, University of Iowa; and Cindy Gramm, Cornell University.

CHAPTER TABLE OF CONTENTS

PART I. The Context of American Labor Relations   1

      Chapter 1. **American Labor–Management Relations: A Broad Perspective**   **3**

      Chapter 2. **The Historical Development of the American Labor Movement**   **17**

      Chapter 3. **Labor and Employment Law**   **55**

                  Appendix: Landmark Cases   **97**

      Chapter 4. **Union Structure and Government**   **106**

      Chapter 5. **Comparative Labor Relations**   **133**

PART II. Unions and Collective Bargaining   165

      Chapter 6. **Collective Bargaining: The Process**   **167**

                  Appendix: A BLS Wage Survey   **194**

      Chapter 7. **Wages and Collective Bargaining**   **198**

      Chapter 8. **Collective Bargaining for Economic Supplements**   **234**

Chapter 9. **Institutional Issues in Collective Bargaining   263**

Chapter 10. **Administrative Issues in Collective Bargaining   276**

PART III. Labor Disputes and Their Resolution   307

Chapter 11. **Grievance Procedures and Arbitration   309**
             Appendix: Arbitration Cases   324

Chapter 12. **Alternative Dispute Resolution Techniques   358**

Chapter 13. **The Strike   376**

Chapter 14. **Labor–Management Disputes: Union Boycotts and Corporate Campaigns   399**

PART IV. Unionization in the Public Sector   425

Chapter 15. **The Political and Legal Framework in the Public Sector   427**

Chapter 16. **Public Sector Unionism: The Federal Government   451**

Chapter 17. **Public Sector Unionism: State and Local Government   467**

PART V. The Future of Labor–Management Relations   487

Chapter 18. **Current Issues, Future Concerns   489**

Chapter 19. **The Future Shape of Labor–Management Relations   510**

Appendix: **The Negotiating Exercise   519**

Index   553

CONTENTS

PART I.   **The Context of American Labor Relations**   **1**

    Chapter 1   **American Labor–Management Relations:**
                A Broad Perspective   **3**

The Key Players: Who They Are, What They Want   3
    The Workers, Many and Diverse   4
    The Managers, Changing with the Times   5
    The Government, Industrial Peacekeeper   6
The Mutual Dependency of Labor and Management   6
Why Workers Join Unions   7
    The Psychology of Unionization   7
    What the Studies Show   9
Why Management Resists Unions   10
    Loss of Flexibility   10
    Outside Interference?   10
    Wages Are Not an Issue   11
Trends in Union Membership   11
Discussion Questions   13
Vocabulary List   14
Footnotes   14
References   15

Chapter 2   The Historical Development of the American Labor Movement   17

Labor in Colonial America   17
    The Economy and Labor in the Colonies   18
    Colonial Labor Conditions and Regulations   18
A New Economic Order   20
    The Merchant Capitalists and the Factory System   20
    The Rise of Worker Associations   21
The Rise of an Industrial Workforce, 1860–1914   24
    Captains of Industry, Workers, and the Modern Corporation   24
    The Emergence of National Unions   26
Urban Industrialism   32
    Reaction and Progressive Reform   33
    Prosperity and the Decline of Organized Labor in the 1920s   36
The Development of a New Labor Relations System   39
    Prelude: The National Industrial Recovery Act   39
    The National Labor Relations Act   40
    John L. Lewis and the Rise of the CIO   41
    Union Power After the War   41
Organized Labor in the Affluent Society   43
    Labor Gains   44
    Labor Losses   45
    The End of the Postwar Affluence?   46
Discussion Questions   47
Vocabulary List   48
Footnotes   49
References   52

Chapter 3   Labor and Employment Law   55

Common Law and the Foundation of Labor Relations   56
    Common Law and English Labor   56
    Common Law Comes to the New World   57
Antitrust Acts: The Legislature Joins the Fray   58
    The Sherman Act: Strikes at Monopolies   58
    A Sherman Backlash: The Clayton Act and the Federal Trade
    Commission Act   59
The Railway Labor Act: Keeping the Engines Rolling   61
    RLA Forerunners   61
    Why the RLA Works   62
The Norris–LaGuardia Act: Labor's Magna Carta   63
The National Industrial Recovery Act: Labor in the New Deal   64
The National Labor Relations Act and Its Amendments   65
    The Wagner Act (National Labor Relations Act): Supporting Employees'
    Rights   65

The Taft–Hartley Act (Labor–Management Relations Act): Supporting Employers' Rights   66

The Landrum–Griffin Act (Labor–Management Reporting & Disclosure Act): Protecting Union Members   70

The National Labor Relations Board   70

Federal Mediation and Conciliation Service   74

Other Important Laws—Setting the Boundary Conditions   75

The Fair Labor Standards Act   75

The Social Security Act   77

A Federal Stake in Equal Rights   79

The Occupational Safety and Health Act   85

The Employee Retirement Income Security Act   86

The Worker Adjustment and Retraining Notification Act   87

RICO: The Racketeering Influenced and Corrupt Organizations Act   88

The Controversy over Workers' Privacy   88

The Future for Employment Law   90

Discussion Questions   91

Vocabulary List   92

Footnotes   93

References   96

Appendix: Landmark Cases   97

The Danbury Hatters' Boycott: *Loewe v. Lawlor*   97

Double Standard: *Bedford Cut Stone Company v. Journeymen Stone Cutters' Association of North America*   99

In Defense of "little" Norris–LaGuardias: *Senn v. Tile Layers Protective Union*   101

Across State Lines: *NLRB v. Reliance Fuel Oil Corp.*   102

A Question of Stereotypes: *Price Waterhouse v. Hopkins*   104

Chapter 4   Union Structure and Government   106

Craft and Industrial Unions   107

Similar Skills, Similar Jobs: The Monopolism of Craft Unions   107

Various Skills, Various Jobs: The Diversity of Industrial Unions   107

Merger: Monopoly Meets Diversity   107

The Structure of the American Labor Movement   108

The Federation   108

The National/International Union   112

The Local Union: Where Workers and Union Meet   118

Power and Union Government   120

Union Power Centers   120

Who Leads the Unions?   122

Union Democracy   125

Workers' Rights   125

For the Common Good: Individual Versus Collective Rights   126

Discussion Questions   127
Vocabulary List   127
Footnotes   128
References   131

Chapter 5   Comparative Labor Relations   133

Labor Relations in Neighboring Countries   133
    Canadian Labor Relations   133
    Mexican Labor Relations   135
Labor Relations in Western Europe   136
    British Labor Relations   136
    German Labor–Management Relations: The EC model?   138
    Labor Relations in Scandanavia: Sweden   141
Labor Relations in Japan   142
    Trade Unionism in Japan   143
    The Firm and the Worker   143
    The Japanese Wage System and Spring Labor Offensive   144
    The Japanese System in Transition   145
Labor Relations in the Soviet Union and Eastern Europe   146
    The Soviet Union: Labor Relations and the State   146
    Eastern Europe: A Revolution   147
Labor Relations Along the Pacific Rim   148
    Labor Relations in China   149
    Labor Relations in the Four "Tigers"   151
    Australia: The West in the East   157
Discussion Questions   158
Vocabulary List   159
Footnotes   159
References   162

PART II.   Unions and Collective Bargaining   165

Chapter 6   Collective Bargaining: The Process   167

Organization and Certification   167
    The Organizing Campaign   167
    The Election Campaign   169
Political Pressures in Collective Bargaining   171
    Politic Pressure and the Union   172
    Political Pressures and Management   173
Bargaining Behavior   173
    Preparing for Negotiations   174
    Stages of the Bargaining Process   176
    Establishing a Bargaining Strategy   178
Bargaining Power   180
    Union Power in Terms of Employer Costs   181
    Employer Power in Terms of Union and Worker Costs   184

Bargaining Structure   186
    Multi-Tier Bargaining   186
    Multi-Party Bargaining   188
Discussion Questions   189
Vocabulary List   190
Footnotes   190
References   193
Appendix: A BLS Wage Survey   194

Chapter 7   Wages and Collective Bargaining   198

The Theory of Union Wage Policy   199
    The Economic Theory: The Union as a Monopoly Power   199
    The Political Theory: A Matter of Comparison   203
    Combining Economic and Political Theories   206
Setting the Level of Wages   206
    Classical Microeconomic Theory   207
    The Ability-to-Pay and Wage Levels   208
    The Equity Basis for Wage Levels: What Is Fair?   210
Wage Adjustments During the Term of the Contract   212
    Negotiated Annual Wage Increments   213
    Cost-of-Living Adjustments   214
    Wage Reopeners   216
Determining the Wage Structure   217
    Internal Wage Differentials   217
    Two-Tier Wage Structures   218
    Job Evaluation: Toward an Objective Ranking   220
The Relative Wage Effect of Unionism   221
    Wage Differentials Independent of Unionism   221
    Wage Differentials Associated with Unionism   223
    Measuring the Pure Union Wage Effect   226
Discussion Questions   227
Vocabulary List   228
Footnotes   229
References   231

Chapter 8   Collective Bargaining for Economic Supplements   234

The Package Approach   234
    Meeting a Wide Range of Worker Needs   235
    Fringe Benefits Grow in Diversity and Cost   236
Pensions   237
    Pension Plan Types   238
    Issues Involving Pensions   239
Health Care Coverage   241
    Cost and Exclusion: The Problems of Health Care Benefits   241

Guaranteed Income Plans   243
    Supplemental Unemployment Benefits   244
    The Guaranteed Income Stream   245
Other Fringe Benefits, Old and New   246
    Supplemental Pay   247
    Leave Programs   248
    Personal Services   249
    Family Benefits   251
    Flexible Benefit Plans   254
Discussion Questions   255
Vocabulary List   256
Footnotes   257
References   261

Chapter 9   Institutional Issues in Collective Bargaining   263

The Union and the Security Clause   263
    Why Union Security Clauses?   264
    Negotiated Union Security Arrangements   265
    Union Finances and Cash Flow   269
Defining Management Rights   269
    The Residual Theory of Management Rights   270
    The Explicit View of Management Rights   270
    A Flexible Approach to Management Rights   271
Sharing Management Rights   271
    Joint Problem Solving   272
    Joint Decision Making   272
Discussion Questions   273
Vocabulary List   273
Footnotes   274
References   275

Chapter 10   Administrative Issues in Collective Bargaining   276

Seniority: The Keystone of Labor Contracts   276
    The Width of the Seniority Unit   277
    Seniority and Labor Mobility   279
    Seniority and Affirmative Action   281
    Superseniority   282
Work Rules   282
    Production Standards   283
    Job Classifications   286
    Subcontracting Rules   288
Technological Change and Work Rules   290
    Major Technological Advances   291
    Union Response to Technological Advances   293

Discipline and the Grievance Procedure   297
    Changes in Administering Discipline   297
Discussion Questions   298
Vocabulary List   298
Footnotes   299
References   303

PART III. Labor Disputes and Their Resolution   307
    Chapter 11   Grievance Procedures and Arbitration   309

What Is a Grievance?   310
    Contract Violation Grievances   310
    Shop Problems Grievances   310
    Other Reasons for Grievances   310
    The Grievance as Protected Protest   311
The Grievance Procedure   311
    The First Step: The Shop Floor   312
    The Second Step: Formalizing the Grievance   312
    The Third Step: The Top Level   312
    The Fourth Step: Arbitration   313
How Arbitration Works   313
    What Is Arbitration?   313
    The Arbitration Process   315
    Problems with Arbitration   318
Discussion Questions   319
Vocabulary List   320
Footnotes   320
References   322
Appendix: Arbitration Cases   324
Case #1, *Social Security Administration, Westminister Teleservice
    Center* and *American Federation of Government Employees,
    Local 3302*   324
Case #2, *Burns International Security* and *UPGWA, Local No. 538*   327
Case #3, *Capitol Plastics of Ohio, Inc.* and *Amalgamated Clothing
    and Textile Workers Union, AFL–CIO/CLC and Local 1901*   329
Case #4, *United Food and Commercial Workers Union, Local 775
    and Levitz Furniture Company of the Pacific, Inc.*   335
Case #5, *Housing Authority of Louisville* and *Service Employees
    International Union, Local 557*   337
Case #6, *G.C.I.U., Local 261* and *Harry Hoffman and Sons Printing*   344
Case #7, *Ohio Valley Coal Company* and *United Mine Workers
    of America, District No. 6, Local Union 1810*   348
Case #8, *Shell Oil Company, Deer Park, Texas Complex* and *Oil,
    Chemical and Atomic Workers International Union, Local 8–367*   352

Chapter 12   Alternative Dispute Resolution Techniques   358

Nonunion Complaint Resolution   358
    Appeals to Management   359
    Appeals to Peer Review Boards   360
    Appeals to Organizational Ombudspersons and Referees   362
Methods of Contract Impasse Resolution   363
    Actions of the Third-Party Neutral   363
    Governmental Actions under Emergency Provisions   365
    Contract Impasse Arbitration (Interest Arbitration)   369
Discussion Questions   371
Vocabulary List   372
Footnotes   372
References   374

Chapter 13   The Strike   376

Economic Strikes and Lockouts   377
    Why Economic Strikes?   377
    Case: The Anatomy of a Dispute—The Eastern Airlines Strike   382
    Carrying Out a Strike   385
    Trends in Work Stoppages   388
    The Lockout   390
Other Types of Strikes   391
    Strikes Protected by Law: Unfair Labor Practice Strikes   391
    Wildcat Strikes   391
    Sympathy Strikes   392
    Strikes Prohibited by Law   392
Strike Prevention   394
    Prevention Through Government Seizure   394
    Prevention Through Strike Fines   394
    The Problems of Strike Prevention Plans   395
Discussion Questions   395
Vocabulary List   396
Footnotes   396
References   398

Chapter 14   Labor–Management Disputes: Union Boycotts and Corporate Campaigns   399

Union Boycotts   399
    The Primary Boycott   400
    The Secondary Boycott   410
Corporate Campaigns   412
    The Basic Elements of a Corporate Campaign   412
    The Eastern Airlines Dispute: A Case Study   415
    A Unique Union Response to Management Actions   418

Discussion Questions   420
Vocabulary List   421
Footnotes   421
References   423

PART IV. Unionization in the Public Sector   425

Chapter 15 The Political and Legal Framework in the Public Sector   427

The Growth of Public Sector Unionism   428
Federal Executive Orders and Statutes   428
   The Gag Rules   428
   The Kennedy Promise: Executive Order 10988   429
   Correcting the Problems: Executive Order 11491   430
   The Postal Reorganization Act: "Privatizing" the Postal Service   431
   The Civil Service Reform Act: Keeping Civil Services
      Workers Happy   431
Public Employee Rights at the State and Local Level   433
   The Scope of Public Sector Laws: A Model   433
   Procedures to Resolve Impasses   433
   California Laws—An Example   434
The Right of Public Employees to Strike   443
   Federal Employees: Without the Right to Strike   443
   The State and Local Government Employees' Right to Strike   443
   Case: The Workers Can Strike, and That's No Garbage (*County
      Sanitation District No. 2 of Los Angeles v. Los Angeles County
      Employees Association, Local 660*)   444
Emerging Trends   445
   Drug Testing   446
   Wrongful Discharge   446
   Free Speech   447
Discussion Questions   447
Vocabulary List   448
Footnotes   448
References   450

Chapter 16 Public Sector Unionism: The Federal Government   451

The Development of Federal Government Unionism   452
   Labor Relations Prior to 1962: Lack of Activity   452
   Labor Relations, 1962 to the Mid-1970s: High Growth   453
   Labor Relations Since the Mid-1970s: Stability   455
The Power of Federal Government Unionism   456
   Bargaining Activities   456
   Case: Federal Unionism Battered: The Rise and Fall of PATCO   458
   Political Activities   459

Is Federal Government Unionism Different?   459
    The Legal and Political Framework   460
    The Economic Environment   461
    The Nature of the Business   462
Discussion Questions   464
Vocabulary List   464
Footnotes   465
References   466

Chapter 17   Public Sector Unionism: State and Local Government   467

The Development of State and Local Government Unions   467
    The Explosion in Demand for Public Services   467
    The Spurt in Public Sector Collective Bargaining Laws   469
    The Slowing of Public Sector Unionization   469
    The Public Sector Unions   470
Major Issues in State and Local Government Labor Relations   474
    Infringing on the Sovereign Power of the State   474
    Fiscal Responsibility   475
    The Government as a Monopoly Supplier   475
    The Right to Strike   476
Impasse Procedures as Alternatives to the Strike   478
    Mediation and Conciliation   478
    Fact Finding   478
    Arbitration   479
Is State and Local Government Unionism Different?   480
    The Legal and Political Framework   480
    The Economic Environment   481
    The Nature of the Business   482
Discussion Questions   483
Vocabulary List   483
Footnotes   484
References   485

PART V.   The Future of Labor–Management Relations   487

Chapter 18   Current Issues, Future Concerns   489

Unions and Inflation   490
    Wages and Prices: Cost-Push Inflation   490
    Wages, Prices and Employment: The Phillips Curve   493
Labor–Management Cooperation   494
    The International Experience   494
    The American Experience   495
Comparable Worth: Equal Money for Equal Value   500
    The Earnings Gap   500
    The Goal of Comparable Worth   501
    Comparable Worth in Place   501
    Comparable Worth in the Future   503
Discussion Questions   504

Vocabulary List   505
Footnotes   505
References   507

Chapter 19   The Future Shape of Labor–Management Relations   510

The End of American Unions?   511
What Does "More of the Same" Mean?   512
Turning It Around   513
     Effectively Representing Current Members   513
     Recruiting New Members   514
Discussion Questions   516
Vocabulary List   516
Footnotes   517
References   517

Appendix: The Negotiating Exercise   519

Bargaining Objectives and Strategies   519
     Define Areas   519
     Develop Ranges   520
     Assign Priorities   520
The Background   521
     The Company   521
     The Union   524
     Labor–Management Relations at ACP   525
     Labor and Pay Issues   527
     Labor and Benefits   527
     Management and Pay Issues   527
     Management and Benefits   528
Roles and Rules   528
     The Union Negotiating Team   528
     The Management Negotiating Team   529
     Some Basic Ground Rules   530
The Present Contract   531
Statistical Information   539
The Computer Program   544

Index   553

PART ONE

THE CONTEXT
OF AMERICAN
LABOR RELATIONS

T he United States has a unique system of labor relations. In no other country is there such a highly decentralized decision-making system within a complex legal web of common law decisions and statutes. To begin the analysis of this dynamic system, we will explore its uniqueness and its roots. First, we examine the participants, their goals and motivations, and the basic nature of American labor relations. Next, we briefly analyze the growth of American unionism during the last 90 years and its decline during the last 20 to 30 years.

The broad overview of the system presented in Chapter 1 is followed in Chapter 2 by a concise history of American unionism, starting in colonial times and moving through the major periods of labor movement growth and change to the present. The next chapter explores the development of the legal framework of American labor–management relations. Then an examination of the present structure and governance of American unions, viewed in the context of their historical development and present trends affecting them, follows. Finally, in Chapter 5, an analysis of labor–management relations systems in other countries rounds out the context of American labor relations. Discussion of these systems in Western Europe, Japan, the Soviet bloc, and the emerging nations, especially of the Pacific Rim, gives some interesting insights into the American system now and in the future.

CHAPTER 1

AMERICAN LABOR–MANAGEMENT RELATIONS: A BROAD PERSPECTIVE

The American system of unionization, as it exists today, originated in the 1880s, but its legal framework was not shaped until the 1930s. Unlike many American institutions, our labor relations system evolved very differently from that of England, especially in its political and statutory dimensions. In fact, the evolving English system is borrowing heavily from ours in the latter respect. Our system of laws and practices is particularly American.[1] It has grown into a structure of complex interrelationships that must be viewed in its own historical, philosophical, and economic context. It is now undergoing substantial changes that must be seen in the same context, especially with regard to the economic changes that are occurring in the United States and the world.

Because the dynamics of labor–management relations reflect the changing structure of the economy and the competitive environment, they have raised many interesting problems and challenges for unions and workers, management, and the system in which they interact. This chapter notes some of these problems, and the next four chapters lay the background for analyzing these problems in the final four parts of the book.

THE KEY PLAYERS: WHO THEY ARE, WHAT THEY WANT

On the surface, labor–management relations would appear to involve only two parties. On one side is the union, representing the workers; on the other side is management, representing the employing organization. In democratic systems, unions are independent of the organizations with which they deal, although in some countries, such as Japan, they work very closely with management. In spite of these differences, the players remain the same.

Not nearly as apparent, but important nonetheless, is a third party—the government. Its presence is felt in many ways: it sets the legal ground rules and boundary conditions for labor–management relations as will be discussed in detail in Chapter 3. Sometimes it is physically present, for example, as a mediator. At other times it forbids strikes, while keeping the two parties bargaining. The shadow of this third participant is, therefore, a presence to be reckoned with.

The Workers, Many and Diverse

The workers, represented by their union in the organizations where unionization exists, are the most numerous participants in the labor–management relationship as well as the most heterogeneous.[2] Blue-collar workers may perform unskilled, semiskilled, or highly skilled tasks. White-collar workers may hold clerical jobs or professional/technical positions that require four or more years of college. Workers of all kinds may have no high school degree, advanced university degrees, or anything in between; they range in age from the teens to the 60s and 70s.

Although workers are a heterogeneous group, they share two major goals: job security and pay. Historically, in times of prosperity and economic growth, workers have set their sights mainly on higher pay. Recessions, on the other hand, force their attention to shift to job security. But union workers have traditionally pushed for job retention without pay cuts, whereas nonunion workers have tended to accept pay cuts in hard times.[3]

In the 1980s, the economy grew steadily, and we just ended our longest postwar growth period.[4] However, the primary goal of the vast majority of workers, especially unionized workers, was not large pay increases but job security. In many cases, this quest has been accompanied by pay cuts or changes in the rules of the workplace designed to increase productivity, allowing firms to meet competition and stay in business.*

For example, in 1988, the United Mine Workers (UMW) exchanged pay for job security in their new contract with the coal industry. The contract requires (1) producers to fill 60 percent of their open jobs at nonunion mines with laid-off UMW members and (2) all subleasing and subcontracting jobs to go to UMW members. The miners did receive a pay increase, but the hike was far less than that under earlier contracts.

This signals a shift in worker goals and priorities, mirroring the shift in the structure of the labor force and the changes in international competition. Furthermore, an expanding list of legislation at the federal and state level and of court rulings protects workers' job security. These court rulings include a growing number of decisions limiting *dismissal without just cause* or the *employment-at-will* doctrine, which holds

---

* Productivity gain is loosely defined as increased output per labor unit input (e.g., per labor hour), which would tend to reduce labor cost per unit of output, assuming the gain in productivity exceeds any increase in wages or salaries.

that employees are hired and fired at the will of their employers. Also included are measures to soften the loss of job and enhance reemployment opportunities, such as plant closure notice and severance pay for affected workers.[5] Further protected by these laws and rulings are employee privacy, health and safety, pensions and other benefit plans, hours of work and other working conditions, the right to participate in union activities, and more.[6]

Job security and pay are still important to most workers, but, for many, these goals have been attained and, to some extent, protected. Now, as some surveys indicate, many workers place job satisfaction ahead of job security or higher pay.[7]

The Managers, Changing with the Times

Managers form a smaller and much more homogeneous group than workers. Their function is to run their organization as they see fit, within accepted legal and moral bounds. Their decisions help to determine the profitability of a business and the success of a nonprofit organization. Their primary goal is therefore to manage with minimal interference and maximum cooperation from labor.* This goal usually means motivating workers, individually and in small groups, without continually having someone or something looking over their shoulders and questioning their every move.

In the past, managerial success, especially in large corporations clustered in oligopolistic industries, meant keeping labor costs down in bad economic times and keeping growth in labor costs reasonable in good economic times when many of the cost increases could be passed on to the customer through increased prices. This approach translated into major confrontations with organized labor. In good times unions and employee associations tried to achieve pay increases greater than the increases in the price level, that is, the inflation rate. In bad times, unions and employee associations tried to maintain pay scales and even increase them to exceed the rise in prices.** Confrontation was the norm, and rarely was it replaced by cooperative efforts.

The economic environment of the 1980s and 1990s has changed this traditional scenario. Increased global competition and heightened domestic competition growing out of deregulation have made the manager's job more challenging, to say the least. This environment has shown that a necessary ingredient for organizational success is the cooperation of the workers and their representative or bargaining agent. Cooperative labor–management programs increased substantially in the 1980s, as they did in the 1930s when American business was faced with hard times marked by many bankruptcies and plant closures. The record of cooperation between the United Auto Workers (UAW) and General Motors (GM) in the 1980s on issues such as increasing productivity, shifting production between plants, and worker job security is well documented (but has begun to wear thin in the 1990s).[8]

---

* This concern can be boiled down to job security (and job satisfaction). In a profitable organization, managers are rewarded for job performance, as reflected by organization profits, and usually receive higher pay and bonuses based on those profits.

** Inflation has accompanied every recession since the 1954 downturn (the 1958, 1961, 1970, 1975, 1980, 1982 and 1991 downturns).

The Government, Industrial Peacekeeper

The third player, government, represents the public. Its goal, as stated in the National Labor Relations Act (NLRA) of 1935, is "to eliminate the causes of certain substantial obstructions to the free flow of commerce and to mitigate and eliminate these obstructions when they have occurred."[9] The government stake in the labor–management relations system is simply to pursue the public interest by striving for industrial peace, which should lead to maximum economic welfare, other things being equal.

Three major legislative acts form the basis for the government's peacekeeping role: the NLRA, or, as it is more popularly known, the Wagner Act, passed in 1935; the Labor–Management Relations Act (LMRA), or the Taft–Hartley Act, in 1947; and the Labor–Management Reporting & Disclosure Act (LMR&DA), or the Landrum–Griffin Act, in 1959. The Wagner Act moved to increase the power of employee associations to better balance the relationship of labor and management, while the Taft–Hartley Act swung in the opposite direction to balance that relationship. The Landrum–Griffin Act was aimed primarily at cleaning up union corruption and securing the rights of union members within their unions.

Two major government agencies charged with securing industrial peace are the National Labor Relations Board (NLRB), set up to administer the Wagner Act, and the Federal Mediation and Conciliation Service (FMCS), set up in the Taft–Hartley Act to provide services to labor and management as requested to help avert industrial strife caused primarily by collective bargaining impasses. Other federal agencies also contributing to the government goal are the Railway Labor Board (RLB) and the National Mediation Board (NMB), which are similar to the NLRB and the FMCS but deal only with labor–management relations in the rail and airline industries, and the Federal Labor Relations Authority (FLRA), which is also similar to the NLRB but deals only with labor–management relations in the federal government. These agencies will be discussed again in Chapters 3 (RLB, NMB) and 15 (FLRA).

THE MUTUAL DEPENDENCY OF LABOR AND MANAGEMENT

The labor–management relationship is basically one of **mutual dependency.** Without labor, we have no work, no output, and therefore no need for management. Without management, we have no planning, directing, and coordinating, and therefore no jobs. However, the economic goals of labor and management may be perceived as diametrically opposed. The higher the labor share of output, the lower the ownership and management share. If output or revenue is growing, higher wages and salaries are compatible with higher profits and management pay and bonuses. If not, something has to give!

The conflicting economic goals of labor and management can make the relationship between an organized workforce and management an adversarial one. Traditionally, confrontation has been the norm rather than the exception. The usual procedure in collective bargaining has been for one party (customarily labor) to lay its demands on the table, the other party to counter these, the first party to counter, and so on. The procedure includes much **compromise,** give-and-take without a shared approach to problem solving. Rarely is the relationship a pure power struggle.* Only when one party is powerful enough to be totally dominant and impose its will completely on the other party will compromise be absent.

In many instances, however, recent developments in labor–management relations point toward a more accommodating relationship. Under pressure from increased competition, and away from the bargaining table, confrontation is not the norm between labor and management. **Cooperation,** involving shared problem solving, is becoming more common, supplanting the tradition of confrontation and compromise. For instance, the managers and workers at the Campbell Soup Company in Omaha, Nebraska, meet regularly to work out problems. Company officials cite these cooperative efforts as a factor in the plant's improved productivity, which is essential if the company is to survive in the increasingly competitive food processing industry.[10]

In some relationships, **joint decision making** is appearing, which is a truly participatory style of interaction. More will be said about these last two relationships in Chapter 18.

WHY WORKERS JOIN UNIONS

Joining a union or a labor association was a common step for many workers from the 1930s to the 1970s, but it has not been as customary since the early 1980s. Why do workers join, and why has union membership tapered off so drastically in recent years?

The Psychology of Unionization

Basic motivation theory can help shed some light on why workers unionize. **Maslow's hierarchy of needs,** the classical form of this basic model, describes five need levels, as shown in Figure 1.1.[11] The lowest, or basic level needs, are those that people seek

---

* Work stoppages have not exceeded 470 in a year (1952) with a maximum loss of just 0.43 percent of estimated total working time (1959) since 1947. See, "Major Work Stoppages: 1990," Bureau of Labor Statistics (BLS) *Bulletin 91–32*, February 5, 1991. See also Chapter 13 of the present volume.

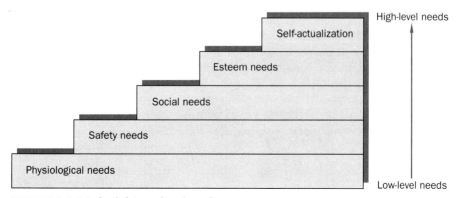

FIGURE 1.1 Maslow's hierarchy of needs

most intensely if they have not achieved them. The intensity of pursuit decreases, however, as lower level needs are met and as people turn their attention to higher levels requirements. According to Maslow, satisfied needs are no longer motivators, although they were once more intensely sought than the needs that replaced them.

Satisfying Lower Level Needs

Maslow's theory provides a good explanation of why workers joined unions during the late nineteenth century. In this period, many workers joined in order to meet the physiological needs of food, clothing, and shelter and the safety needs of health, security, and certainty. These are the human needs that are most intensely desired.

Through a union, people could collectively increase their pay to achieve a standard of living that provided for the basic needs of life, a standard of living that many immigrant workers in mines, factories, and mills had not achieved. In many families of the late 1800s, all members had to work, even ten-year-old children, to make enough to feed themselves. Safety standards were at best lax and at worst non-existent.

The labor laws of the 1920s and 1930s represented the first steps in ensuring that lower level needs would be met. The Occupational Safety and Health Act (OSHA) of 1970, the Employee Retirement Income Security Act (ERISA) of 1974, and the Worker Adjustment and Retraining Notification Act (WARN) of 1988 capped off this effort. Today the only lower level need that unions can meet is the uncertainty of job security and fair treatment by superiors. But even in this area unions may not be strongly needed, for court decisions in unlawful discharge cases, limiting the employment-at-will doctrine, are beginning to increase job security in our society.

Satisfying Social Needs

Unions have always been able to provide for the social needs of workers. From their earliest days, unions emphasized camaraderie among their members. Many unions were even called brotherhoods or fraternal orders. Group relationships are a natural consequence of working together, and this commonality is enhanced by shared membership in a union.

As other social groups have proliferated and workers have joined them, the impact of unions on workers' social needs has been diluted. These other groups are taking up an increasing portion of workers' leisure time. This is especially true of the younger workers who are becoming more important in unionization drives. These groups, include bowling leagues and other sports clubs, neighborhood social groups, and similar organizations, are fulfilling the social needs function that unions once performed.

Satisfying Higher Level Needs

Unions can also help fulfill the higher level need for esteem. The ability of workers to voice their concerns at the workplace, particularly when they feel management has treated them poorly, enhances self-respect. Workers can also earn the respect of their colleagues by holding union office, and especially by moving up the union hierarchy, from local to state/regional to national levels.

Unions, however, can provide little satisfaction at the highest need level, self-actualization. The structure of the union movement may provide self-actualization for a handful of workers, such as officers of national unions and the Federation (AFL–CIO). But the nature of the American union movement, based on the view that the collective good is paramount, does not permit the development of the individual if it is not in the group interest.

New techniques in organizing unions and developing union policies and programs are needed for self-actualization. The AFL–CIO recognizes this need, as noted in its 1985 report, "The Changing Situation of Workers and Their Unions." The reformulation of union policies and programs will, among other things, attempt to provide for the growth and fulfillment of the individual, which is a strong motivator for a large portion of today's and tomorrow's workforce.

What the Studies Show

Thomas Kochan's report on the Department of Labor's Quality of Employment Survey provides an interesting perspective on the reasons why workers join unions and labor associations.[12] A majority of workers noted that they join or seek to form a union "when (1) greatly dissatisfied with their job and economic conditions, (2) they desire more influence over their job conditions."[13] Jeanne Brett and two labor law professors reported the same findings in a study done with the cooperation of the National Labor Relations Board.[14] Over 80 percent of their study participants felt that unions were effective in "(1) protecting their members against unfair practices of employers, (2) improving members' job security, (3) improving the wages of their members."[15] In this survey white-collar workers, though not anti-union, did not fully share these views and were "especially concerned with the threats unionization might pose to their individual autonomy and independence."[16] Many of these white-collar workers have a strong affiliation with their profession.

In other words, the most important reason why workers willingly join unions or labor organizations is to improve their working conditions, primarily to (1) make sure they get fair treatment on the job; (2) achieve some influence in determining work conditions; and (3) get protection against unjust dismissal. Wages also seem to be a fairly important reason for unionization.

If management does not meet these needs, workers may well unionize. Arbitrary action by management in promotion, job or shift assignment, and the like is not fair treatment; the usual union solution is to employ seniority (years on the job with the organization) to regularize these decisions. The inability to communicate with management about problems on the job or in the plant makes workers feel they have no say about working conditions; the union solution is the grievance procedure. Arbitrary dismissal of workers, though limited in recent years by legislation and court rulings, continues; if dismissal involves the worker's union activities, the union solution is the grievance procedure or an unfair labor practice charge.

Workers join unions for several other reasons as well. First, they may have to join the union as a condition of keeping their jobs. This requirement, known as a union shop, is discussed further in Part II. Second, group or peer pressure might lead workers to join a union, especially if recognized leaders among the workers' reference group join a union. Finally, some workers join because they feel it offers them an opportunity to become a leader by attaining local union office and possibly moving up to national office. These last two reasons address the need to fulfill social and esteem needs as described by basic motivation theory.

WHY MANAGEMENT RESISTS UNIONS

Management has resisted unions and labor organizations in the workplace since the very beginning of unionization in the United States. Outright hostility was the norm until the middle of this century when it was replaced by grudging acceptance of unions as a fact of life, not as a benefit to the company and its workers.

Managers resist unions and labor organizations for two basic reasons. First, and most importantly, they believe that unions and labor organizations reduce their ability to operate their companies and agencies: unionization is equated with inflexibility. Second, they see unions and labor organizations as outsiders, and their workers as insiders: they feel they can solve their workers' problems without outside interference.

Loss of Flexibility

Most workers join unions and labor organizations primarily to have some say in their working conditions, especially in regard to management actions they consider to be unfair. But these actions are part of management's prerogative to operate the organization in a way that will maximize profits, which is the primary (but not the only) goal of the organization. Management must allocate resources, including labor, to meet this goal. Flexibility in responding to a rapidly changing environment is therefore critical. By protecting its members and their jobs, a union limits this flexibility.

Union work rules, union grievances, and other union policies can significantly limit management decision making with respect to the workforce.[17] Unions demand a share in management's right to direct workers and set the rules of the workplace. Every managerial action that affects the workers can therefore be second-guessed by the union. For example, in the United Mine Workers' strike with Pittston Corporation in 1989, both sides sought control over the power to subcontract and to schedule irregular and Sunday shifts.[18]

Outside Interference?

Managers also resist unionization because they do not like a third party, the union, acting as an intermediary between them and their workers. Most managers feel that they are fair and that they take their workers' needs into account in their decisions. The company gives the worker a job and expects his or her loyalty in return.

Unions tend, at best, to split worker loyalty. A unionized worker is a member of both the company's labor force and the union. Even in an environment of good labor–management relations, workers will look to the union, not their managers, to represent their interests. The worker who is not happy with the decision of a manager will have the union question that decision rather than talking directly to the manager. This is the primary purpose of the grievance procedure. Unions always attempt to place themselves between workers and managers.

Wages Are Not an Issue

Contrary to popular belief, wages are not a major factor in management's anti-union stance. For a few smaller companies in areas that are predominantly nonunion, union wage demands may be a major problem. However most companies, especially larger ones, are not fighting unionization to avoid union wage scales.

In areas where some companies are unionized, firms trying to maintain their nonunion status usually pay wages that are approximately the same as those at unionized firms. This effect on nonunion wages is sometimes called the **threat effect;** the threat of unionization causes companies to meet union wage levels in order to stay nonunion. It also causes nonunion companies to develop various communications programs that allow workers to voice their concerns about management decisions without risking their jobs.

Chrysler Corporation took this approach to stave off further unionization in its ranks. In 1988, it established a formal grievance procedure for its nonunion white-collar employees similar to the traditional union grievance procedure. Such a procedure, which allows employees to question perceived irregularities in business operations, is rare for nonunion workers at major private companies.[19]

TRENDS IN UNION MEMBERSHIP

In 1954, 39.2 percent of the private sector workforce of wage and salary workers were union members.[20] In 1989, this figure had dropped by almost 60 percent; the number of employed union and employee association members was down to 16.96 million, or 16.4 percent of the employed wage and salary workers in the United States.[21] As reported by the Bureau of Labor Statistics, this decline has been going on for about four decades (see Table 1.1). Membership declined most sharply during the early 1980s with less precipitous drops since then.

What happened? Several contributing factors are well documented, and others are widely shared conjectures. The major factors relate to the increasingly competitive environment and the changing structure of the economy and the workforce. Another major factor, increasing management opposition, may be the most important of all.

The competitive environment is now marked by two trends that impinge heavily on unions and labor associations: (1) heightened foreign competition, which is increasingly coming from low-wage but relatively high-productivity countries like Korea and Taiwan, and (2) increased domestic competition, especially nonunion, owing primarily to the major deregulations of the 1980s. These trends have seriously weakened union power and have caused major losses of business in industries where unions have traditionally been the strongest, for example, heavy industry such as steel and autos, and transportation such as trucking. As of 1989, union membership rates were highest in two industries: government (36.7 percent) and communications and public utilities (34.2 percent).[22] Both of these industries are generally immune to foreign competition, although communications was not, and is not, immune to deregulation.

The changing structure of the economy and labor force has affected union strength longer than increased foreign and domestic nonunion competition have. Since World War II, the U.S. economy has been shifting from a mass-production to a mass-

Table 1.1   *Union Membership in the United States*

Year	Number of Union Members[a]	Number as Percentage of the Work Force[b]
1960[c]	17.1 million	31.4%
1970	21.2 million	30.0%
1980	20.1 million	23.0%
1985	17.0 million	18.0%
1986	17.0 million	17.5%
1987	16.9 million	17.0%
1988	17.0 million	16.8%
1989	17.0 million	16.4%
1990	16.7 million	16.1%

Sources: BLS Bulletins 77–771 (9/77), 79–605 (9/3/79), 89–45 (1/27/89), and 90–59 (2/7/90); *Monthly Labor Review*, May 1986, May 1987; *Wall Street Journal*, January 25, 1988, p. 3, April 4, 1991, p. A9B.

[a] Members of unions and employee associations that represent workers in collective bargaining (*employed* members since 1980).

[b] Work force means *employed* wage and salary workers from 1980 on.

[c] Union members only; other years include members of employee associations as well.

consumption economy, with a parallel shift from mining, construction, and manufacturing to service industries. Because unions have traditionally been strongest in the production industries and weakest in services, they have lost their power base.

Unions have made only minor inroads in the relatively unorganized service sector, with the exception of government where they have been very successful. The union membership rate is very low in the private sector service industries as shown in Table 1.2. In 1989, union membership accounted for only 6.3 percent of employment in wholesale and retail trade; 2.3 percent in finance, insurance, and real estate; and 5.8 percent in services. In addition, for part-time workers and women, who make up a

Table 1.2   *Unionization in the Service Sector*

Industry	Members of Unions	Represented by Unions
Wholesale and retail trade	6.3%	7.0%
Wholesale trade	6.8%	7.8%
Retail trade	6.1%	6.8%
Finance, insurance and real estate	2.3%	3.1%
Services	5.8%	7.0%
Government	36.7%	43.6%

Source: "Union Membership in 1989," Bureau of Labor Statistics *Bulletin 90–59*, U.S. Department of Labor, February 7, 1990, Table 2.

significant portion of the service sector labor force, membership was, respectively, 6.7 percent and 12.6 percent of employment.[23] Significantly, between 1980 and 1986 over three-fourths of new jobs were created in the service and retailing industries, most of them in companies with less than 100 employees.[24]

Unions have traditionally had problems with, or simply refrained from organizing, white-collar workers, women, part-time workers, and workers in small companies. The organization of white-collar workers presents special problems, as they are more likely to identify with their profession and tend to work more closely with management than blue-collar workers. However, analysis has shown that white-collar workers are as willing to join unions as blue-collar workers.[25] Unions are also striving hard to overcome organizational shortcomings with respect to women, who are more likely to support unionization than men.[26] The economics of organizing part-time workers and workers in small companies is, however, difficult to overcome.

The last major factor contributing to the decline of unionization in the private sector is hardening management attitudes. Richard Freeman, in a National Bureau of Economic Research report, concludes that "half of the decline can be accounted for by increases in management opposition, as indicated by a quadrupling of **unfair labor practice** charges against management since 1960."[27] Accompanying this outright opposition has been an upsurge in the use of anti-union consultants.

Another aspect of this opposition includes a significant increase in enlightened personnel or **human resource management** policies in many nonunion organizations. As a result, workers feel no need for union representation or a unionized environment.

No doubt such policies in unionized companies, combined with an attitude of outright management opposition, have contributed to the drastic increase in unfair labor practice charges as companies have tried to bypass the unions with which they deal. In response to heightened economic concerns, some companies have demanded concessions in bargaining. If their unions refuse these, management provokes a strike and operates the company with nonstriking personnel, a stance popularly referred to as "playing hardball." A favorable political climate since 1980 has played no small part in the stiffening of management opposition to unions and unionization.

As union representation in the American labor force shrinks, some very fundamental institutions and beliefs are being called into question. Before dealing with these, we will further explore the context of American labor relations, the institution and process of collective bargaining, the nature and resolution of labor disputes, and the growth of unionization in the public sector.

DISCUSSION QUESTIONS

1. Who are the key players in labor–management relations and how do their goals differ or coincide?

2. How would you expect the goals of a union worker to differ from those of a nonunion worker in times of economic hardship? In times of prosperity?

3. In what ways are the goals of management diametrically opposed to those of labor? What allows them to arrive at agreements in spite of this opposition?

4. Use Maslow's hierarchy of needs to explain the high rate of union affiliation in the late nineteenth century and its decline in recent years.

5. List three reasons why workers may want to join unions and provide specific examples to illustrate each.

6. How would you answer the charge that managers are anti-union because they are "just too cheap"? Be sure to provide specific reasons to support your position.

7. Briefly describe the trend in union and labor association membership over the past ten years or so. Can you explain this trend?

VOCABULARY LIST

mutual dependency   Maslow's hierarchy of needs

compromise   threat effect

cooperation   unfair labor practice

joint decision making   human resource management

FOOTNOTES

1. Theodore W. Kheel, "Exploring Alternatives to the Strike—Is the Strike Outmoded?," *Monthly Labor Review* (September 1973): 35.

2. In 1989, the civilian labor force numbered 123.87 million—117.34 million employed and 6.53 million unemployed. See *Monthly Labor Review* (February 1990): 23.

3. Milton Friedman, "Some Comments on the Significance of Labor Unions for Economic Policy" in David M. Wright, *The Impact of the Union* (Kelley & Millman, 1956), especially pp. 226–227, where Friedman proposes a wage rigidity theory of collective bargaining.

4. The economy's growth rate in the United States, however, averaged about 2 percent from the 1970s into the 1980s, about one-half the growth rate of 3.8 percent from 1953 to 1973, as noted in Richard Edwards, et al., *Unions in Crisis and Beyond* (Auburn House Publishing, 1986), p. 2.

5. These are the aims of the 1988 Worker Adjustment and Retraining Notification Act (WARN).

6. See John Hoerr, et al., "Beyond Unions," in Alan M. Glassman, Naomi Berger Davidson, and Thomas G. Cummings, eds., *Labor Relations: Reports from the Firing Line* (Business Publications, 1988), p. 495; *Wall Street Journal*, November 8, 1988, p. B1.

7. *Wall Street Journal*, January 12, 1988, p. 1, commenting on a survey of human resource officials by the *Personnel Journal*.

8. *Wall Street Journal*, March 30, 1990, p. A3.

9. Federal Regulation of Employment Service, Binder 6, NLRA Scope, S44:2 (p. 5), October 1980 revision.

10. *Omaha World-Herald*, September 5, 1989, p. 1.

11. Abraham H. Maslow, "A Theory of Human Motivation," *Psychological Review* 50 (1943): 370–396.

12. Thomas A. Kochan, "How American Workers View Labor Unions," *Monthly Labor Review* (April 1979).

13. Ibid., p. 30.

14. Jeanne M. Brett, "Why Employees Want Unions," *Organizational Dynamics* (Spring 1980): 51.

15. Kochan, "How American Workers View Labor Unions," p. 24.

16. Ibid., p. 30.

17. Robert E. Allen and Timothy J. Keaveny, *Contemporary Labor Relations* (Addison–Wesley, 1988), p. 144.

18. *Business Week*, October 9, 1989, p. 144.

19. *Wall Street Journal*, March 16, 1988, p. 34.

20. William T. Dickens and Jonathan S. Leonard, "Accounting for the Decline in Union Membership, 1950–1980," *Industrial and Labor Relations Review* (April 1985): 323. This figure is based on nonfarm and nonconstruction workers; the authors note that the BLS peak for union membership as a percentage of the entire labor force occurred in 1945.

21. BLS *Bulletin 90–59*, February 7, 1990. Employed membership was given as 16.96 million (16.4 percent of employed wage and salary workers); representation was 19.2 million (8.6 percent), showing representation of about 2.25 million workers who were not union or association members.

22. Ibid.

23. Ibid.

24. *Wall Street Journal*, April 27, 1988, p. 27.

25. Kochan, "How American Workers View Labor Unions," pp. 27–28.

26. Ibid.; see also Maryellen Kelley's comments in *Proceedings of the Thirty-ninth Annual Meeting* (Industrial Relations Research Association Series, December 28–30, 1986), p. 287.

27. *Wall Street Journal*, February 16, 1988, p. 1.

REFERENCES

BRETT, JEANNE M. "Why Employees Want Unions," *Organizational Dynamics* (Spring 1980): 47–59.

CHALYKOFF, JOHN, and PETER CAPPELI, " 'Union Avoidance': Management's New Industrial Relations Strategy," *Monthly Labor Review* (April 1986): 45–46.

CULLEN, DONALD E. "Recent Trends in Collective Bargaining in the United States," *International Labour Review* (May–June 1985): 299–322, especially 316–319.

DICKENS, WILLIAM T., and JONATHAN S. LEONARD, "Accounting for the Decline in Union Membership, 1950–1980," *Industrial and Labor Relations Review* (April 1985): 323–334.

EDWARDS, RICHARD, PAOLO GARONNA, and FRANZ TODTLING, *Unions in Crisis and Beyond,* Auburn House, 1986.

GARBARINO, JOSEPH W. "Unionism Without Unions: The New Industrial Relations?" *Industrial Relations* (Winter 1984): 40–51.

HOERR, JOHN, WILLIAM G. GLABERSON, DANIEL B. MOSKOWITZ, VICKY CAHAN, MICHAEL A. POLLOCK, and JONATHAN TASINI, "Beyond Unions," in ALAN M. GLASSMAN, NAOMI BERGER DAVIDSON, and THOMAS G. CUMMINGS, eds., *Labor Relations: Reports from the Firing Line.* Business Publications Inc., 1988, pp. 493–505.

KAHN, SHULAMIT, "Union Membership Trends: A Study of the Garment Workers," *Monthly Labor Review* (June 1986): 33–35.

KHEEL, THEODORE W. "Exploring Alternatives to the Strike—Is the Strike Outmoded?" *Monthly Labor Review* (September 1973): 35–37.

KOCHAN, THOMAS A. "How American Workers View Labor Unions," *Monthly Labor Review* (April 1979): 23–31.

KOKKELENBERG, EDWARD C., and DONNA R. SOCKELL, "Union Membership in the United States, 1973–1981." *Industrial and Labor Relations Review* (July 1985): 497–543.

CHAPTER 2

THE HISTORICAL DEVELOPMENT OF THE AMERICAN LABOR MOVEMENT

F rom our nation's inception, labor has played a pivotal role in the growth and development of the economy. Its quest for justice and equality has had a major impact on society as a whole. The U.S. labor movement, which gained momentum in the nineteenth century, promoted improvements in working conditions and gained a higher standard of living for its members. It also prompted major reforms in society. The advances in the workplace, which were controversial and uneven in their impact on the U.S. workforce, were the result of conflict, often violent, between management and workers. Indeed, one of the salient themes that recurs throughout the history of U.S. labor relations is the tension and adversarial climate found in the nation's workplaces. This climate was less of a problem in the colonial period when skilled workers had a degree of autonomy and control over their work. It became a serious problem with the emergence of urban industrial capitalism and reached crisis proportions in the mass-production industries of the twentieth century. Although history cannot help us predict the future, it does enable us to see what happened in the past, the decisions and programs that worked and those that failed.

LABOR IN COLONIAL AMERICA

The British colonies in North America were primarily extractive economies dependent on agriculture, fishing, harvesting of timber, mining, animal husbandry, hunting, and related occupations that tapped the New World's ample resources. The colonies grew and were nurtured by a government whose economic policy emphasized the security and prosperity of the mother country. This policy was consistent with seventeenth- and eighteenth-century mercantilist principles and beliefs that held out as a goal for nation-states the achievement of a favorable balance of trade in precious metals and self-sufficiency through trade with imperial colonies.

European colonization, then, was an outgrowth of the Old World's search for new sources of gold and silver. Ultimately, the English colonies became valuable sources of raw materials such as rice, tobacco, iron, lumber, pitch, tar, turpentine, deer skins, and other commodities. Colonial settlements in the New World also served as a captive market for British manufactured goods. Through such an autarchic relationship, carefully administered and controlled through London, the power and prestige of England could be advanced in a world where commercial rivalry for raw materials and markets was intense.

The Economy and Labor in the Colonies

The overwhelming majority of colonial inhabitants was engaged in agriculture and other extractive industries. At the same time, the colonial economy employed skilled and unskilled laborers in small-scale manufacturing and handicraft occupations, in building houses and barns, in constructing ships to carry raw materials, and in providing other goods and services essential to everyday life. These activities were carried on mainly by free laborers and by indentured servants who, in return for passage to the New World, bound themselves to serve a master for an agreed upon number of years. The indentured servants consisted of emigrant volunteers seeking new opportunities, the unemployed, convicts, debtors, and others who could not pay their own transportation costs. Approximately one-half of those who emigrated to the colonies initially came over as indentured servants. Because the period of bondage was fixed by law to no more than seven years, indentured servants and their descendants eventually entered the free labor market.[1]

As the colonies developed from primitive settlements to thriving enterprises, their economies became more diversified and specialized. Prosperity through trade with England spurred the growth of towns and cities, increasing both their size and the diversity of their populations.[2] Consequently, local markets became large enough to support workshops owned and operated by craftspeople and, in some cases, merchants who, in turn, hired master craftspeople to supervise journeymen and apprentices. The increasing demand sustained craft workers in such skilled trades as furniture and cabinet making, printing, shipbuilding, hat making, brewing, and the making of jewelry and other decorative artifacts. Local crafts flourished to such an extent that Carl Bridenbaugh, a modern historian, titled the eighteenth century "the great age of the colonial craftsman."[3]

Colonial Labor Conditions and Regulations

Highly skilled craftspeople as well as unskilled itinerant workers, who exchanged their labor for lodging, board, or wages, found labor conditions in the North American colonies an improvement over those that existed in the Old World. Because of an inadequate labor pool, wages were higher and treatment was generally better. Moreover, geographical mobility enabled the skilled and unskilled to escape cruel employers and harsh conditions. Nevertheless, it would be a mistake to romanticize the lives of colonial workers. Most work in the colonial period was physically demanding, and mistreatment by masters and other employers occurred, as is evidenced throughout the colonial period by frequent strikes, slowdowns, conspiracies to desert, and free laborers summarily quitting their jobs.

In England, labor conditions were regulated to ensure that agricultural and manufacturing interests had access to a supply of cheap labor as well as to protect the worker from excessive cruelty. Similarly, in the colonies, labor policies were influenced by English laws and practices as developed in the **Tudor Industrial Code.** This body of laws regulated labor conduct, employer–employee relations, and the labor supply, and served to protect the consumer by ensuring quality work through the apprenticeship system. The major provisions of the code specified the following:

1. All able-bodied persons were compelled to work.
2. Wrongful dismissal of employees was unlawful.
3. Justices of the peace set maximum wages based on the labor supply and condition of the economy.
4. Combinations of workers for the purpose of raising wages were unlawful.
5. Workers were to honor contracts as to length of service and to produce letters asserting that they were free to be hired out.
6. The term of apprenticeship was seven years.

Additional eighteenth-century amendments were aimed at maintaining the supply of English skilled craftspeople by restricting their freedom to emigrate.[4]

Colonial Regulation of Labor

Colonial attempts to apply all or part of the Tudor Industrial Code met with mixed results. Compulsory labor was enforced through publicly supported workhouses and, in the mid eighteenth century, also through the creation of local manufacturing establishments to provide jobs for the unemployed. Both institutions upheld the principle that labor was required of all, a norm that was vital in the labor-scarce colonies. Although colonial courts attempted to regulate wages and prices, their efforts ended in failure. The reason was simple: labor scarcity. Nevertheless, the principles of regulation died out slowly as colonial towns continued to set the fees charged by occupations that had a quasipublic function (e.g., porters, cartsmen, millers, smiths, gravediggers, ships pilots). Throughout the colonial period, authorities passed laws that imposed restraints on the employers' right to dismiss laborers. Unlike their British counterparts, however, colonial administrators were less concerned about *combinations,* whether created by employers, master craftspeople, journeymen, or other groups such as the licensed trades. It was not unusual for colonial tradespeople, acting as a group, to petition colonial governments or to strike for either higher wages or prices. Punishment for strike activities was inconsistent and often mild.[5]

Colonial Labor Organizations

Labor unions, as we know them in the twentieth century, did not exist in the colonies in the seventeenth and eighteenth centuries. Skilled tradespeople, however, had common interests, and to advance those interests they established **mechanic societies.** These colonial organizations provided members of the same trade with sickness, accident, and death benefits, promoted the self-improvement and competence of fellow artisans, lent money, and settled disputes. Mechanic societies were descendants of the medieval guilds through which craftspeople set conditions of entry into the craft, standards of production and quality, wages and prices, and regulations relating to the marketing of goods and services. Unlike the medieval guilds, however, mechanic societies were not very effective in enforcing regulations and controlling the behavior of their members because of the geographical mobility of artisans and the shortage of labor.[6]

A NEW ECONOMIC ORDER

The American Revolution disrupted the colonies' profitable commercial nexus with the mother country, and it initiated long-range social, political, and economic changes. From the nation's inception its founders recognized two inherent weaknesses: (1) a critical shortage of labor, both skilled and unskilled and (2) a lack of investment capital. Yet, the country possessed almost limitless natural resources. In responding to the challenges of building a nation, America's political leaders reestablished old commercial ties and added new ones. They developed economic policies that dealt with protection from foreign competition, and they set out to develop banking, agriculture, transportation, and manufacturing. A steady stream of immigrants and the natural increase of its own inhabitants stimulated economic development. A transportation revolution, which included the construction of roads, turnpikes, canals, and eventually railroads in the first half of the nineteenth century, tied wilderness settlements to urban centers, linked markets, and stimulated the growth of enterprises that were larger and more complex than those of the colonial period.[7]

The transformation of basic institutions that occurred after the war affected how work was organized, coordinated, and controlled. The emergence of the factory system with its large-scale mechanization and the increase in competition from domestic and foreign firms made merchant capitalists cost conscious. Because of greater competition and an unstable economy, characterized by wide cyclical swings, workers were constantly threatened by wage reductions and a higher cost of living. Many did not earn wages sufficient to provide for the bare essentials of life. In addition, new technology eliminated skilled jobs and diminished what contemporaries believed was the dignity associated with work. The new technology challenged the worker's autonomy and control over the workplace, conditions once enjoyed by colonial craftspeople. The loss of status in the community and economic insecurity and deprivation led to increased labor militancy and the development of trade unions in the first half of the nineteenth century.[8]

The Merchant Capitalists and the Factory System

In the early nineteenth century, **merchant capitalists** became leading figures in organizing the factors of production. Profits earned in commercial ventures were reinvested to acquire raw materials; to hire skilled and unskilled workers in order to convert raw materials into finished products; and finally, to obtain the services of distributors such as jobbers, wholesalers, and retailers, who got the products to the customer. Improved transportation, in which merchant capitalists had invested, enabled this entrepreneurial class to manufacture goods for regional and international markets. As the size of these markets grew, their firms expanded, requiring larger outlays of capital, sizable labor forces, machinery, and natural and mechanical sources of power. Wholesale goods replaced custom goods which were now produced mainly for local markets. To satisfy demand, manufacturing had to be reorganized. Resources that included land, labor, and capital had to be used efficiently to take advantage of economies of scale and scope. The **factory system** helped merchant capitalists achieve these objectives. Factories located near powerful streams used water power so effectively to run machines that by 1850, for instance, this method of manufacturing predominated in the production of cotton textiles.[9] The factory system and the mechanization of manufacturing spread to other industries so that products such as nails, tacks, files, boots and shoes, rifles, and other goods were machine produced. While the factory system helped revolutionize manufacturing, steam power altered the nation's transportation system. By 1860, it was commonplace to see steamboats, railroads, and steam elevators and inclines delivering and helping distribute the flow of factory inputs and outputs.

The Rise of Worker Associations

While mechanized factories eliminated the need for skilled labor, the factory system itself created an organizational setting in which laborers lost control over what they did, how they did it, and how much they earned. In response to these changes, workers established "societies" and "associations." In the late eighteenth and early nineteenth centuries, these organizations were local and were restricted to a particular craft. Tactically, workers attempted to raise wages by setting an agreed upon wage scale and vowing not to work for less. Employers who failed to meet the demands of workers usually faced a strike. Workers also tried to establish closed shops by having employers agree only to hire trade association members.

That worker associations and societies were sometimes effective in combating low wages and rising living costs can be inferred from the growing number of employers' associations that were formed in the first half of the nineteenth century to hold down wages and destroy labor combinations. Employers' appeals to the courts are also testimony to a degree of labor effectiveness, even though the decisions undermined labor's efforts to organize. From 1806 through the 1820s, employers took labor groups to court to defeat their attempts to establish a minimum wage.

The Conspiracy Cases

The judicial proceedings came to be known as the **Conspiracy Cases.** The first group of cases involved journeymen cordwainers (shoemakers) who sought higher wages to combat rising living costs. In 1806, the Philadelphia court ruled that a combination of workers formed to raise wages was illegal. Decisions in New York (1809) and Pittsburgh (1815), however, set aside the question of illegality of combinations to raise wages, but addressed the issue of whether or not the striking cordwainers had used unlawful means to obtain higher wages. In sum, the cordwainers were found guilty of engaging in an unlawful conspiracy because of the tactics they employed: strikes, closed shops, boycotts, and so on. Later cases, such as those involving New York hatters (1823), Philadelphia tailors (1827), and Philadelphia spinners (1829), elaborated and reinforced the earlier court decisions, which condemned the means workers used to obtain higher wages rather than whether or not combinations were illegal conspiracies. Nonetheless, workers and their organizations continued to fight in the courts for the right to organize and strike. Their efforts were rewarded in 1842 when Chief Justice Lemuel Samuel Shaw of the Massachusetts Supreme Court declared, in *Commonwealth v. Hunt*, that workers' associations were lawful, as were strikes. Other state courts gradually accepted the principles on which Chief Justice Shaw based his decision.[10]

Commonwealth v. Hunt represented a victory for labor and its right to organize. Overall, however, the period between the Revolutionary War and the Civil War was a difficult one for workers. Unfavorable court decisions, unsympathetic legislatures, ethnic divisions among workers, immigrants eager to work for low wages, and the power and authority of employers, backed by local police and state militias, undermined labor's unity and efforts at concerted action. Nevertheless, labor made progress in raising workers' consciousness, influencing political and social movements, and establishing labor organizations.

Organizational Innovation: City Federations to National Associations

The relative strength of labor waxed and waned with the nation's economic fortunes. A postrevolutionary depression, economic disruption between 1800 and 1816 caused by warfare in Europe that eventually involved the United States, and financial panics in 1819, 1837, and 1857 followed by several years of depression made the establishment and sustenance of labor organizations difficult. Workers frequently lost their jobs and were forced to work for whatever wages employers offered. Nevertheless, numerous trade associations and unions emerged during years of prosperity. Between 1821 and 1828 shoemakers, printers, hatters, tailors, carpenters, house painters, stone cutters, and other crafts established local trade associations. These groups of skilled workers fought, sometimes successfully, for higher wages and for the ten-hour day to replace the twelve-and-a-half-hour day "sunrise-to-sunset" system then in effect.

The workers' recognition of strength in numbers and their desire to create permanent institutions led to the formation in 1827 of the **Philadelphia Mechanics Union of Trade Associations,** the nation's first **city federation** of labor, a citywide confederation of craft associations and unions. Subsequently, workers established similar institutions in other urban centers. Further experiments in institution building followed. These organizations were predicated on labor's realization that greater size gave financial strength and the power to conduct successful strikes. In 1831, for instance, the New England Association of Farmers, Mechanics, and Other Workmen was founded for the purpose of uniting all producing classes, both skilled and unskilled. During the 1850s, the skilled crafts established national organizations. The first, the National Typographical Union, was created in 1852 and was followed by the Stone Cutters in 1853, the Hat Finishers in 1854, the Molders in 1859, and the Machinists in 1859. The most significant institutional development was the formation in 1834 of the **National Trades' Union,** an organization consisting of members of the various city federations. Initially an advisory body, the National Trades' Union became directly involved in the ten-hour day movement for federal employees.[11]

Labor Involvement in Politics and Social Reform

To advance the cause of labor, particularly that of skilled workers, and to improve their status which had diminished with the advent of the factory system, workers turned to politics. Sometimes they worked through existing parties and their candidates, and other times they formed workingmen's parties and ran their own candidates. Among the issues labor fought for in the three decades before the Civil War were

1. A ten-hour day: the sunrise-to-sunset system included twelve-and-a-half-hour days and seventy-five-hour weeks.
2. Universal male suffrage: property qualifications prohibited the poor from having a say in the affairs of society.
3. Abolition of imprisonment for debt: the poor, many of whom were working class, were most affected by this practice which gave judges discretion to imprison debtors; unequal justice was a fact of life, and the poor suffered disproportionately.
4. Abolition of the militia system: this burden fell most heavily on workers, since the wealthy could hire a substitute or pay a fine for not showing up for periodical militia drills.
5. A mechanics' lien law: workers lost thousands of dollars when firms went bankrupt or the owner died; the proposed law would give laborers preferred creditor status.
6. Abolition of all chartered monopolies: monopolies were associated with privilege and reduced competition.
7. Equal and universal education: workers recognized the importance of education in achieving a measure of dignity and respect and thus fought hard on this issue.[12]

In addition to political activities, workers were engaged in a variety of social reform movements that included the founding of communistic settlements and producer cooperatives. Some social reform movements led by labor attacked the wage system, the sanctity of private property, and the ideal of rugged individualism, core values and institutions in the merchant capitalists' society. Other efforts at reform, such as offering workers access to cheap land in the West, were attempts to create artificial labor shortages in the East and, consequently, higher wages.

By the 1850s, some labor leaders began to recognize that politics and social reform not only were ineffective strategies, but also led to bitter disagreements among workers. If workers were to improve their lot, labor advocates reasoned, they would have to concentrate on creating strong institutions that were efficiently administered. Similarly, they realized that direct efforts to improve wages, hours, and working conditions would yield more positive results than political activities or efforts to reform society. To such individuals, trade unions had to eschew politics and reform schemes and instead become "pure and simple." This debate over strategic issues would continue into the twentieth century.

Labor Gains and Losses: 1800–1860

To assume that labor prior to the Civil War was impotent, ineffectual, or lacking working-class consciousness is inaccurate. What is striking is that the antagonism and adversarial spirit between workers and merchant capitalists emerged early in the industrialization process. In protesting long hours, low pay, loss of autonomy, and inhuman working conditions, laborers organized, conducted strikes and slowdowns, and engaged in other activities involving resistance to authority. Throughout the nineteenth century, the high turnover rate in the nation's factories is testimony to the deeply rooted unhappiness of workers.[13]

At the same time labor made some gains. Federal employees achieved the ten-hour day, as did other employees; wages in some industries improved; and the variety of social benefits given to trade union members provided institutional support to those who were injured, sick, or family members of deceased workers. Perhaps most important was the establishment of a tradition of action by laborers whereby they would have a voice in determining their economic destiny.

THE RISE OF AN INDUSTRIAL WORKFORCE, 1860–1914

The secession of southern states from the Union in 1860 and 1861 caused economic uncertainty and a serious disruption of trade between North and South. Initially, the split in the nation resulted in high unemployment, but all-out war stimulated demand and accelerated the trend toward what eventually became a national urban-industrial economy.

Captains of Industry, Workers, and the Modern Corporation

The dominant businesspeople of the new era of industrial capitalism were neither shop owners nor merchants but manufacturers. The workers they employed increasingly found themselves in jobs that were semiskilled or unskilled.

Between 1880 and 1900, large organizations, which had mechanized production and further rationalized the factory system, began to dominate the economy. The Standard Oil Company, Carnegie Steel (later U.S. Steel and now USX), the American Tobacco Company, the New York Central Railroad, Armour and Swift, and others became synonymous with the rise of big business. Founders of these enterprises, such as John D. Rockefeller, Andrew Carnegie, James B. Duke, Cornelius Vanderbilt, and others accumulated wealth beyond anyone's imagination. Under their leadership, the managers and directors of these firms created new forms of organization and new methods of marketing. Alfred D. Chandler, a modern business historian, underscored the unprecedented nature of these changes:

The great modern corporation, carrying on the major industrial processes, namely, purchasing, and often production of materials and parts, manufacturing, marketing and finance—all within the same organizational structure—had its beginnings in that period. Such organizations hardly existed, outside of the railroads, before the 1880s. By 1900 they had become the basic business unit in American industry.[14]

In this new environment workers were at a disadvantage. Forced to bargain for jobs and wages with large enterprises, they lost power, independence, and ultimately dignity and status in their community. Meanwhile, employers had huge investments tied up in plant and machinery. To be competitive, they sought to keep costs down by paying as little as possible for labor. The arrival of unprecedented waves of immigrants between 1870 and 1914 provided them with a large, unskilled labor pool willing to work long hours for low wages. Thus, the surplus labor pool exacerbated unemployment, intensified competition for jobs, and pitted recent immigrant against native born. It also made organizing labor difficult: in an age that emphasized specialization, unskilled work, and mechanization; each worker, unlike machinery which represented a large capital investment, was easily and cheaply replaced.

Adding to the uncertainty and anxiety for both labor and big business was the erratic behavior of the economy. Although the United States had experienced financial panics, depressions, and economic crises since its founding, the emergence of an integrated, national urban economy after the Civil War magnified the consequences of these events. Depressions or financial panics occurred in each decade between 1870 and 1914. In the last three decades of the nineteenth century, there were serious depressions between the years 1873 and 1878, 1882 and 1885, and 1893 and 1897, with brief intervening periods of revival, expansion, and prosperity.

Consequently, life for the industrial worker, skilled and unskilled, was filled with uncertainty. Frequent wage cuts and intermittent employment, not to mention unhealthy and unsafe working conditions, were characteristic in the late nineteenth and early twentieth centuries. When employed, workers faced long hours, frequently twelve or more a day, six or seven days a week. Workers had neither retirement benefits, unemployment compensation, nor accident insurance. Health and safety codes governing the workplace did not exist. Men, women, and children (child labor was the norm in some industries) faced an autocratic management whose authority was absolute.

For these reasons and others, labor dissatisfaction was expressed through formal and informal protest. Resistance to management control and regimentation occurred through spontaneous actions that undermined managerial authority and through deliberate collective action that sought greater control over the production process and the conditions of employment. The spontaneous actions involved individual actions, such as disobedience or recalcitrance, that undermined the authority of a foreman; the collective actions sought change favorable to the workers through boycotts, strikes, and collective bargaining.[15]

The Labor Problem

Symptomatic of the century's labor problems were the violence and discord that characterized the period between the Civil War and the beginning of World War I. In response to labor's efforts to organize for higher wages and better working conditions, employers practiced **blacklisting,** that is, publicizing the names of union organizers and strikers (labor troublemakers) throughout the region so that they would have difficulty finding employment. They instituted ironclad oaths that prohibited employees from joining a union or striking. Management also resorted to the courts to have injunctions served on striking unions.

Contributing to the dismal relations between labor and management was the tendency for strikes to degenerate into violent confrontations between employers using Pinkerton detectives and scabs (strike breakers) to end strikes and laboring men and women who, in retaliation, destroyed property, disrupted production and distribution, and also indulged in violence against others.

Industrial Violence

Between 1865 and 1914, industrial violence was a common occurrence, leading some middle-class observers to fear that the nation was on the verge of class warfare and social revolution. Most notable was the great railroad strike of 1877, precipitated by a wage reduction put into effect by many of the nation's railroads. The ensuing strike was marked by arson, murder, and rioting in several states, and it paralyzed almost two-thirds of the country's railroad mileage, including four major trunk lines and many shorter ones that were forced to discontinue operations. The strike spread to other industries, making it truly national in scope and the first in which federal troops were used.[16]

Major strikes in the 1880s and 1890s underscored the enormity of what observers called "the labor problem." The Homestead Strike of 1892 was one of the most violent labor–management confrontations in the nation's history. The strike between members of the Amalgamated Association of Iron and Steel Workers and Carnegie Steel lasted all summer and was marked by a day-long pitched battle between armed guards hired by Carnegie Steel's general manager, Henry C. Frick, and disgruntled steel workers.[17] Likewise in 1894, a strike between the Pullman Palace Car Company and Eugene V. Debs' American Railway Union quickly deteriorated into a violent confrontation between the two antagonists, resulting in the issuance of an injunction against the strikers and the calling out of federal troops by Grover Cleveland.[18] These instances and the thousands of other strikes that marked the last four decades of the nineteenth century dramatized the disenchantment of American workingmen and -women.

The Emergence of National Unions

In the late nineteenth century, the creation of an economy that was national in scope, the emergence of a factory system that utilized machine power, and the related loss of worker independence, autonomy and skills led to efforts to establish labor unions that also were national in scope. Indicative of this trend after the Civil War was the formation of the National Labor Union in 1866 and the Knights of Labor in 1869 (Table 2.1).

The National Labor Union

The **National Labor Union (NLU),** a confederation of skilled craft unions, was founded to obtain higher wages and the eight-hour day, as well as to abolish the

Table 2.1 *The Emergence of National Unions*

Organization	Founding Date	Major Characteristics
National Labor Union	1866	"One big union" (but all craft workers); social reform orientation
Knights of Labor	1869	"One big union"; social reform or uplift unionism
American Federation of Labor	1886	Federation of independent unions (primarily of skilled workers); business or "bread-and-butter" unionism
Industrial Workers of the World	1905	"One big union"; radical (syndicalism) unionism

use of convict labor and restrictions on immigration. In addition, the union advocated the establishment of producer and consumer cooperatives, equal rights for women and Afro-Americans, and an inflationary monetary policy. Its first leader, William Sylvis, was committed to political action. He believed that the wage system should be abolished and that the nation's economy ought to consist of small, self-employed producers. After Sylvis died in 1869, the NLU leadership was taken over by middle-class reformers who lost interest in practical ways to improve the workers' lot. Instead, they sought to institute a variety of reforms, some of which involved taxation, banking, currency, and federal land policy.

The Knights of Labor

During its short life, the NLU faced competition from a rival union, the Order of the **Knights of Labor (KOL),** founded by Uriah H. Stephens in 1869. Unlike the NLU which consisted of crafts and skilled trades, the Knights were an all-inclusive industrial union that reflected its founder's dream of organizing all workers into one "great brotherhood." The union admitted unskilled workers, women, blacks, and immigrants as well as skilled craftspeople and workers. It excluded only professional gamblers, bankers, lawyers, stockholders, and those who sold or manufactured distilled spirits.

The organizational structure of the Knights was simple. It consisted of local assemblies, that is, individual members from one or more occupations or trades; district assemblies that included five or more local assemblies; and a general assembly that drew its elected members from the district assemblies. The General Executive Board and officers of the Knights were elected by the general assembly. To protect its members from employer harassment and reprisals, the Knights adopted secrecy and elaborate rituals, earning the union the condemnation of the Catholic Church, which disapproved of the Order's oath-bound secrecy and rituals.

The leadership of the Knights was reformist in its outlook and social philosophy. Uriah Stephens, a tailor, and his successor, Terence V. Powderly, a railroad worker, were inspired by the social idealism and reform movements of the 1840s and 1850s. Consequently, they were less concerned with such bread-and-butter issues as collective bargaining, higher wages, the eight-hour day, and improved working conditions than with reforming American society along egalitarian and humanitarian lines. For Powderly and other leaders of the Knights, improvements for workers would come only when fundamental changes occurred in the institutions and organization of society. Reflecting this reformist orientation, A. W. Wright, a member of the Knight's Executive Board, noted that the union did not believe "that the emancipation of labor will come with increased wages and a reduction in the hours of labor; we must go deeper than that, and this matter will not be settled until the wage system is abolished." Similarly, Terence Powderly claimed that "there is no good reason why labor cannot through cooperation own and operate mines, factories, and railroads." Thus, the leadership of the Knights ignored issues involving organizational development and economic betterment.[19]

In the aftermath of the great railroad strike of 1877, workers found the idea of one great brotherhood attractive. Membership in the Knights of Labor increased as skilled, semiskilled, and unskilled workers became more militant. In 1879, the union had more than 9,000 members, by 1882 more than 42,000, and, by 1885, more than 110,000. Although Powderly disavowed the use of strikes, believing that they wasted valuable resources and did not solve fundamental problems like child labor, monopoly power, and the inequitable distribution of wealth, he and the others who made up the hierarchy of the Knights could not control the rank-and-file.

In 1884–1886, the nation experienced a number of major strikes as working men and women resisted wage reductions. Although Powderly and his colleagues had little to do with the wave of strikes, the union grew rapidly when, in the spring of 1885, it successfully overturned management's decision to cut wages on three railroads—the Missouri Pacific; the Missouri, Kansas, and Texas; and the Wabash—all owned and controlled by the speculator Jay Gould. Membership suddenly soared to 700,000. Sentiment for a general strike for the eight-hour day to be held on May 1, 1886, added to a heightened atmosphere of militancy. Powderly urged caution but could not control the ill-advised actions of the members. A strike in the spring of 1886 against Gould's southwest system ended in defeat. Powderly's caution and lack of support for the general strike of May 1, 1886, was not well received by the rank-and-file. As a result, membership in the Knights began to decline. From 700,000 members (after the victory over Gould's railways), the Knights declined to 75,000 in 1893 and disappeared entirely by the turn of the century.

The American Federation of Labor

Most significant for the future of labor were the independent trade union groups that sprang up in this period, the **American Federation of Labor** (**AFL**) being the most important of these. These groups rejected the radical programs of the socialists as well as those of the social reformers. Leaders of the independent trade unions possessed a narrow vision of what their organizations could do for workers. Typical of their attitude were the sentiments expressed by Adolph Strasser of the Cigarmakers, a founder of the AFL, when questioned by U.S. Senator Henry W. Blair at a committee meeting on relations between labor and capital. In reply to Senator Blair's inquiry concerning the ultimate ends of the trade union movement, Strasser replied: "We have no ultimate ends. We are going on from day to day. We are fighting only for immediate objects—objects that can be realized in a few years." Samuel

Gompers, another of the founders of the AFL and its president for almost 40 years, also emphasized limited, short-term goals. "Whatever ideas we may have as to the future of society . . . ," he said, "they must remain in the background and we must subordinate our convictions . . . to the general good that the trades union movement brings to the laborer."[20]

It was upon this modest philosophy of "pure and simple" trade unionism that the American Federation of Labor was founded in 1886. The AFL was a group of autonomous national, state, and local trade unions and assemblies, loosely associated since 1881 in the **Federation of Organized Trade and Labor Unions (FOTLU)**. Rejecting the Knights' idea of one big union for everyone, Gompers, the AFL's founding father, and his associates committed the Federation to encouraging skilled workers to organize into craft unions. Although Gompers was not opposed to industrial unions (the Mine Workers and Brewery Workers were affiliated with the AFL), the Federation was dedicated primarily to organizing the skilled trades.

Gompers felt that skilled workers were the best targets for trade union (craft union) membership for several reasons.

1. Skilled workers had the necessary education (skills) and discipline, as well as higher pay, to form and maintain, especially financially in terms of ability to pay dues regularly, an organization like a union.

2. Skilled workers had to protect their investment in their skills, which gave them the commitment to support a union.

3. There were a much smaller number of skilled than unskilled workers, thereby increasing the chances that the union would control the labor supply and thus have monopoly power.

4. The much smaller number of skilled workers made it easier to obtain higher wages from employers, as the impact on costs would be less than obtaining those wages for the mass of unskilled workers in large corporations.

The AFL also differed with the KOL in its approach to improving relations between labor and capital. Discarding the reformist philosophy of the National Labor Union and the Knights, the Federation sought such immediate objectives as shorter hours, higher wages, and better working conditions. Gompers and his followers accepted the major tenets of capitalism and the basic institutions that evolved in the system, arguing only that labor wanted a larger share of the economic pie. Consequently, the AFL rejected trying to change the existing economic system through reform. They saw no benefit in forming a separate labor party. The way to achieve tangible results, Federation leaders believed, was through collective bargaining. If this did not work, they were ready to use the strike as a weapon. Their unionism was **business, or bread-and-butter unionism.**

Gompers' belief that economic issues had first priority, and should not be diluted at all by social reform or any long-run political ends, formed the basis for **voluntarism**: unions are voluntary organizations, and so they should not be regulated by government. The nineteenth century government philosophy of *laissez faire* for business should extend to labor, and so Gompers steered the AFL away from any political program, even support of such important laws as child labor laws.

During the late nineteenth and early twentieth centuries, labor made some head-way in organizing workers. By 1900, one in fourteen workers belonged to unions. This was a larger number than ever before in the nation's history. However, approximately 15 million workers, mostly unskilled, were unorganized.

The American Railway Union

Despite limited success, workers faced significant impediments in gaining recognition of their right to organize and bargain collectively. These difficulties are illustrated in the rise of the **American Railway Union (ARU),** an industrial union that welcomed all railroad workers.

In the late nineteenth century, the railroad industry was organized into autonomous brotherhoods such as the Brotherhood of Locomotive Firemen and the Brotherhood of Locomotive Engineers. These craft organizations were exclusive, and they jealously guarded their autonomy. On the other hand, switchmen, maintenance and roundhouse workers, brakemen, and other unskilled workers were not organized. To strengthen the position of railroad workers, Eugene V. Debs, former secretary of the Locomotive Firemen, founded the American Railway Union in 1893. This organization would ultimately represent all railway employees, including the factious brotherhoods. An easy victory against James J. Hill's Great Northern Railroad in January 1894 helped increase membership in the ARU. But in May 1894 a boycott and strike against the Pullman Palace Car Company brought defeat and eventual destruction of the union.[21]

The reasons for the ARU's defeat showed the weaknesses labor would have to overcome before it could gain legitimacy. When the ARU struck, railway managers had no difficulty finding replacements. At the same time the Brotherhoods, jealous of their exclusivity, did not support the strike. Management, recognizing the threat they faced to their authority, began coordinating their labor policies and their actions whenever one of them faced a strike. In Chicago, the General Managers' Association worked together to defeat the Pullman strikers. Finally, the use of injunctions against the striking ARU and the employment of federal troops to enforce them and protect the U.S. mail ended the dispute. For violating the injunctions issued by two federal judges in Chicago, Eugene V. Debs was sentenced to six months in jail.

The *injunction* became an effective device with which to end strikes, for it avoided a jury whose members could easily side with the union. The most effective type of injunction was one based on the **Sherman Antitrust Act of 1890,** which prohibited any combination or conspiracy in restraint of trade between the states. Although the Sherman Act was initially passed to halt the growth of large monopolies, it was used effectively against unions.

The Industrial Workers of the World

The rise of the **Industrial Workers of the World (IWW)** was emblematic of labor discontent prior to World War I (Table 2.1). The IWW or **Wobblies** (as members of the IWW were commonly called) was founded in 1905 by Daniel DeLeon, Eugene V. Debs, and other radicals. Its leadership consisted of revolutionaries who believed that unions existed to abolish capitalism and the political state. Their **syndicalist philosophy** called for revolution to overthrow the system, but offered no alternative goals for the new society. The leadership believed that societal goals would come out of the revolution itself, like the phoenix rising from the ashes of the old system. The rhetoric and actions of IWW members aroused fear in the middle classes that labor agitators would actually destroy the nation's economic and political system. William D. Haywood, an IWW ideologue and activist, reinforced these fears. "Big Bill" Haywood was at the center of many of the strikes initiated by the IWW. As a participant, he made it clear that he drew inspiration from the notion that revolution would bring a more harmonious and equalitarian society:

> I have a dream . . . that there will be a new society sometime in which there will be no battle between capitalist and wage earner . . . there will be no political government . . . but . . . experts will come together for the purpose of discussing the welfare of all the people and discussing the means by which the machinery can be made the slave of the people instead of a part of the people being made the slave of machinery.[22]

Haywood's new order included the abolition of child labor, the emancipation of women, and better treatment of the aged.

The IWW with its anarchist-syndicalist-socialist program appealed to textile workers, migratory farmers, miners, dock workers, and lumberjacks. It was an industrial union of the poor and unskilled, and it had no compunction about using strikes, boycotts, and sabotage to win concessions from employers. In the first 15 years of the twentieth century, the IWW challenged the AFL's claim to speak for working men and women. Fundamentally, the AFL, whose membership consisted mainly of workers in the skilled trades, was a conservative institution that accepted industrial capitalism and its institutions. What the AFL sought for its members was a larger share of the economic pie through higher wages, shorter working hours, and other tangible benefits. Conversely, the IWW was devoted to the overthrow of capitalism, using violence if necessary. IWW leaders like Haywood, Vincent St. John, Joe Hill, and others saw class warfare as an inevitable byproduct of capitalism. This did not mean, however, that workers should suffer injustices until the day a new order was established. The IWW leadership was pragmatic, and while it could dream of a classless utopia in which all industry was administered by workers themselves, it could not ignore the specific grievances of its members. Consequently, the IWW worked hard to make immediate improvements in the industries in which its workers were employed.

In the 1912 textile strike in Lawrence, Massachusetts, for example, IWW leaders sought to improve the lot of the industry's unskilled, immigrant constituency. At that time, the textile industry was one of the most highly mechanized in the country. Its labor force consisted of a small number of highly skilled workers, represented by the United Textile Workers, which was affiliated with the AFL, and a larger number of unskilled laborers, mostly immigrants, who were regarded by the United Textile Workers as socially inferior and therefore unfit for union membership.

Working conditions in the mills were unhealthy and unsafe, the workday was long, and wages were low. The mills' operators, who frequently controlled the political and economic institutions of the town in which the operatives lived, shamelessly exploited their workforce. When a Massachusetts law went into effect in January 1912, limiting the workweek of women and children who worked in the mills to 54 hours, the mills' operators decided to cut what already were low wages. Mill workers resented this decision, and within three days 25,000 men, women, and children went on strike. The IWW, meanwhile, sent one of its best organizers, Joseph Ettor, to Lawrence, where he set up a strike committee. They demanded from mill owners a 15 percent increase in wages and double pay for overtime work. Ettor also established a relief committee to solicit strike funds from supporters and ordered demonstrations against the two mills still operating. The state's militia was called out to restore order. In one of the demonstrations organized by Ettor, a woman was killed. Even though he had nothing to do with the death, Ettor was arrested and accused of being an accessory to the murder. The mill owners (and city officials) hoped that jailing Ettor would end the strike. But other IWW leaders, including Big Bill Haywood, more than adequately took Ettor's place. The headlines worked to the advantage of the strikers and their IWW leaders, as it was a striker that was killed, not any soldiers. The workers gained allies they never knew they had. By March 1912, the mill owners decided to negotiate with the union. Subsequently, mills throughout New England granted wage increases.[23]

The militant IWW was active in other parts of the country, especially in the agricultural and extractive industries. IWW representatives could be found organizing migratory farmers on the Great Plains, lumber and timber workers in the Pacific Northwest, and copper miners in Jerome and Bisbee, Arizona. Between its founding in 1905 and America's entrance into World War I in 1917, the IWW focused attention on the deplorable economic conditions that unskilled and semiskilled workers faced. Their campaigns for higher wages, shorter hours, and better working conditions appealed to a broad spectrum of the population who believed that industrial reform was necessary if the country was going to remain committed to democratic ideals and institutions. To others, the IWW's revolutionary rhetoric and bombast, which included appeals to violence and sabotage, was simply a threat that had to be suppressed. In dramatizing the grievances of labor, the IWW and the labor movement in general provoked collective responses from the owners of big and small companies and members of such middle-class professions as law, social work, education, health, and journalism. Through associations and organizations, they in turn advocated a variety of solutions to America's labor problems.

URBAN INDUSTRIALISM

The growth of industry, the rise of cities, and the influx of immigrants irrevocably altered a nation that was envisioned by its founders to be primarily rural and agricultural. The emergence of the factory system and the use of steam, and later electricity and gas, as sources of power increased productivity and diminished the role of skilled labor. The size and structure of business also grew enormously as firms expanded through a process of integration and combination. The nation's first big business, the railroads, pioneered in developing modern management techniques and new administrative structures. More importantly, the railroads created a national market, enabling firms to sell products nationwide to consumers in locations as diverse as large metropolises and isolated hamlets. It was in this highly competitive and technologically advanced environment that Standard Oil, American Tobacco, DuPont, and other large firms increased their productive capacities under the direction of salaried professional managers.[24]

Cities also grew in a spectacular fashion as immigrants and native, rural Americans in search of jobs were drawn to urban places. New York City's population grew from 1 million inhabitants in 1860 to 3 million in 1900. Chicago, meanwhile, experienced a tenfold population increase during the same period. Other cities, large and small, experienced rapid growth at the expense of rural areas. Overall, the population growth of the entire country was boosted by the arrival of hundreds of thousands of immigrants annually. The total population of the United States in 1900 was 76 million, of which 10 million had been born in Europe and roughly 26 million were of foreign parentage.

By 1900, the United States was one of the wealthiest countries in the world. Its productive capacity evoked envy and admiration from foreign observers and visitors. The factors responsible for this growth included technological and organizational innovation; vast quantities of natural resources; a supply of cheap, unskilled labor (11 million more immigrants would come to America between 1900 and 1915); and an entrepreneurial spirit typified by such individuals as Levi Strauss, George Eastman, Richard W. Sears, and Andrew Carnegie. Although economic expansion would continue into the first three decades of the twentieth century, labor strife and general discontent became a source of disruption to the economy and, ultimately, a grave concern to employers and citizens in general. Labor disturbances hurt profits. They also challenged what middle-class professionals viewed as the fundamental values and institutions on which democratic capitalism was founded: the rule of law, respect for the rights of property, and individual liberty.

Reaction and Progressive Reform

Some Americans believed that the labor movement, whether it reflected Gompers' conservative philosophy or the IWW's revolutionary pronouncements, was inconsistent with American values and institutions. Such individuals and groups saw trade unions as the primary cause of the nation's labor relations problems, and they formed organizations whose objective was to undermine the labor movement.

One such group was the **National Association of Manufacturers (NAM)**, an organization made up primarily of small businesses. The NAM lobbied Congress and organized efforts at the polls to defeat congressmen sympathetic to labor. They also fought labor's right to exist in the courts. Two court cases, one involving the United Hatters of America and D. H. Lowe and Company of Danbury, Connecticut, and the other, employees of Buck's Stove and Range Company of St. Louis, are examples. The courts called into question not only the use of the boycott as a union tactic but also, in the first case, the very legality of the trade union itself on the grounds that its actions interfered with interstate trade. Union leaders, therefore, were liable for damages from labor disputes (see Chapter 3).

The National Civic Federation

The **National Civic Federation (NCF)**, an organization representing the views of "big business," was more moderate in its approach to labor and trade unions. Although basically anti-union, many members of the NCF believed that unfettered capitalism was basically destructive, and they looked to government to solve the problems of unfair competition and economic instability. The group included such captains of industry as Andrew Carnegie and Cyrus McCormick; Mark Hanna, the U.S. senator and powerful chairman of the Republican National Committee; the presidents of Columbia and Harvard universities; Samuel Gompers of the AFL; and middle-class professionals who believed that *laissez-faire* capitalism was insufficient and unstable because of its cyclical nature.

The NCF reflected the views of conservative and moderate elements in American society that challenged the political and economic philosophy of limited government, rugged individualism, and ruthless competition. Members of the NCF, along with others, believed that the economic progress gained during the nineteenth century came at the cost of the concentration of economic power, inequitable taxation, political corruption, waste of the nation's natural resources, child labor, and other abuses. Historians have given the name **Progressives*** to these proponents of reform and have designated their activities and accomplishments during the first two decades of the twentieth century as the **Progressive Movement.**[25]

Progressive Labor Legislation

One object of scrutiny by Progressive reformers was employer–employee relations. The Pullman Strike, the emergence of the radical IWW, and a multitude of other incidents involving brutality and disregard for civil liberties, as well as the use of Pinkertons, union spies, city police, state militias, and federal troops to end labor disputes, alarmed enlightened business leaders and appalled civic leaders and others. Muckraking journalists covering a variety of industries aroused the public's conscience as they exposed unsafe working conditions, unbearably long hours, exploitation of children, abusive and tyrannical foremen, price gouging in company stores, and the wretched living conditions of working men and women.** These revelations helped generate support for important labor legislation in the early

* The Progressives fought for an expansion of government regulatory activity. Through legislative efforts on the national level, they were responsible for the Hepburn Act (1906), which gave the Interstate Commerce Commission the power to regulate the freight rates of railroads; the Pure Food and Drug Act (1906), which created the Food and Drug Administration; the Meat Inspection Commission Act (1906); the Federal Reserve System (1913); the Federal Trade Commission Act (1914) and the Clayton Antitrust Act (1914), which classified certain types of corporate activities as monopolistic; and passage of the Sixteenth Amendment, authorizing a federal income tax.

** Between 1870 and 1920, America led the world in work stoppages. Moreover, strikes in the United States were more violent and bitter than anywhere else in the world. Hundreds were killed in the great railway strike of 1877. The beginning of a new century did not bring enlightenment. In 1913, the United Mine Workers organized a strike against the Colorado Fuel and Iron Company, one of the largest coal producers in the Rocky Mountain area. Ultimately, federal troops were sent out to restore order, but before that could happen the state militia attacked a miners' tent colony at Ludlow, Colorado, killing miners, their wives, and their children. According to historian William O'Neill, the Colorado militia "left a trail of bloodshed and savagery across the southern part of the state reminiscent of the genocidal Indian Wars."

twentieth century. States passed laws regulating child labor and governing maximum hours and minimum wages for women. As a result of the publicity and outcry following the 1911 Triangle Shirt Waist Factory fire in New York City in which 100 young women, locked in their factory loft, lost their lives, states passed laws defining factory safety regulations. Employer liability for industrial accidents was strengthened, and workmen compensation systems for job-related injuries, the most significant accomplishment of the Progressive Era, were established in 30 states.

Managers and Factories

While progressive labor laws were being enacted, employers initiated changes in the workplace aimed at solving labor problems. These involved exerting greater control over the workforce through *centralized management*. Such efforts, Daniel Nelson shows in his recent study of the factory system, were aimed at increasing productivity and efficiency.[26] The adoption of new technology, the imposition of order and system in the manufacturing organization through the application of scientific management techniques, and the establishment of welfare programs within companies revolutionized factory management practices by locating authority and responsibility for decision making with experts rather than with foremen and first-line supervisors. The development of welfare programs, for instance, was based on the conviction that the labor problem could be solved by the voluntary efforts of employers who would establish paternalistic programs encouraging employee self-improvement, loyalty, and cooperation. Under the supervision of welfare secretaries (the predecessors of the directors of personnel), lunchrooms, restrooms, medical departments, and insurance and savings plans were provided in some of the nation's textile mills, iron and steel plants, machine producers, and other manufacturing firms.

Other changes, dictated by self-interest and supported by the development of new managerial practices, reflected employers' desires to reach new levels of efficiency and productivity by improving labor relations. For example, by increasing the number of middle managers with line authority, large manufacturing companies could reduce the power that foremen and first-line supervisors had over the workforce. As a consequence, personnel decisions were less subject to the whim and caprice of an autocratic supervisor. What emerged in the new factory environment were identifiable personnel policies and procedures. Consistent with the reform spirit of the times, some companies also saw to it that factory renovation and construction met health and safety codes. These changes and others complemented the efforts of middle-class reformers to solve the labor problem.

The Five Dollar Day

It was in the spirit of paternalism and self-interest that Henry Ford announced his Five Dollar Day Plan, for which he earned a reputation as a great American humanitarian, philanthropist, and friend of labor. The impetus for the plan emerged from the experiences Ford engineers had on the production line. In developing the assembly line process and refining mass production techniques, Ford engineers were still confronted with what they referred to as "the human element of production."

As Stephen Meyer III notes in *The Five Dollar Day*, "these [human] problems included preindustrial immigrant attitudes and forms of behavior, worker lateness and absenteeism, high rates of labor turnover, soldiering and output restriction, and craft and industrial unionism."[27] To eliminate behavior that interfered with the efficient operation of the assembly line, Ford officials developed and implemented in 1914 the **Five Dollar Day Plan.** A key component in the plan was the Ford Sociological Department, which was in charge of investigating Ford workers and advising them on how to improve their lives. The Five Dollar Day, contrary to myth, was not a high minimum wage but a profit-sharing plan that tied worker eligibility to character traits, personal habits, and obedience to company rules and regulations. In this way, Henry Ford sought to maintain a disciplined and orderly workforce.

To be eligible for the Ford plan, a worker had to meet the company's standards of good character. The Sociological Department investigated the personal lives of each worker and then recommended whether or not the employee should be allowed to participate in the profit-sharing scheme. A pamphlet published in 1914 explained profit sharing in the following manner to Ford employees: "A worker is only put on the list of profit sharers after he has been carefully looked up, and the company is satisfied he will not debauch the additional money he receives."[28] Those who were ineligible were subjected to advice from the Sociological Department investigators on how to improve their morals and everyday living habits.

Ford workers resented the company's paternalism, and the plan was eventually abandoned after World War I. Growing labor militancy, postwar inflation which eroded the financial attractiveness of the Five Dollar Day, and union efforts to organize the automotive industry brought about a change in Ford labor policies. No longer interested in using moral suasion to change the workers' personal habits and culture, the company turned to repressive measures to obtain a disciplined workforce. They employed spies, discharged workers, and pressured others who were suspected of being trade unionists, radicals, or simply objectors to the regimented work routines in Ford plants. In the 1920s, the Ford Motor Company adopted labor policies that were repressive, authoritarian, and thoroughly anti-union.

Prosperity and the Decline of Organized Labor in the 1920s

Social historians have viewed the 1920s as a harbinger of the mass-consumption society that emerged in the 1950s. For labor unions, however, it was a decade of decline. In 1920, union membership was at 5 million, of which 4 million were affiliated with the AFL. By 1930, overall union membership had declined to 3.4 million and AFL membership dropped to 2,770,000 while the labor force grew.[29] More importantly, workers in the growth sectors of the economy, the automobile, electrical, rubber, and other mass-production industries, were largely unorganized.

Although some workers' wages had increased significantly, enabling them to purchase houses, appliances, and even automobiles, conditions in the nation's mass-production industries left much to be desired. Fatigue, boredom, and the pressure brought about by the relentless pace of mechanized production lines took their toll on the longevity, health, and overall quality of workers' lives.[30] Efforts by industrial unions in the AFL such as the United Mine Workers, the International Ladies'

Garment Workers Union, and the Amalgamated Association of Iron, Steel, and Tin Workers to organize the masses of the unskilled in major industries like autos and steel were met with indifference by the Federation leadership. With Gompers' death in 1924, William Green took over the presidency of the AFL and continued the policy of craft unionism. Similarly, the labor movement met resistance from employers who were unwilling to recognize the legitimacy of unions, collective bargaining, and worker grievances. In the first half of the 1920s, employers followed a policy of repression and coercion, and in the second half one of conciliation.

The American Plan

Ford's shift away from paternalism and social uplift after World War I to one of repression and direct attack was repeated in many other industries. In response to postwar strikes and the rise of radical groups in the United States, management launched the so-called **American Plan,** an aggressive anti-union policy that successfully employed such tactics as the use of the **yellow-dog contract** (a contract a worker signed to obtain a job, pledging he or she would not organize, support, or join a union) and the **labor injunction** to undermine union-organizing efforts.

Large companies operating in isolated communities established their own private police systems to thwart union activity and to break strikes. Some formed company unions to counter trade union organizing. Others established employer associations whose main objective was to undermine and destroy the labor movement through collective action. As one witness reported concerning the activities of those associations,

> The belligerent association may fight the union in actual battles with machine guns; it may oppose the union in legislative and political matters; it may combat all union strikes; it may carry on a continual propaganda against the union in every particular or only against certain practices . . . it may effectively blacklist all union members by means of a card-index system; it may attempt to destroy all the sentimental appeal in the betterment activities of the union by doing welfare work; or it may combine a few or all of these activities in its general campaign against the union. The secret service system . . . is characteristic . . . [31]

Advocates of the American Plan believed that they were fighting the *closed shop,* where only union members could get jobs and work, which in their minds was the antithesis of the American tradition of free association. To them, the *open shop* meant liberty, equal opportunity, and no special privileges. In the open shop environment, union and nonunion workers were treated alike. In reality, however, the open shop was, as Irving Bernstein (1970, 1972) notes in his study of the period, usually a closed *nonunion* shop, where a trade union member who overtly advertised his or her affiliation was denied a job or, if employed, summarily fired.

Company Unions

Workers' discontent, as expressed in labor strife, frequent absenteeism, lethargy, uncooperative behavior, and a high turnover rate, was extremely costly to firms, something that industry leaders recognized. Although they rejected collective bargaining by independent unions, industry leaders recognized that a nonadversarial labor relations system had to be found to address the interests and concerns of both capital and labor. The American Plan obviously failed to do this in any way that would ever lead to a harmonious relationship between labor and capital.

John D. Rockefeller, Jr., genuinely shocked by the violence associated with industrial relations, saw poor communications as the root cause of mistrust between employer and employee. "When men get together and talk over their differences candidly," he explained, "much of the ground for dispute vanishes."[32] Rockefeller recognized that when businesses were small, the manager-owner had daily contact with his employees. Large industry, however, made such interaction impossible. One of Rockefeller's recommendations for what he believed was fundamentally a human relations problem was the establishment of **employee representation plans** or **company unions.** These organizations were controlled by management, but employees could elect representatives to discuss grievances, plant safety, and other problems relating to production. Strikes were prohibited, and management reserved the right to hire and fire and determine wages and hours.[33]

Rockefeller's solution emerged in the 1920s as a popular alternative to trade unions (and collective bargaining). Standard Oil, Bethlehem Steel, International Harvester, Proctor and Gamble, the Pennsylvania Railroad, and many other firms, large and small, adopted this solution. Neither workers nor labor leaders were enthusiastic supporters, however. They charged that companies influenced elections, prohibited independent meetings of (and intimidated) worker representatives, and failed to recognize these representatives as true equals.

Welfare Capitalism

Company unions or employee representation plans were part of a larger labor relations strategy that became known as **welfare capitalism.** Its implementation resulted in company-provided health care, housing, recreational facilities, cafeterias, libraries, cooking and sewing classes, kindergartens, and other services.[34] Another facet of welfare capitalism was *employee stock ownership.* Advocates of this program hoped that ownership of shares would make "the worker a capitalist in viewpoint" who rejected unions and radical solutions.[35]

Also given a boost by welfare capitalism was the **personnel management movement.** Its advocates argued that employee relations should become the function of high-level management professionals. The tasks of hiring, firing, and disciplining workers as well as determining promotions and transfers became the responsibility of personnel managers. This group argued that cleaner, safer, and better lighted and ventilated factories were socially desirable and led to higher levels of productivity.

Welfare capitalism was offered to the workers in place of trade unions and the improvement in working conditions they obtained through them. David Brody, one of the preeminent historians of the twentieth-century labor movement, has suggested that if it had not been for the Great Depression, which brought welfare capitalism practices to an end, American labor relations might have followed a paternalistic course rather than developing into a tripartite system of big business, big government, and big labor.[36] Whether this would have actually happened is open to conjecture, but what is clear about the decade of the 1920s is that organized labor had lost ground.

There were several reasons for the decline of the labor movement at this time. First, the AFL under Samuel Gompers and his successor, William Green, had become conservative and bureaucratic. The craft unions, which defined the organizational structure of the AFL, jealously guarded their autonomy and authority. They were not interested in organizing workers in the mass-production industries. This activity involved industrial groupings that would cut across crafts and blur jurisdictional lines between them. Unions with large numbers of unskilled workers would also weaken the older craft unions' influence. Consequently, working-class solidarity was not fostered in the 1920s.

Second, there was little government support for labor, as reflected in a number of court decisions. Although the **Clayton Act of 1914** exempted unions from prosecution under the nation's antitrust laws, court rulings in the 1920s took away or severely curtailed labor's right to strike, picket, and conduct boycotts. In the 1921 *Duplex Printing Press Co. v. Deering* and the 1927 *Bedford Cut Stone Co. v. Journeymen Stone Cutters' Association of North America*, the courts held that labor boycotts were unlawful and granted injunctions to stop them (see Chapter 3). In addition to the widespread use of injunctions, the courts' willingness to uphold the legality of yellow-dog contracts seriously threatened the survival of trade unionism in the United States.

Third, private sector actions associated with the American Plan and the paternalism of welfare capitalism were effective anti-union strategies. Finally, the stock market crash in 1929 and the beginning of the Great Depression further weakened organized labor. In 1932, one of the nation's foremost experts on the labor movement predicted that unions would be of little importance in the American economy of the 1930s.[37]

THE DEVELOPMENT OF A NEW LABOR RELATIONS SYSTEM

The moribund labor movement of the 1920s and early 1930s experienced a revival beginning in 1933 and continuing through America's involvement in World War II.[38] A number of circumstances, both internal to the labor movement itself and external, were responsible for this upsurge. These included the growth of AFL affiliates and the establishment of a new national federation, the Congress of Industrial Organizations (CIO), whose members, in industrial unions, came primarily from the mass-production industries. Behind the growth of the CIO was the dynamic leadership of United Mine Workers president John L. Lewis. The AFL, faced with the loss of millions of potential members from the nation's core industries to the CIO, became more aggressive and flexible in its attitude toward organizing the unskilled. Externally, the policies of the New Deal, and later the exigencies of war with its labor shortage and military production demands, provided a favorable environment for organized labor.

Prelude: The National Industrial Recovery Act

The new Democratic administration of Franklin Delano Roosevelt in 1933 sought to extricate the nation from its worst economic depression ever. One of the earliest legislative efforts involved passage of the **National Industrial Recovery Act (NIRA)** on June 16, 1933.[39] The act created the **National Recovery Administration (NRA),** an agency through which the Roosevelt administration could exempt employers from the operation of the antitrust laws. Ultimately, through NRA prescribed codes, the administration hoped to stabilize prices, promote employment, raise wages, and provide emergency relief to the unemployed.

The NIRA also gave new hope to labor. In Section 7(a), which John L. Lewis helped draft, labor gained the right to bargain collectively with employers through representatives elected by the workers themselves. Although doubts were raised concerning the NIRA's constitutionality, its passage encouraged Sidney Hillman of the Amalgamated Clothing Workers, David Dubinsky of the International Ladies' Garment Workers Union, and John L. Lewis of the United Mine Workers to revive and rebuild their unions. In assessing their efforts, Irving Bernstein writes that "the rebuilding of the UMW, the Amalgamated, and the ILGWU in 1933 was of the utmost significance...to the future of the American labor movement. These developments formed an axle upon which trade unionism was to turn for most of a decade."[40]

The National Labor Relations Act

The bureaucratic and legalistic AFL could not control the labor unrest and militancy that arose after passage of the National Industrial Recovery Act. In 1934, work stoppages and strikes occurred throughout the nation, often involving whole communities. Auto parts workers struck in Toledo, Ohio; longshoremen in San Francisco; and truckers, freight-handlers, and produce-loaders in Minneapolis. Violent clashes with authorities, resulting in deaths and injuries on both sides, characterized all three strikes. The culmination was a general strike involving textile workers in New England and the South.

The NRA's enforcement powers were too weak to make anti-union companies abide by Section 7(a)'s provision for collective bargaining. In addition, widespread feeling among business leaders that the NIRA itself was unconstitutional encouraged numerous violations. Senator Robert F. Wagner, an influential and respected Democrat, was aware of the NIRA's weaknesses. He sought to remedy them through legislation that would establish a federal agency to protect labor's right to organize and seek resolution of disagreements through collective bargaining. To Wagner, strong unions meant higher wages, which would increase consumer purchasing power and lead to recovery and a strong economy.[41] Meanwhile, Roosevelt sought to strengthen the NRA's role in labor relations by creating a **National Labor Board (NLB)** to investigate and solve labor disputes. On May 27, 1935, however, the U.S. Supreme Court ruled the NIRA unconstitutional.

The prospect of unregulated labor–management relations was one the administration and congressional leaders did not want to deal with. Therefore, President Roosevelt and key congressional leaders supported passage of the **Wagner (National Labor Relations) Act** which became law on July 5, 1935. The act created the **National Labor Relations Board (NLRB)**, defined employer unfair labor practices, and protected labor from such practices as blacklisting and company unions. In essence, the Wagner Act committed the federal government to safeguarding and encouraging collective bargaining through independent unions. Passage of the Wagner Act marks a watershed in the history of American labor relations.

John L. Lewis and the Rise of the CIO

Although public policy measures created a better environment for labor, its leaders recognized that much work had to be done. John L. Lewis, a rough, burly man who could be a forceful and eloquent speaker, recognized that workers in the core industries of the U.S. economy had to be organized if labor was going to be a vital force in America. In this respect he disagreed with the veteran leadership of the AFL which argued that new recruits from the mass-production industries would destroy the labor movement.[42] Late in 1935, Lewis, Sidney Hillman, David Dubinsky, Charles Howard, and leaders from several small AFL affiliates founded the **Committee for Industrial Organization.** The name was later changed to the **Congress of Industrial Organizations (CIO)** when, three years after its founding, the CIO officially broke with the AFL.

From the beginning, the CIO carried on an aggressive campaign to organize the unskilled. In June 1936, the Steel Workers Organizing Committee was established. Rejecting the AFL's ambivalence toward political activism, the CIO supported the reelection of Franklin Delano Roosevelt in 1936. The president's resounding victory gave encouragement and a sense of momentum to the CIO's rank-and-file. In February 1937, the United Automobile Workers, after a six-day sitdown strike at various General Motors' Fisher Body plants in Flint, Michigan, won a union contract with the huge automotive company. This victory over one of the most powerful corporations in the world paved the way for the organization of other core industries.[43] Three weeks after the victory over General Motors, United States Steel recognized the Steel Workers Organizing Committee, a CIO affiliate.

Success in other basic industries followed, and membership soared. More than just achieving recognition and growth in numbers, the CIO brought a militancy and energy to the labor movement that had an impact on the day-to-day operation of plants and shops. "With the coming of the CIO," Robert H. Zieger writes in his *American Worker, American Unions, 1920–1985*, "struggles for shopfloor power rippled through scores of industrial plants, as triumphant activists now tried to redefine basic relationships." This **brass-knuckles unionism** was particularly characteristic of the United Automobile Workers and the Rubber Workers. Adding to the strength of the CIO was its appeal to a broad spectrum of workers. The CIO unions encouraged Afro-American membership and welcomed anticapitalist radicals, which included socialists, communists, and others.[44]

Union Power After the War

Strikes and bitter disputes over restrictive labor legislation characterized the period following World War II. The strikes signaled the growing power of organized labor, and the restrictive legislation disputes reflected the desire of management, political conservatives, and others to limit labor's influence on the shop floor as well as in American society. Indeed, in 1945, organized labor was stronger than it had ever been, having 14.5 million members, which was 35 percent of the civilian labor force. It had achieved the goal John L. Lewis had set in the 1930s—organization of the workers in the nation's industrial core. Moreover, federal legislation in the 1930s gave unions the legal standing and legitimacy that they never had before. Consequently, the AFL and the CIO became powerful institutions in the American economy.

Under William Green's leadership, the AFL embraced industrial unionism as well as supporting the growth of such old-line craft affiliates as the Machinists, Carpenters, Electrical Workers, and Teamsters. Unions in growing sectors of the postwar economy enabled the AFL to dominate the labor movement into the next decade. In addition, the AFL and the CIO had a group of young leaders who were superb organizers and excellent tacticians. Among the new generation of leaders were George Meany, an AFL officer; Dave Beck and James Hoffa, both Teamsters; A. Phillip Randolph, president of the Brotherhood of Sleeping Car Porters; and Walter and Victor Reuther, dynamic forces in the United Auto Workers.

The Postwar Strikes

The sudden end of the war meant cancellation of military orders, massive layoffs of workers, and the return of soldiers looking for permanent employment. Fear of a postwar depression similar to the one that followed World War I brought new worries to a nation that was war weary. Labor's rank-and-file, having been denied raises during the conflict, grew restless. Union leaders and workers were convinced that once wartime price controls ended, inflation would send the prices of goods and services soaring. In bargaining with employers, union officials sought substantial wage increases.

Impatient with management's intransigence, work stoppages and strikes began immediately after the war and reached a peak in the winter of 1946. Hundreds of thousands of automotive, steel, electrical appliance, and other mass-production workers went on strike. Confrontations between management and labor resulted in general strikes in cities such as Rochester, New York; Oakland, California; and Pittsburgh, Pennsylvania. The year 1946 ranks as one of the most strike-ridden in the nation's history. Unlike the railroad strike of 1877 or the sitdown strikes of 1937, however, these strikes were orderly. In the main, workers were willing to let their union leaders fight for higher wages and protection from inflation rather than reacting violently themselves.

Restrictive Labor Regulation: The Taft–Hartley Act

Leaders of major corporations, public officials, and members of the middle class, reacting to the epidemic of strikes in 1945 and 1946, sought to limit the power of organized labor. In bargaining with unions, management hoped to regain traditional prerogatives by including company-rights provisions in contracts. These contracts detailed the disciplinary measures taken in the event a union member violated its provisions; they also spelled out management rights such as setting production standards and schedules and imposing discipline in the workplace.

As anti-union sentiment grew after the war, labor's critics focused their attacks on the Wagner Act, arguing that it had made federal labor policy decidedly pro-union. When the Republican party gained control of both houses of Congress in 1946, support for new labor legislation became more vocal. Congress debated restrictive labor legislation in 1946 and early 1947. Eventually, it passed the **Taft–Hartley (Labor–Management Relations) Act** over President Truman's veto.

Sponsors of the bill sought to balance more equitably the interests of employers, workers, unions, and the general public by making the National Labor Relations Board a neutral body rather than an advocate for unionism. The act gave workers the right to reject unionism or to get rid of a union through decertification proceedings. Other provisions, for example, (1) outlawed the closed shop; (2) allowed employers to sue unions for failure to abide by contracts or for damages done during a strike; (3) prohibited union dues from being used for contributions to political campaigns; and (4) allowed states to pass laws prohibiting compulsory union membership clauses in collective bargaining.

Organized labor strenuously objected to the Taft–Hartley, arguing that the law placed labor in the same position it had occupied in the 1920s. Some, however, found consolation in that it had not repealed the right to organize, nor did it diminish federal government support for collective bargaining. Failing to prevent passage of the legislation, labor intensified its activities in the political arena. Although unions were forbidden to use dues for political donations, the CIO through its political action committee and the AFL through its Labor's League for Political Education, created in 1947, provided money and personnel for the 1948 election. Both federations recognized that the victory of pro-labor candidates was essential to labor's future. Organized labor's 15 million members and its many sympathizers made up an important voting bloc that could transform American politics. Support for Truman in 1948 demonstrated the power of the labor vote.

That labor's influence had limitations became apparent when it was unable to effect a revision of the Taft–Hartley Act, even though it had helped elect a Democratic president and Congress. Nonetheless, labor did have an impact on public policy issues involving education, civil rights, Social Security, medical care, economic growth policies, and foreign policy in the Truman and succeeding administrations. Labor was aided, of course, by an expanding postwar economy that promised a constantly rising standard of living.

Labor's public image, however, suffered in the immediate postwar period as charges of communist infiltration were leveled at certain unions, such as the International Longshoreman and Warehousemen and the United Electrical Workers. Although radical elements could be found in trade unions throughout the history of the labor movement, the periods following World Wars I and II were characterized by vigorous crusades to root out anti-American elements. Immediately after World War II, fundamental differences between the United States and Russia led to an intense rivalry for ideological supremacy and for global hegemony. What eventually became the cold war lasted more than four decades and had serious repercussions in the United States as citizens and public officials debated the nature and extent of the Soviet threat. Membership in the Communist party or sympathy with the Soviet experiment was enough to label one a traitor. The issue of communists and their involvement in the labor movement dominated public attention in the late 1940s and the 1950s.[45]

ORGANIZED LABOR IN THE AFFLUENT SOCIETY

The 1950s and 1960s were decades of economic prosperity, rising worker income, and success for the labor movement as a whole. A "no raiding" pact between the AFL and CIO in 1954 led to their merger in 1955, strengthening organized labor and enabling it to obtain for its members significant contract gains that altered working-class lifestyles as well as workers' behavior on the shop floor.

Labor Gains

Path-breaking contracts in the automotive industry led to automatic cost-of-living adjustments (COLAs) and increases for productivity gains (see Chapter 7 for details of these). Other outcomes of the collective bargaining process gave workers a level of economic security that no generation of workers ever had. In 1955, the UAW, under the leadership of Walter Reuther, was able to get auto companies to establish a special fund that would be used to pay workers unemployment benefits. This benefit was supplementary to funds provided by the states, and it eventually enabled laid-off workers to receive up to 95 percent of their normal wages (see Chapter 8 for the details of Supplementary Unemployment Benefits, or SUBs).

At the same time unions won other impressive nonwage benefits. Prior to 1945 such benefits as pensions, group insurance, and health plans were an outgrowth of corporate paternalism and were aimed, where they existed, at discouraging the growth of unions. In the 1950s, such benefits became major bargaining issues.

Not all workers, of course, obtained such generous benefits. Between organized and unorganized labor especially, there existed an ever-widening gap. Those in the nation's service, light manufacturing, and casual labor sector made less progress. The victories of organized labor, however, did set a standard for employers throughout the nation. As Zieger states:

> By the early 1970s, pensions, health insurance, and the like had become so commonplace that millions of Americans took these hard-won benefits for granted. Few remembered the generations of militancy that paved the way for the UMW's 1947 health plan, the sacrifices of striking steel workers in 1949 that gained the first substantial pension plan, or the strikes and shrewd bargaining of the UAW in 1949 and 1950 that created auto industry pensions.[46]

While contract negotiations in the 1950s and 1960s became well-publicized rituals, the real struggle between management and labor occurred on the shop floor. No matter how comprehensive contracts were, they could not cover all contingencies involving job assignments, work rules, discipline, grievances, and seniority rights. Consequently, the shop floors of local plants became "contested terrain," with management pushing for greater flexibility and control and labor arguing for limits to managerial authority.[47] What emerged through collective bargaining was a system in which employee grievances and employer-imposed discipline were covered in negotiated contracts. When disputes arose that were not covered, a grievance procedure ending in outside binding arbitration by a neutral third party was used. Issues that previously were settled through wildcat strikes, slowdowns, and other tactics now were subject to procedures that brought order and a measure of fairness to the workplace. This was an important outcome of the labor movement, one that imposed a **workplace rule of law** in major U.S. manufacturing plants.[48]

Labor Losses

An important consequence that all these developments had on organized labor was the creation of a huge bureaucracy. Accountants, lawyers, economists, health and safety experts, investment analysts, and other professionals became important in the everyday operations of labor organizations as well as in setting their long-term goals. Contracts that covered pay and economic supplements, defined the content and pace of work, established discipline and grievance procedures, and dealt with other issues were complex and lengthy documents that gave labor relations a highly legalistic and inflexible character. The federal government's efforts to rid unions of corruption and to restore democratic rights to its members further exacerbated this tendency by adding to the complexity governing union activities. Important in this vein was the **Landrum–Griffin (Labor–Management Reporting & Disclosure) Act** (1959), which imposed strict financial reporting requirements and regulations governing internal standards of conduct for unions.

Organized labor also faced the challenge of declining membership. As a percentage of the labor force, unionized workers had begun to decline in the late 1950s. An unalterable fact was that the expanding postwar economy was creating more jobs in the service sector than in manufacturing. The overwhelming majority of what became known as white-collar jobs was found in banking, insurance, retailing, and government. Many involved clerical and sales work. These nonunion jobs were generally low-paying and often dead-end positions. Offsetting the decline in union membership, however, was the organization of the rapidly expanding public sector, which consisted of government workers, many in white-collar jobs. The efforts of the American Federation of State, County, and Municipal Employees (AFSCME), the American Federation of Teachers (AFT), and other unions consisting of firefighters, police, nurses, postal employees, and other civil servants brought in millions of new members. By the early 1970s, the AFSCME became one of the largest AFL–CIO affiliates. Strikes, once a rarity in the public sector, became commonplace in the late 1960s.

Other problems surfaced. Critics, among them labor's supporters, charged that as trade unions became bureaucratic institutions, they had lost their sense of social purpose and commitment to the workers' welfare. To a certain extent, such criticism was justified. Success and prosperity diminished idealism and common purpose among labor's leadership. But the same could be said for workers, too. However precarious union gains in the mass production sector were, the obvious fact was that the rise of an affluent working class had no historical precedent. For many assembly line workers and others, affluence meant a change in lifestyle. As incomes rose, blue-collar workers abandoned ethnic, working-class neighborhoods for the suburbs. Less important in their lives were the union halls, saloons, and social centers—institutions that nurtured solidarity and community. Consumption, a solitary activity, became an important focus of suburban living, and the struggles of the 1930s and 1940s faded to a distant dream.

Also complicating labor relations was the entrance in the 1960s of a new generation of workers. Rather than supporting the leadership on traditional bread-and-butter is-sues, this group, a product of postwar affluence, was concerned with the quality of life in the workplace. They rebelled against the boredom, tedium, and relentless pace of mass-production work. They resented, as did older workers, the heavy toll the assembly line took on their emotional and physical well-being. Union leaders failed to understand the complaints that were at the heart of the "blue-collar blues." In spite of high wages and excellent benefits, absenteeism, drug abuse, and alcoholism began to plague the nation's factories and, ultimately, affected the quality of products that consumers purchased. A special task force appointed by Elliot Richardson, Secretary of Health, Education, and Welfare, reported in its investigative study, *Work in America* (1973), that large numbers of workers were dissatisfied with their jobs. Where such discontent existed, the taskforce concluded:

> The productivity of the worker is low—as measured by absenteeism, turnover rates, wildcat strikes, sabotage, poor quality products, and a reluctance by workers to commit themselves to their work tasks. Moreover, a growing body of research indicates that, as work problems increase, there may be a consequent decline in physical and mental health, family stability, community participation and cohesiveness, and "balanced" sociopolitical attitudes, while there is an increase in drug and alcohol addiction, aggression, and delinquency.[49]

By the 1970s, pervasive discontent over the way work was organized affected all segments of the labor force: blue collar and white collar.

The End of the Postwar Affluence?

Worker discontent was not the only problem facing organized labor. The vaunted U.S. economy's performance began to weaken as productivity declined, inflation increased, unemployment grew, and other problems in major economic institutions surfaced. Domestic manufacturing faced stiff competition from foreign firms, which produced higher quality products more cheaply. As a result, the economic engines that drove the powerful twentieth-century American economy began to atrophy. USX, General Motors, RCA, and many other core industry companies suffered from declining profits and diminishing market share. Unemployment soared in the 1970s and early 1980s as companies eliminated jobs and shut down plants. Some firms, looking to cut costs, relocated manufacturing operations abroad, where unions did not exist, or established plants in states that had right-to-work laws that weakened unions. According to one estimate, such corporate-level decisions involving private disinvestment in plant and equipment during the 1970s and early 1980s cost the nation 32 million jobs. New jobs were created, but many of these were in the low-wage, nonunion service sector.[50]

Intense global competition, structural changes in the U.S. economy and labor force, a shift in public policy favoring deregulation, and other domestic and international changes put organized labor in a position comparable to the 1920s. The general public questioned whether contemporary unions had any meaningful social purpose in American life. Other setbacks accompanied organized labor's declining image. Organizing campaigns failed; established unions were decertified; labor's political influence waned; and its membership dwindled. In 1954, 35 percent of the workforce was unionized; in 1980, 21 percent; and in 1989, 16 percent.[51]

The accession of Ronald Reagan to the presidency accelerated organized labor's decline. The appointment of conservative members to the NLRB helped management not only block union organization, but also displace unions where they already existed. Seven months into his presidency, Reagan set the tone for his administration's labor policy by firing and permanently replacing 11,500 striking federal air traffic controllers after they defied a back-to-work order. As a result of Reagan's actions, the controllers' union collapsed. The new president's action set a precedent that became popular with private as well as public sector management throughout the 1980s. Permanent replacements, drawn from the ranks of the unemployed or from those holding low-paying jobs, became part of management's arsenal when faced with striking unions.[52] Such actions were reminiscent of management's use of scabs, who were temporary replacements rather than permanent ones. Overall, the labor relations environment of the Reagan era was similar to that which existed in the 1920s under the American Plan.

On a more positive note, leading union and nonunion companies in the United States began developing new relationships that involved, in varying degrees, employee participation in problem solving and production decisions, the creation of flexible teams, job enrichment and enlargement policies, gain-sharing, and other innovative practices that encouraged cooperative work systems.[53] Whether these new management tools and techniques are the basis of a new labor relations system will depend on whether the adversarial tradition, based on irreconcilable differences and competing interests, can be overcome. The outcome, it seems, will also depend on whether management and labor can identify mutual interests and develop relationships based on respect and trust, shared goals, and a willingness to form mutually advantageous partnerships rather than continuing their traditional adversarial relationship. The bloody ground of U.S. labor history suggests that the birth of a new era in labor relations will be a difficult one.

DISCUSSION QUESTIONS

1. Why did England's efforts to regulate colonial labor markets, employer–employee relations, and economic activity in general fail?

2. Compare the Tudor Industrial Code with today's labor laws. In particular, what are the differences between the two, and why do the differences exist?

3. What are the differences between today's unions and colonial mechanic societies?

4. Explain how new technology and the factory system in the nineteenth century led to a changed status for skilled and unskilled workers.

5. Historically, the labor movement worked for the achievement of social and economic goals. Labor's appeal rested on a vision of America in which the economic risks of a free market economy were reduced and public policy supported a form of democratic capitalism that had equalitarian elements. Give examples from the nineteenth and twentieth centuries of specific labor groups and goals sought.

6. Compare and contrast the overall philosophy and goals of the Knights of Labor, the American Federation of Labor, and the Industrial Workers of the World.

7. Samuel Gompers believed that only skilled (craft) workers could support a trade union and a trade union federation. What was his reasoning for this belief?

8. Name three possible advantages of organizing *unskilled* workers.

9. How did employers in the late nineteenth and early twentieth centuries meet the challenge of the trade union movement?

10. This chapter explained how the NAM battled organized labor. Given its differing philosophy and membership, how do you think the NCF battled organized labor?

11. The failed unions mentioned in this chapter had in common the ideas of "one big union" and some reform orientation. How did these two points contribute to their downfall?

12. Explain voluntarism, and the reasons for its final rejection by the AFL in the 1920–1930 period.

13. Define paternalism. Henry Ford's Five Dollar Day Plan combined paternalism and self-interest. Why did it fail?

14. Describe the tactics used by management in the so-called American Plan of the 1920s.

15. Define welfare capitalism and explain why, despite good intentions, it failed as an alternative to trade unions.

16. Why do historians regard the 1935 National Labor Relations Act as a watershed in the history of U.S. labor relations?

17. Discuss the philosophy and goals of the Congress of Industrial Organizations (CIO).

18. How did the merger of the AFL and the CIO strengthen organized labor?

19. Discuss the successes and failures of the labor movement in the 1950s and 1960s.

20. What is meant by the term *blue-collar blues*. How was this condition resolved?

21. Discuss changes in the U.S. economy that have occurred between 1973 and the present, and the impact these changes have had on U.S. labor-management relations during this period.

22. How did the decades of Ronald Reagan and the American Plan resemble each other in terms of labor relations? How did they differ? Do you think the decade after Reagan's presidency will similarly reflect the decade after the American Plan? Why or why not?

VOCABULARY LIST

Tudor Industrial Code
mechanic society
merchant capitalist
factory system
Conspiracy Cases

Philadelphia Mechanics Union of Trade Associations
city federation
National Trades' Union
blacklisting

National Labor Union (NLU)

Knights of Labor (KOL)

American Federation of Labor (AFL)

Federation of Organized Trade and Labor Unions (FOTLU)

business (bread-and-butter) unionism

voluntarism

American Railway Union (ARU)

Sherman Antitrust Act of 1890

Industrial Workers of the World (IWW)

Wobblies

syndicalist philosophy

National Association of Manufacturers (NAM)

National Civic Federation (NCF)

Progressives

Progressive Movement

Five Dollar Day Plan

American Plan

yellow-dog contract

labor injunction

employee representation plan

company union

welfare capitalism

personnel management movement

Clayton Act of 1914

National Industrial Recovery Act (NIRA)

National Recovery Administration (NRA)

National Labor Board (NLB)

Wagner (National Labor Relations) Act

National Labor Relations Board (NLRB)

Committee for Industrial Organization

Congress of Industrial Organizations (CIO)

brass-knuckles unionism

Taft–Hartley (Labor–Management Relations) Act

workplace rule of law

Landrum–Griffin (Labor–Management Reporting & Disclosure) Act

FOOTNOTES

1. Joseph G. Rayback, *A History of American Labor* (Free Press, 1966), pp. 7–11; Henry Pelling, *American Labor* (University of Chicago Press, 1960), pp. 3–6.

2. Carl Bridenbaugh, *Cities in the Wilderness* (Oxford University Press, 1966), pp. 175–205; Gary B. Nash, *The Urban Crucible* (Harvard University Press, 1979).

3. Carl Bridenbaugh, *The Colonial Craftsmen* (University of Chicago Press, 1966), p. 6.

4. Rayback, *A History of American Labor*, p. 12.

5. Ibid., pp. 13–23; Gary B. Nash, "The Failure of Female Labor in Colonial Boston," in Daniel J. Leab, ed., *The Labor History Reader* (University of Illinois Press, 1985), pp. 42–65; Richard B. Morris, *Government and Labor in Early America* (Harper & Row, 1965), p. 20.

6. Rayback, *A History of American Labor*, pp. 4, 17, 47.

7. Henry C. Dethloff, *Americans and Free Enterprise* (Prentice-Hall, 1979), pp. 69–86; George Rogers Taylor, *The Transportation Revolution, 1815–1860* (Harper & Row, 1968).

8. See Norman Ware, *The Industrial Worker, 1840–1860* (Quadrangle Books, 1964); Jonathan Prude, *The Coming of Industrial Order: Town and Factory Life in Rural Massachusetts, 1810–1860* (Cambridge University Press, 1983); Alan Dawley, *Class and Community: The Industrial Revolution in Lynn* (Cambridge University Press, 1976).

9. See Caroline F. Ware, *The Early New England Cotton Manufacture: A Study of Industrial Beginnings* (Houghton Mifflin, 1931).

10. Rayback, *A History of American Labor*, pp. 56–59.

11. Ibid., pp. 75–128.

12. Ibid., pp. 92–103; Pelling, *American Labor*, pp. 21–47.

13. Prude, *The Coming of Industrial Order*, pp. 217–237.

14. Quoted in Dethloff, *Americans and Free Enterprise*, p. 148. For a description and analysis of these developments, see Alfred D. Chandler, Jr., *The Visible Hand: The Managerial Revolution in American Business* (Harvard University Press, 1977), pp. 285–314; John A. Garraty, *The New Commonwealth* (Harper & Row, 1968), pp. 78–127; Ray Ginger, *Age of Excess* (Macmillan, 1965), pp. 19–34; Edward C. Kirkland, *Industry Comes of Age* (Quadrangle Books, 1967), pp. 163–180 and 195–215.

15. See David Montgomery, *Workers' Control in America* (Cambridge University Press, 1979); Herbert G. Guttman, *Power and Culture* (Pantheon Books, 1987), pp. 70–92.

16. For a description of the strike, see Robert V. Bruce, *1877: Year of Violence* (Bobbs–Merrill, 1959); Phillip S. Foner, *The Great Labor Uprising of 1877* (Monad Press, 1977).

17. Leon Wolff, *Lockout: The Story of the Homestead Strike of 1892* (Harper & Row, 1965).

18. Almont Lindsey, *The Pullman Strike* (University of Chicago Press, 1964) describes and analyzes the strike with the events leading up to it. Stanley Buder, *Pullman: An Experiment in Industrial Order and Community Planning, 1880–1930* (Oxford University Press, 1967) focuses on George Pullman's social philosophy and how it was reflected in the town he built and the company he ran.

19. Gerald N. Grab, *Workers and Utopia: A Study of Ideological Conflict in the American Labor Movement, 1865–1900* (Quadrangle Books, 1969), p. 38; Garraty, *The New Commonwealth*, p. 162. The Knights of Labor are also discussed extensively in Norman Ware, *The Labor Movement in the United States, 1860–1895* (Vintage Books, 1964); Leon Fink, *Workingmen's Democracy: The Knights of Labor and American Politics* (University of Illinois Press, 1983).

20. Rayback, *A History of American Labor*, p. 194.

21. Lindsey, *The Pullman Strike*.

22. Melvin Dubofsky, *We Shall Be All: A History of the Industrial Workers of the World* (Quadrangle Books, 1969), p. 156.

23. Ibid., pp. 227–262; Ettor was acquitted later.

24. Chandler, *The Visible Hand*, pp. 81–121 and pp. 337–483.

25. Discussion of the Progressive Movement is based on William L. O'Neill, *The Progressive Years: America Comes of Age* (Dodd, Mead & Co., 1975).

26. Daniel Nelson, *Managers and Workers: Origins of the New Factory System in the United States, 1880–1920* (University of Wisconsin Press, 1975).

27. Stephen Meyer III, *The Five Dollar Day: Labor, Management and Social Control in the Ford Motor Company, 1908–1921* (State University of New York Press, 1981), pp. 5–6.

28. Ibid., p. 115.

29. Pelling, *American Labor*, p. 136; Rayback, *A History of American Labor*, p. 312.

30. Robert H. Zieger, *American Workers, American Unions, 1920–1985* (Johns Hopkins University Press, 1986), pp. 3–10; Irving Bernstein, *A History of the American Worker, 1920–1933: The Lean Years* (Houghton Mifflin, 1972).

31. Bernstein, *A History of the American Worker*, pp. 153–154.

32. Ibid., p. 165.

33. Ibid., pp. 171–174.

34. Stuart D. Brandes, *American Welfare Capitalism, 1880–1940* (University of Chicago Press, 1970), pp. 5–6.

35. Bernstein, *A History of the American Worker*, p. 183.

36. David Brody, *Workers in Industrial America: Essays on the 20th Century Struggle* (Oxford University Press, 1980), p. 47.

37. Zieger, *American Workers*, p. 26; Bernstein, *A History of the American Worker*, pp. 83–143.

38. For a history of the rebirth of the labor movement, see Irving Bernstein, *A History of the American Worker, 1933–1941: Turbulent Years* (Houghton Mifflin, 1970); Zieger's summary in *American Workers, American Unions* provides a solid overview (pp. 26–61).

39. Bernstein, *A History of the American Worker, 1933–1941*, pp. 30–36.

40. Ibid., p. 89.

41. Ibid., pp. 330–333.

42. See Melvyn Dubofsky and Warren Van Tine, *John L. Lewis: A Biography* (New York Times Book Co., 1977).

43. For an account of the strike and its consequences, see Sidney Fine, *Sit Down: The General Motors Strike of 1936–1937* (University of Michigan Press, 1969).

44. Zieger, *American Workers, American Unions*, p. 51.

45. For a thoughtful history of the 1940s and 1950s, see John Patrick Diggins, *The Proud Decades* (W. W. Norton, 1988).

46. Zieger, *American Workers, American Unions*, p. 153.

47. See Richard Edwards, *Contested Terrain* (Basic Books, 1979).

48. Brody, *Workers in Industrial America*, pp. 173–211.

49. Quoted in Harry Braverman, *Labor and Monopoly Capital* (Monthly Review Press, 1974), p. 31.

50. Barry Bluestone and Bennett Harrison, *The Deindustrialization of America* (Basic Books, 1982), p. 26.

51. *Business Week*, May 7, 1990, p. 24.

52. *New York Times*, March 13, 1990, p. A12.

53. For these new developments in U.S. labor relations, see Thomas A. Kochan, Harry C. Katz, and Robert B. McKersie, *The Transformation of American Industrial Relations* (Basic Books, 1986).

REFERENCES

BERNSTEIN, IRVING. *A History of the American Worker, 1920–1933: The Lean Years.* Houghton Mifflin, 1972.

————. *A History of the American Worker, 1933–1941: Turbulent Years.* Houghton Mifflin, 1970.

BLUESTONE, BARRY, and BENNETT HARRISON. *The Deindustrialization of America.* Basic Books, 1982.

BRANDES, STUART D. *American Welfare Capitalism, 1880–1940.* University of Chicago Press, 1970.

BRAVERMAN, HARRY. *Labor and Monopoly Capital.* Monthly Review Press, 1974.

BRIDENBAUGH, CARL. *The Colonial Craftsmen.* University of Chicago Press, 1966.

BRODY, DAVID. *Steelworkers in America: The Nonunion Era.* Harper & Row, 1969.

————. *Workers in Industrial America: Essays on the 20th Century Struggle.* Oxford University Press, 1980.

BRUCE, ROBERT V. *1877: Year of Violence.* Bobbs–Merrill Co., 1959.

BUDER, STANLEY. *Pullman: An Experiment in Industrial Order and Community Planning, 1880–1930.* Oxford University Press, 1967.

CANTOR, MILTON, ed. *American Workingclass Culture.* Greenwood Press, 1979.

COCHRAN, THOMAS C., and WILLIAM MILLER. *A Social History of Industrial America.* Harper & Row, 1961.

DAWLEY, ALAN. *Class and Community: The Industrial Revolution in Lynn.* Harvard University Press, 1976.

DERTOUZOS, MICHAEL L., RICHARD K. LESTER, ROBERT M. SOLOW et al. *Made in America.* MIT Press, 1989.

DETHLOFF, HENRY C. *Americans and Free Enterprise.* Prentice-Hall, 1979.

DIGGINS, JOHN PATRICK. *The Proud Decades.* W. W. Norton, 1988.

DUBOFSKY, MELVYN. *We Shall Be All: A History of the Industrial Workers of the World.* Quadrangle Books, 1969.

EDWARDS, RICHARD. *Contested Terrain.* Basic Books, 1979.

EHRLICH, RICHARD L., ed. *Immigrants in Industrial America, 1850–1920*. University Press of Virginia, 1977.

FINE, SIDNEY. *Sit Down: The General Motors Strike of 1936–1937*. University of Michigan Press, 1969.

FINK, LEON. *Workingmen's Democracy: The Knights of Labor and American Politics*. University of Illinois Press, 1983.

FONER, PHILLIP S. *The Great Labor Uprising of 1877*. Monad Press, 1977.

GARRATY, JOHN A. *The New Commonwealth*. Harper & Row, 1968.

GINGER, RAY. *Age of Excess*. Macmillan, 1965.

GRAB, GERALD N. *Workers and Utopia: A Study of Ideological Conflict in the American Labor Movement, 1865–1900*. Quadrangle Books, 1969.

GUTTMAN, HERBERT G. *Power and Culture*. Pantheon Books, 1987.

———. *Work, Culture, and Society*. Random House, 1977.

KIRKLAND, EDWARD C. *Industry Comes of Age*. Quadrangle Books, 1967.

KOCHAN, THOMAS A., HARRY C. KATZ, and ROBERT B. MCKERSIE. *The Transformation of American Industrial Relations*. Basic Books, 1986.

LEAB, DANIEL J., ed. *The Labor History Reader*. University of Illinois Press, 1985.

LINDSEY, ALMONT. *The Pullman Strike*. University of Chicago Press, 1964.

LIVESAY, HAROLD C. *Samuel Gompers and Organized Labor in America*. Little, Brown, 1978.

MAGAZINER, IRA C., and ROBERT B. REICH. *Minding America's Business: The Decline and Rise of the American Economy*. Harcourt Brace Jovanovich, 1982.

MEYER, STEPHEN, III. *The Five Dollar Day: Labor, Management and Social Control in the Ford Motor Company, 1908–1921*. State University of New York Press, 1981.

MONTGOMERY, DAVID. *Workers' Control in America*. Cambridge University Press, 1979.

MORRIS, RICHARD B. *Government and Labor in Early America*. Harper & Row, 1965.

NELSON, DANIEL. *Managers and Workers: Origins of the New Factory System in the United States, 1880–1920*. University of Wisconsin Press, 1975.

O'NEILL, WILLIAM L. *The Progressive Years: America Comes of Age*. Dodd, Mead & Co., 1975.

PELLING, HENRY. *American Labor*. University of Chicago Press, 1960.

PRUDE, JONATHAN. *The Coming of Industrial Order: Town and Factory Life in Rural Massachusetts, 1810–1860*. Cambridge University Press, 1983.

PUSATERI, C. JOSEPH. *A History of American Business*. Harlan Davidson, 1984.

RAYBACK, JOSEPH G. *A History of American Labor*. Free Press, 1966.

REICH, ROBERT B. *The Next American Frontier*. New York Times Books, 1983.

SCHATZ, RONALD W. *The Electrical Workers: A History of Labor at General Electric and Westinghouse, 1923–1960*. University of Illinois Press, 1983.

SILVERMAN, BERTRAM, and MURRAY YANOWITCH, eds. *The Worker in "Post-Industrial" Capitalism.* The Free Press, 1974.

TAYLOR, GEORGE ROGERS. *The Transportation Revolution, 1815–1860.* Harper & Row, 1968.

WARE, CAROLINE F. *The Early New England Cotton Manufacture: A Study of Industrial Beginnings.* Houghton Mifflin, 1931.

WARE, NORMAN J. *The Industrial Worker, 1840–1860.* Quadrangle Books, 1964.

————. *The Labor Movement in the United States, 1860–1895: A Study in Democracy.* Vintage Books, 1964.

WOLFF, LEON. *Lockout: The Story of the Homestead Strike of 1892.* Harper & Row, 1965.

ZIEGER, ROBERT H. *American Workers, American Unions, 1920–1985.* Johns Hopkins University Press, 1986.

CHAPTER 3

LABOR AND EMPLOYMENT LAW

L abor law in the United States is composed of common law decisions, statutory enactments, and administrative rules and regulations. In addition to state and federal laws, private agreements have also helped to mold employers' and employees' rights, duties, and responsibilities. Through the years labor law has evolved with the changing demands of society.

Labor relations, or **collective bargaining,** was initially governed by common law. Only in the last decade of the nineteenth century did statutes begin to regulate the labor–management relationship and the status of trade unions. The Sherman Act (1890), followed by the Clayton and Federal Trade Commission Acts (1914), were the first laws to address this area. All three, however, were designed primarily to regulate the trade practices of business, mainly antitrust activities.

The first of several labor laws that dealt primarily or exclusively with labor–management relations was the Railway Labor Act of 1926. This law was followed by the Norris–LaGuardia Act of 1932 and the National Industrial Recovery Act of 1933. This legislation set the stage for the passage of the National Labor Relations (Wagner) Act of 1935, the basic law that, with its amendments, now governs labor–management relations.

In this chapter we will first review the early history of labor law from its beginnings in English common law to 1935. We follow this with a discussion of the National Labor Relations Act which forms the modern context of labor law and other laws that continue to affect labor relations today.

COMMON LAW AND THE FOUNDATION OF LABOR RELATIONS

Common law, or **case law,** originated in England and was brought to this country by the early settlers. It requires that all cases follow precedent, that is, the rules established by a judge in a previously litigated case based on the same or similar issues.

Common law develops by a simple procedure. Let's say a dispute arises between two or more individuals or groups of individuals. One party, called the plaintiff or petitioner, depending on the type of relief being sought from the court, sues the other party, called the defendant or respondent.* After hearing the parties' arguments, the judge states the law either orally or in a written decision. If either party desires, the decision may be appealed to a higher court within that jurisdiction. Once all appeals are completed and a final judgment is rendered, the case terminates. Each appellate court usually writes a statement explaining the legal rationale used in reaching its decision; this writing is called the **opinion** and becomes part of the common law of that area or jurisdiction.

The legal reasoning used by the highest court ruling on the case is binding on all future cases dealing with similar legal issues. It becomes the precedent for other cases: this principle is known as **stare decisis,** which means "to stand by decided matters." Only when social views or economic conditions require it does a court overrule a precedent.[1] Thus, when the first labor cases were tried in the United States during the 1800s, the court relied heavily on decisions rendered by the English courts which dealt with similar issues. The decisions in those English cases were only guidelines. The U.S. courts did not have to follow them, but they tended to do so because of the *stare decisis* principle. Only later did changing social views demand a different approach.

Common Law and English Labor

Under English common law (except during the feudal period), individual employees were generally able to negotiate with their employers and often obtained **at-will contracts** by which either party could terminate the agreement at any time desired. But the English courts had a less equitable attitude toward employees who attempted to bargain as a group.

The roots of labor law as it relates to collective bargaining date back to 1348 when the Black Death ravaged the workforce. In order to help employers survive this troubled time, ordinances were passed in 1349 and 1351 to fix wages, regulate terms of employment, and prohibit third persons from enticing away another's employee. In 1562, the Elizabethan Statute of Laborers, the first comprehensive code, was enacted.[2] After that, laborers had great difficulty obtaining any rights or benefits from employers. Any attempts to better their lot in life by collective bargaining were thwarted.

---

* A plaintiff is a person primarily seeking monetary relief from a defendant. A petitioner is a party primarily seeking an equitable remedy, that is, requesting the court to force the respondent to specifically do an act or refrain from doing an act. Courts are reluctant to give equitable relief unless monetary damages fail to cure the petitioner's problem.

When employees attempted to bargain collectively, employers asserted that statutes were being violated and employees were charged. When the English courts did not find that statutes were violated, employers claimed that collective bargaining itself was a criminal conspiracy. One famous case based on that theory was *Rex v. Journeymen Tailors of Cambridge*, decided in 1721.[3] The tailors agreed not to work for less than a set salary, and after trial, the court convicted them of common law conspiracy.

Common Law Comes to the New World

In the United States some of the early courts followed the arguments established by the English courts. Often the courts found that workers refusing to work for less than a specified rate and attempting to stop others from reaching independent contracts for employment were involved in criminal conspiracies. In approximately 17 trials between 1806 and 1842, labor unions were charged with conspiracies. In some cases, employees were indicted and convicted of criminal conspiracies, and many received jail terms.

Most of the cases held that a broad range of employees' activities that intended to interfere with the right of an employer to manage the business constituted criminal conspiracy. One case, however, held that employees attempting only to bargain collectively for themselves still constituted a criminal conspiracy. That case was *Commonwealth v. Pullis* (Philadelphia Mayor's Court, 1806), more commonly referred to as the Philadelphia Cordwainers case. In that case a group of shoemakers were charged with criminal conspiracy because they struck to increase their rate of pay. They were convicted.[4]

Although most cases found labor's activities illegal, one did not: In *People v. Melvin* in 1809, journeymen were allowed to work as a group as long as they did not "deprive their fellow citizens of rights as precious as any contended for."[5] The courts' conflicting decisions caused great confusion for workers and impeded the development of the labor movement.

Finally, there was a public outcry that criminal punishment was an inappropriate means for controlling workers' activities. In the landmark decision of 1842, *Commonwealth v. Hunt*, the Massachusetts Supreme Court dismissed a criminal indictment against a group of bootmakers for refusing to work for their employer until the employer discharged a journeyman who did not belong to the Boston Journeymen Bootmakers' Society. The trial court found the journeymen guilty of criminal conspiracy, but on appeal Chief Justice Lemuel S. Shaw, writing for the court, stated that unions or associations

> may be entered into, the object of which is to adopt measures that may have a tendency to impoverish another, that is, to diminish his gains and profits, and yet so far from being criminal or unlawful, the object may be highly meritorious and public spirited. The legality of such an association will therefore depend upon the means to be used for its accomplishment. If it is to be carried into effect by fair or honorable and lawful means, it is, to say the least, innocent; if by falsehood or force, it may be stamped with the character of conspiracy. It follows as a necessary consequence, that if criminal and indictable, it is so by

reason of the criminal means intended to be employed for its accomplishment; and as a further legal consequence, that as the criminality will depend on the means, those means must be stated in the indictment.[6]

Thus, the court adopted a position now referred to as the **ends/means test,** which simply required proof of either an illegal purpose (end) or use of an illegal method (means) in order for a conviction to stand. The results of this case encouraged the shift from criminal to civil liability as a means of controlling labor association activities. This ends/means test was subsequently used in civil actions (noncriminal cases) where parties wanted to stop certain conduct.

ANTITRUST ACTS: THE LEGISLATURE JOINS THE FRAY

Although the Sherman, Clayton, and Federal Trade Commission (FTC) Acts were aimed primarily at regulating monopolies and monopolistic actions, they also covered some aspects of labor–management relations. The 1890 Sherman Act did not specifically govern labor unions, but its antitrust provisions were applied to them and thus impeded the spread of unionization. The Clayton and FTC Acts (1914) specifically addressed the question of unions and unionization, especially to protect labor organizations from prosecution as monopolies under the Sherman Act.

The Sherman Act: Strikes at Monopolies

Pursuant to the Commerce Clause of the U.S. Constitution (Article I, Section 8, Clause 3) and the Necessary and Proper Clause (Article I, Section 8, Clause 18), Congress had the authority to regulate labor relations in interstate commerce.[7] In 1890, Congress passed the **Sherman Antitrust Act** (15 U.S.C. Sections 1-7), better known as the Sherman Act, to prohibit restraint of trade and monopolization. Although it was passed in response to activities by large companies, the act was applied in numerous federal cases to all kinds of anticompetitive actions, including union activities.

Sections 1 and 2 of the act are the substantive provisions and most important.

- *Section 1* states that "[e]very contract, combination in the form of trust or otherwise, or conspiracy, in restraint of trade or commerce" is illegal. This language, though very broad, was intended to apply to individual groups that conspired together, rather than to monopolies.

- *Section 2* states that "every person who shall monopolize, or combine or conspire to monopolize any part of the trade or commerce among the several states . . . shall be deemed guilty of a felony." Thus, monopolizing was made illegal.

Section 1 of the act was applied to a number of cases. In the landmark case of *Loewe v. Lawlor* [208 U.S. 274 (1908)], better known as the Danbury Hatters' case, the court used the Sherman Act against union activity. At issue was a nationwide boycott by the American Federation of Labor (AFL) of retail stores that sold hats produced by the D. E. Loewe Company of Danbury, Connecticut. The AFL was trying to help the Hatters' Union organize. The company filed suit under the Sherman Act asserting that the boycott was a conspiracy in restraint of trade and that treble damages, in the amount of $240,000, should be awarded. The district court dismissed the case, but it was then appealed. The U. S. Supreme Court reversed the decision and sent the case back to the trial court. The union's activities were found to be in restraint of trade under the Sherman Act. (An abridged copy of the Court's decision can be found in the appendix following this chapter.)

Another landmark decision was *Gompers v. Bucks Stove and Range Company* [221 U.S. 418 (1911)]. In that case the Supreme Court held that it was illegal under the Sherman Act to encourage a boycott by either spoken or printed words. The facts in the case were quite simple: the American Federation of Labor printed the name of a company in the "We Don't Patronize" list in its publication. This was illegal. Again, this type of result encouraged the public to seek an amendment to the Sherman Act.

During the same year, Chief Justice Edward D. White adopted a **rule of reason** in the important case of *Standard Oil Company v. United States*.[8] The rule of reason condemned only restraints that in effect were unreasonably anticompetitive. In applying the rule of reason, a court had to determine what harm was done to the competition from the alleged restraint, what the purpose of the restraint was, and whether a less restrictive alternative could have been used to attain the same result. The rule of reason is still applied in most cases today.

Finally, in *Coronado Coal Company v. United Mine Workers of America* [268 U.S. 295 (1925)], the U.S. Supreme Court held that when the intent of those preventing the production of an item is to control the supply of items entering or moving in interstate commerce, then the action is a direct violation of Section 1 of the Sherman Act. It should be noted that if the Sherman Act, Section 1, were given a literal interpretation, every contract dealing with goods in interstate commerce would violate it.

Currently, if a person is criminally prosecuted under either sections 1 or 2 of the Sherman Act, he or she can be found guilty of a felony, fined up to $100,000, and/or imprisoned up to three years. A corporation could be liable up to $1 million. In a civil action remedies include divestiture or dissolution.

A Sherman Backlash: The Clayton Act and the Federal Trade Commission Act

Cases such as *Loewe v. Lawlor* led to growing displeasure with the failure of the Sherman Act and its application not only to unfair trade practices or methods of competition, but also to union activities. Thus, in 1914 there was sufficient interest in Congress to pass the **Clayton Act**[9] and the **Federal Trade Commission Act**.[10]

The Clayton Act has four substantive sections:

- Section 2, which was subsequently amended by the Robinson–Patman Act, prohibits certain types of price discrimination.[11]
- Section 3 prohibits tying agreements* and other exclusive dealing agreements.

* A tying agreement is an arrangement whereby one party agrees to supply a product if the other party takes another of its products, usually unwanted.

- Section 7 prohibits certain corporate mergers.

- Section 8 prohibits interlocking directorates (that is, no individual can serve on the board of any two competitive companies over a specified size).

The Justice Department, the Federal Trade Commission, and private parties may bring actions for equitable relief under Section 16 of the act. Any person may also sue for treble damages, the cost of the suit, and reasonable attorney's fee pursuant to Section 4 of the act.[12]

The Federal Trade Commission Act was enacted primarily to establish the Federal Trade Commission (FTC). The FTC has five commissioners whose job is to monitor business conduct, to advise Congress regarding antitrust matters, and to enforce the Clayton and Federal Trade Commission Acts. The commission has the authority to issue cease and desist orders to stop "unfair methods of competition" and "unfair or deceptive acts or practices in or affecting commerce."[13] The cease and desist orders require offenders to stop pursuing the unlawful conduct; violators accept them through consent orders, rather than go through lengthy administrative hearings. Violation of a cease and desist order can result in a $10,000 per day fine. In 1938, the Wheeler–Lea Act added the language making "unfair or deceptive acts or practices" illegal. In 1975, the section was again amended to makes acts "affecting" commerce unlawful conduct.

Recently, the FTC has been unusually inactive, especially during the Reagan administration. In the eight years of that administration, the FTC filed an average of less than half the number of cases filed annually in the 17 previous years, and many of the largest mergers went unchallenged by the FTC on antitrust grounds. States have responded to this lax federal enforcement by becoming more active in areas such as antitrust and consumer protection.[14]

Although Congress desired to reduce the unions' exposure to antitrust liability by passing these acts, the courts continued to give the law a narrow interpretation and often issued injunctions *ex parte* (one-sided or without both sides first having a right to a hearing). In effect, the court would stop a union strike or other activity first, and even though the issues were given a full hearing at a later date and sometimes the union was vindicated, the momentum for unionizing was broken.

In *Duplex Printing Press Co. v. Deering* [254 U.S. 443 (1921)], the Supreme Court gave a narrow interpretation of the Clayton Act to provisions protecting labor activity. It held members of a labor union guilty of a conspiracy to obstruct commerce by boycotting their employer's product in states other than where manufactured. In essence, the union members wanted a *closed shop*—an agreement between employer and union under which only union members could be hired—rather than an *open shop* in which employees were free to decide whether or not to join a union. Union members attempted to restrain the employer's interstate trade by a variety of means. They organized a **secondary boycott*** against the products of Duplex, threatened sympathetic strikes if customers in other states purchased the items, threatened

---

* A secondary boycott is basically a union method to coerce third parties, such as customers or suppliers, into not doing business with the "primary" employer who is in a labor dispute with the union.

trouble if truckers shipped the presses, and threatened blacklisting if repair shops worked on the presses.

Another such case was the landmark *Bedford Cut Stone Company v. Journeymen Stone Cutters' Association of North America* [274 U.S. 37 (1927)], in which the Court directly applied the *Duplex* decision. Justice Louis Brandeis, in his vigorous dissent, asserted that the Court established a double standard for big business versus unions: the Sherman Act and Clayton Act were interpreted more strictly against unions than big business. The majority of the Court held that, although a union may have a legal purpose in organizing and unionization when issuing a directive (to boycott) to its members, the activity (a boycott in constraint of trade) may still be illegal because of the means used to comply with the directive. The companies were entitled to an injunction against the union because the conduct violated the Sherman Antitrust Act. (The appendix reprints part of the majority opinion.)

THE RAILWAY LABOR ACT: KEEPING THE ENGINES ROLLING

The passage of the **Railway Labor Act (RLA)** in 1926 was a long time in coming.[15] Many legislative attempts had been made over an almost 40-year period to harmonize labor–management relations on the railroads, but for one reason or another they were not successful. The Railway Labor Act finally seemed to meet this goal.

RLA Forerunners

Railroad employees had been among the earliest groups to unionize. After bloody strikes in 1888, Congress enacted the Arbitration Act which provided for voluntary arbitration of disputes by a three-person panel requested by either party to a dispute or by a state governor or the president.[16] The act also included an investigative section giving the president the power to investigate a railroad labor problem. During the Pullman strike of 1894, a panel was convened, but the strike was terminated by federal troop action.

As a result of the failure of the act, as seen during the Pullman strike, the Erdman Act of 1898 was passed. It had the authority to require mediation of disputes and to encourage arbitration if mediation failed. It also prohibited employers from discriminating against union members. The antidiscrimination section of the act carried a penal remedy. In *Adaira v. United States* (1908),[17] the Court held that the prohibition against discrimination, which carried a prison sentence, was unconstitutional. The demise of the Erdman Act led the way to yet another act.

In 1913, Congress passed the Newlands Act. Although it retained most of the Erdman Act's mediation and arbitration requirements, it established a permanent three-member Board of Mediation. It was a short-lived act, however, owing to strike threats by firemen and engineers who refused to arbitrate on the issue of an eight-hour workday. In order to avoid a serious strike by railroad employees over this issue, Congress enacted the Adamson Act which provided for the eight-hour workday.[18]

During the First World War, the government took control of the railroads in order to facilitate troop movements. When control was returned to private industry, the

Transportation Act of 1920 was passed.[19] The act established the Railroad Labor Board. Unfortunately, having no enforcement power, the Board was ineffective.

Why the RLA Works

After this string of ineffective laws, the Railway Labor Act was finally passed. It helped in many ways to bring some harmony to labor–management relations in the railroad industry. The RLA required management to meet and negotiate with labor on a variety of matters relating to working conditions—to agree not only on a collective bargaining contract, but also on changes in those working conditions during the term of the contract. If labor challenges those changes, management must bargain over them. The purpose of the act was to avoid work stoppages.

Two recent (June 1989) U.S. Supreme Court rulings have diluted the power of unions under the law. In the first ruling, the union opposed the railroad's unilateral announcement that urinalysis drug testing of railroad (and airline) employees would be conducted as periodic and return-from-leave exams. The Court held this to be a "minor" dispute in which an employer could act unilaterally and need not bargain over the change with the union.[20]

The procedures for negotiations stipulated in the Railway Labor Act are extremely complex, however; and unions have been able to use the unclear language to block such moves as attempts to modernize work practices. In 1988, for example, unions successfully wielded the act to force the Pittsburgh and Lake Erie Railroad to operate with five-man train crews where two men would have sufficed. Such a move contributed to the railroad's bankruptcy.[21]

The second court decision allows a railroad (or airline) to reorganize and sell assets, if that action is approved by the Interstate Commerce Commission (or the Federal Aviation Administration), without extended bargaining over the issue with its union(s), if that bargaining might postpone the action beyond the scheduled closing date of the sale.[22] A federal appeals court applied this reasoning in the Eastern Airline dispute in 1988, when the court allowed the airline to close its Kansas City hub and lay off workers. (See, in Chapter 13, The Anatomy of a Dispute—The Eastern Airlines Strike.)

A method for settling disputes at impasse was included in the RLA. The **National Mediation Board** (**NMB**) was established to help mediate disputes. If, after the NMB's intervention, the parties fail to resolve the dispute, the NMB can then declare negotiations at an impasse. From this point, the parties can take no further action for 30 days, during which the old (present) contract remains in force. After the 30 days, they can take whatever actions they deem appropriate (e.g., strike or impose a new contract). The NMB asks the parties to present their case to binding arbitration. However, arbitration is completely voluntary. If the parties choose not to arbitrate, the U.S. president, with or without the advice of the board, can call an investigatory board. If a presidential board is established, a mandatory 60-day cooling-off period is implemented in order to maintain the status quo.

The act is enforced by the Interstate Commerce Commission (ICC), the Federal Aviation Administration (FAA), the National Mediation Board (NMB) and the **National Railroad Adjustment Board** (**NRAB**). Each has its unique duties. The ICC deals with rail transportation operating as a general transportation system, not as commuter trains. It must approve any sale, merger, or consolidation of railroad property. The FAA deals with these matters for airlines. The NMB mediates bargaining impasses and arbitrates these if necessary. It also answers bargaining unit questions. The NRAB has 34 members and 4 separate arbitration boards to resolve different occupational and jurisdictional disputes. The airlines are not subject to the NRAB. They seek assistance from special boards of arbitration. In 1966, the Railway Labor Act provided for the establishment of special boards of adjustment when necessary to resolve disputes pending with NRAB for over a year or those disputes not subject to NRAB jurisdiction.

Employees affected by the Railway Labor Act have the right to strike once they have complied with specific procedures set forth in the act. Failure to follow the procedures can result in the issuance of an injunction, that is, a court order requiring the employees to return to work. Injunctions are seldom granted because the Norris–LaGuardia Act usually prohibits them.

The RLA has been amended four times over the years.[23] These amendments expanded its authority to airline employees, required parties to bargain in "good faith," established the National Railroad Adjustment Board, and prohibited yellow-dog contracts.* The amendments covered other minor issues, including the requirement of criminal penalties for violations of certain provisions of the act.

THE NORRIS–LAGUARDIA ACT: LABOR'S MAGNA CARTA

The **Norris–LaGuardia Act,** passed in 1932, has often been described as the Magna Carta for labor organizations.[24] It reversed numerous court opinions restricting union activities, establishing a *laissez-faire* attitude instead. Commonly called the Anti-Injunction Act, it restricted the federal courts' power to issue injunctive relief in labor disputes, except as specifically permitted in the act. In the preamble of the act, Congress specifically stated its intent: "To amend the Judicial Code and to define and limit the jurisdiction of courts sitting in equity, and for other purposes."

Some of the more important sections include:

- Section 1, which prohibited the federal courts from issuing injunctions, "except in strict conformity with the ... Act."
- Section 3, which declared yellow-dog contracts unenforceable by any federal court.
- Section 4, which listed certain activities that were permitted by law and could not be the subject of an injunction.
- Section 7, which specified the procedures that had to be complied with before a court issued an injunction. (A full hearing was required, with proof of substantial and irreparable injury resulting to the requesting party, if the injunction was to be issued.)
- Section 13(c), which specifically defined various terms, including "labor dispute."

* A yellow-dog contract is an agreement between an employer and an employee in which the employee, upon taking a job, promises not to organize, support, or join a union.

Numerous states enacted their own Norris–LaGuardia Acts since the federal law applied only to interstate commerce and the federal courts. In *Senn v. Tile Layers Protective Union* [301 U.S. 468 (1937)], the U.S. Supreme Court upheld Wisconsin's little Norris–LaGuardia Act as constitutional.[25] The result in *Senn* was also interpreted as settling the issue as to the constitutionality of the federal act. (A copy of part of the decision is found in the appendix to this chapter.)

Numerous cases were brought under the Norris–LaGuardia Act. Two important ones were *Lauf v. E. G. Shinner & Co.* and *New Negro Alliance v. Sanitary Grocery Co., Inc.*

In *Lauf v. E. G. Shinner & Co.* (1938), the act came under legal scrutiny.[26] This was a suit to restrain the union (1) from picketing the company's place of business and (2) from forcing the company to discharge any of its employees who did not belong to the petitioning union or to compel them to become members of the union and to accept it as their bargaining agent (a requirement called a union shop agreement— see Chapter 9). The district court granted a preliminary injunction against the union. The circuit court of appeals affirmed this injunction. The Supreme Court reversed the lower court's decisions, finding that there was a labor dispute within the meaning of Section 13(a) of the act and that the Court would follow the expressed provisions of the act barring use of the injunction.

In *New Negro Alliance v. Sanitary Grocery Co., Inc.* (1938), the employees requested that black clerks be hired in certain of its stores.[27] The employer failed to respond to the request, and so the employees picketed the stores. Although the employer attempted to obtain an injunction, the Supreme Court found that there was a labor dispute as defined by the act, even though no union was involved. No injunction was issued.

THE NATIONAL INDUSTRIAL RECOVERY ACT: LABOR IN THE NEW DEAL

In 1933, the U.S. economy was in dismal straits. It was the time of the Great Depression, and approximately 15 million people were unemployed. In response to this crisis, President Roosevelt established the **New Deal** program. Congress, supporting the president's recommendations, enacted the **National Industrial Recovery Act (NIRA),** along with the National Recovery Administration, to establish codes of fair competition with which large industries would voluntarily comply.[28]

Although compiled without labor input, the NIRA was the first government legislation that specifically encouraged the formation of unions for the purpose of collective bargaining. Unfortunately, it had little enforcement power. Employees continued to unionize, and employers continued to refuse to recognize and bargain with them. Thus, numerous strikes resulted.

In an attempt to settle the disputes, the National Labor Board (NLB) was created in August 1933. The seven-member board was initially used for mediation but lost its effectiveness quite rapidly. It had few sanctions available and relied mainly on the power of persuasion. It did, however, establish some important principles: it required secret ballots for the election for union representation, and it considered strikers to be employees even while on strike, if the employer violated the NIRA.

In 1934, Congress authorized the president to establish boards to investigate certain disputes under the NIRA. The NLB was then abolished, and the "old" National Labor Relations Board was established. This body, too, had a short life span because the NIRA, the source of its authority, was found to be unconstitutional in the Supreme Court case of *Schechter Poultry Corp. v. United States* (1935).[29]

THE NATIONAL LABOR RELATIONS ACT AND ITS AMENDMENTS

The time had come for Congress to encourage peaceful settlement of disputes between labor and management in private industry. Since Congress had had little success with the *laissez-faire* approach to labor relations, it now took a more direct approach. It encouraged the formation of unions and their right to collectively bargain. In 1935, Congress passed the **National Labor Relations Act** (**NLRA**), better known as the **Wagner Act**.[30] Subsequently, in 1947, the NLRA was amended by the Labor–Management Relations Act,[31] better known as the Taft-Hartley Act, and in 1959 by the Labor–Management Reporting and Disclosure Act,[32] better known as the Landrum–Griffin Act. Together, the acts form the primary modern body of federal law regarding labor–management relations.

The Wagner Act (National Labor Relations Act): Supporting Employees' Rights

The Wagner Act was passed in 1935 by a concerned Congress. Many legislators feared that this act, like those preceding it, would be found unconstitutional. One of the dominant issues was that the act, when applied to manufacturing businesses, allegedly violated the Tenth Amendment of the U.S. Constitution by allowing Congress to exceed its authority under the commerce clause and invaded the powers reserved to the states.

When tested, however, in the case of *NLRB v. Jones and Laughlin Steel Corp.* (1937), the majority of the Supreme Court found the act to be constitutional.[33] The Court decided that the **National Labor Relations Board** (**NLRB**) had jurisdiction over unfair labor practices and issues of representation "affecting commerce." It further stated, "it presents in a most striking way the close and intimate relation which a manufacturing industry may have to interstate commerce and we have no doubt that Congress had constitutional authority to safeguard the right of respondent's employees to self-organization and freedom in the choice of representatives for collective bargaining." The Court held that the industrial strife would cause a serious impact on interstate commerce. Thus, labor relations could be regulated pursuant to the interstate commerce clause.

Making Union Activities Legal

The Wagner Act was the federal government's first effective law that not only supported and encouraged employees' rights to unionize and collectively bargain, but also legalized those activities. Section 7 provides employees with the right "to self-organize, to form, join, or assist labor organizations, to bargain collectively through representatives of their own choosing, and to engage in concerted activities, for the purpose of collective bargaining or other material aid or protection."

Table 3.1   *The Wagner Act, Unfair Labor Practices of Employers*

Interference with employees' rights to organize and bargain collectively.
Domination or interference in organizing or administering a labor organization.
Discrimination in employment to discourage (or encourage) membership in a labor organization (union shop allowed).
Discrimination in employment because an employee files charges or gives testimony under the Act.
Refusal to bargain collectively, in good faith, with the representative of employees.

Forbidding Unfair Labor Practices

The Wagner Act goes on in Section 8(a) to define **unfair labor practices** forbidden to employers. The act states that "it shall be an unfair labor practice for an employer:

(1) to interfere with, restrain, or coerce employees in the exercise of the rights guaranteed in Section 7 [to organize and bargain].

(2) to dominate or interfere with the formation or administration of any labor organization or contribute financial or other support to it.

(3) to discriminate in regard to hiring or tenure of employment or any terms or conditions of employment to encourage or discourage membership in any labor organization.

(4) to discharge or otherwise discriminate against an employee because he or she has filed charges or given testimony under this act.

(5) to refuse to bargain collectively with the representatives of his or her employees, subject to the provisions of Section 9(a).

The unfair labor practices of employers are summarized in Table 3.1.

All prohibitions defined in the act up to this time referred solely to an employer's activities, but there was no prohibition of an employer's right to go out of business. If only part of a business was terminated or a plant relocation was planned, then the employer's motives had to be reviewed. If the closing was based on economic reasons, then the action was legal; if the action was aimed at escaping unions, it was not legal.

The Wagner Act created the National Labor Relations Board to administer and enforce the law. It was first composed of three members and later expanded to five, appointed by the president. Its powers include issuing rules and regulations, investigating unfair labor practices, prosecuting such illegal conduct, and holding administrative hearings for violations of the NLRA. It also conducts secret ballot elections to determine union representation.

The Taft–Hartley Act (Labor–Management Relations Act): Supporting Employers' Rights

Unionization grew enormously after the enactment of the Wagner Act to the point that, by 1947, employers were felt to be the victims of unfair labor practices perpetrated by labor unions rather than vice versa. Congress therefore acted to change the law to develop more balance in labor–management relations by passing the **Taft–Hartley Act.** As noted earlier, Congress passed the act over President Truman's veto.

Protecting Employers from Union Abuses

The Taft-Hartley Act amended the Wagner Act to incorporate a finding that industrial strife resulted in part from certain undesirable practices by labor unions.[34] The term *unfair labor practice* was amended to include activities engaged in by employees and unions as well as employers.

Section 7, defining the basic rights of employees "to form, join, or assist labor organizations, to bargain collectively, through representatives of their own choosing, and to engage in other concerted activities" was amended with the statement that they "shall also have the right to refrain from any or all of such activities." In essence, if the workers do not want a union, they have the right to reject the union.

The new Section 8(b) of the act made it unlawful for a union

1. To interfere with employees' rights to organize and bargain or refrain from these activities or to choose their bargaining representative.
2. To cause or attempt to cause an employer to discriminate against an employee in violation of the act because of union membership or nonmembership.
3. To refuse to bargain collectively with an employer.
4. To engage in, or to induce or encourage or coerce the employees of any employer to engage in actions such as secondary strikes, boycotts, or refusals to handle goods as in a hot cargo clause (defined later in this chapter), or to force an employer to bargain with an uncertified union, or to assign work not within a union's certification.
5. To require employees to pay an initiation fee which the board finds excessive or discriminatory.
6. To cause or attempt to cause an employer to pay or deliver or agree to pay or deliver any money or other thing of value, for services that are not performed or are not to be performed.
7. To picket an employer to force recognition.

These unfair labor practices are summarized in Table 3.2.

This act also made some major changes in the representation elections covered in Section 9. For example, a certification election could be held only once a year, and economic strikers would lose their voting rights after being out on strike 12 months. It also reorganized the National Labor Relations Board and increased the membership from three to five members. Unfair labor practices were prosecuted by the new office of General Counsel at the NLRB.

The President Steps in: National Emergency Legislation

When a national emergency looms (when the health and safety of the public is imperilled by a labor dispute of an entire industry or a substantial part of one), the president of the United States has the authority under the Taft-Hartley

Table 3.2   *The Taft-Hartley and Landrum-Griffin Acts, Unfair Labor Practices of Labor*

1. a. No interference with employee rights to choose their bargaining representative or to choose not to have one.
    b. No interference with employer in choice of a bargaining representative.
2. No causing or attempting to cause an employer to discriminate in employment because of labor organization membership (union shop allowed).
3. Bargaining collectively in good faith with representatives of the employer.
4. No actions (strikes, inducing strikes, boycotts) or threats of these to
    a. Force an employer or self-employed person to join a labor or employer organization, or to agree to a hot-cargo clause [8(e); see (8) below].
    b. Mount a secondary boycott, or force an employer to bargain with an uncertified union.
    c. Force an employer to bargain with a labor organization other than the one certified as the bargaining representative of its employees.
    d. Force an employer to assign work to its members if its certification does not entitle them to that work.
    (Refusal to cross picket lines is allowed; informational picketing is allowed if it affects only primary employer.)
5. No excessive initiation fees if a union shop agreement exists.
6. No pay for work not performed or not to be performed.
7. No picketing of an employer by an uncertified union to force recognition if there is a presently certified union and the act bars a new election or if the picketing union does not file for a representation election within 30 days (purely informational picketing allowed).
8. No hot-cargo clauses (binding employer from dealing with another organization as dictated by the labor organization).

Act to intervene. The national emergency dispute provisions are found in Sections 206–210.

The act requires that the president appoint an independent board to investigate the situation. After a full but timely investigation of the dispute, a report is submitted to the president. The board has subpoena power to allow it to develop a comprehensive report.

The president may at this point decide to intervene. If this course is taken, the attorney general files the appropriate petition to stop the labor dispute. If an injunction is issued, it is for 80 days. To date, the 80-day injunction has been issued in 29 cases.[35]

During this cooling-off period, the parties are required to bargain in good faith. The Federal Mediation and Conciliation Service (FMCS), established by the Taft–Hartley Act, helps in this bargaining. (The FMCS will be discussed later in this chapter.)

If the dispute is not resolved through the continued bargaining of the two parties (with the assistance of the FMCS), the NLRB takes a vote of the employees at the end of the cooling-off period. If they reject the employer's final offer, the injunction is dissolved at the end of the 80-day period, and the employees are free to strike or the employer is free to lock out the workers. At this time the president makes a full report to Congress, which may contain recommendations for legislative action.

Other emergency legislation can be found in the Railway Labor Act, which applies to most railroad and airline employees.[36] When parties have a serious contract dispute, they may use the National Mediation Board to help settle the problem. The board may make recommendations as to how to settle the dispute. If this fails to resolve the problem and the parties refuse to go to arbitration, the board will declare an impasse. Once this happens, there is a 30-day freeze on employer and employee actions. The president may convene another emergency board to hear the dispute and make recommendations. It can recommend a 60-day cooling-off period, after which the workers can strike or the employer may unilaterally change the terms and conditions of employment.

The Right-to-Work Clause and Other Amendments

The Taft-Hartley made several other changes. Some involved additional statements in the various sections to balance the picture. For example, in Section 8(a)(3), employer discrimination designed to encourage or discourage union membership was prohibited.

Much to the chagrin of unions, the Taft-Hartley Act contained Section 14(b), which is known as the **right-to-work clause.** This section allows state law to override federal law (the Taft–Hartley Act, in this case) with respect to compulsory unionism. Federal law allows unions to bargain for compulsory membership clauses in their collective bargaining agreements, which would require all workers in the bargaining unit to be union members to keep their jobs (see Chapter 9 on the various forms of these clauses). Some states (21 as of 1991, as noted in Table 3.3) have laws that say no worker must be a union member or support a union financially to get and hold a job; these are referred to as "right-to-work" laws. Section 14(b) allows states to forbid compulsory unionism. (We will discuss this subject later in this chapter as well as in Chapter 9.)

Collective bargaining agreements became enforceable in the federal district court. Breach of contract remedies could be pursued in court. Furthermore, private parties could seek a civil remedy—damages—if they were injured as a result of a secondary boycott, that is, certain unlawful union activities aimed at employers not involved in a labor dispute with the union.

Table 3.3 *Right-to-Work States*

Alabama	Nevada
Arizona	North Carolina
Arkansas	North Dakota
Florida	South Carolina
Georgia	South Dakota
Idaho	Tennessee
Iowa	Texas
Kansas	Utah
Louisiana	Virginia
Mississippi	Wyoming
Nebraska	

The Landrum–Griffin Act (Labor-Management Reporting and Disclosure Act): Protecting Union Members

Over the years, unions had become quite powerful in their own right. In the 1950s, Congress held hearings into union activities and procedures and uncovered corruption within the union leadership. After two and a half years of investigation and public hearings, the Senate Select Committee on Organized Crime (the McClellan Committee) disclosed irregularities in union activities, especially in the use of union funds for union officials' salaries and benefits, and in the exercise of members' rights in their unions. Members did not have the right to free speech, nor were union officials democratically elected.

Thus, in 1959, the **Landrum–Griffin Act** was passed to remedy the fiscal problems and members rights. The act includes a complicated system for reporting financial information, a bill of rights for members to protect them against their union, and procedures for elections of union officers. A fiduciary duty is imposed on union officers, and they are required to file reports with the Secretary of Labor regarding any conflicts of interest. The law gives the Secretary of Labor the power to investigate and enforce the act. It also provides civil and criminal remedies for financial abuses by union leaders.

Amendments to the NLRA/LMRA

In addition to addressing these labor issues, the Landrum–Griffin Act also amended the Wagner and Taft–Hartley Acts, giving employers some impressive advantages, including:

1. Giving state authorities jurisdiction of cases brought to the NLRB but rejected by the board as not meeting its jurisdictional standards.
2. Closing some "loopholes" in secondary boycotts.
3. Outlawing, as an unfair labor practice of unions, hot-cargo provisions in collective bargaining agreements, except where permitted in the garment industry and construction industry.
4. Making it unlawful for a union to picket for recognition under most circumstances.

Hot-cargo agreements or clauses are contracts in which the employer agrees not to require employees to handle or work on goods that are products of plants employing strike breakers, nonunion employees, or workers hostile to a union. These forms of secondary boycotts are discussed further in Chapter 14.

The unfair labor practices and the election provisions of the Wagner, Taft–Hartley, and Landrum–Griffin Acts comprise most of the law discussed in this book and are at the heart of labor law. These three acts are summarized in Table 3.4.

The National Labor Relations Board

The NLRB, composed of five members, is nominated by the president and confirmed by the Senate for staggered five-year terms of office. The members have the power to adjudicate unfair labor practices. They determine appropriate bargaining units in representation cases (the size and composition of a group of workers for election

Table 3.4   *The Three Major Labor–Management Relations Laws*

Law	Date	Major Provision(s)
National Labor Relations (Wagner) Act	1935	Guaranteed rights to unionize; listed unfair labor practices of management
Labor–Management Relations (Taft–Hartley) Act	1947	Added unfair labor practices of unions
Labor–Management Reporting and Disclosure (Landrum–Griffin) Act	1959	Added an unfair labor practice of union officials; specified regulation of internal union affairs and rights of workers as union members

purposes) and conduct these elections. The board appoints the general counsel whose duty it is to investigate and prosecute violations of the law.

Much of the NLRB's work is resolved in regional offices by investigators, prosecutors, and administrative law judges. These judges are independent, life appointees and conduct hearings on labor disputes. Their findings may be appealed for review to the board in Washington.

Jurisdiction

The NLRB has the authority to adjudicate labor disputes affecting interstate commerce, involving employer or employee activities covered under the acts.

Many cases have reviewed the meaning of interstate commerce. In 1939, in *NLRB v. Fainblatt*, the Supreme Court focused on determining if *any* raw or finished materials were transported across state lines, rather than on the amount of materials.[37] If there was transportation across state lines, the NLRB had authority.

The Supreme Court's 1963 decision in *NLRB v. Reliance Fuel Oil Corp.* [371 U.S. 224 (1963)] took the issue a step further.[38] The Court extended the board's jurisdiction to any case that could affect the free flow of commerce. Theoretically the board could hear almost any labor case, unless it was specifically exempt under the act. However, the board deliberately chose not to exercise its broad authority. It actually limited its jurisdiction by setting a minimum standard based on the dollar amount of gross annual revenue in any particular industry. These standards are based on a particular industry and were basically set in the case of *Siemans Mailing Service* when the Board gave specific gross dollars per industry.[39] (The *Reliance Fuel Oil Corp.* case can be found in the appendix to this chapter.)

When Congress became concerned that the board would continue to increase the minimum dollar amount to fall under its jurisdiction, the legislature took steps to stop the trend at its first opportunity. Section 14(c)(1) of the Landrum–Griffin Act prohibited a further restriction of the board's jurisdiction "prevailing upon August 1, 1959." Therefore, for example, if a labor dispute developed in a retail firm, $500,000 gross annual volume of business would be necessary in order to have the NLRB consider the case.

Through the years, Congress and the NLRB expanded jurisdiction to include groups such as the U.S. Postal Service, subject to the Postal Reorganization Act; private hospitals, in the 1974 health care amendments; private universities; law firms; sheltered workshops; and charitable institutions.

Some employers and employees are specifically exempt from the law. Among the exempt employers are the federal government, along with the Federal Reserve Bank; a state (or other government); an employer subject to the Railway Labor Act (railroads and airlines); and labor unions when acting as the employer. Exempt employees include persons covered by the Railway Labor Act, supervisory employees, independent contractors, people employed by spouse or parents, domestic help, and agricultural laborers.

How the NLRB Works

A private party initiates all actions brought before the NLRB. Most of the cases are based on unfair labor practices; the rest involve the right of employees to use the representative of their choice in collective bargaining.

Unfair Labor Practice Procedures   An unfair labor practice case must be initiated within six months of the alleged unlawful practice. A charge is filed, and the regional office follows up with an investigation of the allegation. Upon completion of the investigation, a determination must be made regarding the merits of the case. If it has no merit, it is dismissed. If it does have merit and the charging party has not voluntarily withdrawn, the regional director decides whether to issue a complaint. If the director fails to issue a complaint, the charging party can appeal to the general counsel's office in Washington, D.C., which is the "court of last resort" on this issue. Most often the appeal is denied.

When a complaint is issued in an unfair labor practice case, the regional office attorney prosecutes the case. A public hearing is held before an administrative law judge, selected by the Civil Service Commission. This judge hears the case and issues detailed findings of fact and a recommendation for a decision based on the law. This report is sent to the NLRB in Washington, D.C., and to all the parties. If a party does not file an "exception" to the judge's report within 20 days, the report becomes final. When there are exceptions, the parties file written briefs with the NLRB arguing their respective positions. Usually three members of the board review each case.

The board has no power to force compliance. However, under Section 10(e) of the act, the board can petition the U.S. Court of Appeals in the appropriate region to enforce the board's order. A defendant can also seek relief in that court. In the renowned case of *Universal Camera Corp. v. NLRB* (1951), the Supreme Court established guidelines for review of the board's findings.[40] In essence, the Court stated that judicial review of "the whole record" was required and that the administrative law judge's conclusions could be better than the board's since the judge was more impartial.

An unhappy party to an unfair labor practice case may upon receipt of a decision from the federal appeals court file a *writ of certiorari* (a request for a hearing) to the U.S. Supreme Court. The Supreme Court is not required to take the case. If the writ is granted, the Supreme Court will hear the case.

Procedures for Representation Cases   Under Section 7 of the NLRA, employees are entitled "to bargain collectively through representatives of their own choosing." This section is at the heart of the act. Section 9(a) also states that the representative chosen "by the majority of the employees in a unit appropriate for such purposes, shall be the exclusive representative... for purposes of collective bargaining in respect to rates of pay, wages, hours of employment, and other conditions of employment." These are mandatory negotiation subjects. The term *other conditions of employment* has been interpreted to mean, among other things, pensions, stock-purchase plans, profit sharing, retirement rules, and cost of food and housing provided by the employer.

Given these powers to negotiate, the workers' representative is a powerful and important position from the employees' point of view. The choice of representative is a critical issue under the NLRA. How does the NLRB proceed in governing the representation election process?

Basically, when employees are trying to decide if they should choose a union as their bargaining agent, they follow the explicit procedures set by the NLRA. The intent is to permit free choice of representation in the work place. Usually unions have big campaigns to encourage enrollment in their organizations prior to petitioning the NLRB to start the procedures for an NLRB representation election.

Though the representatives are often elected, this is not required. If a union claims to represent a majority of the employees' and there is no doubt of the employees' choice of the union, the employer can voluntarily accept the union as bargaining representative. If, on the other hand, there is an election for a bargaining representative, an employer will deal with that duly elected union for at least 12 months. No other union or any of the employees can file a new request for a certification or decertification election within that time period.

In order to hold an election, an employee or union must file a petition seeking certification (or decertification). If two or more unions are claiming exclusive representation, then even the interested employer can file a petition with the Board along with proof of the union's demand for recognition. When the petition is filed by the employees or union, it must be supported by authorization cards signed and dated by at least 30 percent of the employees. The regional director then notifies all the interested parties and asks the employer for certain information, such as the nature and volume of the business (for jurisdictional purposes) and statements regarding the petition.

At this juncture an investigator is assigned to the case to determine:

1. If the NLRB has authority.
2. If a representation issue has been posed.
3. If the bargaining unit is appropriate.
4. If authorization cards show that at least 30 percent of the employees want the petitioning union as the bargaining representative.

If there is an insufficient claim for an election, the petition can be dismissed. This dismissal can be appealed to the board. If a petition is withdrawn, a six-month waiting period is imposed on that party before another petition can be filed.

If there is sufficient evidence for an election, a hearing is held, unless waived, to decide issues related to composition of the bargaining unit, exempted employees, poll locations, and other such items. If there is agreement on these issues, a **consent**

election will be held. If there is no agreement on the issues, then a hearing will be held. At the hearing a union with 10 percent or more of the employees' support can participate, if desired. Such unions can even force a hearing when a consent election has been agreed upon by the major union trying to become the employees' bargaining representative.

Upon completing the hearing, the regional director receives the hearing officer's report and decides whether to hold the election to certify that the union is the bargaining representative, or dismiss the petition. This authority was delegated to the regional director in the early 1960s. The decision can be appealed to the board in Washington, D.C., if it is inconsistent with legal precedence, if there is a serious factual error, or if there was an unfair hearing (i.e., prejudice to the appealing party or other compelling reasons). The board acts quickly on such issues. An election is held 25 to 30 days after the decision is rendered even if an appeal is being pursued.

Disputes sometimes arise over which union should represent a particular group or whether a union should represent a particular group of individuals with different concerns from those of the majority of employees. The NLRB will often require that a group show some "uniqueness" in order to be represented by another representative.

Right-to-Work Laws: Who Decides?

If the union is certified, then it must negotiate for all employees in the unit, even if some employees are not union members. The union will probably try to negotiate a **union shop clause** with management, which would require all affected employees to become members of the union within a set period or forfeit their jobs (see Chapter 9).

Under Section 14(b) of the Taft–Hartley Act, the states can choose to prohibit compulsory union membership arrangements. As noted earlier, as of 1991 a total of 21 states have some type of law regarding union membership (see Table 3.3). A few of these state laws allow an **agency shop,** which does not require membership in the union but just a fee paid for the union's services as a bargaining representative. Most, however, require an **open shop,** which allows the employee complete freedom to decide. These states often call their statutes **right-to-work laws.**

Federal Mediation and Conciliation Service

In the Taft–Hartley Act, Congress established the **Federal Mediation and Conciliation Service (FMCS),** an independent administrative agency that was designed to help in the bargaining process. Its services can be utilized by any party involved in a labor dispute that may endanger public health or safety or that may have a substantial impact on interstate commerce if it results in a union strike or management lockout.

The FMCS supplies arbitrators in national emergency disputes as required by the Taft-Hartley Act or if the parties so desire (see Chapters 11 and 12), from a list they maintain of third-party neutrals.

Private agreements and certain state laws have mandatory and/or permissive arbitration clauses for certain types of labor disputes. The FMCS is a ready source of assistance in resolving bargaining disputes.

OTHER IMPORTANT LAWS—SETTING THE BOUNDARY CONDITIONS

A number of laws have a direct impact on labor relations. We will review a few of them here to provide a more complete perspective on the working legal environment of labor–management relations. Some of these laws are listed in Table 3.5.

The Fair Labor Standards Act

On June 25, 1938, the **Fair Labor Standards Act (FLSA)** was signed into law.[41] Its intent was to regulate child labor, minimum wages, and overtime pay. There are numerous exceptions to the act, but it regulates most businesses involved in production for interstate commerce, with at least two employees.

Child Labor Regulation

The FLSA specifically prohibits oppressive child labor. In general, the law defines the term *oppressive* in terms of excessive hours or hazardous work. Congress did not want children to be deprived of education and/or health by working long hours in unsafe environments. Thus, the act spelled out restrictions for minors in the workplace.

The standard is basically as follows: a minor aged 16 to 18 may work any length of time in nonhazardous positions; a minor aged 14 to 16 may work limited hours in nonhazardous, nonmanufacturing, or nonmining jobs; younger children have special rules, as do those children employed on farms. There are, of course, exceptions to the law, such as children delivering newspapers, actors or entertainers, and those working for their parents.

The Minimum Wage

The **minimum wage** is a base fee of not less than a certain dollar amount per hour. Problems develop when different rules are set for various types of employees such

Table 3.5 *Other Important Labor and Employment Laws*

Law	Date	Major Provision(s)
Fair Labor Standards (Wages and Hours) Act	1938	Regulation of child labor, overtime hours and pay, minimum wage
Social Security Act	1935	Retirement and survivors benefits, health programs for retirees, unemployment compensation, public assistance
Civil Rights Act	1964	Prohibition of discrimination in the job market
Occupational Safety and Health Act	1970	Regulation of safety and health at the workplace
Employee Retirement Income Security Act	1974	Regulation of pension programs and benefits

as waiters (tips involved) or musicians. Executives, administrators, professionals, and outside salespeople are exempt from the law.

In 1989, President George Bush and Congress, after much controversy, reached an agreement to raise the federal minimum wage from $3.35 to $4.25.[42] The $3.35 figure has been the minimum since 1981; the new figure will become effective in April 1991. The new law also provides for a subminimum **training wage** of $3.61 for youngsters 19 and younger, which may be paid for up to 180 days.

Many states also regulate child labor and the minimum wage. In 1988 alone, Guam, the Virgin Islands, the District of Columbia, Puerto Rico, and 13 states passed laws affecting the minimum wage. Sixteen states have increased the minimum wage above the prevailing $3.35 per hour federal standard. The state of California has the highest minimum wage in the nation at $4.25 an hour, which is soon to be matched by the federal minimum.

Overtime Pay

An employee is entitled to overtime pay based on one and a half times his or her regular pay for hours worked in excess of 40 per week. Furthermore, under the Portal to Portal Act of 1947, certain activities undertaken before and after work, such as driving to and from work, can be included for the purpose of calculating overtime if such activities were included in an employment agreement or were customary in an industry. The Equal Pay Act of 1963, discussed in a later section of this chapter, has much in common with this law.

Enforcement

The federal government has the power to enforce the FLSA. The Department of Labor is authorized to seek injunctive relief and restitution of back pay for injured employees.

Employees are allowed to sue on their own behalf and to seek recovery of back wages, overtime, liquidated damages, reinstatement, and legal fees. The action, however, must be brought within two years of the inquiry, or three years if there is an intentional violation.[43]

Other Acts Regulating Wages

Other statutes have been enacted to cover employees who do not normally qualify under the Fair Labor Standards Act. When airports, defense personnel housing, highways, and other federal projects are undertaken, minimum standards are usually required by contract.

Several other federal statutes have established a minimum wage to be paid workers in particular industries. For example, the Walsh–Healy Act[44] requires manufacturers and dealers that supply goods valued at $10,000 or more to the federal government to use a specified wage guideline. The Davis–Bacon Act[45] requires a similar minimum wage rate if an employer has a building contract with the federal government for more than $2,000; this wage scale is made up of the usual wages, on the average, paid to construction workers in the area. This has typically been the union wage.

The Social Security Act

In 1935, Congress passed one of the nation's most extensive and controversial pieces of legislation, the **Social Security Act.**[46] It was originally intended to provide an income for retired workers and unemployment insurance. Every year the Congress threatens to revise and/or abolish the act owing to financial problems, but it continues to exist. In 1983, the act was greatly amended in hopes of strengthening the program.

The Retirement Program

Social Security retirement benefits were originally intended to supplement other sources of retirement income and not to replace all lost earnings. In 1989, approximately 26.5 million people received monthly cash Social Security retirement benefits; 3.5 million were payments to eligible family members.[47]

A person can begin receiving benefits at the age of 62. Benefits can be assigned to an unmarried child under 18, or 19 if the child is still a full-time student in high school or grade school. The benefits can also be awarded to unmarried children who are severely disabled, to a spouse over 62, to a spouse caring for a child under 16 years of age or disabled, or to certain divorced spouses. In order to receive benefits, an eligible person must apply to the Social Security Administration.

In order for a person or that person's family to qualify for benefits, he or she must have earned at least six credits and worked for at least ten years. Currently, one credit of coverage is received for each $500 of annual earnings; however, a maximum of four units may be earned each year. But having enough units to be fully insured does not ensure the maximum amount of dollar benefits under the program.

To determine the actual benefits a person or his/her family receives, actual earnings over a period of years are adjusted to take into account changes in average wages since 1951. The adjusted earnings are averaged, and a formula is applied. Increases in the future are automatic once benefits are initiated. If the insured begins to receive payments at 62, the benefits will be reduced permanently. Most people therefore begin benefits at 65 years of age. By the year 2000 the age at which full benefits are payable will be increased to 67.

If a person works after benefits begin, he or she may lose some or all of these benefits under the program. For example, people from 65 to 69 years of age may earn $8,880 per year without losing any benefits. Any amount over this is subject to withholding based on a formula used to determine how much of a person's benefits are lost when his or her earnings exceed the given limit.

The programs are supported by taxes imposed on an employer and employee from the 1954 Federal Insurance Contributions Act (FICA).[48] In 1990, an employee contributed 7.65 percent of his or her gross annual wage (up to $51,300). The employer matches these withholdings and is responsible for paying the full amount to the federal government even if the employer fails to withhold funds from the employee. Failure to pay can result in a penalty and criminal liability on the part of the employer.

Employers are very concerned about the high cost of Social Security. According to reports, this is becoming one of the hottest and touchiest issues facing corporate America.[49]

Through the years, the act has been amended and extended to a variety of individuals and for a number of purposes. In 1939, Congress decided that the dependents of a deceased worker should be entitled to some monetary benefits, often referred to as survivors or unmarried minors insurance. For example, the spouse or unmarried minors of a deceased worker may qualify for benefits. In 1956, Congress amended the law to provide benefits for disabled workers and their families. In 1965, the Medicare and Medicaid programs were enacted.

Medicare/Medicaid

Medicare provides basic coverage for hospital and certain medical expenses for qualified disabled individuals, retirees, and individuals over the age of 65. It is administered by the Health Care Financing Administration and not by Social Security offices. The funding of the programs comes partly from Social Security taxes assessed on wages and voluntary medical insurance plan fees paid via monthly premiums by the covered individual. About three-fourths of its funding comes from general revenues of the federal government. Enrollees pay a basic premium of $31.90 a month (through December 1989).[50]

During the Reagan administration, the Medicare Catastrophic Coverage Act became law. It was intended to shield the elderly and disabled Medicare beneficiaries from the financial ruin of major illness. In 1988, it enjoyed wide support. However, by the end of 1989 Catastrophic Health Insurance was ended.[51] The rapid reversal in opinion was due to the cost of the program to individuals. Approximately 40 percent of the 33 million people eligible for Medicare were to pay a surtax, based on their income tax owed, of up to $800 in 1989. This was to be increased to 28 percent or a maximum amount of $1,050 in 1993. A flat fee, $4 a month, was taken out of Social Security checks. It was primarily the surtax, as well as the flat fee, that caused the repeal of the program.

Medicaid is a federally sponsored program that encourages states to provide financial assistance for the medical expenses of needy individuals. Some hospital, laboratory, and professional nursing and doctor fees are covered under most programs. All 50 states have some form of Medicaid. Title XIX of the Social Security Act permits a variety of programs and will provide money to the states to help fund the respective programs, as long as the states follow the federal guidelines.

Providing for the Ineligible

In 1974, Congress created the **Supplemental Security Income program** to assist needy individuals who were not qualified to receive Social Security. Funded by general revenues, it expanded the original old age protection, survivors, insurance, and disability insurance. Generally, only individuals who are over 65, blind, or disabled, and have less than the minimum dollar income set yearly by the federal government qualify to receive monetary benefits under the program.

Providing for the Unemployed

The United States was not interested in **unemployment compensation** for many years. Everyone from politicians to employers to union leaders encouraged the concept of full employment, and unemployment insurance was considered likely to inhibit full employment. However, in 1932–1933 when unemployment reached approximately 25 percent of the workforce, the idea of unemployment compensation was taken under advisement. President Roosevelt appointed a Committee on Economic Security to explore this issue, among others. The committee recommended a joint state–federal program for unemployment compensation.

Acting on the committee's and the president's recommendations, Congress enacted Titles III and IX of the Social Security Act (1935), establishing a federal–state unemployment compensation program. The law permitted states to join the system and to adopt a program that fit within the federal guidelines. Although the states were not required to join the federal program, it was more advantageous for employers. Employers would be taxed on a percentage of their payroll and given a tax credit on their federal tax returns. If a state was not a member of the federal program, no credit would be given to an employer on the federal tax return for any state tax levied.

Today all 50 states have programs. Although they all differ, they have some basic similarities as well. The 1954 Federal Unemployment Tax Act[52] requires that all employees in the private sector be covered. Certain farmworkers and domestic employees earning an insufficient salary may be exempt, as may self-employed individuals. In 1990, self-employed individuals also began to be covered, as required by the Self-Employment Contributions Act.[53] All states require a basic earnings level for eligibility. The duration of benefits in all states cannot exceed 26 weeks.

A Federal Stake in Equal Rights

Four federal laws attempt to prohibit discrimination by employers and unions: (1) the Civil Rights Act of 1964, Title VII, as amended by the Equal Employment Opportunity Act of 1972 and the Pregnancy Discrimination Act of 1978; (2) the Equal Pay Act of 1963; (3) the Age Discrimination in Employment Act of 1967; and (4) the Vocational Rehabilitation Act of 1973 and the Americans with Disabilities Act of 1990.

The Civil Rights Act of 1964

Discrimination in employment based on sex, race, color, religion, or national origin was prohibited by the **Civil Rights Act of 1964,** Title VII, as amended by the Equal Employment Opportunity Act of 1972. The bill was introduced by President John F. Kennedy after racial violence erupted in Alabama in 1963. It was designed to stop discrimination in the labor market, in hiring and in promotions. The law covers most private and public employers, including state governments and unions.

The EEOC In the Civil Rights Act, Congress created the **Equal Employment Opportunity Commission (EEOC),** giving it the authority to enforce the law, to conduct investigations, and to attempt conciliations. If an agreeable settlement in a dispute cannot be reached, the commission can then decide whether to litigate the issues. If reasonable cause is found a suit can be filed in the U.S. District Court by legal counsel for the EEOC. The commission even has the authority to litigate **class actions** on behalf of too numerous a group of individuals to name personally for a pattern or practice of discrimination. The time limitation for filing a suit is very complicated, and anyone bringing action must be extremely careful to comply with such rules or lose the right to bring the suit.

Remedies   As remedies for violation of the law, courts award injunctions, reinstatement of employees, and back pay and seniority as far back as two years prior to the filing of the action.[54] The courts can also give other relief as they deem appropriate.

If the EEOC chooses not to sue, a **right-to-sue letter** will be issued to the injured party. This authorizes the injured party to bring a private action, suing on its own behalf.

An organization must have at least 15 employees or members to be covered by the act. Hiring halls or employment agencies, however, can have a single employee.[55]

Educational institutions must also comply with the law. In May 1989, for example, 24 nonacademic employees of the University of California at Riverside filed a complaint with the U.S. Department of Labor alleging discrimination, harassment, and retaliation on the job by the university from 1980 to 1989. As of this writing, the U.S. Department of Labor is reviewing the complaint to determine if a formal investigation should be held.[56]

Cases in Discrimination   In 1989, the U.S. Supreme Court delivered a major blow to **affirmative action**—a plan to remove discriminatory barriers to employment and education. In five cases the Court reversed approximately 20 years of liberal decisions, making it tougher for plaintiffs to win job **discrimination** claims. However, in 1991, a sixth case barred sex discrimination under the guise of a "fetal protection" policy.

On January 23, 1989, the Court held in *Richmond v. Cronson*[57] that the Constitution limits the power of state and local governments to reserve a percentage of their business for minority contractors. To justify racial quotas or similar programs, there must be a well-documented showing of past discrimination now being corrected by the specific program.

In *Wards Cove v. Atonio*[58] on June 5, 1989 the Court held that those bringing charges of racial bias must prove that the employer has no business reason for imposing the restriction. The Court reversed *Griggs v. Duke Power Co.* [401 U.S. 424 (1971)], which had construed Title VII to prohibit "not only overt discrimination but also practices that are fair in form but discriminatory in practice." The new decision declares that "statistical disparities or racial imbalances in one segment of an employer's work force does not, without more, establish a *prima facie* case."*

Then the Supreme Court held on June 12, 1989, in *Martin v. Wilks*,[59] in a 5 to 4 decision, that court-approved affirmative action settlements can be reopened when white male employees allege **reverse discrimination** (that is, discrimination against one group in an effort to help another) or when third parties to the settlement have their rights violated. In this case, white firefighters in Birmingham, Alabama, challenged a court-approved settlement intended to increase the number of blacks hired and promoted in the department. This decision could open a new round of litigation for disputes thought to be settled.[60]

---

* A *prima facie* case is one in which the plaintiff will win if no contradictory evidence is admitted in court.

The concept of reverse discrimination comes from a famous California case, *Regents of the University of California v. Bakke* [438 U.S. 265 (1978)]. In the *Bakke* case, the plaintiff was a white male who alleged he was unlawfully discriminated against when he applied for admission to medical school at the University of California at Davis. He asserted that the school used race as a criterion for admission and that he was denied admission solely because he was not black. The Court held that race may be taken "into account when it acts not to demean or insult any racial group, but to remedy disadvantages cast on minorities by past racial prejudice." The Court held that Bakke, was, however, improperly denied admission since the school used race as the *sole* basis for the preferential treatment. Bakke subsequently went to medical school at the University of California at Davis.

In the case of *Patterson v. McLean Credit Union*[61] on June 15, 1989, the Supreme Court also held that one of our oldest civil rights statutes, the Civil Rights Act of 1866, does not apply to cases of racial harassment or other discriminatory activity by an employer *after* hiring, but rather only in the interviewing stage. The Court, however, did not reverse its decision in *Runyon v. McCrary* [427 U.S. 160 (1976)], which in essence held that the 1866 civil rights statute forbids discrimination in making private contracts.

The fifth major case, on May 1 of 1989, was the case of *Price Waterhouse v. Hopkins*.[62] In this case, the accounting firm of Price Waterhouse denied a woman a partnership because the other partners thought she was too masculine. The Supreme Court remanded the case, sending it back to the lower court for further hearings consistent with its opinion. In May of 1990, U.S. District Court Judge Gerhard Gesell ordered Price Waterhouse to make Ms. Hopkins a partner and reimburse her for lost income, approximately $350,000. This is the first time a woman has been ordered to be made a partner based on illegal sexual stereotyping.

Many employers feel that the Court decision in this case will make it difficult to fire or fail to promote a woman.[63] However, the case has made it easier to discriminate. In the 6 to 3 ruling, the Court held that employers in sex discrimination suits must show that they would have reached the same employment decision even if they had not considered the sex of the candidate. In essence, the Court diminished the burden of proof. The employer has to prove that by the "preponderance of the evidence" the same employment decision would have resulted even if there had not been any bias. The lower courts used a higher standard of proof (clear and convincing evidence), but this was not upheld in this Supreme Court case. The Court also reconfirmed that Title VII covers and prohibits sexual stereotyping. (Part of the Supreme Court opinion can be found in the appendix to this chapter.)

In March 1991, the Supreme Court overturned lower court decisions that women could be prohibited from working in certain hazardous jobs. In the case of *United Automobile Workers of America, U.A.W. v. Johnson Controls, Inc.*, the plaintiffs (union and employees) challenged, under Title VII of the Civil Rights Act, a "fetal-protection policy" issued by Johnson Controls, Inc.[64] In essence the company had prohibited any women of child-bearing age from working in the battery division, at relatively higher paying jobs, because of possible exposure to hazardous lead chemicals that could cause damage to a fetus and expose the company to substantial liability. The Court held that such fetal protection policies, currently used by more than a dozen major corporations including GM, DuPont, and Monsanto as well as Johnson Controls, are sex discrimination prohibited by the Civil Rights Act of 1964 and the Pregnancy Discrimination Act of 1978.

Exceptions to the Act   As mentioned earlier, discrimination is generally prohibited by law, but it is sometimes permitted. Discrimination on the basis of sex, religion, or national origin may be permitted because of a statutory exception or case determination; that is, if the discriminatory activity is based on a bona fide occupational qualification necessary to that particular job. A church, for example, could require a person to be of a certain religion in order to be hired.[65] On the other hand, airlines cannot require that "stewardesses" be only women. This is not a bona fide occupational qualification. In *Diaz v. Pan American World Airways, Inc.* the Court did not believe sex was a bona fide occupational qualification.[66] It ruled that the airline discriminated against males. Today it is common to see male cabin attendants. Currently, a controversy is growing over weight restrictions for female stewardesses; it is argued that older women are naturally a few pounds heavier, as are pregnant stewardesses. The restrictions may be found to violate the law.

Sexual Harassment   If an employee is sexually harassed (i.e., sexual advances are made or sexual favors are requested or actual sexual acts are performed) while on the job, the harasser is guilty of a violation of Section 703 of Title VII. In the case of *Meritor Savings Bank v. Vinson* [106 S. Ct. 2399 (1986)], the Supreme Court confirmed that sexual harassment is a violation of Title VII. In this interesting case, an employee testified to over 40 instances of sexual favors with her employer, a bank vice-president, from 1974 to 1977. She asserted that her career advancement ended when she stopped having sex with him. The Court found that a "hostile environment" sex discrimination case is actionable under Title VII. The case was remanded for further proceedings.

In addition, requiring employees to wear sexually provocative uniforms when the employer should know that it will encourage sexual harassment by nonemployees will also result in employer liability. Such an employer may be liable for civil damages.

The Pregnancy Discrimination Act of 1978   In 1978, Congress amended Title VII again in order to prohibit pregnancy discrimination. The **Pregnancy Discrimination Act of 1978 (PDA)**[67] prohibits an employer from discharging or refusing to hire or promote a woman solely on the basis that she is pregnant. As just noted, the PDA was used by the Supreme Court to ban fetal protection policies. Pregnancy is to be treated in the same manner as any other disability. Mandatory leave is permitted only if a woman is unable to continue working.

The states have taken the lead in legislation regarding parental leave. In 1988, Maine and Wisconsin, for example, passed laws requiring certain private sector employers and state governments to provide unpaid family medical leave for the birth or adoption of a child or the serious illness of the employee, child, spouse, or parent. In the previous year, Connecticut, Minnesota, Oregon, and Rhode Island enacted family leave laws covering pregnancy leaves. The exact periods of leave differ from state to state, as does the size of the employers covered.

In Maine, the law covers employers of 25 or more people and requires a grant of up to 8 weeks leave. In Wisconsin the law covers employers of 50 or more and requires granting up to 6 weeks "maternity" leave.[68]

The Equal Pay Act of 1963 and Other Salary Issues

The **Equal Pay Act of 1963** prohibits employers from paying one sex a lower wage for equal work, such as paying a woman less than a man for the same work.[69] This has been a very controversial area. The act sets out exceptions for deviations in salaries such as wages based on seniority, merit, production of an individual worker, or a differential based on a factor other than sex.

In *Hodgsen v. Robert Hall Clothes, Inc.* [473 F. 2d 589 (3rd Cir. 1973)], the Third Circuit Court of Appeals held that male salespersons could be paid higher salaries than women because there was a greater profit in men's clothing. Thus, the differential was a permitted variance because the pay was not based on sex but rather on a factor other than sex. It appears, then, that one sex can be paid less than another if the two do not do "equal" work.

Under current federal guidelines, **pay equity,** also referred to as **comparable worth,** is not an acceptable measure for charging sex discrimination. Comparable worth deals with occupations, comparing jobs that are "traditionally" held by males (construction workers, truck drivers) with those "traditionally" held by females (nurses, secretaries). At issue are standardized job skills, requirements, and duties that are arbitrarily weighted differently for compensation purposes between the two groups. Comparable worth theory holds that skills, training, responsibilities, and other factors should be rated on a sexless basis.

Thus, arguments concerning comparable worth can be made only in relation to jobs that are predominantly male or female. In addition, comparable worth does not cover individual cases, but instead deals with the entire field.

As of 1989, a few states had begun pay equity adjustments for some of their female state government employees, but the entire subject of comparable worth was still being fought out in the courts (see Chapter 18).[70]

The Age Discriminaiton in Employment Act of 1967

The **Age Discrimination in Employment Act of 1967** (and appropriate executive orders) prohibits employers, including the federal government and states, from discriminating based on age.[71] The law protects employees between the ages of 40 and 70.

If a job has a bona fide occupational qualification related to age, an employer may apply this qualification and, in essence, discriminate. Furthermore, if there is a reasonable factor other than age as to why an individual between 40 and 70 years of age was not hired or promoted or was fired, then there has been no discrimination under the act. Thus, if a man is 50 years old and fails to do his job, he can be fired without violating the act. The age of 70 can be a mandatory retirement age in the private sector but not for federal employees.

In 1979, the EEOC became the enforcement agency for this act, replacing the Department of Labor. Age discrimination cases are filed quite frequently. All types of employers have been found to "inadvertently" discriminate on the basis of age.

In one interesting case, 19 tenured professors between the ages of 48 and 69 filed suit in May 1989 against Memphis State University claiming age discrimination. Apparently, they were among 27 faculty members who filed complaints with the EEOC or the Tennessee Human Rights Commission earlier in the year. The lawsuit alleges that the professors were deprived of fair salary increases and benefits that were given to younger faculty. They are seeking, among other relief, back pay and pension plan adjustments.[72] The case is still being decided.

The Vocational Rehabilitation Act of 1973

The **Vocational Rehabilitation Act of 1973** encourages the employment of the handicapped.[73] Under this law, federal contractors that have contracts in excess of $2,500 are required to make "good faith" efforts to hire the handicapped. It also prohibits discriminating against a worker solely by reason of his or her handicap in any program or activity with federal funding.

The act defines a handicapped individual as "any person who (A) has a physical or mental impairment, which substantially limits one or more of such person's major life activities, (B) has a record of such impairment, or (C) is regarded as having such an impairment." To find discrimination, however, this impairment must not interfere with the requirements of the job.

If a handicapped individual is discriminated against, he or she had the burden of proving that all duties of the job can be performed. An employer is expected, however, to make a reasonable accommodation for the individual.

Several cases have reviewed the rights of the handicapped. For example, in *Southeastern Community College v. Davis* [442 U.S. 397 (1979)], the Supreme Court held that a federally funded nursing college program did not violate the law when it refused to admit a student with a severe hearing disability. The redesigning of the program that would have been necessary to accommodate the student's problem was not a "reasonable accommodation."

The Americans with Disabilities Act of 1990

The **Americans with Disabilities Act (ADA)** of 1990 basically extends the coverage of the Vocational Rehabilitation Act of 1973 to all employers, including those in the private sector. The ADA goes into effect on July 26, 1992. Employers with fewer than 15 employees are exempt. The ADA does not have an affirmative action requirement or the limited application to federal contractors or federally funded programs as does the Vocational Rehabilitation Act.

Violations of the ADA can be enforced under Title VII of the Civil Rights Act of 1964. Those filing under this title would be eligible for injunctive relief as well as other remedies such as attorneys' fees, court costs, and back pay. The widespread application of this law promises to spawn a multitude of court cases defining the ways in which employers must accommodate the handicapped in hiring, promotion, and other conditions of employment.

The Occupational Safety and Health Act

In order to protect the worker from hazards on the job, Congress passed the **Occupational Safety and Health Act of 1970.**[74] The intent of the law was to provide a safer environment for employees. The act created the Occupational Safety and Health Administration (OSHA) in the Department of Labor to regulate and enforce the law, the National Institute of Occupational Safety and Health (NIOSH), a research institute, and the Occupational Safety and Health Review Commission (OSHRC), the adjudicatory arm that hears violations of the law. OSHRC decisions may be appealed to the Federal Court of Appeals.

OSHA has the authority to adopt safety standards, which are classified as interim, permanent, and emergency. All are subject to comment (and attack) by interested parties.

Employer Responsibilities: Keeping Workers Safe

Employers have the duty to comply with safety standards and maintain a hazard-free environment. According to the act, employers must keep their businesses free of recognized hazards likely to cause death or great bodily injury, and must comply with the OSHA standards.[75] For example, battery-producing companies must keep lead exposure and the lead blood levels of employees at a relatively safe level; irradiation plants must keep cobalt-60 and cesium-137 contained.

An employer of eight or more employees must keep records of any work-related injury or illness. This could assist in determining dangerous environmental conditions or substances. If employees report violations, refuse to work due to dangers on the job, or exercise other similar rights, the employer may not retaliate against them; Section II(c) protects the employees' rights.

OSHA Inspections

OSHA has the authority to do on-site inspections. Visits are commonly made to locations where serious injury or death has occurred, where a formal complaint by an employee has been filed, and where dangerous industries are functioning. An inspection is usually unannounced.

A warrant may be necessary if the employer refuses to consent to the inspection. If the site is private and not in public view and the employer refuses, and/or no emergency exists, a warrant will be required to visit the site.[76] For example, a warehouseman can refuse to have an inspection without a warrant if no emergency is known.

When an inspection is made, both the employees and employer must have a representative accompany the inspector, who is called a compliance officer.[77] Upon completion of the tour of the work environment, the officer will give a closing conference explaining where possible violations may exist. These will be discussed by the three parties. A report will subsequently be drafted. The OSHA area director, upon review, has six months to notify the employer of the violations found.

Meeting the Timetable

Employers must correct any problems within a specified period. If an employer is unhappy about the timetable that has been set to abate a violation or a penalty, he or she must contest the issue in writing within 15 days of receipt of the citation. This is called a **notice of contest.** The employees are entitled to learn of the employer's intent to contest the finding; the employer must post a notice of such intent.

An administrative hearing will subsequently be held to review the issues. Any findings may be appealed to the OSHRC for review within 30 days of the administrative law judge's ruling. OSHRC is not, however, required to hear the case. Once all administrative remedies have been exhausted, appeal may be made to the U.S. Court of Appeals.

Remedies for Violations

For certain types of violations a criminal prosecution may be pursued. If an employer willfully made false statements, certifications or representations, or had unauthorized advanced notice of inspections, he or she may be heavily fined and/or jailed. Any violations, citations, and penalties are sent to the employer via certified mail.

Many states also have passed their own laws to protect worker safety. These are usually administered in conjunction with the federal law.

The Employee Retirement Income Security Act

Over the years many private employers have instituted employee pension plans. Because of numerous abuses in handling funds for employee benefits, Congress enacted the **Employee Retirement Income Security Act** (**ERISA**) in 1974.[78] Although the act is known primarily for benefits related to pension plans, it also established guidelines for health and welfare plans, such as medical coverage, vacation pay, and death benefits.

What ERISA Does

ERISA established fiduciary standards of conduct for pension plan administrators. It set rules for the vesting of pensions with employees, a point discussed in detail in Chapter 8. It required all types of disclosure, including financial, to employees and the government. It also provided a standard for special tax treatment for the pension funds. Furthermore, it provided employees and beneficiaries with a remedy when violations occur.

The **Pension Benefit Guaranty Corporation** (**PBGC**) was established under ERISA to insure benefits in the event a pension plan fails. In recent years, owing primarily to the bankruptcy of firms in the steel industry, the corporation has been operating with a $3 billion deficit. The PBGC collects premiums for its services from employers and, when necessary, makes payments on an employer's behalf. It also has the authority to seek reimbursement from the defaulting employer.

A plan can be voluntarily terminated if proper notice is given to the Pension Benefit Guaranty Corporation. A ten-day notice is required. The plan's assets are allocated to the interested parties. If all claims are paid, any excess may be returned to the employer. If, however, the assets are inadequate to cover the liabilities, they are allocated *pro rata*, distributed proportionally. Thus, an employer can relieve itself of future (but not present) liability by terminating its plan. Plan termination is not allowed in the case of inadequate funds for present benefit claims. In this case, the employer is liable for 100 percent of the insufficient funds with an upper limit of 30 percent of its net worth.

In the 1980s, pension termination was not a rare event. About 1,900 companies, including the Exxon Corporation and the American Red Cross, diverted money from pension accounts, often to finance mergers. The companies usually replaced their pension funds with less generous plans or with no plans at all. In response, in 1989 Congress began working on legislation that would require all companies that terminate pension plans to establish replacement plans that have enough money to meet both current and projected obligations.[79]

The act covers only private employers, not government or tax-exempt organizations, that offer defined benefit retirement plans. (This topic is discussed further in Chapter 8.) In December 1987 Congress passed major amendments to ERISA to coordinate ERISA's 1974 provisions with the 1986 Internal Revenue Code.[80]

Remedies for Violations

If a violation of the act takes place, numerous parties can take action in pursuit of various remedies. Before bringing a legal action, individual beneficiaries or participants must first exhaust all administrative remedies. They can then bring a civil action in federal court for breaches by the administrator and recover damages due the plan. A penalty can also be imposed if an administrator fails to provide requisite information.

The Department of Labor and the Internal Revenue Service can also seek relief in federal court. Criminal penalties are available for intentional violations. Fines up to $5,000 and/or up to a year in jail can be awarded for reporting and disclosure violations. Fiduciary violations can cost up to $100,000 in fines.

The Worker Adjustment and Retraining Notification Act

In July 1988, a plant closing bill was signed into law.[81] The **Worker Adjustment and Retraining Notification Act** (**WARN**) requires a 60-day advance notice to employees prior to the closing of a factory or facility. WARN provides employees with early notice that they soon will be out of jobs and with some security while looking for new positions.

Xerox, Pillsbury, and Merrill Lynch have been among the companies to file advance notices under WARN. In many cases, WARN notifications lead to state- and company-sponsored taskforces to help employees find new work.[82]

Traditionally, little if any notice was given to employees prior to a major business layoff. Congress felt this was a more equitable solution to major layoffs and plant closings. Notice could help employees prepare for the future.

RICO: The Racketeering Influenced and Corrupt Organizations Act

The **Racketeering Influenced and Corrupt Organizations Act (RICO)** was passed in 1970 to prevent organized crime from moving into legitimate businesses and labor organizations. The thrust of the act was primarily criminal in nature. It also has civil "remedies" that are applied against individuals rather than organized crime members.

Under RICO, it is a federal crime to conduct the affairs of an enterprise engaged in or affecting interstate commerce through a pattern of racketeering. Essentially all that is necessary for an indictment is that two or more crimes be committed related to one criminal purpose. The crimes must be perpetrated within a ten-year period, with the most recent crime being committed within five years of indictment.

The act is being applied quite liberally. In 1989, the International Brotherhood of Teamsters was being prosecuted under RICO but settled just prior to trial. The Longshoremen's union is now under suspicion.[83]

Some feel that RICO is being too broadly applied. In October 1989, for example, the U.S. Supreme Court let stand a lower court ruling applying RICO to "pro-life" supporters who violated an abortion clinic's business activities.[84] Both the U.S. Chamber of Commerce and the AFL–CIO, which are not usually on the same side of any issue, are lobbying for amendments to this law to prevent its very broad application.

The Controversy over Workers' Privacy

Some serious issues involving privacy rights are daily confronting the employee and employer at the workplace. These may become the subject of negotiation and/or a lawsuit, and the law is not yet settled. What are the privacy rights of an employee? What rights does an employer have to information about workers? The issues are very broad. Legal actions have already been brought in an attempt to resolve the parties' legal rights and duties.

We will briefly review five areas of employment privacy here: **drug testing; AIDS; polygraph tests; computer surveillance;** and **genetic screening.**

Drug Testing

Employee drug testing is becoming more common in the United States, for drug use appears to be growing. Although it is not always obvious that substance abuse interferes with work, studies have found that the user may suffer impaired judgment. As seen in the major Alaskan oil tanker spill when the captain of the Exxon tanker was too drunk to steer the ship out of port, alcohol can have a devastating cost to the environment and the employer. Thus, employers have pushed for the right to test.

The federal constitutional right of privacy appears to apply only to government actions. Many legal issues are involved in testing. In 1989, the U.S. Supreme Court resolved some of the constitutional issues when it decided two cases, *Skinner v. Railway Labor Executives Association*[85] and *National Treasury Employees Union v. Von Raab.*[86]

In the *Skinner* case, employees of the railroad were subject to the Federal Railroad Administration's regulations. The federal regulations in question required blood and urine testing of employees involved in major accidents and of those who violated certain safety rules. The unions representing the employees challenged the regulations, asserting that they violated the Fourth Amendment and the right to privacy and that individualized suspicion of wrongdoing is essential prior to a search. The Supreme Court held that blood tests, urine samples, and breath testing are Fourth Amendment searches and that governmental interest in the safety of society is a compelling reason for the "minimal" intrusion. No individualized suspicion is necessary.

In the *Von Rabb* case, the U.S. Customs Service required employees seeking transfers or promotions to positions involving drug interdiction or to positions handling classified materials or firearms to submit to urinalysis tests. Except for the positions handling classified materials, the Court found a compelling state interest in "safeguarding our borders." It stated that "the safety outweighs the privacy expectations of employees." The testing was reasonable under the Fourth Amendment.

These two decisions indicate that employees working for the federal government or those highly regulated by government may be searched if there is a compelling state interest intended to protect society. In the private sector, employers can require testing unless prohibited by agreements or law.

Drug testing has been restricted in approximately a dozen states, but exceptions continue to occur. It is not clear whether such testing violates a person's Fourth Amendment right under the Constitution, for in some cases such activity has been permitted when the public safety is at issue.[87]

AIDS

Employees suffering from acquired immune deficiency syndrome (AIDS) are covered by laws protecting the handicapped, but many employers and employees wrongfully discriminate against such affected people. Currently, employers' attempts to avoid hiring a person affected by the disease seem to focus on finding some other basis for denying employment. Compounding the concern of employing workers with AIDS is the increased cost employers might have to absorb owing to increases in group medical premiums.

In 1988, Circle K Corporation revised its employee health care plan, adding a clause that denied new employees medical coverage for illnesses and accidents related to "personal life-style decisions." These included health problems resulting from AIDS as well as from alcohol and drug abuse. The change was proposed as a way of controlling company medical costs, particularly after an executive found that the company paid nearly 4 percent of its health care budget for the treatment of nine AIDS cases. However, public outcry led to the forced suspension of the change.[88]

Polygraph Tests

Lie detector tests as a requirement for employment have been restricted in approximately 40 states. However, they are still being used. Many employees feel compelled to submit to such tests. This is not considered "voluntary" submission and may cause problems in court.

In 1988, the Employee Polygraph Protection Act was passed.[89] The act essentially prohibits the use of a variety of lie detector tests in the private sector when hiring.

There are a number of exceptions to this rule, and employers may use them randomly if, for example, they are conducting an investigation involving economic loss or injury to the business.

Businesses are seeking alternatives to polygraphs to determine the character of job applicants. One booming industry is the honesty test. Companies purchase questionnaires that call for "yes" or "no" answers to ethical questions. After the applicants complete the questionnaires, the forms are scored by computer. The "riskiness" of each candidate is assessed, and the companies use the assessments in their hiring procedures.

Another rapidly spreading substitute for polygraphs is handwriting analysis. Handwriting analysts examine a candidate's writing in order to develop a personality profile. Handwriting analysis is generally less expensive and faster than other tests for discerning a potential employee's personality. However, the reliability of both honesty tests and handwriting analyses as predictors of job performance has not been convincingly proven.[90]

Computer Surveillance

Employers are increasingly using computer surveillance to obtain information on employees. They are also utilizing computers to monitor work and telephone conversations. Currently, this is considered legally acceptable behavior.

For example, Delta Airlines uses computers to track which employee records the most reservations. A recruiting firm in Chicago watches computerized schedules to see who interviews the most candidates. Safeway Stores, Inc., installed dashboard computers on its trucks that record such data as driving speed and length of time a truck is stopped. On the basis of the computer data, Safeway tries to discharge or suspend up to 20 drivers a year.[91]

Genetic Screening

Genetic screening can determine whether a person is susceptible to certain diseases. This type of information can be helpful if a person is working in a potentially dangerous environment. If can also be utilized to make employment decisions that focus on holding future medical plan costs down, a point made above when discussing AIDS. To date, there does not appear to be any legislation prohibiting its use, and thus this technique will probably be used more often in the future. The far-reaching ramifications, however, can be frightening because employers may use this method to discriminate against qualified candidates.

THE FUTURE FOR EMPLOYMENT LAW

The legal environment of labor–management relations has changed drastically through the years. Public policy has dictated the direction it has taken. Although court decisions have reflected some of the changes, legislation has been the catalyst and the most effective method of change.

Again, some of the laws that affect employment rights are the Railway Labor Act, the Norris–LaGuardia Act, the National Labor Relations Act (the Wagner Act), the

Labor–Management Relations Act (the Taft–Hartley Act), the Labor–Management Reporting and Disclosure Act (the Landrum–Griffin Act), the Social Security Act, the Federal Unemployment Tax Act, the Fair Labor Standards Act, the Walsh-Healy Act, the Davis–Bacon Act, the Civil Rights Act, the Equal Employment Opportunity Act, the Equal Pay Act, the Age Discrimination Act, the Vocational Rehabilitation Act, the Pregnancy Discrimination Act, the Occupational Safety and Health Act, the Employee Retirement Income Security Act, and the Worker Adjustment and Retraining Notification Act.

A brief review shows a movement from the at-will employment contract to contracts set by free collective bargaining through unionization in the workforce. As the extent of unionization in the United States decreases, employment law seems to extend into areas that were once the purview of unions. Public policy is at the heart of employment law, and it will continue to be refined as long as the society believes in employee rights secured through collective bargaining or government oversight.

DISCUSSION QUESTIONS

1. Discuss the major trend in the law governing labor organizations from the early 1700s to the Sherman Act. Why was the Sherman Act enacted?

2. Why do you suppose early courts were so anti-union?

3. Why was the Railway Labor Act enacted? What did it establish? To whom does it apply?

4. Which act is often referred to as the Magna Carta for labor organizations? Why does it have that reputation? Discuss the importance of this act.

5. What legal concept was reviewed in the case of *Loewe v. Lawlor*? Discuss in full.

6. The Wagner Act defines unfair labor practices for an employer. Discuss the five activities that constitute unfair labor practices.

7. How did the Taft–Hartley Act change labor law? Why was it enacted? What was unlawful under Section 8(b) of the act?

8. What are the functions of the National Labor Relations Board?

9. What is the legal issue reviewed in *NLRB v. Reliance Fuel Oil Corp.*?

10. What was the purpose of enacting the Social Security Act? What benefits does the act offer? Who qualifies under the act to receive benefits?

11. What is the purpose of the Fair Labor Standards Act? What does the law specifically prohibit? Discuss.

12. Discrimination in employment is attacked in a variety of ways. There are five federal laws that specifically deal with equal rights in employment. Name them and briefly discuss each one.

13. What is the purpose of the Occupational Safety and Health Act? What does it do?

14. What does ERISA stand for? Discuss its purpose. What does the Pension Benefit Guaranty Corporation have to do with ERISA?

15. Explain the purpose of the Worker Adjustment and Retraining Notification Act.

16. What privacy issues may become serious problems in the future?

17. On what basis did the U.S. Supreme Court remand *Price Waterhouse v. Hopkins?*

18. What are right-to-work laws? Have any states enacted this kind of legislation?

19. Describe the activities of two government panels discussed in this chapter that are involved in labor–management relations?

VOCABULARY LIST

labor relations

collective bargaining

common law

case law

opinion

stare decisis

at-will contract

ends/means test

Sherman Antitrust Act

rule of reason

Clayton Act

Federal Trade Commission Act

secondary boycott

Railway Labor Act (RLA)

National Mediation Board (NMB)

National Railroad Adjustment Board (NRAB)

Norris–LaGuardia Act

New Deal

National Industrial Recovery Act (NIRA)

Wagner Act (National Labor Relations Act)

National Labor Relations Board (NLRB)

unfair labor practice

Taft–Hartley Act (Labor–Management Relations Act)

right-to-work clause

Landrum–Griffin Act (Labor–Management Reporting & Disclosure Act)

hot-cargo agreement

consent election

union shop clause

agency shop

open shop

right-to-work laws

Federal Mediation and Conciliation Service (FMCS)

Fair Labor Standards Act (FLSA)

minimum wage

training wage

Social Security Act

Medicare

Medicaid

Supplemental Security Income program

unemployment compensation

Civil Rights Act of 1964

Equal Employment Opportunity Commission (EEOC)

class action

right-to-sue letter

affirmative action

discrimination

reverse discrimination

sexual harassment

Pregnancy Discrimination Act of 1978

Equal Pay Act of 1963

pay equity

comparable worth

Age Discrimination in Employment Act of 1967

Vocational Rehabilitation Act of 1973

Americans with Disabilities Act (ADA) of 1990

Occupational Safety and Health Act of 1970

notice of contest

Employee Retirement Income Security Act (ERISA)

Pension Benefit Guaranty Corporation (PBGC)

Worker Adjustment and Retraining Notification Act (WARN)

Racketeering Influenced and Corrupt Organizations Act (RICO)

drug testing

AIDS

polygraph test

computer surveillance

genetic screening

FOOTNOTES

1. In *Massachusetts Bonding and Insurance Co. v. U.S.* [352 U.S. 128 (1956)], Justice Felix Frankfurter quoted T. H. Huxley's statement regarding the fact that a bad rule can become embedded in the law; under *stare decisis* "a theory survives long after its brains are knocked out."

2. Statute of Laborers, 5 Eliz., c. 4 (1562).

3. 8 Mod. 10 (1721).

4. Transcripts of testimony, arguments of attorneys, and jury instructions of early criminal conspiracy cases can be located in Volumes III and IV of John R. Commons et al., *A Documentary History of American Industrial Society* (A. H. Clark Co., 1910).

5. 2 Wheeler Criminal Case 262 (1809).

6. 4 Metcalf 3, 45 Mass. 111 (1842). There are some interesting articles and books that discuss the economic developments surrounding the prosecution of these types of cases. For more information, see Walter Nelles, "Commonwealth v. Hunt," *Columbia Law Review* 32 (1932): 1128.

7. Numerous cases have upheld the power of Congress to regulate commerce pursuant to the Commerce clause, the Necessary and Proper clause (which provides Congress with the power to enact laws that are necessary and proper for enforcing the other powers granted in the Constitution), and the Supremacy clause (which makes federal law the supreme law of the land—Article VI, Clause 2). Some cases of note are *Gibbons v. Ogden* [9 Wheaton 1 (1824)] and *U.S. v. E. C. Knight Co.* [155 U.S. 685, 156 U.S. 1, 15 S.Ct. 249, 39 L.Ed. 325 (1895)].

8. *Standard Oil Company v. United States* [221 U.S. 1, 31 S.Ct. 502, 55 L.Ed. 619 (1911)].

9. The Clayton Act, 15 U.S.C. Sections 12–27 (1914).

10. The Federal Trade Commission Act, 15 U.S.C. Sections 41-58 (1914).

11. Passed in 1936, the Robinson–Patman Act, 15 U.S.C. Sections 13(a)–13(f), was aimed at protecting small competitors.

12. The Clayton Act, Section 4 (15 U.S.C. Section 15) states that actual injuries are necessary.

13. 15 U.S.C. Section 45(a)(1).

14. *New York Times,* December 18, 1988, p. 1.

15. Railway Labor Act, 44 Stat. 577, Ch. 347 (1926).

16. Arbitration Act, 30 Stat. 424, Ch. 370 (June 1, 1898).

17. 208 U.S. 161 (1908).

18. Adamson Act (Eight Hour Act), Ch. 436, 39 Stat. 721 (September 3 and 5, 1916).

19. Transportation Act, Ch. 91, 41 Stat. 456 (February 28, 1920) and Ch. 172, 41 Stat. 590 (May 8, 1920). This act was subsequently amended.

20. *Consolidated Rail v. Railway Labor Executive Assn.* [109 S.Ct. 2477 (1989)].

21. *Forbes,* May 30, 1988, p. 224.

22. *Pittsburgh and Lake Erie Railway Co. v. Railway Labor Executives Assn.* [109 S.Ct. 2585 (1989)].

23. The act was amended in 1934, 1936, 1951, and 1966.

24. The Norris–LaGuardia Act, 29 U.S.C. Sections 101–115 (1932).

25. 301 U.S. 468, 57 S.Ct. 857, 81 L.Ed. 1229 (1937).

26. 303 U.S. 325, 58 S.Ct. 578, 82 L.Ed. 872 (1938).

27. 303 U.S. 552, 58 S.Ct. 703, 82 L.Ed. 1012 (1938).

28. National Industrial Recovery Act, Ch. 90, 48 Stat. 195 (June 16, 1933).

29. 295 U.S. 495, 55 S.Ct. 837, 79 L.Ed. 1570 (1935).

30. National Labor Relations Act (Wagner Act), 49 Stat. 449–57 (1935).

31. Labor–Management Relations Act (Taft–Hartley Act), 61 Stat. 136–52 (1947).

32. Labor–Management Reporting and Disclosure Act (Landrum–Griffin Act), 73 Stat. 25–41 (1959).

33. 301 U.S. 1, 57 S.Ct. 615, 81 L.Ed. 893 (1937).

34. For a discussion of the Taft-Hartley amendments to the NLRA, see Archibald Cox, "Some Aspects of the Labor Management Relations Act, 1947," *Harvard Law Review* 61 (1947–1948): 1 and 274.

35. U.S. Department of Labor, Bureau of Labor Statistics, "Summary Report—National Emergency Disputes Under the Labor–Management Relations (Taft–Hartley) Act, 1947–1972" (no date).

36. The publicly funded rail commuter services, such as Amtrak, are subject to the 1981 amendment to the Railway Labor Act. There are significant differences, such as a 240–day cooling-off period while two consecutive emergency boards attempt to settle the dispute [95 Stat. 681, Section 1157 (1981)].

37. 306 U.S. 601 (1939).

38. 297 F. 2d 94 (2d Cir. 1962), reversed, 371 U.S. 224 (1963).

39. *Siemans Mailing Service,* 122 NLRB 81 (1958).

40. 340 U.S. 474, 71 S.Ct. 456, 95 L.Ed. 456 (1951). The Court stated that the board is "one of those agencies presumably equipped or informed by experience to deal with a specialized field of knowledge, whose findings within the field carry the authority of an expertness which courts do not possess and therefore must respect."

41. 29 U.S.C. Sections 201 et seq. (1938).

42. *Wall Street Journal*, November 1, 1989, p. A3 and *New York Times*, November 1, 1989, p. A1. President Bush had vetoed a bill in June 1989 that would have increased the federal minimum wage to $4.55.

43. See *Marshall v. Brunner* [668 F. 2d 748 (3rd Cir. 1982)] for a case reviewing this issue.

44. Walsh–Healy Act, 41 U.S.C. Sections 35–45 (1936).

45. Davis–Bacon Act, 40 U.S.C. Section 276a (1931).

46. Social Security Act, 42 U.S.C. Section 301 et seq. (1935).

47. U.S. Department of Health and Human Services, Social Security Administration, "Retirement" (SSA Publication No. 05–10035, January 1989), p. 7.

48. 26 U.S.C. Sections 3101–3126 (1954)

49. *Wall Street Journal*, June 30, 1989, p. B1.

50. U.S. Department of Health and Human Services, "Retirement," p. 7.

51. *New York Times*, December 5, 1989, p. A1.

52. Federal Unemployment Tax Act, 26 U.S.C. Sections 3301-3311 (1954).

53. Self-Employment Contributions Acts, 26 U.S.C. Sections 1401 et seq. (1990).

54. 42 U.S.C. Section 706(q) (1964).

55. 42 U.S.C. Section 701(b)–(e) (1964).

56. *The Chronicle of Higher Education*, May 24, 1989, p. A2.

57. 109 S.Ct. 706 (1989).

58. 109 S.Ct. 2115 (1989).

59. 109 S.Ct. 2180 (1989).

60. *Wall Street Journal*, June 13, 1989, p. A1.

61. 109 S.Ct. 2363 (1989).

62. 109 S.Ct. 1775 (1989).

63. *Wall Street Journal*, May 2, 1989, p. B1.

64. *New York Times*, March 21, 1991, p. A1.

65. For a current review of religious discrimination, see Laura S. Underkuffler, "'Discrimination' on the Basis of Religion: An Examination of Attempted Value Neutrality in Employment," *William and Mary Law Review* 30 (1989): 581–625.

66. 442 F. 2d 385 (Fifth Circuit, 1971).

67. Pregnancy Discrimination Act, 42 U.S.C. Section 200(e)–(k) (1978).

68. Miranda S. Spivack, "A New Coalition Is Winning on Family Leave," *Governing* (September 1988): 69; see also the section on family leave programs in Chapter 8 of the present volume.

69. 29 U.S.C. Section 206(d)(1) (1963).

70. *Working Woman*, May 1989, p. 40.

71. 29 U.S.C. Section 623 (1967).

72. *The Chronicle of Higher Education*, May 24, 1989, p. A3.

73. 29 U.S.C. Sections 701–794 (1973).

74. 29 U.S.C. Section 651 et seq. (1970).

75. 29 U.S.C. Section 654(a) (1970).

76. *Marshall v. Barlow's, Inc.* [436 U.S. 307(1978)] held that an inspector must obtain a warrant.

77. *Chicago Bridge v. OSHRC* [535 F. 2d 371 (7th Cir. 1976)] found that the right to have employer and employee representatives accompany the compliance officers on an inspection was mandatory.

78. 29 U.S.C. Sections 1001–1461 (1974).

79. *Business Week*, July 3, 1989, p. 31.

80. For more information, see David L. Gregory, "COBRA: Congress Provides Protection Against Employer Termination of Retiree Health Insurance," *San Diego Law Review* 24 (1987): 77.

81. The Worker Adjustment and Retraining Notification Act, 29 U.S.C. Sections 2101 et seq.

82. *New York Times*, March 19, 1989, p. 1 (Business Section).

83. *Wall Street Journal*, July 19, 1989, p. B11.

84. *McMonagle v. Northeast Women's Center, Inc.* [110 S.Ct. 261 (1989)].

85. 109 S.Ct. 1402 (1989).

86. 109 S.Ct. 1384 (1989).

87. *Wall Street Journal*, November 21, 1989, p. B1.

88. *Wall Street Journal*, August 18, 1988, p. 23.

89. 29 U.S.C. 2001 et seq.

90. *Fortune*, December 19, 1988, p. 7 and *Wall Street Journal*, August 25, 1988, p. 19.

91. *Business Week*, January 15, 1990, p. 74.

REFERENCES ══════

COMMERCE CLEARING HOUSE. *Labor Law Course*. 1976.

COMMONS, JOHN R., U. B. PHILLIPS, E. A. GILMORE, H. L. SUMNER, and J. B. ANDREWS. *A Documentary History of American Industrial Society*. A. H. Clark Co., 1910–11, Volumes III and IV.

Cox, Archibald. "Some Aspects of the Labor Management Relations Act, 1947." *Harvard Law Review* (November 1947): 1–49.

———. "Some Aspects of the Labor Management Relations Act, 1947." *Harvard Law Review* (January 1948): 274–315.

Getman, Julius G. *Labor Relations: Law, Practice and Policy.* Foundation Press, 1978.

Gorman, Robert A. *Basic Text on Labor Law, Unionization, and Collective Bargaining.* West Publishing Co., 1976.

Gregory, David L. "COBRA: Congress Provides Protection Against Employer Termination of Retiree Health Insurance." *San Diego Law Review* 24 (1987): 77.

Henderson, Richard. *Compensation Management: Rewarding Performance.* Prentice–Hall, 1989.

Kenny, John J. *Primer of Labor Relations.* Bureau of National Affairs, 1986.

Leslie, Douglas L. *Labor Law in a Nutshell.* West Publishing Co., 1986.

Nelles, Walter. "Commonwealth v. Hunt." *Columbia Law Review* 32 (1932): 1128.

Sloane, Arthur A., and Fred Witney. *Labor Relations.* Prentice–Hall, 1988.

Taylor, Benjamin, and Fred Witney. *Labor Relations Law.* Prentice–Hall, 1987.

Twomey, David. *A Concise Guide to Employment Law EEO & OSHA.* South-Western Publishing Co., 1986.

Underkuffler, Laura S. " 'Discrimination' on the Basis of Religion: An Examination of Attempted Value Neutrality in Employment." *William and Mary Law Review* 30 (1989): 581–625.

A P P E N D I X

LANDMARK CASES

The Danbury Hatters' Boycott

Loewe v. Lawlor
208 U.S. 274 (1908)

Facts This action was brought in the Circuit Court for the District of Connecticut under Paragraph 7 of the Anti-Trust Act of July 2, 1890, c. 647, 26 Stat. 209, claiming treble damages for injuries inflicted on plaintiffs by a combination or conspiracy. The defendants filed a demurrer, which is a motion basically stating that the facts alleged fail to state a cause of action. The motion was sustained and the case was dismissed upon plaintiffs' failure to amend the complaint.

The case was brought to the Circuit Court of Appeals for the Second Circuit by writ of error, and that court certified the question to be brought to the U.S. Supreme Court. At that juncture all the parties applied to the U.S. Supreme Court to hear the case. The Court accepted the case and carefully reviewed sections one, two, and seven of the Sherman Act.

The defendants were members of the United Hatters of North America, a union with approximately 9,000 members, and affiliated with 1,400,000-member AFL. In what was an attempt to unionize the shops of fur hat manufacturers, particularly the plaintiffs, the defendants declared a boycott of wholesale dealers of the fur hats. They distributed circulars containing notices of such dealers and customers to be boycotted. These activities injured the plaintiffs business.

Court Discussion   Mr. Chief Justice Fuller delivered the opinion of the court. The question is whether, upon the facts presented, this action can be maintained under the Sherman Act.

The first, second, and seventh sections of that act are as follows:

1. "Every contract, combination in the form of trust or otherwise, or conspiracy, in restraint of trade or commerce among the several states, or with foreign nations, is hereby declared to be illegal. Every person who shall make any such contract or engage in any such combination or conspiracy, shall be deemed guilty of a misdemeanor, and, on conviction thereof, shall be punished by fine not exceeding five thousand dollars, or by imprisonment not exceeding one year, or by both said punishments, in the discretion of the court.

2. "Every person who shall monopolize, or attempt to monopolize, or combine or conspire with any other person or persons, to monopolize any part of the trade or commerce among the several States, or with foreign nations, shall be deemed guilty of a misdemeanor, and, on conviction thereof, shall be punished by fine not exceeding five thousand dollars, or by imprisonment not exceeding one year, or by both said punishments, in the discretion of the court."

7. "Any person who shall be injured in his business or property by any other person or corporation by reason of anything forbidden or declared to be unlawful by this act, may sue therefor in any Circuit Court of the United States in the district in which the defendant resides or is found, without respect to the amount in controversy, and shall recover three fold the damages by him sustained, and the costs of suit, including a reasonable attorney's fee."

In our opinion, the combination described in the declaration is a combination "in restraint of trade or commerce among the several states," in the sense in which those words are used in the act, and the action can be maintained accordingly.

And that conclusion rests on many judgments of this court, to the effect that the act prohibits any combination whatever to secure action which essentially obstructs the free flow of commerce between the States, or restricts, in that regard, the liberty of a trader to engage in business.

The combination charged falls within the class of restraints of trade aimed at compelling third parties and strangers involuntarily not to engage in the course of trade except on conditions that the combination imposes; and there is no doubt that (to quote from the well-known work of Chief Justice Erle on Trade Unions) "at common law every person has individually, and the public also has collectively, a right to require that the course of trade should be kept free from unreasonable obstruction." But the objection here is to the jurisdiction, because, even conceding that the declaration states a case good at common law, it is contended that it does not state one within the statute. Thus, it is said, that the restraint alleged would operate to entirely destroy plaintiff's business and thereby include intrastate trade as well; that physical obstruction is not alleged as contemplated; and that defendants are not themselves engaged in interstate trade.

We think none of these objections are tenable, and that they are disposed of by previous decisions of this court....

We think a case within the statute was set up and that the demurrer should have been overruled.

Judgment reversed and cause remanded with direction to proceed accordingly.

Double Standard

Bedford Cut Stone Company v. Journeymen Stone Cutters' Association of North America
274 U.S. 37 (1927)

Facts This suit was brought by petitioners, Bedford Cut Stone Company and 23 other companies, all in the business of quarrying or fabricating Indiana limestone, against an association of mechanics, the Journeymen Stone Cutters' Association of North America (hereafter referred to as the General Union). The petitioners' annual aggregate sales amounted to about $15,000,000, more than 75% of which was made in interstate commerce to customers outside the State of Indiana. The General Union, respondents, had members in various states and Canada. The petitioners brought an action in federal district court to enjoin the union and affiliated unions from conspiring to commit acts in restraint of interstate commerce in violation of the federal Anti-Trust Act. It was alleged that the union issued a notice to all its locals and members directing members not to work on stone "that has been started—planned, turned, cut, or semifinished—by men working in opposition to our organization," with the exception of one employer holding an injunction against the union. This notice was persistently adhered to by the members.

The federal district court refused a preliminary injunction and subsequently dismissed the action. The court of appeals affirmed that decree, and the action was brought before the Supreme Court.

Court Discussion Mr. Justice Sutherland delivered the opinion of the court....

From a consideration of all the evidence, it is apparent that the enforcement of the general order to strike against petitioners' product could have had no purpose other than that of coercing or inducing the local employers to refrain from purchasing such product. To accept the assertion made here to the contrary would be to say that the order and the effort to enforce it were vain and idle things without any rational purpose whatsoever. And indeed, on the argument, in answer to a question from the bench, counsel for respondents very frankly said that, unless petitioners' interstate trade in the so-called unfair stone were injuriously affected, the strikes would accomplish nothing....

Interstate commerce was the direct object of attack "for the sake of which the several specific acts and courses of conduct (were) done and adopted." And the restraint of such commerce was the necessary consequence of the acts and conduct and the immediate end in view (*Swift & Co. v. United States*, 196 U.S. 375, 397). Prevention of the use of petitioners' product, which, without more, might have been a purely local matter, therefore, was only a part of the conspiracy, which must be construed as an entirety; and, when so regarded, the local transactions become a part of the general plan and purpose to destroy or narrow petitioners' interstate trade. In other words, strikes against the local use of the product were simply the means adopted to effect the unlawful restraint. And it is this result, not the means devised to secure it, which gives character to the conspiracy....

A restraint of interstate commerce cannot be justified by the fact that the ultimate object of the participants was to secure an ulterior benefit which they might have been at liberty to pursue by means not involving such restraint....

With a few changes in respect of the product involved, dates, names and incidents, which would have no effect upon the principles established, the opinion in *Duplex Co. v. Deering*...might serve as an opinion in this case. The object of the boycott there was precisely the same as it is here, and the interferences with interstate commerce, while they were more numerous and more drastic....The conclusion was reached that complainant was entitled to an injunction under the Sherman Act as amended by the Clayton Act, and that it was unnecessary to consider whether a like result would follow under the common law or local statutes....

In *Gompers v. Bucks Stove & Range Co.*, 221, U.S. 418, 438–439, this court said that the restraining powers of the courts extend to every device whereby commerce is illegally restrained; and that—"To hold that the restraint of trade under the Sherman Anti-Trust Act, or on general principles of law, could be enjoined, but that the means through which the restraint was accomplished could not be enjoined would be to render the law impotent."...

Whatever may be said as to the motives of the respondents or their general right to combine for the purpose of redressing alleged grievances of their fellow craftsmen or of protecting themselves or their organizations, the present combination deliberately adopted a course of conduct which directly and substantially curtail, or threatened thus to curtail, the natural flow in interstate commerce of a very large proportion of the building limestone production of the entire country, to the gravely probable disadvantage of producers, purchasers and the public; and it must be held to be a combination in undue and unreasonable restraint of such commerce within the meaning of the Anti-Trust Act as interpreted by this court. An act which lawfully might be done by one, may when done by many acting in concert take the form of a conspiracy and become a public wrong, and may be prohibited if the result be hurtful to the public or to individuals against whom such concerted action is directed....

From the foregoing review, it is manifest that the acts and conduct of respondents fall within the terms of the Anti-Trust Act; and petitioners are entitled to relief by injunction under paragraph 16 of the Clayton Act, c. 323, 38 Stat. 730, 737, by which they are authorized to sue for such relief "against threatened loss or damage by a violation of the anti-trust laws," etc. That the organizations, in general purpose and in and of themselves, were lawful and that the ultimate result aimed at may not have been illegal in itself, are beside the point. Where the means adopted are unlawful, the innocent general character of the organizations adopting them or the lawfulness of the ultimate end sought to be attained, cannot serve as a justification. Decree reversed.

In Defense of "Little" Norris–LaGuardias

Senn v. Tile Layers Protective Union
301 U.S. 468 (1937)

Facts   Senn, a contractor, had a small business setting tile. He did much of his own work. The Tile Layers Union tried to unionize his shop and he was willing; however, under the union agreement he would be prohibited from working since he did not qualify as a union member. Upon his refusal to sign the contract, two men picketed his business, which was also his home. Two banners were carried stating he was unfair to the tile union.

Senn brought an action for an injunction. The trial court denied a remedy solely on the ground that the acts were permitted in the course of a labor dispute within the meaning of the Wisconsin Labor Code.

The case was appealed. The Supreme Court of Wisconsin sustained the dismissal of the action against the labor unions and their agents, thus permitting the picketing. The State Supreme Court also denied a motion for rehearing, with two judges dissenting. The case was appealed to the United States Supreme Court. Mr. Justice Brandeis delivered the opinion of the Court.

Court Decision   This case presents the questions whether the provisions of the Wisconsin Labor Code, which authorize giving publicity to labor disputes, peaceful picketing and lawful patrolling, and prohibit granting of an injunction against such conduct, violate, as here construed and applied, the due process clause or equal protection clauses of the Fourteenth Amendment.

FIRST. The defendants moved to dismiss the appeal for want of jurisdiction. They contend that the federal question presented is not substantial. . . .

SECOND. The hearings below were concerned mainly with questions of state law. . . . The question for our decision is whether the (state) statute, as applied to the facts found, took Senn's liberty or property or denied him equal protection of the laws in violation of the Fourteenth Amendment. . . .

The unions concede that Senn, so long as he conducts a nonunion shop, has the right to work with his hands and tools. . . . The question for our determination is whether either the means or the end sought (by the union) is forbidden by the Federal Constitution.

THIRD. Clearly the means which the statute authorizes—picketing and publicity—are not prohibited by the Fourteenth Amendment. Members of a union might, without special statutory authorization by a state, make known the facts of a labor dispute, for freedom of speech is guaranteed by the Federal Constitution. The State may, in the exercise of its police power, regulate the methods and means of publicity as well as the use of public streets. If the end sought by the unions is not forbidden by the Federal Constitution the State may authorize working men to seek to attain it by combining as pickets, just as it permits capitalists and employers to combine in other ways to attain their desired economic ends. . . . In the present case the only means authorized by the statute and in fact resorted to by the unions have been peaceful and accompanied by no unlawful act. It follows, that if the end sought is constitutional—if the unions may constitutionally induce Senn to agree to refrain from exercising the right to work in his business with his own hands, their acts were lawful.

FOURTH. The end sought by the unions is not unconstitutional. Article III, which the unions seek to have Senn accept, was found by the state courts to be not arbitrary or capricious, but a reasonable rule "adopted by the defendants out of the necessities of employment within the industry and for the protection of themselves as workers and craftsmen in the industry." The sole purpose of the picketing was to acquaint the public with the facts and, by gaining its support, to induce Senn to unionize his shop. There was no effort to induce Senn to do an unlawful thing. There was no violence, no force was applied, no molestation or interference, no coercion. There was only the persuasion incident to publicity. . . .

The laws of Wisconsin, as declared by its highest court, permits unions to endeavor to induce an employer, when unionizing his shop, to agree to refrain from working in his business with his own hands—so to endeavor although none of his employees is a member of a union.

FIFTH. There is nothing in the Federal Constitution which forbids unions from competing with non-union concerns for customers by means of picketing as freely as one merchant competes with another by means of advertisements in the press, by circulars, or by his window display. Each member of the unions, as well as Senn, has the right to strive to earn his living. Senn seeks to do so through exercise of his individual skill and planning. The union members seek to do so through combination. Earning a living is dependent upon public favor. To win the patronage of the public each may strive by legal means. Exercising its police power, Wisconsin has declared that in a labor dispute peaceful picketing and truthful publicity are means legal for unions.

SIXTH. It is contended that in prohibiting an injunction the statute denied to Senn equal protection of the laws. . . . But the issue suggested by plaintiff does not arise. For we hold that the provisions of the Wisconsin statute which authorized the conduct of the unions are constitutional. One has no constitutional right to a "remedy" against the lawful conduct of another.

Affirmed.

Across State Lines

NLRB v. Reliance Fuel Oil Corp.
371 U.S. 224 (1963)

Court Decision   The Reliance Fuel Oil Corporation, respondent herein, was found by the National Labor Relations Board to have committed certain unfair labor practices in violation of the National Labor Relations Act, 49 Stat. 449, as amended, 29 U.S.C. 151 et seq. Jurisdiction before the Board was predicated upon the fact that Reliance, a New York distributor of fuel oil whose operations were local, purchased within the State a "substantial amount" of fuel oil and related products from the Gulf

Oil Corporation, a supplier concededly engaged in interstate commerce. In 1959 Reliance purchased a few hundred dollars worth of truck parts in New Jersey, but the Board did not rely on such transactions to sustain its assertion of jurisdiction. Most of the products sold to Reliance were delivered to Gulf from without the State of New York and prior to sale and delivery to Reliance were stored, without segregation as to customer, in Gulf's tanks located within the State. During the fiscal year ending June 30, 1959, Reliance had gross sales well in excess of $500,000 (the Board treated Reliance as a "retail" concern, and this amount of gross sales met its self-imposed standard for exercise of jurisdiction: 129 N.L.R.B. 1166, 1170–1171).

The Board adopted its trial examiner's findings that the operations of Reliance "affected" commerce within the meaning of the Act and that the unfair labor practices found tended "to lead to labor disputes burdening and obstructing commerce and the free flow of commerce...." (129 N.L.R.B. 1166, 1171, 1182). The Court of Appeals reversed, 297 F. 2d 94, because, in its view, the record before the Board did not adequately demonstrate the existence of jurisdiction and remanded the case to the Board so that it might "take further evidence and make further findings on the manner in which a labor dispute at Reliance affects or tends to affect commerce." The only issue before this Court is whether on the record before it the Board properly found that it had jurisdiction to enter an order against Reliance; the substantive findings as to the existence of the unfair labor practices are not here in dispute.

Under Section 10(a) of the Act, the Board is empowered "to prevent any person from engaging in any unfair labor practice (listed in Section 8) affecting commerce." Section 2(6) defines "commerce" to mean "trade, traffic, commerce, transportation, or communication among the ... States ... " and Section 2(7) declares:

> The term "affecting commerce" means in commerce, or burdening or obstruct- ing commerce or the free flow of commerce, or having led or tending to lead to a labor dispute burdening or obstructing commerce or the free flow of com- merce.

This Court has consistently declared that in passing the National Labor Relations Act, Congress intended to and did vest in the Board the fullest jurisdictional breadth constitutionally permissible under the Commerce Clause.... The Act establishes a framework within which the Board is to determine "whether proscribed practices would in particular situations adversely affect commerce when judged by the full reach of the constitutional power of Congress. Whether or not practices may be deemed by Congress to affect interstate commerce is not to be determined by con- fining judgment to the quantitative effect of the activities immediately before the Board. Appropriate for judgment is the fact that the immediate situation is repre- sentative of many others throughout the country, the total incidence of which if left unchecked may well become far-reaching in its harm to commerce." (*Polish Alliance v. Labor Board*, 322 U.S., at 648. See also *Labor Board v. Fainblatt*, 306 U.S., at 607–608).

That activities such as those of Reliance affect commerce and are within the con- stitutional reach of Congress is beyond doubt. Through the National Labor Relations Act, "... Congress has explicitly regulated not merely transactions or goods in interstate commerce but activities which in isolation might be deemed to be merely local but in the interlacing of business across state lines adversely affect such commerce." (*Polish Alliance v. Labor Board*, 322 U.S. 648). This being so, the jurisdictional test is met here: the Board properly found that by virtue of Reliance's purchases from Gulf, Reliance's operations and the related unfair labor practices "affected" commerce, within the meaning of the Act. The judgment of the Court of Appeals accordingly must be and is reversed.

Mr. Justice Black concurs in the result.

A Question of Stereotypes

Price Waterhouse v. Hopkins
109 S. Ct. 1775 (1989)

Court Discussion   Congress' intent to forbid employers to take gender into account in making employment decisions appears on the face of the statute. In now-familiar language, the statute forbids an employer to "fail or refuse to hire or to discharge any individual, or otherwise to discriminate with respect to his compensation, terms, conditions, or privileges of employment," or to "limit, segregate, or classify his employees or applicants for employment in any way which would deprive or tend to deprive any individual of employment opportunities or otherwise adversely affect his status as an employee because of such individual's ... sex." [42 USC Sections 2000e–2(a)(1),(2)]. We take these words to mean that gender must be irrelevant to employment decisions. To construe the words "because of" as colloquial shorthand for "but-for causation," as does Price Waterhouse, is to misunderstand them.

We have, in short, been here before. Each time, we have concluded that the plaintiff who shows that an impermissible motive played a motivating part in an adverse employment decision has thereby placed upon the defendant the burden to show that it would have made the same decision in the absence of the unlawful motive. Our decision today treads this well-worn path. . . .

In saying that gender played a motivating part in an employment decision, we mean that, if we asked the employer at the moment of the decision what its reasons were and if we received a truthful response, one of those reasons would be that the applicant or employee was a woman. In the specific context of sex stereotyping, an employer who acts on the basis of a belief that a woman cannot be aggressive, or that she must not be, had acted on the basis of gender. . . .

As to the employer's proof, in most cases, the employer should be able to present some objective evidence as to its probable decision in the absence of an impermissible motive. Moreover, proving "that the same decision would have been justified . . . is not the same as proving that the same decision would have been made." Givhan, 439 US, at 416, 58 L Ed 2d 619, 99 S Ct 693, quoting *Ayers v. Western Line Consolidated School District*, 555 F2d 1309, 1315 (CA5 1977). An employer may not, in other words, prevail in a mixed-motives case by offering a legitimate and sufficient reason for its decision if that reason did not motivate it at the time of the decision. Finally, an employer may not meet its burden in such a case by merely showing that at the time of the decision it was motivated only in part by a legitimate reason. The very premise of a mixed-motives case is that a legitimate reason was present, and indeed, in this case, Price Waterhouse already has made this showing by convincing Judge Gesell that Hopkins' interpersonal problems were a legitimate concern. The employer instead must show that its legitimate reason, standing alone, would have induced it to make the same decision.

Although Price Waterhouse does not concretely tell us how its proof was preponderant even if it was not clear and convincing, this general claim is implicit in its request for the less stringent standard. Since the lower courts required Price Waterhouse to make its proof by clear and convincing evidence, they did not determine whether Price Waterhouse had proved by a preponderance of the evidence that it would have placed Hopkins' candidacy on hold even if it had not permitted sex-linked evaluations to play a part in the decision-making process. Thus, we shall remand this case so that that determination can be made.

CHAPTER 4

UNION STRUCTURE AND GOVERNMENT

The structure of the American labor movement is, in large measure, the structure of the AFL–CIO (the Federation) and its constituent national unions. The AFL and AFL–CIO have been synonymous with the American labor movement for over 100 years. The discussion in this chapter will go beyond the static perspective of organization structure and look at trends in union structure, especially mergers. We will also analyze the power center in unions. The bargaining or economic and political decision-making center of all trade unions is not at the national level as Samuel Gompers visualized in his 1886 model of a trade union movement, but may appear at lower levels, even the lowest level, the local.

The topic of union leadership is closely related to that of structure and power; thus, the next focus of discussion is on structure, organization, and governance within the American labor movement. Specifically, we will analyze the nature of union leadership and corruption in unions. We will also talk about how units like the Federation and its national/international unions and their regionals and locals are related and how they function. The chapter ends with a brief discussion of union democracy, with special emphasis on how unions achieve their goals with respect to the workers they represent and the management with which they bargain. The organization and structure of collective bargaining are covered in Chapter 6.

CRAFT AND INDUSTRIAL UNIONS ===

Trade unions (another name for labor unions) are typically classified as craft or industrial unions. This distinction is based on the grouping of workers together in the national union and down through to the locals, the smallest units of the national.

Similar Skills, Similar Jobs: The Monopolism of Craft Unions

Craft unions are composed of workers in a single craft with similar skills doing similar jobs; for the most part, they are skilled workers or apprentices learning their craft. Examples of craft unions are the carpenters, electricians, machinists, and plumbers. The unions are usually geographically organized; the building trades are the best examples of this organization, and they are also the classic examples of craft unions.

A local union that has organized most of the workers practicing its craft in its area of operations is fairly powerful. This power is based on controlling the labor supply in the craft and is therefore a form of monopoly power.

The craft local would be the major (and if it organized all those in the craft in the area, the *only*) seller of that category of labor service, forcing users (employers) to deal with it. Present trends show that many craft unions have little monopoly power. In the building trades, nonunion competition has caused a substantial erosion of this power.[1] Today nonunion carpenters, plumbers, electricians, and other construction workers are building more housing in many locations than union workers.

Craft unions were the basis of the American Federation of Labor in the nineteenth century. Samuel Gompers laid the craft union framework for the AFL by specifically calling for organizing only skilled workers, sharing common interests, in AFL-chartered national unions.

Various Skills, Various Jobs: The Diversity of Industrial Unions

Industrial unions are made up of all workers in an industry. They do a variety of jobs, and they have a range of skills varying from unskilled to semiskilled to skilled. An electrician working in an automobile assembly plant is likely to be a member of the United Auto Workers (UAW), an industrial union, rather than the International Brotherhood of Electrical Workers (IBEW), a craft union. Examples of industrial unions are the auto workers, steel workers, (coal) mine workers, and clothing and textile workers.

Unlike craft unions, industrial unions are organized along industry lines. To gain some semblance of monopoly or economic market power, an industrial union would have to organize all the companies in an industry. Since it cannot control the labor supply like a craft union's locals, to be in a position to attain any monopoly power—that is, to become the major seller or price-maker for labor services—it must possess power apart from labor market power. This power, if attained, would be a power primarily of the national union rather than its locals.

Merger: Monopoly Meets Diversity

Industrial unions were reluctantly chartered by the craft union-oriented AFL. An early example was the United Mine Workers in 1890.[2] The handful of major industrial unions in the old AFL, led by the UMW, split off to form the Congress of Industrial Organizations in 1936, primarily over the issue of industrial unionization.[3]

The merger of the AFL and CIO brought the major craft and industrial unions together in 1955, with the exception of those specifically expelled by each federation. The AFL–CIO now represents all major craft and industrial unions in the United States.[4]

THE STRUCTURE OF THE AMERICAN LABOR MOVEMENT

The Federation

The **AFL–CIO, the Federation**, is an umbrella organization. (The structure of the organization is shown in Figure 4.1.) It does not bargain with management except for those few independent locals that have not affiliated with a national union. It has little economic power, other than the power of expulsion, which is a dubious power at best.[5] The chartered national unions, the central units in the labor movement, are completely autonomous. The Federation's primary purpose is political. It also resolves internal disputes that arise between its constituent unions, and it attempts to assure that these unions' policies are in compliance with the general policies of the AFL–CIO. Another important function of the Federation is to promote labor's public image. It is also active in education and research to further the aims and image of American labor and as a service to its constituent unions. The Federation interfaces with foreign labor movements and supports their development in less developed nations.

Politics and the Federation

Historically, the AFL shunned national political involvement, under the general concept of voluntarism, as explained in Chapter 2. With the passing of Samuel Gompers as leader, the AFL became more active politically. From its beginning, the CIO was more active in the political arena. The New Deal enactments involved the government and the labor movement in labor–management legislation to a substantial degree, and by the end of World War II both the AFL and CIO were politically involved in a regular, ongoing fashion.[6]

The Federation supports, and lobbies for, legislation that (1) benefits the union movement, in terms of union rights and protection, (2) benefits workers in general, and (3) benefits the public, in terms of social welfare. These goals sometimes conflict, as would be true for protectionist legislation that might benefit workers but not the public in general.

In the first category are measures such as the repeal of several provisions of the Taft–Hartley Act, for example, the prohibition of secondary actions like boycotts*

---

* One of the last major labor law reform attempts of the Federation was the passage of a Common–Situs Picketing Law to allow a construction union to picket a general contractor at a construction site and have all other construction unions working for subcontractors involved in the job join the picket line to force the general contractor to take some action, for example, not use nonunion labor for certain jobs. The Supreme Court has ruled that such picketing is a violation of Section 8(b)(4)(B) of the Taft–Hartley Act. A common-situs picketing bill was passed by Congress in 1976 but vetoed by President Gerald Ford, causing the resignation of then Secretary of Labor John Dunlop.

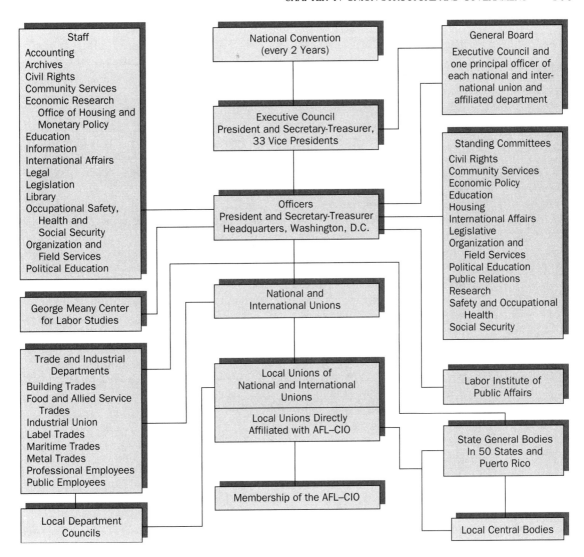

FIGURE 4.1 Structure of the AFL–CIO.
Source: American Federationist, the official monthly magazine of the AFL–CIO.

and Section 14(b), which allows state right-to-work laws to take precedence over the provisions in the National Labor Relations Act that allow collective bargaining contracts to have compulsory union membership clauses (see Chapter 3). Moreover, the Federation lobbies for trade protection legislation for industries like the automobile industry which are particularly hard hit by imports. In some instances, this lobbying, when successful, also benefits nonunion workers whose jobs are saved by trade legislation.

In the second category are laws like OSHA, ERISA, and WARN (the 1988 Worker Adjustment and Retraining Notification Act, requiring advance notice of plant closing). Also included is legislation protecting specific groups of workers, like women, children, and the handicapped: these laws relate to discrimination in employment. The AFL–CIO was a major supporter of the 1972 Equal Employment Opportunity Act and all civil rights legislation. In 1988, they were a major factor in getting the polygraph (lie detector) protection bill passed.

These efforts to benefit workers in general are closely related to the third category of legislation, that benefiting the general public. Examples of such laws are those promoting full employment (such as the Humphrey–Hawkins Equal Opportunity and Full Employment Act of 1976 and CETA, the Comprehensive Education and Training Act of 1973), education, and universal health care. Social welfare legislation is high on the AFL–CIO agenda.

Another aspect of the AFL–CIO's political activities, as well as many national unions and labor associations both within and outside the Federation, is its election activities. It is a large contributor to campaigns, in terms of both money and volunteer helpers. State federations and local labor councils are particularly instrumental in mobilizing volunteers. Campaign contributions are funneled through the Federation's Committee on Political Education (COPE). Since COPE is a political action committee (PAC), its funding comes from voluntary contributions by union members and not from dues that legally can be used only to support representation activities, primarily collective bargaining. Federal Election Commission figures show, however, that the funds COPE raised for the 1988 election placed it 48th on the list of political fundraisers, whereas the then-independent Teamsters' PAC was number one.[7]

The Federation also keeps track of the voting records of members of Congress on legislation relating to labor and social welfare. Its Department of Legislation publishes these records annually, tallying the "right" and "wrong" votes of each legislator on each bill or key issue the AFL–CIO is following.[8] For example, Senators Edward Kennedy of Massachusetts and Howard Metzenbaum of Ohio constantly rank high on the Federation tally, while Senators Larry Pressler of South Dakota and Phil Gramm of Texas rank near the bottom.

Resolving Internal Disputes

A second major function of the Federation is to resolve internal disputes between member unions, which usually involve organizational jurisdictions. Many of these disputes arose as a result of the 1955 merger when craft and industrial unions sought to organize and represent the same or overlapping groups of workers.

The merger guidelines and the 1954 "no-raiding" pact discussed in Chapter 2 laid the groundwork for a mechanism to adjudicate such disputes. A board of arbitration of union leaders was established after the 1955 merger to settle all jurisdictional disputes. A recent board decision awarded the newly affiliated Teamsters the right to organize the Coors brewery workers whom the International Association of Machinists originally held to be in its jurisdiction. A new procedure adopted in 1986 includes mediation and impartial binding arbitration.[9]

Closely related to organizational dispute resolution, but actually the opposite side of that coin, are the Federation's efforts in merging affiliate unions. In 1986, the AFL–CIO adopted new merger guidelines for this purpose.[10] (Mergers are discussed later in this chapter.) Finally, another function closely related to organizational and merger issues is the organizational help the Federation makes available to its constituent unions.

Promoting Labor's Public Image

A third major function of the Federation is to promote the American labor movement's public image. Since the turn of the century, when Samuel Gompers, as president of the AFL, claimed to be "spokesman for the House of Labor," the Federation has been committed to waging a public relations campaign. To bolster the image, both the AFL and CIO ousted many unions in 1950–1955. The AFL expelled its corrupt affiliates with open ties to racketeers and gangsters (e.g., the International Longshoremen's Association),[11] while the CIO ousted its allegedly communist-dominated unions (e.g., the United Electrical Workers and the International Longshoremen's and Warehousemen's Union).[12] The AFL–CIO moved again to bolster its image by expelling the International Brotherhood of Teamsters (IBT) in 1957 for "reputed underworld ties."[13] The IBT reaffiliated with the Federation in 1987.

The present policy of the AFL–CIO was clearly stated over 30 years ago by the Federation leadership: to protect the American labor movement from corrupt practices and communist influences. It fulfills this pledge through its Executive Council, by investigating any affiliated union that the Council considers to be corrupt or communist influenced. If the investigation shows the charges of corruption or communist infiltration to be true, and the union does not cleanse itself of the problem, the Council may act to suspend it. This abridgment of national union autonomy was felt to be necessary to support the image of an independent, democratic labor movement, and to forestall any legislative action that would be aimed at these problems.

Besides these cleansing moves, the AFL–CIO carries on active public relations campaigns, many of which are pointed directly at organizing workers (see below). Some campaigns, however, are aimed purely at bolstering labor's public image, as the Federation's recent, two-year "Union, Yes" television campaign was.[14]

Education and Research

The Federation has traditionally carried on education and research projects in three areas. The first grouping relates to the major social issues with which they are involved. The second area is the labor force in general and the union movement specifically. Third, the Federation serves as a research and education resource for its affiliated unions, especially smaller ones that have limited capabilities to carry on these functions themselves.

Many of the AFL–CIO's educational efforts are concentrated at its George Meany Center for Labor Studies. The Center also offers courses for developing union leaders. The Federation's 1985 report, "The Changing Situation of Workers and Their Unions," suggested a greater role for the Center in educating and developing union leaders, especially local leaders such as shop stewards.[15] As part of its educational efforts, the Federation provides speakers for the public, especially schools and colleges. It also makes available films to educate the public about the American labor movement, primarily the AFL–CIO.

International Dimensions

The AFL–CIO interfaces with international labor movements and organizations. It has become particularly concerned with labor movements in developing countries. The Federation is a member of the International Confederation of Free Trade Unions (ICFTU), and its president heads the union advisory group to the Organization for Economic Cooperation and Development (OECD). Through the U.S. government, the Federation maintains an avid interest in and some influence over the ongoing programs of the United Nations' International Labor Organization.*

The Federation's growing interest in international labor affairs parallels the growth of multinational businesses in both the United States and other countries. The movement of work and jobs across national borders is an increasingly common occurrence, as multinationals locate plants where they see an economic advantage, which usually includes low labor costs and weak or no unions. It is becoming increasingly clear to labor movements and unions in all countries, especially developed countries, that some form of labor coordination is needed to offset the multinationals' ability to move work rather easily from country to country.

A second concern of the Federation with respect to foreign unions and labor organizations is the spreading influence of communism in these countries, especially in developing countries. In the wake of the 1955 merger, the AFL–CIO withdrew from international labor organizations because of communist domination. Now, the Federation's leadership has decided that it would be wise to rejoin these organizations to help stop the spread of communist influence in the labor movements of developing countries and thus help ensure free trade unions in free countries.

The National/International Union

The Federation's **national** (or **international,** if they have Canadian affiliates) unions are the central units in the labor movement. Since the formation of the AFL in 1886, each national or international union has been chartered as an *autonomous* unit by the Federation. It develops its own constitution, bylaws, policies, and programs, in line with general Federation guidelines. The union also sets its own collective bargaining agenda. It organizes workers in its particular craft or industry as defined by its charter from the Federation, chartering them in locals. It has total control over its financial resources, including the strike fund which can be used to support its members when they are on a nationally sanctioned strike. It supports legislation and candidates for office that are important to and supportive of the union, through lobbying, campaign contributions, and supply of campaign volunteers. It is also a resource that its locals can call on when they need help. The national/international has many important functions, and carries them out both independently and in coordination with the Federation.

* Prior to the 1955 merger, the CIO belonged to the World Federation of Trade Unions, but it withdrew from this organization to placate the AFL's anticommunist sentiments. These same feelings caused the AFL–CIO to withdraw from the ICFTU (and the United States from the ILO), but both of these organizations were rejoined (*Christian Science Monitor*, February 18, 1988, p. 3).

Collective Bargaining on the National Level

Collective bargaining is a key function of the union. The locus of the major collective bargaining effort in the union can be at the national level or the local level, or at an intermediate point. The extent of the market for the product(s) produced by the union's members generally determines the appropriate level. In large industrial unions dealing with large employers, collective bargaining is carried out primarily at the national level. Examples of this centralized **bargaining structure** are the UAW (bargaining with each of the auto companies) and the United Steel Workers (USW) (bargaining with each of the major steel companies since the breakup of the steel producers' bargaining group). Locals at each plant also negotiate but primarily over local (plant-specific) issues. Figure 4.2a illustrates this bargaining and negotiating structure.

Collective bargaining by the national union assures similar pay for its members doing the same or similar jobs, no matter where they work. If the products involved are sold in a national market (e.g., automobiles, chemicals, and petroleum), and the union has organized a significant portion of the workers in that industry to the extent that the union-negotiated wage is the industry wage, this strategy "takes labor out of competition." That is, the difference in the cost of production would not include the labor costs.[16] This has been a long-sought goal of the labor movement: to base competition on differences in managerial costs rather than labor costs.

a. The traditional stucture

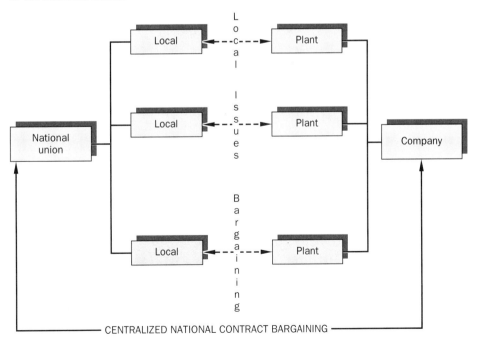

FIGURE 4.2 Large industrial union bargaining structure.

In an environment of economic growth and relatively low unemployment, unions have traditionally bargained vigorously for this goal, especially in centralized situations where the national does the collective bargaining. The 1980s environment was one of relatively low unemployment and growth. With these conditions we would expect **centralized bargaining** to have flourished. On the contrary, centralized bargaining situations were compromised by the differences in various economic provisions in contracts with one company versus another in the same industry, as in the auto industry starting in the early 1980s. Bargaining concessions made in the early 1980s are still having their impact, as unions strive to enhance employment security in negotiations rather than higher, industry-standardized pay. However, in 1989, the USW reversed the impact of concessions in the steel industry, especially those made in the 1986 bargaining round. The union won back wage and cost-of-living concessions from four major producers, moving closer to uniform industry wage rates for its workers.[17]

Fragmentation of bargaining is progressing at an increasing rate.[18] Different auto companies, steel companies, and trucking companies, for example, pay different wages to workers doing the same jobs.[19] The threats of plant closings have persuaded many nationals to let their threatened locals negotiate pacts to save jobs rather than union wage scales. (Figure 4.2b illustrates this changing picture.) The enhanced global competitive environment and the greater domestic competition partially stemming from deregulation of several industries have put unions and labor

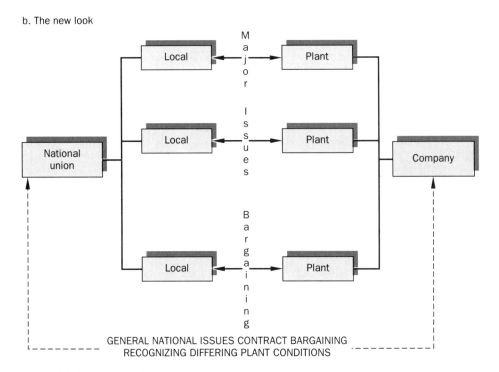

b. The new look

GENERAL NATIONAL ISSUES CONTRACT BARGAINING
RECOGNIZING DIFFERING PLANT CONDITIONS

FIGURE 4.2 (*Continued*)

associations much more on the defensive, in opposition to a much harder dealing management acting in a political environment favorable to them.

One cause of this favorable political environment is the shift in the NLRB's attitudes during the 1980s. During the Reagan administration, the NLRB decided a much smaller fraction of disputes in the unions' favor. For example, according to the AFL–CIO, the NLRB sustained unfair labor practice charges against employers 84 percent of the time in the mid-1970s, but that rate dropped to 50 percent by the early 1980s.[20]

Because most craft unions deal with products produced and sold in a local market, the primary collective bargaining function falls on the local in such cases. The national aids its locals in carrying out this function and tries to ensure that the local's contract is in line with national union policies and with the contracts of other locals. However, as noted above, present trends show a greater divergence of contract terms, especially in wages, among locals of the same national craft union. A primary example of this divergence is in the building trades, where locals are granting major concessions and waivers in wages and work rules to combat a growing use of nonunion workers in their construction crafts.

Union Organizing: On the Decline

The national is responsible for **organizing** new workers and thus expanding the union. Over the last 15 to 20 years, union success in this function has been, on the average, dismal. The decline in union membership since the 1950s as a percentage of the labor force is well documented. As we learned in Chapter 1, the changing structure of the economy and the labor force is partly responsible. As the economy and the labor force shifted from mining, construction, and manufacturing to services, the union movement began to witness an erosion of its membership base and thus its power. The mass-production industries (steel, autos, etc.) were the highly unionized ones, as were construction and mining. The service industries, with the exception of government, were not.

The union organizing tactics successful in the large-scale unionization of the mass-production industries from the 1930s through the 1960s were not effective in organizing the service workers of the 1970s and 1980s. Many of these service workers are women and teenagers employed as part-timers working in relatively small establishments, such as local stores or restaurants.

Another major factor in this lack of success is increased management opposition to unions, both within the law (better, more sophisticated personnel policies) and beyond it (unfair labor practices under Section 8(a) of the Taft–Hartley Act).[21] From 1950 to 1980, the number of workers organized through National Labor Relations Board representation elections as a percentage of workers in those elections dropped from 84 to 37 percent.[22] Table 4.1 shows clearly this growing lack of success in organizing new workers. Innovative approaches to union organizing are needed, and both the Federation and various unions are developing and implementing such approaches.

The AFL–CIO's 1985 report, "The Changing Situation of Workers and Their Unions," noted many new ways under discussion to increase the organizational power and scope of unions.[23] The report highlights two general approaches. First is the

Table 4.1 *Success of Unions in NLRB Representation Elections*

Year	New Workers Won in Elections as a Percentage of Workers in Those Elections	New Workers in Union-Won Elections as a Percentage of the Workforce
1950	84%	2.0%
1960	59%	0.7%
1970	52%	0.6%
1980	37%	0.2%

Source: Adapted from Richard B. Freeman, "Why Are Unions Faring Poorly in NLRB Representation Elections?" in Richard L. Rowan, ed., *Readings in Labor Economics and Labor Relations* (Richard D. Irwin, 1985), p. 130.

recommendation that the Federation develop new methods of increasing worker interest in joining a union, by, for example, establishing new categories of membership for workers who are not in an organized bargaining unit, or by providing direct services and benefits to workers outside of a collective bargaining structure completely (as those employed in nonunion companies). The second recommendation is to improve the organizing activity of the AFL–CIO and its affiliates directly. The report felt that this objective could be accomplished, among other ways, by better selection and training of organizers, greater use of modern communications technology, and increased targeting of small establishments for organizing (and developing economical ways to service these when unionized). The report was optimistic about the resurgence of the union movement, especially through the use of new methods to increase the organization and unionization of workers.

Politics and the National

Like the Federation, national unions are active in the political arena. They lobby for legislation that is beneficial to them, and they actively support candidates sympathetic to their goals. Recently, they have followed the Federation's lead and broadened their support to a variety of political issues as they strive to appeal to a wider spectrum of workers. They hope in this way to counter the drop in union membership.

Many national unions have **PACs** (**political action committees**) that are designed along the lines of the Federation's COPE, the original labor movement PAC. The Teamsters' Democratic Republican Independent Voter Education (DRIVE) committee was the top PAC for the 1988 political campaign, raising $5.3 million.[24]

Besides raising money for political purposes, nationals provide volunteer workers for campaigns. Union campaign workers canvas electoral districts, man phone banks, and perform related grass-roots political activities.

The National As a Resource

National unions also provide a myriad of services to their locals. They sponsor education and research programs, many of which are done for locals in general (e.g., training programs for local officials) and for locals specifically (e.g., asking for assistance in some research or educational area).

Nationals also aid locals in grievance and arbitration matters. They may send staff members, who are typically assigned to regional or district offices of the national, to work with local grievance committees in processing grievances at higher levels—for example, at the level of the plant manager or company vice president for industrial relations. With regard to arbitration matters, they may provide staff legal assistance in arbitration proceedings.

National craft unions and industrial unions whose locals do the bulk of collective bargaining with management usually get assistance from the national staff, again typically from union experts who work out of regional or district offices. The national may conduct research on many economic issues like wages and fringe benefits for its various locals in preparation for collective bargaining. Except in the case of the largest locals, the national union has more staff and financial resources available to perform these various activities for its locals, and it is one of its important functions.

Union Mergers: Strength in Unity

Before closing this discussion of the place of the national (international) union in the structure of the labor movement, the changing picture of national unions through mergers deserves some attention. In the face of declining union power, and as a continuation of the meshing of the AFL and CIO unions since the 1955 consolidation, **union mergers** have been accelerating.

After the AFL and CIO merged, unions that had obvious jurisdictional overlaps (CIO and AFL unions chartered to organize the same or similar workers) were encouraged to merge. Financial considerations also played an important part in encouraging these mergers. As suggested earlier, merger activity in the first 15 years or so after the consolidation was not very vigorous, however, as unions protected their turf. Furthermore, the onset of concession bargaining, followed by the unfavorable climate of the Reagan years, was still in the future.

The pace accelerated in the 1979–1984 period as 30 mergers occurred.[25] Today, merger discussions continue between several pairs of unions.[26] This wave of mergers has been motivated by efforts to bolster sagging union power, to cut union costs, and even to assure union survival. The drop in union membership has impacted many unions. To avert their demise, several of the smaller of these unions have merged or joined larger unions. Some of the larger unions that have lost a substantial number of members (such as the UAW, which has seen a 30 percent drop in membership in the last dozen years) have had to cut staff drastically.

The largest of the mergers in recent years occurred in 1979 when the Retail Clerks International Union joined with the Amalgamated Meat Cutters and Butcher Workmen of North America to form the United Food and Commercial Workers, which had a membership of over 1.2 million at that time.[27] A recent (1989) large-scale merger involved the joining of the National Union of Hospital and Health Care Employees with the Service Employees International Union (SEIU), pushing the SEIU to almost 1 million members.[28]

The Local Union: Where Workers and Union Meet

The **local union** is the point of contact of the workers with their union, and as such it is a very important level in the structure of the labor movement. The local's two major functions are (1) collective bargaining to represent workers dealing in a local-ized product market and bargaining over plant (local) issues in a national collective bargaining environment, and (2) the day-to-day administration of the contract.

Collective Bargaining on the Local Level

Craft and industrial locals have many differences, one significant one being the part they play in collective bargaining. All locals are involved in collective bargaining, but the extent of topics bargained over is usually greater for the craft than for the industrial locals.

Craft union locals, like those in the building trades, usually have a significant role in collective bargaining. Their bargaining committees negotiate local (or re-gional) area contracts on wages and related topics with local employers, for example, contractor associations. Since the product is offered in the local market, national coordination is of importance for general policies such as work rules rather than for the specifics of pay and similar items. The craft local has substantial independence from the national, especially when compared to an industrial union local.

Typically, the national unions impose many more constraints on industrial union locals with regard to the scope of their collective bargaining. The negotiating com-mittees of the industrial union locals usually concern themselves with local (or plant) issues, and wages and other economic issues are generally set by bargaining at the national level. However, some larger industrial locals are more significantly involved in the range of topics encompassed by collective bargaining. In an industrial union like the United Food and Commercial Workers (UFCW), locals do the primary col-lective bargaining, because (1) they comprise local market-oriented service workers in supermarkets and other commercial establishments (as department stores), and (2) several of the original unions that merged to form the UFCW were craft unions that had a strong tradition of local collective bargaining (such as the Meatcutters and Butchers, and Barbers and Beauticians).

Contract Administration

Both types of locals are primarily responsible for **administering the contract**; as such, they oversee grievance processing and arbitration (see Chapter 11). In a craft local, the **business agent** is the main officer and handles the grievances (complaints) of the members at the various sites in the area at which they are working. The agent may appoint an employee as shop steward at each site to handle the initial step or steps in the grievance procedure. The business agent, a full-time employee of the local, travels from site to site to administer the contract and handle grievances, especially those at the final steps in the process. He or she also administers the local's affairs, holding meetings, and so on.

In an industrial local, the on-site administrators are the **shop stewards**, elected representatives in each area of the plant. The shop stewards handle employee grievances at the shop floor level and start these complaints through the grievance steps specified in the collective bargaining agreement. If lower level supervisors and shop stewards cannot resolve the grievance, it moves upward in the organization, ultimately becoming the responsibility of the local's **grievance committee**. This elected committee of the local plays an important role in processing grievances once they proceed beyond the shop stewards and lower level managers such as line supervisors.

Operating the Local

The local union's operation is a key element in maintaining the labor movement in the United States, for it is the organization with which the rank-and-file members interact on a daily basis. In carrying out its major day-to-day functions, the typical industrial local has two hierarchies. First, contract administration involves shop stewards and plant grievance committees, elected officials who have the responsibility of assuring that management abides by the collective bargaining contract and provides a safe workplace. Second, running the organization is the responsibility of the elected officers of the local, the president, vice-president (if there is one), and the secretary and treasurer (offices commonly combined into one, a secretary-treasurer). These operating officers often make up the bargaining or negotiating committee of the local.

Operating the organization involves many considerations. A primary concern of local officers is maintaining contact with the members to get feedback on their needs and desires. The major communications channel between officers and members is the local's regular union meetings. But only 5 to 10 percent of members attend local meetings, except for those meetings when a vote is to be taken: a strike vote (usually the best attended meeting), contract ratification (if voted upon), and local officer elections.[29] The meeting competes with many other activities that fill a member's evening hours: bowling, local sporting events, the movies, and other recreation. However, shop stewards are expected to be present at the local's meetings, and they provide a communications channel between the officers and the members with whom they are in daily contact on the job.

Because meeting attendance is so poor, many locals try different approaches to keep in contact with their membership. Many have recreation leagues, and sponsor bowling, softball, and other sports teams. They use other social and recreational activities to maintain membership interest and contact. Larger locals issue a regular newsletter, while smaller ones attempt to maintain visibility in the national's newspapers and other mailings to the union members.

Running the local union is a major, time-consuming job. In larger locals it is a full-time, paid position. If the local has a business agent, he or she is a full-time, paid union official. In the majority of cases, however, the local president is a full-time employee of the company. Time spent on union business during working hours may be paid by the employer or the union; this issue is covered in the collective bargaining agreement. Union functions performed after working hours, such as holding the regular union meetings, are done on a voluntary basis. Local officers, especially the president, have a tough, poorly rewarded job. They serve for many reasons: some out of a sense of duty, and some to satisfy their own ambitions, hoping to climb the union ladder to district or regional posts and national positions. Whatever their motive, the vast majority serve well.

POWER AND UNION GOVERNMENT ═══════

The people who run unions are people with power, and how they use that power is a major public concern. A large segment of the public is aware of national unions and their leaders primarily through media coverage. For example, the late Walter Reuther, as president of the United Auto Workers and vice-president of the AFL–CIO at the time of the 1955 merger, was a well-known union leader. His honesty and integrity, his fight for democracy in unions, and his support of social legislation in the United States made him and the UAW a model of a progressive union leader and union. His untimely death in May 1970 in a plane crash was a major loss to his union and the American labor movement.

In contrast to the public image of Walter Reuther is the public image of the late Jimmy Hoffa and the International Brotherhood of Teamsters. From the same city (Detroit) in the same era as Reuther, Hoffa built a reputation that was the exact opposite of Reuther's. In 1957, as he assumed the presidency of the Teamsters, Hoffa was a prime target of the McClellan Committee (Senate Committee on Improper Activities in the Labor Field) and its general counsel, Robert Kennedy. His lack of cooperation and his overt cues to his fellow officials of the Teamsters to "take the Fifth (Amendment)" created a totally negative image for him, the union, and the American labor movement. His behavior also contributed to the passage of the Landrum–Griffin Act in 1959. When Kennedy became attorney general of the United States, he was finally successful in obtaining federal convictions against Hoffa—for mail fraud ("conspiring to lift money from the Central States Pension Fund") and jury tampering.[30] Hoffa went to prison in 1967, giving up the presidency of the IBT but remaining president of the Detroit local he had headed for years. In 1971, the Nixon administration commuted his sentence. Hoffa mysteriously disappeared in 1975; his disappearance is generally believed to have been the work of Mafia figures involved with New Jersey and New York Teamster locals.

National union leaders, whether or not they are media figures, usually sit in the seat of power, and they sit there for a long time. In most cases the union president remains in that office until he chooses to retire or dies—as was the case for both Reuther and Hoffa. The power of unions and the power of union leaders are rather controversial issues, as will be discussed in the next section.

Union Power Centers

One of Samuel Gompers' founding principles of the AFL was the autonomy and supremacy of the national unions: he visualized a national that controlled its own finances and internal affairs. It would charter locals and control them. He saw the power of the labor movement residing within the national unions. They would be the **power centers** because they held and controlled the economic or financial resources, and they controlled the collective bargaining decision making of their locals. They also held the political power in the union. Gompers' model fit the geography of his times.

In the last quarter of the nineteenth century, especially in the long depression decade of 1873–1878, most union activity was on the East Coast. There was some union activity in the Midwest (Ohio, Illinois) and only a smattering in places like

St. Louis, New Orleans, San Francisco, or the Rocky Mountain mines organized in local miners unions, which became the Western Federation of Miners (WFM).[31] Thus, a national might have six locals in New York, Newark, Philadelphia, Pittsburgh, Cleveland, and Cincinnati and could easily oversee them. As national markets expanded to encompass the whole country, locals began to proliferate. The growth of industrial unionism in the 1930s, primarily in the mass-production industries, expanded even more the national unions' geographic spread. However, national craft (versus industrial) union power did not grow rapidly with the development of the national market, as the products of their workers were usually sold in a local market.

Finding the Center: Where Does Power Reside?

The power center of a union is determined by the nature of the product markets for the outputs produced by the union members. For most craft unions, the product is sold in a small geographic area. In the building trades, construction is done in a given local area. Buildings are not constructed in a factory and shipped nationwide to where they are needed (except for certain pre-fabs). Longshoring services (stevedoring) are localized at given port areas. Thus, for a craft union, the power center tends to be the local. The need for wage uniformity is local; the locals of the union do the bulk of the collective bargaining on the bread-and-butter issues of wages, fringe benefits, and related topics.

There are exceptions to craft locals holding substantial power and decision-making authority. The Teamsters, in their core craft (over-the-road trucking), compete primarily in a regional area, which is larger than a local one but smaller than the nation. Historically, their power centers tended to be regional rather than local or national units. However, under Hoffa the Teamsters national centralized collective bargaining and power in the 1960s and negotiated National Master Freight Agreements.[32] Interestingly, Hoffa's rise to the presidency of the IBT was based upon his powerful position as head of the midwestern regional unit of the Teamsters, based in Detroit.

Most industrial unions of any notable size organized large, mass-production industries, with companies producing output sold in a national market. Autos, steel, and rubber products, for example, are manufactured in many locations and are shipped nationwide. The need for uniform wages and similar working conditions is obvious. Uniform wages and fringe benefits should yield uniform labor costs in an industry, taking labor out of the competition. Thus, the bread-and-butter issues are usually negotiated on a national scale. The national bargains with each company, such as the UAW with GM, or with a coalition of all the companies in the industry, such as was the case in the steel industry until the mid-1980s. The power center is the national (or international). A notable exception is the United Food and Commercial Workers (UFCW), in which the locals deal primarily with, for example, an area's supermarkets. Unlike most industrial union locals, the UFCW locals use business agents, as do craft unions. As was noted earlier in this chapter, policies and practices reflect to a great extent those of the craft unions (for example, the Meat Cutters) that merged to form the UFCW. Competition is primarily at a local level, and much of the negotiations are areawide—for example, citywide.

The Changing Nature of Union Power

In the past decade, enhanced competition from imports and an ever-larger domestic nonunion sector has undercut the power of unions in general, especially the power of large national unions. Union numbers (both absolutely and as a percentage of the labor force) have been steadily declining, showing a weaker trade union movement in general and some areas of substantial loss of power. These losses are concentrated in mass-production industries, where, for example, the United Auto Workers has shrunk by several hundred thousand members.

The shrinkage in membership of large industrial unions like the UAW, where the power center has been at the top, has caused this power to diffuse downward to locals. These locals now seek to negotiate terms and conditions of employment to meet the local needs both of the local union and the plant involved. Survival has become a major point of contention for many locals and plants. Uniformity of wages, to take labor out of competition, may still be a major goal of American unions, but it is not the operating principle of locals negotiating for their survival in the face of plant closings.

Who Leads the Unions?

Union leaders are, by law, elected officials.[33] At the local level, presidential turnover is not uncommon. However, at the national level, as we have said, presidential turnover is very rare. **Entrenched leadership** at the national level may be good or bad, but the long tenure in this powerful position naturally sets up situations that are questionable.

Local Leadership

At the local level, the president is in direct contact with members of the union. As mentioned earlier, attendance at regular union meetings is sparse, but members are in contact with their local leaders through their shop stewards and at the workplace. The actions of local leaders have an immediate, traceable impact on the local members. Dissatisfaction with the union is usually aimed at the local leaders because they are close at hand and relatively easily unseated. Entrenchment—long tenures—of local leadership is uncommon.

National Leadership

At the national level, the president is not in contact with the union membership. The governing body of the national is the **convention**, which is usually held every year or two. Federal law requires that conventions and elections be held at least every five years, but most unions hold theirs more often. In the past the Teamsters was an exception, but it is now holding elections and operating under the purview of a court-appointed independent administrator and two other overseers. This reform was the result of a 1989 settlement of a racketeering suit filed against the union by the Department of Labor.[34]

Delegates from all locals and regionals attend the convention primarily to formulate policy, to plan programs, and to attend to other related business. They also nominate officers, which usually means electing them, for almost all unions operate under a one-party system.[35] Rarely are minority rights, especially in terms of active dissent, protected. (The issue of union democracy is discussed later in this chapter.)

Between conventions, the national is governed by an executive board. In most cases, the executive board gives the president substantial leeway to run the affairs of the union, including appointing staff, managing the union media (papers, newsletters, etc.), and regulating locals. With these powers, the president can co-opt most active dissenters through staff appointments. Using the union media (newsletters, the union magazine), the president can promote himself, keep his name and accomplishments in the minds of the membership, and even paint negative pictures of his opponents.

Union Corruption: When the System Fails

Entrenched leadership in big organizations means power. National union leadership is entrenched, and unions are big organizations. Most union leaders are capable of handling this powerful position with dignity and integrity, but, of course, there are exceptions. As Rees noted in 1977, "Corruption and racketeering have long been present in some American unions."[36] These words were a reflection on the results of the Senate investigation into racketeering and **union corruption** by the McClellan Committee held in 1957.

Two targets of the committee investigation were the International Longshoremen's Association (ILA) and the Teamsters. The Teamsters union was expelled from the AFL–CIO in 1957 and reaffiliated with the Federation in 1987. It has been operating under the long-term oversight of three court-appointed officials since March 1989. The ILA was expelled from the AFL several years before the Teamsters' expulsion. The federal government has filed a suit against it, similar to the one against the Teamsters which was settled in March 1989. Like that earlier suit, the U.S. attorney is using the Racketeering Influenced and Corrupt Organizations (RICO) law as a means of reforming the union.[37]

Rees looked at four areas of union corruption:

1. *The misuse of operating funds* involves the embezzlement and misappropriation of funds by union officers. These actions tend to involve relatively small amounts of money. When the local treasurer pockets the week's petty cash reserves, little money is usually involved. This type of corruption might be found at any level: national, local, and intermediate units like regionals.

2. *Bribery* commonly comes in the form of employers' payoffs, gifts, and so on, for concessions at the bargaining table (negotiating so-called **sweetheart contracts**). It tends to involve union officers at both the local and national level who lead the collective bargaining team of the union. One recent case involved major concessions to U.S. Steel in 1983 at its Fairfield, Alabama, plant; the local union negotiators ended up with large pensions for which they were not eligible.[38]

3. *Racketeering* involves doing union business with firms which enriches union leaders. In some cases, union leaders get kickbacks from these firms for giving them union contracts. In other cases, they or members of their family own the firms. The McClellan Committee investigations, particularly those aimed at the Teamsters and their leaders, found this to be a common area of labor racketeering.

They were particularly interested in looking at instances where union business went to firms linked to organized crime. This line of investigation, targeting the Teamsters' Jimmy Hoffa, continued into the Kennedy administration when the McClellan Committee's general counsel, Robert Kennedy, became U.S. Attorney General. As mentioned earlier, it resulted in prison for Hoffa. The latest government investigation of the Teamsters caused a suit to be filed against the union. Just before coming to trial (in March 1989), the union and government settled. The settlement, as noted in the previous section, reformed the union's election procedures and set up three court-appointed administrators to oversee union affairs.

4. *The misuse of moneys paid into funds for the union membership by the companies for which they work, and administered by national union leaders*, is the fourth type of corruption. The building trades and longshoring unions administer these types of funds as do the Teamsters. These are mainly pension and health or welfare funds, and involve hundreds of millions of dollars. This type of corruption, like the previous one, has been particularly identified with the Teamsters.[39] The use of these funds for the building and remodeling of officers' homes was one reported abuse.

The problems of corruption in unions are magnified when organized crime figures are involved. In the case of the Teamsters, the ascent of Hoffa to power substantially increased the presence of organized crime figures in the Teamsters. Some allege that Hoffa used these figures to consolidate his power in the union.[40] In the case of the Longshoremen, organized crime on the New York (and New Jersey) docks has a long history. (It inspired the 1954 film *On the Waterfront*, an early Marlon Brando movie.)

How prevalent are corrupt acts by union leaders? Richard Freeman and James Medoff, in their landmark book, noted that very few unions are plagued by corruption and that most of it is concentrated in four areas: Teamsters, Longshoremen, Hotel and Restaurant Workers, and the Building Trades.[41] The corruption in the Teamsters seemed to derive from the leadership's perception of the best way to consolidate power. In the other three areas, the corruption is at the local level, particularly in New York, and the three industries mentioned have been noted for local pockets of corruption for many years.[42] The presence of corruption in the unions dealing with these companies prone to dishonesty and criminal influences is not surprising.

Freeman and Medoff conclude that "the amount of union corruption is no more than, and probably less than, business corruption."[43] Corruption in government, which may be a better comparison for unions because leaders are elected, has been a fact of life from William (Boss) Tweed's Tammany Hall in mid-nineteenth century New York, to the national scandals of Watergate, Wedtech, and the Iran–Contra case in the 1970s and 1980s. It is still upsetting to find corruption in unions, but no more so, and probably less, than finding it in government and business.

Why has corrupt union leadership, especially over long periods of time, been tolerated? Union leaders are elected officials, and unions are democratic institutions. To understand the need for and support of strong, singleminded, and sometimes not totally honest leadership, we must take a close look at the meaning of democracy in the context of labor–management relations.

UNION DEMOCRACY

To most of us, democracy means freedom, or the power of the people to govern where there is equality of rights without arbitrary differences in class rank. A democratic system utilizes the instrumentalities of government to protect the rights of its people. In labor–management relations, a democratic labor association would protect the rights of its members, the workers. What are those rights? How do labor associations protect them? What is **union democracy**?

Workers' Rights

Union members have two major groups or sets of rights. The first includes the rights they have relative to their jobs and employers, and the second includes the rights they have relative to their union, as their duly elected representative at the workplace.

Collective Action Protects Job Rights

The first set of rights, and for most workers the more important, are their job rights. The union's function is to protect these rights against encroachment by management, especially "arbitrary" managerial actions that might deprive workers of their jobs. Also of importance to workers is the right to protest treatment on the job that they feel is unjust. The union protects them against these actions through negotiated items like a grievance procedure, usually with neutral, third-party decisions if labor and management can't work out the problem. This **voice function**, as Freeman and Medoff call it, is a major accomplishment of unions.[44]

In addition to the voice function, unions seek to protect workers' standard of living, or the workers' pay and perquisites. This is accomplished through the union's **monopoly face**, as Freeman and Medoff call this functional exercise of union economic power.[45]

The Rights of Individuals as Union Members

The workers' individual rights as members of their union include the right to dissent from union policies, both those determining the internal working of the union and its collective bargaining programs.

These rights are not exercised in most unions. At the local level, attendance at union meetings is sparse. As noted earlier in this chapter, regular union meetings draw about 5 percent of the membership. At the national level, dissent is difficult against an entrenched leader, especially if that leader has been successful in protecting and enhancing workers' rights related to their jobs.

If workers don't like what the union is doing or for what it stands, they lose interest in having the union remain as their bargaining agent. This means one of two things: either the union goes or the worker goes. The union can be removed as the bargaining agent through the process of decertification (see Chapters 3 and 6). Decertifying a union requires that a majority of the workers in the bargaining unit be involved. If over half the membership in the unit dislikes the union's actions and stance, the union may be removed as the bargaining representative. If, however, the majority of the workers are not dissatisfied with the union, the alternative for the individual worker is to quit the union. In some cases, this might mean giving up the job, if the union and management have a collective bargaining contract with a compulsory union membership clause. This type of clause requires that all workers in the bargaining unit be members of the union while the contract is in force. In the absence of a compulsory union membership clause, the worker may quit the union and keep his or her job. This, however, usually brings peer pressure to rejoin, as the majority do support the union.

The individual is protected against many possible abuses at the hands of his or her union by law. The Landrum–Griffin Act contains a bill of rights for union members which guarantees freedom of speech and assembly and other rights. It also requires that members have the opportunity to speak freely on matters of union business. The act also contains other safeguards against union abuse (due process types).

For the Common Good: Individual Versus Collective Rights

To maximize the union's ability to collectively secure job rights for the workers, individual rights or freedoms may have to be compromised. Without the protection of collective action through unions or labor associations (or the threat of this type of protection), the power of the individual worker is negligible compared to that of the employer. John Kenneth Galbraith forcefully presented this concept of unions balancing the power of management in his *American Capitalism: The Concept of Countervailing Power* almost 40 years ago.[46] This concept is sometimes referred to as **industrial democracy**.*

Why might individual rights or freedoms have to be compromised for the collective rights of the whole group of workers? Is this tradeoff necessary?

In collective bargaining, management has increasingly been speaking with a united voice. In their recent book on the American industrial relations system, Kochan, Katz, and McKersie discuss the management structure for collective bargaining. Reflecting a basic anti-union value, the management position in negotiations is more frequently filtered and constrained by the values of chief executive officers who are intervening directly in the negotiating process.[47] The managerial ranks present a uniform collective bargaining stance, as determined by the firm's executives.

The union's management must match this unified front to secure a balance of power. If a dissident group in the union openly disagrees with the union's collective bargaining stance and tries to do something about it, company management can

---

* This term characterizes the grievance procedure (often referred to as industrial jurisprudence) that allows workers to freely protest job dissatisfaction as well as the power balance between organized labor and management; see, for example, John F. Witte, "Industrial Democracy," in Clark Kerr and Paul D. Staudohar, *Industrial Relations in a New Age* (San Francisco: Jossey–Bass, 1986), pp. 135–138. The term also describes worker participation in workplace management.

quickly take advantage of this crack in union solidarity. The balance of power swings to their side at the expense of the workers. A union weakened by minority dissent, having to spend time and effort continually to align its members behind union goals, will be easy pickings for a determined management that doesn't face that problem. Industrial, or **external democracy**, the upholding of collective rights, and individual, or **internal democracy**, the upholding of individual rights, are seldom compatible in this type of setting.

Union and management power will be discussed in further detail in Chapter 6, within the framework of the process of collective bargaining. The issue will be examined in the context of union and management costs, as the basis of the theory of bargaining power.

DISCUSSION QUESTIONS

1. What are the major functions of the Federation (AFL–CIO) as the umbrella organization of the American labor movement?

2. Discuss the term *spokesman for the House of Labor.*

3. Discuss the trend in union organizing results, and give some of the basic reasons for this trend.

4. Two unions, the International Brotherhood of Brass Workers and the United Fastener Appenders, are thinking about merging. Describe possible factors for and against merging.

5. Describe two possible economic environments, one in which central bargaining would encounter difficulty and one in which it would flourish.

6. What is the difference between a craft and an industrial union?

7. Give a specific example of (a) a craft union and (b) an industrial union that behave atypically in some way and explain why they do not behave in "textbook" style.

8. What determines where (at which level) the center of power is in a union?

9. Why are national union presidents entrenched in their positions? Why are local presidents not as solidly ensconced?

10. What type of corruption occurs in American unions?

11. Which unions seem to be the corrupt ones?

12. Compare and contrast external democracy and internal democracy in American unions. (Define each concept as best you can.)

VOCABULARY LIST

craft union

industrial union

AFL–CIO (the Federation)

national/international union

collective bargaining

bargaining structure

centralized bargaining

fragmentation of bargaining

organizing

political action committee (PAC)

union mergers

local union

administering the contract (contract administration)

business agent

shop steward

grievance committee

power center

entrenched leadership

convention

union corruption

sweetheart contract

union democracy

voice function

monopoly face

industrial democracy

external democracy

internal democracy

FOOTNOTES

1. *Wall Street Journal*, August 2, 1988, p. 24.

2. The United Mine Workers was the first major industrial union chartered by the AFL. It was affiliated with both the AFL and the Knights of Labor; the KOL affiliation explains the industrial union organization (Norman J. Ware, *The Labor Movement in the United States, 1860–1895* (Vintage Book, 1929), pp. 209–221).

3. Melvin W. Reder, *Labor in a Growing Economy* (John Wiley, 1957), p. 68.

4. As of this time, the United Electrical Workers (UE) is practically the only national of any size not in the Federation. Large labor associations like the National Education Association (NEA) and the American Nurses Association (ANA) are not AFL–CIO affiliates. See *Monthly Labor Review* (December 1989): 56.

5. The expulsion of the IBT (the Teamsters) in 1957 led to the growth of that non-affiliated union to over 2 million members by 1974 (*Wall Street Journal*, October 23, 1987, p. 8), making it the largest American union or labor association. The IBT rejoined the Federation in October 1987, swelling AFL–CIO membership by over one-eighth, from 12.7 to 14.3 million (*Business Week*, November 9, 1987, p. 110).

6. William H. Miernyk, "Labor and Politics," in E. Wright Bakke, et al., *Unions, Management and the Public* (Harcourt, Brace & World, 1967), pp. 335-341. Miernyk notes that the passage of the Taft–Hartley Act in 1947 forced this political activism on the labor movement. It should be noted that voluntarism was not the prevailing doctrine at the state level, and state AFL councils were instrumental in the passage of child labor laws and laws protecting women in the workplace during the Progressive Era of the early 1900s.

7. *Business Week*, July 4, 1988, p. 3; the number two PAC was that of the American Medical Association.

8. See, for example, "The People's Lobby," AFL–CIO Department of Legislation, March 1985.

9. Charles J. McDonald, "The AFL–CIO's Blueprint for the Future—A Progress

Report," *Proceedings of the Thirty-Ninth Annual Meeting* (Industrial Relations Research Association, December 28–30, 1986), pp. 281–282. The procedure worked very well in resolving about 20 disputes between the Teamsters (after their rejoining the AFL–CIO in October 1987) and other unions (see *Wall Street Journal*, April 19, 1988, p. 1).

10. Ibid.

11. John Hutchinson, *The Imperfect Union* (E. P. Dutton, 1972), p. 297.

12. Reder, *Labor in a Growing Economy*, pp. 81–82.

13. "The AFL–CIO: A Tougher Team with the Teamsters," *Business Week*, November 9, 1987, p. 110. The Teamsters reaffiliation with the AFL–CIO is the major focus of this article.

14. "AFL–CIO Plans TV Ads to Boost Labor's Image," *Wall Street Journal*, May 11, 1988, p. 28; the AFL–CIO Committee on the Evolution of Work report, "The Changing Situation of Workers and Their Unions" (February 1985), p. 20, advocated this approach, expanded use of the electronic media, through the work of the Federation's Labor Institute of Public Affairs (see Figure 4.1).

15. Ibid., p. 24.

16. Albert Rees, *The Economics of Trade Unions* (University of Chicago Press, 1977), p. 57. Rees notes that unions dealing with diverse employers selling in different product markets have a different outlook.

17. *Wall Street Journal*, May 30, 1989, p. C18; the contract with USX, the largest American steel producer, does not expire until 1991.

18. Richard Edwards and Michael Podgursky, "The Unraveling Accord: American Unions in Crisis," in Richard Edwards et al., eds., *Unions in Crisis and Beyond* (Auburn House, 1986), p. 16. The authors point to the breakdown of centralized bargaining by the Teamsters.

19. In three of Armco's steel plants, hourly labor costs varied from $19.63 to $20.63 to $22.88 (*Wall Street Journal*, May 3, 1989, p. A8).

20. *New York Times*, October 30, 1988, p. 4.

21. Jack Fiorito, Christopher Lowman, and Forrest D. Nelson, "The Impact of Human Resource Policies on Union Organizing," *Industrial Relations* (Spring 1987): 113; *Wall Street Journal*, February 16, 1988, p. 1, noted the astounding increase of unfair labor practice charges against management.

22. Richard B. Freeman, "Why Are Unions Faring Poorly in NLRB Representation Elections?," in Richard L. Rowan, *Readings in Labor Economics and Labor Relations* (Richard D. Irwin, 1985), p. 130.

23. AFL–CIO Committee on the Evolution of Work, pp. 18–22, 27–29; Charles Heckscher, "Crisis and Opportunity for Labor," *Proceedings of the 1987 Spring Meeting* (Industrial Relations Research Association, April 29–May 1, 1987), p. 468.

24. *Business Week*, July 4, 1988, p. 43; *Wall Street Journal*, July 14, 1988, p. 26.

25. Larry T. Adams, "Labor Organization Mergers 1979–84: Adapting to Change," *Monthly Labor Review* (September 1984): 23–24.

26. See, for example, "Today the Mine Workers—Tomorrow, the AFL–CIO?," *Business Week*, February 25, 1988, p. 27, about the proposed merger between the United Mine Workers (UMW) and the Oil, Chemical and Atomic Workers (OCAW), which as of early 1990 remained up in the air.

27. Adams, "Labor Organization Mergers," p. 23. The UFCW then absorbed three smaller unions: Barbers, Beauticians and Allied Industries International (1980); Retail Workers (1981); and Insurance Workers (1983). In 1989, it absorbed the National Brotherhood of Packinghouse and Industrial Workers.

28. *Wall Street Journal*, November 21, 1988, p. B7A.

29. John C. Anderson, "Local Union Participation: A Reexamination," *Industrial Relations* (Winter 1979): 30.

30. Steven Brill, *The Teamsters* (Simon and Schuster, 1978), p. 35.

31. Melvyn Dubofsky, *We Shall Be All: A History of the Industrial Workers of the World* (Quadrangle Books, 1969), pp. 24–25; the WFM was the forerunner of the IWW.

32. Edwards and Podgursky "The Unraveling Accord." The authors note, however, that this centralization broke down in the 1980s, being an aspect of the changing environment of labor–management relations.

33. The Landrum–Griffin Act (1959) requires that elections for all union officers be held at least every five years.

34. *Wall Street Journal*, March 14, 1989, p. A3; *New York Times*, March 14, 1989, p. A1, March 15, 1989, p. A10, March 16, 1989, p. A3, March 17, 1989, p. A19, and June 1, 1989, p. C19 (where it was noted that, in addition to an independent administrator, an independent investigations officer and an independent elections officer were named).

35. Clark Kerr and the authors noted almost 30 years ago that, at the level of the national officers, only one American union has a two-party system; see Seymour M. Lipset, Martin Trow, and James Coleman, *Union Democracy* (Anchor Books, 1962), Foreword and Preface.

36. Rees, *The Economics of Trade Unions*, p. 175.

37. *Wall Street Journal*, July 19, 1989, p. B11, and February 15, 1990, p. 82.

38. *New York Times*, November 20, 1989, p. A1; *Business Week*, December 25, 1989, p. 48 and January 8, 1990, p. 44. Charged in this "sweetheart" deal were USX, the two union officials, and USX's executive vice-president of employee relations at the time.

39. *Wall Street Journal*, June 11, 1987, p. 2; June 3, 1988, p. 36; June 29, 1988, p. 3 (which noted that the March 1986 Report of the President's Commission on Organized Crime concluded that "The leaders of the nation's largest union [the Teamsters] have been firmly under the influence of organized crime since the 1950s"); July 1, 1988, p. 17.

40. Brill, *The Teamsters*, p. 35.

41. Richard B. Freeman, and James L. Medoff, *What Do Unions Do?* (Basic Books, 1984), pp. 214–217.

42. See, for example, *Wall Street Journal*, December 16, 1988, p. C12.

43. Freeman and Medoff, *What Do Unions Do?*

44. Ibid., p. 6.

45. Ibid.

46. John Kenneth Galbraith, *American Capitalism: The Concept of Countervailing Power* (Houghton Mifflin, 1952), especially pp. 121–123.

47. Thomas A. Kochan, et al., *The Transformation of American Industrial Relations* (Basic Books, 1986), pp. 12–13, 131–132.

REFERENCES

ADAMS, LARRY T. "Labor Organization Mergers, 1979–84: Adapting to Change." *Monthly Labor Review* (September 1984): 21–27.

AFL–CIO Committee on the Evolution of Work. "The Changing Situation of Workers and Their Unions." AFL–CIO, February 1985.

ANDERSON, JOHN C. "Local Union Participation: A Reexamination." *Industrial Relations* (Winter 1979): 18–31.

BRILL, STEVEN. *The Teamsters*. Simon and Schuster, 1978.

CHAISON, GARY N. *When Unions Merge*. Lexington Books / D. C. Heath & Co., 1986.

DUBOFSKY, MELVYN. *We Shall Be All: A History of the Industrial Workers of the World*. Quadrangle Books, 1969.

EDWARDS, RICHARD, and MICHAEL PODGURSKY. "The Unraveling Accord: American Unions in Crisis." In Richard Edwards, Paolo Garonna, and Franz Todtling, eds., *Unions in Crisis and Beyond*. Auburn House, 1986, pp. 14–60.

FIORITO, JACK, CHRISTOPHER LOWMAN, and FORREST D. NELSON. "The Impact of Human Resource Policies on Union Organizing." *Industrial Relations* (Spring 1987): 113–126.

FREEMAN, RICHARD B. "Why Are Unions Faring Poorly in NLRB Representation Elections?" In Richard L. Rowan, ed., *Reading in Labor Economics and Labor Relations*. Richard D. Irwin, 1985, pp. 129–141.

FREEMAN, RICHARD B., and JAMES L. MEDOFF. *What Do Unions Do?*, Basic Books, 1984.

GALBRAITH, JOHN KENNETH. *American Capitalism: The Concept of Countervailing Power*. Houghton Mifflin, 1952.

HECKSCHER, CHARLES. "Crisis and Opportunity for Labor," *Proceedings of the 1987 Spring Meeting*. Industrial Relations Research Association, April 29–May 1, 1987, pp. 465–470.

HUTCHINSON, JOHN. *The Imperfect Union.* E. P. Dutton, 1972.

KOCHAN, THOMAS A., HARRY C. KATZ, and ROBERT B. McKERSIE. *The Transformation of American Industrial Relations.* Basic Books, 1986.

LIPSET, SEYMOUR M., MARTIN TROW, and JAMES COLEMAN. *Union Democracy.* Anchor Books/Doubleday & Co., 1962.

McDONALD, CHARLES J. "The AFL–CIO's Blueprint for the Future—A Progress Report." *Proceedings of the Thirty-Ninth Annual Meeting.* Industrial Relations Research Association, December 28–30, 1986, pp. 276–282.

MIERNYK, WILLIAM H. "Labor and Politics." In E. Wright Bakke, Clark Kerr, and Charles W. Anrod, *Unions, Management and the Public*, Harcourt, Brace & World, 1967, pp. 335–341.

REDER, MELVIN W. *Labor in a Growing Economy.* John Wiley, 1957.

REES, ALBERT. *The Economics of Trade Unions.* University of Chicago Press, 1977.

WARE, NORMAN J. *The Labor Movement in the United States, 1860–1895.* Vintage Books/Random House, 1929.

WITTE, JOHN F. "Industrial Democracy." In Clark Kerr and Paul D. Staudohar, *Industrial Relations in a New Age.* Jossey-Bass, 1986, pp. 135–138.

CHAPTER 5

COMPARATIVE LABOR RELATIONS

N ow that you have gained some familiarity with the American system of labor–management relations and American unions and the legal framework within which they operate, we can make contrasts with labor relations in other areas of the world. The areas we cover will include

1. Canada and Mexico, our neighbors in this hemisphere.
2. Western Europe, primarily the British, the expected EC (European Community or the Common Market), and the Scandinavian systems.
3. Japan, with its changing system.
4. The Soviet Union and Eastern Europe, where labor relations and economic and political systems are rapidly changing.
5. The other areas of the Pacific Rim (besides Japan and the United States), primarily Australia, China, and the newly industrialized economies (NIEs) of South Korea, Taiwan, Singapore, and Hong Kong.

LABOR RELATIONS IN NEIGHBORING COUNTRIES

Canadian Labor Relations

To most observers, especially non-Canadians, "the labor relations systems in Canada and the United States look very much alike."[1] They share many institutions:

- Companies and trade unions (primarily American-based) that operate in both countries, such as the Big 3 auto companies (GM, Ford, and Chrysler) and the United Auto Workers.

- A labor policy based on government support for unionization and collective bargaining as exemplified by the 1935 Wagner Act in the United States.
- Economies that are closely linked, especially since the 1989 adoption of the free trade pact. (However, the U.S. economy is about ten times larger than Canada's, so economic relations between the two are dominated by it.)

But the systems differ.

Stability in Canadian Unionization

One very discernible difference between labor relations in Canada and the United States shows up in the statistics on union membership. Membership in American unions dropped from about 30 percent in 1970 to 16.1 percent in 1990 (see Chapter 1, Table 1.1). In Canada, the membership rate has been very stable, about 37 percent since 1975.[2] This stability seems to be related to employer attitudes and the government's role with respect to unions in Canada.

Management, in general, accepts the right of unions to exist and to negotiate agreements to benefit their members. The government, both provincial and federal, insures the right of employees freely to choose to unionize and collective bargain, and also sees to it that this bargaining will be in good faith. Since most workers are covered by provincial labor law, these governments are the major insurers of "fair play." Some have come up with innovative approaches to fulfill this function, such as arbitration of first agreements when there is bad faith bargaining or compulsory dues checkoff for workers.[3]

Overall, Canadian employers have not practiced union avoidance as American employers have. Furthermore, the Canadian governments, both provincial and federal, have sought to protect labor union power, which the obsolete National Labor Relations Act has not.[4] The 1985 Royal Commission on the Economic Union and Development Prospects for Canada reaffirmed the government's commitment to protect union power by directing that "all Canadian governments provide a supportive legislative environment for the labor movement and for collective bargaining."[5]

A Decentralized System in Change

Another major difference between labor relations in the two countries, and specifically collective bargaining, is the greater decentralization of this activity in Canada than in the United States. This reflects (1) the difference in the legal framework with Canadian provincial (state) law dominating, not federal; and (2) the geographical spread of Canada in combination with the regional concentration of resources and production.

Strong union growth in the public sector, offsetting a decline in private sector union membership, has prompted the Canadian federal government to take a greater (and more centralized) role in labor relations.[6] Although the government's increased role might, at first, seem to make labor relations more similar in the two countries, it does not have this effect. At both provincial and federal levels, the government is still committed to the protection of labor union power. The basis of that commitment is the proposition that unions and collective bargaining are necessary components of modern democratic political systems, allowing employee–citizens to participate in the making of decisions affecting their working lives.[7]

The Canadian government's position in developing a tripartite system of cooperation and consensus by labor, management, and government is moving Canadian labor relations closer to the European model. The expansion of workers' participation, by legislation when necessary, is a hallmark of Western European industrial relations systems. Canada is adopting this model and is moving away from the U.S. model whereby worker participation tends to occur in management-controlled and -initiated schemes.[8]

Mexican Labor Relations

Labor relations in Mexico, as in most of Latin America, are characterized by **state authoritarianism.**[9] The Mexican unions have grown powerful by allying themselves with the ruling Institutional Revolutionary Party (PRI). Since most industries in Mexico are run by the state, all workers in these industries belong to unions, most of which are tied together by the Confederation of Mexican Workers (akin to the American AFL–CIO). In exchange for maintaining labor peace and lending political support, Mexico's presidents have backed the powerful union presidents.[10] For example, the leaders of the powerful Oil Workers Union were given control of the distribution of contracts for 40 percent of the outside work done at Pemex, the state's oil monopoly; this greatly enriched these union leaders, since corruption ran rampant.[11]

When Carlos Salinas de Gortari became president of Mexico at the end of 1988, he took on the unions, starting with the oil workers. His motivation was to stem corruption in Mexico and carry out economic (and political) reform. In addition, the unions, especially the Oil Workers Union which is the largest of them, did not lend much support to his campaign for president. Before his plans to privatize large sectors of the economy are actualized, he must overcome union resistance, which is spearheaded by corrupt and entrenched leadership. Salinas has been successful in battles with the leaders of the Oil Workers, the Telephone Workers, and the National Education Workers (teachers and other school employees), unions with over 1.2 million members. His campaign has also aroused dissident leaders in many unions to rally the rank-and-file in grass-roots movements that have unseated old-line leaders in unions such as the Musicians, the Automobile Workers, and the Government Workers.[12]

Unions in Mexico are avidly striving for union democracy, encouraged by President Salinas's anticorruption campaign. However, they are also seeking wage increases in the neighborhood of 100 percent to try to keep up with the country's high rate of inflation; these wage increases would upset the Salinas administration's economic reform program. The strikes and confrontations of 1989–1990 secured some advances for workers and unions, but they also upset many government leaders. As the move toward private ownership continues, the role of the government will diminish as labor unions become more independent. Unionism in Mexico, as in Latin America in general, faces an optimistic future as manufacturing shifts to Third World countries with cheap labor costs, increasing employment opportunities, and prospects for greater development overall.[13]

LABOR RELATIONS IN WESTERN EUROPE

Not all the labor relations systems in Western European countries are cast in the same mold. However, when compared with the United States in particular, they can be characterized by **political involvement** of unions (through the Labor and Socialist parties), **worker participation** (primarily mandated by law), and high levels of union membership. As the European Community's planned economic integration (by 1992) progresses (see Figure 5.1), the labor relations systems of the 12 Common Market countries will converge. EC employment law has been aimed at harmonizing social (and labor) legislation and policy among the member states for the past 20 years, prodded by the European Trade Union Confederation.[14]

British Labor Relations

British unionism is characterized by a "highly fragmented and competitive craft union structure, coupled with highly conflictual tendencies in industrial relations."[15] Deeply seated class conflicts have made the labor–management relationship in Great Britain a very adversarial one. Prior to the 1980s, labor relations were marked by constant industrial actions, especially wildcat strikes, for grievance arbitration is not utilized in Britain. Furthermore, employers are not legally required to recognize unions and to bargain with them.[16] The labor agreements that are negotiated, traditionally in a multi-union multi-employer setting (reflecting the dominant craft union

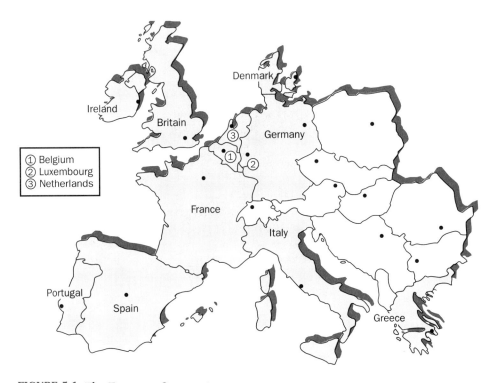

FIGURE 5.1 The European Community.

structure), are not legally enforceable. Great Britain's labor–management relations are quite volatile, as the year-long (1984–1985) coal miners' strike and the short but crippling nationwide Ford Motor strike (1988) illustrate.

The Thatcher "Revolution"

Margaret Thatcher's Conservative government, which was in office from May 1979 to 1990, extensively overhauled the British labor relations system. Pre-Thatcher, labor–management relations were governed, for the most part, by common law and conflict. The 1980s saw the passage of four major labor laws and two supplemental laws (see Table 5.1).[17] The thrust of these laws and the accompanying high levels of unemployment in the 1980s has been to rein in union power. For example, they have made the union shop (called the closed shop in Britain) and any industrial actions, such as strikes, to require union membership unlawful. They have also imposed a major restriction on industrial actions (strikes, refusals of overtime, slowdowns, and work-to-rule, which is a form of slowdown) officially called for or supported by a union's national leaders by requiring majority support by secret ballot no more than four weeks before the planned action. The new laws do not cover "unofficial" actions, mainly wildcat strikes that the national union leadership has nothing to do with. Moreover, union members who refuse to take part in official industrial actions are protected against any discipline by their union. The laws also require that all the national leaders of unions be elected by secret ballot of the membership at least every five years, a requirement similar to that in America's Landrum–Griffin Act.

The European Community legislation that British labor relations falls under has moved to enhance union and worker power. This legislation covers procedures for consultation with unions on a host of issues; employee involvement in decision making; and antidiscrimination and equal pay (especially for women) provisions that actually were included in British law because of EC requirements. But British unions, like America's, are in decline; however, they represented about 42 percent of the labor force at the end of 1987.[18]

A Centralized System in Change

Although the British labor relations system is highly fragmented, collective bargaining between coalitions of unions and employers is centralized. For example, negotiations between the Engineering Employers' Federation and the Confederation

Table 5.1 *British Labor Laws of the Thatcher Government*

Law	Date
Employment Act	1980
Employment Act	1982
Trade Union Act	1984
Wages Act	1986
Sex Discrimination Act	1986
Employment Act	1988

of Shipbuilding and Engineering Unions involved 4,500 plants and 34 unions representing over 2 million employees.[19] The Trade Union Congress, the national federation with which most British unions are affiliated, has traditionally been a force for centralization.

When the negotiated agreements, though not legally enforceable, are administered at the plant level, the primary concerns involve work rules and area-specific issues. Fringe benefits are not important, for many have been established by law and are provided by the government. **Shop stewards** and **steward councils,** usually the most influential local officials in the union, and a **works council** representing workers of the plant's (and company's) various divisions along with national union representatives, will often negotiate plant-level agreements to supplement the national agreement.

The members of the works council are often not union officials, and as a result of the 1980s' laws weakening compulsory union membership, union officials have become even rarer. Under the EC model of labor participation in decision making in the labor–management relations system, which will probably be based on the system of co-determination, the works councils will assume a greater role as the conduit for this participation at the shop floor level. Let's now turn to a discussion of that system.

German Labor–Management Relations: The EC Model?

The German labor relations system has two components: worker participation in organization decision making, commonly referred to as co-determination; and collective bargaining, the more traditional area of labor–management interaction.

Worker Participation in Running the Organization

The German system of worker participation, **co-determination,** involves workers in an organization at three levels:

1. The shop floor.
2. Middle to top operating and executive management.
3. The board of directors (board of supervisors in Germany).

The co-determination (*Mitbestimmung*) model is mandated by law in Germany, with three legal participation ratios coexisting, giving workers one-third to one-half the seats on boards.[20] Table 5.2 summarizes the major features of Germany's co-determination model.

The Works Council   At the shop level, workers' representatives are organized in a **works council.** This group participates on an equal footing with management in decision making at the lowest level in the company. All private companies with five or more workers must have a council.[21]

The primary responsibility of the works council is to administer all laws, regulations, safety rules, and collective bargaining agreements, especially as they relate to

Table 5.2 *Co-Determination in Germany*

Level	Representation Group	Participation
Top	Board of supervisors	1/3 to 1/2 of elected members
Mid	Executive (management) board	Labor director
Low	Works council	Equal say with management

workers' rights. In cooperation with management, the works council also deals with matters such as

- Job evaluation.
- Piece rates and wage structures.
- Working hours, overtime, breaks, and holiday schedules.
- Worker recruitment, selection, and training.
- Worker dismissal and layoff and compensation to these workers.
- Safety, accident prevention, and welfare schemes.

Any disputes over these issues between management (employer) and the works council can be brought to arbitration (an internal but neutral committee), or a conciliation committee with a neutral, outside chairperson, or the labor courts.

Union officials function separately from the works councils. However, they may serve on them (as a "separate" job), and, in fact, they commonly do. The vast majority of council members are union members, even in plants where the union has a low membership rate.

The Labor Director   At the middle to top operating management level, workers' representatives sit on executive or management boards (policymaking committees) as **labor directors.** These full-time positions are usually filled by union members.

The executive board conducts a company's day-to-day business. Financial or marketing decisions are usually reserved for management, but staff, personnel, and social policies and practices involve the labor director who has equal status with the other members of the board. Like other top managers, the labor director is elected by the board of supervisors (or at least the labor members on it).

The Board of Supervisors   At the highest level in the company, workers participate in the **board of supervisors** (called the board of directors in the United States) whose labor members comprise one-third to one-half its seats. The labor members are chosen by the works council (from among the blue-collar and white-collar workers), the trade union (from among outsiders) with approval from the works council, and the Federation of German Unions (*Deutscher Gewerkschaftsbund*, DGB). For example, if labor has five seats on the board, the works council fills two, the trade union with approval of the works council fills two, and the DGB fills one. Five members would be elected by the shareholders if membership was half labor, half owners. The two groups would select the eleventh member.

Table 5.3   *The 12 European Community (EC) Countries*

Belgium	Italy
Denmark	Luxembourg
France	Netherlands
Germany	Portugal
Greece	Spain
Ireland	United Kingdom (Great Britain)

The board of supervisors, like the American board of directors, meets quarterly. It appoints the executive board, which includes the company's top managers and the labor director. It oversees the executive board's activities and determines overall company policy.

The Spread of Co-determination   The shared authority system of worker participation is more fully developed in Germany than in any other EC country. However, other countries have legislated worker participation in the management of companies. This is usually through works councils with varying levels of authority. The EC countries besides Germany with this type of legislation are Denmark, France, Luxembourg, and the Netherlands; works councils and other forms of participation also exist, but not by law, and are on the increase in the EC countries of Belgium, Italy and the United Kingdom.[22] With only Greece, Ireland, Portugal, and Spain yet to adopt co-determination, we can see that the European Community (see Table 5.3) is likely to make this system its model for worker participation in decision making at the plant and/or company level.

Unionism and Collective Bargaining in Germany

In conjunction with the co-determination model, unions and employers' associations carry out collective bargaining on an industrial basis, regionally or nationally (depending on the industry). The major subjects of this bargaining are wage levels, wage differentials, and the length and distribution of working time.[23] Most fringe benefits are mandated by law, as is true in the majority of European nations.

In the 1980s, Germany's strong economic performance worked in favor of the unions, even in the presence of rather high rates of unemployment. Major wage gains were made, making Germans the highest paid workers in the EC, working among the fewest hours per week (see Table 5.4).

The German unions, though worried about the effect the 1992 EC integration and removal of all trade barriers would have on their membership, pushed for a shorter workweek (to 35 hours) and the continuation of the ban on Sunday work as well as healthy wage increases in the 15 percent range, led by IG Metall (Germany's largest union, with 2.6 million members).[24] The 1990 round of bargaining promised to be a rough one. However, in the May 1990 settlement between IG Metall and the Metal Industry Association, the union settled for a 6 percent increase for 1990, and the 35-hour week was pushed to 1995. The availability of the 9 million worker East German labor force, with an average hourly wage of $5.40 (about one-fourth that of West Germany), was the main reason the union backed away from its demands.[25]

Table 5.4 *Wages and Workweeks in the Common Market (1988)^a*

Country	Average Wage (U.S. $/hr)	Average Workweek (hours)
West Germany^b	$18.29	38.4
Netherlands	15.14	40
Denmark	14.99	38
Belgium	14.42	38
Italy	13.59	40
France	12.37	39
Great Britain	10.80	39
Ireland	9.94	40
Spain	9.70	40
Greece	4.97	40
Portugal	3.10	45

Sources: *New York Times*, October 9, 1989, p. C8; *Business Week*, May 21, 1990, p. 60.

^{a} Excluding Luxembourg.

^{b} By 1990, the hourly wage had increased to $21, while workweek hours decreased to 38.

The close relationship between Germany's unions, industry, and government, a key factor in the country's postwar economic success, is changing. German reunification followed by the economic unification of the European market promises to change labor relations in Germany. With membership declining and even some labor leaders questioning the rigid union stance on work rules and working hours, the German unions will have to develop a new strategy for the 1990s to maintain and enhance German competitiveness in Europe and the world.

Labor Relations in Scandinavia: Sweden

The Swedish model of labor relations, now undergoing major change, was a very unusual one.[26] As in most European systems, collective bargaining was centralized. However, the unions, in conjunction with government and industry, took into consideration wider, macroeconomic issues (such as full employment and price stability) beyond higher pay for their members. Social issues also played a major role. Wage solidarity was a key feature: equal pay for equal work, regardless of an industry's or firm's profitability. Interunion wage rivalry was minimized. This cooperative model was aimed at full employment, low inflation, and rapid change coupled with steady economic growth in a global economy.

The highly centralized collective bargaining initially took place between the Swedish Confederation of Trade Unions (LO),* representing 90 percent of blue-collar workers, and the Swedish Employers Federation (SAF), representing 40,000

* The letters used in the abbreviations of foreign organizations match the foreign-language spelling of the association, which may be different from the English translation.

firms in private industry. However, structural changes in the labor market, mirroring those in the economy, took place between the 1950s and the 1980s. These were similar to changes occurring in the United States and, indeed, in most industrialized economies of the world. The main feature was the growth of the service sector and the shrinking of manufacturing: the service sector, which employed 40 percent of the Swedish labor force in 1950, now employs two-thirds of it, while the industrial (export) sector employs under 20 percent. Collective bargaining now involves not only LO, but also the Central Organization of Salaried Employees (TCO) and the Central Organization of Professional Employees (SACO/SR). The three union confederations represent 80 percent of the white-collar workers in Sweden's public and private sector.

The coordination between unions, industry, and government increased with the labor market changes, which in turn increased centralization of union policymaking and collective bargaining. Coming on the heels of the energy crisis of the 1970s, this move prompted worker discontent. Strikes not sanctioned by the unions occurred in the early 1970s, breaking Sweden's postwar labor peace, as economic prosperity gave way to economic scarcity. This led to legislation decentralizing labor relations. Concern also grew over the growing size of the public sector, which today accounts for about 65 percent of gross domestic product (the largest of the Western industrialized nations).

The changing structure of the economy and industrial restructuring to meet international trade considerations have caused a fragmentation of collective bargaining. This fragmentation and decentralization have made Sweden's macroeconomic planning more difficult. The growing pressures of international marketing in an export-dependent country like Sweden have altered its labor relations system. Union rivalry has replaced union solidarity as employer competition and trade-mandated issues have replaced employer coordination. The government has had to contend with its own employment problems and pressures from public sector unions for *more*, in the face of inflationary pressures and concern over growing public expenditures.

The present drift of government in the labor market is to push both sides into showing some concern for the national economy. Continued intervention in collective bargaining in a less formal way than in the past is likely. The unions will continue to press publicly for government legislation on social policies to remove these considerations from collective bargaining so that they can speak more for their members than for the public at large. For their part, employers will continue to advocate more flexibility as they continue to restructure to meet international competition. The Swedish model, characterized by a high degree of centralization and tripartite cooperation in the common interest, has been supplanted by one of self-interest but accommodation, with continued free collective bargaining.

LABOR RELATIONS IN JAPAN

Whereas industrial relations in Western Europe and the United States stem from the tradition of horizontal competition between trade unions and employers, Japan's harmonious labor relationships rely on the vertical bonds between the paternalistic company and its loyal employees. The Japanese employment system has been shaped by government policies, the nation's industrial growth since the 1950s, business strategies, and, most importantly, the attitudes and activities of the workers themselves.[27] Another major factor in the system is the interaction between the labor union movement and the state.[28]

Trade Unionism in Japan

Japan has four national trade union federations: Sohyo (General Council of Trade Unions of Japan), which is the largest; Domei (Japanese Confederation of Labor), the second largest; and two smaller organizations, Churitsuroren (Federation of Independent Unions of Japan) and Shinsanbetsu (National Federation of Industrial Organizations). They have unionized about 28 percent of the employed workforce. However, in the large industrial companies, the rate is closer to 60 percent.[29] The proportion of the workforce in unions has fallen some from over 35 percent in 1970, reflecting the decline of heavy industries where unions are strong and the growth in private sector services where they are not, the same as in the United States. Two recent studies also suggest that the decline in both countries is due to the workers' loss of faith in the unions' ability to solve any and all problems the workers may have, and to the unions' perceived ineffectiveness in the face of stronger, government-supported resistance by management.[30] The highest rates of unionization are in utilities, transport, and telecommunications.

Enterprise Unionism

Most unions in Japan are organized by enterprise or establishment, not by occupation or by job. Today enterprise unions account for nearly 90 percent of all union organizations. An **enterprise union** consists of only regular employees of a single firm, regardless of their job classification. This type of unionism is characterized by the close relationship between management and workers, resulting in a participative management system that is different from those of all other industrialized countries. Because of the mixed representation of blue-collar and white-collar workers, enterprise unions are less likely to be viewed as only a negotiating body, but also as a forum for employees to participate in a company's managerial and operational decisions. Enterprise unions generally have a cooperative attitude toward management as a result of such participative management. Workers view their interests as being best served by the company for which they work. This viewpoint, in turn, weakens the overall union movement since the existence of the union is dependent on the existence of the enterprise.

Furthermore, because unionism is predominantly on an enterprise basis, collective bargaining is highly decentralized. Approximately 50,000 unions conclude collective bargaining agreements with their companies. This is not to say that bargaining is totally decentralized. Almost all enterprise-level unions are affiliated with one of the trade union confederations like Sohyo and Domei. Although they do not directly participate in negotiations, they do influence these transactions and increasingly so.

The Firm and the Worker

The Japanese system is known for its lifetime employment and worker participation. Both components, however, are restricted to the larger companies in the economy.

These companies employ less than half the labor force. The others, the majority of workers, are found in smaller workshops and stores where employment is relatively unstable.

Lifetime Employment

Lifetime employment is somewhat of a myth in Japan. Only companies with 1,000 or more employees, such as Sony and Toyota, offer lifetime employment, and only to the elite, primary corps of employees. Mainly clustered in manufacturing, these enterprises now employ less than 5 percent of Japan's total labor force.[31] This component of the economy has been and is still shrinking relative to the "secondary" economy in which employment is sporadic. Lifetime employment never covered more than 25 percent of Japan's labor force, but even this limited system has been eroded by the recent trend of job hopping among young, aspiring junior managers and professionals.[32]

As the technological revolution sweeps through Japan, more and more firms are automating. The Japanese blue-collar worker is being replaced by robots and the like. White-collar workers are increasingly using machines with growing levels of microelectronics built in as computer-integrated systems take hold.

Worker Participation

Workers and unions in the large firms characterized by lifetime employment are also heavily involved in decision making at the shop floor levels. Unions, however, vary in their support for extensive co-participation with management:

> Domei-affiliated unions favor full worker participation with co-determination of basic management strategies, but Sohyo unions commonly are cautious, fearing to dilute the identity of the union as a separate force, and the Japanese employers' federation Nikkeiren, while favoring joint consultation, does not greatly favor worker directorships or co-determination as in the West German model.[33]

However, the microelectronics revolution in these firms has substantially curtailed worker participation just as it has lifetime employment.

The Japanese Wage System and Spring Labor Offensive

There are relatively modest wage differentials between managers, white-collar, and blue-collar workers in most large Japanese business organizations. The traditional **seniority system,** which stems from lifetime employment, determines both wages and the timing of promotion. Besides wages and salaries, Japanese workers in the larger firms receive seasonal bonus payments worth about five months' salary.[34] In addition to basic salary, these workers receive compensation supplements in the form of housing or a housing allowance, daily living support, recreational benefits, and medical care. In a comparison of hourly pay, Japanese pay is among the highest in the world (see Table 5.5).[35]

Since the 1960s, Japanese trade unions have organized coordinated industrywide **Spring Labor Offensives (the Shunto).** Annual wage demands are presented to all

Table 5.5 *Average Monthly Wages and Workweek in Manufacturing in the Pacific Rim, 1986*

Country/"Colony"	Average Monthly Wage, Mfg. (U.S. $)	Average Mfg. Workweek (hours)
Singapore	$ 737	47
Hong Kong	420	45.2
South Korea	401	54.7
Taiwan	385	48.2
Japan	1,935	40
United States	1,515	36.4

Sources: Yearbook of Labor Statistics (United Nations, 1987); *Abstract of Employment and Earning Statistics in Taiwan Area Republic of China, 1987* (Directorate General of Budget, Accounting and Statistics, Executive Yuen, ROC, 1987).

major employers in a concentrated period, with a peak in April. Instead of independent actions by each enterprise union, the Shunto is a simultaneous effort and has industrywide impact. The agreements reached affect wage levels for all workers, including nonunion ones.[36]

The impact of the Spring Labor Offensive has weakened since the early 1980s owing to slow growth and increased unemployment. In 1986, major unions accepted relatively low wage increases of 3 to 4 percent, which grew to just over 5 percent by 1989.[37] The Offensive, however, is important in the Japanese labor–management relationship. This is the uniquely Japanese form of collective bargaining, for the negotiating power of the enterprise union is rather limited by itself.

The Japanese System in Transition

Traditionally, the Japanese workers and their unions believed that three sacred trusts united them and their firms: lifetime employment, the traditional wage and seniority system, and enterprise unionism. Lifetime employment is being shaped by two contemporary forces:

1. The postwar baby-boom generation is more Westernized, more receptive to greater challenges; they will not wait 10 to 20 years to realize their career goal, and the shrinking number of midlevel management positions also results in greater competition.

2. The old, group-oriented approach worked well for mass-production systems, but the future lies in creative corporate strategies in high-technology environments.

Bringing in midcareer managers from outside gives companies a greater competitive edge. Sony hired about 70 midcareer switchers in 1987.[38]

Many companies are modifying their traditional employment and wage system to introduce more flexible personnel management practices. Nissan Motors and Nippon Kayaku (a pharmaceutical giant) have started to link pay and performance.[39] The older paternalistic traditions still have a dominant influence on many people in Japanese industries, but the major characteristics of the Japanese labor relations model (lifetime employment, seniority-based wages, and enterprise unions) are changing. These characteristics were major factors in the postwar Japanese economic miracle, but we should also realize that adaptability to change helped the large Japanese industries survive substantial economic crises (the energy crisis of the early 1970s, for instance). The future Japanese model of industrial relations will continue to change, eliminating barriers to economic growth, which will enable the Japanese to extend the postwar economic miracle.

LABOR RELATIONS IN THE SOVIET UNION AND EASTERN EUROPE

In this section, we discuss events in what was once the Soviet or Eastern bloc. These events and the bloc can only be characterized as rapidly changing. The years 1989–1990 were marked by (1) the unseating of hard-line communist governments in Poland, Czechoslovakia, Hungary, Romania, Bulgaria, and East Germany (with the reunification of Germany taking place in December 1990); and (2) strong nationalistic outpourings and independence movements in the USSR itself, for example, Soviet Georgia, Armenia, the Baltic Soviet Republics of Lithuania, Latvia, and Estonia, and even the Ukraine, the second largest of the Soviet Socialist Republics. Mikhail Gorbachev's twin policies of *perestroika* (restructuring) and *glasnost* (openness) have led to amazing and far-reaching results so far, such as the declaration of independence by Lithuania. These events promise to continue to amaze.

The Soviet Union: Labor Relations and the State

Trade unions in the USSR are officially sanctioned by the state and party as independent organizations. Theoretically, they have two functions, which are carried out through trade union committees at the workplace: the defense of workers' rights and participation in the management of production.[40] In practice, the function of Soviet trade union leaders was to keep worker efforts and productivity high and maintain industrial peace by exhorting the workers to do their utmost for the state and party. Another important function was political indoctrination.

As unofficial arms of the state and party, trade unions in the Soviet Union (and the Eastern bloc) have been controlled by the management of the enterprises for which their members work. As a Soviet critic noted several years ago, labor relations in the USSR (and, until recently, Eastern Europe) are "peaceful": (1) absolute power has been concentrated in the hands of the party and absolute control in the hands of the secret police; (2) labor unions have been required to be subservient to the state; and (3) a nonmarket, bureaucratic economy has been imposed where all real values, including the value of work, are lost.[41]

This picture changed dramatically in the Soviet Union in 1989. The Siberian coal strikes in July, which quickly spread to the Ukraine, were said to have involved as many as 150,000 miners.[42] In an unusual move, the officially sanctioned Council of Trade Unions publicly supported the strikes, and the government carefully avoided any confrontations with the strikers. In fact, President Gorbachev praised the strikers for taking things into their own hands to force changes in line with *perestroika* and promised to speed consideration of the strike settlement, with its many economic and political concessions, in the Supreme Soviet.[43] He stated that ineffective union leaders must share in the blame for allowing conditions to deteriorate in the minefields, and he called for restructuring of the union organizations. The coal strikes, and the concessions they gained, may have laid the foundation for a free and independent union (like Solidarity in Poland).

In October 1989, the Soviet Union passed legislation permitting, on a limited basis, economic strikes.[44] At the end of the month, a work stoppage in the Siberian coalfields above the Arctic Circle, which quickly spread to the Ukraine, occurred in defiance of the law that forbids strikes in energy industries.[45] Workers on strike complained that concessions made in the wake of the summer strikes were not put into effect. Again, the government avoided confrontation. The coal miners struck again in March and April of 1991, and yet again the government avoided confrontation; they even agreed to double miners' pay over the next 12 months.

The reforms that are sweeping the Soviet Union promise to move the country to a less bureaucratic economic structure. Trade unions will gain some independence from management. However, as political reform appears to be less radical in the USSR than in Eastern Europe, the retention of power by the Communist party leads us to the conclusion that the state and party will continue to attempt to keep all economic activity under control. Trade union freedom of action will likely be achieved through compromises with the state, on a case-by-case basis.

Eastern Europe: A Revolution

The Eastern bloc, in no more than "the wink of an eye," was transformed from countries run by communist governments as Soviet satellites into democracies striving to effect reforms that would move their economies to the levels represented by the capitalist nations of Western Europe. This transformation was nothing short of a revolution. However, the seeds of this revolution were planted as many as 35 years ago, with brief but startling uprisings such as Hungary's in 1956 and the Prague Spring of 1968. And the rise of Poland's Solidarity started ten years ago, in 1980.

Solidarity Triumphs

In the summer of 1980, a trade union strike committee in Poland's Gdansk region issued a series of demands to present to the communist government. These demands, posted in the huge Lenin Shipyard in the city of Gdansk, started with: "Recognition of the Free Trade Union, independent of the Party and employers...."[46] Sit-in strikes were carried out to back the demands, and the government bowed to the strike committee, popularly referred to as **Solidarity,** and negotiated. As a result of the negotiations, Solidarity became an independent self-governing trade union, with the strike committee chairperson, Lech Walesa, becoming chairperson of its national coordinating commission. Solidarity was divided by region, unlike the Soviet (and Polish state) model which is grouped by industry.

At the end of 1981, martial law was declared in Poland, Solidarity's leaders were arrested, and Solidarity was dissolved by the Polish government, sending the organization underground. A new state–party labor organization was formed, the Polish

Trade Union Alliance (OPZZ). Support for Solidarity was maintained by outsiders, including the AFL–CIO, Pope John Paul II, and many Western leaders. However, Poland's workers continued to push for legalizing Solidarity, and in 1988, they showed their support through two waves of strikes and demonstrations.

In April 1989, responding to workers' pressures and the refusal of Western nations and international agencies to grant economic assistance to Poland's ailing economy until Solidarity was legalized, the government did just that. The union, which the regime now needed to gain Western economic aid and trade, was allowed to assume a political role, and won 260 seats (out of 261 contests) in June's parliamentary election.[47] This was the first democratic election in the Eastern bloc in almost 45 years, since the immediate postwar period.

Today, as an integral part of the government, Solidarity leaders (ex-leaders actually) have to cope with the economic woes of the country, such as inflation and unemployment, as well as the needs (and rights) of the workers. Thus, the goals pursued are often in conflict, especially in light of Poland's austerity program to curb inflation and continue economic reform. Even before joining the government, Solidarity officials worked to halt the coal miners and copper miners' strikes.[48] And recently Walesa settled a rail strike.[49]

The story of Solidarity is a story of both a trade union and a nationalist movement. It is a story that is certainly not over yet, and one that is being repeated, on a smaller and less dramatic scale, in other Eastern bloc nations.

Other Eastern Bloc Developments

The five other countries of Eastern Europe are well on the road to democratic governments with free and independent trade unions. Hungary recognizes free trade unions and has paved the way for opposition political parties.[50] Unfortunately, like Poland (and the other four in the Eastern bloc), it is staggering under a heavy debt load, and inflation is very high. This problem is a great challenge to the unions, which are trying to maintain the purchasing power of their members in a fragile economy undergoing reform and moving toward a market orientation. Austerity versus worker living standards is the chief problem for now and the near future.

Perhaps the most astounding East (or East–West) bloc development is the reunification of Germany. German Chancellor Helmut Kohl visualizes a reunified Germany as a major linchpin in a European free market for Eastern as well as Western Europe.

LABOR RELATIONS ALONG THE PACIFIC RIM

The Pacific Rim is the fastest growing region in the world, and its countries are leaders in the world economy and in international trade. In this section we discuss labor relations in China, the four "tigers" (the newly industrialized economies—NIEs—of South Korea, Taiwan, Singapore, and Hong Kong), and Australia. (Labor relations in the Asian economic giant of the region, Japan, have already been discussed. The other regional giant, the United States, is the subject of the rest of the book.)

Labor Relations in China

The complex, intertwined relationship between Chinese labor unions and the communist power structure poses great challenges for those who are trying to analyze it from the vast amount of information available, ranging from published statistics to fabricated propaganda materials. Traditionally, Western observers have relied largely on official publications to study trade unionism and labor–management relations in the People's Republic of China (PRC). This approach imparts a certain degree of bias. Furthermore, the close association between many so-called China experts and the Chinese government has also alienated them from the truth and reality in China.

The Development of Trade Unionism in the PRC

In 1948, the Communist party (CPC) organized the All-China Federation of Trade Unions (ACFTU). ACFTU functions as the sole trade union center for China's 15 national unions which have 536,000 branches and 100 million members, representing 90 percent of the labor force.[51] Many of China's grass-roots trade unions are inseparable from the CPC structure. Union representatives are typically party cadres. The unions are not independent by nature.

The interactions between workers, management, and the government (and party) are very different in China than in the United States and other Western nations or Japan. These interactions are schematically illustrated in Figure 5.2. Chinese labor–management relations are unique because (1) the grass-roots trade union organizations branch out from the party structure; hence, the government/party directly supervises the unions, and (2) management people often identify themselves as part of the labor force, as is evident in China's state-owned enterprises. In the 1989 pro-democracy movement, the leader of China's first independent, nationwide labor union was the plant manager of an aluminum factory in Shanxi. The system is best illustrated by the following official comments:

> In China, the fundamental interests of trade unions and the government are identical. Trade unions should safeguard the government's authority, which in return should respect and protect the trade unions' legal rights and interests, expanding their rights to participate in state affairs and exercise social supervision.[52]

A Weak Labor Class Awareness

Unlike the close relationship between the labor movement and the stages of economic development witnessed in many developing and NIEs, workers' expectations in China are drastically different from those of their counterparts both in Asia and the Eastern bloc. Those who are puzzled by the initially similar but strikingly different outcomes between China and Eastern Europe in 1989 have simply overlooked the lack of workers' support in China's pro-democracy movement. Although China's 536,000 grass-roots trade union organizations have a combined membership of 100 million workers, many of them are peasants. Forty years of a socialist public ownership system brought them a slightly better life than rural farmers. In general, the

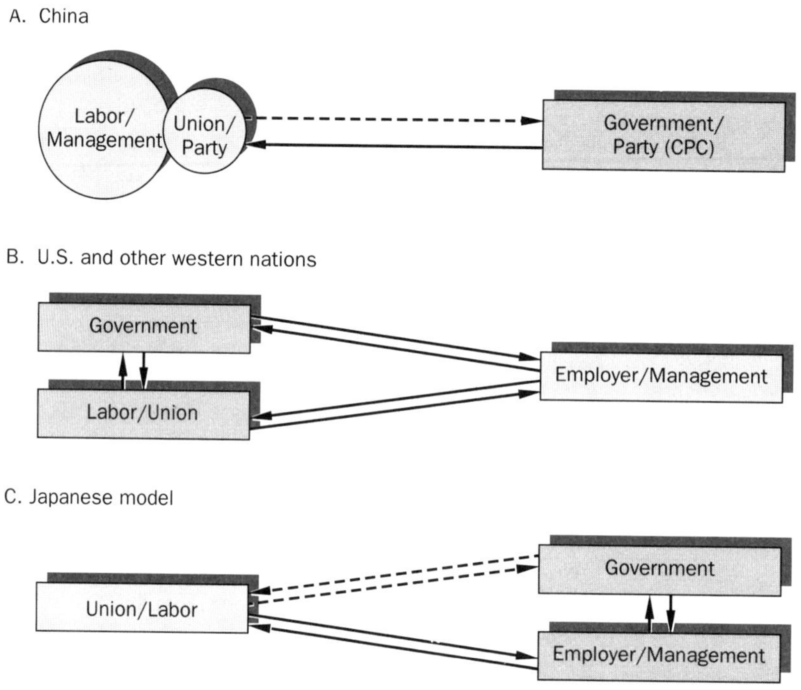

A. China

B. U.S. and other western nations

C. Japanese model

FIGURE 5.2 Three models of labor–management relations.

workers' class awareness and cohesiveness are low. In the better days of economic reform, even official sources admitted that trade union work was not at all satisfactory. Measures to safeguard workers' interests have been weak, and their leadership and administration remain overly bureaucratic.

Changes in the System: Labor and Management Working Together

Before the June 1989 crackdown, enterprise managers were gaining decision-making autonomy as China's reform program grew. On the surface, it appeared that trade unions had also become more independent, but most unions were far from being free from party and state control. Unions were more involved in helping to raise productivity and defusing potential conflicts. There was talk about unions of management and workforce, which by no means resembled any significant organized labor movement.[53] It was more like the concession and cooperation sentiment that blossomed in the United States in the 1980s amid the decline of industrial competitiveness in the international economy.

The quest for change, however, gradually spread within the organization, from managerial autonomy to union independence. A local union in Shenyang declared itself "Solidarity" in 1988. Some unions turned down government subsidies in order to gain more independence. In the Special Enterprise Zone (SEZ) of Shenzen, unions got directly involved in settling labor–management disputes by, for example, negotiating grievances of workers directly with management. The first secretary of the ACFTU, Zhu Houze, argued that the unions should (1) become independent,

(2) truly represent workers' interests, and (3) establish collective bargaining power against the enterprise and the government.[54]

But the pendulum has momentarily swung back to the other extreme. Although the Beijing government boasts that two workers' movement colleges and five workers' universities under the trade unions have set up a labor protection department, trade unions are for the time being back under full state/party supervision.[55]

In short, enterprise autonomy with independent decision making in many state-owned enterprises has become a phenomenon of the past as a result of the current government crackdown and austerity program. Unions striving for independence have once again been silenced. Ironically, for those workers who fought for economic and political freedom, the 1989 unrest in China was not between labor and management. It was the struggle of united labor and management against the state—the biggest, and the only, employer. It will be this coalition that revives the move to independent decision making and free unions when the time is right.

Labor Relations in the Four "Tigers"

While organized labor has been on the decline in the United States and Japan, labor movements in the four Pacific Asia NIEs—South Korea, Taiwan, Singapore, and Hong Kong—are experiencing important changes and unionism appears to be on the rise. This turn of events has surprised many analysts who saw Asian workers as forever obedient and believed no widespread strikes were likely to take place.

The contrast between East and West exhibits an interesting reflection of the cyclical nature of labor movements. Pacific Asia's four NIEs share two commonalities: a strong presence of U.S. multinationals, and export-oriented growth strategies with the United States as the major market. Consequently, there seems to be a strong U.S. influence on management styles in the region. Labor–management relations in the four NIEs lie somewhere between the two extremes of the Japanese and U.S. models but more closely resemble the distrustful one found in the United States.[56]

Nonetheless, the differences between these four NIEs should not be ignored. What we are witnessing today are two opposite trends of labor movements on the two sides of the Pacific Basin. Labor–management tensions in the two regions are strikingly similar, but the countries' (and colony's) economic conditions and stages of economic development cause opposite ramifications. Although the degree of unionization, types of unions, government involvement, historical background, and current political environment vary considerably among the four NIEs, labor–management relations in the region can be grouped into two categories: (1) Singapore and Hong Kong—relatively stable and peaceful, and (2) Taiwan and South Korea—highly unsettling and rapidly changing in the next year or two.

Stable Relations: Singapore and Hong Kong

If the problems of limited natural resources and labor shortages are alleviated, Singapore and Hong Kong will thrive even more on their highly educated and adaptable workforce. Both have tried to move from labor-intensive to capital-intensive industries, and from manufacturing-dominated to service-oriented economies. Their greatest advantage is their small size. Labor issues become extremely sensitive when a land's economic structure is undergoing major changes. The problems, however, are less complicated and more easily dealt with if they are restricted to a very small geographical area.

Singapore   Singapore, an independent republic within the British Commonwealth with a population of approximately 2.5 million, has experienced rapid economic growth since independence. This has given it the second highest per capita GDP (gross domestic product) in Asia since the early 1980s. Statistics on the labor force, especially in manufacturing during the 1980s, indicate a declining labor supply, while demand is rising as a result, for example, of an increasing number of U.S. and Japanese subsidiaries.

Trade unions in Singapore developed after World War II. A Singapore Trade Union Congress appeared in the 1950s and split in 1961 into the National Trades Union Congress (NTUC) and a leftist Singapore Association of Trade Unions which collapsed in 1963. In the mid-1980s, there were 83 registered employee trade unions with 200,613 members; 96 percent of these workers belong to unions affiliated with the NTUC, which has a close relationship with the government, the ruling People's Action party.[57] The federation and its unions have adopted policies of industrial cooperation intended to promote growth and attract foreign investment. In 1986, NTUC agreed to an indefinite wage freeze, following the 1985 recession, in line with a recommendation of the National Wage Council (NWC).

The NWC, founded in 1972, is made up of representatives from the government, employers, and unions. It sets annual wage guidelines, providing a framework for decentralized collective bargaining. Although these recommendations are not legally binding, they are followed by the government for its large number of public sector employees, clearly setting a precedent and virtually imposing conformity for all others.[58] The NWC system has kept union demands in line and contributed to industrial peace. The government, leaning toward democratic socialism, tends to be protective of workers' interests.

As a result of the 1985 economic downturn, the high wage policy introduced in 1979 was abandoned in early 1986 in favor of wage restraint. Two NWC flexible wage models were designed to link pay hikes to increases in productivity or corporate profitability in 1986.[59] After two years of wage restraint, NWC recommended moderate pay gains for 1988.[60] Wage gains now comprise a small basic raise and a variable bonus dependent on company and individual performance. Employers and workers negotiate on the basis of productivity, profit, and competitiveness. This gives market forces a larger role in setting wages than in the past. Although workers welcomed the recent pay raise and employers viewed the recommendations as giving them greater management autonomy, productivity measurement difficulties and fluctuating profits are inevitable and will continue to generate labor–management relations problems. On a positive note, greater flexibility in Singapore's decentralized collective bargaining will give each individual firm or union more leeway to resolve its own problems.

Hong Kong   Hong Kong, a British colony due to revert in its entirety to China in 1997, had a population of more than 5.6 million in 1988. The number of people leaving Hong Kong in fear of the change of administration after 1997 has been increasing annually. This has become a blessing for the remaining workforce. With the shortage of workers, especially the skilled and professional (which promises to intensify), employees' expectations are being more generously met.

Hong Kong has two politically opposed trade union federations, both formed after trade unionism was legalized in 1948: the Hong Kong Federation of Trade Unions (FTU) and the Hong Kong and Kowloon Trade Union Council (TUC). FTU supports China, whereas TUC favors Taiwan. In 1988, a total of 458 registered trade unions were affiliated with these federations, consisting of 415 employees' unions, 29 employers' associations, and 14 mixed organizations of employers and employees, with a total declared membership of about 405,000.[61] Only about 14 to 15 percent of the labor force is unionized, but this is growing. Workforce and union activities have been increasing considerably as a result of migrating Chinese and Southeast Asian refugees. Hong Kong's labor shortage problem is different from that of Singapore. Skepticism over Beijing's promises has spurred an exodus of professionals and managers and some skilled workers.

Collective bargaining is poorly developed in most Hong Kong companies. Labor regulations, updated in June 1988, cover a large portion of the subject matter of collective bargaining. For example, they stipulate maximum hours of work for women and children as well as holidays, severance pay, and other benefits.[62] The government has attempted to improve working conditions and terms of employment through an extensive program of labor legislation. Much of the effort was made in the late 1970s when the potential for labor trouble was great. Between 1978 and 1987, 135 pieces of legislation were enacted to improve conditions of employment, particularly health and safety at work.[63] Regulations cover most hazardous industrial activities. Industrial safety in general is promoted through the use of the mass media, and relies heavily on the cooperation of employers and workers.

Most labor–management disputes are settled through the intervention of the Labor Department. Strikes are relatively uncommon, and striking workers may be dismissed for breach of contract. During 1987, the Labor Department dealt with 16,372 labor problems, most of which were worker grievances. Annual working days lost per 1,000 employees in the late 1980s have been a relatively low one or two days. In contrast, the figure was as high as 20 in the late 1970s.[64] There is no legal minimum wage in Hong Kong, and the prevailing wage level is essentially the result of market forces.

The lack of significant worker unrest and a relatively weak labor movement in Hong Kong seems to be the result of three factors: (1) different political loyalties (China versus Taiwan), (2) a large number of small unions, and (3) the absence of labor class consciousness among most Chinese.

Changing Relations: South Korea and Taiwan

South Korea and Taiwan are rapidly moving toward a new era of labor–management relations. Until 1987, strikes and lockouts were completely banned under Taiwan's martial law. In South Korea labor unrest occurred only as an isolated incident and was dealt with severely by the government. Recent labor movements in these two countries are principally the result of the easing of decades of political suppression. The transition from highly centralized and tightly controlled regimes to more democratic governments apparently stirred up workers' desires for greater political freedom. The new leaders of South Korea and Taiwan appear to be more tolerant than before. Rapid economic growth and rising corporate profitability have also intensified workers' desires to share in the gains.

Labor–management harmony is a thing of the past, however. Major changes in the substance and structure of labor–management relations took place in Taiwan and South Korea in the late 1980s, and are continuing in the 1990s. A wave of widespread labor unrest (nearly 4,000 strikes) struck Korean enterprises in 1987, and the first strike in Taiwan after 40 years of industrial peace broke out in early 1988. Workers slowing down production, walking out (or going "on leave," since strikes are outlawed in Taiwan), and participating in riots and disturbances have occurred everywhere. Long-established company rules are being swept aside, and independent employee unions are developing. The government is rapidly acting to amend, rectify, and enact labor regulations.

South Korea   Its 40 million plus population makes South Korea the largest of Pacific Asia's four NIEs. GNP has increased 50-fold in the last 25 years. South Korea is now one of the world's 12 biggest exporting nations.

In contrast to this glowing picture of development and growth, the average Korean worker puts in almost a 55-hour workweek, compared with just over 36 for U.S. workers and 40 for Japanese workers (see Table 5.5 as well as Table 5.4 which has comparative figures for European Community countries). South Korea has no Social Security system, and few companies provide for worker retirement or workers compensation as a result of job-related injuries. The protests against low wages, unemployment, and corrupt union officials following the assassination of President Park in 1979 led the Chun government to tightly limit the scope of union activities.[65]

Legislation enacted in 1980 by the administration of Chun Doo Hwan defined the status of trade unionism. Under this legislation, only one union was permitted in each enterprise, and only enterprise-level unions could negotiate with employers. No national union representatives could participate. Disputes were to be settled directly between unions and employers, under the authority of tripartite labor committees representing employers, workers, and the government. The government, however, nominated the members of these committees. The revised labor law enacted by the Chun government can best be described as a unique labor–management relations model designed to solidify the government's central role in labor relations.

Eighty-five percent of the approximately 1 million organized workers belong to the 16 unions affiliated with the Federation of Korean Trade Unions (FKTU). But the FKTU and its unions were substantially weakened under 1980 legislation that excluded them from direct involvement in industrial disputes and collective bargaining. Until 1987, FKTU's role was reduced to representing the interests of organized labor to the government.

FKTU became increasingly active in 1987, pressing the government for major labor reforms. These included specific constitutional guarantees of workers' rights, an end to the ban on union members engaging in politics, and giving workers a greater say in management decisions.[66] These demands extended beyond the basic traditional negotiating items such as wage hikes, decent working hours, and safe work environments, to the quality of work life such as participation and job enrichment.

These actions of Korean unions may set an example of challenges to improve employees' rights for other developing Asian countries.

Toward the end of Chun's reign, Korean labor grew more and more enraged. In 1987, incidents of labor unrest skyrocketed prior to the presidential election. Workers engaged in more than 3,600 wildcat strikes, recording one of the most violent periods in the country's labor history. The wave of labor unrest in 1987 pushed the nation into deep political crisis. Independent unions were born, and union membership soared. A new president was elected in Korea's first democratic transition of power. Workers' gains were phenomenal. On January 1, 1988, the minimum wage law was enacted, setting a monthly floor of W 111,000 (754 Won equaled U.S. $1 at that time) for workers in a dozen low-paying manufacturing industries including food, textiles, garments, and leather, and a monthly minimum of W 117,000 in other areas.[67] The new pay levels, based on eight-hour workdays and excluding bonuses, apply to all firms with ten or more employees; some 100,000 workers are expected to benefit. A new national pension scheme was also established in January 1989, affecting companies employing more than ten permanent staff.

In general, salary increases averaged better than 19 percent in 1987. In that one year, more than 1,400 unions were formed after 4,000 strikes and labor disputes, many of them violent. There were 3,400 strikes from late July through mid-September alone. In the first six months of 1988, more than 1,000 fresh labor disputes occurred. Labor disputes broke out at the giant anti-union Hyundai and Daewood conglomerates and continued through 1988. At the height of the confrontation, Hyundai Motors suffered a three-week strike in April 1988 that resulted in a 26 percent wage increase. This was a surprisingly generous outcome, even though it met only about one-half of the workers' original demand for a 55 percent increase.[68] Strikes continue in Korea; in 1990, two major ones, stopped by government intervention, were against Hyundai's Ulsan Shipyard and the Korea Broadcasting Service.[69] Most companies now realize they must negotiate.

Union leaders are also learning to improve their skills and effectiveness. They are joining training sessions sponsored by universities, the American AFL–CIO, and international labor groups. The results have been better organized and more disciplined unions.[70]

The strikes in the spring of 1988 raised serious concern, for they were instrumental in establishing the practices and procedures for future Korean labor–management relations. What now seems to be taking shape in South Korea is very different from Japan's relatively strike-free labor relations system, resembling more the basically adversarial one found in the United States. One major contribution of the recent labor movement, however, is the changing governmental attitude as a result of the aggressive labor offensive. As long as there is no violence, President Roh's government is likely to sit on the sidelines, allowing labor and management to work out their differences through free collective bargaining.

Taiwan Taiwan and Korea have traveled nearly identical economic development paths and share certain similar industrial policies. While thousands of violent labor disturbances were being staged in South Korea in the late 1980s, foreign observers in Taiwan did not anticipate any surge in labor unrest that would seriously affect the country's economy. However, they were wrong. The handsome payoff for the Korean workers apparently emboldened their counterparts in Taiwan to follow suit.

Taiwan, with a population of 19 million, recognizes only one trade union federation, the Chinese Federation of Labor (CFL), which is closely tied to the ruling Kuomintang government and with which all unions are affiliated. The right to form trade unions is accorded under the constitution and the labor code, but all union branches are effectively controlled by committees of the Kuomintang. In 1987, there were 2,471 unions with 1.87 million members.[71] All were workplace unions organized on both an occupational and an enterprise basis, closely resembling the Japanese model.

Membership in trade unions is not compulsory. Strikes have been forbidden under martial law since 1949, and no significant strikes had been recorded until May 1, 1988, when 400 railroad workers took simultaneous one-day vacations. Collective bargaining, though legally protected, is poorly developed, and wage rates are generally set unilaterally by employers. The unions are active in providing social, recreational, and credit union services, but not improvements in health and safety standards. These are stipulated in the Labor Standards Law as employers' responsibilities. Since its first passage in 1984, however, the law has been almost totally ignored. Although the percentage of the labor force that is unionized is relatively high, union membership is not similar to that in other industrialized countries. Unions are more allies of management than representatives of labor's interests.

Most labor–management disputes in Taiwan have involved back wages, severance pay, and layoffs. The Labor Standards Law of 1984 was aimed at calming worker discontent and discouraging labor votes from going to the opposition. The law's implementation has been slowed by constant reviews and attempts at clarification. Management objects that the law imposes too many obligations on employers; workers object that it leaves them in a weak negotiating position in the absence of the right to strike. Furthermore, relatively light penalties for noncompliance have led to doubts about whether the law will be rigorously enforced. Industrial relations experts claimed that nonenforcement of basically adequate legislation may be the source of most labor–management disputes in Taiwan.[72]

The argument has proven to be highly accurate. On May 1, 1988, railroad workers used Article 37 of the Labor Standards Law ("Workers should be granted leaves on Memorial Day, Labor Day, and other public holidays") as an excuse to walk out on their duties, causing a complete halt in the island's rail transportation system and recording the first strike in 40 years in the Republic of China (ROC). Because Taiwan's labor laws still ban strikes, even after a decade of martial law ended in 1987, most workers use work slowdowns as a major weapon in labor disputes.

Most labor experts agree that Taiwan's recent disputes indicate a new awakening on the part of workers. The island's labor force is becoming more aggressive. The use of street demonstrations to test the government's tolerance has almost become a norm. Many experts advise that companies follow the regulation in the Labor Standards Law that calls for regular monthly meetings between management and labor. It is expected that as workers grow more sophisticated, companies will come under even greater pressure to adopt some form of collective bargaining, and monthly meetings could help smooth the transition.[73] The predominance of small (under 100 employees) companies in Taiwan, which reduces the distance between top management and factory workers, makes this interaction much easier than in Korea, where firms tend to be much larger: Daewood and Hyundai employ more than 200,000 workers between them.

Australia: The West in the East

Discussions of the Pacific Rim countries tend to focus on Japan and South Korea, Taiwan, Singapore, and Hong Kong (as well as the United States). However, on the eastern edge of the rim is Australia, an important participant in the region and its only "Western economy." Australia's labor relations system is unusual for a developed country, and, as is the case of labor relations throughout the world, it is undergoing major changes.

The Australian System

Australia's **industrial tribunals** make its labor–management relations system unique in the industrialized world. Most other countries have government agencies to deal with problems between labor and management, but none has so many (107 tribunals for a labor force of about 6 million) that are so involved with day-to-day labor–management relations.[74] Australia's system is aimed at regulating economic and industrial problems through tribunals, the leading example being the federal Conciliation and Arbitration Commission.[75] These industrial tribunals are quite independent of federal and state (and territorial) governments, for their members hold lifetime appointments. The tribunals resolve contract impasses, and thus they have the power to set wages and conditions of employment, and rule on managerial rights, a power upheld by the Australian High Court in two cases in 1983.[76] The actions of the tribunals make the system a centralized and standardized one.

The unions in Australia, with a membership of over 50 percent of the labor force, are organized on a craft or occupational rather than an industrial or enterprise basis.[77] Thus, in a midsized plant of 500 or so workers, there may be five to ten unions. Most of Australia's 300 or so unions are affiliated with the Australian Council of Trade Unions (ACTU), a coordinating body which, like the AFL–CIO in the United States, has little power itself. However, its political clout when the Labor party is in power is significant.

The State of the Unions

The 1980s witnessed the decline of unions in most Western economies. This was not the case in Australia. Unions have been able to maintain their membership and a relatively high percentage of the labor force that is organized. They have also enhanced their standing with workers by making gains in nonwage issues, like the 35-hour week push that shortened the workweek (but to 38 hours only).[78]

In the area of wages, the unions have worked quite successfully within the constraints of wage setting by the industrial tribunals. In bad times, the tribunals have protected wages from the natural downward pressures of the market. In good times, unions, through bargaining, have been able to push workers' wages above tribunal-set levels or awards. These increases, beyond officially set wage levels, are a kind of **wage drift** that is common in countries with centralized wage-setting systems.[79]

The maintenance of union power can be traced to the tribunal system, as exemplified by the Arbitration Commission. The centralization of decisions in labor relations has caused a decline in the influence and power of employers but an increase in that of unions. The political success of the Labor party federally and in a majority of the states has been another important factor in maintaining union power.

DISCUSSION QUESTIONS

1. What shared factors would lead you to believe that Canadian and American labor relations are pretty much the same?

2. What are the two basic underlying elements that are so different in Canada and the United States that seem to be causing Canadian unions to grow and American unions to shrink?

3. What was the relationship of Mexican unions and the government, and why is it changing?

4. What are the three general characteristics of labor relations in Western Europe that differentiate it from the American system?

5. Margaret Thatcher changed British labor relations. How did she do it, and what has, in general, been the thrust of her changes?

6. What are the levels at which workers participate in the German system of co-determination, and how do they participate at each of the levels?

7. What is the function of a German works council?

8. Who performs the various functions of the German works council in the U.S. labor relations system? What are the pluses of the U.S. approach to shop-level labor relations? What are the minuses?

9. Would you say German collective bargaining is centralized? Why?

10. What made Sweden's trade unions (and management) so different from most trade unions in the 1950s through the 1960s?

11. Most European nations mandate fringe benefits for workers by law. What are the advantages and disadvantages of this route?

12. Discuss the structuring of the Japanese labor movement in enterprise unions and how it is related to industrywide Spring Labor Offensives, the Shunto.

13. How is the Japanese wage (and seniority) system different from that of other industrialized countries?

14. What has been the major function of Soviet trade unions?

15. Why did the communist government in Poland legalize Solidarity in early 1989? How did this move lead to democratic elections in Poland?

16. What is the unique relationship in China between labor and management, and between labor–management and the government/party?

17. Why are Chinese workers, unlike Eastern Europe's, not supportive of economic and political reform?

18. How would you characterize labor relations in Singapore and Hong Kong? In South Korea and Taiwan? Why are these characterizations different?

19. What is the role of industrial tribunals in the Australian labor relations system?

20. Looking over the various labor relations systems described in this chapter, name the characteristics of a country and its labor system that lead to the adoption of a centralized collective bargaining system. How about a decentralized one? Examining only those characteristics, what type of system would you guess the United States had? Why?

VOCABULARY LIST

state authoritarianism	board of supervisors
political involvement	enterprise union
worker participation	lifetime employment
shop steward	seniority system
steward council	Spring Labor Offensive (the Shunto)
works council	Solidarity
co-determination	industrial tribunals
labor director	wage drift

FOOTNOTES

1. Roy J. Adams, "North American Industrial Relations: Divergent Trends in Canada and the United States," *International Labor Review*, No. 1 (1989): 47.

2. Henry P. Guzda, "First Industrial Relations Congress of the Americas," *Monthly Labor Review* (May 1989): 50.

3. William H. Holley and Kenneth M. Jennings, *The Labor Relations Process* (Dryden Press, 1988), p. 603.

4. Guzda, "First Industrial Relations Congress of the Americas," p. 51.

5. Adams, "North American Industrial Relations," p. 58.

6. Holley and Jennings, *The Labor Relations Process*, pp. 602–603.

7. Adams, "North American Industrial Relations," p. 49. In the United States, the proposition that unions are unnecessary where employers "do right willingly" is widely held (it is claimed).

8. Roy J. Adams, "Industrial Relations and the Economic Crisis: Canada Moves Towards Europe," in Hervey Juris et al., eds., *Industrial Relations in a Decade of Economic Change* (Industrial Relations Research Association, 1985), p. 115.

9. Guzda, "First Industrial Relations Congress of the Americas," p. 51.

10. *Wall Street Journal*, February 23, 1989, p. A19.

11. *Business Week*, January 23, 1989, p. 52; *Wall Street Journal*, October 19, 1989, p. A15.

12. *New York Times*, February 27, 1989, p. A4.

13. Guzda, "First Industrial Relations Congress of the Americas," p. 50.

14. Herbert R. Northrup et al., "Multinational Union–Management Consultation in Europe: Resurgence in the 1980s?," *International Labor Review*, No. 5 (1988): 528–529.

15. Michael Emerson, *What Model for Europe?* (MIT Press, 1988), p. 17.

16. Brian Towers, "Running the Gauntlet: British Trade Unions Under Thatcher, 1979–1988," *Industrial and Labor Relations Review* (January 1989): 168–169; between 1975 and 1980, legal recognition was available to unions.

17. Towers, "Running the Gauntlet." The discussion of the details of the laws are from pp. 168–171.

18. Ibid., p. 174.

19. Holley and Jennings, *The Labor Relations Process*, p. 607.

20. Everett M. Kassalow, "Employee Representation on U.S., German Boards," *Monthly Labor Review* (September 1989): 39.

21. Gerhard Leminsky, "Worker Participation: The German Experience," in Benjamin Martin and Everett M. Kassalow, eds., *Labor Relations in Advanced Industrial Societies, Issues & Problems* (Carnegie Endowment for International Peace, 1980). The details on works councils (pp. 146–149), labor directors (pp. 150–151), and board of supervisors labor members (pp. 151–152) are from this selection.

22. Holley and Jennings, *The Labor Relations Process*, p. 608.

23. Otto Jacobi, "World Economic Changes and Industrial Relations in the Federal Republic of Germany," in Hervey Juris et al., eds., *Industrial Relations in a Decade of Economic Change* (Industrial Relations Research Association, 1985), p. 231.

24. "Affluent German Unions Fear 1992," *New York Times*, March 8, 1989, p. C1; and "Shorter Workweek a Volatile Issue for Germans," October 9, 1989, p. C8; *Wall Street Journal*, April 10, 1989, p. A9B.

25. *Wall Street Journal*, May 7, 1990, p. A10; *Business Week*, May 21, 1990, p. 60.

26. Kristina Ahlen, "Recent Trends in Swedish Collective Bargaining: The Collapse of the Swedish Model," *Current Sweden* (Swedish Institute, March 1988). Much of this section comes from this source and a second piece by Ahlen, "Recent Trends in Swedish Collective Bargaining: Heading Toward Negotiated Incomes Policy?" (Swedish Institute, March 1988).

27. A. Gordon, *The Evolution of Labor Relations in Japan: Heavy Industry, 1853–1955* (Harvard University Press, 1985).

28. Sheldon Garon, *The State and Labor in Modern Japan* (University of California Press, 1987).

29. Koji Taira and Solomon B. Levine, "Japan's Industrial Relations: A Social Compact Emerges," in Hervey Juris et al., eds., *Industrial Relations in a Decade of Economic Change* (Industrial Relations Research Association, 1985), p. 279.

30. *Wall Street Journal*, July 27, 1989, p. A10.

31. Taira and Levine, "Japan's Industrial Relations," p. 255.

32. *Business Week*, September 5, 1983, p. 98.

33. J. F. Harper, *Trade Unions of the World* (Gail Research, 1987), p. 233.

34. Yasuo Kuwahara, "Japanese Industrial Relations," in G. J. Bamber and R. D. Lansbury, eds., *International and Comparative Industrial Relations* (Allen & Unwin, 1987).

35. *Business Asia*, June 19, 1989, p. 199.

36. Harper, *Trade Unions of the World*, p. 245.

37. *Business Week*, July 24, 1989, p. 32.

38. *Wall Street Journal*, October 11, 1988, p. A12.

39. *Wall Street Journal*, March 14, 1989, p. A1.

40. Bruno Grancelli, *Soviet Management and Labor Relations* (Allen & Unwin, 1988), p. 107.

41. *Wall Street Journal*, March 16, 1988, p. 27.

42. *New York Times*, July 20, 1989, p. A1.

43. *New York Times*, July 24, 1989, p. A1.

44. *New York Times*, October 10, 1989, p. A8.

45. *New York Times*, October 28, 1989, p. A8.

46. Robert A. Senser, "How Poland's Solidarity Won Freedom of Association," *Monthly Labor Review* (September 1989): 34.

47. Ibid, p. 37.

48. *New York Times*, February 9, 1989, p. A7; May 10, 1989, p. A4.

49. *New York Times*, May 29, 1990, p. A4.

50. *Business Week*, February 16, 1989, p. 51.

51. *Beijing Review*, February 13–26, 1989, p. 32.

52. *Beijing Review*, November 7–13, 1988, p. 7.

53. *Beijing Review*, February 13–26, 1989, p. 31.

54. *China Times Weekly*, January 6–12, 1990, p. 48.

55. *Beijing Review*, July 17–23, 1989, p. 28.

56. *Wall Street Journal*, April 26, 1988, p. 12.

57. Harper, *Trade Unions of the World*.

58. *Business Asia*, July 15, 1985, p. 215.

59. *Business Asia*, December 1, 1986, p. 384.

60. *Business Asia*, June 20, 1988, p. 199.

61. *Hong Kong: The Facts, Employment* (Hong Kong Government Information Services, June 1988).

62. "Summary of Labor Regulations in Hong Kong," *Wage Rates, General Employment Information, Rental and Purchase Prices of Flatted Factories* (Hong Kong Government Industrial Promotion Office, August 1988).

63. *Hong Kong: The Facts, Employment.*

64. Ibid.

65. *Business Asia*, May 1, 1981, p. 139.

66. *Business Asia*, May 3, 1987, p. 248.

67. *Business Asia*, March 28, 1988, p. 104.

68. *Business Week*, May 2, 1988, p. 45.

69. *Wall Street Journal*, May 2, 1990, p. A10.

70. *Wall Street Journal*, April 26, 1988, p. A10.

71. Harper, *Trade Unions of the World.*

72. *Business Asia*, June 30, 1986, p. 207.

73. *Business Asia*, April 4, 1988, p. 112.

74. Braham Dabscheck and John Niland, "Australian Industrial Relations and the Shift to Centralism," in Hervey Juris et al., eds., *Industrial Relations in a Decade of Economic Change* (Industrial Relations Research Association, 1985), p. 42.

75. Ibid., pp. 42–43; the tribunal is referred to as the Arbitration Commission.

76. Ibid., p. 45.

77. John Niland, "How Do Australian Unions Maintain Standing During Adverse Periods?," *Monthly Labor Review* (June 1986): 37.

78. Ibid., p. 39.

79. Dabscheck and Niland, "Australian Industrial Relations," pp. 47–48.

REFERENCES

ADAMS, ROY J. "Industrial Relations and the Economic Crisis: Canada Moves Towards Europe." In Hervey Juris et al., eds., *Industrial Relations in a Decade of Economic Change.* (Industrial Relations Research Association, 1985), pp. 115–150.

———. "North American Industrial Relations: Divergent Trends in Canada and the United States." *International Labor Review*, No. 1 (1989): 47–64.

BLAIN, NICHOLAS, JOHN GOODMAN, and JOSEPH LOWENBERG. "Mediation, Conciliation and Arbitration: An International Comparison of Australia, Great Britain and the United States." *International Labor Review* (March–April 1987): 179–198.

BRUCE, PETER G. "Political Parties and Labor Legislation in Canada and the U.S." *Industrial Relations* (Spring 1989): 115–141.

DABSCHECK, BRAHAM, and JOHN NILAND. "Australian Industrial Relations and the Shift to Centralism." In Juris et al., eds., *Industrial Relations*, pp. 41–72.

EMERSON, MICHAEL. *What Model for Europe?* MIT Press, 1988.

GARON, SHELDON. *The State and Labor in Modern Japan.* University of California Press, 1987.

GORDON, A. *The Evolution of Labor Relations in Japan: Heavy Industry, 1853–1955.* Harvard University Press, 1985.

GRANCELLI, BRUNO. *Soviet Management and Labor Relations.* Allen & Unwin, 1988, Ch. 7.

GUZDA, HENRY P. "First Industrial Relations Congress of the Americas." *Monthly Labor Review* (May 1989): 50–52.

HARPER, J. F. *Trade Unions of the World.* Gail Research, 1987.

HELBURN, I. B., and JOHN C. SHEARER. "Human Resources and Industrial Relations in China: A Time of Ferment." *Industrial and Labor Relations Review* (October 1984): 3–15.

HOLLEY, WILLIAM H. and KENNETH M. JENNINGS. *The Labor Relations Process.* Dryden Press, 1988, Ch. 16.

JACOBI, OTTO. "World Economic Changes and Industrial Relations in the Federal Republic of Germany." In Juris et al., eds., *Industrial Relations,* pp. 211–246.

JURIS, HERVEY, MARK THOMPSON, and WILBUR DANIELS, eds. *Industrial Relations in a Decade of Economic Change.* Industrial Relations Research Association, 1985, Chs. 2, 4, 7, and 8 (all cited as separate references).

KASSALOW, EVERETT M. "Employee Representation on U.S., German Boards." *Monthly Labor Review* (September 1989): 39–42.

KUWAHARA, YASUO. "Japanese Industrial Relations." In G. J. Bamber and R. D. Lansbury, eds., *International and Comparative Industrial Relations.* Allen & Unwin, 1987.

LEMINSKY, GERHARD. "Worker Participation: The German Experience." In Benjamin Martin and Everett M. Kassalow, eds., *Labor Relations in Advanced Industrial Societies, Issues & Problems.* Carnegie Endowment for International Peace, 1980, pp. 139–160.

NILAND, JOHN. "How Do Australian Unions Maintain Standing During Adverse Periods?" *Monthly Labor Review* (June 1986): 37–39.

NORTHRUP, HERBERT R., DUNCAN C. CAMPBELL, and BETTY J. SLOWINSKI. "Multinational Union–Management Consultation in Europe: Resurgence in the 1980s?" *International Labor Review,* No. 5 (1988): 525–543.

RICO, LEONARD. "The New Industrial Relations: British Electricians' New-Style Agreements." *Industrial and Labor Relations Review* (October 1987): 63–78.

SENSER, ROBERT A. "How Poland's Solidarity Won Freedom of Association." *Monthly Labor Review* (September 1989): 34–38.

TAIRA, KOJI, and SOLOMON B. LEVINE. "Japan's Industrial Relations: A Social Compact Emerges." In Juris et al., eds., *Industrial Relations,* pp. 247–300.

TOWERS, BRIAN. "Running the Gauntlet: British Trade Unions Under Thatcher, 1979–1988." *Industrial and Labor Relations Review* (January 1989): 163–188.

WEISZ, MORRIS. "A View of Labor Ministries in Other Nations." *Monthly Labor Review* (July 1988): 19–23.

PART TWO

UNIONS AND COLLECTIVE BARGAINING

At the heart of American trade unionism is collective bargaining—negotiating with management concerning the terms and conditions of employment. Since their earliest days, this activity has been the major function of almost all American unions. It is the essence of collective action, a dynamic process of give-and-take.

We begin the discussion of collective bargaining in Chapter 6 by developing the framework of the process, and we cover the subject matter of collective bargaining in the next four chapters. Setting pay is probably the most popularly held notion of what collective bargaining is all about, and wages are the first topic we examine. A wide-ranging discussion of economic supplements to pay (fringe benefits) follows, inasmuch as fringe benefits are a wide-ranging topic. For the past four decades the dollar amount and variety of fringes have been growing, and now make up approximately 40 percent of the compensation package. We next take up the two major institutional issues in collective bargaining: the needs of unions to survive and prosper as an institution (union security) and the needs of management to run the operation (management rights). Finally, we discuss the administrative issues in collective bargaining, primarily seniority and work rules. These have become a central issue dividing union and management, being perhaps the major factor in the debate over flexibility and productivity.

CHAPTER 6

COLLECTIVE BARGAINING: THE PROCESS

T he collective bargaining process is long and complex. It includes legitimization of the union as the workers' bargaining agent and lengthy preparations for the actual negotiations, which might go on for a year or more. The outcome of these negotiations depends on the balance of power between the two parties and their bargaining stances. Each party's stance depends on its behavior in reaching its goals, coupled with the internal political pressures with which it is contending.

ORGANIZATION AND CERTIFICATION

As a prelude to bargaining, the union (or labor organization) must attain the legally defined status of **exclusive,** or sole, **bargaining agent**. An organization campaign typically ending in an NLRB election accomplishes this objective. As was noted in Chapter 3, the National Labor Relations Act provided the mechanism for union certification through election. After certification, the union assumes the duty to bargain for all workers in the defined bargaining unit.

The Organizing Campaign

The process of organizing new workers is a critical activity for unions. It brings in new members, who constitute the lifeblood of the national union and the union movement. It extends the reach of union influence, or, in present times when unions are in decline, it aids them in maintaining their status by helping to offset this decline.

Starting the Organizing Process

The first step in the union organizing procedure, when the union starts its **organizing campaign**, involves meeting with key workers in the target unit. If the workers contact the union because they want it to organize them, the identification of key employees is easy. However, if the union targets the employees because they want to organize them, the union organizers must pinpoint these key people, leaders in the plant or company to whom others will listen.

This first contact is usually made without the knowledge of the employer. A vigilant employer, however, will probably get wind of the drive as small groups of employees discuss it and meet with the union organizers. Secrecy will disappear for sure as more people learn of the contact with the union, as information is widely distributed, and as the union organizers call ever larger meetings of employees.

The Organizing Campaign in High Gear

Once the organizing campaign is in the open and swings into high gear, the union organizers will distribute authorization cards to the employees. **Authorization cards** (see Figure 6.1) are not official votes for union representation but show support for the union. The union organizers will urge the workers, primarily through the key employees they have been working with from the start, to sign and return these cards.

USW, LOCAL 680, SEIU, AFL-CIO
Authorization for Membership

Name _____

Signature _____
(please sign)

Telephone _____

Address _____

City _____ State _____ Zip _____

Employer _____ Work Location _____

Job Title _____

NOTE: PLEASE READ BEFORE SIGNING Date_____

FIGURE 6.1 Union authorization card.
Source: United Stanford Workers, Local 680, Service Employees International Union, AFL–CIO.

The union organizers collect signed authorization cards from workers and submit them to the NLRB in support of their petition for certification. Typically, organizers will collect authorization cards from over 50 percent of the employees they are trying to organize before filing an election petition with the NLRB. As the cards express only interest, and not commitment to the union, some workers who sign them may change their minds during the election campaign. Conversely, nonsigners may vote for the union after the campaign. If the union has signed authorization cards from at least 30 percent of the employee group they seek to organize, however, they can still petition the NLRB to conduct a certification or representation election. Section 9 of the NLRA contains the procedures for representation elections (choice of bargaining agent), including the "30 percent rule" [9 (e) (1)].

At the Nissan Motors assembly plant in Tennessee, employees in 1989 rejected by a 2 to 1 margin the United Auto Workers (UAW) bid to represent them. Although the union had gotten more than half the plant's workers to sign authorization cards, it received only 30 percent of the votes. In Nissan's favor, workers at the plant made 37 percent more than the average manufacturing wage in the area, and there had not been a layoff at the plant since its 1983 opening. Thus, the union had difficulty selling unionization to the workers.[1]

Customarily, the union first requests recognition as bargaining agent from the employer. This request is usually denied, even if the union has authorization cards from a substantial majority of the employee group. Once the certification petition is filed with the NLRB, the election process and campaign officially begin.

The Election Campaign

For the union, the **election campaign** is an extension of the organizing campaign. The union organizers will continue their efforts to align employee support behind the union, trying to reach all the employees using employer-supplied information such as addresses and phone numbers.

Management will typically stiffen its opposition to the union at this time. If management was aware of organizing efforts prior to the election petition, which it probably was, it will already have formulated a strategy for the election campaign. Increasingly, this strategy has involved labor relations consultants to help defeat the organizing drive.[2]

The 17-month campaign that the UAW started in January 1988 to unionize the Nissan Motors assembly plant in Tennessee was especially earnest, as the union was trying to recapture lost power and reverse a decline in membership by organizing a Japanese-owned plant in the United States. For example, the UAW purchased half an hour of air time from a local television station right before the election to run a pro-UAW program criticizing the plant's managers and charging poor employee safety. Nissan countered such moves by airing promotional messages on its closed-circuit television system that associated the UAW with layoffs and called the union an outsider.[3]

The Employees Involved

The NLRB will first convene a meeting with employer and union and obtain a list of employees. At the meeting, the NLRB will find out if the two parties agree on the appropriate **bargaining unit** (the group of workers to be represented by the union), workers in the unit who are eligible to vote in the representation election, and the details of the election (date and time and place). If there is agreement, the election, known as a **consent election** as all parties have agreed (or consented) to the unit and details, is set to be held.

If union and employer disagree on any of the issues noted above, the NLRB will hold a hearing to come to a decision and set, or direct, the election to be held. The board's hearing is a fact-finding proceeding. A frequent matter of contention is the composition of the bargaining unit; the inclusion or exclusion of a group of employees sympathetic to the union may assure winning or losing the certification election, and management is aware of this potential. Resolving this question is important to both parties.

The bargaining unit can be very broad (multi-plant or plantwide) or narrow (department, work group). The board's hearing officer will determine a contested grouping based on several factors. Probably the most important consideration is the similarity of skills, pay, and other working conditions of the employees involved. A second consideration is the preferences of these employees. A separate election may be held to determine preference. If the parties have had a collective bargaining relationship in the past, the grouping used then will be a consideration. Other technical reasons may be utilized to exclude workers from a bargaining unit; for example, plant guards or confidential employees (those having access to information on an employer's labor relations, as clerks in a company's labor or industrial relations department) will be excluded.

The issue of the bargaining unit can be very acrimonious. The hearing can be long, with many conflicting views vigorously pressed by labor and management. After the issues in contention are settled, and the **directed election** particulars are set, the campaign can start in earnest.[4]

Election Campaign Rules

After setting the details of the election, the employer, within seven days, must provide the NLRB with the names and addresses of the employees in the bargaining unit eligible to vote. This list is made available to the union so that it has a reasonable chance of reaching these workers in its election campaign.

The campaign is run under rules defined (broadly) in the law. Both union and employer tend to use persuasive campaign material. But as long as the campaign propaganda is not fraudulent or coercive, it is allowed.[5] Other similar restrictions prevail, especially in the 24-hour period prior to the election.[6]

Election Results: Certification

The election itself is conducted through secret ballot (see Figure 6.2), by NLRB personnel. If the union wins the election, gaining a majority of the votes, it is duly certified as the exclusive bargaining agent for the workers in the bargaining unit. As exclusive bargaining agent, the union is certified by the NLRB as the employee's duly elected representative. The employer *must* bargain with the union. Certification is binding for 12 months, and the union may not be replaced as bargaining

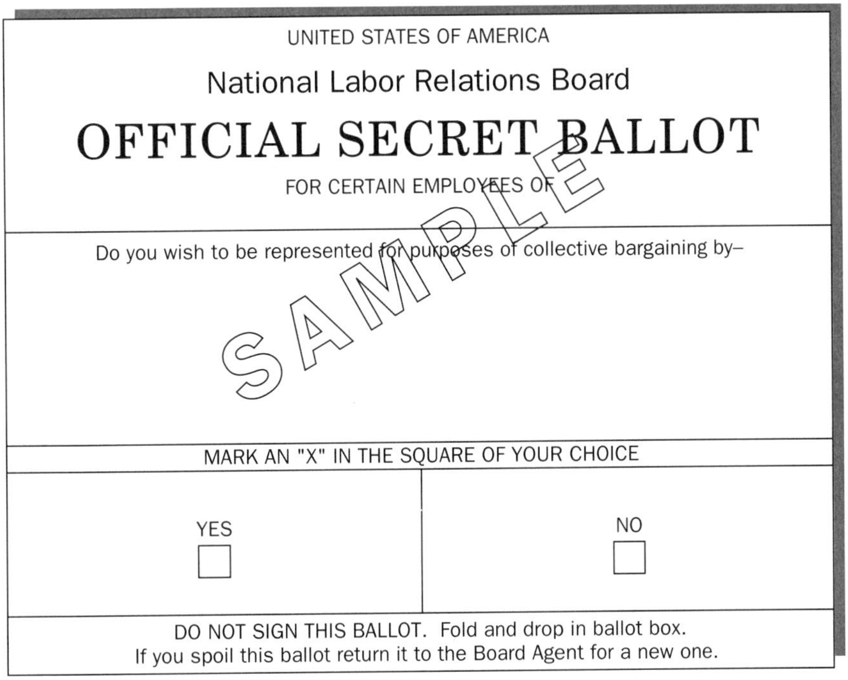

UNITED STATES OF AMERICA

National Labor Relations Board

OFFICIAL SECRET BALLOT

FOR CERTAIN EMPLOYEES OF

Do you wish to be represented for purposes of collective bargaining by–

SAMPLE

MARK AN "X" IN THE SQUARE OF YOUR CHOICE

YES	NO
☐	☐

DO NOT SIGN THIS BALLOT. Fold and drop in ballot box.
If you spoil this ballot return it to the Board Agent for a new one.

FIGURE 6.2 Sample National Labor Relations Board ballot.
Source: NLRB

representative during that time, not even by the employees. If the employer does not bargain in good faith with the newly certified union, the board may extend certification beyond one year. The signing of a contract will bar any new election for certification during the term of that contract, for up to three years.

If the union is the exclusive bargaining agent, as certified by the NLRB, it is the representative of all the workers in the bargaining unit. If the union does not negotiate a union security clause requiring workers to belong to the union to maintain their job with the organization, it must still act as agent for nonmembers as well as members in the unit. This means the union bargaining agreements cover *all* workers in the unit. It must process and pursue nonmember as well as member grievances. The union must generally treat nonmembers as it would any member in the bargaining unit.[7]

POLITICAL PRESSURES IN COLLECTIVE BARGAINING

The process of collective bargaining is affected by both economic and political considerations. The political factors sometimes dictate bargaining goals and strategies that seem far removed from the economic conditions that prevail. Some appreciation of these political elements is necessary to understand the bargaining stance of both parties.

Political Pressure and the Union

As a voluntary coalition of workers, the union is quite susceptible to political pressures from various groups in this coalition. Unions are not strongly structured democracies, but nonetheless, they are basically democratic institutions. The leaders must respond, in some measure, to rank-and-file pressures, even if some of those pressures are not reasonable in the environment in which the union is dealing with management.

A Cause of Pressure: The Requirement to "Deliver"

In Chapter 4 we noted that unions, though theoretically democratic institutions, might well sacrifice individual for collective rights. We also observed that almost all unions have a one-party system and that dissident factions tend to be short-lived. But this is true only if the union leader "delivers," that is, negotiates collective bargaining agreements that keep the rank-and-file happy. This means keeping wages high, or at least higher than the reference groups of the bulk of the membership, and continually improving economic supplements, all the while protecting the workers' jobs.

The requirement to "deliver" is manifested in two ways. First, if the leadership does not meet the expectations of the rank-and-file, they will not approve the contract, if they have that option. Rank-and-file ratification is not required by law. Most unions require ratification of proposed contracts because of the traditional democratic basis of union organizations and because ratification shows support for the union's collective bargaining leaders. A few unions don't have ratification votes, probably because it means they must negotiate collective bargaining agreements without final authority to agree to a contract.[8]

Second, if the leadership does not keep the rank-and-file happy, they will oust it through the election process. This option may take a long time, as the road to unseating national leaders starts with local elections to unseat local officers loyal to the leadership and then proceeds through state or regional elections. At any point in this process, the ouster campaign can go astray, but if the leadership continues to disappoint the rank-and-file, the leaders of the movement to change will maintain their local support and will eventually unseat a leader who does not deliver.*

The Effect of Pressure: An Example

The requirement to deliver places some major constraints on union leaders in the collective bargaining process, even firmly entrenched individuals who have headed their unions for decades. Thus, a collective bargaining situation could develop where the economic facts dictate a modest pay raise, or even none, but the political

---

* The Teamsters are a classic example of a union with entrenched leadership. Teamsters for a Democratic Union, gathering strength from the concessions made by the leadership over the past eight years, and from the specter of government control of the union, were pushing for direct member voting for officers of the national. This method was in contrast to the present method whereby local leaders elect the national officers at the convention, held every five years, which may be years after they are elected locally (*Wall Street Journal*, April 19, 1988, p. 1; January 20, 1989, p. B6). Government control (actually, federal court control) was imposed in March 1989 (*Wall Street Journal*, March 14, 1989, p. A3).

pressures on the union leader require securing a relatively rich package of pay raises and fringe benefits.

For example, the Teamsters, caught in the trucking deregulation of the early 1980s, made major concessions to employers and, in the 1985 negotiations, agreed (1) to have a two-tier wage system, with new hires paid 70 percent of the union wage, (2) to give up its cost-of-living clause that increased wages in line with the Consumer Price Index, and (3) to allow lower wages and no fringe benefits for part-time drivers.[9] This situation brought to the fore a dissident faction in the IBT, Teamsters for a Democratic Union (TDU), which put substantial pressure on the union leadership to negotiate a relatively rich contract in 1988. Thus, the Teamsters bargained for big pay hikes and benefit increases, reinstatement of the cost-of-living clause, a phase-out of the two-tier wage system, and the return of fringe benefits to part-time drivers.[10]

Political Pressures and Management

Managers of organizations, especially in the private sector, are most affected by economic pressures. The primary goal of business firms, unlike that of trade unions, is the maximization of profit or the wealth of their stockholding owners. Firms have other goals, encompassing issues related to social responsibility, for example. In the main, however, management works with a relatively defined set of objectives, headed by profit maximization, and determines the overall programs to reach these objectives. With this relatively narrow focus, the management team is not very susceptible to political pressures generated within the organization. Business firms are not normally democratic institutions. However, managers are susceptible to external political and social pressures. Some pressures may emanate from government, especially local area government trying to pursue its own industrial policy and image. Pressures may also come from the managers' external peer group. This type of peer pressure can be very effective.

In a given geographical area, firms and their management are linked together in an economic and social web. Actions taken by the management in one company will affect not only that company but also others in the local area, even if the various firms are in totally different lines of business. If a firm's pay scale is higher, on the average, than that of the other firms in the area, it develops a reputation as a high-paying company. Lacking that reputation, the other companies in the area suffer in the local job market, especially for skilled workers.

The pressure to hold the line in labor negotiations, then, may come not from the economic facts of the company's situation, but from the company's need to fit in with other firms in its local area. Furthermore, pressure to maintain wage rates and employment may come from local government and not the economic position of the company. These pressures are a combination of political and social pressures and can be very effective in shaping the general stance of management in collective bargaining.

BARGAINING BEHAVIOR

Collective bargaining is both an emotional and a rational process. Its highly emotional aspect makes it difficult to describe the typical contract negotiation. Yet, the rational aspects, based on extensive information gathered prior to the actual negotiations, allows us to describe, in general terms, the negotiation process.

Preparing for Negotiations

Prior to actual negotiations, both parties will undertake extensive preparations for bargaining; as noted earlier, these preparations may last as long as a year. All unions and employers go through similar steps to prepare for negotiations. Selecting the negotiating teams and issues that should be included in the bargaining are important decisions. Both sides will define, sometimes with little sharing of information, a series of positions, or proposals and counterproposals, based on studies of comparable situations as well as the economic facts of the organization's competitive position in its market or markets. For each subject under negotiation, both sides will set upper and lower limits, and assign that subject a priority. The collection of large amounts of information to support the arguments is crucial, and much of the preparation time and energy will go into this task. In addition to formulating a bargaining stance, they will also develop a bargaining strategy. These activities will require comprehensive knowledge of the economic situation and depend on the immediate political pressures on union and management.

Establishing a Bargaining Stance: Political Factors

With respect to the union especially, the political pressures that bear on the development of bargaining stances and strategies will have a substantial impact on the composition of the negotiating team and the list of initial demands. Surveys of rank-and-file desires and preferences may add all sorts of bargaining items to the list, especially if the union has a dissident faction. The leadership would not want to upset members and possibly enhance the dissidents' position. In-house surveys will also include detailed input from the union's shop stewards and the company's first-level managers. These surveys are designed to pinpoint problem areas in the existing (prior) contract which have been brought to the parties' attention during the life of that contract, usually through the grievance procedure. These problems should be addressed in the upcoming negotiations.

Establishing a Bargaining Stance: Economic Factors

Economic factors are the basis for the wage and fringe benefit demands made by each side. These factors also relate to labor productivity and job security issues that lately have been of major importance to labor and management. Three general areas of the economic situation can be delineated: (1) the company's "ability-to-pay" or financial health, (2) the economics of the local area and industry, especially prevailing wage rates, and (3) the general economic health of the country.

Company Information Information relating to a company's present financial health is found in its financial accounts, such as the income (profit and loss) statement. If the firm claims it cannot meet wage demands, or wants wage cuts, it must supply the union with the financial information behind its claims or demands.[11]

A collective bargaining contract may run for three (or more) years, and the company's financial health for this three-year period is as important as for the present.

Future information is based on forecasts, and companies don't have to share this information with the union with which they deal. If a company demands concessions or no wage increase based on poor profitability (or losses) over the past several years, it will show the union that information, as it is usually available to anyone through published financial statements. If concessions or no wage increase demands are based on forecasts of poor performance over the coming three years or so, the company may not want to share its forecasting models and methodology with the union. Then the union must develop its own forecasts.

Unions can get some information on the industry from government sources, especially Bureau of Labor Statistics (BLS) data which are published every month in the *Monthly Labor Review*.[12] However, these are industry averages and may not be representative of the company position. Past income statements can be used to develop trends in sales and earnings, and, as noted, these past statements are readily available. If no major changes are expected to occur in the firm's operations or competitive situation, trend analysis can be very useful. But if major changes are and will be occurring, the trend may not be useful. Without a sharing of information, within a cooperative labor–management environment, firm financial information can become a major stumbling block in negotiations.

Local Area and Industry   Data on the economics of the local area and industry may be gathered from a variety of sources. As noted in the previous paragraph, the BLS publishes a large amount of monthly industrial data. In addition, it issues occasional bulletins on union wage rates and supplementary benefits by industry and even area, summary bulletins on earnings by occupation and other characteristics of workers, and area wage surveys (see the appendix to this chapter). State labor departments, such as California's Employment Development Department, also publish statistical summaries for local area labor markets.[13]

The BLS also publishes the **Consumer Price Index (CPI)** for major cities and the U.S. city average on a monthly basis (see Figure 6.3). Less frequently, it publishes CPIs for smaller metropolitan areas. The various Federal Reserve District Banks publish economic data for their districts.

Labor and management can utilize all these sources and any other to develop the basis for their economic demands, especially wages. Because of the huge amount of data available, and the relatively neutral nature of data gathering and sorting, management and union have sometimes joined forces in this undertaking. This approach is becoming more common—a sign of and a result of a more cooperative collective bargaining environment in labor–management relations.

National Economic Information   The general economic situation of the country will affect the parties, even though it is not as important as the economic situation of the company, the local area, and the industry.

The CPI, as mentioned earlier, is a major factor in wage adjustments. The overall unemployment rate can affect demands, as well as bargaining stances in general. Many of the sources of national economic data were noted above, especially the publications of the BLS. National economic data are also published by the Federal Reserve District Banks and Federal Reserve System, and the Department of Commerce.

‣◦

CONSUMER PRICE INDEXES
PACIFIC CITIES AND U. S. CITY AVERAGE
ALL ITEMS INDEXES
(1982-84=100 unless otherwise noted)
MARCH 1991

		ALL URBAN CONSUMERS							URBAN WAGE EARNERS AND CLERICAL WORKERS					
				PERCENT CHANGE								PERCENT CHANGE		
				Year ending		1 Month ending						Year ending		1 Month ending
		INDEXES								INDEXES				
MONTHLY DATA	MAR. 1990	FEB. 1991	MAR. 1991	FEB. 1991	MAR. 1991	MAR. 1991		MAR. 1990	FEB. 1991	MAR. 1991	FEB. 1991	MAR. 1991	MAR. 1991
U. S. City Average............	128.7	134.8	135.0	5.3	4.9	0.1		127.1	132.8	133.0	5.1	4.6	0.2
(1967=100)...............	385.5	403.8	404.3	–	–	–		378.5	395.7	396.1	–	–	–
Los Angeles-Anaheim-Riverside..	134.5	139.9	139.7	4.7	3.9	-0.1		130.5	135.5	135.3	4.4	3.7	-0.1
(1967=100)...............	397.3	413.2	412.8	–	–	–		385.6	400.4	399.8	–	–	–
San Francisco-Oakland-San Jose.	130.0	136.1	136.3	5.3	4.8	0.1		129.0	134.5	134.7	4.9	4.4	0.1
(1967=100)...............	399.7	418.5	418.9	–	–	–		392.8	409.7	410.1	–	–	–
West	129.6	135.9	135.8	5.5	4.8	-0.1		127.9	133.9	133.7	5.3	4.5	-0.1
(Dec. 1977 = 100)	209.4	219.7	219.6	–	–	–		205.8	215.4	215.1	–	–	–
West - A	131.5	137.5	137.4	5.3	4.5	-0.1		128.3	133.9	133.7	4.9	4.2	-0.1
(Dec. 1977 = 100)	214.4	224.2	224.1	–	–	–		207.7	216.8	216.5	–	–	–
West - C	126.0	133.1	133.2	5.8	5.7	0.1		125.2	132.0	132.1	5.6	5.5	0.1
(Dec. 1977 = 100)	195.4	206.4	206.7	–	–	–		193.1	203.5	203.7	–	–	–

Size classes: A = 1,250,000 and over, B = Not available for West, C = 50,000 to 330,000, D = Not available for West.

Release date April 12, 1991. For more information call (415) 744-6600 or (213) 252-7521. CPI 24 hour hotline numbers for the pacific cities are as follows:

Anchorage	(907) 271-2770	Los Angeles	(213) 252-7528	San Diego	(619) 557-6538	Seattle	(206) 553-0645
Honolulu	(808) 541-2808	Portland	(503) 326-4132	San Francisco	(415) 744-6605		

FIGURE 6.3 Monthly Consumer Price Index (CPI).
Source: BLS

Both union and management must have the relevant data for these three areas to formulate their proposals, counterproposals, and **limits of acceptance**.* These economic data are gathered and sorted for relevancy. The parties use the data to support their proposals, especially those relating to wages and fringe benefits. (This is a major feature of the negotiating exercise found at the end of the book.)

Stages of the Bargaining Process

The bargaining itself involves a series of meetings, with the offering of proposals and counterproposals, both those prepared prior to negotiation and variations of these. Typical negotiations involve a substantial amount of give-and-take. By law, both parties must bargain in good faith, a term not at all well defined as we noted in Chapter 3.

The bargaining process can be divided into three stages: initial, middle, and final. Although these stages are not truly distinct from each other, certain characteristics differentiate them. These differentiations are useful in describing the rational process of contract negotiation, as well as seeing where the emotional aspects are at their most intense. They are summarized in Table 6.1.

The Initial Stage of Negotiations

In the initial stage of negotiations, the party that is pressing for a new contract presents its demands. This stage is technically the start of the collective bargaining

* Each party has a lower limit, beyond which it normally cannot be driven; these can be called limits of acceptance.

Table 6.1 *Stages of the Bargaining Process*

Stage	Major Characteristic	Nature of Demands
Initial	Emotional "show," much posturing	Extreme
Middle	Serious discussions, much compro- mising and problem solving	Moderated, start to converge
Final	Pressure of deadline, rapid pace of negotiations marked by flexibility of both parties	Converge

process. Traditionally, this party has been the union. As required by the NLRA/LMRA, it must notify the other party (the employer) at least 60 days prior to the expiration date of the present contract that it wants to modify the contract. Over the past ten years, however, management has frequently been the party pressing for new contract terms, in an attempt to gain concessions from labor.

The initial stage is usually somewhat emotional and politically motivated. Initial demands are generally extreme, encompassing economic proposals that would bankrupt the company if granted and other proposed items that may seem very strange at face value. At this stage, however, the union is actually using the negotiating process to meet a diverse set of needs.

The union makes use of excessive initial demands that have been put forth strongly (and emotionally) to set the stage for later trading off and compromising. The union negotiators are trying to gain leverage and are perhaps setting a tone for later bargaining sessions. They may also be trying to hide their goals and objectives, as well as their priorities. It is important to get all these desires across to management, but the initial stage is usually not the right time to do it. Establishing the climate of negotiations and a base for bargaining tradeoffs is important at this stage. Timing is important in negotiating.

The union negotiators may, for political reasons, present items that management is unlikely to accept in any settlement. These items may be ideas from members, and not including them in the negotiations may endanger the leadership of the union. The leaders will let management dispose of these requests, so management will assume the blame for rejecting them. Moreover, the early meetings often have invited onlookers, especially from the union ranks, and the laying out of an enormous variety of demands, as well as much of the posturing and theatrics accompanying this presentation, is for their benefit. These guests do not sit in at later sessions. However, the union negotiators must be careful in stating their excesses, so as not to build up too high expectations in the rank-and-file which may cause the membership to reject the final contract.

Another objective of presenting unusual items is to expose them to management, and, once rejected, bring them back in future years when negotiating future contracts. Once put forth, a proposal seems less strange three or six years down the line.

The Middle Stage of Negotiations

The initial stage of negotiations moves into the middle stage when the posturing stops and more serious discussions start. Each party seriously considers the proposals and counterproposals of the other, trying to find common ground and areas of compromise.

Priorities start to emerge. The list of demands has been narrowed from the initial proposal(s), and, even though a hundred items might be under discussion, their relative importance to the party proposing them starts to emerge.

Furthermore, the dollar value of the economic components of the package that each party is targeting begins to converge. For example, if management wants to grant no more than $4.00 per hour (and hopes to settle at about $2.50) and the union wants to obtain at least a $3.50 per hour compensation increase (and hopes to gain as much as $5.00), the dollar value of proposals starts to converge at $3.50 to $4.00 per hour. This increase may be bargained over in many forms, as part wage increase and part fringe benefit (for example, increased holidays and/or hospital-medical insurance coverage and/or life insurance coverage), but the total dollar value of the offers will be in the $3.50 to $4.00 range.

Thus, in the middle stage of the process, each party clarifies the estimates that it set going into negotiations, and definitely establishes the worst offer it will accept (usually a minimum figure for the union and a maximum figure for management). Through much compromising and problem solving, the pattern of a settlement emerges.

The Final Stage of Negotiations

The final stage of negotiations involves more compromising and trading off. The primary difference here is the looming of a deadline—contract expiration. When the contract expires, if there is no settlement, a strike or lockout (a "strike" by the employer, with plant operations utilizing management and/or replacement workers if there is no shutdown) may occur.

Thus, in the final stage negotiating proceeds at a more rapid pace. Flexibility is a key at this point, with discussions between negotiators occurring at the table and away from it. By now each party has a good feeling for the lower limits acceptable to the other, and seeks to find areas of agreement with these limits in mind. In a political sense, both parties may have to go further than they want to in granting concessions on different items to each other. Saving face may become important, especially in the ratification process when the union members discuss the contract's benefits.

The vast majority of negotiations produce settlements. In 1987 and 1988, about 0.02 percent of estimated working time was lost to major work stoppages in collective bargaining situations. This percentage rose to 0.07 in 1989, still under a tenth of a percent.[14] Both parties strive hard to avoid a strike. When an impasse is reached, many times union and management will call in a mediator (a third-party neutral) to help them reach an agreement and avert a strike. But more will be said about mediation in Chapter 12.

Establishing a Bargaining Strategy

The bargaining process will be affected by the differing attitudes of the parties toward the main issues under discussion. The strategies of each party will be a function not only of its goals, issue by issue, but of the other party's goals as well. The two parties may be in direct conflict, or they may agree on an issue or the existence of a problem to which both want a solution acceptable to each side. Different perceptions of the attitudes of the opposite side to an issue will evoke different negotiating behavior. Bargaining behavior also changes over the period of negotiations. One analysis of this complex process breaks it down by the nature of the divergence or congruence of the parties' goals and the function of the negotiating activity. In that analysis, Walton and McKersie identify four bargaining activities or strategies—distributive bargaining, integrative bargaining, attitudinal structuring, and intraorganizational bargaining.[15]

Distributive Bargaining

Distributive bargaining is the set of strategies, tactics, and activities utilized by negotiators when their goals or objectives are in *direct conflict*. In a traditional sense, it is the essence of collective bargaining, based on the adversarial relationship between labor and management. The outcome of this type of negotiating will usually have one party as the winner and the other as the loser.

Numerous items are subject to distributive bargaining, and they typically include almost all economic issues such as wages and fringe benefits. When labor bargains over wages, or wage increases, it asks for as much as it can while management seeks to grant as little as it can. Much of the negotiating activity is centered on modifying the other party's opposition to what is being sought. The tactics used tend to have emotional elements, typically involving threats and/or bluffing.

Integrative Bargaining

Integrative bargaining is the set of strategies, tactics, and activities employed by negotiators when their goals or objectives are not in conflict, but rather focus on a problem of *common concern*. It is basically joint problem solving, as the goals of the opposing parties can be integrated. The solution allows both parties to be winners.

An example of an issue that would be settled by integrative bargaining might be the establishment of a substance abuse program when both labor and management recognize that substance abuse is a growing problem in the company. The company wants to retain its trained workforce, and the union wants to maintain its members' jobs. The substance abuse program as an employer-provided benefit meets these two goals. The details of the program may bring the parties into conflict (e.g., under a one-week residency program, should that week off from work be paid or unpaid leave, or should sick leave be used for that purpose), but these details can be ironed out as both parties seek congruent ends. The emotional content of this type of bargaining is typically low.

Attitudinal Structuring

Attitudinal structuring is the set of activities carried on in negotiating that is aimed at influencing the *relationship* between the two parties. Unlike distributive and integrative bargaining which are joint decision-making processes, attitudinal structuring is an emotional, interpersonal process, with a social basis. Economic issues are not directly involved, and, in fact, no bargaining issues per se are in contention.

In collective bargaining, the two parties will not only negotiate an agreement but will also administer it over its term (typically three years) and negotiate succeeding contracts every three or so years. Both parties must work on this long-term relationship. Attitudinal structuring during the negotiating process is part of this maintenance function and is particularly important in the context of bargaining when conflicting goals are abundant.

Intraorganizational Bargaining

Intraorganizational bargaining involves the set of strategies, tactics, and activities utilized by both parties to gain *consensus* among the people in their respective organizations. It involves the efforts by both sets of negotiators to align the expectations of their constituents with theirs. Intraorganizational bargaining is, therefore, primarily aimed at the political elements of the bargaining process already discussed. The union, in particular, is prone to these types of pressures as it is a political organization whose leaders are elected and in which the contract typically has to be ratified by the rank-and-file.[16]

BARGAINING POWER

Collective bargaining is a give-and-take process, with each side trying to maximize its goal attainment. The proposal–counterproposal process involves compromise and cooperation, and the outcome is very difficult to predict. The interplay of the relevant economic factors and the political pressures under which the parties are working makes prediction almost an impossibility. However, certain factors can be used to define the power each party theoretically holds in a given bargaining situation. This may allow a guess at the favorableness of the outcome to the parties involved.

The **bargaining power** of each party relative to the other can be defined as the costs it can cause the other party relative to the costs it bears in imposing those costs on the other party. In ratio form, this measure would be:

$$\text{Bargaining Power } (X) \quad \frac{\text{Costs Imposed on } Y}{\text{Costs Incurred by } X}$$

In essence, this is a ratio of the costs of disagreement.[17] It is similar to the Chamberlain bargaining power model, which involves the cost of disagreement relative to the cost of agreement.[18]

In most bargaining situations, these costs would relate to the costs of a **work stoppage** that could be imposed on Y, management (the employer) by X, the workers (union). If the ratio is greater than one, the union (X) has more bargaining power than the employer. However, this holds for this one time. In the next round of collective bargaining, the ratio may change. The union strike or management lockout is the part of collective bargaining that occurs when the parties no longer make compromises and concessions, and they disagree on the terms of the bargain. The definition of the strike (or lockout) and the various uses of these work stoppages are the subject of Chapter 13. At this juncture, the costs to each party are of interest.

Union Power in Terms of Employer Costs

The major costs imposed on the employer depend on the extent and timing of any production disruption, the nature of the product involved, the competitive situation, and the economic situation in general. These costs would be manifested most directly in terms of lost sales and profits.

In addition, lost sales may mean lost customers, which amounts to a longer run cost. Customers may be lost as they are forced to find new suppliers during a strike, and they may stay with those suppliers after the strike. This loss of customers happened to an entire industry in the late 1950s and 1960s. Industrywide strikes in basic steel caused customers to turn to foreign steel producers, and they stayed with them.[19]

The Extent of a Work Stoppage and Employer Cost

The first determinant of the cost to the employer is the extent of any production disruption. A work stoppage that shuts down operations completely imposes the greatest cost on the company. If the production process was labor intensive, and the company did not try to hire replacements for strikers (commonly referred to as scabs) to operate the plant or use supervisory personnel to operate, employer cost would be at a maximum.

This assumes, however, no stockpiling of products in inventory before the stoppage that could be used to meet sales requirements during the stoppage. But more will be said about this topic below, as it relates to the nature of the product.

Traditionally, plants were not operated extensively, if at all, during a work stoppage.[20] Supervisory personnel might try to keep things going, but at a very diminished pace. The hiring of replacements for strikers was almost unheard of. However, the last several years has seen a change. Strike replacements are now used in many instances, especially in highly automated industries such as oil, chemicals, and communications, which are more easily operated by supervisory personnel during strikes. With the increased use of these tactics, management has become more willing to take a harder line with labor.

The Timing of a Work Stoppage and Employer Cost

The timing of a production disruption is a second determinant of the cost of that disruption. As most products have some seasonal pattern of sales, a disruption of production is most costly during the peak season.

For example, a bathing suit producer has a peak season in the first third of the year, and by summer production has tapered off sharply.* A work stoppage would be most effective in the first third of the year and least effective in the last third. For a toy manufacturer, a work stoppage in the fourth quarter (October–November–December) would be disastrous, while one in January or February would cause

---

* Bathing suit manufacturers must allow for a month or two of distribution time before their product is sold to the final consumer. Thus, their peak production period would be March/April, with peak sales of suits in May/June.

relatively small problems. Related to seasonal sales patterns are cyclical patterns. These will be discussed shortly.

The Nature of the Product and Employer Cost

As noted earlier, the nature of the product is another important determinant of the costliness of a production disruption.

If the product is a service, a work stoppage will have a dramatic effect unless service delivery is highly automated. The telephone system is an example of a highly automated service that would continue at a slightly diminished rate during a work stoppage. However, maintenance of phone lines and equipment is not highly automated, and a work stoppage would cause severe service disruptions. Teaching is a service with little automation, and work stoppages usually cause total service disruption.

If the product is a nondurable good, especially a perishable one like food, a work stoppage will have a major effect. The normal service or perishable good cannot be inventoried, so a work stoppage will effectively cut revenue to zero. Customers will have to go elsewhere to satisfy their needs unless the service is a monopoly.

If the product is a durable good like a refrigerator or car, however, it can be inventoried. An alert management that can see a power struggle with the union looming in the near future will attempt to stockpile a significant amount of the product in the months leading up to that struggle. This will normally be done by using overtime or adding more shifts if the plant is not already on three-shift operations. A substantial inventory buildup could tide a firm over a long work stoppage, maintaining sales and profitability.

Using overtime to build up inventories, however, dilutes some of the gain in employer power by increasing worker cash balances, through overtime pay, and augmenting the power of the union and workers. This point will be discussed below in the next section.

The Competitive Situation and Employer Cost

Another important determinant of the cost to employers of a production disruption is the competitive situation. Other things being equal, the more competitive the industry is, the greater effect a work stoppage will have on plant sales and profits.

If there is substantial foreign competition, a work stoppage will most likely mean lost sales and may even allow foreign producers to capture and retain a significant proportion of the market, as was the case in basic steel in the 1950s. A foreign product whose quality is high, or even higher, than that of a domestic product or brand, and similarly priced, is a threat in a normal competitive situation. It is a much greater threat if the domestic product or brand is not available owing to a production disruption.

Even if there is little or no foreign competition, being in a competitive industry of domestic producers can have the same effect on a struck firm with product availability severely restricted. For this reason, firms in a single industry may try to bargain collectively, through an employers' association.[21] The union representing the workers in these firms, on the other hand, may try to bargain with each firm individually and at different times.

Bargaining with each firm in a competitive industry, the union could pick what it feels is the "weakest" of the major firms in the industry and negotiate a favorable contract with that firm. A strike, or even the threat of a strike, should be sufficient to bring this "weak sister" to agree to the terms that the union wants. Then it can move on to the next firm and attempt to negotiate a contract with the same terms just obtained from the first firm. The union can argue that if one firm in the industry accepted those terms, all should. Using a production disruption in this second firm as a veiled threat, especially in a highly competitive industry (and in the wake of a successful strike, if it was needed, against the first firm), the union should be able to do as well in bargaining with the second as the first firm. This is called **whipsawing**. In many industries whipsawing became the major reason for multi-employer bargaining, especially in the highly competitive trucking industry.

The General Economy and Employer Cost

A final major determinant of employer cost from a production disruption is the state of the economy in general. In boom times, of course, most firms have more to lose, given a high level of sales and the attraction of the market to foreign producers, and so on. Workers in a tight labor market (low unemployment rate) will find it easier to get part-time, temporary work while on strike, a point we will make again below.

In slack times, during a recession, plants usually operate at a lower level of activity, with lower sales and profits. A strike at that time will be less costly to the firm. Furthermore, if the level of activity before the disruption is low enough, supervisory personnel might be able to continue operations at this low level. In a loose labor market, the firm will also find it easy to hire strike replacements. As noted above, operating plants with replacement workers has become more common in the last five to ten years.

Whistleblowing and Employer Cost

A new factor in the power balance is the threat of employee **whistleblowing**—the reporting to the relevant government agency or commission the company's violation (or alleged violation) of a regulation or law. This factor is especially effective if the company is regulated by a government agency or does substantial business with some branch of government. This action can cause the firm to incur substantial costs in fines and the like, even without a production disruption.

The employees (or union) can report safety violations to the Occupational Safety and Health Administration (OSHA), invoking an inspection that might uphold these violations or even find others, which could result in a fine. This happened at both IBP, Inc., and John Morrell & Co., when the United Food and Commercial Workers union (UFCW) went to OSHA with safety complaints, resulting in a $5.6 million fine for IBP and a similar one for Morrell.[22] In addition, UFCW complaints about violations of the overtime requirements of the Fair Labor Standards Act resulted in large back-pay awards to workers at both companies.

Employees of an airline can report safety violations to the Federal Aviation Administration (FAA), which might cause inspections and an assortment of other problems for the company. In the Eastern Airlines dispute (which resulted in a strike and bankruptcy in March 1989), the machinists union (International Association of Machinists) complained to the FAA of the falsification of aircraft maintenance records at Eastern's Kennedy (New York) Airport facilities. The airline's repair station certificate for Kennedy was suspended in May 1989 following an FAA investigation.[23]

In general then, the employers' costs will be highest, and union power greatest, when a production disruption

1. Shuts down production completely.
2. Occurs at a peak season (time of year) for the company.
3. Involves nonautomated services or perishable goods.
4. Is in a competitive industry.
5. Occurs in boom times.
6. Results from whistleblowing when the company is in violation of some law or regulation.

Employer Power in Terms of Union and Worker Costs

Many of the factors discussed above affect the bargaining power of union and workers in terms of the cost to management of a work stoppage or strike. However, a work stoppage also carries a cost to the union and workers, and this cost increases employer power. Three cost factors will be singled out for discussion in this section: the loss of wages, the divisiveness the union may face, and the loss of members.

The Loss of Wages and Union Cost

The first major concern of the workers out on strike is loss of wages. During a strike, union members get no pay and they get no fringe benefits. This leaves them and their families with no health care insurance and other related coverage provided through their jobs. The greater the loss of pay, the greater the employer bargaining power.

This loss can be tempered by several factors. First is the availability of strike benefits to replace some of the lost wages. A union with a large strike fund, or "war chest," will enhance its bargaining power. The national union is responsible for amassing and dispensing strike funds to its locals. Local unions only receive strike funds for work stoppages approved by the national or intermediate union-governing bodies.

A second factor is the income that can be earned working at an alternative job. As noted in the preceding section, in boom times, in a tight labor market, alternative job income is available; in recession, it usually is not. In the 1980s, the unemployment rate stayed above 5 percent, and in the early part of this period it was over 6 percent. Alternative employment income was not easily obtained. However, a major provider of alternative income is a working spouse. The spread of dual-earner families enhances the bargaining power of unions, as long as the two don't work in the same bargaining unit at the same company. If they do, the loss of income is doubled.

A third factor is the availability of public assistance to replace lost income. Federal public assistance benefits are increasingly being denied strikers, as a 1988 Supreme Court decision ruling that strikers are ineligible for food stamps illustrates.[24] The present political climate suggests that laws and court decisions will continue the denial of federal public assistance program benefits to strikers. State public assistance program benefits are available to striking workers in some states and are denied in others.

The problem of lost wages for strikers is exacerbated if a significant fraction of the union membership is in an illiquid financial position. If they have a high level of debt (house mortgage plus payments on a car, boat, large appliances, furniture, etc.) claiming a high proportion of their income, the loss of that income can mean losing the assets that are being purchased through credit. If they have little savings (cash balances) compared to this debt, these assets will be lost. Unions whose members are deeply in debt will have problems calling a strike, particularly if many believe it will not be a short one.

Union Divisiveness and Union Cost

A second major concern of the union, as an institution, is the deepening a strike may cause of any divisiveness that exists in the rank-and-file. The leaders of a union with dissidents who have some backing from a portion of the membership would be hesitant to call a strike, other things being equal. Dissidents could easily undermine a militant union leadership, especially if the rank-and-file were not behind a strike. Even when the union members aren't opposed to a strike being advocated by a militant leadership, the dangers posed by a popular dissident group may endanger the leaders. The greater the divisiveness, the greater the employers' bargaining power.

Conversely, a leadership that tries to avert a strike when a militant faction is advocating one might also be in a risky position. In this instance, the leadership might be more inclined to call a strike in order to show the rank-and-file how tough they, the leaders, really are.

Even if there is no dissident faction, the emotions and financial problems of a striking rank-and-file that only halfheartedly supports a strike can create forces that can tear the union apart. Unless the membership widely and wholeheartedly backs a work stoppage, that stoppage could threaten the very existence of the union or, at least, the tenure of the leaders. This point brings us to the union's next major concern.

Membership Loss and Union Cost

The third concern of unions on strike is membership loss. During a strike, members have the right to resign from the union and return to work, and the union can do nothing about it.[25] The greater the likelihood of membership loss, the greater the employer bargaining power.

Another threat to the union and its membership ranks is the increasingly common use of strike replacements by management. This tactic puts the members' jobs in jeopardy and increases the risk to the union of lost membership. If a strike is settled without members guaranteed their jobs back, those who don't get their old jobs back will have to seek employment elsewhere and will leave the union. The union will then have to enroll the replacements as members, if they can. During a strike, replacement workers may also call for decertification of a union, replacing it as a bargaining agent by another union or no union at all.[26] However, strikers are normally eligible to vote in this decertification election.[27] Loss of certification is a definite threat and is becoming more so as management is increasingly likely to replace strikers. This means that job loss becomes more and more probable.

In general, then, union and worker costs are highest, and management power is greatest, when a production disruption or work stoppage

1. Causes member income to drop with little replacement from strike funds or income from alternative jobs, for example, and if the members in general are in an illiquid financial position.

2. Occurs when dissident factions can heighten union divisiveness, and if members are not widely and strongly supportive of the action.

3. Causes membership loss because of lukewarm support, causing members to resign and return to work or leave to find other employment, especially if they are replaced by strike breakers. These actions could even lead to decertification of the union.

BARGAINING STRUCTURE

Most collective bargaining scenarios feature a one-on-one situation—a union bargaining with a company. Although this is typically the case, other bargaining structures are used to fit the needs and desires of the parties. In some instances, these other bargaining structures are used simply for convenience sake. The savings in using such bargaining structures will be the dominant factor in their utilization. In other cases, however, a type of bargaining structure may be used to enhance the bargaining power of one of the parties.

Multi-Tier Bargaining

Multi-tier bargaining is utilized when a large national union negotiates with a large national company with plants spread across a large area, for example, the country. This structure is very similar to the typical one-on-one bargaining arrangement. A national contract is negotiated in a one-on-one fashion. At the same time, however, local contracts will be negotiated to supplement the national agreement.

This structure was traditionally used because it equalized the power of union and management. A large company bargaining separately with relatively small locals at its various plants would give the employer the upper hand. Large national unions centralizing collective bargaining, but still allowing plant-level negotiations over some issues, offer greater opportunity to balance employer power. Furthermore, a centrally bargained wage scale would tend to result in equal pay for equal work throughout the company. This is a major union goal.

An Example of the Traditional Multi-Tier Process

An example of multi-tier bargaining is the negotiations between the UAW and any one of the Big 3 U.S. auto makers, GM or Ford or Chrysler. The national union and the company will negotiate a basic (or master) contract covering items standardized across all plants, such as wages, fringe benefits, institutional arrangements (e.g., union security clauses and management rights clauses), and general administrative procedures like the grievance procedure and many work rules.

At the plant level, contract bargaining for the local and the plant will focus on issues specific to that site, including negotiating some variations in work schedules and work rules. For example, plant conditions might dictate that winter schedules have a later starting time because of weather conditions or, in a plant with a hot and dusty environment, that worker breaks might have to be more frequent.

Recent Developments in Multi-Tier Bargaining

Concessions and the National Contract   An increasing number of national collective bargaining structures include plant-level bargaining. These plant-level negotiations are becoming more important in setting a wide variety of employment terms and conditions. In recent years, companies have been able to get plant-specific concessions, under the threat of plant closure, that have included wage cuts, major work rule changes, and even changes in seniority provisions.[28] In addition to divergence of contract terms plant-to-plant within a company, another recent trend in several industries has been the divergence of contract terms company-to-company in an industry. This breakdown in closely duplicated contracts in an industry has occurred with relatively large companies negotiating individually, usually sequentially, with a large union.

Concessions and Pattern Bargaining   Traditionally, when a large union like the UAW bargained with the companies in an industry like the auto industry (GM, Ford, and Chrysler), they used the bargaining outcome from the first negotiation as the model for the bargain they obtained from the others in that industry. This is called **pattern bargaining**. If they set the first bargain with one of the weaker companies in a competitive industry by applying pure bargaining power which they have vis-à-vis that company, and if they use that first outcome to force the same terms on the other companies in the industry, one-by-one, the result is whipsawing, as discussed above.

The economic environment of the last ten years or so has caused major changes in this strategy of setting patterns, starting with the October 1979 settlement between the UAW and Chrysler, which most people consider the first major "concession bargain" in this wave of concession bargaining.[29] By the mid-1980s, the break in pattern bargaining had been cited many times in the media, in articles with titles like "The Beginning of the End for Industrywide Wages?"[30] Unions were forced to accept unequal pay for equal work across the plants of many a company and to put wages back in competition. The fact was that imports and domestic nonunion competition were doing just that. The breakdown has even extended to multi-employer bargaining, a structure that "formalizes pattern bargaining."[31] A discussion of this form of structure follows.

Multi-Party Bargaining

Multi-party bargaining occurs when the employers or unions, or both, form a coalition to negotiate. This type of bargaining is sometimes called **coalition bargaining**.[32] In most cases, this structure is utilized for reasons relating to bargaining power.

Multi-Employer Bargaining

Multi-employer bargaining denotes a coalition of employers in an industrywide grouping. Examples include the Freight Haulers Association in trucking, the Bituminous Coal Operators Association in coal mining, and the now defunct Coordinating Committee Steel Companies.[33]

Most employer coalitions are formed to enhance the bargaining power of companies in a relatively competitive industry facing a powerful union that has organized the vast majority of workers in that industry. This is especially important to employers when the industry has weaker companies that would allow the union to whipsaw the industry.

Recent trends, however, have pointed to the breakdown of pattern bargaining in general, as noted above, and the breakup of multi-employer coalitions. The basic steel companies disbanded their coalition in 1985. The Bituminous Coal Operators Association (BCOA) has dropped from a high of 130 members to just 15.[34] Many defections from the Freight Haulers Association, as well as many new, independent (and usually nonunion) operators, have been spawned by deregulation.

In 1988, however, the United Mine Workers and the Bituminous Coal Operators Association, for the second straight time, were able to reach a contract agreement without a major industry work stoppage. Nevertheless, several companies were expected to continue to seek more favorable terms. These companies, which include metallurgical coal companies, follow different market economics than those of the majority of coal companies, and they do not believe the BCOA fights for their particular interests.[35]

Multi-Union Bargaining

Employer negotiating associations are more common than union associations. Union groupings for **multi-union bargaining** have usually been formed for convenience rather than for reasons relating to bargaining power. An example of this type of structure is the multi-union bargaining of the construction craft unions, given their mutual needs from employers, who also tend to bargain as a general contractors association.[36]

Since much craft union bargaining is local, these types of coalitions are easier to maintain. They involve much fewer workers than would be involved in a large national union organized along industrial lines. Moreover, the craft unions are not in competition with each other, leading to rather stable coalitions.

Coordinated Bargaining

Coordinated bargaining is a multi-union structure in that it involves several unions, and yet it has some major differences from the multi-union arrangement. It customarily involves one employer, whose workers are organized in several bargaining units represented by these several different unions. This structure is utilized when a company has several craft unions rather than a single industrial one representing its workers, or when the company produces outputs that are heterogeneous, placing it in several diverse industries.

The situation of a company operating in diverse industries and thus dealing with different industrial (and craft) unions probably represents the most popular example of a coordinated bargaining structure. This example involves General Electric (and Westinghouse) and the 12 unions representing its workers, bargaining as the Coordinated Bargaining Committee of GE (and Westinghouse) Unions, which include the International Brotherhood of Electronic Workers, the United Electrical Workers, the Sheet Metal Workers, and the United Auto Workers.[37] In their coordinated bargaining, all the unions' contracts expire at the same time. They all bargain with the employer for uniform wage rates for given job classifications and uniform fringe benefits and other terms of employment. The unions don't necessarily bargain physically as one entity, and each has its own contract. But they coordinate their proposals and counterproposals to end up with a uniform outcome.

Now that we have some idea of the process of negotiating, we can move on to a discussion of the subject matter of collective bargaining.

DISCUSSION QUESTIONS

1. Once a union and a group of workers at a company decide to try to unionize that company, what must they do?
2. What is an authorization card, and how is it used?
3. Define the term *exclusive bargaining agent*.
4. In 1988, the Teamsters got relatively favorable terms in their settlement with the Freight Haulers Association, although the economic situation for the companies was not much better than it was in 1985 when the Teamsters made several major concessions. Why did the Teamster leadership bargain "so tough" in 1988?
5. Compare distributive and integrative bargaining.
6. Why might union negotiators undertake intraorganizational bargaining?
7. How might you define the bargaining power of party X relative to that of party Y when those two are collective bargaining with each other?
8. Explain how the cost to a company of a production disruption varies with the timing of that disruption.

9. Explain how the cost to a company of a production disruption varies with the nature of the product produced.

10. Explain how the cost to a company of a production disruption by its workers varies with the general health of the economy.

11. What three major costs are borne by workers and their union when they exert their bargaining power and go out on strike?

12. What is multi-tier bargaining? What are its advantages for unions? For management?

13. What is causing the abandonment, evident over the last five to ten years, of multi-employer bargaining?

14. In preparing for collective bargaining, what type of economic information would a union find especially helpful?

15. What uses might a union in collective bargaining make of the Consumer Price Index (CPI)?

VOCABULARY LIST

exclusive bargaining agent
organizing campaign
authorization card
election campaign
bargaining unit
consent election
directed election
Consumer Price Index (CPI)
limits of acceptance
distributive bargaining
integrative bargaining
attitudinal structuring

intraorganizational bargaining
bargaining power
work stoppage
whipsawing
whistleblowing
multi-tier bargaining
pattern bargaining
multi-party bargaining
coalition bargaining
multi-employer bargaining
multi-union bargaining
coordinated bargaining

FOOTNOTES

1. *Wall Street Journal,* July 28, 1989, p. A3.

2. *Wall Street Journal,* February 16, 1988, p. 1; August 23, 1988, p. 1; January 10, 1989, p. A1; see also Cheryl L. Maranto, "Corporate Characteristics and Union Organizing," *Industrial Relations* (Fall 1988): 354–355.

3. *Wall Street Journal,* July 29, 1989, p. A3; July 25, 1989, p. A1.

4. The details of formal designation of the terms of the election can be found in many sources, for example, Commerce Clearing House's *1989 Guidebook to Labor Relations,* Ch. 4. This chapter in the Guidebook also gives most of the

details of matters covered in this section, as well as procedures for decertifying (getting rid of) a union.

5. Commerce Clearing House, *1989 Guidebook to Labor Relations*, p. 120.

6. Ibid., p. 121.

7. Union security clauses will be discussed in Chapter 9, particularly the union shop which requires union membership to keep one's job; the duty of fair representation for grievances is discussed in Ch. 11.

8. The United Steel Workers, for example, moved to membership ratification of contracts in basic steel in 1986 (*Wall Street Journal*, January 17, 1986, p. 38); the Teamster ratification vote used to require that only one-third of the members vote "yes" for contract acceptance (*Business Week*, May 23, 1988, p. 59), but this was changed to majority approval (*Wall Street Journal*, October 20, 1988, p. A13).

9. *Business Week*, May 23, 1988, p. 59 and March 21, 1988, p. 90. However, some of the smaller, weaker carriers could not pay the increases in wages and benefits; therefore, the union allows profit-sharing and stock ownership plans to substitute for the increases. In fact, a special provision of the contract would have all workers at a weak trucking firm take a 15 percent pay cut if 75 percent of the members at that company voted to do so. The cut would be made up in the future through profit sharing, given, of course, the company made profits to share (*Wall Street Journal*, April 19, 1988, p. 1).

10. *Business Week*, March 21, 1988, p. 90; these types of concessions in collective bargaining have been and will be mentioned and discussed throughout the book.

11. Section 8 (a) (5) of the NLRA/LMRA requires disclosure of this information as an act of good faith bargaining (see Ch. 3).

12. The *Monthly Labor Review* has monthly industry data on Employment of Workers, Average Weekly Hours, Average Hourly and Weekly Earnings, and the Employment Cost Index, and quarterly Major Collective Bargaining Settlements/Average Compensation and Wage Adjustments.

13. The California Economic Development Department puts out a quarterly labor market bulletin for major labor markets (Metropolitan Statistical Areas), mainly on employment and unemployment by industry.

14. *Monthly Labor Review* (March 1989): 82, Table 29; (March 1990): 102, Table 30.

15. Richard E. Walton and Robert B. McKersie, *A Behavioral Theory of Labor Negotiations* (McGraw–Hill, 1965), pp. 4–6.

16. Ibid., p. 6.

17. Melvin W. Reder, *Labor in a Growing Economy* (John Wiley & Sons, 1957), pp. 164–165; as a student of Professor Reder, I obtained substantial elaboration on this model.

18. Neil W. Chamberlain and James W. Kuhn, *Collective Bargaining* (McGraw–Hill, 1965), Ch. 7.

19. I. W. Abel, "Steel: Experiment in Bargaining," in Richard L. Rowan, *Readings in*

Labor Economics and Labor Relations (Richard D. Irwin, 1980), p. 173, where Abel notes that "the 116-day strike in 1951 . . . provided foreign steel makers an initial opportunity to acquire and cultivate American customers."

20. Donald E. Cullen, "Recent Trends in Collective Bargaining in the United States," *International Labor Review* (May–June 1985): 311; Cullen notes that "many small employers have operated during strikes in the past, but few large companies attempted to do so from around 1950 until fairly recently."

21. This is the case with the Teamsters and trucking firms, whose industry association is called Trucking Management, Inc. (*Business Week*, March 21, 1988, p. 90). It was also the case with the USW and Big Steel, where multi-employer bargaining broke down in 1985 (*Wall Street Journal*, May 6, 1985, p. 12, and April 7, 1986, p. 6).

22. *Business Week*, August 29, 1988, p. 82; *Wall Street Journal*, October 25, 1988, p. A24.

23. *Wall Street Journal*, May 5, 1989, p. A8. The Texas Air battle with its unions and the Eastern dispute are examined more closely in Chs. 13 and 14.

24. *Wall Street Journal*, March 24, 1988, p. 14.

25. In 1977, the NLRB ruled that a union cannot fine or otherwise place restrictions on workers who quit the union and return to work. The Supreme Court upheld the NLRB in 1985 (*Wall Street Journal*, June 28, 1985, p. 10).

26. If the striking union was certified as bargaining agent over a year ago, the workers, whether or not they are strike replacements, can call for a decertification election (*1989 Guidebook to Labor Relations*, pp. 128–129).

27. Ibid., p. 117. The law allows a replaced striker to vote on decertification up to 12 months after the start of the strike as long as "the striker has (not) abandoned his interest in his struck job." Unreplaced strikers can vote in decertification elections held more than 12 months after the strike starts, under the same condition of job interest. This relates to an economic strike, which is the subject of this section. (See Ch. 13 for a discussion of other types of strikes.)

28. *Wall Street Journal*, April 16, 1987, p. 1.

29. Cullen, "Recent Trends in Collective Bargaining," p. 299.

30. *Business Week*, March 5, 1984, p. 78; see also Audrey Freedman and William E. Fulmer, "Last Rites for Pattern Bargaining," *Harvard Business Review* (March –April 1982), and Robert B. Hoffman, "The Trend Away from Multiemployer Bargaining," *Labor Law Journal* (February 1983). But also see Kathryn J. Ready, "Is Pattern Bargaining Dead?," *Industrial and Labor Relations Review* (January 1990): 272–279.

31. Cullen, "Recent Trends in Collective Bargaining," p. 310; Cullen notes that multi-employer bargaining has deteriorated in coal, trucking, and steel. The total breakdown of the structure in steel was noted above (*Wall Street Journal*, May 6, 1985, p. 12 and April 7, 1986, p. 6).

32. Alan Balfour, *Union–Management Relations in a Changing Economy* (Prentice–Hall, 1987), p. 186.

33. I. W. Abel, "Basic Steel's Experimental Negotiating Agreement," *Monthly Labor Review* (September 1973): 40, and *Wall Street Journal*, May 6, 1985, p. 12; April 7, 1986, p. 6.

34. *Wall Street Journal*, November 12, 1987, p. 6, and February 1, 1988, p. 36.

35. Ibid., p. 12.

36. Balfour, *Union–Management Relations in a Changing Economy*, pp. 186–187.

37. *Business Week*, December 14, 1987, pp. 102–103; *Wall Street Journal*, June 29, 1988, p. 30.

REFERENCES

ABEL, I. W. "Basic Steel's Experimental Negotiating Agreement." *Monthly Labor Review* (September 1973): 39–42.

———. "Steel: Experiment in Bargaining." In Richard L. Rowan, *Readings in Labor Economics and Labor Relations*. Richard D. Irwin, 1980, pp. 172–176.

BALFOUR, ALAN. *Union–Management Relations in a Changing Economy*. Prentice–Hall, 1987, Ch. 9.

CHAMBERLAIN, NEIL W., and JAMES W. KUHN. *Collective Bargaining*. McGraw–Hill, 1965, Ch. 7.

COMMERCE CLEARING HOUSE. *1989 Guidebook to Labor Relations*. 1989, Ch. 4.

CULLEN, DONALD E. "Recent Trends in Collective Bargaining in the United States." *International Labor Review* (May–June 1985): 299–322.

FREEDMAN, AUDREY, and WILLIAM E. FULMER. "Last Rites for Pattern Bargaining." *Harvard Business Review* (March–April 1982).

FREEMAN, RICHARD B. "Why Are Unions Faring Poorly in NLRB Representation Elections?" In Rowan, *Readings in Labor Economics and Labor Relations*, 1985, pp. 129–141.

GOMPERS, SAMUEL. *Labor and the Common Welfare*. E. P. Dutton, 1919, p. 20.

HOFFMAN, ROBERT B. "The Trend Away from Multiemployer Bargaining." *Labor Law Journal* (February 1983).

INDUSTRIAL UNION DEPARTMENT, AFL–CIO. "Coordinated Bargaining: Labor's New Approach to Effective Contract Negotiations." In Rowan, *Readings in Labor Economics and Labor Relations*, 1980, pp. 161–166.

MARANTO, CHERYL L. "Corporate Characteristics and Union Organizing." *Industrial Relations* (Fall 1988): 352–370.

MISHEL, LAWRENCE. "The Structural Determinants of Union Bargaining Power." *Industrial and Labor Relations Review* (October 1986): 90–104.

READY, KATHRYN J. "Is Pattern Bargaining Dead?" *Industrial and Labor Relations Review* (January 1990): 272–279.

REDER, MELVIN W. *Labor in a Growing Economy*. John Wiley, 1957, Ch. 6.

WALTON, RICHARD E., and ROBERT B. MCKERSIE. *A Behavioral Theory of Labor Negotiations*. McGraw–Hill, 1965, Chs. 1 and 10.

APPENDIX

A BLS WAGE SURVEY

Area Wage Survey
Stockton, CA
August 1990

U.S. Department of Labor
Bureau of Labor Statistics
Summary
October 1990

This summary presents results of an August 1990 survey of occupational wages in the Stockton Metropolitan Statistical Area, which consists of San Joaquin County. This is 1 of over 110 areas which the Bureau of Labor Statistics surveys annually or every other year at the request of the Employment Standards Administration of the U.S. Department of Labor for use in administering the Service Contract Act of 1965. In addition, the Bureau conducts more extensive studies of occupational wages and related benefits in 90 other areas throughout the United States. For information on these reports and other Bureau publications, contact any BLS regional office identified on the back page.

This study covered establishments employing 50 workers or more in manufacturing; transportation, communication, and other public utilities; wholesale trade; retail trade; finance, insurance, and real estate; and selected services. A sample of 94 establishments employing 25,353 workers was selected to represent 270 establishments employing 48,870 workers in the area. Data collected in the sample of establishments were projected to represent all establishments within the scope of the survey.

Table 1 provides hourly earnings information on office and plant workers employed in selected occupations common to a variety of industries. Occupational classification was based on a uniform set of job descriptions designed to take account of variations in job duties among establishments. The job descriptions used in the survey are available on request. (See table 2 for further information on the scope of the survey.)

Number of workers receiving straight-time hourly earnings (in dollars) of —

Occupation[1]	Number of workers	Hourly earnings (in dollars)[1] Mean	Median	Middle range	4.00 and under 4.50	4.50–5.00	5.00–5.50	5.50–6.00	6.00–6.50	6.50–7.00	7.00–7.50	7.50–8.00	8.00–8.50	8.50–9.00	9.00–10.00	10.00–11.00	11.00–12.00	12.00–13.00	13.00–14.00	14.00–15.00	15.00–16.00	16.00–17.00	17.00–18.00	18.00–19.00	19.00–20.00	20.00–21.00	21.00 and over
Secretaries	119	10.52	9.33	8.80–12.02	-	-	-	-	1	-	-	3	23	7	30	15	10	12	5	5	3	3	2	3	-	-	-
Secretaries II	9	10.19	10.25	8.19–10.27	-	-	-	-	-	-	-	-	-	1	4	3	1	-	-	-	-	-	-	-	-	-	-
Secretaries III	80	9.61	9.14	8.19–10.27	-	-	-	-	-	-	-	3	23	5	24	12	3	3	2	2	1	1	-	-	-	-	-
Secretaries IV	19	12.74	12.41	11.63–13.99	-	-	-	-	-	-	-	-	-	-	-	-	4	8	3	2	1	1	-	-	-	-	-
Secretaries V	8	15.72	16.88	-	-	-	-	-	-	-	-	-	-	-	-	-	-	-	-	1	2	1	3	1	-	-	-
Word processors	8	9.92	9.81	-	-	-	-	-	-	-	-	-	-	-	2	2	-	2	-	-	-	-	-	-	-	-	-
Key entry operators	44	7.04	6.75	6.09–6.79	-	-	-	-	10	19	-	1	1	-	2	-	-	-	-	-	-	-	-	-	-	-	-
Key entry operators I	21	6.52	6.66	6.06–6.79	-	-	-	5	5	9	-	-	1	-	1	-	-	-	-	-	-	-	-	-	-	-	-
Key entry operators II	21	7.11	6.75	6.75–8.58	-	-	-	5	5	10	-	-	-	-	1	-	-	-	-	-	-	-	-	-	-	-	-
Switchboard operator-receptionists	100	6.69	6.35	6.00–6.83	-	2	-	11	43	25	5	-	4	3	6	1	3	-	-	-	-	-	-	-	-	-	-
Order clerks	63	7.56	6.92	6.69–7.75	-	-	-	1	9	22	4	12	4	-	9	1	-	-	-	-	-	-	-	-	-	-	-
Order clerks I	60	7.38	6.92	6.55–7.50	-	-	-	1	9	22	4	12	4	-	9	-	-	-	-	-	-	-	-	-	-	-	-
Accounting clerks	279	9.06	9.00	7.82–9.96	-	-	3	-	5	4	7	58	24	33	80	47	5	6	2	1	1	-	-	-	-	-	-
Accounting clerks II	133	8.42	7.85	7.50–9.00	-	-	1	-	5	4	7	52	10	19	21	9	4	2	-	-	1	-	-	-	-	-	-
Accounting clerks III	90	9.34	9.35	8.51–10.01	-	-	-	-	4	4	-	6	14	10	34	22	1	1	-	-	-	-	-	-	-	-	-
Payroll clerks	28	9.62	9.68	8.33–11.78	-	2	2	-	2	1	-	-	2	-	7	5	5	1	1	-	-	-	-	-	-	-	-
Computer systems analysts	16	16.38	16.49	15.03–18.46	-	-	-	-	-	-	-	-	-	-	-	-	-	-	-	4	3	1	-	4	-	-	1
Computer systems analysts I	7	14.25	15.03	-	-	-	-	-	-	-	-	-	-	-	-	2	-	1	1	3	2	-	-	-	-	-	-
Computer systems analysts II	6	18.20	17.64	-	-	-	-	-	-	-	-	-	-	-	-	2	1	-	-	1	2	1	2	-	2	1	1
Computer programmers	23	14.09	12.69	11.54–15.84	-	-	-	-	-	-	-	-	-	-	1	3	4	4	4	2	1	1	-	-	-	1	2
Computer programmers II	12	11.52	11.54	-	-	-	-	-	-	-	-	-	-	-	1	3	3	1	4	1	-	-	-	-	-	-	1
Computer programmers III	6	13.68	13.56	-	-	-	-	-	-	-	-	-	-	-	-	-	1	1	4	1	-	-	-	-	-	-	2
Computer operators	25	9.96	9.81	8.57–10.87	-	-	-	-	-	-	-	-	3	5	5	3	3	1	1	1	-	1	-	-	-	-	-
Computer operators II	15	9.33	8.68	8.57–10.51	-	-	-	-	-	-	-	-	-	5	3	2	1	1	1	-	-	1	-	-	-	-	-
Computer operators III	7	10.89	10.00	-	-	-	-	-	-	-	-	-	1	-	2	2	-	1	-	1	-	-	-	-	-	-	-
Drafters	13	10.38	10.45	-	-	-	-	-	-	-	-	-	1	-	2	2	3	2	5	2	3	-	-	-	-	-	-
Electronics technicians	173	13.99	16.46	8.75–16.46	-	-	-	-	-	10	10	-	13	7	-	4	2	2	5	2	3	91	-	3	2	-	12
Electronics technicians I	39	7.87	7.00	6.76–8.48	-	-	-	-	-	10	10	-	8	7	-	1	1	1	2	-	-	-	-	-	-	-	-
Electronics technicians III	20	18.45	21.04	14.40–21.04	-	-	-	-	-	-	-	-	-	-	-	1	1	1	2	1	2	1	-	2	2	-	12
Registered industrial nurses	6	14.48	13.97	-	-	-	-	-	-	-	-	-	-	-	-	-	1	1	1	1	-	-	1	-	1	-	-
Maintenance carpenters	7	13.55	14.67	-	-	-	-	-	-	-	-	-	-	-	-	-	-	3	-	2	2	-	-	-	-	-	-
Maintenance electricians	147	15.22	14.64	14.03–14.94	-	-	-	-	-	-	-	-	-	-	-	3	3	12	14	82	4	-	-	20	12	-	-
Maintenance mechanics (machinery)	615	14.07	14.64	12.75–14.67	-	-	-	-	-	-	-	-	-	-	4	34	126	-	9	402	14	-	5	21	-	-	-
Maintenance pipefitters	11	16.86	18.70	-	-	-	-	-	-	-	-	-	-	-	-	-	-	-	-	14	-	-	21	6	6	-	-
Motor vehicle mechanics	108	15.50	14.64	12.72–19.87	-	-	-	-	-	-	-	-	-	-	-	11	17	8	31	5	-	-	1	6	32	-	-
Tool and die makers	21	14.01	14.03	12.84–14.23	-	-	-	-	-	-	-	-	-	-	-	-	4	9	4	9	-	-	1	6	-	-	-
Stationary engineers	31	14.31	14.64	13.00–14.64	-	-	-	-	-	-	-	-	-	-	-	-	1	-	9	21	-	-	1	-	-	-	1

See footnotes at end of table.

195

Occupation[2]	Number of workers	Hourly earnings (in dollars)[1]			Number of workers receiving straight-time hourly earnings (in dollars) of —																							
		Mean	Median	Middle range	4.00 and under 4.50	4.50–5.00	5.00–5.50	5.50–6.00	6.00–6.50	6.50–7.00	7.00–7.50	7.50–8.00	8.00–8.50	8.50–9.00	9.00–10.00	10.00–11.00	11.00–12.00	12.00–13.00	13.00–14.00	14.00–15.00	15.00–16.00	16.00–17.00	17.00–18.00	18.00–19.00	19.00–20.00	20.00–21.00	21.00 and over
Truckdrivers	587	11.16	10.30	9.00–12.17	–	–	–	–	6	17	10	2	60	42	87	101	30	114	12	23	1	77	5	–	–	–	–
Truckdrivers, heavy truck	45	10.12	12.05	8.75–12.05	–	–	–	–	–	–	10	–	–	–	–	–	11	24	4	–	–	–	–	–	–	–	–
Truckdrivers, tractor-trailer	386	10.41	10.30	9.00–12.17	–	–	–	–	–	11	–	1	44	31	68	93	29	77	2	23	–	–	5	–	–	–	–
Shippers	49	9.40	8.84	6.79–12.71	–	–	–	5	5	10	1	–	–	8	1	–	–	16	2	–	–	–	–	–	–	–	–
Receivers	19	10.50	12.13	7.45–12.13	–	–	–	–	–	–	5	–	–	–	1	1	–	9	2	–	–	–	–	–	–	–	–
Shippers and receivers	46	10.51	10.53	9.62–10.91	–	–	–	–	–	–	1	–	–	4	11	28	2	–	–	–	–	–	–	–	–	–	–
Warehousemen	55	8.39	8.00	6.79–9.60	–	–	–	6	7	5	2	6	3	14	15	–	–	1	–	–	–	–	–	–	–	–	–
Order fillers	53	7.50	7.95	6.50–8.64	–	–	–	10	–	10	–	8	11	14	–	–	–	–	–	–	–	–	–	–	–	–	–
Shipping packers	164	8.58	7.91	6.05–12.76	–	10	10	–	22	12	19	11	19	–	–	–	–	44	–	–	–	–	–	–	–	–	–
Material handling laborers	301	8.48	9.10	8.37–9.13	2	–	–	–	–	–	5	–	43	39	210	–	–	–	5	–	–	–	–	–	–	–	–
Forklift operators	686	11.61	11.98	10.42–12.16	–	–	–	–	–	11	5	9	13	1	16	133	131	287	–	–	–	48	–	–	–	–	–
Guards	618	5.27	5.00	4.80–5.35	23	169	287	66	39	3	4	9	1	1	4	4	–	–	–	–	–	–	–	–	–	–	–
Guards I	606	5.21	5.00	4.80–5.35	23	169	287	66	39	3	4	9	1	–	14	–	–	–	–	–	–	–	–	–	–	–	–
Janitors, porters, and cleaners	212	8.52	8.29	6.95–8.95	–	5	10	5	24	19	1	22	40	36	14	4	1	2	–	–	–	–	–	–	–	–	–

[1] Excludes premium pay for overtime and for work on weekends, holidays, and late shifts. Also excluded are performance bonuses and lump-sum payments of the type negotiated in the auto and aerospace industries, as well as profit-sharing payments, attendance bonuses, Christmas or year-end bonuses, and other nonproduction bonuses. Pay increases—but not bonuses—under cost-of-living allowance clauses and incentive payments, however, are included. Hourly earnings reported for salaried workers are derived from regular salaries divided by the corresponding standard hours of work. The wages of learners, apprentices, and handicapped workers are excluded. The mean is computed for each job by totaling the earnings of all workers and dividing by the number of workers. The median designates position—one-half of the workers receive the same as or more than this rate and one-half receive the same as or less than this rate. The middle range is defined by two rates of pay; one-fourth of the workers earn the same as or less than the lower of these rates and one-fourth earn the same as or more than the higher rate. Middle ranges are not provided when fewer than 15 workers are reported.

[2] For occupations with more than one level, data are included in the overall classification when a subclassification is not shown or information to subclassify is not available.

[3] All workers were at 21.00 to 22.00.

Industry division[1]	Minimum employment in establishments in scope of survey	Number of establishments		Workers in establishments		
		Within scope of survey[a]	Studied	Within scope of survey[a]		Studied
				Number	Percent	
All divisions	50	270	94	48,870	100	25,353
Manufacturing	50	92	34	22,853	47	12,951
Nonmanufacturing[b]	50	178	60	26,017	53	12,402

[1] The Stockton Metropolitan Statistical Area, as defined by the Office of Management and Budget through October 1984, consists of San Joaquin County. The "workers within scope of survey" estimates shown in this table provide a reasonably accurate description of the size and composition of the labor force included in the survey. The estimates are not intended, however, to serve as a basis for comparison with other statistical series to measure employment trends or levels since (1) planning of wage surveys requires the use of establishment data compiled considerably in advance of the payroll period studied, and (2) small establishments are excluded from the scope of the survey.

[a] The Standard Industrial Classification Manual was used in classifying establishments by industry. All government operations are excluded from the scope of the survey.

[b] Includes all establishments with total employment at or above the minimum limitation. All outlets (within a metropolitan area or nonmetropolitan county) of nonmanufacturing companies are considered as one establishment when located within the same industry division.

[a] Includes all workers in all establishments with total employment (within the area) at or above the minimum limitation.

[b] Includes transportation, communication, and other public utilities (excluding taxicabs and services incidental to water transportation); wholesale trade; retail trade; finance, insurance, and real estate; hotels and other lodging places; personal services; business services; automotive repair services and garages; motion pictures; membership organizations (excluding religious organizations); and miscellaneous services. Major industries excluded from this survey are agriculture; mining; construction; and some services (notably educational institutions and medical services).

CHAPTER 7

WAGES AND COLLECTIVE BARGAINING

W ages have traditionally been the central focus of collective bargaining. The wage rate* has been (and to a great extent still is) the major concern of the average worker. In the approximately 40 years from the late 1930s to the late 1970s, union leaders did not sign contracts involving pay cuts if they valued their jobs. Unemployment was an acceptable alternative to decreased wage rates!

With the late 1970s came concession bargaining, stemming primarily from increased rivalry with both domestic and international competitors, coupled with a stiffening of managerial opposition, apparently encouraged by the prevailing political climate. This development has changed the unions' almost religious fervor to avoid pay cuts; instead, job security has become a focal issue.[1] All the same, wages remain a key point in collective bargaining, and they are becoming even more important for unions trying to gain back concessions granted in the 1980s.

This chapter discusses union wage policy and examines three aspects of wages related to collective bargaining: setting the level of wages, determining increases in wage levels, and establishing the wage structure in an organization. The chapter ends with an analysis of the wage effect of unionism.

Setting the level of wages is especially important when the first contract is negotiated or new jobs are defined. Typically, most unions are continually involved

---

* Two wage systems are normally used in the workplace. The first, the *day rate* system, bases pay on an hourly wage rate, for a standard eight-hour day, five-day week. It is used in the vast majority of cases. The second, the *piece rate* system, bases pay on ouput (pieces produced by the worker). This system is not used much today, except in agriculture and in less developed countries.

with establishing wage changes or adjustments during the term of the contract. The **wage structure,** or relative wage levels in an organization, encompasses competing institutional goals as well as economic realities. Some of these economic realities spawned two-tier wage structures in the wave of concession bargaining of the 1980s. These structures are discussed here, along with other aspects of intraorganization and interorganization wage structures.

All three aspects—wage levels, wage changes, and wage structure—are closely interrelated and are all results of similar forces.

THE THEORY OF UNION WAGE POLICY

Union wage policy is the underlying rationale employed by unions in negotiating wage rates. The theory of union wage policy has been a major topic of debate in labor and industrial relations for many years. Over the last 50 years the debate has focused on theories of the union as an economic maximizing institution versus the union as a politically motivated force.

The Economic Theory: The Union as a Monopoly Power

At the base of the **economic theory of union wage policy** is the concept that unions are rational economic maximizers with **monopoly** (or **market**) **power.**[2] They face a downward-sloping demand curve for their product, labor services. Like a monopolist or a seller in a market structure such as imperfect or monopolistic competition, they set the price for this product to maximize their objective.

Several interrelated concepts are important in this economic theory. First, some basic terms relating to the labor market must be defined. Then, it is important to determine what the unions maximize and how the unions monopolize the selling of their product, labor services.

Some Basic Terms Defined

In an economic theory of union wage policy, several definitions relating to the labor market need to be explicitly examined. These should be set in the framework of market supply and demand analysis as illustrated in Figure 7.1.

The **units of labor** sold by workers through their union and purchased by companies and agencies are usually measured in labor-hours. However, it is common to hire workers in large blocks of time, for example, 40-hour weeks.

The price of labor, the **wage rate,** is in dollars/labor-hour. However, the cost of labor goes beyond wages and includes a variety of fringe benefits. Some of these have specific costs, in the form of insurance premiums and Social Security taxes. Others have contingent or probabilistic costs, in the form of sick leave. Still others have deferred costs, in the form of pensions, for which employers must put aside a portion of expected pension benefits in the present but can defer fully funding these benefits. In general, economic theories of union wage policy assume that fringe benefits or economic supplements are a fixed proportion of wages.

The **demand curve for labor** (*DD* in Figure 7.1) denotes the amount of labor services employers will purchase at different wage rates. It is assumed that unions have some market power. If they had no power to set wage rates above the competitive

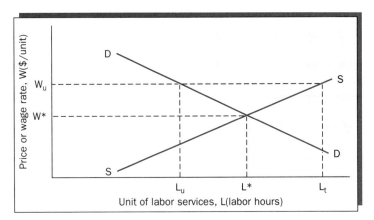

FIGURE 7.1 Labor market supply and demand.

level, why would workers join unions? Thus, the union can raise the wage rate above the market clearing level (denoted W^* in Figure 7.1).

The higher the unions push the wage rate, however, the lower will be the labor-hours employed; this tradeoff is called the **employment effect.** If all workers in the labor market are union members, then higher union wage rates mean higher unemployment among union members.

The **supply curve for labor** (SS in Figure 7.1) denotes the amount of labor services (traded off against leisure) workers will offer at different wage rates. If unions have some market power, this means they control some (or if a monopolist, all) of the supply of labor services in the market. At the least, they control that portion composed of their members, which they try to differentiate from nonunion workers. The claim that union workers are more productive and more loyal (lower quit rates) is not unfounded.[3] As recent trends suggest, however, this claim is becoming increasingly more difficult to sell to management.

What Do Unions Maximize?

Within the framework of a market analysis, sellers set prices to maximize their objective. In the product market, price and production are set to maximize the profit of the seller. In a labor market, where the seller is the union acting as an agent for its members, profit is not the objective.

The union and its members are concerned with two variables within the framework of a labor-market analysis: jobs (employment) and pay (the wage rate, assuming a standard 40-hour week). The union, then, wants to maximize the wage rate and employment for its members. However, as the wage rate goes up, employers want to hire fewer workers; this is how the employment effect works. Employment increases can be obtained by cutting the wage rate. However, unions traditionally have not done this.

If the union bargains for a higher wage rate than the market rate (W^*), say W_u, employment will be L_u (see Figure 7.1). If union membership exceeds the number of workers denoted by L_u, some of these members will be unemployed. This means not only that some present members are unhappy, but also that membership growth will be limited, as new workers who join the union can look forward to unemployment. This started to occur in some building trades unions in the 1980s and stopped the fairly large increases in the union wage rate that had been gained in the 1970s. Short-run pay maximization has long-run growth implications for the union. At the extreme, union wage rate maximization implies employment of very few workers, possibly just one. But the bankruptcy of the firm would probably precede this highly reduced employment. Pay maximization would have to be accompanied by some constraint limiting the unemployment of members.

If the union wishes to maximize the employment of its members, wage cuts may be in order. If, in fact, the union is growth oriented, severe wage cuts coupled with some compulsory membership arrangement (like the union shop, discussed in Chapter 9) will be its strategy. However, this approach might push the wage rate below the market-clearing competitive rate (where supply equals demand) if union membership exceeded L^* (see Figure 7.1). If this is the case, workers, seeing job opportunities that pay higher in other labor markets, will leave the union and move to those other markets where they will be paid at least the market rate. Again, however, union leaders have traditionally avoided cuts in the nominal wage rate, even in bad times. The concession bargaining of the early and mid-1980s has changed this aversion, but in many industries the granting of major concessions by unions seems to have abated substantially in the last several years.

Dunlop combined wage rate and employment in an objective he called the **wage bill,** the income of the union's membership.[4] This product of wage rate times the number employed is what unions maximized as economic agents. This combination recognized the action of the employment effect, the tradeoff between pay and jobs.

How Do Unions Sell Labor Services?

Given the objective to be maximized, how do unions sell labor services in negotiations with employers? If moving up and down the labor market demand curve causes changes in both wage rate and employment, what combination will a union choose? That is, what wage rate will it negotiate, and, given market forces, what employment level will this mean for its membership? The answer depends on the market power of both the employer in the product market and the union in the labor market.

The demand curve for labor services is a **derived demand,** derived from the demand curve for the product those labor services produce. If the employer has monopoly power in the product market, a price change will cause a proportionally smaller change in the quantity of the product purchased. This is termed **inelastic demand** (see Figure 7.2). As an example, if the producer raised price by 10 percent, quantity might drop by only 5 percent, causing revenue to go up by 5 percent. If the demand for the product is inelastic, the demand for the labor to produce it will be inelastic.

Under conditions of inelastic demand, union wage gains will generate little, if any, unemployment. A 10 percent wage increase may cause a few layoffs (1, 2, maybe 3 percent of the workforce). Furthermore, if the union has monopoly power in the labor market, these gains may generate no membership unemployment, but rather unemployment of nonunion workers. This type of union monopoly power comes

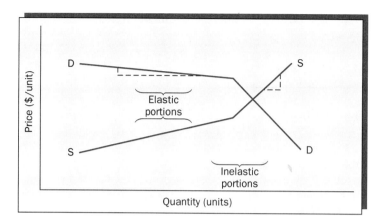

FIGURE 7.2 A demand and supply curve with different price elasticities.

from differentiating union labor from nonunion labor. Unions have attempted to make product markets less competitive so that wage increases can be passed on with little effect on member employment. They do so by actions such as trying to organize whole industries and lobbying for protective trade legislation.[5]

If demand is **elastic,** that is, a wage change will cause a proportionately larger change in employment, the union faces a problem. In fact, under conditions of elastic demand in the labor market, a wage cut would cause an increase in the income of the membership because of the relatively large jump in employment, given that the newly employed were or became union members. However, a union with substantial market power could still get wage increases under these conditions, at least in the short run. They could make an all or nothing offer to the employer: a wage increase with no layoffs. This would push the firm above its demand curve. In Figure 7.1, this would mean a wage above W_u with employment at L_u (or a wage of W_u and employment greater than L_u). The union would not only set wages through negotiations, but would also set the employment level. The unneeded employees ($L_t 2L_u$) would be, for all practical purposes, idle. In the not so long run, this strategy would result in the bankruptcy of the firm. The high union wages and fringe benefits of American steel workers, gained by the United Steel Workers' highly aggressive bargaining backed by strikes in the 1950s to the 1970s, helped push companies like Republic Steel and Wheeling-Pittsburgh Steel into bankruptcy.

Problems of Implementation

Under the economic theory of trade union behavior, wage determination is a matter of rationally maximizing an objective like the income of the union membership, given some constraints on employment maintenance and avoidance of wage cuts. However, like all theories based on rational economic actions, implementing the wage policy theory is not without problems.

The first problem is definitional. If the union maximizes the income of its membership, how are we to define membership? Does the membership include presently employed members, or all present members? Does it include future members? There is a tradeoff between maximizing for present members and union growth, a point examined earlier. In economic theory, short-run actions (involving present members) are important, but the theory really works in the longer run (involving future members). Defining membership is a real problem in this sense.

Another problem relates to the simplifying assumption (or definition) of fringe benefits. If fringe benefits are assumed to be a given proportion of wages, **nonmonetary union goals** have no place in the model. Yet seniority, grievance procedures, and work rules are important subjects in collective bargaining.

Related to these omitted nonmonetary concerns is the subject of union security, a serious omission. Although unions may trade off a portion of a wage increase for a security arrangement (compulsory membership) like the union shop, the economic theory only treats wage–employment tradeoffs. Union security enhances union power, and union power (market power) is an important element in the economic theory of union wage policy.

A much debated problem with the economic theory centers on the demand curve for labor services, primarily the recognition of the employment effect by a union.[6] Dunlop's approach assumes that unions are not only aware of the labor market demand curve they face, but also have some feeling for the curve's elasticity. That is, they are assumed to have a feeling for the magnitude of the wage–employment tradeoff.

Arthur Ross brought up several other problems in his work, *Trade Union Wage Policy*.[7] His observations are discussed in the following section.

The Political Theory: A Matter of Comparison

The **political theory of union wage policy** starts with the premise that unions do not perceive a wage–employment tradeoff. As articulated by Ross, the theory characterizes unions more as political than as economic institutions. Union leaders are not economic agents maximizing incomes for their membership; rather, they are politically motivated individuals. Their behavior, and hence union behavior, is based on a union's interactions as an organization with government and other unions, as well as interactions as an agent with its own members and the employer. These elements, organizational interactions, are the determinants of union wage rates.

Under the political theory, union objectives are tied to the success of the union as an organization. This involves success in dealing with government, other unions, and the community at large as well as the firm and its own membership. This approach to explaining union behavior does not preclude income maximizing, for this may well meet the union goal of successfully dealing with membership preferences. The interests of the union as an organization are not usually in conflict with those of its members.[8]

As a political institution, the union must reconcile the conflicting pressures of the groups with which it interacts. It develops its objectives based on what is fair and equitable to those groups. In turn, fairness and equity are based on comparisons. The political theory of union wage policy is a theory of comparisons.

Orbits of Coercive Comparison

In reconciling conflicting pressures from interest groups, union leaders seek a collective bargaining settlement that is fair and equitable. This settlement can be found by making comparisons to negotiated settlements throughout the economy. This array of negotiated settlements in the economy forms **orbits of coercive comparison** for the union leader seeking a fair and equitable settlement for his or her members.[9]

Orbits of coercive comparison are illustrated in Figure 7.3. The innermost orbits contain settlements negotiated by similar parties (union and management) in similar circumstances (same industry, same or similar skills or occupations, etc.). Settlements A, B, and C would be the closest comparisons for the union seeking a model settlement. The terms of those bargaining agreements would be the ones most likely to meet the conflicting pressures on the union in its negotiations. Because settlements D and E involve less similar parties and circumstances, obtaining terms similar to those in collective bargaining will be less likely to meet the interest group pressures on the union and its leaders. Similarly, settlements F, G, and H involve even fewer similarities, and I, J, and K, the fewest.

The union leadership would be best served in meeting its objectives by negotiating a settlement similar to that labeled A, B, or C in Figure 7.3, if the perceptions of the interest groups, especially the membership, coincide with those of the union leaders. Thus, one of the union leader's major functions is to sell the "right" comparison to the rank-and-file. If the union leader picks settlement A as the target for the collective bargaining agreement, he or she must mold the membership's expectations so that they perceive A as a good settlement. This acceptance assures maintaining the leadership position by making the members happy when obtaining results the members expect. This is the political reality in a union.

In addition to molding membership expectations, the union leader's choice of target must be tolerable to the firm. The firm must have the ability to pay the cost of the settlement. If the target settlement involves a competitor, this aspect is particularly critical. Choosing a target settlement whose costs outstrip the firm's financial ability to meet it will result in very hard bargaining. If that settlement can't be imitated, the leader's position in the union may be jeopardized, especially after selling the target to the membership. **Ability-to-pay**, then, is an economic precondition or constraint in selecting a target settlement.

Pattern Bargaining

An interesting corollary of the political theory of union wage policy is **pattern bargaining.** A key settlement or bargain is established, and falls in inner orbits of comparison of other unions, who imitate it. Their settlements are in turn imitated. This creates a pattern of similar collective bargaining settlements that ripples through the economy.

The starting points, or **key bargains,** are usually highly visible ones between large unions and large corporations. Since they get substantial media coverage, their terms are well publicized. It is not hard to mold rank-and-file expectations to these targets. Firms are also hard pressed to buck the pattern, unless they simply can't afford to pay, as Chrysler couldn't in the late 1970s.

In 1988, however, Chrysler was coming off its fourth straight year of billion-dollar profits, and the United Auto Workers union could demand a contract matching those reached the previous year at Ford and General Motors. The Ford and GM settlements constituted the key bargains for the Chrysler workers. In fact, so similar

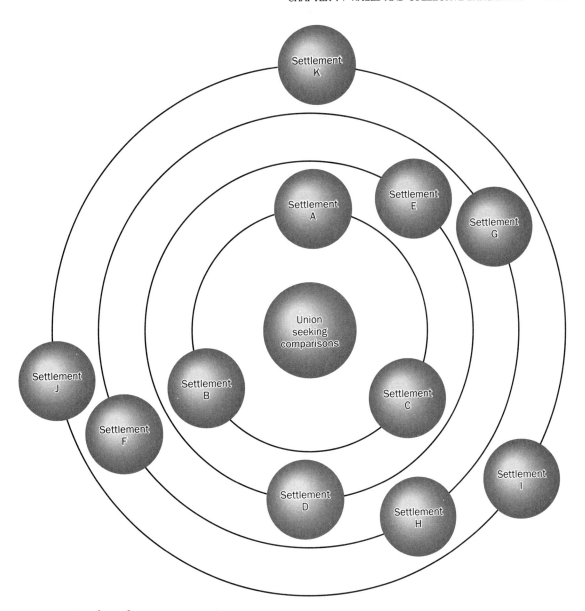

FIGURE 7.3 Orbits of coercive comparison.

were the circumstances among the three auto makers that Chrysler executives had little choice but to accept the contract signed at Ford and GM.[10]

As collective bargaining becomes more decentralized, a point made in Chapter 4, patterns disappear. The supply of key bargains and the financial ability of companies to meet set targets diminish. Fragmentation occurs as specific plants of large companies, treated as profit centers, become the focus of bargaining, generating more divergent and less visible settlements. Pattern bargaining exists in more centralized power situations.

Combining Economic and Political Theories

The two theories of union wage policy seem to contrast sharply in their suppositions concerning union behavior. Is union wage policy a function of economic variables like the wage rate and membership employment, and do unions try to maximize total membership income? Or is union wage policy a function of political pressures exerted by the interest groups that interact with the union like its members, the company, other unions, and the government, and do unions try to enhance the well-being of the union as an organization for its leaders as well as its members?

A review of both the economic and the political theories shows that neither posits behavior based totally on economic or political factors. For example, the economic theory of union wage policy recognizes constraints like no wage cuts except under extreme circumstances where this would result in substantial member unemployment (as a plant closing). This constraint is political—wage cuts would generate rank-and-file displeasure, especially of older union members who typically are insulated from layoff because of their substantial seniority. Furthermore, given the constant rise in the cost of living, a wage cut would be very upsetting to the members. On the other hand, a major constraint of the political theory is ability-to-pay, an economic variable.

The theories also overlap in terms of the short and long run. In the short run, political pressures might well tend to dominate the decision-making process of unions and their leaders. Union leaders may not recognize the employment effect in any single contract negotiation with a company. The union may be able to push the company to a higher wage than it wanted to grant, and to keep the membership employed—in the short run. The United Steel Workers were able to do this in basic steel from the 1950s into the 1970s with aggressive bargaining backed by long, tough strikes.

In the long run, however, economic limits dominate. The survival of the firm is at stake in the long run. The employment effect will become clearly visible. Employer resistance to union demands in the short run, if continually overcome, translates into capital investment in the long run to substitute for expensive labor. The wage–employment tradeoff is in operation, given enough time for economic forces to work. The situation in basic steel since the 1970s illustrates this principle: large-scale unemployment and fewer American firms in the industry.

SETTING THE LEVEL OF WAGES

Determining the level of wages is a very complex and subjective process. Both political and economic factors are at work in wage negotiations. The organization would like to pay a wage rate that is related to the worker's productivity and that is within its ability to pay. The workers, through their labor organization, want a wage that supports their standard of living, compares favorably with what their reference group is paid, and is equitable. These employee and employer concerns are blended together in wage bargaining, with some dominating in certain bargaining environments and others in other environments. Moreover, they are always balanced with the administrative and institutional issues being negotiated at the same time.

Classical Microeconomic Theory

The classical microeconomic theory of wages is based on **marginal productivity theory,** which states that the marginal physical product (MPP) is derived from the total physical product function—the MPP is the addition to total output obtained from hiring one more worker. As Figure 7.4 illustrates, the hiring of each additional unit of labor causes additions to output to increase (1) first at an increasing rate and (2) then at a decreasing rate (the law of diminishing returns). In the third stage, added labor units cause a decline in total output (negative returns).

In classical microeconomic theory, the organization's demand curve for labor, the basis of the economic theory of union wage policy, is a schedule of labor employed and the marginal revenue product (MRP) of this workforce. The MRP is equal to the MPP of the workforce times the average revenue (price) at each point of production (determined by the amount of labor employed).

The microeconomic theory of wages is a theory of market supply and demand. Simply put, the wage rate is determined by the intersection of labor supply and labor demand curves. Synthesized eloquently by John Hicks, the marginal productivity theory of wages is a model of classical economic thinking.[11]

The Demand Curve for Labor

The downward sloping portion of the marginal product curve in Figure 7.4 becomes the organization's demand curve for labor. The figure shows a clear tradeoff between wages and employment: the higher the wage, the lower the level of employment. Earlier, in the discussion of the economic theory of union wage policy, we named this the employment effect.

The classical model is built on many assumptions. It applies to the competitive model, with all its assumptions of perfect information, perfect factor mobility, and so on. Under perfect or pure competition, price is a given. Therefore, the wage rate is easily defined under the assumption that the organization knows its total product curve, based on the further assumption that the labor input is homogeneous; that is, all workers are equally skilled/efficient/motivated. Obviously, the real world is far from this theoretical world.

Applying Marginal Productivity Concepts

Given the many assumptions of the marginal productivity theory of wages, it seems likely that most firms do not know their demand curve for labor with any precision. However, this does not mean that firms do not try to link wages with worker productivity. The concept of **productivity** (output per unit of input) is an important one and carries over into decisions relating to wage levels, wage adjustments, and wage structure.

An interesting article relating to the use of productivity theory posits that firms set pay, a wage rate, for a given job classification. They then hire workers who pass a "test" (which could be an apprenticeship program) that shows they meet the minimum requirements for the job classification. The firms also include a probationary period of employment to ensure work performance meets the minimum requirements.[12]

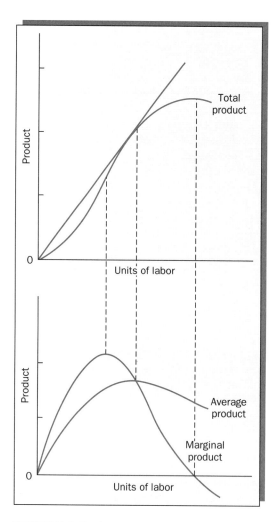

FIGURE 7.4 Productivity curves.

Thus, a ballpark productivity–wage relationship is established, and the heterogeneity of the workforce is taken into account and is actually measured through testing and observation.

The Ability-to-Pay and Wage Levels

The business firm that is profitable is more capable of paying higher wages than one that is not. The ability-to-pay argument of unions is basically a form of profit sharing: a firm making good profits should share this money with its workers, who are a major reason for this profitability. Unions feel very strongly that this sharing is only fair. The concessions that the UAW made to Chrysler in the late 1970s were not granted to GM and Ford, because they were profitable. Higher wages at these two auto companies were reflections of union feelings of fairness. The actual profit sharing negotiated at Ford and GM in the 1980s directly reflected this union belief.

Unions have strongly fought "loss sharing" (pay cuts); however, in the past decade or so, when truly threatened by companies on the brink of bankruptcy, facing massive plant closing and even the end of the company itself, have they come around to accepting it. Again, an example of this truly threatening scenario started on a large scale with the troubles of Chrysler Corporation in 1979. This situation launched the round of concession bargaining of the 1980s.

Unions Address the Ability-to-Pay

The union position on connecting wage levels with ability-to-pay is based on both economic and fairness (or **equity**) grounds. In classical economics, excess profits are economic rent, above and beyond competitive payments such as market wage rates.[13] As economic rent, these profits can be claimed by factors of production that help generate this excess. Unions have the power (compared to nonorganized factors of production) to lay a claim to the excess.

Trade unions argue that union labor is a special factor deserving of a share of the excess profits. Unions believe that their members are more highly trained and motivated than nonunion labor, and thus more productive.[14] Accordingly, it is only fair that they share in the firm's profits which they had so large a role in generating.

Management Addresses Ability-to-Pay

The management position on ability-to-pay is very different from the union position. However, management shows less resistance to high wages if (1) the labor cost to total cost ratio is low, which is usually true if there is a small workforce, for example, in a capital-intensive company, (2) the supply of labor is relatively inelastic, which is usually true for skilled workers,* and (3) the higher labor cost can be passed on to the consumer, minimizing loss of sales and layoffs.[15]

Let's expand on the second point. Since skilled workers need time to develop skills, they are considered to be in inelastic supply, unless there is a pool of unemployed workers in the labor market. Without a pool of unemployed skilled workers, wage increases would tend to send workers into training to acquire the needed skills. Some skilled workers may be drawn from other labor markets, usually other geographical locations. But the shift requires information transfers to these other areas, movement of workers and families (if they have them), and other mobility-shifting adjustments. This is costly to management.

The third point, the ability to pass higher labor costs through to the consumer, usually holds for companies with monopoly power. These tend to be the companies with extensively unionized workforces structured in industries characterized as oligopolies. However, the pass-through effect (price increases), even for a firm with

---

* Gompers understood the first two points quite well, and these formed the basis for his philosophy at the founding of the AFL: organize only skilled workers (small in number compared to the unskilled so that the union labor cost/total cost ratio would be low, and inelastic in supply as skilled workers need a training period, like an apprenticeship, to learn their trade).

substantial economic power, will be limited by the product market price elasticity of demand.* Figure 7.2 illustrates the elasticities of demand and supply. If the firm is faced with strong competition (i.e., lacks substantial economic power), high labor costs, if not shared by all competitors, will cause the firm to become less profitable, even unprofitable, and to lose its ability to pay high wages. In the present environment, where traditional oligopolies (e.g., steel and automobiles) face strong competition worldwide from foreign competitors, high wage rates are being cut and brought more into line with wage rates of foreign competitors in newly industrialized countries.**

The Equity Basis for Wage Levels: What Is Fair?

The equity basis for wage levels is based on two classical trade union goals: (1) taking labor out of competition; and (2) narrowing the pay differences within an organization.[16] This last goal is manifested by unions aiming for equal dollar increments for all members, narrowing the relative (percentage) differences between higher paid skilled workers and lower paid unskilled ones. The vast majority of cost-of-living adjustments are made this way. (Wage adjustments during the term of the contract are discussed later in this chapter).

The equity concept is the basis for the political theory of union wage policy. The idea of fairness is important to unions in a political sense and it has a strong philosophical basis in trade union history. The idea is also linked to worker standards of living.

Equal Pay for Equal Work

The most basic union statement of wage level equity is "a fair day's pay for a fair day's work." This basic goal, being so broad, is not very operational as a wage-setting guideline. However, it succinctly states trade union philosophy, and it implies that large pay differences within an organization are not compatible with union philosophy.

A closely related and more operational basic union objective is **equal pay for equal work.** This is a basic principle of trade union wage policy, especially as a political factor. It has been, and it remains, the basis for the union equity position on wage levels. As an operational guideline, equal pay for equal work is based on comparisons of a given worker in one organization with a comparable worker in another. These comparisons are of workers in similar circumstances, usually (1) in the same or a like industry and (2) doing approximately the same job, two factors that tend to be related.

---

* The price elasticity of demand measures the response in quantity sold to a change in price; if the relative (percentage) increase in quantity is greater than the relative decrease in price, we say that the demand is elastic in that part of the curve.

** U.S. wage rates will continue to exceed substantially those in developing countries like Korea or Taiwan. However, as the productivity differences narrow between U.S. labor and labor in these countries (as the productivity differences have narrowed between U.S. labor and labor in Western Europe and Japan), the wage rate differences will narrow.

If the industry is competitive, a strong economic argument exists for equal or similar wage levels. If the union has organized the major companies in the industry, a good possibility exists that there will be equal or similar wage levels. This would be a result of pattern bargaining in one form or another, a natural outcome of trade union wage policy based on equity. The union or unions in the industry would be taking labor out of competition.

Union leaders would have a clear and explicit target to shoot for in setting wage levels (and wage changes): the first contract negotiated in a company in the industry in question becomes the key bargain and the pattern for all other contracts to be negotiated in that industry. Having a clear and explicit target also allows union leaders to mold member expectations, selling the terms of the first contract to members in the other companies in that industry as a good settlement for them. This is what the leaders of the United Steel Workers attempted in their 1989 round of bargaining with Bethlehem, National, Inland, and Armco; the first settlement with Bethlehem Steel set the pattern for the terms of the other three.[17]

If other companies in the industry lack the ability to pay wages at the level negotiated with the first company, union leaders have to be careful in molding member expectations based on that first contract. If it can't be repeated at other companies, the leaders may be in big trouble. Or, if "external shocks" occur, such as foreign and/or nonunionized competition, concessions may have to be made to weaker companies in the industry. This is what happened in the auto and steel industries, to name but two examples, in the 1980s. The patterns broke down, and bargaining involved a whole array of concessions by the unions in these (and other) industries. In transportation, primarily trucking and airlines, the pattern breakdown and concessions occurred as the extent of unionization in the industries fell, owing to deregulation spawning substantial nonunion domestic competition. Table 7.1 presents a comparison of the equity basis for setting the level of wages, and the first two bases (the microeconomic theory of marginal productivity and ability-to-pay).

Before moving on to another concept related to equity that unions espouse, we should include a brief note on managerial equity bases for setting wage levels. Management's basis for comparisons consists primarily of external wage surveys, as

Table 7.1 *Bases for Setting the Level of Wages*

Basis	Theoretical Objective	Value to Parties
Microeconomic theory (marginal product)	Economic efficiency	Wage maximizes economic welfare
Ability-to-pay	Economic affordability and fairness (sharing)	Firms can pay, labor shares in excess profits
"A fair day's pay for a fair day's work"	Equity	Not an operational concept
Equal pay for equal work	Equity	Takes labor out of competition

discussed in Chapter 6, and internal job evaluations. Conceptually, wage surveys are akin to union comparisons. They are pointed to setting the level of wages for a given job based on levels paid by other firms in similar situations (e.g., geographic area and industry). Job evaluations are internal organizational instruments that try to set wage levels for a job based on various characteristics required of the worker doing that job. However, as job evaluations are more applicable to wage structure than to wage level, they will be discussed in the wage structure section of this chapter.

Wage Levels and the Standard of Living

The last level-of-wage concept related to equity we will discuss is the **standard of living** concept. Trade unions, especially in the first half century of the AFL's existence (1886 to about 1940), aimed much of their efforts at elevating workers' pay to the point where they could enter the mainstream middle class of America, in an economic sense. They were very successful in this endeavor. Since World War II, most union members have ascended to the middle class, and union pay scales still assure them of a standard of living above the modest but adequate level defined by the federal government.[18]

Basic standard of living needs are now of little concern to most union members; instead, their concern is with maintaining the standard of living they have attained. This has more to do with keeping up with the increasing cost of living, which has more to do with wage adjustments than setting the level of wages. We turn to that subject now.

WAGE ADJUSTMENTS DURING THE TERM OF THE CONTRACT

When trade unions are preparing to negotiate another collective bargaining contract, one of their major concerns centers on establishing **wage adjustments** over the term of that contract. This concern will be greater, the greater (1) the duration of the contract and (2) the economic uncertainty during that duration, especially uncertainty related to inflation. With regard to the first factor, in the private sector the contract is usually for about three years, and so the discussion will assume approximately a three-year contract.

Most contracts use one or a combination of three popular adjustment mechanisms:

1. The negotiated annual wage increment.*
2. The automatic cost-of-living adjustment or escalator clause.
3. The wage reopener.

---

* Many companies are pushing for annual lump-sum payments that do not increase the wage base, which wage rate increases do, and thus will not add to fringe benefits pegged to wages or generate larger dollar raises for a given percent raise in the future (*Wall Street Journal*, November 3, 1988, p. A2; June 29, 1988, p. 1).

Negotiated Annual Wage Increments

The **annual wage increment,*** sometimes called the **annual improvement factor,** has been a fixture in trade union contracts for many years. It is a negotiated change in wage rates that will go into effect for the first year of the contract, the second (for a two-year contract), the second and third (for a three-year contract), and so on.

A Historical Perspective

In the early postwar period, the annual wage rate increases were linked to productivity increases, particularly in the large mass-production industries that dealt with large industrial unions. In that period, annual productivity increases were averaging over 5 percent in these industries. Unfortunately, the 1950s also introduced a continuous inflation of the general price level, even during the two recessions of that decade.** So the wage increases were linked to escalator clauses (cost-of-living adjustments, discussed later in this chapter).

The linkage to productivity gains assured the labor force a share in that increase, without, theoretically, causing unit labor costs to increase. If the percentage increase in wages doesn't exceed the percentage increase in productivity, unit labor costs won't increase. For example, if wages (hourly labor cost) go up 5 percent, and productivity (hourly labor output) increases by 5 percent, the labor cost per unit stays the same.

The inflationary pressures of the 1950s and 1970s, accompanied by a decrease in productivity gains (especially in the 1970s), caused increases in wage rates, particularly union wage rates, and higher unit labor costs.[19] These spurts have been called **wage–price spirals,** and they worked this way: the annual improvement factor raised wages in an attempt to keep up with prices, which then spurted ahead, supposedly propelled by rising costs partially attributable to the overly generous wage increases, which in turn caused wages to spurt again to keep up with prices, and so on. Figure 7.5 illustrates this spiral.

Annual Improvement Factors Today

In the 1980s, the increased foreign and domestic competition forced many firms, primarily unionized firms, to seek cuts in labor costs. Annual wage increments, no longer linked to productivity, were prime targets. A substantial number of firms substituted lump-sum payments for wage increases. This kept wage rates down, lowering future labor costs and economic supplements tied to wage rates. At many of

---

* Many companies are still negotiating wage cuts (concessions). In the heavy bargaining year of 1988, Safeway Stores in Oklahoma and Kansas City got a $2.50/hour (20 percent) wage "rollback" from the United Food & Commercial Workers; Uniroyal Goodrich Tire got a $0.63/hour pay cut (and other concessions) at its Eau Claire, Wisconsin plant from the United Rubber Workers; and the Teamsters' trucking contract with Trucking Management, Inc., has provisions allowing for 15 percent wage cuts in exchange for stock at weaker companies if these weaker companies need the cuts to remain in business and maintain employment (*Wall Street Journal*, November 3, 1988, p. A2; June 29, 1988, p. 1, and *Business Week*, March 21, 1988, p. 90).

** During the troughs of the two recessions (1954 and 1958), inflation of the general price level occurred, marking a major deviation from prior economic recessions which were accompanied by *deflation;* this "deviation" still holds true.

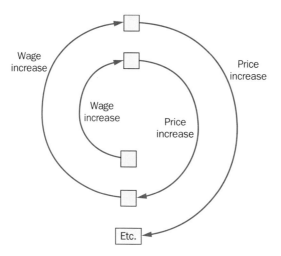

FIGURE 7.5 The wage-price spiral.

the hardest hit firms, wage increments turned to wage cuts, as concession bargaining took hold.

Overall, average annual wage increases in collective bargaining fell to record low levels: 1.8 percent per year in 1986 negotiations (1.2 percent for the first year of the contract), 2.1 percent in 1987 (2.2 percent for the first year), and 2.4 percent in 1988 (2.6 percent for the first year).[20] Furthermore, in the late 1980s the United Food and Commercial Workers and the United Rubber Workers granted pay cuts, with the Teamsters contract set up to grant pay cuts if weaker companies in the trucking industry asked for them.[21] Thus, in several instances improvement factors are becoming negative and might better be termed survival factors.

Cost-of-Living Adjustments

Cost-of-living adjustment (COLA) or **escalator clauses** are automatic wage rate adjustments. They index the wage rate to the rate of inflation, which is usually measured by the **Consumer Price Index** (see Figure 6.3, Ch. 6).

Price index adjustments in collective bargaining have been used for over 70 years in negotiations, but they were first used to automatically adjust wages based on changes in the CPI in the 1948 GM–UAW contract.[22] The drop in the general price level in the 1949 recession caused the UAW to oppose a COLA in its 1950 negotiations with GM, but when GM tied the annual improvement factor to the COLA, the UAW bought it in a five-year contract.[23] This historic contract popularized the COLA, and soon it became a standard feature of most contracts with durations of two or more years.[24]

In an era of ever-present inflation (the 1950s to the present), a COLA is a straightforward way to protect the purchasing power of workers' wages. As contract negotiations become more complex and expensive, a COLA, by decreasing the uncertainty of longer contract durations, is a benefit to both union and management.

How COLAs Work

A COLA is usually set up to adjust wage rates *periodically*, typically on a *quarterly basis*. A *formula* is utilized to increase wages, usually by a given number of cents per hours for every percentage point change in the *price index*. The most commonly used index is the CPI.

For example, assume the average wage rate in an organization is $8.50 per hour. The CPI in January 1989 was 121.1 (1982–1984 = 100).[25] A 1 percent increase in the average wage would be 8.5 cents. A one-point rise in the CPI would be about 0.83 percent (1/1.211). Thus, a one-point CPI increase should be matched by about a 7 cents per hour wage rate increase (8.5 cents/1.211 or 8.5 cents 3 0.83) to maintain average real wages, or purchasing power, of the workers at the January 1989 level.

The escalator clause in the contract (signed, let's say, on January 31, 1989) might specify that wages will increase 7 cents per hour for every one-point increase in the CPI, adjusted quarterly and rounded off to the nearest cent. In April, the CPI was at 123.1, a 2.0 point jump (123.1 2 121 .1). This would signify a quarterly wage increase of 14 cents per hour (2.0 points 3 7 c ents). No roundoff is needed for the quarterly wage increase. This would give a full adjustment of purchasing power, maintaining real wages at the January 1989 level.

COLA Caps

In addition to the formula, price index, and timing of adjustments, many COLAs have caps. A cap specifies the maximum wage adjustment (COLA payment) that will be made. In a period of inflationary uncertainty, management may want to protect against unexpectedly high inflation causing unexpectedly high wages. If the union, for one reason or another, agrees to a cap, management can plan for the future with labor cost, at the maximum, calculated using the wage rate with the COLA increase capped out at the agreed upon figure.

Going back to our example above, we see that the formula matches a one-point increase in the CPI with a 7 cents per hour wage rate increase. Now assume that quarterly adjustments are capped at 15 cents per hour. If the CPI increased from the January level of 121.1 to a level of 123.4 in April (instead of 123.1), an uncapped COLA would give a 16 cents per hour wage increase. However, with the 15 cent cap, the quarterly wage increase would be limited to the cap, 15 cents per hour.

Another recent variation on limiting COLA payments is to set a lower limit on the increase in prices (inflation rate) before the COLA kicks in. The newest (1989) steel workers' contract with Bethlehem, National, Armco, and Inland Steel sets such a limit. The COLA provision pays wage increases only when the annual inflation rate exceeds 3 percent; if inflation is 3 percent or less during a year, no cost-of-living adjustment is made to wage rates.[26]

In the last ten years, the number of capped COLAs has increased. During this period, special delays and diversions of COLA payments have also been negotiated. Furthermore, more COLAs are moving to an annual adjustment period from the traditional quarterly period. Finally, there has been a decrease in COLA coverage, but this may be reversed in the face of higher inflation rates.[27] These developments are all part of the concessions granted by unions to management, as well as the shift of unions from an emphasis on pay to an emphasis on job security.

Wage Reopeners

Wage reopeners are clauses that allow periodic renegotiation on the wage rate section of the collective bargaining contract. For a three-year contract, the parties usually agree to negotiate wages on an annual basis, or at the end of years 1 and 2. The predetermined date, however, might be set at 18 months, so wage renegotiation might occur only once, after the initial contract negotiations, in the three-year period. The wage reopener clause does not automatically change wages, but only allows the parties to bargain over pay while the rest of the contract remains in force.

A practical problem with wage reopeners is that they subject the whole contract to renegotiation. In theory, the clause only allows for renegotiation of wage rates. In practice, however, if one of the parties wants a change in another part (or parts) of the contract that is not up for renegotiation, they might make outrageous wage-change demands. This party would then explain that these demands might be toned down if changes were agreed to in the other part (or parts) of the contract that they want altered. Thus, practically the whole contract can be reopened for renegotiation.

Under the law, wage reopener clauses are treated as terminations of the wage section of the contract, which would allow strikes over wage issues while the rest of the contract is technically in force.* This would lend credence to demands of the party wishing to make wholesale changes. To this date, no strikes have occurred under wage reopener clauses.

Wage reopeners are the least popular of the three major wage adjustment mechanisms commonly used in collective bargaining.[28] However, with the decline of COLAs and the increasing economic uncertainties of the early 1990s, their use can be expected to increase. Contract durations show no significant decrease and, if anything, an increase. To cope with uncertainties and to minimize negotiation expenses, intracontract adjustments, especially with respect to wages, are needed. It is usually much less expensive to renegotiate the wage section of a contract than the entire contract.

The three adjustment mechanisms discussed above are compared in Table 7.2.

---

* A strike over the wage issue would require a 60-day notice by one of the parties to modify the contract, as is required at the termination of the entire contract (see Ch. 3).

Table 7.2 *Methods to Adjust Wages During the Term of a Contract*

Method or Clause	Type of Mechanism	Basis of Adjusting
Improvement factor	Automatic	Annual increases set in contract negotiations
COLA	Automatic (formula)	CPI or similar price index, using a negotiated formula for periodic increases
Wage reopener	Contract partially reopened	Periodic negotiation of wages

DETERMINING THE WAGE STRUCTURE

Within every organization, wage rates vary over a wide range. This is known as the internal wage structure. **Wage differentials** are based on many factors, including the characteristics of the workers and the characteristics of the job. Another type of variation, the two-tier wage structure, stems from concession bargaining.

Internal Wage Differentials

In every organization, workers will be paid different wages for doing their jobs. Internal wage differentials exist for similar jobs as well as for different jobs. Wage differentials for similar jobs can be attributed to the characteristics of the workers or to their working hours or to the lower pay given entry level workers in a two-tier wage structure which will be discussed in the following section. Wage differentials that vary over a wide variety of jobs can be attributed to the requirements of that job.

Wage Differentials for Similar Jobs

When comparing pay for a given job, differences are usually attributable to three factors. Other factors are rare. One that comes to mind, discrimination, is unlawful. Another, two-tier wage structures, will be discussed separately.

Shift differentials   A worker on the "graveyard" shift (midnight to 8 a.m.) would be paid a premium, additional hourly pay, over a worker doing the same job on the "swing" shift (4 p.m. to midnight), who in turn would be paid a premium over a worker in that job classification on the "day" shift (8 a.m. to 4 p.m.). The further working hours deviate from the norm, the greater the premium would be. A worker on the graveyard shift has his or her life turned completely around, working while others are sleeping and sleeping when others work.

Seniority   In most organizations, the longer workers are with the organization, the higher their pay will be. Since they get step raises, their pay increases even without promotions or across-the-board pay increases. **Seniority** also increases other valuable aspects of the job, primarily economic supplements (fringe benefits) and job security (subjects covered in detail in the next chapter and Chapter 10, respectively). This job enhancement tends to build loyalty to the organization. Another variation of this differential, in craft unions, is the lower pay given apprentices compared to journeymen in the same job classification.

Baseball is an industry where seniority is important. In fact, a study by a Harvard doctoral candidate in 1988 showed that pay in baseball is based more on seniority than on individual performance. The study found that performance is more important than tenure only when management and the player work out a salary through arbitration.[29]

Overtime Pay   In this instance of wage differentials, base wage rates may be the same for two workers, but if one employee works **overtime** he or she will have a higher weekly pay than the other. For most employees, hours worked beyond 40 a week are paid at time and a half (1 1/2 times the regular wage rate), as required by the Fair

Labor Standards Act. It is also typical, especially in a unionized environment, to pay double time and even triple time for Sunday and holiday work. In many companies, overtime is awarded based on seniority, so these two factors work together to enhance the pay of those workers who have been with the organization the longest.

Wage Differentials for Different Jobs

The greater differences in pay in an organization are probably attributable to the requirements of the job. These are referred to as **occupational** or **skill differentials.** Jobs requiring more skill and training pay higher than unskilled positions.

The skill differential can be substantial, and one of the concerns in industrial unions, whose bargaining units contain skilled, semiskilled, and unskilled workers, is this differential. As the bulk of union members will be unskilled or semiskilled, there is a tendency to flatten out this aspect of the wage structure by shrinking skill differentials. However, if the skill differential is cut too much, the skilled workers in the bargaining unit will be upset. They may form a dissident faction and try to unseat the union leadership, or, in the extreme, they may leave the union and join (or form) another that pays more attention to their "unique" position.

The skill differential is based on the characteristics of the job. However, skill is not the only characteristic of a job that differentiates its pay from that of other jobs. Evaluating a job to place it in the wage structure of an organization is a complex task but an important one, and will be discussed shortly.

Two-Tier Wage Structures

Two-tier wage structures are plans in which new hires are paid on a separate and lower wage scale than employees doing the same job but who are already with the firm. These structures became widespread in 1983 and 1984, as a component of concession bargaining. Unions, forced into granting concessions, accepted the imposition of two-tier wage plans as it protected present workers at the expense of new hires.[30]

The Two Basic Approaches

Two-tier plans are typically categorized as permanent or temporary. As most plans are in unionized companies and are set by collective bargaining contracts, however, this classification is not that clear cut.[31] Permanent plans contained in a three-year contract may not be resumed at the end of the three years, particularly if the union can avert a two-tier plan.

Permanent plans are characterized by a permanent difference in wages for new workers hired after a specified date, which is usually the starting date of the collective bargaining contract, and workers employed in a given job classification prior to that date. No provision is made to move the lower pay up to merge with the pay scale of existing workers.

After the contract expires, however, the union may not agree to a continuation of the two-tier structure. It may attempt to align the pay scales and do away with all differences except for those occurring because of seniority. This union stance is in line with previous discussions of the union goal of flattening the wage structure, which is an equity concept. The stance is particularly likely if the lower paid new hires become numerous enough to exert pressure on the union's bargaining demands.

Temporary plans provide for a merging of the new hires' lower pay with the pay of existing workers in the job classification. At specified intervals over the term of the contract, the pay differential of the two-tier plan is reduced, until it disappears, other than normal differences due to, for example, seniority. However, if the merging takes place over an interval exceeding contract duration, a new contract might push the final date of equalization further into the future, making the two-tier plan less temporary.

Problems with Two-Tier Plans

Two-tier wage plans are labor cost reduction plans. As such, management views them favorably.[32] Unions, on the other hand, see several major problems with these pay structures. Early plans, negotiated in the retail food industry in the late 1970s, followed by similar adoptions in trucking, airlines, aerospace and the Postal Service, have been phased out or changed because of these drawbacks.[33]

A major problem connected with a two-tier wage structure is the feeling of discrimination it causes among employees in the lower tier. Working side by side with higher paid people doing the same job, the lower tier workers often have morale problems and are less productive.

Related to the feeling of discrimination is the problem that two-tier wage structures might, in fact, be discriminatory. If new hires were primarily minorities or women under, for example, an affirmative action plan, they would be paid less for equal work. Although not tested in the courts, this structure could present a major legal problem.

Two-tier systems also create political problems for the union. Lower tier workers might well resent the union sacrificing their interests for those of older workers. This could result in a dissident faction within the union, made up of a growing number of newer employees if the organization is expanding, and thus hiring. The UFCW locals probably agreed to more two-tier plans than any other union. In 1989, lower tier worker demands for pay equality led to an 81-day strike against a Seattle supermarket chain.[34] In addition, the lower tiered workers might claim that the union is not carrying out its legally required duty of fair representation, for it has put the interests of the older, higher tiered members above those of the newer, lower tiered members.

One other interesting problem associated with two-tier plans is the incentive they give management to replace higher tiered workers with lower tiered workers to reduce labor costs even more. Such actions have been attempted. In one case, a Los Angeles area supermarket chain began substituting lower paid clerks for higher paid ones.[35]

These types of problems, as well as somewhat improved economic conditions, caused a decline in the implementation and use of two-tier wage structures in the latter half of the 1980s. This trend is shown in Table 7.3. However, in line with Jacoby and Mitchell's findings, the drop in the frequency of two-tier pay plans has been much slower than the rise; management's positive attitude toward these plans will probably result in their maintenance into the future.

Table 7.3   *The Frequency of Two-Tier Wage Structures*

Year	Frequency of Two-Tier Pay Plans in Nonconstruction Settlements
1983	5%
1984	8%
1985	11%
1986	10%
1987	9%
1988	5%
1989	6%

Sources: Sanford M. Jacoby and Daniel J.B. Mitchell, "Management Attitudes Toward Two-Tier Pay Plans," *Journal of Labor Research* (Summer 1986): 225; *Wall Street Journal*, June 16, 1987, p. 1, April 18, 1989, p. A1, and Friday, April 20, 1990, p. B1; *Business Week*, April 25, 1988, p. 16.

Job Evaluation: Toward an Objective Ranking

Job evaluation is the grading of jobs in an organization to rank them objectively and rationally in a wage structure. Many organizations feel that a substantial number of their jobs are specific to the company or agency, and market comparisons are not available to set wages for those jobs. Or the jobs might require substantial knowledge and skills specific to the organization, making market comparisons to set wages somewhat invalid. Thus, pay should be assigned by relating the value of the job to the organization, using job evaluation.

The evaluation is done in several dimensions, with points assigned to each factor and then totaled for the job. This total will give relative rankings of jobs; by using these rankings with benchmark jobs and their pay, wage rates can be assigned. These base wage rates will make up the organization's wage structure, measuring the relative worth of jobs to the organization. Job evaluation to set wage rates is typically utilized in a nonunion environment.

How Job Evaluation Works

In job evaluation, analysts work with the characteristics or requirements of the job. Defining these factors yields a job description. Each of the factors is then graded on a point system. Some common job factors used are (1) the skill required, including education and/or training and certification in the trade, previous experience, manual dexterity, and so on; (2) the effort needed, including the physical demands, monotony and fatigue, and stress related to the job; (3) the responsibility involved, including workers supervised, involvement with the safety of others, machinery and equipment used, recordkeeping, and contact with the public; and (4) working conditions, including exposure to dangerous materials and machinery, noise levels, temperature extremes, and unpleasantness in general.

Once the relevant dimensions of the job are defined and graded, or assigned points, the points can be totaled to yield the ranking of the job within the organization. Next, some wage index must be defined to relate to the points for each job. A common approach to relating wage rates to job value or points is to use a benchmark job with a well-defined market wage rate. Since this is often an entry-level job found in many organizations, there is a large sample of well-publicized wage rates for the job. The ratio of wage rate to point value for the benchmark job is then applied to all the other jobs graded for job evaluation to set their wage rate.

Problems with Job Evaluation

Job evaluation is a relatively expensive method used to develop an organization's wage structure, compared to, for example, wage and salary surveys. An evaluation analyst is a highly trained human resource (wage and salary) administrator. In many instances, the organization will hire a consultant or purchase the package (method) to do the evaluation. But if the organization feels that its job requirements are unique, and they are relatively free to set wages (e.g., they are nonunion), job evaluation is often used. It allows valuing jobs in terms of their worth to the organization.[36]

The use of job evaluation has been in the headlines recently in relation to comparable worth and the issue of pay for women versus men doing comparable work. However, because job evaluation wage setting abstracts from the market, it is felt that comparable worth job evaluation studies are not bases for overturning market-determined wage rates. Unionized firms rarely use this approach to determine wage rates, and the resulting wage structure, as noted earlier, is a major point in collective bargaining.

THE RELATIVE WAGE EFFECT OF UNIONISM

What effect do unions (and labor organizations) have on wages? Is there a union–nonunion wage differential? Research has shown that unions do have an effect on wages, but the measurement of this effect requires correcting for many other factors that cause wage differentials. Finally, measuring the relative wage effect of unions is made more difficult because it varies over time.

The **relative wage effect of unionism** is a complex subject, important in both a policy sense and for individual choice, and richly researched. The discussion below will be relatively brief. The references at the end of this chapter list many works on the relative wage effect, and the student is encouraged to consult them, especially the seminal work by H. Gregg Lewis (1963) and his followup piece (1986).[37]

Wage Differentials Independent of Unionism

In the absence of unions, economic theory would predict wage differentials based on a variety of factors. Occupational or skill differentials exist within the firm, as was noted above. Across firms, geographic wage differentials would be expected, and across industries, interindustry wage differences would exist.

Individual characteristics also generate wage differentials. Education, which is somewhat related to occupation, and age and job tenure (seniority) also affect wages. Two other characteristics of individuals affect wages as well as seniority in general—sex and race. Although discrimination is unlawful, it is still a reality in the labor market.

Occupational Wage Differentials

Skilled workers are paid a higher wage than unskilled workers. Occupational or skill differentials are an expected return on one's investment in acquiring skills—a return on human capital.

A second occupational consideration affecting wages relates to the conditions of the job. Some occupations are inherently risky (protective services like police or fire); others are somewhat unpleasant (garbage collector, sewer worker); still others require long absences from home (merchant marine, traveling salesman). Occupations that involve risk, unpleasant surroundings, and the like, require higher pay to attract workers.

In the presence of unions, particularly industrial unions, skill differentials tend to be narrowed, especially in terms of percentage differences in wage rates. Industrial unions approach one of their goals, equity, through greater wage equality. Thus, absolute wage increases (dollars per hour) rather than relative increases (percent) are typically the bargaining target. However, economic pressures limit this narrowing, as too low an occupational or skill differential will not attract the skills needed.

Geographic Wage Differentials

Economic theory would predict that wages in pleasant geographic locations (climate, scenery, and other characteristics of areas) would be lower than in locations that are not as geographically pleasant, other things being equal. Attracting workers to Alaska requires a premium compared to California.

Wage rates, however, might well be higher in rather pleasant areas as compared to unpleasant ones owing to other than pure geographical characteristics. Cost-of-living differences might account for this paradox, as they certainly do in California's Santa Clara ("Silicon") Valley. Wages are high there, even though the location is superb in terms of weather, surroundings (including proximity to one of the great cities of the world, San Francisco), and so on. But the cost of living in this region is very high. In the late 1950s, the Valley started to develop rapidly, moving from an agricultural to an industrial base. Industry was concentrated in aerospace and electronics/"high tech," which were and are relatively high-paying industries. Thus, the **geographic wage differential** in this area was to some extent an industrial (interindustry) wage differential.

High-wage areas tend to have high costs of living. The cause and effect relationship is not well defined here—do high wages push up the cost of living, or does the cost of living push up wages? These conditions are correlated and yield some interesting intercity/interarea wage differentials.

Industrial Wage Differentials

Pure **industrial (interindustry) wage differentials** should not exist in a competitive economy. They should be differences attributable to skill mix and geography if an industry is geographically concentrated. However, industry differentials do exist independent of skill and geographical differentials, and they are attributable primarily to industry structure.

In a concentrated industry (for example, an oligopoly), firms make excess (monopoly) profits that may be shared with labor. As noted above, in discussing the determinants of wages related to ability-to-pay, unions bargain for higher wages as their rightful share of monopoly profits. In the absence of unions, wages should not exceed the competitive or market level; in the presence of unions, they do. It has been found that concentrated, high-wage industries are highly unionized and have a union-induced higher level of capital per worker tending to raise skills, productivity, and wages.[38] Interindustry wage differentials grew throughout the 1970s, owing primarily to this cycle of unionism-wage increases.

Individual Characteristics and Wage Differentials

Several individual characteristics that affect pay have been mentioned above, as they relate to occupational wage differentials. Education is definitely related to occupational or skill differentials. Age and seniority (job tenure) are important elements in and of themselves, but they, too, are related to skills. Marital status seems to be strongly correlated with seniority; married people exhibit greater job stability.

Some individual characteristics that affect pay, however, are not highly correlated with occupation or skill. These are race and sex, two variables that do generate wage differentials in the labor market. Discrimination in pay (and job opportunities) based on sex and race is illegal, but it does seem to be present, based on past discriminatory acts as well as less, but still lingering, discrimination today. In the presence of unions, especially industrial unions, the differential is less. A strongly held goal of equity and a relatively long history of nondiscriminatory policies have alleviated, and in many cases, eliminated wage differences and differences in job opportunities owing to race and sex. Unions like the UAW have been in the forefront of the civil rights battle for many years.

Wage Differentials Associated with Unionism

Before measuring the relative wage effect of unionism, we must correct for other factors causing wages to differ. Earlier, we discussed some of the obvious factors — occupation, geography, and industry. However, unionism generates indirect wage effects that must be taken into account. The discussion of industrial wage differentials began to address this subject; unions induce productivity-enhancing investment by the firm which in and of itself increases wages. Other factors linked to unionism that have a wage effect include the effect of unions on worker quality and on nonunion wages.

Higher Quality, Higher Pay

It has been argued that union workers are better qualified and more productive than nonunion workers.[39] Besides the reasons noted above (productivity-enhancing investments), it can be argued that the protection a union gives workers against job loss (related to the lower quit rates noted by Freeman and Medoff) makes them better workers.

This increased job security also makes management more selective in its hiring. A marginal, and perhaps even a bad, worker is more difficult to terminate after the firm's normal probationary period ends. The union will require just cause for discharge and will contest terminations that don't clearly meet this requirement. Thus, it is important for management to screen out poorer workers in the selection process and hire only higher quality labor, paying them higher wages.

Union Effect on Nonunion Wages

In many cases nonunion organizations pay their workers wages that are higher than the competitive or market level. They do so to keep their workers happy, to retain them, and to forestall their unionization. Thus, an indirect union effect on relative wages operates on the nonunion side, tending to understate the purely union–nonunion wage differential. These union impacts on nonunion wages are called the threat effect and the demonstration effect.[40]

The **threat effect** is the matching (paying) of union wage rates by a nonunion firm in an attempt to avoid unionization. As wage rates are highly visible to workers in discussions with their friends and neighbors, higher wages in a unionized company can be a powerful stimulus to workers in a nonunion company to seek to unionize. Accordingly, nonunion employers may well keep their wage rates in line with union rates in their area to remain unorganized. As noted in Chapter 1, the primary reason most nonunion firms want to stay nonunion is to maintain their flexibility of operations, not to pay lower wages.

The **demonstration effect** is the matching of union wage rates by a nonunion firm to retain its workers and to avert widespread labor discontent. At the extreme, it may also be a move to avoid unionization, making it no different from the threat effect. The demonstration effect is especially operative when a unionized company locates in an area in which the companies are predominantly nonunion. Its higher, union wage scale demonstrates the feasibility of pay wages at this level. The older, lower paying firms will be forced to match these higher wages to keep their workers, especially skilled workers, from moving to the new, unionized company.

Both the threat effect and the demonstration effect are very difficult to measure, yet they have an important influence on the union–nonunion wage differential. If not taken into account in measuring it, the differential will be understated.

Other Union-Induced Effects on Wages

Several other factors caused by union actions or decisions will affect the union–nonunion wage rate differential. These include the effect unions have on the supply of nonunion labor, the unions' conscious tradeoff of higher wages for nonpecuniary benefits like work rules and union security arrangements, and the concentration of unions on increasing fringe benefits rather than wages for one reason or another.

Under certain conditions, unions can have an impact on nonunion wages through increasing the supply of nonunion labor. If an area has segmented labor markets for union and nonunion labor, and a union can control membership and exclude workers, it can have this impact, as traditionally was the case in the building trades unions. By excluding workers from union membership and having a strong union hold on a substantial amount of construction in an area, the building trades unions caused excluded workers to shift to the nonunion construction market. As a result, the supply curve of labor in this nonunion market was pushed out, depressing the market wage level. This **crowding effect** is illustrated in Figure 7.6. The effect tends to widen the union–nonunion wage differential in these markets, driving the nonunion market wage down and keeping the union wage up. In fact, in all the studies he surveyed, Lewis found that the relative wage effect of building trades unions was greater than that in any other industry.[41]

Another factor that is difficult to take into account is the unions' decision to temper their wage demands in collective bargaining and instead obtain noneconomic benefits from management. Bargaining for added work rules and/or increased job security will require tradeoffs for the union, which may mean lower wage rates. The same is true for added union security arrangements like strong compulsory membership requirements for all workers holding jobs in the bargaining unit or the checkoff (a payroll withholding of union dues and fees by the employer for the union). Besides the benefit of these items to employees and the union itself, their visibility to the public tends to be less than a large wage increase would be. This fact might result in good public relations for the union, especially if union wages and unemployment are felt to be high.

A last factor that might cause the understatement of the relative wage effect of unionism is the unions' concentration in collective bargaining on increasing fringe benefits at the expense of wage rates. Studies have shown that, as compared to nonunion establishments, unions do in fact raise the share of compensation (wages and fringes) going to fringe benefits.[42] They do so for many reasons, which will

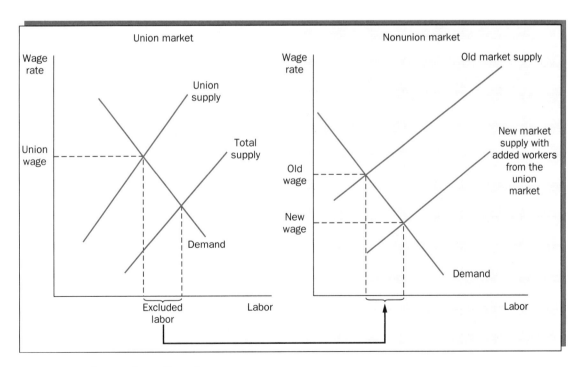

FIGURE 7.6 The crowding effect of unions.

be discussed in the next chapter. But the effect of this bargaining strategy is to bias downward the measurement of the relative wage effect, as fringe benefits are excluded.[43]

Measuring the Pure Union Wage Effect

After making all possible adjustments for the factors discussed above, we can estimate the pure relative wage effect of unionism. Lewis summarized estimates for all data sources he utilized in his calculations and came up with a mean of 15 percent for the pure union–nonunion wage differential for the years 1967 to 1979.[44] The estimates for each of the 13 years are shown in Table 7.4.

Lewis's survey also includes relative wage effect estimates by sex, color, marital status, industry, occupation, region, city size, schooling, experience, age, and seniority. In addition, he includes wage effect estimates from many other studies.

Trends in the Union–Nonunion Wage Differential

A quick look at Table 7.4 reveals that the union–nonunion wage differential grew steadily in the 1970s, but dropped drastically in 1979, falling back to the 1970 level. It was in 1979 that Chrysler gained major wage concessions from its unionized workforce, heralding the start of a decade of concession bargaining.

The year 1983 marked the widening of the wave of concessions granted by unions in many industries. The relatively large wage differential was a contributing factor in the onset of concession bargaining. Larger wage and salary advances for nonunion workers started in 1983 and continued through the 1980s to 1990, as shown in Table 7.5. This trend further narrowed the union–nonunion wage differential.

Table 7.4   *The Relative Wage Effect of Unionism, 1967–1979*

Year	Mean Wage Effect	Low Estimate of Range	High Estimate of Range
1967	14%	9%	27%
1968	15%	3%	22%
1969	13%	5%	22%
1970	13%	6%	19%
1971	14%	2%	22%
1972	14%	9%	22%
1973	15%	10%	21%
1974	15%	9%	20%
1975	17%	7%	22%
1976	16%	8%	24%
1977	19%	13%	27%
1978	17%	9%	20%
1979	13%	11%	17%

Source: H. Gregg Lewis, *Union Relative Wage Effects: A Survey* (Chicago: University of Chicago Press, 1986), p. 186.

Table 7.5 *Annual Wage and Salary Increases by Union Status, 1980–1990*

	Wage and Salary Increases	
Year	Union Workers	Nonunion Workers
1980	10.9%	8.0%
1981	9.6%	8.5%
1982	6.5%	6.1%
1983	4.6%	5.2%
1984	3.4%	4.5%
1985	3.1%	4.6%
1986	2.0%	3.5%
1987	2.6%	3.6%
1988	2.2%	4.5%
1989	3.1%	4.5%
1990	3.4%	4.2%
Average	4.7%	5.2%

Sources: *Employment Cost Index*, BLS/USDL *News Bulletins 81–104*, Table 2 (February 27, 1981); *83–48*, Table 5 (February 3, 1983); *85–40*, Table 5 (January 29, 1985); *87–39*, Table 6 (January 27, 1987); *89–36*, Table 7 (January 24, 1989); *90–29*, Table 7 (January 25,1990); *91–31*, Table 9 (January 29, 1991).

Will the wage differential disappear? First, unions traded off wage gains for job security during most of the 1980s, and this trend is not likely to continue. Second, union-won fringe benefits, especially in health care, have been substantial. Third, union wage concessions are rapidly becoming much rarer. Looking at all these factors, we can guess that the relative wage effect of unionism will remain, albeit at a lower level than in the 1970s.

DISCUSSION QUESTIONS

1. If unions were economic agents for their members and exhibited maximizing behavior, why would they not maximize the wage rate? The number of workers employed?

2. How might a union attempt to make a product market less competitive (and thus demand for labor more inelastic)?

3. Why might a union, operating in a market with elastic demand, seek a wage increase for its members in the short term, knowing that such a strategy will in the long term lead to the bankruptcy of the business? Why might a business be forced to give in?

4. Define orbits of coercive comparison and discuss their place in union wage theory.

5. This chapter discusses several problems with the economic theory of union wage policy. Name two possible problems associated with the *political* theory of union wage policy.

6. Discuss the marginal productivity theory as the basis for wage rates in an organization. Use a diagram relating wage rates and labor employed.

7. What makes the marginal productivity theory difficult to utilize for setting wages in the typical company?

8. Compare the ability-to-pay basis for setting wage levels with equity bases for setting wages, such as equal pay for equal work.

9. Explain how a COLA works to adjust wage rates during a multiyear collective bargaining contract.

10. What has been the trend, over the past ten years, in the use of COLAs in collective bargaining contracts?

11. What might be a major problem in using a wage reopener clause to adjust wages during the life of a collective bargaining contract?

12. What would cause pay differences between workers doing the same job in an organization? Would any of these factors create problems?

13. What is the difference between a permanent and temporary two-tier wage plan? Is this a real difference, given how two-tier systems are established?

14. What would cause pay differences between workers doing different jobs in an organization? And how might you measure the value that generates these pay differences?

15. What would cause workers to have different pay for the same job in different organizations, assuming the organizations compared were nonunion?

16. What would cause workers to have different pay for the same job in different organizations, if one were unionized and the other wasn't? List the reasons in two groups, one for union-induced differences not based on union monopoly power and the other based on this monopoly power.

VOCABULARY LIST

wage structure
union wage policy
economic theory of union wage policy
monopoly/market power
units of labor
wage rate
demand curve for labor
employment effect
supply curve for labor
wage bill
productivity
equity

derived demand
inelastic demand
elastic demand
nonmonetary union goals
political theory of union wage policy
orbits of coercive comparison
ability-to-pay
pattern bargaining
key bargain
marginal productivity theory
seniority
overtime

equal pay for equal work

standard of living

wage adjustment

annual wage increment/annual improve-
    ment factor

wage–price spiral

cost-of-living adjustment (COLA)/
    escalator clause

Consumer Price Index (CPI)

wage reopener

wage differential

occupational/skill differential

two-tier wage structure

job evaluation

relative wage effect of unionism

geographic wage differential

industrial (interindustry) wage differen-
    tial

threat effect

demonstration effect

crowding effect

FOOTNOTES

1. *Wall Street Journal*, June 29, 1988, p. 1; part of the headline reads "The New Focus: Job Security."

2. The economic theory of union wage policy is typically associated with John Dunlop. His *Wage Determination Under Trade Unions* (Macmillan, 1944) is the seminal work on this topic.

3. Richard B. Freeman and James L. Medoff, in *What Do Unions Do?* (Basic Books, 1984), found that unionized workers are much less likely to quit then nonunion workers (p. 95) and are more productive (p. 163), partially because of lower quit rates. However, over time, unionism may decrease productivity. See Steven G. Allen, "Productivity Levels and Productivity Change Under Unionism," *Industrial Relations* (Winter 1988): 94.

4. M. W. Reder, "The Theory of Union Wage Policy," in Walter Galenson and Seymour Martin Lipset, *Labor and Trade Unionism* (John Wiley, 1960), p. 3; Daniel Quinn Mills, *Labor–Management Relations* (McGraw–Hill, 1989), p. 380.

5. Reder, "The Theory of Union Wage Policy," p. 11. The UAW lobbied heavily, with American auto companies, in support of trade legislation limiting foreign car imports, especially Japanese, in the 1980s.

6. Andrew J. Oswald, "New Research on the Economics of Trade Unions and Labor Contracts," *Industrial Relations* (Winter 1987): 33; Daniel J. B. Mitchell, "Union Wage Polices: The Ross–Dunlop Debate Reopened," *Industrial Relations* (February 1972): 48–49, 51–52.

7. Arthur M. Ross, *Trade Union Wage Policy* (University of California Press, 1948).

8. Reder, "The Theory of Union Wage Policy," pp.3–4.

9. Ross, *Trade Union Wage Policy*, p. 55; Levinson, *Determining Forces in Collective Bargaining* (John Wiley, 1966), p. 4.

10. *Wall Street Journal*, April 15, 1988, p. 12, and May 5, 1988, p. 4.

11. J. R. Hicks, *The Theory of Wages*, 2nd ed. (Macmillan, 1932), Ch. VII.

12. J. Luis Guasch and Andrew Weiss, "Self-Selection in the Labor Market," *American Economic Review* (June 1981): 275–284.

13. Profits above the level that is required to attract capital to insure the long-run survival of the firm (this "base level" is classified as a cost by classical economists) are excess profits.

14. Freeman and Medoff, *What do Unions Do?*, p. 163.

15. Alfred Marshall, *Principles of Economics* (Macmillan & Co., Ltd., 1910), Book VI; Freeman and Medoff, *What Do Unions Do?*, pp. 50–52.

16. Ibid., Ch. 5.

17. George Ruben, "A Review of Collective Bargaining in 1989: Old Problems, New Issues," *Monthly Labor Review* (January 1990): 21.

18. AFL–CIO Committee on the Evolution of Work, "The Changing Situation of Workers and Their Unions" (AFL–CIO, February 1985), p. 15.

19. Freeman and Medoff, *What Do Unions Do?*, pp. 51–52; and *Wall Street Journal*, July 17, 1985, p. 6, which showed U.S. unit labor costs in 1984 increasing while unit labor costs fell in Japan, France, West Germany, Italy, and Britain (all with higher levels of productivity gain *and* lower levels of hourly pay increases).

20. *Wall Street Journal*, January 28, 1987, p. 12; January 27, 1988, p. 4; July 27, 1988, p. 16; January 27, 1989, p. A8.

21. *Wall Street Journal*, June 29, 1988, p. 1, and November 3, 1988, p. A2.

22. Henry Lowenstern, "Adjusting Wages to Living Costs: A Historical Note," *Monthly Labor Review* (July 1974): 23; adjustments were quarterly.

23. Ibid., p. 24.

24. Wallace E. Hendricks, and Lawrence M. Kahn, "The Future of Wage Indexation in Collective Bargaining Contracts," *Monthly Labor Review* (May 1985): 30.

25. All CPI figures are from the monthly BLS mailings for Pacific cities and U.S. city average, as illustrated in Figure 6.3, Ch. 6.

26. *Wall Street Journal*, May 30, 1989, p. C18.

27. Hendricks and Kahn, "The Future of Wage Indexation," pp. 30–31; the COLA coverage declined sharply in 1985 and 1986, so that by October 1987, 38 percent of private industry workers under major collective bargaining agreements were covered versus 61 percent in 1977; see Joan D. Borum, et al., "The Outlook for Collective Bargaining in 1988," *Monthly Labor Review* (January 1988): 12. By March 1989, however, this had climbed to 40 percent (*Wall Street Journal*, March 9, 1989, p. A2).

28. In 1986, annual improvement factors were found in 80 percent of major collective bargaining contracts, COLAs in over 40 percent, and reopeners in only 10 percent. See William H. Holley and Kenneth M. Jennings, *The Labor Relations Process* (Dryden Press, 1988), p. 485.

29. *Wall Street Journal*, February 16, 1988, p. 1.

30. Sanford M. Jacoby and Daniel J.B. Mitchell, "Management Attitudes Toward Two-Tier Pay Plans," *Journal of Labor Research* (Summer 1986): 224.

31. Ibid.

32. Ibid., p. 237.

33. Donald E. Cullen, "Recent Trends in Collective Bargaining in the United States," *International Labor Review* (May–June 1985): 303–304.

34. *Wall Street Journal,* April 20, 1990, p. B1.

35. Jacoby and Mitchell, "Management Attitudes Toward Two-Tier Pay Plans," p. 223.

36. The preceding discussion of job evaluation is brief, and further information can be found in any book on personnel/human resource administration, or wage and salary (or compensation) administration. See, for example, Morris M. Kleiner et al., *Labor Markets and Human Resource Management* (Scott, Foresman, 1988), pp. 321–324.

37. H. Gregg Lewis, *Unionism and Relative Wages in the United States* (University of Chicago Press, 1963) and *Union Relative Wage Effects: A Survey* (University of Chicago Press, 1986); see also Reder's review of the second Lewis book in *Industrial and Labor Relations Review* (January 1988): 309–313.

38. Lawrence M. Kahn, "Unionism and Relative Wages: Direct and Indirect Effects," *Industrial and Labor Relations Review* (July 1979): 530–531; Bruce E. Kaufman and Paula E. Stephan, "Determinants of Interindustry Wage Growth in the Seventies," *Industrial Relations* (Spring 1987): 193.

39. Freeman and Medoff, *What Do Unions Do?*, p. 163.

40. I learned these names and their meaning from Melvin Reder as a student in Professor Reder's labor relations classes; also see Lewis, *Unionism and Relative Wages*, pp. 23–26.

41. Lewis, *Union Relative Wage Effects*, pp. 125–128.

42. Richard B. Freeman, "The Effect of Unionism on Fringe Benefits," *Industrial and Labor Relations Review* (July 1981): 509.

43. Lewis, *Union Relative Wage Effects*, pp. 161–162, where the omission is estimated to lower the differential by 2 to 3 percent, depending on the wage measure used.

44. Ibid., p. 186.

REFERENCES

AFL–CIO Committee on the Evolution of Work. "The Changing Situation of Workers and Their Unions." AFL–CIO, February 1985.

Allen, Steven G. "Productivity Levels and Productivity Change Under Unionism." *Industrial Relations* (Winter 1988): 94–113.

Borland, Jeff. "The Ross–Dunlop Debate Revisited." *Journal of Labor Research* (Summer 1986): 293–307.

Borum, Joan D., James R. Conley, and Edward J. Wasilewski. "The Outlook for Collective Bargaining in 1988." *Monthly Labor Review* (January 1988): 10–23.

CULLEN, DONALD E. "Recent Trends in Collective Bargaining in the United States." *International Labor Review* (May–June 1985): 299–322.

CUNNINGHAM, JAMES S., and ELAINE DONOVAN. "Patterns of Union Membership and Relative Wages." *Journal of Labor Research* (Spring 1986): 127–144.

DUNLOP, JOHN T. *Wage Determination Under Trade Unions.* Macmillan, 1944.

———. "Needed: An Interdisciplinary Approach to Labor Markets and Wage Determination." *Monthly Labor Review* (July 1985): 30–32.

EDWARDS, RICHARD, and PAUL SWAIM. "Union–Nonunion Earnings Differentials and the Decline of Private-Sector Unionism." *American Economic Review Papers and Proceedings* (May 1986): 97–102.

FREEMAN, RICHARD B. "The Effect of Unionism on Fringe Benefits." *Industrial and Labor Relations Review* (July 1981): 489–509.

———. "The Effect of the Union Wage Differential on Management Opposition and Union Organizing Success." *American Economic Review Papers and Proceedings* (May 1986): 92–96.

——— and JAMES L. MEDOFF. *What Do Unions Do?* Basic Books, 1984, Chs. 3, 5, 6, and 11.

GUASCH, J. LUIS, and ANDREW WEISS. "Self-Selection in the Labor Market." *American Economic Review* (June 1981): 275–284.

HENDRICKS, WALLACE E., and LAWRENCE M. KAHN. "Cost-of-Living Clauses in Union Contracts: Determinants and Effects." *Industrial and Labor Relations Review* (April 1983): 447–460.

———. "The Future of Wage Indexation in Collective Bargaining Contracts." *Monthly Labor Review* (May 1985): 29–32.

HICKS, J. R. *The Theory of Wages.* Macmillan, 1963, Ch. VII.

HIRSCH, BARRY T., and ROBERT A. CONNOLLY. "Do Unions Capture Monopoly Profits?" *Industrial and Labor Relations Review* (October 1987): 118–136.

HOLLEY, WILLIAM H., and KENNETH M. JENNINGS. *The Labor Relations Process.* Dryden Press, 1988, Ch. 13.

JACOBY, SANFORD M. "Cost-of-Living Escalators Became Prevalent in the 1950s." *Monthly Labor Review* (May 1985): 32–33.

——— and DANIEL J. B. MITCHELL. "Management Attitudes Toward Two-Tier Pay Plans." *Journal of Labor Research* (Summer 1986): 221–236.

KAHN, LAWRENCE M. "Unionism and Relative Wages: Direct and Indirect Effects." *Industrial and Labor Relations Review* (July 1979): 520–532.

KAUFMAN, BRUCE E., and PAULA E. STEPHAN. "Determinants of Interindustry Wage Growth in the Seventies." *Industrial Relations* (Spring 1987): 186–194.

KLEINER, MORRIS M., ROBERT A. MCLEAN, and GEORGE F. DREHER. *Labor Markets and Human Resource Management.* Scott, Foresman/Little, Brown, 1988, Ch. 15.

LEVINSON, HAROLD M. *Determining Forces in Collective Wage Bargaining.* John Wiley & Sons, 1966, Ch. 1.

LEWIS, H. GREGG. *Unionism and Relative Wages in the United States.* University of Chicago Press, 1963.

————. *Union Relative Wage Effects: A Survey.* University of Chicago Press, 1986.

LINNEMAN, PETER, and MICHAEL L. WACHTER. "Rising Union Premiums and the Declining Boundaries Among Noncompeting Groups." *American Economic Review Papers and Proceedings* (May 1986): 103–108.

LOWENSTERN, HENRY. "Adjusting Wages to Living Costs: A Historical Note." *Monthly Labor Review* (July 1974): 21–26.

MARSHALL, ALFRED. *Principles of Economics*, 6th ed. Macmillan & Co., Ltd., 1910, Book VI.

MILLS, DANIEL Quinn. *Labor–Management Relations.* McGraw–Hill, 1989, Ch. 13.

MITCHELL, DANIEL J. B. "Union Wage Policies: The Ross–Dunlop Debate Reopened." *Industrial Relations* (February 1972): 46–61.

————. "Union vs. Nonunion Wage Norm Shifts." *American Economics Review Papers and Proceedings* (May 1986): 249–252.

OSWALD, ANDREW J. "New Research on the Economics of Trade Unions and Labor Contracts." *Industrial Relations* (Winter 1987): 30–45.

READY, KATHRYN J. "Is Pattern Bargaining Dead?" *Industrial and Labor Relations Review* (January 1990): 272–279.

REDER, M. W. "The Theory of Union Wage Policy." In Walter Galenson and Seymour Martin Lipset, *Labor and Trade Unionism.* John Wiley, 1960, pp. 3–17.

REES, ALBERT. *The Economics of Trade Unions.* University of Chicago Press, 1977, Chs. III and IV.

ROSS, ARTHUR M. *Trade Union Wage Policy.* University of California Press, 1948.

RUBEN, GEORGE. "A Review of Collective Bargaining in 1987." *Monthly Labor Review* (January 1988): 24–37.

————. "A Review of Collective Bargaining in 1989: Old Problems, New Issues." *Monthly Labor Review* (January 1990): 19–29.

SHULENBURGER, DAVID E., ROBERT A. McLEAN, and SARA B. RASCH. "Union-Nonunion Wage Differentials: A Replication and Extension." *Industrial Relations* (Spring 1982): 248–255.

SOLNICK, LOREN M. "The Effect of Blue-Collar Unions on White-Collar Wages and Fringe Benefits." *Industrial and Labor Relations Review* (January 1985): 236–243.

VROMAN, WAYNE. "Cost-of-Living Escalators and Price-Wage Linkages in the U.S. Economy." *Industrial and Labor Relations Review* (January 1985): 225–235.

WALSH, DAVID J. "Accounting for the Proliferation of Two-Tier Wage Settlements in the U.S. Airline Industry, 1983–1986." *Industrial and Labor Relations Review* (October 1988): 50–62.

CHAPTER 8

COLLECTIVE BARGAINING FOR ECONOMIC SUPPLEMENTS

conomic supplements, or **fringe benefits,** are the second economic component of the collective bargaining package. Like wages, they are direct or explicit costs to the organization. They have been the fastest growing part of the package for the past four decades, in terms of both dollar value and diversity.[1] Even so, workers continue to push for expansion of the benefits package. This trend has become a major concern of both union and management and a major issue in contract negotiations.

Why have fringe benefits burgeoned over the years? What are some of these benefits? And what are the major issues of contention in collective bargaining concerning fringe benefits? These questions will be answered in the pages that follow.

THE PACKAGE APPROACH

Prior to the growth of industrial unionism, the trade unions in the United States were concerned primarily with wages and hours of work. The dominant type of organization, the craft union, was a relatively homogeneous group of workers, all doing similar work (the craft). Wage spreads were relatively small, with apprentices at the bottom and full-fledged journeymen at the top of the scale. Some structure was present because of seniority pay differentials. But all workers, if they stayed with the company and the craft, would move up to the top worker ranks and earn the top wage. As skilled workers in a given craft, they shared common concerns.

Meeting a Wide Range of Worker Needs

Industrial unionism is very different from craft unionism. An industrial union includes a wide variety of workers ranging from the unskilled to the skilled, and from the very young who can move into an unskilled job without having to go through a lengthy training program or apprenticeship to the very old.

The heterogeneous nature of the industrial union's workers brings with it a very diverse set of interests and concerns. This diversity poses a problem for both union leaders and organization managers: what will make workers happy? The unskilled, with low wages, are concerned about pay raises, whereas the skilled may be concerned about keeping their wages substantially above those who don't possess their skills and training. The old are concerned about retirement; the young are not. Those in the 25 to 35 age group may be concerned about family care, for they are in the early stages of family formation; the younger and much older workers are not.

Because of this great diversity, the CIO unions developed the **package approach** to collective bargaining in the postwar years.[2] They shifted bargaining from negotiating over wage rates to negotiating over compensation structures, including paid holidays and vacations, pensions and health care, income and job guarantees, and profit sharing.

Something for Everyone: Advantages for Union Leaders

Utilizing this broader approach to the economic issues in collective bargaining, CIO union leaders hoped to get something (maybe just a little) for everyone. They bargained to establish and enhance pensions and sick leave, benefits of special interest to the old, and they fought for family health care and life insurance, benefits of special interest to those at the family formation stage. The union leaders also worked to get vacations and paid holidays, and income and job guarantees, benefits valued by all.

By getting equal fringe benefits for all workers, they were in essence flattening the compensation structure, if not the wage structure, in the organization. Overall pay (wages and fringes) was being made more equal in a disguised fashion. Minimizing the unhappiness of the rank-and-file maximizes leadership tenure.

Lower Costs, Happier Workers: Advantages for Management

Management soon embraced the package approach, because it saw obvious benefits to this type of pay structure. First and traditionally the most important advantage to management was the enhancing of worker loyalty to the organization, reducing turnover and the cost of recruiting, hiring, and training. Seniority systems always held this advantage: the longer workers were with the organization, the greater were their job **property rights** or the values inherent in the job. In many cases, too, longevity led to greater wages. With the addition of various fringe benefits, especially pensions and vacations, these property rights increased substantially.

As a worker builds up a pension with a given organization, his or her ties to that organization increase in value. Leaving the job may mean giving up the pension entirely,[3] or at the least, it will mean a smaller pension from the organization as most pension benefits are based on both years of service and average pay over the last several years of employment with that organization.

The most commonly used length of vacation plans also enhances the job property rights over time. Collective bargaining contracts usually call for increases in vacation time as a worker's seniority increases. For example, a worker may be awarded two weeks vacation each year for the first five years with the organization, then three weeks for each of the next ten years, and finally four weeks a year for over fifteen years of service.

The package approach also gave management the ability to provide benefits that would be rather costly for the worker to purchase individually but not for the organization, which could buy them at substantially reduced group rates. Thus, management can provide a hundred dollars worth of compensation for a fraction of the amount it would pay out in equivalent wages.*

Nontaxable Compensation: Advantages for Workers

Workers also saw some significant benefits to the package approach. First, almost all types of workers got something they wanted. What they got might be small in comparison to their wish list, but it fit their needs. The diversity of the package also helped deemphasize the specifics aimed at workers with diametrically opposed needs.

In addition, the lowest paid workers got about the same level of benefits that the highest paid received, which tended to equalize compensation if not wages. This greater equity was not obvious, however, assuaging some of the problems with the skilled and higher paid workers that occur when flattening the wage structure.

Benefits had one definite advantage for the highly paid worker: they were not taxable. A hundred dollars of wage increases will yield an after-tax benefit of $72 under the 1986 Tax Reform Act (28 percent tax rate), whereas a hundred dollars more of life insurance gives a $100 after-tax benefit. However, $72 is money in hand, whereas the added payoff of $100 of life insurance is payable only under the worst circumstances, death or dismemberment. But if the worker wanted to purchase the insurance as an individual, and he or she did it with after-tax wages, the $100 wage increase would buy only $72 more of insurance. The life insurance fringe benefit substituted for the wage increase would be of advantage to the worker if the benefit was over $72, and a benefit increase equal to a wage increase would be 39 percent better (100/72). Furthermore, if the organization could get better group rates than the individual, the advantage of desired benefits substituted for wage increases gets even better.

Fringe Benefits Grow in Diversity and Cost

With all these advantages (summarized in Table 8.1), it is not surprising that fringe benefits have increased as a proportion of compensation. They now make up about 40

---

* This benefit advantage, like that for pensions, has diminished significantly over time as workers are offered life insurance, health insurance, and so on, at low group rates from the myriad groups they belong to and can join through an avalanche of mail solicitations.

Table 8.1 *Advantages of Fringe Benefits Versus Wages*

To Union Leaders

  A. Get something for everyone
  B. Flatten the "compensation structure" in the organization

To Management

  A. Enhance worker loyalty to the organization
  B. Through group rates, cut the cost of a given increase
      in compensation

To Workers

  A. Get something they want in the contract
  B. Get nontaxable increases in compensation

percent, on the average, of pre-tax compensation, and a greater amount on a post-tax basis. Matching the rise in the dollar value of fringes has been a major expansion in the variety of benefits offered. Many of these benefits have probabilistic costs, such as Supplemental Unemployment Benefits (SUB) and severance pay. The organization pays these benefits only if they are used (see discussion below). Some have deferred costs, such as pensions, but require some present commitment of funds to prepare for the future payments.

These aspects of fringe benefits have made labor particularly expensive to have and very expensive to get rid of! Fringe benefits, together with COLAs, have also made it difficult to forecast labor cost for planning purposes. Unions have exacerbated this problem by not only directly increasing fringe benefits and their costs, but also indirectly increasing them by increasing (1) wages, which will increase the cost of benefits such as holidays, vacation, and sick pay, and (2) tenure on the job, which will increase the cost of deferred benefits such as pensions and life insurance.[4]

In the environment of the 1980s, management wrought concessions in the area of fringe benefits as well as wages. For example, the average family medical coverage under an employer-sponsored plan cost workers five times as much in 1988 as in 1980, and it had higher deductibles as well as increased worker premiums (co-payments).[5] Worker co-payments and deductibles have been growing as health insurance costs accelerated over the past decade.[6] Many organizations are "canceling or curtailing once-generous (pension) plans."[7] These and other trends in specific fringe benefits will be discussed later in this chapter.

PENSIONS

Pension benefits are a form of deferred payment received by the worker after retirement, given that he or she has met specified age and service requirements. **Pension plans** in the private sector were first introduced in the late nineteenth century (public pensions in the United States date back to those given the Revolutionary War veterans), when they were established by some railroads, banks, and public utilities.[8] It was not until after World War II, however, that they were popularized by CIO unions. Today private sector coverage is about 80 percent for unionized workers and about one-half that for nonunion workers, while public sector coverage is about 90 percent for state and local government workers and 100 percent for federal employees.[9]

Pension plans come in all shapes and varieties. Even with the passage of ERISA in 1974, much of the flexibility of the plans remains: the law was not meant to change the characteristics of the wide variety of pension plans, but rather to insure that covered workers received their benefits. Although pension plans remain a major part of the benefit package, they have caused some problems in their administration and economic impact. These will be discussed after a general introduction to pension plans.

Pension Plan Types

Pension plans may vary widely in their characteristics, but they can be categorized into two basic types: defined contribution and defined benefit. Defined contribution plans are relatively simple. Defined benefit plans will vary across many dimensions, including the plan formula determining the worker's retirement benefit, maximum benefit allowable, meshing with Social Security, ages for both early and normal retirement, benefit reductions for early retirement, and vesting provisions (given they meet the requirements of ERISA as discussed below). The method of payout of the pension benefits will also differ.

Defined Contribution Plans: Smaller and Simpler

Smaller organizations with relatively few employees commonly use **defined contribution pension plans.** Thus, they make up the vast majority of plans, but they provide coverage for less than 20 percent of pension plan participants.[10]

These plans are rather straightforward, with the employer contributing a given amount at set intervals to an employee's pension account. In some instances, the employee, too, can (or is required to) contribute to the account. The administrators of the pension plan invest the money in the account and the accumulation of capital and return on investment determines the benefit.

In defined contribution plans, the account belongs to the employee.[11] There is no plan formula, benefit maximum, integration with Social Security, retirement age specifications, benefit reduction for early retirement, or vesting provisions. A choice of payout methods is usually available—namely, lump-sums, annuities, and combinations of these methods.

Defined Benefit Plans: Larger and More Complex

The **defined benefit pension plan,** the type that larger employers commonly use, is more complex than the defined contribution plan. Usually, too, it is more heavily regulated by the federal government.

The benefit is determined by years of service and/or earnings; the most common formula utilizes years of service and an average of the last three to five years' earnings.[12] The organization must set aside, on an annual basis, enough money to fund these pension benefits, based on sound actuarial practices. Most plans set some limit on maximum benefit, usually by limiting years of service to some maximum number, such as 30, but some even limit benefits to a fixed dollar amount.[13]

Firms using defined benefit plans can reduce pension benefits by including the worker's Social Security payments as part of the total calculated benefit. This reduces the firm's funding of the pension, but, like all private firms, it must pay into the Social Security trust fund.

Age requirements for retirement are built into over 80 percent of defined benefit plans. About 45 percent of these plans use 65 as the normal retirement age, while 40 percent specify the ages between 60 and 64. All plans allow early retirement, usually at age 55. Benefit reductions for early retirement are usually less than actuary calculations would dictate, and encourage retirement prior to the normal retirement age.[14]

The Employee Retirement Income Security Act (ERISA) of 1974 and the provisions of the 1986 Tax Reform Act have severely limited the **vesting** requirements for making recipients eligible to receive pension benefits at retirement age. ERISA originally required pension benefit vesting by organizations at a minimum using one of three rules: (1) 100 percent after ten years, (2) 25 percent after five years, increasing to 100 percent after fifteen years, and (3) 50 percent when employee age plus years of service added up to 45, increasing to 100 percent five years later. The Tax Reform Act, code Section 411(a)(2), changed this requirement, specifying only two vesting rules: (1) 100 percent after five years, and (2) 20 percent per year after years 3 through 7.[15] The characteristics of the two types of pension plans are summarized in Table 8.2.

Issues Involving Pensions

Three major longstanding issues concerning pensions are:

1. The effect of pensions on worker mobility.
2. The question of who should administer (and control the use of) pension funds.
3. The use of pension funds.

Pensions and Labor Mobility

In the last 40 years, as pension plan inclusion in collective bargaining contracts became widespread, the question of the effect of pensions on **labor mobility** attracted the interest of economists, businesspeople, the government, and other groups. All these groups generally acknowledge that pensions reduce turnover and labor mobility.[16]

Prior to ERISA and vesting, most analysts felt that the total loss of any pension benefits upon leaving the company before retirement kept workers at their jobs until retirement. Further research since the enactment of ERISA, however, indicates that reduced mobility owing to pension coverage is not attributable primarily to vesting provisions but rather to factors such as capital loss, higher compensation levels in organizations with pensions, and a sorting mechanism that draws low-turnover workers to organizations with pension plans.[17]

Table 8.2 *Pension Plans*

Type	Benefit	Vesting	Common Users
Defined contribution	Determined by account principal and yield on investment	Not applicable; belongs to employee	Smaller organizations with relatively few employees
Defined benefit	Determined by plan formula; based on years of service and/or earnings in relevant years	Per ERISA and 1986 Tax Reform Act: (1) 100% vesting after 5 years or (2) 20% vesting after years 3 to 7	Large organizations; covers over 80% of employees with pensions

This question is important from both a macroeconomic and microeconomic perspective, and so research on it continues. Reduced labor mobility can disrupt the workings of an economy. If workers disregard the wage mechanism that allocates their services efficiently, drawing them to growth sectors where wages are increasing to attract the needed labor force from nongrowth (and declining) sectors where wages are decreasing, economic growth is stymied. Workers, acting as individuals to protect their pensions, can cause labor shortages in growth sectors and labor surpluses in declining sectors. At the extreme, individual declining-sector companies may find that their pension liabilities drive them into bankruptcy, endangering the pensions of all their workers.[18] Thus, reduced mobility can have negative macroeconomic and microeconomic results.

The Administration Controversy

A second issue swirling around pension plans involves the administration of these plans. Most single-employer plans are administered by the employer or jointly by the employer and union, using either internal staff or outside specialists. Multi-employer plans are commonly administered by the union, whose leaders usually choose the administrators.

The power of unions to administer pension funds, which may amount to billions of dollars, has led to some abusive and even criminal actions.[19] Several of these actions, dealing with the pension plans of locals of the Teamsters Union and building trades unions, have involved kickbacks to union officials and investments linked to organized crime.* Pension plan administration linked to union corruption (see Chapter 4) is a controversial issue that may continue for some time.

---

* The *Wall Street Journal*, June 11, 1987, p. 2, reported loans to organized crime leaders from the Teamsters' central states pension fund; and the *Wall Street Journal*, June 3, 1988, p. 36, reported that an administrator of pension plans for Teamsters Local 810 and the Sheet Metal Workers Local 38 pleaded guilty to racketeering and tax evasion, including kickbacks to Local 810 officials.

The Issue of Use

Unlike the previous issues of corruption and criminal activity, the issue of use concerns investments geared to overall (and legitimate) union goals and social goals.

Many union leaders have voiced a desire to directly invest the pension plan funds of their members to enhance the union movement, particularly their union's growth, and to advance the social aims endorsed by the U.S. trade union movement. A 1980 Policy Goal of the Executive Council of the AFL–CIO opposed the investment of union pension plan funds in companies "whose policies are hostile to workers' rights."[20] Building trades unions in several states have organized construction trades pension fund consortia to invest in union construction projects.[21] Some unions, such as the International Ladies' Garment Workers, have even invested union pension funds in housing for retired unionists.

How and for what purposes the billions of dollars in pension funds are invested will continue to be an issue between labor and management, as well as the government which sets the requirements for investing pension funds.

HEALTH CARE COVERAGE

Health care insurance, commonly including hospital, surgical, medical, and prescription drug coverage, has become a standard part of the benefit package. It is now the fastest growing part in terms of cost,[22] especially in some newer areas of health care coverage, such as psychiatric and substance abuse treatment.[23]

The traditional health care benefit package (hospital, surgical, medical, and drugs) has been undergoing major modification in recent years. Workers have made clear to their union leaders their desires for coverage of more health programs. The result has been increased union pressure at the bargaining table to extend and expand the scope of the programs.

A large number of organizations have also expanded coverage to include dental, vision, mental health (and substance abuse) treatment, maternity (and paternity) benefits, and wellness or physical fitness programs.[24] One of the newest health care benefits is nursing home care. A few employers have added this option to their coverage, and a recent survey indicates that many more will do so in the next five years.[25]

The expansion of health insurance coverage benefits, in variety and dollar value, has become one of the major concerns of management, unions, and government. Bills have been introduced to require health insurance for almost all private sector workers. Companies are now faced with substantial union pressure to extend health care coverage to retirees; presently, it is being offered by only one-third of companies, primarily as a supplement to Medicare.[26] Surviving spouses have also been included as eligible for coverage.[27]

Cost and Exclusion: The Problems of Health Care Benefits

Recent trends in this component of the fringe benefit package show two clear problems: cost and the exclusion of part-time workers.

The Upward Spiral of Insurance Costs

As the variety of health care benefits expands, so does the cost of the health care package premiums. In the traditional health care areas, the cost of a given level of coverage has been increasing at a rate significantly greater than the rate of inflation; in the areas of psychiatric and substance abuse treatment, costs are climbing twice as fast as in the basic areas.[28] Thus, a major concern of labor and management with regard to health care coverage is cost containment, coupled with maintenance of benefit diversity and levels.

Two common approaches to these problems are (1) sharing the increasing cost between employee and employer, as was noted earlier, through increased co-payments (with increases as great as 400 percent between 1980 and 1988) and larger deductibles—a relatively short-run solution, and (2) trying to lower costs by changing the methods of delivering health care, through substitution of Health Maintenance Organizations (HMOs) and similar restricted-choice plans like physician networks for free choice health plans,[29] and by requiring second opinions before allowing surgery and mandating that many of these operations, as well as substance abuse treatment, be done in outpatient clinics—longer run solutions.

Another solution currently being discussed is a national health care plan. Both unions and corporations are uniting behind this idea; in fact, union contracts recently reached at AT&T and Bethlehem Steel included labor–management agreements to lobby for a national health care system. In 1989, a National Leadership Commission endorsed a major restructuring of the health care system, including a guarantee of basic coverage for everyone. The specific structure of a national health care program is still a subject of debate. For guidance, many people are studying Canada's system, which is privately run but government funded.[30]

Many organizations are introducing and extending other cost-containment programs that share costs as well as try to lower costs overall. Because of the critical nature of health care, many of these programs are the cooperative efforts of both parties, as labor and management jointly seek solutions to this problem.

The Exclusion of Part-Timers

Another growing problem with health care benefits parallels the growing use of part-time and free-lance workers, or the contingent workforce as it is sometimes called. It has been estimated that only 16 percent of part-time workers get health benefits, but they make up about 25 percent of the workforce, and their numbers are growing.[31] Coverage for these workers would add substantially to employer costs.

At this point in time, labor is pushing strongly for mandated benefit coverage for this group, while employers are just as vigorously opposing it. A bill introduced in Congress would mandate pro-rata medical (and pension) benefits for any worker employed less than 30 hours a week.[32] Presently, support for this type of legislation is insufficient to insure its enactment.

The health care areas of coverage, including some that will be discussed later as personal services and family benefits, are summarized in Table 8.3.

Table 8.3   *Health Care Coverage*

Basic Area Coverage

Hospital/surgical/medical insurance
Major medical insurance
Prescription drug plans
Dental insurance
Vision care insurance
Mental health benefit plans
Wellness programs (smoking control, stress
   management, physical fitness, high blood
   pressure control, weight control)
Maternity/paternity benefit plans
At-home nurse and nursing home care plans
Elder care programs

Income Maintenance

Sick leave
Long-term disability

Retiree Benefits (Supplements to Medicare)

Hospital/surgical/medical insurance
Major medical insurance
Prescription drug plans
Hearing and vision care insurance
Mental health benefit plans
Nursing home care plans
Long-term custodial nursing care plans

GUARANTEED INCOME PLANS

Employment security is an issue that goes beyond fringe benefits. The basic approach to this problem is through job guarantees; these are not fringe benefits per se (see Chapter 10). A second approach to employment security is **income maintenance.** Income maintenance plans would be classified as economic supplements.

The most basic and widespread income maintenance plans are the mandated ones. These plans include **Unemployment Compensation** which provides some income during periods of unemployment between jobs, and **Workers' Compensation** which provides some income for inability to work owing to injuries incurred on the job. Many states also have **Disability Insurance** programs that cover long-term inability to work owing to injuries and sickness, but the workers, not their employers, usually pay the premiums for these programs. The Unemployment Compensation program is, by far, the most widely used program to provide income in the event of job loss.[33]

Income maintenance plans that go beyond those mandated by the government are not very widespread in collective bargaining contracts. However, a majority of these contracts provide for some income protection, usually a form of **severance pay** (separation or termination pay).[34] Longer term income maintenance is rare.

In collective bargaining in the auto industry, union leaders have innovated two approaches to income maintenance, or the **guaranteed annual wage.** The first innovative program was a Supplemental Unemployment Benefit (SUB) plan, and the latest program is the Guaranteed Income Stream (GIS).

Supplemental Unemployment Benefits

The UAW popularized **Supplemental Unemployment Benefit (SUB) plans** in its 1955 contracts with the major auto companies. Those plans were picked up by other unions, such as the steel (USW) and rubber workers (URW), in industries prone to cycles of large-scale layoffs.[35]

These plans attack two major problems associated with state unemployment compensation payments, which operate in about the same way as they did when first implemented in 1935 with the Social Security Act: (1) they are quite low, replacing, on the average, 33 to 35 percent of a unionized worker's pay, and (2) they last only 26 weeks under "normal" economic circumstances, which can be extended another 13 weeks if the state's economic circumstances (primarily unemployment rate) warrant.[36] Most SUB plans at least double the payment received and make payments for about two years.[37]

The Evolution of SUBs

Initially (1955), the SUB payment, when coupled with state unemployment compensation benefits, paid a UAW member enough to replace 60 to 65 percent of his or her take-home pay. If take-home pay was $200 a week and unemployment compensation paid $70, the SUB would be $50 at the 60 percent replacement level and $60 at the 65 percent level.[38]

Over time SUB benefits, like most other fringes, have been liberalized. Coverage was extended to more workers, and in several industries eligibility starts with just one year of seniority. The range of replacement levels has increased. In the auto industry contract of 1967, this level reached 95 percent, while other industries have replacement levels that vary from about 70 to about 90 percent, with a small amount deducted for "work-related expenses."[39]

Where SUBs Fall Short

Although SUBs were planned to aid workers over cyclical unemployment spells for one to two years, they are short-run programs. They commonly require the employer to pay a specified amount per labor-hour into the SUB fund, with a maximum set for the fund. Once that maximum is reached, payments stop; they resume only when the fund is tapped and falls below the maximum. They are replenished, of course, at the specified rate.

The early use of SUBs created few problems, but during the deep recessions of 1974–1975 and 1981–1982, SUB funds ran out in the mass-production industries in the face of large-scale layoffs and plant closings. As the total SUB fund drops, the employer replenishes it. In a prolonged period of unemployment, however, the outflow accelerates while the inflow decelerates as fewer labor-hours are being used.

This combination of longer term mass layoffs and decreasing replenishment of SUB funds creates a strange situation. Low-seniority workers, laid off early in a downturn, collect maximum SUB payments for the duration of the benefit (a year or two), while older, higher seniority and usually higher paid workers, laid off in the later periods of a deep downturn, face a depleted SUB fund and collect small or no SUB payments. Older, higher seniority workers usually have the most influence in the union. Consequently, many SUB plans have been changed, with employer payments toward benefits placed in individual accounts, so that an employee has a vested right to his or her account. In some plans, these accounts can be used to pay workers for other than layoff owing to lack of work.

SUBs, introduced in the 1950s and refined in the intervening 35-odd years, were designed as a temporary replacement of worker income lost in layoffs that occurred with short-term cyclical adjustments. These adjustments had traditionally been a hallmark of the large, mass-production industries. However, SUBs cannot handle the longer term unemployment such as occurred in the 1980s, resulting from structural changes in industry and the workforce.[40] A longer run income maintenance solution is needed.

The Guaranteed Income Stream

The **Guaranteed Income Stream (GIS) plan** was also an innovation of the UAW and auto industry, in their 1982 collective bargaining contracts. This plan attempts to attack the problem of longer term structural unemployment. It was a *quid pro quo* received by the union for concessions granted Ford and GM, and, in 1984, a "jobs bank" was added to it, guaranteeing up to six years of income maintenance or reemployment for workers displaced and subject to long-term layoff.[41]

The GIS seeks to provide a guaranteed lifetime wage, whereas SUBs aim at a guaranteed annual wage; if necessary, the GIS provides benefits to eligible workers until retirement.[42] Eligibility is limited to employees with at least 15 years of seniority; in the case of plant shutdowns, however, eligibility is extended to those with 10 years of seniority.

How GIS Works

GIS benefits start when the employee uses up his or her SUB benefits. The benefits are based on both pre-tax wages before layoff and seniority. The base amount of the benefit is 50 percent of the employee's pre-tax wages plus 1 percent per year for each year of seniority above the eligibility level (15 years), up to 75 percent, which can be paid until retirement.[43]

A worker on layoff with pre-tax earnings of $500 per week would get $250 per week with 15 years of seniority (the base 50 percent). One with 25 years of seniority would get $300 per week (60 percent of earnings). He or she would get the 50 percent base + 10 percent for the extra 10 years of seniority, totaling 60 percent.

The GIS plan has a unique feature. Workers on layoff receive benefits even if they find alternative employment paying as much as their GIS benefit.[44] Only 80 percent

Table 8.4 *Income Maintenance Plans*

Plan	Eligibility	Benefit	Duration	Alternative Income Offset Rate
Supplemental unemployment benefits	As little as 1 year of seniority	Up to 95% of post-tax (take-home) pay when combined with state unemployment insurance benefits	One year (52 weeks) for workers with over 2 years seniority[a]	100%
Guaranteed income stream	Minimum of 15 years of seniority	Up to 75% of pre-tax pay for workers with 40 years of seniority	Starting with depletion of SUB and/or state unemployment benefits, until retirement	80%[b]

[a] Arthur A. Sloane and Fred Witney, *Labor Relations* (Prentice–Hall, 1985), p. 367.

[b] Peter Cappelli, "Auto Industry Experiments with the Guaranteed Income Stream," *Monthly Labor Review,* (July 1984): 38.

of alternative employment earnings offset the benefits. Thus, the plan encourages the finding of alternative employment rather than tying the unemployed worker to the company. Because of the long-term nature of the benefits, the company also has an incentive to help the laid-off worker find alternative employment. If the alternative job pays 125 percent (1/80 percent, or 1 over the offset rate if the rate was other than 80%) or more of the GIS benefit, the benefit is no longer paid.

Income and Job Security

SUB and GIS plans, summarized and compared in Table 8.4, are strong income maintenance measures. When joined with the so-called job banks of the 1984–1985 contracts and the far-reaching guaranteed employment plans of the 1987–1988 contracts in the auto industry, worker security against job and income loss is greatly enhanced.[45]

Both SUB, a short-term guarantee of up to 95 percent of a worker's income, and GIS, a long-term guarantee of up to 75 percent of that income, are major fringe benefits in the industries that use them. This is especially true in light of the fact that economic uncertainty is relatively high and will most likely increase as foreign competition intensifies in markets that continually become more global.

OTHER FRINGE BENEFITS, OLD AND NEW

The variety of fringe benefits offered by organizations is sometimes astounding. Some fringe benefits are mandatory and legally require payments by employers and sometimes by employees as well. These have already been mentioned, and include Social Security, Workers Compensation, and Unemployment Compensation.

The vast majority of fringe benefits are voluntary, however, agreed to by workers and management. Some of the major ones have already been discussed: pensions, health care plans, and guaranteed income plans. In this section, we discuss other benefits, as well as recent trends in their use and changes in their nature.

Supplemental Pay

Fringe benefits are normally regarded as payments that are economic supplements to a person's wages, usually for plans and programs that are offered by organizations equally to all employees. However, the government (Bureau of Labor Statistics, Department of Labor) classifies certain cash payments for work and bonuses as fringe benefits, categorizing them as **supplemental pay**.[46] Profit-sharing plans also fall in this category.

Overtime Pay

Premium pay (**overtime pay**) is the first and largest of these pay supplements. In most companies, workers (excluding managerial and many professionals) must be paid a premium for working over 40 hours a week.

This pay premium, which is at least 50 percent of the regular wage rate, is mandated by the Fair Labor Standards Act. In many collective bargaining contracts, time-and-a-half, the 50 percent premium, is used for only the first two to four hours per day of overtime, with double-time, a 100 percent premium, common for overtime hours beyond that and for Sunday and holiday work.

Shift Pay

Shift pay or **shift differentials** also fall within the supplemental pay category. Workers on swing shift (commonly 4 P.M. to midnight, with time added for dinner) are usually paid a higher wage rate than those on the regular, or day shift. Workers on the graveyard shift (commonly midnight to 8 A.M., with time added for "breakfast") are usually paid a higher rate than those on swing shift. If a company operates on an eight-hour day, with a single shift, there will be no shift pay.

Bonuses

Nonproduction bonuses are also categorized as a supplemental pay fringe benefit. Production bonuses, incentive earnings, and commission payments are included as wages and salaries. Nonproduction bonuses would include Christmas or other holiday bonuses and year-end bonuses not granted as incentive pay. They would also include contract signing bonuses.

Newly popularized payments that fall into the supplemental pay category, and are very similar to nonproduction bonuses, are **lump-sum payments.** The BLS bulletin, *Employer Cost for Employee Compensation*, terms these "lump-sum payments provided in lieu of wage increases." In this era of concession bargaining, management favors lump-sum payments over wage increases because they don't raise a worker's base wage rate.

Profit-Sharing Plans

Profit-sharing plans have been a managerial benefit for many years. Recently, some firms have extended them to nonmanagerial employees as well. In the automobile and steel industries, profit sharing has been extended as a benefit in return for cost-cutting concessions gained from workers. However, some of the newer profit-sharing plans for workers are not in exchange for wage cuts, but rather are designed to enhance worker loyalty and increase productivity.[47]

Most of the profit-sharing plans award cash to employees when the company's profits surpass a preset level. Others award stock. In some cases, the cash versus stock is a controversial issue: the USW sued LTV Corporation which claimed its profit-sharing formula allowed the awarding of stock, not cash, which the union contended should be paid to its numbers.[48]

In 1989, the DuPont Company introduced a pay-incentive plan for all 20,000 of the employees in its fibers business. The plan is novel for large companies in that it applies the pay incentives to lower level supervisors and rank-and-file workers, and not just managers, as is usually the case. The program was engineered to help sustain the company's recent high profit levels. Employees begin collecting monetary bonuses if the fibers business meets at least 80 percent of its profit goals.[49]

Profit sharing as a fringe benefit should continue to grow. A recent survey found that about a fourth of employees ranked this type of fringe benefit as one of their top three choices.[50] Many companies also favor this type of benefit because of its flexibility and productivity-enhancing feature.

Leave Programs

Almost all organizations give workers paid time off in one form or another. **A leave program** is usually required to maintain workers' health, both physical and mental, and workers' productivity.

Holidays and Vacations

Probably the most widely available fringe benefits in organizations are **holidays** and **vacations.** As parts of a leave program, holidays and vacations are recognized as necessary to maintain worker physical and mental health, which in turn results in higher productivity workers.

The number of paid holidays has grown steadily over the years. Some organizations give workers "personal" days off, which might include a worker's birthday or just days off for personal business. The median number of paid holidays provided for in major collective bargaining contracts is 11.[51]

Paid vacations, too, have undergone a steady growth in terms of length and eligibility requirements. Not very long ago, the one-week paid vacation, after a year of service, was common. Two-week vacations usually required five years of service. Now the two-week paid vacation is the more common for the low-seniority worker, with three-week entitlement available to many with as little as five years of service (but more commonly ten years).

The expansion of vacation lengths and eligibilities as well as paid holidays was pioneered by unions in the industries that have been especially hard hit over the past two decades by foreign and other competitive pressures: autos, rubber, and steel. The unions fought for these holidays to preserve jobs. As a result of the visibility of benefits in these major industries, expanded vacations and holidays have spread to other union contracts and to workers in nonunion organizations wishing to remain nonunion.

Sick Leave

Sick leave is a common fringe benefit related to paid holidays and vacations. (They are all "earned time.") It is also related to health care programs. Like holidays and vacations, sick leave pays for itself because it results in healthier, more productive workers. Having a sick worker report in could cause a minor epidemic. Many organizations give special awards to the worker who hasn't missed a day of work all year, or in 5 years, or 10, or even 20. Organizations should realize that this worker deserves no award, for he or she has probably caused a slew of co-workers to miss work. The perfect attendance champion spreads colds, sore throats, and what not. Paid time off is a sound investment for any organization.

Most organizations allot an employee a given number of paid sick days for each month worked, which is commonly a half or one day per month. Some organizations allow workers to accumulate sick leave from year to year, while others do not, either wiping unused sick days off the books at the end of the year so that the healthy workers lose out, or paying the workers for unused sick leave. If the workers are going to lose sick days unused during the year, there is a definite incentive to be "sick"; after all, the paid time off is theirs only if they take it.

New Trends in Leave Programs

Holidays, vacations, and sick leave, as well as personal days off if separately granted, are all paid time away from work. As such, they can be lumped together as leave programs. Some companies today are treating all three or four benefits as one.

An increasingly common approach is to combine these traditionally separate benefits into one, calling them a **leave bank**.[52] All leave time is put into a single account, and workers can draw days off from this account as they need, as long as they give some advance notice to management. Concord Hospital in New Hampshire awards starting employees 28 days a year for leave, plus 7 days for extended illnesses.[53]

Workers typically get fewer days off than under separately categorized leaves, but the added flexibility tends to make up for it. In addition, the organizations using leave banks generally allow workers to cash in unused earned time if they leave. Though not widespread, the use of leave banks instead of separate blocks of paid time for sick leave, vacations, holidays, and personal days off is expected to increase, especially as more organizations move to flexible benefit plans.

Personal Services

Fringe benefits in the form of personal services are not new. Given the upward trend of multiple-worker or two-income families and an aging population, these types of benefits are being offered and will continue to be offered at an increasing rate.

Personal services benefits include traditional life insurance coverage as well as newer programs such as prepaid legal services, physical fitness programs, nursing and nursing home plans, and elder care plans. These benefits can also be defined to include family-oriented benefits. As the list above implies, some of the personal services benefits can also be classified as health care plan programs. A sampling of personal services plans follows.

Life Insurance

Life insurance has been a fringe benefit for many years. Traditionally, workers were covered by term insurance annual policies that had only a death or dismemberment benefit, rather than an investment component. Insurance coverage for higher level management was more likely to have an investment component.

Today life insurance coverage for workers is more likely to have protection and investment elements. In a recent survey, almost 60 percent of personnel directors charged with overseeing the benefit programs of their companies felt that a major growth area in the fringe benefit package would be group universal life insurance. Group universal life insurance has both a protection and an investment component. The investment earns at a variable rate tied to market interest rates; this major point differentiates it from the older whole life policies.

Legal Services Plans

Prepaid legal plans have spread very rapidly as a fringe benefit in the last six or seven years and now cover 14 million workers.[54] As the cost of legal services climbs, so will the expansion of these plans. But the increase in legal costs will make these plans more expensive for the employer or union if it provides the benefit.

The plans typically cover basic legal services such as drafting wills, writing letters on behalf of clients, reviewing documents such as leases, and providing telephone consultations. They provide for referrals and discounts in the case of more serious and complex legal matters. The annual fees generally range from $100 to $200 per year.[55]

We are a litigious society, and the cost of litigation continues to climb. These two related facts will cause these types of plans to expand, perhaps even to the point of covering court proceedings and related matters.

Physical Fitness Plans

Physical fitness or **wellness programs** do not treat illness per se, but rather promote good health to prevent it. A recent survey found that about two-thirds of companies include in their benefits at least one health promotion activity for their workers. These activities include smoking control, health risk appraisals, back care, stress management, exercise and physical fitness, off-the-job accident prevention, nutrition education, high blood pressure control, and weight control.[56]

The trend of heightened health awareness in the United States denotes a significant increase in these programs as fringe benefits. Furthermore, they are a good investment for companies. Maintaining and improving the health of workers increases their productivity.

Nursing Home Care Plans

A small percentage of organizations now offer extended-care group plans for **nursing home care.** For most of these plans, the employee pays all premiums.[57]

As the already high cost of nursing home care and nursing services at home continues to increase, and as the population ages, with a greater number in the over 65 category, more companies are considering offering such plans.[58] Extended-care programs can therefore be expected to become an important and expensive part of the fringe benefits package.

Elder Care Plans

Closely related to nursing home care is **elder care.** In fact, most of the corporate nursing home care plans also allow coverage of employees' parents and in-laws.[59] But elder care programs per se, those just covering aged relatives, are starting to appear at several corporations. Some compensation experts claim that "company support for elder-care is likely to become the new pioneering benefit of the 1990s."[60]

In 1987, fewer than ten companies offered elder care programs; in 1989, that number had jumped to 20 percent of all corporations with 1,000 or more employees. Demand is pushing the trend upward. It has been estimated that at least 20 percent of the 100 million people who work have some responsibilities for elderly relatives. The desirability of elder care plans can be seen at Philip Morris Company, where, only one year after elder care services were first offered, requests for such assistance exceeded those for child care by two to one.[61]

A few larger corporations have instituted comprehensive elder care programs that include not only insurance for aged dependents requiring extended care, but also workshops and seminars, resource material, individual consultations with experts, and telephone hotlines to help with the myriad problems that care for the aged brings.[62] Organizations are beginning to recognize that worker productivity can be greatly affected by elder care concerns. More companies will be instituting elder care programs as the need for them becomes more apparent and pressing.

Family Benefits

Probably the fastest growing group of benefits in the 1990s will be those that relate to the needs of the working family. The developments of the last 30 to 40 years clearly indicate that a majority of families, especially at the formative stage (20 to 30 years of age), will have both spouses in the job market. Two-income families are now the norm. If we also take note of the growth in single-parent families, family needs and work become even more intermingled.

Major **family benefits** that will be common in the 1990s will include those dealing with (1) having children (primarily leave programs and maternity benefits under health care plans), (2) caring for children (both well and sick children), and, at the other extreme, (3) caring for aged dependents. Another family benefit, related to all three categories mentioned above, is flexible work schedules and plans, including part-time work at home.

Maternity/Paternity Leave Programs

Today **maternity and paternity leave** programs are quite common. Most **parental leaves** are unpaid. In some states, these leaves are mandated by law and coordinated with state disability benefits. New Jersey was the thirteenth state to require a parental leave option.[63] Programs cover absences of six weeks to six months. They usually require the employer to continue health care coverage for the worker and to guarantee a comparable job upon the worker's return from the unpaid leave. U.S. Senate bill S. 249 (the Parental and Medical Leave Act) would have mandated unpaid parental leave for up to ten weeks with continued health insurance coverage; it died in the Senate at the end of 1988, and in 1990 President Bush vetoed a resurrected version of it.[64]

Many unions have aggressively lobbied for state- and federally-mandated, expanded parental leave programs. They have also sought these programs at the bargaining table. Unions are now focusing on paid leave options, starting with continuation of fringe benefits for those on leave. The Communication Workers of America (CWA) and the International Brotherhood of Electrical Workers (IBEW) made a major breakthrough in company-provided parental leave programs, and family benefits overall, in their three-year contracts with AT&T signed in May 1989.[65]

The CWA and IBEW contracts provide for parental leaves (including care for seriously ill dependents) of up to one year. The leave is unpaid, but full benefits continue for the first six months. Some benefits, primarily health care, continue for the full year. At the end of the leave, the employee is guaranteed a return to his or her old job.

The issue of **maternity benefit** inclusion in health insurance plans is not as pressing as leave, for most companies now offer maternity benefits. However, the issue is important for women who leave work months before delivery, which, under many plans, would cause them to lose health care coverage.

Child Care Programs

Child care is a second major issue for the dual-worker or two-income family, and probably the most important one. Very few organizations offer child care programs.[66]

The major child care program is **day care.** Good, affordable day care centers are rare, and pressure for them is mounting. Workers with babies and young children are utilizing two options to obtain this service.

The first option is through employers, as a fringe benefit. Thus far, there has been limited success in this direction, but some organizations, primarily government agencies, have provided day care services. In a recent BLS survey, these services were categorized as (1) employer-sponsored day care, provided by 2 percent of the establishments surveyed, (2) assistance, usually financial, with day care costs, provided by an additional 3 percent, (3) information and referral programs, provided by 10 percent, and (4) miscellaneous services.[67] The BLS survey results are shown in Table 8.5. A new twist to this benefit is contained in the 1989 CWA/IBEW contracts with AT&T, in which the company set up a $5 million fund to help employees obtain child care. This fund could be used to develop child care centers to meet the needs of

Table 8.5 *Survey of Employers Providing Some Type of Child Care Benefit*

Child Care Benefits and Work-Schedule and Leave Policies	Total	Industry Sector	
		Private	Government
Total establishments (in thousands)	1,202	1,128	74
Percent providing benefits	11.1	10.1	26.4
Day care	2.1	1.6	9.4
Financial assistance	3.1	3.1	2.9
Information and referral	5.1	4.3	15.8
Counseling services	5.1	4.2	18.2
Other child care benefits	1.0	.9	2.3
Percent with favorable work-schedule or leave policies	61.2	61.4	57.2
Flextime	43.2	43.6	37.5
Voluntary part time	34.8	35.3	26.7
Job sharing	15.5	15.0	23.5
Work at home	8.3	8.5	4.0
Flexible leave	42.9	42.9	43.7
Other work-schedule policies	2.1	1.8	7.1
Percent with no benefits or policies aiding child care	36.8	36.6	39.6

Source: "Employment in Perspective: Women in the Labor Force," Bureau of Labor Statistics, U.S. Department of Labor Report 752, First Quarter 1988.

company employees. Day care benefits are on the increase; a recent survey showed that 15 percent of all firms furnished them in 1989, up from 11 percent in 1988.[68]

The second option for workers seeking to obtain decent day care is through their unions. Union-sponsored day care centers have been established by a few unions, and, though not a fringe benefit, they have been used in several instances as a solution to the day care problem.[69]

The issue of child care also includes attending to seriously ill children. Under maternity/paternity leave, parental leave to care for sick children is becoming more common. As with maternity leaves for births, most are unpaid. So again the major issue becomes that of continuing health care insurance of a parent on leave to care for a seriously ill child, as the new union contracts with AT&T do.

Flexible Work Schedules

Flexible work schedules or plans are spreading as firms recognize that helping workers balance family and job needs pays in terms of more productive workers. An increasingly female workforce coupled with forecasted labor shortages will most likely assure the continuation of this trend. Flexible work schedules are usually thought of as a "woman's perk," but some companies are reporting their use by men as well.[70]

The flexible work plans now in use usually provide for parental leaves, some for over a year, with benefits. The worker on a long leave usually does part-time work with the company during a portion of the leave time, sometimes at home. He or she may return from leave as a full-time or part-time worker. Starting and stopping time at work is also flexible, as long as the worker puts in his or her day. Many of the programs in place are geared to professional workers and are found in nonunion companies (e.g., IBM).[71]

Flexible work schedules will become a popular fringe benefit in the next decade, as will be true for most family benefits. These programs will have components such as expanded leaves, more flexible working hours, some work being done at home, and workers sharing alternating schedules or shifts and even sharing jobs as part-timers. A recent survey of major companies found that over 70 percent of benefits directors predicted a major growth in flexible schedules in the next five years.[72]

Flexible Benefit Plans

With two workers in a family, many economic supplements result in duplicate benefits. This has led to **flexible benefit plans,** often called **cafeteria plans.** Under this plan, the employer stipulates a certain dollar amount available for fringe benefits, and the employee chooses the fringe benefits he or she wants from a given "menu" of benefits, up to the dollar amount allotted to the worker. These plans are becoming quite popular; in 1990, 55 percent of the nation's top 100 firms let workers help decide the benefits they receive.[73]

Flexible Benefit Plan Advantages

A flexible benefit plan enriches the fringe benefit package of the dual-earner family. Duplicate benefit coverage can be traded off for new benefits. For example, if both workers have health insurance, and this insurance covers the spouse and other dependents, one of the two doesn't need this coverage. They can eliminate it for one spouse, who can then elect a new benefit they previously didn't have from the menu of benefits offered.

Flexible benefit plans also have advantages for the employer, who can better control voluntary fringe benefit costs by negotiating a lump sum for them. If they offer a health insurance plan as a separate fringe, for example, a 10 percent jump in the cost of the plan forces negotiation on deductibles, co-payments, and so on. Or negotiations on other fringes may become more difficult if management tries to hold the total increase in benefit costs down to, say, 5 percent, as other benefits may have to be cut to do this. However, if the voluntary benefit allotment under a cafeteria plan is $4,000, the 5 percent target is well defined ($200).

Flexible Benefit Plan Problems

Flexible benefit plans are not in widespread use at this time. A recent survey found that about 25 percent of companies use them, but predicted this figure would reach one-third by 1990.[74] Most organizations using these plans have primarily professional employees. For example, accounting firms utilize them, because most of their employees are professionals, and, incidentally, they are nonunion. This reflects a major problem with cafeteria plans: workers must know what fringe benefits are available, and they must understand them. A recent survey of companies found that their biggest problem in informing workers about benefits was in getting the workers to read the information given them. Almost half the companies in the survey felt that their communications programs relating to benefits just didn't work.[75] However, if faced with a flexible benefit plan, it is felt that the workers will read the information, but employers must make the information more readable.

Another problem with cafeteria plans is the more complex administration they require.[76] Different benefits are going to different employees. Keeping track of who gets what adds a significant administrative burden to the company's personnel group. Furthermore, benefit switching must be allowed, which represents yet another administrative task; however, it is probably more than offset by consolidation and control of fringe benefit costs.

A further problem associated with flexible benefit plans is the loss of economies of scale that typically occur when benefits are purchased for a large number of workers. Under a cafeteria plan, fringe benefit funds are spread over many options, with fewer workers signed up for any one of them. With a fixed dollar amount allotted to each employee, however, the added cost of buying the benefits will fall on the employee. Employees will either get a lower level of coverage for each benefit they choose, or they will pay to supplement the employer's contribution to obtain the greater coverage.[77]

One last interesting problem that crops up with flexible plans for some companies that can offer rather unique benefits is to determine how to include these benefits in a cafeteria plan and how to cost them out. Among these companies are airlines that allow employees free flights on a space-available basis, or department stores and similar consumer goods outlets that give employees discounts on merchandise, or a university that waives tuition (or a substantial portion of it) for employees. The first and last example are costless benefits, and the second would be if the merchandise was discounted to its cost. This problem emphasizes the most basic fact about fringe benefits: their amazing diversity.

DISCUSSION QUESTIONS

1. Why did CIO union leaders in the 1950s expand the focus of collective bargaining from primarily wages to a combination of wages and economic supplements?

2. Why might workers prefer fringe benefit increases to wage increases?

3. What might be some disadvantages of the package approach for union leaders? For management? For workers?

4. What are the two major kinds of pension plans, and which is the most popular? Why?

5. Can reduced worker mobility have any benefits?

6. What does vesting mean in terms of pensions, and what controls pension vesting?

7. What is a SUB plan, and what is its major shortcoming in a changing economy like ours?

8. In a guaranteed income plan like that adopted by the UAW and the U.S. auto industry, what incentives do laid-off workers and management have to seek and get employment?

9. For both employees and employers, give two reasons why profit-sharing plans should be popular.

10. What traditional programs relating to earned time are usually lumped together in a leave program like a leave bank?

11. Why is elder care becoming an important issue in fringe benefit discussions, and what are some of the specific programs that fall under the category of elder care?

12. Family care benefits are growing rapidly. Why? What are some examples of these types of benefits?

13. What is a fringe benefit cafeteria plan? Do you think it will become popular? Why?

14. Describe four fringe benefits that particularly appeal to a company's newest employees; to family formation-age employees; and to the oldest employees. Which group of plans do you think is most costly to the employer?

15. Give three examples from this chapter that demonstrate a trend toward increased flexibility in fringe benefit programs.

VOCABULARY LIST

economic supplements/fringe benefits

package approach

property rights

pension plans

defined contribution pension plan

defined benefit pension plan

vesting

labor mobility

health care insurance

employment security

income maintenance

Unemployment Compensation

Workers Compensation

Disability Insurance

severance pay

guaranteed annual wage

Supplemental Unemployment Benefit (SUB) plan

Guaranteed Income Stream (GIS) plan

parental leave

maternity benefit

supplemental pay

premium pay or overtime pay

shift pay or shift differentials

nonproduction bonuses

lump-sum payments

profit-sharing plan

leave program

holiday

vacation

sick leave

leave bank

personal services benefits

life insurance

prepaid legal plan

physical fitness/wellness program

nursing home care

elder care

family benefits

maternity and paternity leave

flexible work schedules

flexible benefit plan (cafeteria plan)   day care

child care

FOOTNOTES

1. In 1986, employee benefits were 39.3 percent of payroll costs, a new high (*Wall Street Journal*, January 26, 1988, p. 1); from September 1987 to September 1988 they increased 7 percent, over twice the rate of increase of wages and salaries (*Wall Street Journal*, January 11, 1989, p. B10).

2. Jack Barbash, "The Theory of Industrial Unionism" (p. 650) and Irving Bernstein, "The Historical Significance of the CIO" (p. 660), *Proceedings of the 1985 Spring Meeting* (Industrial Relations Research Association, April 18–19, 1985). Since the late 1930s, certain fringe benefits have been and are mandated by the government, and include legally required contributions to Social Security, Unemployment Compensation, and Workers Compensation; these made up about one-third of fringes in 1986. See Olivia S. Mitchell, "Employee Benefits in the U.S. Labor Market," *Proceedings of the Fortieth Annual Meeting* (Industrial Relations Research Association, December 28–30, 1987), p. 213.

3. Prior to the 1974 Employee Retirement Income Security Act (ERISA), few organizations vested pensions (see the section on pensions in this chapter).

4. Richard B. Freeman, "The Effect of Unionism on Fringe Benefits," *Industrial and Labor Relations Review* (July 1981): 490 and 492–493.

5. *Wall Street Journal*, July 12, 1988, p. 1, and August 11, 1988, p. 25; *Business Week*, August 8, 1988, p. 18 (which notes that the average employee premium for family coverage jumped from $97 in 1980 to $484 in 1988, with higher deductibles and less tax advantages due to the Tax Reform Act of 1986), and October 31, 1988, p. 120.

6. John T. Dunlop, "The Changing Health Care System," *Proceedings of the 1987 Spring Meeting* (Industrial Relations Research Association, April 29–May 1, 1987), p. 526.

7. *Wall Street Journal*, August 26, 1987, p. 1.

8. Steven G. Allen and Robert L. Clark, "Pensions and Firm Performance," in Morris M. Kleiner et al., eds., *Human Resources and the Performance of the Firm* (Industrial Relations Research Association, 1987), p. 196.

9. Ibid., pp. 196 and 198; in medium and large firms, pension coverage was 81 percent of all employees in 1989 (BLS *News Bulletin USDL–90–160*, "Employee Benefits Focus on Family Concerns in 1989," March 30, 1990).

10. Allen and Clark, "Pensions and Firm Performance."

11. Ibid., p. 203.

12. Ibid., p. 204.

13. Ibid., pp. 205–206.

14. *Wall Street Journal*, January 3, 1989, p. B1.

15. Commerce Clearing House, *Tax Reform Act of 1986* (1986), pp. 471–472 (paragraph 3161); these rules apply to single-employer plans. Multi-employer plans must vest unionized employees 100 percent after ten years, and nonunion employees must be vested under one of the two rules used for single-employer plans; see also Avy D. Graham, "How Has Vesting Changed Since Passage of Employee Retirement Income Security Act?," *Monthly Labor Review* (August 1988): 20.

16. Steven G. Allen et al., "Why Do Pensions Reduce Mobility?," *Proceedings of the Fortieth Annual Meeting* (Industrial Relations Research Association, December 28–30, 1987), p. 204; see also, Allen and Clark, "Pensions and Firm Performance," p. 223.

17. Allen et al., "Why Do Pensions Reduce Mobility?," pp. 211–212.

18. ERISA created the Pension Benefit Guaranty Corporation (PBGC) to "pick up coverage when a member's pension plan goes broke" (*Wall Street Journal*, August 26, 1987, p. 1), but the PBGC is in financial trouble owing to some large pension plan liabilities with which it has been saddled (*Wall Street Journal*, August 1, 1985, p. 42, and June 23, 1988). However, some covered companies have been able to switch pension plans, cutting their costs but reducing pensions for their workers (*Wall Street Journal*, March 26, 1986, p. 31; July 22, 1988, pp. 21 and 31).

19. Private trusteed pension funds had assets of $1.7 trillion in 1989 (*New York Times*, August 3, 1989, p. A8); estimates of the funds in private and government pension plans were as high as $2 trillion in 1987 (*Wall Street Journal*, August 26, 1987, p. 1).

20. Richard B. Freeman and James L. Medoff, *What Do Unions Do?* (Basic Books, 1984), p. 75.

21. Ibid., pp. 75–76; all these investments have met the legal requirements of ERISA relating to sound investment of workers' pension funds.

22. *Wall Street Journal*, April 22, 1988 (a special section on Medicine and Health), p. 22R, notes that 98 percent of all companies in its sample provide hospital, surgical, medical, and major medical coverage, at an average cost of over $1,600 per year (almost 16 percent of the cost of all benefits). A survey of small businesses in June 1988 ranked soaring health insurance rates as their number one problem (*Wall Street Journal*, December 6, 1988, p. B1). A 21.5 percent increase in medical-benefit costs was predicted for 1989 (*Wall Street Journal*, October 25, 1988, p. A1).

23. *Wall Street Journal*, December 20, 1988, p. B1; December 27, 1988, p. A1.

24. Richard F. O'Brien, "Health Care Cost Containment: An Employer's Perspective," *Proceedings of the 1985 Spring Meeting* (Industrial Relations Research Association, April 18–19, 1985), p. 470, and *Wall Street Journal*, April 22, 1988, pp. 22R–23R, where it is noted that over one-half the sample had dental coverage, over 60 percent had maternity/paternity benefits, and "wellness" or preventative programs (including smoking control, stress management, and weight control) were found in about two-thirds of "the nation's working sites with fifty or more

workers"; dental coverage especially has grown, with 68 percent of full-time employees in medium and large firms participating in employer-financed plans in 1986. See Rita S. Jain, "Employer-Sponsored Dental Insurance Eases the Pain," *Monthly Labor Review* (October 1988): 18.

25. *Wall Street Journal*, June 30, 1988, p. 23.

26. *Wall Street Journal*, April 22, 1988, p. 22R. (The average cost of retiree coverage in the sample was less than 10 percent of the cost for this benefit for employees, but it has the potential to mushroom as the population ages, a definite trend as the "baby boomers" reach retirement age around the turn of the century.) It has been estimated that the potential cost of health benefits for retirees is $400 billion, and firms are trying to reduce this figure by canceling or reducing the benefits of these programs (*Wall Street Journal*, December 8, 1988, p. B1). The issue of mandatory health care insurance generated two bills in Congress, the second of which was slated for vigorous debate in 1989 (*Wall Street Journal*, August 11, 1988, p. 27).

27. O'Brien, "Health Care Cost Containment," p. 469.

28. Ibid., pp. 469–470; *Wall Street Journal*, October 25, 1988, p. B1; December 27, 1988, p. A1; *Insight*, January 16, 1989, pp. 54–55.

29. *Wall Street Journal*, May 11, 1988, p. 25; the cost savings from HMO use, however, may be "slim or hard to find" (*Wall Street Journal*, July 12, 1988, p. 1); outpatient service costs are now exploding because of their required use in many plans (*Wall Street Journal*, October 25, 1988, p. B1).

30. *New York Times*, May 8, 1989, p. C1 and May 30, 1989, p. C1; *Newsweek*, August 28, 1989, p. 46.

31. *Wall Street Journal*, June 6, 1988, p. 40.

32. Ibid.; *Wall Street Journal*, January 3, 1989, p. A1.

33. The use of Workers Compensation, especially for the stress-related maladies of many jobs, is growing rapidly (*Wall Street Journal*, April 7, 1988, p. 27).

34. William H. Holley and Kenneth M. Jennings, *The Labor Relations Process* (Dryden Press, 1988), pp. 489–490.

35. Robert M. MacDonald, "Collective Bargaining in the Postwar Period," in Ray Marshall and Richard Perlman, *An Anthology of Labor Economics: Readings and Commentary* (John Wiley, 1972), p. 541; Arthur A. Sloane and Fred Witney, *Labor Relations* (Prentice–Hall, 1985), p. 366.

36. *Insight*, September 12, 1988, p. 42.

37. Peter Cappelli, "Auto Industry Experiments with the Guaranteed Income Stream," *Monthly Labor Review* (July 1984): 38.

38. Sloane and Witney, *Labor Relations*, p. 368.

39. Holley and Jennings, *The Labor Relations Process*, p. 490.

40. Cappelli, "Auto Industry Experiments," p. 38.

41. Thomas A. Kochan et al., *The Transformation of American Industrial Relations* (Basic Books, 1986), pp. 119–121.

42. Cappelli, "Auto Industry Experiments," p. 38; the details of the 1982 GIS plan given in the discussion are from this article.

43. *Wall Street Journal*, July 21, 1987, p. 6.

44. Under the SUB plan negotiated at this time by the UAW with the auto companies, benefits were reduced dollar for dollar by outside earnings (*Wall Street Journal*, July 21, 1987, p. 6).

45. See, for example, *Wall Street Journal*, July 21, 1987, p. 6; August 12, 1987, p. 4; August 13, 1987, p. 4; September 1, 1987, p. 7; September 8, 1987, p. 7; September 18, 1987, p. 3; September 21, 1987, p. 2; October 2, 1987, p. 5; October 6, 1987, p. 20; October 9, 1987, p. 2; October 13, 1987, p. 2; May 12, 1988, p. 26; and *Business Week*, October 26, 1987, p. 32; May 9, 1988, p. 118. The job guarantee programs will be discussed in more detail in Chapter 10.

46. See, for example, BLS, *News Bulletin 88–293*, "Employer Costs for Employee Compensation–March 1988," June 16, 1988.

47. *Wall Street Journal*, October 3, 1988, p. B1; October 6, 1988, p. A4.

48. *Wall Street Journal*, December 27, 1988, p. A1.

49. *Wall Street Journal*, October 6, 1988, p. A4.

50. *Wall Street Journal*, September 7, 1988, p. 27.

51. Holley and Jennings, *The Labor Relations Process*, p. 491.

52. Janet L. Norwood, "Employee Benefits: Measurement Problems," *Proceedings of the Fortieth Annual Meeting* (Industrial Relations Research Association, December 28–30, 1987), p. 222; also Janet L. Norwood, "Measuring the Cost and the Incidence of Employee Benefits," *Monthly Labor Review* (August 1988): 4.

53. *Wall Street Journal*, July 5, 1988, p. 1.

54. *Wall Street Journal*, January 24, 1989, p. B1; July 25, 1988, p. 15.

55. Ibid.

56. *Wall Street Journal*, April 22, 1988, p. 22R; December 15, 1988, p. A1.

57. *Wall Street Journal*, June 30, 1988, p. 23.

58. In 1980, 25 million people in the United States were 65 or older; in 20 years that number is expected to be 50 million (*Wall Street Journal*, June 30, 1988, p. 23).

59. Ibid.

60. *Wall Street Journal*, August 8, 1988, p. 14.

61. *New York Times*, June 4, 1989, p. 19.

62. *Wall Street Journal*, August 8, 1988, p. 14.

63. *Wall Street Journal*, March 27, 1990, p. A1.

64. U.S. General Accounting Office, *Parental Leave: Estimated Cost of Revised Parental and Medical Leave Act*, Report GAO/HRD–88–103, May 1988, pp. 1–4, and Report GAO/HRD–88–132, September 1988, pp. 2–3; *Wall Street Journal*,

July 19, 1988, p. 1, August 5, 1988, p. 38, October 10, 1988, p. A12, and April 5, 1991; *Governing* (September 1988): 66–70; *New York Times*, May 8, 1990, p. A1.

65. *Wall Street Journal* and *New York Times*, May 30, 1989, p. B12 and A8, respectively.

66. Norwood, "Employee Benefits," p. 227 and "Measuring the Cost," p. 6. Howard V. Hayghe, "Employers and Child Care: What Roles Do They Play?," *Monthly Labor Review* (September 1988): 38.

67. Ibid., p. 40.

68. *Wall Street Journal*, December 19, 1989, p. A1.

69. *Wall Street Journal*, July 19, 1988, p. 1.

70. *Wall Street Journal*, October 18, 1988, p. A4; November 1, 1988, p. B1; November 18, 1988, p. A1; January 10, 1989, p. B1.

71. Ibid.

72. *Wall Street Journal*, September 7, 1988, p. 27.

73. *Wall Street Journal*, March 6, 1990, p. A1.

74. *Wall Street Journal*, April 4, 1989, p. 1 (by benefits consultant A. Foster Higgins & Co.).

75. *Wall Street Journal*, July 26, 1988, p. 1.

76. Norwood, "Employee Benefits," p. 222 and "Measuring the Cost," p. 4.

77. *Wall Street Journal*, September 7, 1988.

REFERENCES

ALLEN, STEVEN G., and ROBERT L. CLARK. "Pensions and Firm Performance." In Morris M. Kleiner, Richard N. Block, Myron Roomkin, and Sidney W. Salsburg, eds., *Human Resources and the Performance of the Firm*. Industrial Relations Research Association, 1987, pp. 195–242.

———, and ANN A. McDERMED. "Why Do Pensions Reduce Mobility?" *Proceedings of the Fortieth Annual Meeting*. Industrial Relations Research Association, December 28–30, 1987, pp. 204–212.

BARBASH, JACK. "The Theory of Industrial Unionism." *Proceedings of the 1985 Spring Meeting*. Industrial Relations Research Association, April 18–19, 1985, pp. 648–654.

BERNSTEIN, IRVING. "The Historical Significance of the CIO." *Proceedings of the 1985 Spring Meeting*. Industrial Relations Research Association, April 18–19, 1985, pp. 654–658.

CAPPELLI, PETER. "Auto Industry Experiments with the Guaranteed Income Stream." *Monthly Labor Review* (July 1984): 37–39.

COMMERCE CLEARING HOUSE. *Tax Reform Act of 1986*. 1986, Code Section 411 (a), paragraph 3161, pp. 471–472.

DUNLOP, JOHN T. "The Changing Health Care System." *Proceedings of the 1987 Spring Meeting.* Industrial Relations Research Association, April 29–May 1, 1987, pp. 524–527.

FREEMAN, RICHARD B. "The Effect of Unionism on Fringe Benefits." *Industrial and Labor Relations Review* (July 1981): 489–509.

———, and JAMES L. MEDOFF. *What Do Unions Do?* Basic Books, 1984, Ch. 4.

GRAHAM, AVY D. "How Has Vesting Changed Since Passage of Employee Retirement Income Security Act?" *Monthly Labor Review* (August 1988): 20–25.

HAYGHE, HOWARD V. "Employers and Child Care: What Roles Do They Play?" *Monthly Labor Review* (September 1988): 38–44.

HOLLEY, WILLIAM H., and KENNETH M. JENNINGS. *The Labor Relations Process.* Dryden Press, 1988, Ch. 13.

IGNAGNI, KAREN. "Organized Labor's Perspective on Rising Health Care Cost." *Proceedings of the 1985 Spring Meeting.* Industrial Relations Research Association, April 18–19, 1985, pp. 473–476.

JAIN, RITA S. "Employer-Sponsored Dental Insurance Eases the Pain." *Monthly Labor Review* (October 1988): 18–23.

KOCHAN, THOMAS A., HARRY C. KATZ, and ROBERT B. MCKERSIE. *The Transformation of American Industrial Relations.* Basic Books, 1986, Ch. 5.

MACDONALD, ROBERT M. "Collective Bargaining in the Postwar Period." In Ray Marshall and Richard Perlman, *An Anthology of Labor Economics: Readings and Commentary.* John Wiley, 1972, pp. 527–544.

MITCHELL, OLIVIA S. "Employee Benefits in the U.S. Labor Market." *Proceedings of the Fortieth Annual Meeting.* Industrial Relations Research Association, December 28–30, 1987, pp. 213–219.

NORWOOD, JANET L. "Employee Benefits: Measurement Problems." *Proceedings of the Fortieth Annual Meeting.* Industrial Relations Research Association, December 28–30, 1987, pp. 220–230.

———. "Measuring the Cost and Incidence of Employee Benefits." *Monthly Labor Review* (August 1988): 3–8.

O'BRIEN, RICHARD F. "Health Care Cost Containment: An Employer's Perspective." *Proceedings of the 1985 Spring Meeting.* Industrial Relations Research Association, April 18–19, 1985, pp. 468–473.

SLOANE, ARTHUR A., and FRED WITNEY. *Labor Relations.* Prentice–Hall, 1985, Ch. 8.

SOLNICK, LOREN M. "The Effect of Blue Collar Unions on White Collar Wages and Fringe Benefits." *Industrial and Labor Relations Review* (January 1985): 236–245.

CHAPTER 9

INSTITUTIONAL ISSUES IN COLLECTIVE BARGAINING

C ollective bargaining is concerned primarily with setting the terms and conditions of employment and is oriented toward worker rights. However, part of the collective bargaining contract deals with both union and management as institutions with particular needs that must be met to insure their success and, indeed, even their survival. On the one hand, the contract approaches the labor organization's (usually the trade union's) rights, and its responsibilities and duties as an institution, apart from the workers who compose its membership. As the duly elected and certified bargaining agent of these workers, some of these duties are spelled out under the law (in the National Labor Relations Act and its amendments). On the other hand, part of the contract deals with the rights and, to a lesser and more implicit extent, the responsibilities of management in directing the operations of the organization.

THE UNION AND THE SECURITY CLAUSE

Theoretically, the trade union as an institution is a voluntary coalition of individual workers who band together to bargain over the terms and conditions of their employment. The workers can choose to join or not to join the union that is charged with representing them, their exclusive bargaining representative. A union security clause, mandating membership (or financial support), changes this worker option.

Why Union Security Clauses?

Why do unions want **union membership security clauses?** First, a duly certified union, as a bargaining representative, must act in good faith for all workers in the bargaining unit, whether or not they are members. Moreover, stable labor–management relations may be difficult to attain if union leaders must continually worry about losing members.

Meeting the Duty of Fair Representation

Under the **fair representation** requirement of the NLRA/LMRA, a duly certified union, as exclusive bargaining representative, must fairly represent all workers in the bargaining unit. The law does not require that all members of the bargaining unit be members of the union. Those who are not must still be represented as the members are by the exclusive bargaining agent, the union. Even though they pay no money to support the bargaining and negotiating activities of the organization, the law entitles them to the same results of these activities as it does members. In essence, they get a "free ride." Even union members who choose to leave the union and stop paying for its activities cannot be discriminated against. Thus, quitting the union because of a disagreement with its actions becomes an obvious way to protest.

For example, in a union, as in most voluntary and democratic organizations, workers elect representatives to speak for them: the union officers. They may also elect other officials, or, in many cases, the union leadership appoints other officials: shop stewards or business agents, and the union grievance committee. When election procedures are used, not all members get what they want, as is true in any election held for any purpose. If a union member doesn't like the outcome of a union election, should he or she be free to disassociate from the union and no longer support it financially or in any other way?

Again, the union negotiates with the employer to set the terms and conditions of employment. If a union member doesn't like the collective bargaining agreement negotiated by the union with management, and ratified by the rank-and-file, should he or she be free to disassociate the union? Negotiated union security clauses in the collective bargaining contract answer these questions.

Achieving Stability in Labor–Management Relations

A second important reason for union security arrangements is stability in labor–management relations. A union that has no security clause in its contract with management must continually prove itself to its members. If it negotiates a contract that some members don't like, those workers might choose to leave the union.*

---

* If enough members don't like the way a union is representing them, such as negotiating and signing contracts they don't like, they can decertify the union and replace it with another or no union altogether (see Chapters 3 and 6), or they can refuse to ratify a contract. Even as we write about concession bargaining and its effect on the union movement, the rank-and-file of many unions are refusing to ratify contracts, sending their officers back to the bargaining table: "The resulting turmoil has threatened to unseat several union leaders and caused confusion for employers" (*Business Week*, July 18, 1988, p. 103).

In order to maintain membership and strength, the union leaders may have to be continually aggressive over the years in their contract negotiations and grievance processing, and may have to aim for results that are not warranted by the facts of the situation. If union leaders slip up in the eyes of their members, and there is no union security arrangement, membership defections may threaten the viability of the union. This union aggressiveness in keeping workers happy so that they remain union members will not result in stable labor–management relations; a maturing of that relationship would not be possible. It has been observed that "An assured status for the union is not a guarantee of successful union-employer relations but it is a prerequisite."[1]

Negotiated Union Security Arrangements

As we all know, there is strength in numbers. Union membership security clauses are designed to enhance union strength through numbers. They generally tend to make union membership a condition of employment. Some form of compulsory membership insures that the workers support the union that is their sole collective bargaining agent or representative. The law allows a duly certified union an important measure of union security except in those states that have passed right-to-work laws, superseding this allowance under federal law. The more common forms of union security clauses are summarized in Table 9.1.

Table 9.1 *Forms of Union Security*

Arrangement	Worker Membership Requirement	Worker Financial Support Requirement
Closed shop[a]	Must be a union member to obtain job	Must pay union dues, fees, etc.
Preferential shop[a]	Must be a union member to obtain job; if no qualified union member available, anyone can be hired and need not join the union	Union members must pay dues, fees, etc.; nonmembers pay nothing
Union shop	Must join the union to retain job	Must pay union dues, fees, etc.
Agency shop	None	Must pay fees equivalent to union dues; no fines
Maintenance of membership	Must remain in the union if a member;[b] nonmembers need not join	Union members must pay dues, fees, etc.; nonmembers pay nothing

[a] The closed shop and preferential shop are unlawful under the Taft–Hartley Act but are allowed in "modified" form.

[b] There is an "escape period" at the beginning of the contract's duration during which members may leave the union (and nonmembers can join).

The Closed Shop—Using the Hiring Hall

The **closed shop** is the strongest union security arrangement that can be negotiated between union and management. It requires that the worker already be a member of the recognized union to get (and hold) a job. The union is, in essence, doing the hiring for the firm, and to a great extent it controls employment. It usually does so through a **union hiring hall**, where the various categories of workers represented by the union sign up to obtain work, and the employers seeking these types of workers go to obtain their services. When employers who have signed a collective bargaining agreement with the union require work of the type done by workers represented by the union, they contact the hiring hall. A qualified worker (union member) is referred to them from a list kept by the union at the hall.

The closed shop arrangement fits the needs of craft unions, especially in the construction and longshoring (stevedoring) industries. In these industries, the employers need a dependable source of labor in a locale where they do not have their own workforce, because, for instance, they operate sporadically in that area. Take the example of a major construction company based in New York that wins a contract to build a bridge in California. It would be quite inconvenient, not to mention very expensive, to move their entire construction crew across the country to work on this bridge. They can't build the bridge in New York and then transport it to California. They would go to the bridge site, sending a management team, and hire the needed work crews there. A local hiring hall, run by a union, could supply them with the skilled labor they need.

The closed shop was made unlawful by the Taft–Hartley Act in 1947. Before this law, about one-third of workers covered by collective bargaining contracts were in closed shops.[2] After 1947, this figure decreased dramatically, but because of the usefulness of the hiring hall arrangements, closed shops did not disappear—they simply became disguised. The Landrum–Griffin Act of 1959 allowed the use of a modified closed shop in the building and construction industry.[3] Under this modification, hiring halls still refer workers to employers, but they cannot keep a qualified worker's name off the referral list because he or she is not a union member. If the nonmember gets referred and gets the job, he or she must join the union after seven days.[4] In theory, the modifications allow for nondiscriminatory hiring of workers, but in actuality the names at the top of the referral lists always seem to be union members in good standing.

The Preferential Shop—A Modified Closed Shop

The **preferential shop** is an open-ended form of the closed shop. Under this negotiated security arrangement, the union runs a hiring hall, with referral lists of qualified workers (union members) they represent. When an employer who has signed a collective bargaining agreement with the union needs a specific type of worker represented by the union, it asks the hiring hall to supply one. If the union cannot furnish the needed worker within a short period of time, usually 24 hours, the employer is free to hire anyone.

The preferential shop was popular in the garment industry, an industry that evolved slowly from handicraft to mass production, resulting in many small shops that were craft–oriented and became subcontractors to the larger companies in the industry.[5] The two major unions in this industry, the International Ladies' Garment Workers (ILGWU) and the Amalgamated Clothing Workers (ACWU), deal with both the large, integrated producers and small subcontractors, the latter existing in a rather chaotic competitive environment. Thus, the preferential shop served the employers (especially the smaller ones) well by providing skilled workers in the tailoring trades, but allowed them to hire nonunion workers when needed to meet peak seasonal demands. The preferential shop, like the closed shop, was outlawed by the Taft-Hartley Act but was resurrected in modified form by the Landrum–Griffin Act.

The Union Shop—Members Only

The **union shop** is a negotiated union security arrangement that requires that all workers hired by a company join the union representing the employees of that company. The worker does not have to be a union member to get the job, but must become one to retain it. After the passage of the Taft–Hartley Act, the union shop became the most widespread form of union security provision in the private sector.

Under the law, the worker must have at least a 30-day period of employment before becoming a union member. In some cases, this probationary period is set by union and management negotiations at 60 days or even 90. After this period, the worker must join the union and pay initiation fees and dues as required of all members, or lose the job. The union shop provides the trade union with substantial security, requiring membership of all workers in the bargaining unit. It guarantees that the union will maintain its numbers if the company maintains its level of employment.

The Taft–Hartley Act required that a union shop provision be subject to membership vote every year. This provision was dropped by the Landrum–Griffin Act, substituting a requirement that bans a union shop if the membership has voted against it within the previous 12 months. No other restrictions are placed on the union shop arrangement by federal law, other than exemptions for employees for religious reasons.[6]

The Agency Shop—Dues Required

The **agency shop** is a form of union security that does not require a worker either to be or to become a member of the union, but does require the worker's financial support of it. Under an agency shop provision, a worker must make a regular financial payment to the union to support its collective bargaining activities. The payment is typically equivalent to regular initiation fees and dues. However, the amount of dues is limited to those funds needed for collective bargaining: to negotiate and administer the contract.[7]

This negotiated union security arrangement, however, does not require membership, and in that respect it is very weak. The union has no control over the worker. He or she does not have to support union strikes or strike-related activities. Financial support is all that is required. Agency shops are widely used in the public sector where compulsory unionism is often prohibited.

The Maintenance of Membership Clause—In Defense of the Status Quo

One other union security arrangement that is no longer widely used is the **maintenance of memberhsip clause**. Under a maintenance of membership provision, all workers who are union members when a contract is signed must remain members throughout the duration of the contract. An escape period, usually the first 15 days that the contract is in force, is included to allow members to leave the union or nonmembers to join.

The maintenance of membership arrangement does not require membership in or financial support of the union, but it can be regarded as a halfway house between no union security and the union shop.[8] Many employers who have granted the union a maintenance of membership provision go to the next step and grant it a union shop. Maintenance of membership clauses were popular in World War II, when the War Labor Board endorsed them as a compromise between union demands for the union shop and management insistence on no compulsory unionism.[9]

Restrictions on Union Security Arrangements: The Open Shop and Right-to-Work Laws

Under Section 14(b) of the Taft–Hartley Act (LMRA), state laws are allowed to supersede federal law dealing with compulsory unionism. Federal labor law allows union shop, agency shop, and maintenance of membership clauses. States can pass laws prohibiting these arrangements, resulting in compulsory open shops. An **open shop** is one in which no union security arrangement exists. Working under this condition, no worker can be required to join the union or financially support it. The union would still be the exclusive bargaining representative for all workers in the bargaining unit, but none of these workers would be required to fund its negotiating and representational activities.

The open shop is legally mandated in 21 states, the so-called right-to-work states. The 21 right-to-work states are listed in Table 3.3, in Chapter 3. As a quick analysis of the table indicates, 11 of these states are in the South and 6 are in the Rocky Mountain region, areas not known to be overly friendly to unions and unionism. The last state to prohibit compulsory unionism was Idaho, whose law passed in 1985 but did not go into effect until 1986; prior to Idaho's law, the last state **right-to-work law** was enacted by Louisiana in 1976.[10]

Since an open shop arrangement does not require the worker to belong to or financially support a union, carrying out collective bargaining activities is, at best, difficult. If half the workers in an organization are union members, they will be paying to represent all the workers, as the law requires. This normally would not last too long, since nobody likes "freeloaders" or would want to help maintain their well-being. One by one the members will defect, with each defection increasing the share of financial support required of the remaining membership (or decreasing the representational benefits they receive for a given dues payment) and increasing the number of freeloaders. Nevertheless, through hard work and commitment, unions do operate effectively in right-to-work states.

Union Finances and Cash Flow

Compulsory unionism not only increases (or maintains) membership numbers, but also maintains financial support. Without money, the union cannot function as an institution. The modified closed and preferential shop, the union shop, and maintenance of membership arrangements (to a degree) sustain union membership and thus financial support as long as employment in the bargaining unit is up. The agency shop, with respect to financial support, does the same thing. All members and agency shop participants pay monthly dues to support the union's collective bargaining and representational activities. In addition, members make installment payments on their initiation fees.

How Unions Collect Their Funds

A union can collect payments from its members in three ways. First, members can remit their payments voluntarily each period, usually each month. This method is rarely used, for it is easy for members to forget to pay, thereby resulting in a very erratic cash flow. A second method is to have the shop stewards or business agents collect from each member; for some recalcitrant members, this might require several visits. This method can interfere with the work going on at the company. It might also cost the employer money if the contract called for paying shop stewards their regular wages while on union duty, such as grievance handling or dues collecting.

The third, and the preferred method, is to use a system called the **checkoff**. In fact, the checkoff is found in 90 percent of collective bargaining contracts.[11] The dues checkoff, negotiated with management in collective bargaining, is a system in which dues and initiation fee payments are deducted directly from the union member's paycheck and then transmitted to the union. With use of the checkoff, there is no work disruption to collect union dues and fees. In addition, it is of little administrative cost to the employer, who is already set up to make payroll deductions and various employee premium co-payments for fringe benefits. To implement a checkoff, each member must give the employer written approval to make the payroll deduction for regular payments to the union.

From the union's point of view, the checkoff is very important. It represents another step in defining the union as a permanent institutional presence in the company, which management is usually not excited about doing. However, once a union security arrangement exists, the union is assured a large measure of permanence in the organization. The checkoff also helps the union secure financial health. It means a prompt and complete flow of funds every period. It saves much time and energy which union officers have to expend if they had to collect payments from each member personally. The checkoff is used primarily for dues and commonly for initiation fees paid in installments. The law also permits its use for special union assessments but restricts its use for fines.

DEFINING MANAGEMENT RIGHTS

At the heart of the labor–management relationship in collective bargaining is the division of authority to control the workplace. The control of a company rests with management, as the agent of the owners, based on traditional property rights. But the owners own the capital, not the labor. The union, as representative of the workers, is intent on redefining the scope of control as it affects the workers.

A legally certified union, as the bargaining representative of the workers, has the authority—indeed, the requirement—to set the terms and conditions of employment in conjunction with management. This means a redefinition of management's right to be the sole authority on the best way to operate the company. The two parties have very different views of where to draw the line on sharing authority and how to define management's rights.

Theories of **management rights** vary across the spectrum. We will look at three widely divergent views: the residual theory of management rights, the explicit view of management rights, and the flexible approach.

The Residual Theory of Management Rights

One theory holds that management retains all rights to manage the organization's operations and its workforce that it has not specifically given up, modified, or eliminated in the collective bargaining agreement. This view is called the **residual theory of management rights**.[12]

In negotiations, managers who subscribe to the residual theory regard every union demand as an erosion of their rights to carry out their job. This attitude can create rather acrimonious labor relations. It also makes for rather short (and sometimes even a nonexistent) general management rights clause in the contract, such as: "The management (or employer or company) reserves (or retains) all rights to manage (or operate or direct) and control its business, subject to those specifically modified (and/or limited) by the terms of this agreement." This short clause can be very effective in purveying management's philosophy, particularly if it looks on labor–management relations as a pure conflict situation. However, the union would most likely respond with a continuous flow of grievances and work disruptions over the life of the contract.

The Explicit View of Management Rights

At the other pole is the **explicit view of management rights**—the theory that all management actions that might affect the terms and conditions of employment are matters for union–management consultation and negotiation, whether or not they are addressed in the collective bargaining contract. In most labor–management relationships, if a matter concerning the terms and conditions of employment comes up during the life of the contract, and that matter is a bone of contention between labor and management, they will resort to third-party neutrals for a decision. Even in a relatively cooperative relationship, some matters not clearly specified in the collective bargaining agreement will become grievances. Some of them will go to arbitration, to be decided by the third-party neutral. In a less cooperative environment, arbitration may occur quite often over the life of the contract. This leads to a second view of management rights, the use of a long form clause in an attempt to completely spell out managerial prerogatives or rights.[13]

Some contracts contain management rights clauses that try to spell out everything. In one contract, this clause ran over a dozen pages.[14] No clause can cover everything in a given area, however, especially an area that can be as contentious as management rights. Items left out of a long clause that supposedly covers everything may be considered as rights relinquished to labor.

A Flexible Approach to Management Rights

The first two theories are based on the premise that the labor–management relationship is an adversarial one. In practice, a constant state of hostility very rarely exists between labor and management. Although cooperation is not the typical state of labor–management relations, this approach, in conjunction with compromise, is much more common than confrontation. At companies where labor–management relations are amicable and are built on trust, both sides realize that the collective bargaining agreement is a **living document** that cannot cover everything, no matter how hard both sides work on it.[15] A short management rights clause is therefore typical. This represents a third view of management rights under collective bargaining: administration of the contract is a matter of accomodation and cooperation.

No matter what form a management rights clause takes, it is always open to interpretation. Any clause in a contract can be questioned, as can its implementation. Management practice and consistency over the years has as much to do with defining management rights as any clause in an agreement. No clause can really be definitive without reference to all other clauses in the agreement that impinge on it. Again, consistency is all important, in contract drafting and administration.

SHARING MANAGEMENT RIGHTS

The involvement of labor in the management of company operations has a long history in the United States. Recent forms of involvement have encompassed the spectrum from union or labor advisory groups to co-determination with and without equity shares.* One of the major causes for accommodation and cooperation between labor and management is a clear threat to the survival of the company and thus the union. Along with concessions, and as part of them, the union makes an honest attempt to increase productivity and efficiency, especially through changes in work rules (see the following chapter) and even involvement in company operations. Sometimes unions are even involved in strategic management decision making.

Much of this enhanced cooperation between labor and management has come as a *quid pro quo* for union concessions. Although the most publicized concessions have been in the area of wages and fringe benefits, relaxation of work rules to enhance organizational flexibility is found in many agreements. Involving labor in management decision making lends some protection to workers, along with income protection measures as discussed in Chapter 8.

---

* Co-determination usually means labor representation on corporate boards and other management decision–making committees on down through the organization. See, for example, Clark G. Ross, "Labor's Role in Corporate Decision-Making," *The Collegiate Forum*, (Fall 1981): 3; also Ch. 5.

The 1980s have seen a move in this direction, in response to heightened international competition and nonunion domestic competition. Management's hardened anti-union position in this environment is a new assertion of its right to direct and manage, and to win back some of the rights it gave up in this area (especially in terms of work rules). It is unlikely that management, particularly in the mass-production, construction, and transportation industries, where concessions have been great, wants to see an end to unions. Rather, its stance is now dictated by what clearly seems to be the steps that must be taken to survive.

This sharing of management rights is a form of cooperation that can be expected to grow in the next decade as organizations seek more flexibility to increase both productivity and the ability to adapt to market changes in general.

Joint Problem Solving

At this point in time, the sharing of management rights has been manifested primarily in **joint labor–management problem solving**, usually of shop problems, through vehicles like **Quality of Working Life (QWL) programs**.[16] This approach to decision making on the job is a sharing at the lowest level of management, the one closest to the workers and encompassing most of their day-to-day concerns. Although programs like QWL are led by steering committees at higher levels of management, they do not require massive disclosure of information used by management to run the organization. However, they do require the sharing of some of these vital data.

Joint problem-solving approaches are spreading in both unionized and nonunionized organizations. They are a first step in overcoming the many controversies that flare up with regard to interpreting the scope of management rights. The future of labor-management relations will likely be marked by more sharing of authority and control in the workplace.

At Duriron Company, for example, closer ties between management and labor were touted as boosting company productivity by 15 percent in 1988. The Steel Workers Union and National Steel officials meet frequently to plot company production gains. And at Williams Pipe Line, managers and workers conduct regular problem-solving and brainstorming sessions.[17]

Joint Decision Making

Involvement of unions in management decision making, especially at the highest level of the organization, has been much less common than involvement at the lower levels like the shop floor. In only a few cases have unions shared management rights in terms of strategic decision making.

Joint labor–management decision making can have some major drawbacks.[18] First, if the organization does poorly, the union will share the blame with management. This is a particularly important consideration if union involvement was a *quid pro quo* for concessions needed by the company because it was doing poorly. Second, the union leaders' participation in managing the firm may divert them (and the union) from their primary function, the protection of workers' interests. Moreover, the union leaders may be forced to support decisions that may hurt their members in the company's workforce, their members in competing companies, and other unions' members working for competitors.[19] A final problem associated with a union leader's involvement in management decision making is the possibility that he or she will be, or appear to be, co-opted by management. This would discredit the leader with his or her union, leading quickly to that leader's ouster.

Despite all the drawbacks, unions have moved into the highest levels of management decision making. They hold board of director seats at Chrysler (United Auto Workers), Pan Am (flight engineers, as well as a representative of nonunion employees), Wheeling-Pittsburgh Steel, CF & I Steel and Kaiser Aluminum (United Steel Workers), and PIE Nationwide and Transcon (Teamsters, as well as a nonunion employee representative on Transcon's board).[20] As yet, their involvement has not created the major problems outlined above. However, if union strength diminishes any further, the actions of these leaders as business decision makers will fall under increasing scrutiny.

DISCUSSION QUESTIONS

1. Why should a worker be forced to join a union, if that union is legally certified to be the exclusive bargaining agent in a company, to get or hold a job with that company?

2. Imagine a union with a clause requiring all employees at a business to join. In what ways could it placate hostile members and keep them from becoming a source of internal friction?

3. Compare the closed shop and the preferential shop.

4. Compare the union shop and the agency shop.

5. What is a right-to-work state?

6. Why is it unlikely that management, particularly in the industries where concessions have been great, would want to see an end to unionism?

7. Explain the residual theory of management rights.

8. Would you consider items left out of a long management rights clause to be rights given up to management or labor? Why?

9. What is the most common way at this time for management to share rights with labor?

10. What potential drawbacks does union involvement in management decision making have for union management? What are some advantages? Why do you think union involvement in management decision making has not yet led to many problems?

VOCABULARY LIST

union membership security clause

fair representation

closed shop

union hiring hall

preferential shop

union shop

agency shop

maintenance of membership clause

open shop

right-to-work law

checkoff

management rights

residual theory of management rights

explicit view of management rights

living document

joint labor–management problem solving

Quality of Working Life program

joint labor–management decision making

FOOTNOTES

1. Daniel H. Pollitt, "Union Security in America," in Richard L. Rowan, *Readings in Labor Economics and Labor Relations* (Richard D. Irwin, 1976), p. 282.

2. Melvin W. Reder, *Labor in a Growing Economy* (John Wiley, 1957), p. 178.

3. Lee Balliet, *Survey of Labor Relations* (Bureau of National Affairs, 1987), pp. 133–134. Balliet also notes that a 1959 Court decision allowed hiring halls to refer workers, under specific procedures.

4. Commerce Clearing House, *1989 Guidebook to Labor Relations* (1989), p. 233.

5. Balliet, *Survey of Labor Relations*, p. 118.

6. Commerce Clearing House, *1989 Guidebook*, p. 234. Valid religious objections to joining or supporting a union exempt the employee, who must then "contribute" to a nonreligious charity from among those listed in the contract an amount equal to fees and dues paid by union members. The union is allowed to charge this employee for handling his or her grievances.

7. *Wall Street Journal*, June 30, 1988, p. 2. This Supreme Court decision barred collection and use of agency shop payments by a worker for political, legislative, social, and labor–organizing activities by unions if he or she doesn't want to support these activities. The separation of activities and their costs into "chargeable" and "not chargeable" is creating some interesting problems. (See Anna DuVal Smith and John E. Drotning, "Fair Share Fees: Theory, Law and Implementation," *Proceedings of the 1988 Spring Meeting* (Industrial Relations Research Association, March 23–25, 1988), pp. 465–466.

8. Reder, *Labor in a Growing Economy*, p. 179.

9. Ibid.

10. *Monthly Labor Review* (April 1985): 61.

11. William H. Holley, and Kenneth M. Jennings, *The Labor Relations Process* (Dryden Press, 1988), p. 400.

12. This view is sometimes referred to as the reserved rights doctrine (Holley and Jennings, *The Labor Relations Process*, p. 394).

13. Holley and Jennings, *The Labor Relations Process*, p. 395.

14. Arthur A. Sloane and Fred Witney, *Labor Relations* (Prentice–Hall, 1985), p. 421.

15. Reder, *Labor in a Growing Economy,* p. 163.

16. Michael Schuster, "Models of Cooperation and Change in Union Settings," *Industrial Relations* (Fall 1985): 383.

17. *Wall Street Journal,* April 26, 1988, p. 1.

18. Robert B. McKersie, "Union Involvement in Entrepreneurial Decisions of Business," in Thomas A. Kochan, *Challenges and Choices Facing American Labor* (MIT Press, 1985), pp. 151–152; Everett M. Kassalow, "Concession Bargaining: Towards New Roles for American Unions," *International Labor Review,* No. 5 (1988): 586.

19. *Business Week,* December 14, 1987, pp. 127–128.

20. Ibid.

REFERENCES

BALLIET, LEE. *Survey of Labor Relations.* Bureau of National Affairs, 1987, Ch 5.

COMMERCE CLEARING HOUSE. *1989 Guidebook to Labor Relations.* 1989, Ch. 8.

DRAGO, ROBERT. "Quality Circle Survival: An Exploratory Analysis." *Industrial Relations* (Fall 1988): 336–351.

HOLLEY, WILLIAM H., and KENNETH M. JENNINGS. *The Labor Relations Process.* Dryden Press, 1988, Ch 11.

KASSALOW, EVERETT M. "Concession Bargaining: Towards New Roles for American Unions." *International Labor Review,* No. 5 (1988): 573–592.

McKERSIE, ROBERT B. "Union Involvement in Entrepreneurial Decisions of Business." In Thomas A. Kochan, *Challenges and Choices Facing American Labor.* MIT Press, 1985, pp. 149–166.

POLLITT, DANIEL H. "Union Security in America." In Richard L. Rowan, *Readings in Labor Economics and Labor Relations.* Richard D. Irwin, 1976, pp. 281–288.

REDER, MELVIN W. *Labor in a Growing Economy.* John Wiley, 1957, Ch. 6 and 7.

ROSS, CLARK G. "Labor's Role in Corporate Decision-Making." *The Collegiate Forum* (Fall 1981): 3.

SCHUSTER, MICHAEL. "Models of Cooperation and Change in Union Settings." *Industrial Relations* (Fall 1985): 382–394.

SLOANE, ARTHUR A., and FRED WITNEY. *Labor Relations.* Prentice–Hall, 1985.

SMITH, ANNA DuVAL, and JOHN E. DROTNING. "Fair Share Fees: Theory, Law, and Implementation." *Proceedings of the 1988 Spring Meeting.* Industrial Relations Research Association, March 23–25, 1988, pp.464–470.

VERMA, ANIL, and ROBERT B. Mc KERSIE. "Employee Involvement: The Implications of Noninvolvement by Unions." *Industrial and Labor Relations Review* (July, 1987): 556–568.

CHAPTER 10

ADMINISTRATIVE ISSUES IN COLLECTIVE BARGAINING

T he array of issues governing the rules of the workplace and the day-to-day interpretation and application of the labor agreement are known as the administrative issues in collective bargaining. They usually comprise the most complex part of the contract and cover the widest range of subjects. The major administrative issues included in a typical collective bargaining contract are seniority (and superseniority), work rules, discipline, and the grievance procedure. They are aimed primarily at protecting the workers in their jobs and protecting those jobs themselves.

In the past decade, some of these administrative issues have become the focal point in collective bargaining. Management has made productivity and flexibility a key element in the drive to become more competitive in an increasingly competitive international environment. Work rules are a major factor in determining productivity, labor costs, and flexibility.[1] Seniority and discipline also affect these key elements. The shifting of the emphasis in collective bargaining to productivity and flexibility issues, coupled with job security which has become a major issue with workers, has resulted in some innovative approaches to organizing and controlling work. Before moving on to some of these approaches, we will discuss the major administration areas and issues.

SENIORITY: THE KEYSTONE OF LABOR CONTRACTS

Seniority is one of the oldest principles of the workplace, and its use for many job-related or personnel decisions is a deeply held conviction of organized labor.[2]

Table 10.1 *Common Uses of Seniority*

Category of Use	Application
Job security	In layoffs and subsequent rehiring[a]
Work assignments and placement	In work shift assigment, in overtime assignment, and in promotions
Fringe benefits	Vacation times and lengths
Wages	Step increases

[a] Especially strong use through superseniority for union officials critical to the administration of the contract and representation of the bargaining unit members.

Seniority can be simply defined as "length of service in an employment unit,"[3] such as a company or plant or department. Basically, seniority as a system reflects the ethics of the queue (i.e., first come, first served). The longer the worker is at the job, the greater are the job property rights, and thus the greater is the need to protect the incumbent in maintaining those rights. This is the objective of a seniority system.

Seniority, especially when used in a unionized company, governs layoffs and rehiring. In this sense, it truly protects the longer term employee, the high seniority worker who has the greater property rights related to the job. Those property rights usually include preferential work (shift and overtime) assignments, enhanced fringe benefits (preferential selection of and longer vacation times), higher wages,[4] and preferential eligibility for promotion. Greater job security through protection from layoffs is also an important job right that grows with increasing seniority. The proponents of the strict use of seniority for work assignments and other benefits justify these property right enhancements as rewards for the loyal, long-term worker. Some of the common uses of seniority are summarized in Table 10.1.

The Width of the Seniority Unit

One of the major issues involved in seniority is the definition of the **seniority unit,** or employment unit. The controversy in the use of seniority for layoffs and rehiring lies in the management position that seniority units should be narrow and the opposing union position that they should be wide. Since most organizations, including nonunion ones, use seniority for decisions involving layoffs and rehiring, the **seniority unit width** is the bone of contention.[5]

Wide Seniority Units

The wider the unit (or seniority base), the greater the job protection for high seniority workers. In a companywide unit, when a layoff occurs, the senior workers have maximum job protection. If their area (for example, department) bears the major brunt of the cutback, they can "bump" anybody with less seniority in the defined unit, in this case the whole company. **Bumping** is the act of replacing a less senior worker, provided the higher seniority worker can do his or her job. The worker bumped by a more senior worker can, in turn, bump a worker with less seniority, and that worker can then bump a less senior worker, and so on. A chain reaction of bumping results. The wider the unit (or base), the greater the potential for this chain reaction to cause production disruptions and the retention of less able workers.

With a massive number of bumps, wholesale worker displacements occur, and supervisors are diverted from their primary functions to oversee workers who are trying to prove that they can do jobs they have not been doing or may never have done. In a typical bump, the replacement (more senior) workers must show their new supervisors that they can do the job. For example, if a senior worker bumps a machinist, he or she must prove to the supervisor the ability to run the machine, by, for example, doing one or two actual jobs that need machining. The supervisor will usually watch the "new" machinist do the work as well as inspect the machined parts.

Many of the workers end up doing jobs that are relatively new to them, displacing usually younger workers who have been doing those jobs for some time and may possess skills older workers don't.[6] This situation usually results in lower productivity: the replacing workers may end up in jobs they can barely do, jobs at which the replaced workers were good; and the replaced workers may be doing jobs from which they bumped others, jobs that they can barely do.[7]

Narrow Seniority Units

In a narrow seniority unit or base, such as a job, craft, or department, layoffs don't cause much chaos in terms of disruptions stemming from bumping chain reactions and workers doing jobs at which they are relatively unproductive. The bumping that does occur is usually less disruptive because the parties involved work at the same job or in the same or similar units doing the same or similar work.

Narrow units offer the higher seniority workers much less job security, however. As they can only bump other workers within their own unit, for example, department, narrow units provide less of a cushion of lower seniority workers to be bumped. The effects of unit widths are summarized in Table 10.2.

Evaluating Worker Productivity: Seniority Versus Merit

The issue of bumping more productive workers to accommodate older, more senior workers has always been a sore point with management. The union response has

Table 10.2 *Seniority Unit Width*

Seniority Unit or Base	Width	Effect on Company	Protection for Worker
Job	Narrowest	Least disruptive	Least protection, Most restrictive
Craft Department Division Plant	↓	↓	↓
Company	Widest	Most disruptive	Most protection, Least restrictive

always been a questioning of management's evaluation of worker productivity. The union claims that worker productivity, based on the worker and not the capital with which he or she works, is very difficult to measure. Management evaluations of worker productivity are subjective at best and may be colored by all sorts of arbitrary and capricious reasoning. Allowing management to choose who gets laid off and who doesn't, based on its evaluation of worker productivity, is not acceptable to unions. In all unionized and most nonunion organizations, the senior worker is kept "unless a junior employee is a significantly better performer."[8] Unions favor the absolute objectivity of length of service over management-defined merit for most personnel decisions; length of service is an explicit measure, and experience should have something to do with worker productivity.[9]

This difference of opinion carries over to the issue of overtime assignment and promotions. Again, unions argue for choice based primarily on seniority as an objective measure of the worker's value to the organization. Management argues for merit, as defined by management evaluations, to make the choice. Under most collective bargaining contracts, both seniority and management evaluations are factors in promotion decisions.[10] However, promotions out of the seniority unit can cause problems. These problems point to another major issue in the use of seniority, worker mobility.

Seniority and Labor Mobility

An important assumption of classical economics is that factors of production, such as labor, are "perfectly" mobile. If opportunity knocks, in terms of higher pay and better working conditions, workers respond. However, **labor mobility** has never been perfect.

People raise families and settle into neighborhoods, thereby increasing labor inertia. If an area becomes depressed, with wholesale job losses, and stays that way, this inertia is overcome, as basic needs must be met. This occurred in the early 1980s in the Midwest, especially the upper Midwest, which earned the name "Rust Belt." Workers poured out of the Rust Belt in search of jobs, especially in the Sun Belt (the Southwest and California).[11] Overall, however, labor mobility tends to be limited. Seniority, as a major part of the property rights attached to specific jobs, plays a large role in limiting mobility.

Intercompany Mobility

When a worker moves from one company to another, he or she gives up all his or her accumulated seniority. As a low seniority employee in the new company, the worker loses:

1. Job security in the face of any downturn in company sales.
2. Preferential assignment for work shifts and overtime.
3. Some fringe benefits, like choice of vacation time and length of vacation and perhaps even accrued pension benefits.
4. Preferential eligibility for promotion.

A worker would move only if the wages and perceived value of the other aspects of the new job were greater than the previous job's wages and the perceived value of the lost property rights attached to that job. In addition, the value of the new job must compensate for any moving of family and household if the job requires it. This last cost of moving is not related to the property rights of the old job, but it does grow over time along with those property rights.

Intracompany Mobility

Moving permanently from one job to another within a company, through promotion, may also be limited by considerations of seniority. If a transfer is within the seniority unit, it will not affect one's seniority.

If, however, the transfer is out of the unit, a problem does arise. If the transfer involves loss of seniority, only a major promotion with a substantial increase in wages, which would more than offset the lost property rights conferred by seniority, would be accepted. In many organizations, however, workers tapped for transfer can be granted the right to take their accumulated seniority with them to the new unit. Thus, the organization can affect promotions without granting huge wage increases. This type of transfer would still leave the worker in the same bargaining unit.

Transferring out of the bargaining unit to one represented by another union almost always means loss of seniority. It is akin to accepting a job with another company.

If a move is to another of the company's plants, to a different seniority unit represented by the same union but a different local, the question of transferring seniority becomes a sticky one. Large national unions had, for the most part, negotiated multiplant contracts with companies. Under this type of centralized bargaining, the issue of worker movement within the company, between seniority units and even bargaining units represented by the national, could be and were addressed. The movement now to more and more negotiations at the local level has in many cases pushed this issue off the national collective bargaining agenda. Local autonomy has meant that local issues are the focus of the bargaining, and many issues of concern to the national union are no longer applicable. Even management support for such administrative issues may not bring them back to the table, especially if the local union is not supportive of these issues. Plantwide concerns and viewpoints dominate.

Transfers from Bargaining Unit to Management   One type of internal transfer has special problems: promotion not only out of the seniority unit but also out of all bargaining units completely to a supervisory (management) position. Not only are managerial employees, such as supervisors, excluded from the right to unionize; they are also excluded from the protection of the national labor laws.[12] Thus, if management wants to tap a worker for promotion to supervisor because that worker shows leadership potential, it (and that worker) must wrestle with the problem of seniority.

Because workers are hesitant about moving from the bargaining unit into lower level management, some collective bargaining agreements contain provisions allowing workers to retain their seniority in a bargaining unit for a specified time period while holding a supervisorial position. If the person does not work out as a supervisor, he or she can drop back into the bargaining unit at the same seniority level held upon taking the promotion. Some agreements even allow the worker who has dropped back into the unit to add the time spent as supervisor to his or her seniority.

If the worker as supervisor is fired rather than demoted, however, he or she is out of a job. A supervisor can be fired much more easily than a worker who has the protection of his or her union and the grievance procedure. But capricious discharge is now very likely to be overturned by the courts in unlawful discharge cases (see Chapter 3). Promotion to supervisor is a major step for a worker, and the problems involved in seniority can be overcome, allowing the worker to take advantage of a great opportunity.

Seniority and Affirmative Action

The Problem of Discrimination

It has been alleged that the use of seniority rules in personnel decisions, especially in layoffs and promotions, has a negative impact on minority workers.[13] Some claim that because of the historical, and enduring, race and sex discrimination in the labor market, minority workers have lower seniority than they would have had in the absence of that discrimination. As the last hired they are the first to go when layoffs occur, and they are the lowest in eligibility for promotions.

Nonetheless, some civil rights activists involved with labor market issues have supported seniority as a system protecting against discrimination by management. Research conducted 15 years after the Civil Rights Act of 1964 showed that the difference in seniority between black and white union members was under a year.[14]

The Seniority Award as a Solution

In 1976, the Supreme Court ruled that **retroactive seniority** as well as back pay was a legitimate remedy for discrimination. In the famous *Bowman Transportation* case, the Court ruled that federal judges could award retroactive seniority to discrimination victims "who were refused employment for racial reasons, then later hired by the same company."[15] In 1984 and 1985, the Court reaffirmed this stance; retroactive seniority is a proper remedy for discrimination. But the 1984 decision, involving a voluntary affirmative action plan utilizing a form of retroactive seniority, was struck down as it did not award the seniority for proven discrimination, but rather for being in a minority group that traditionally has been subject, as a group, to discrimination.[16]

The courts, then, have ruled that an organization that has been proven to have discriminated against minority employees can be directed to award retroactive seniority to those employees. However, in the absence of proof of specific discrimination, retroactive seniority for minority workers is not a correct remedy. In essence, the rulings indicate that seniority systems are, in and of themselves, nondiscriminatory. They should only be altered, in terms of granting retroactive seniority, if the organization in which they are used was proven to have discriminated, thus denying potential employees and actual employees finally hired access to the seniority system at the point of initial application.

Awarding seniority to workers greater than that held by others who have been on the job longer is a serious and major step. It should be done only under the most pressing circumstances. The next section discusses one of those circumstances.

Superseniority

Superseniority is a status conferred on local union officials who have a major role in administering the collective bargaining contract. These are primarily the officers who are involved in the grievance procedure: union (shop) stewards and/or grievance committeepersons. In some instances, superseniority may be granted the local president and other officers "involved in processing grievances or other on-the-job contract administrative functions."[17]

Superseniority and Contract Administration

A union certified as sole bargaining agent is charged with representing the employees in the bargaining unit. Besides negotiating the collective bargaining agreement, which could well be the major function of the national union and its paid officers, this role primarily means administering the contract, on a day-to-day basis, at the local level.

Contract administration involves interpreting and applying the collective bargaining agreement on the shop floor and in the office. The "point people" in this activity are the shop stewards. Skilled and knowledgeable shop stewards are important to both the employer and the union and its members. Thus, they are almost always granted superseniority to protect them from layoff.[18] If the local also has a grievance committee to handle grievances in the latter steps of the procedure, the members of this committee will usually be granted superseniority.

One controversy dealing with superseniority is its use by local officers as a "perquisite" of the job. The NLRB has ruled that superseniority cannot be conferred on local union officers who are not involved in administering the collective bargaining contract.[19] If the local officers are involved in grievance processing, acting as, say, the plant grievance committee, granting them superseniority is perfectly legitimate. If they are not involved in contract administration, however, the granting of superseniority is not legitimate. Again, the alteration of seniority rights is a very serious matter and should only be done under the most pressing conditions.

WORK RULES ══════════

Work rule changes have been in the forefront of collective bargaining negotiations in the past ten years as companies strive for more flexibility, productivity, and lower costs. In several instances, management has granted labor a great deal in exchange for work rule changes.[20] More commonly, management has obtained these changes by "taking a hard line, threatening to close a plant or invest elsewhere."[21] The traditional governance of work by a myriad of work rules applied to a plethora of job classifications is vigorously under attack, and this type of job protection is loosening.

Production Standards

Work rules have a long history in American labor relations.[22] Most work rules are basically **production standards.** The adversarial nature of the labor–management relationship is very clearly seen in the use of work rules. Many employers in the late nineteenth and early twentieth centuries viewed their workers as inputs to the production process, no different than machines, and treated them as such. Thus, many of these rules were established as standards to protect worker health and safety as much as, and even more than, to protect and control the jobs of union members.

Technological change, which has a substantial effect on workers, together with more enlightened managerial outlooks, changed the need for workers and their unions to contractually set rules to protect themselves against loss of life and limb. As American industry modernized, and government legislation was enacted to protect worker health and safety on the job, many work rules became obsolete. However, many of these rules remained in force, even though they had lost their primary function, worker protection. These work rules now exist more to protect and control jobs than workers, and they are sometimes called "make work" rules.

Unions have gained many of these work rules and retained them by tradeoffs for higher pay and other forms of job security in collective bargaining negotiations. Many union members, especially older ones, are great defenders of work rules that they have "paid for" with lower pay increases, and other concessions, than they could have gotten in the past.[23]

Work rules related to production standards control three elements of the production process: input, output, and method or technique.

Input Work Rules

Since labor is an input in the production process, the most popular and widespread work rules related to production deal with input. These **input control rules** are especially important in job preservation, work creation, and protection of the less able worker. Input standards cover a variety of subjects, including the number of workers assigned to a job, work to be done on a job (especially by union members), the pace of work, and the kind of work a person in a specified job classification can and cannot do.

The Number of Workers on a Job   The setting of **manning requirements,** or **crew size,** for a job is probably the best known input control rule. Management commonly refers to these requirements as "featherbedding," but most don't fit the legal definition of featherbedding per Section 8 (b) (6) of the Taft–Hartley Act.[24] The act makes it unlawful to extract pay for work not done, and if any work is done, even if the action to gain pay is an "extraction," there is no unfair labor practice.

The most widely publicized manning work rules are those on the railroads, especially the rules relating to train crew size. First, the introduction of diesels eliminated the job of the stoker or fireman, but union work rules requiring "three in the cab" kept them on the job for many years without any real work to do. The long, drawn-out process of attrition was the solution to get cab crews down to two, an engineer and a conductor.

Then the elimination of hand brakes made the job of brakeman obsolete. By union-instigated state laws, some large freight trains required as many as seven or eight brakemen. The passing of the hand brake caused most state "full-crew" laws to be taken off the books, but union work rules have succeeded in keeping two brakemen on most trains, for safety reasons, giving a crew of four (including the engineer and conductor). Management has argued that the brakemen are not needed, because sensitive track-side devices along lines make the safety checks of brakemen unnecessary. Many railroads have been able to reduce train crew size to three, and even two on nonstop runs.[25] But it has been a long, hard, expensive fight, and it's not over yet.

Work That Must Be Performed by a Union Member   Another grouping of input control rules are those requiring **duplicate** or **unnecessary work.** Many interesting examples of this rule were (and are) found in the building trades. As Slichter reported, electricians working with electrical apparatus prewired at the factory would rewire them before installing them in buildings.[26] Plasterers would be required by union rules to apply three coats of plaster, even though the building codes specified only two. In some instances, building trades unions have gotten excess work requirements built into local building codes.

Probably the most publicized duplicate/unnecessary work rules were those used by the International Typographical Union.[27] These rules required duplicate typesetting. First, the work rule was applied to items running in more than one newspaper or magazine, such as an advertisement, when an exchange of plates was used by the first printer or was sent by the company or agency that developed the ad. The rule required that the plate be duplicated at each successive site (paper or magazine) receiving it. Then the rule was applied to plates typeset by computer, requiring comparison plates to be set manually to "check" the computer-set plates. These work rules became important bargaining issues at locals that had obtained them, and they were ultimately traded in collective bargaining negotiations for wage increases and/or job guarantees.

The Pace of Work   **Work speeds** are another important input element for which unions develop work rules. These controls include a diverse group of machine-oriented rules that address capital equipment from machine tools (lathes, mills, drills, etc.) through assembly lines.

Many rules focus on rates (time standards) set by management and contested by the union. As any industrial engineer or efficiency (time and motion study) expert knows, setting standards has several subjective elements, and these may cause a wide variation in a time standard for a job set by different experts.* A wide variation might be particularly true if one expert worked for the company and the other for the union. Management-developed standards may err on the side of tightness, while those developed by the union tend to err toward looseness. In addition to this subjectivity issue is the fact that standards will change as different methods, materials, and equipment used on the job are introduced.

* One such subjective step is rating the worker relative to standard pace in a stopwatch time study.

Requiring constant updating of time standards is not usually feasible and, when done, reopens the conflict between management and union as to the correctness of the standard. Workers usually suspect management of speedups, while management is very concerned about workers doing jobs slower than they should be done, commonly called goldbricking or soldiering. In addition, older workers may not be capable of doing a job as rapidly as younger, more able-bodied, and better educated workers, so that a well-set standard for the "average" worker may make them look bad.* The controversy over work speeds, or the pace of production, has abated substantially since the 1970s, but it is still an element in the general work rules–restrictive practices issue in collective bargaining.[28]

Work Designated for a Specific Job   **Work assignments** are yet another major area in which work rules are rampant, and was one of the primary areas of concern to management in the 1980s.[29] Interunion work assignment disputes were common prior to 1947 as unions, especially AFL- and CIO-affiliated unions, had overlapping jurisdictions. The passage of the Taft–Hartley Act practically eliminated work assignment conflicts. However, changing technology alters the nature of work in many companies, and narrowly defined jurisdictions of unions can cause work assignment disputes.

The primary focus of work assignment rules is on **job classification work assignments,** based on job descriptions that can never truly describe what a worker holding a given job should do. Thus, a set of rules is developed to try to delineate what a worker should *not* do. This will have a major impact on flexibility and productivity. Since job classifications will be discussed in the next section, we will continue our discussion of production standards with output control work rules. Production standards to control input are summarized in Table 10.3.

Output Work Rules

Output control rules are rare as formal union rules, but they do exist. Informal restrictions on output are more common. Like informal rules of the shop limiting input, especially the pace of work, output norms are set whenever workers can control their output and are *not* on a piece-rate basis (incentive-pay system). In most work situations, it is easier for work groups to develop input norms, as they are part of the input. However, output norms can also be devised which will require the employment of more workers to meet company output targets and to protect less able workers.

The major purpose of these types of rules is to limit daily or weekly output. For intermittent and seasonal workers, output control rules are important job elements, prolonging the work. Sometimes it is difficult to differentiate between output-limiting rules, which put direct restrictions on the results of the work done, and input-limiting rules, which put restrictions on the work itself, and thus indirectly limit output.

---

* The problems of the less able workers were especially troublesome in the pre–World War II period when incentive-pay systems were widespread. Thus, below-average performance meant below-average pay.

Table 10.3 *Input Control Production Standards*

Input Controlled	Common Usage	Comments
Crew size (manning)	Transportation (railroads, airlines)	Commonly called featherbedding
Duplicate (or unnecessary) work	Printing, transportation (rail, air)	Commonly called featherbedding
Work speeds	Machine shops, assembly line operations	Allows goldbricking, protects slower workers
Work assignments (who can do what)	Many industries	Narrowly defined job classifications
Production machinery and/or technique used	Many industries	Really control of process or method (technology used)

The best examples of output work rules are those found in the railroad industry. One turn-of-the-century rule governing the distance a train can travel in a day can severely limit train movement today. In some cases, the crew of a modern fast-moving freight train can collect three days' pay in one,[30] or, by requiring many crew changes, cause a 100-miles-an-hour train to cover only about 500 miles in an eight-hour period, which represents a 35 to 40 percent loss in possible output. These types of rules defining a day's work in terms of output have carried over to the airlines, with the use of distance and trips. Another example of an output control rule is the load limit used by longshoremen for their sling loads, slowing down the loading or unloading of a ship.

Output work rules represented one area of contention between Pittston Company and the United Mine Workers in a dispute that led to a nine-month strike by miners in 1989. In the eventual settlement, Pittston made big gains in work rules. As a result of the work rule changes, which dealt with the number of hours workers could put in, industry sources estimated the company would save $2 to $3 a ton, for a total annual savings of $10 million to $15 million.[31]

Technique or Method Work Rules

Technique work rules, aimed at controlling method or technique, are very common and almost all are a result of technological changes. New materials, machines, and processes have a profound effect on work. Most work rules that are designed to control methods are rules dealing with the use of these technologies. As such, they are closely related to work rules dealing with inputs, especially when the matter concerns new, improved machinery and materials.

Job Classifications

In addition to production standards, job classifications have been used for over 100 years.

Unit Work and Supervisors

One job classification work rule that is common to almost all unionized industries and companies forbids a supervisor or foreman from doing any work handled by the employees in the bargaining unit. For example, supervisors are prohibited from "taking the place of a worker who goes to the restroom, repairing a tool, or helping when the work falls behind."[32]

This type of rule can cause production to be stretched out when workers who are assigned work through their job classification are not in the immediate area when that work has to be done before other tasks can be undertaken. These workers must be called in while the supervisor and the rest of the work crew wait. The supervisor may well have held that job classification in the past and be perfectly capable of doing the work, but the rule, set up to preserve bargaining unit work, forbids it.

The Purpose of Job Classifications

In many manufacturing plants, there are over 100 job classifications.[33] These restrict many workers to narrowly defined and sometimes mundane tasks that can quickly become drudgery. However, they perform two important functions for the workforce.

First, they preserve jobs and work. In the face of technological change, this is a crucial factor for the worker(s) facing displacement. From the managerial point of view, however, it is a loss of efficiency.

Second, rigidly defined jobs give labor powerful leverage in any dispute with management during the life of the contract. With the contract in force, labor cannot legally strike. However, workers can **"work to rule,"** which means doing only what job descriptions require, and no more. As most workers show some initiative in doing their jobs, working to rule drops productivity significantly. Management would be quickly forced to negotiate with labor to resolve the issue.

Recent Developments in Job Classifications

Work assignment rules based on narrowly defined job classifications slow the production process down and make it quite inflexible. Regaining flexibility to increase productivity has become a management crusade in collective bargaining negotiations. As collective bargaining contracts come up for renewal, job classification work rules have become one of the prime targets for change. Management's insistence on these changes is growing.

In some industries, this crusade has been conducted by shifting work from unionized to nonunion shops. In the building industry, some companies have established nonunion units that sometimes work side by side with the company's unionized unit, a practice called double-breasting.[34]

In addition, an increasing number of contracts with drastically reduced job classifications are being negotiated. A plant that had 217 job classifications now has 69.[35] One new auto plant, Chrysler's Sterling Heights (Michigan) plant, has 16 classifications as opposed to 80 in the company's older plants.[36]

Japanese auto manufacturers have three to five job classifications in their U.S. plants, while GM, Ford, and Chrysler have about 60.[37] Under this competitive pressure, American manufacturers will continue their push to streamline job categories. As new technologies spread through American plants, the breakdown of job assignment work rules will become more critical to overall company efficiency.

Subcontracting Rules

Subcontracting, now often called **outsourcing,** has become a major cost-saving strategy of multinational firms operating in a world economy as much as in a national economy. In the American auto industry, much of Ford's success relative to GM is attributed to Ford's buying 50 to 60 percent of its parts from subcontractors while GM goes outside for only 30 to 40 percent of its parts.[38] The joint application of production standards and job classifications has determined, to a great extent, the allocation of work within the organization; subcontracting rules are aimed at this allocation of work between the organization and other companies.

The Early Union Response to Subcontracting

American unions launched their first vigorous attack on the subcontracting problem in the 1950s. A renewed growth of subcontracting and interplant work movement in the postwar period spurred union interest in trying to put some controls on these management decisions.[39]

Traditionally, some subcontracted work was acceptable to unions, but the subcontracting of work that had been done in the plant by the members of the bargaining unit was another matter, for it threatened the workers' existing jobs. This was especially onerous to unions when the subcontractor did the work at the plant, as with janitorial services. A continuing source of conflict was the disagreement between management and labor as to what were traditionally subcontracted practices that threatened union jobs. The problem was different at the local versus the national union level. The local was concerned about any subcontracting or interplant work transfers that threatened the jobs of the bargaining unit. The national, however, was not very worried about work taken from one of its locals and subcontracted or transferred to another.

In general, unions opposed subcontracting (and work transfer) to "(1) protect normal employment opportunities for its members, (2) preserve the particular union's jurisdiction and strength, (3) enlarge work opportunities of its members, (4) combat escape from unionism, and (5) protect union standards against competition."[40] The unions feel as strongly about these reasons today as they did 30 to 40 years ago.

Contemporary Union Methods to Control Subcontracting

From labor's viewpoint, subcontracting or outsourcing is a transfer of work and jobs from the bargaining unit or the union or even the country to others. Coupled with the application of technological change leading to enhanced productivity (labor-saving innovation), it can cause substantial loss of jobs in a company, especially when implementation leads to plant closings. In many heavy manufacturing industries, this was the case in the 1980s.

Recently negotiated collective bargaining contracts have recognized this fact, with labor extracting some innovative work guarantee measures in the face of "the erosion of jobs through . . . productivity improvements and outsourcing."[41] In 1988, Chrysler Corporation's revelation that it was planning to move the production of one of its lines of cars to nonunion plants in Mexico seriously jeopardized ongoing contract talks with the United Auto Workers. The union uproar led Chrysler to back away from the proposal.[42] In their attempts to control or limit the impact of company subcontracting and work transfer practices, unions utilize three major approaches.[43]

Limiting Subcontracting by Contract   The most direct method to control excessive subcontracting is to establish rules and limitations in the contract through the collective bargaining process. These formal work rules tend to restrict subcontracting and work transfer to situations in which the company lacks the capacity to accomplish the work, or the peculiar skills or machinery to do it. If bargaining unit members are on layoff, subcontracting or work transfer is usually prohibited, particularly if it is to go to nonunion workers.

Limiting Subcontracting by Arbitration   A second approach to controlling subcontracting and work transfers involves the use of the grievance procedure and arbitration. Negotiated subcontracting and work transfer clauses tend to be ambiguous, generally using "established practice" to determine what is allowable and what is not. Because of this ambiguity, unions frequently resort to arbitration to determine, and limit, the validity of specific subcontracting and work transfer attempts by management.

The recognition clause in collective bargaining contracts usually defines the bargaining unit employees and the status of the union to represent them in matters pertaining to "wage, hours, and other terms and conditions of employment" (see Article II, Section 1, of the Negotiating Exercise contract at the end of the book). Unless a subcontracting clause is very explicit and unambiguous, or the management rights clause specifically defines the right of management to subcontract or transfer work out of the plant, any decision of this type is usually grievable.

Limiting Subcontracting by Labor–Management Cooperation   The third way unions deal with subcontracting or work transfer is not actually to control these management decisions, but rather to make these actions less attractive to the company or to limit their impact on the company's labor force. This is more of a cooperative approach to the problem rather than an adversarial one, as was the case with the first two union methods. Enhancing the productivity and the specific skills of the company's labor force so that they can competitively do work targeted for subcontracting is an example of a cooperative approach. In many instances, however, this enhancement may be the result of concessions granted by unions under the threat of plant closing or a similar event.

Another aspect of cooperation on this issue might be the union's acquiescence in subcontracting or outsourcing accompanied not just by loss of jobs, but also by some company action(s) to put the laid-off workers back to work or guarantee their wages for some period of time while they are out of work. The SUB and GIS plans discussed in Chapter 8 do this, as do the 1984 job banks established by the UAW and the Big 3,[44] and the 1987–1988 job security plans, another UAW–Big 3 program.[45] These job security plans contain restrictions on plant closings and work transfers, as well as job guarantees in the face of outsourcing. They are aimed at job loss pressures resulting from technological changes and productivity improvements as much as from work transfers and subcontracting. This brings us to the next topic of discussion, technological change and work rules.

TECHNOLOGICAL CHANGE AND WORK RULES

Technological change has always created new jobs as well as destroying old ones; thus, the introduction of new technology in the workplace requires an adjustment to change. This has always presented a problem for labor: what should its policy be with respect to change? In the past, some unions have fought technological change, trying to prevent it: these battles were not successful, and unions have gone out of existence in the process.[46]

As a second alternative, many unions agree to the introduction of new technology and try to control the jobs created by the change. The attempts at control usually involve work rules in one form or another. Until approximately 1950, technological changes tended to create jobs for the relatively unskilled, like machine operators, while destroying the jobs of skilled craftspeople. In contrast, since 1950, technological change has led to the creation of jobs for highly skilled and professional workers while destroying the jobs of unskilled and semiskilled workers. This has made union control of these jobs more difficult to achieve.[47]

Some unions have chosen a third option: to encourage technological change, while protecting their present members from the impact of its introduction.[48] Encouraging the adoption of new technology may be the only way to keep a company in business. The variation of union response to the introduction of technological change in the workplace is summarized in Table 10.4.

Table 10.4   *Union Responses to Technological Change*

Response	Examples	Usual Outcome
Outright opposition	Window-glass makers union (first quarter of the 20th century)	Union loses and disappears
Cooperation and control	Some rail unions, many industrial unions	Union membership changes, usually grows with the industry if the job control is successful, shrinks if new jobs go to nonmembers
Encouragement and protection	Steel workers and auto workers (last quarter of the 20th century)	Union shrinks, with relatively rapid job displacement if member protection is weak, but slow (e.g., through attrition) if protection is strong

Major Technological Advances

Mechanization

The major technological advances of the Industrial Revolution were characterized by **mechanization**—the replacement of human (and animal) power by machine power. The early textile machines, and then engines (steam and internal combustion in particular), displaced manual labor. The nature of production was altered, with many handicraft workers and skilled artisans replaced by machines. People to run and maintain these machines filled the numerous jobs created. Economic growth was spurred, and new jobs in expanded economies naturally accompanied such growth.

In the short run, job displacement occurred. But as displaced workers found places for their skills in industries that had not been mechanized yet, or as they adjusted to the new, and in many cases lower skill requirements in the mechanized industry, the adjustment to change was made. Most of the impact of mechanization was felt on the shop floor, at construction sites, on railroads, in mines, and on farms. As unions expanded, especially in heavy industry, construction, and transportation, they met the onslaught of technology with work rules aimed at controlling the introduction and use of the innovations and the jobs they created.

Automation

The major technological advances of the information age were and are characterized by **automation**—the replacement of human thinking processes as well as manual labor by machine processes. General-purpose, electronic digital computers are displacing mental as well as physical labor. The nature of production has again been altered, but now computer power is displacing machinists, welders, assemblers, process controllers, clerks, secretaries, operations planners, and even some lower level managers. Economic growth has spurted, and new jobs naturally accompany this growth.

Personnel trained in setting up electronic systems, and in programming, operating, and maintaining them, are filling the numerous jobs created in the information age.* Two other interesting classes of jobs created by the use of computers involve (1) the inputting of data to the machine, which is a rather low-tech, not very exciting job but crucial to any automated system, and (2) analyzing the voluminous output of computers to extract the essential and needed information from the reams of paper generated by computer analysis, an unstructured job requiring substantial education and skills as well as patience.

Unions, seeing the growth in the primarily white-collar labor force in these new occupations, have mounted many campaigns to organize these mostly nonunion workers, but they have not been very successful. (See Chapter 1 which discusses

* The output of computer professionals, especially that of systems analysts, is predicted to be short of the demand for these skills for at least ten years in every survey published by the Department of Labor, including the Occupational Outlook series published quarterly and the bulletins covering specific industries and published intermittently. An article in the *New York Times* pointed to some of these shortages and the large wage increases they are generating for data entry clerks and computer programmers (September 5, 1988, pp. D1 and D4).

trends in union membership.) If unions don't represent a significant number of the workers involved in the newly created jobs, they cannot exert any control over the introduction, use, and spread of the technology, a technology that has and will affect them and their members, as it will all workers.

Comparing Automation and Mechanization

Unlike earlier technological change (primarily mechanization), adjustments to automation have not been and are not short run. The common results of automation are large-scale job displacement in both the short run and the intermediate run, as structural changes in the economy cause technological unemployment that may last five to ten years. New education and skill requirements are substantially different from old skills and require extensive retraining to acquire.[49] In the long run, people adjust to the opportunities that this technological change brings, developing the required knowledge and skills through education and training. In many cases, this means a college education and even graduate work.

Exacerbating the problem is the fact that automation is affecting many industries at the same time, not just one or two. Mechanization generally involved the development of relatively specific machines to replace manual labor in a given application. Its impact was somewhat limited at any one time. Automation, on the other hand, is pervasive and involves the application of a machine, the general-purpose computer, to a wide variety of tasks. Some of these tasks cut across all organizations, private and public—automation in the office, for example.[50] The diverse applications of computers is astounding. Computers dedicated to single applications can be used to control processes in the petrochemical industries, control trains, or control telephone calls. Computers can keep track of thousands of events and control their timing on a 24-hour-a-day basis, without human intervention.

Besides its pervasiveness, the spread of computer applications is very rapid. Innovations diffuse quickly, from leading edge companies to imitators to laggards, in a matter of two or three years. The speed of diffusion of automation results in major substitutions of computers for manual and mental labor, displacing blue-collar workers, especially in the mass-production industries, and white-collar office and even professional and managerial workers. This displacement moves along at an ever-increasing pace.[51] Whole job groupings almost disappear throughout the economy in two to three years, and others are drastically altered (or created) in similar, short time periods, making workers' skills obsolete almost overnight.

The two general types of technological change, mechanization and automation, are compared in Table 10.5 along six different dimensions. There are many important dimensions of technological change, and both union and management have to weigh them carefully in implementing innovation. Because of its diverse nature, automation is more difficult to analyze than mechanization.

The union response to automation has to be broader, and more immediate, than the individual's adjustment. It cannot be blind, however, nor can it be developed with only the union member in mind. Let us now turn to a discussion of the union response to technological change.

Table 10.5 *Comparing Mechanization and Automation*

	Mechanization	Automation
Technology focus	Power systems/engines and production machinery	Electronic computers
Displacement	Replaces manual (physical) labor and craft work	Replaces manual labor and cognition (mental labor)
Characteristics of new jobs created	Many lower skilled, machine operator/mass-production jobs created, as well as some more highly skilled maintenance jobs	Computer/information worker—programmer, analyst, technician—mostly highly skilled professional (white-collar) jobs
Scope of impact	Narrow range of applications, one or two industries at a time affected	Wide range of applications, cuts across almost all industries including government
Speed of diffusion	Other than power systems, moves slowly, usually in very different forms, from industry to industry	Very rapid diffusion within major companies of an industry, and initial impact is economywide (all industries)
Historical perspective	Take off in Industrial Revolution, peaking in 19th and first half of 20th centuries	Take off in information age, last half of 20th century, and accelerating with microcomputers

Union Response to Technological Advances

Technological change is an ongoing process and, especially in the long run, cannot be stopped or forestalled. Historically, technology has increased jobs through economic expansion, as it generally is output-enhancing even when first introduced to save costs. Technology increases standards of living and, on balance, is a positive element for society. Even the displacement of workers in the short or intermediate run has a positive side: many of the jobs made obsolete by technological change were both menial and dangerous.

Unfortunately, job displacement means unemployment for the individual. Even if the unemployment rate is dropping, many displaced workers cannot find jobs because their skills have been made obsolete and thus are not in demand in the labor market. These workers, many of them older union members with little opportunity for major retraining, are those on whom the American labor movement should focus.

Prior union attempts to fight innovation were failures, as noted above. Moreover, union attempts to control the pace of introduction and use of new technology through work rules were at best a short-run remedy. The programs for these workers that union and management have developed in collective bargaining negotiations are designed to soften the impact of technology, and not eliminate it. Union–management programs designed to ease the displacement of workers can be grouped into three categories:

1. Keeping workers employed, using some form of job security.
2. Allowing employers to let workers go, but maintaining worker income for a period of time after they have been "surplused."
3. Allowing surplusing, but requiring advance notice and services for these employees.

Maintaining Employment

Keeping workers employed despite technological change that makes their skills and jobs obsolete requires a relatively strong union, with a well-considered job security program. Early union attempts to this end involved restrictive subcontracting rules. An early example of this type of union strategy was that of the United Mine Workers under John L. Lewis in the 1950s and 1960s. The union encouraged mechanization in the mines, and in exchange the mining companies did not lay off workers. Employment shrunk, as did union membership, through attrition.[52] The jobs "retired" with their incumbents.

Unions can also pursue this strategy by trying to "spread the work." The building trades unions, the United Auto Workers and the United Steel Workers were and, to some extent, still are major proponents of this approach. They are able to spread the work by negotiating shorter workweeks, usually coupled with large overtime premiums or restrictions, even prohibitions, on overtime. They also negotiate longer vacations and added holidays.[53]

The ultimate spreading-the-work strategy is **work sharing,** an idea that unions traditionally opposed in favor of the use of seniority to allow older workers to maintain their jobs as younger ones got laid off. In the presence of massive layoffs and potential plant closings, however, many unions are rethinking their positions on this approach. Furthermore, several states encourage work sharing by allowing workers with reduced workweeks to draw partial state unemployment insurance payments.[54] Though still not a widespread practice, work sharing should increase as it does alleviate the impact of technological change. It fits the needs of many working families in which one or even both parents are seeking a shorter workweek and want to "share" their job with others in similar circumstances.

Recent innovative approaches to maintaining employment levels in a company as new technology is implemented are exemplified by the programs negotiated by the UAW with the Big 3 auto companies in 1984 and 1987. The 1984 program, the **job bank program** (called the Protected Employment Program or PEP at Ford), kept workers on the payroll for as long as six years if their jobs were eliminated by the introduction of new technology or outsourcing (subcontracting). The program also gave these workers extensive retraining and relocation assistance.[55]

In 1987 and 1988, the programs went a step further.[56] An **employment level program** was established in each of the companies; each company was to maintain a set number of workers, except for industrywide sales slumps during which layoffs would be allowed. In addition, for every two UAW workers that retired, the company was to add one new UAW worker. Furthermore, no plant closings were allowed. GM's

Secured Employment Level (SEL), however, could be reduced by early retirement buyouts, and GM has done that. Ford's Guaranteed Employment Number (GEN) could be reduced only through attrition, at the one in for two out pace noted. The companies, however, budgeted a given dollar amount to maintain these employment levels: $500 million at Ford and $1.2 billion at GM. The programs last only three years, the term of the contract.

The combination of the 1984 job bank programs and the 1987 employment level programs shows a new view of employee job security. When coupled with retraining and skill upgrades, these innovative programs portend a new outlook on the utilization of the present workforce.

Maintaining Income

The second approach of unions involves **income maintenance** for displaced and unemployed workers. The use of lump-sum payments to workers being surplused is one direct but short-run measure for extending income beyond the job. Severance payments, as these have traditionally been labeled, have been and are commonly awarded to professionals and management personnel upon termination. They are now becoming more common for all types of workers, and some unions have negotiated very generous payments.[57] Some of these payments are joined with an extension of company-paid medical and life insurance coverage.

An increasingly common form of income maintenance for workers who have lost their jobs is Supplemental Unemployment Benefits (SUB). This program, discussed in Chapter 8, is a relatively short-term approach to income maintenance, typically lasting one year. The Guaranteed Income Stream program, pioneered by the UAW (as was the SUB program), is a longer term approach to income maintenance after job loss. As discussed in Chapter 8, the program was limited to workers with at least 15 years of seniority. These workers could receive payments ranging from 50 to 75 percent of their pay for as long a time as they needed it. In conjunction with these payments, they could also receive testing, counseling, and retraining as well as job placement services.[58]

A widely used approach to maintain worker income after job loss is early retirement. Workers slated for surplusing are offered payments to enhance their pension income or to carry them through until they become eligible for Social Security and company pensions.[59] In many instances, a company's early retirement program is aimed at buying out older workers to implement productivity improvement and cost-cutting programs. This was the aim of the early retirement plan at GM, which was part of the 1987 employment level program discussed above. Interestingly, in recent years, early retirement on a purely voluntary basis has been declining in the United States.[60]

Enhancing Reemployment

A third union strategy designed to contend with technological change in the workplace is basically to "flow with it" and primarily soften its impact on workers. These efforts include negotiated **retraining programs,** usually coupled with job placement (outplacement) services.[61] In many instances, these retraining and outplacement services are linked to short-run income maintenance programs for the newly unemployed workers.

Outplacement services are becoming increasingly popular. By one estimate, revenues from such services leaped from $35 million in 1980 to $350 in 1988, and growth is predicted to continue, although the field is also expected to become more competitive and thus more tumultuous. One reason why corporations employ outplacement services is because the presence of the services makes the task of firing people easier. Besides defusing fired employees' anger, outplacement counselors also help employees with resume writing, interviewing, and financial planning.[62]

A frequent requirement that unions imposed on companies to soften the blow of technological displacements was advance notice of large layoffs and plant closings. A recent survey showed that less than 70 percent of companies provided advance notice of a plant closing or permanent layoff; however, this figure was over 80 percent if the company was unionized and 60 percent if it wasn't.[63] Union efforts toward this end were instrumental in the passage of the 1988 Worker Adjustment and Retraining Notification Act, which requires 60-day notice of a plant closure or mass (500 or more workers) layoff.[64] Federal mandating of **worker displacement advance notice** and retraining points to the widespread nature of this problem. These three traditional approaches are summarized in Table 10.6.

A New Approach to Implementing Technology

A new outlook on this problem of adjustment to technological change may be starting to take hold in the United States. **Sociotechnical systems,** systems for the organization and management of work, focus on blending workers and technology.[65] Initially used in Norway and then Sweden, they have become a primary element in the organizational philosophy of large Japanese companies.

In Japan, it has long been recognized that workers are the key to the successful implementation of new technology. Highly successful Japanese companies invest

Table 10.6 *Labor–Management Programs to Deal with Technological Displacement*

Approach	Focus	Some Specific Programs
Keep displaced workers employed	Job security	Work sharing; UAW job bank/GIS/protected levels of employment; loss of job by attrition only
Provide some forms of income for displaced workers	Income security	Severance pay; SUB; early retirement
Provide some form(s) of employment service for displaced workers	Enhanced reemployment opportunity	Retraining; outplacement services; advance notice of job loss

heavily in human capital by training and retraining their workers. Human factors have a key role in their organization and their management of work, and even in the design of their products. Japanese companies have maintained and upgraded the skills of their workers through extensive training programs, some with durations of a year or more, allowing them to master new machines, methods, etc.[66]

American companies are now implementing such sociotechnical systems, requiring extensive retraining of both workers and managers, in industries as diverse as financial services, engine manufacturing, auto and truck manufacturing, food processing, and consumer products.[67] This move to invest in workers rather than surplus them in order to phase in technological changes effectively will perhaps become part of the new industrial relations policy of companies. A new relationship may well develop between union and management to handle this issue.

DISCIPLINE AND THE GRIEVANCE PROCEDURE

Before leaving the subject of contract administration, a brief note on worker discipline and the place of the grievance procedure in this process is appropriate. Because the grievance procedure is the cornerstone of the day-to-day administration of the labor agreement, it is fitting to end this chapter and Part Two of the book with an introduction to it. The nature and use of the grievance procedure will be the topic of the next chapter.

Changes in Administering Discipline

Discipline cases are the most common ones addressed through the grievance procedure. The traditional philosophy of employment, the common law doctrine of employment-at-will, held that employees kept their position in the organization at the will of the employer. Under this doctrine, the employer could promote, demote, suspend, and terminate (the ultimate organizational discipline) the employee as it saw fit.

With a union present and a grievance procedure in place, this power over the employee has changed drastically.[68] In most discipline cases, management must treat the grievance procedure as a major factor. The union, as representative of the employees, will contest almost all discipline at the behest of its members. This is especially true in the case of discharge. In a unionized setting, discharge is allowed for "just cause."[69] Just cause is a very broad term and can mean many different things to different people. As has been noted in several discussions in this book, unlawful discharge suits are being filed and won with greater frequency. The power to discharge at will has been tempered.

Most human resources administrators agree that the disciplining of employees requires a consistent, systematic approach. **Progressive discipline** is a common term applied to this process. Repeated "violations" or the poor performance of the worker receive progressively greater penalties—for example, verbal to written warnings to suspension to termination, with each step accompanied by a corrective action plan for the employee. An action like termination can be upheld only for the most severe infractions.[70]

DISCUSSION QUESTIONS

1. What job rights are related to seniority?
2. Discuss the diametrically opposed views of management and labor on the width or scope of the seniority unit.
3. If you were a union shop steward and the plant manager asked you to take on the job of supervisor on the condition that you become inactive in the union to become a "solid" member of the management team, what would your response be, and what proposal might you make to the plant manager? Why?
4. What, besides seniority, limits mobility? What spurs it?
5. Were union work rules necessary in the late 1800s and early 1900s? Why?
6. Are union work rules necessary in 1992? Why?
7. What is the primary result of union work rules based on job classifications?
8. Why do unions, for example, a plant local, attempt to restrict subcontracting?
9. How does subcontracting contribute to a company's success?
10. Define mechanization.
11. Define automation.
12. Why are adjustments to mechanization, but not adjustments to automation, considered short-run changes?
13. Discuss the three general policies unions might develop to deal with the introduction of technological change in the workplace.
14. Discuss the three approaches unions might use to deal with the impact of technological change on their members.
15. In Japan, it has long been recognized that workers are the key to the successful implementation of new technology. In comparison, what do you think management in America has focused on as the key to implementing technological change? Explain.
16. Define progressive discipline, and discuss why it is important for management to develop a progressive discipline procedure in a unionized plant.

VOCABULARY LIST

seniority	production standard
seniority unit	input control rule
seniority unit width	manning requirements/crew size
bumping	duplicate/unnecessary work
labor mobility	work speed
retroactive seniority	work assignment
superseniority	job classification work assignment
work rule	output control rule

technique work rule

"work to rule"

subcontracting/outsourcing

technological change

mechanization

automation

work sharing

job bank program

employment level program

income maintenance

retraining program

outplacement services

worker displacement advance notice

sociotechnical system

progressive discipline

FOOTNOTES

1. Thomas A. Kochan et al., *The Transformation of American Industrial Relations* (Basic Books, 1986), p. 86.

2. Anil, Verma and Thomas A. Kochan, "The Growth and Nature of the Nonunion Sector Within a Firm," in Thomas A. Kochan, ed., *Challenges and Choices Facing American Labor* (MIT Press, 1985), p. 108.

3. Richard B. Freeman and James L. Medoff, *What Do Unions Do?* (Basic Books, 1984), p. 122.

4. Higher wages come through seniority (or step) pay increases, granted by many organizations on top of negotiated improvement factors and COLAs.

5. Verma and Kochan, "The Growth and Nature of the Nonunion Sector," p. 108, report a recent survey showing that 80 percent of nonunion plants use seniority in layoff and rehire decisions.

6. Michael J. Piore, "Perspectives on Labor Market Flexibility," *Industrial Relations* (Spring 1986): 148.

7. One union argument in support of seniority is that higher seniority workers, who have longer service with the organization, are higher productivity workers. When moving into new jobs, however, this doesn't seem to be the case. See Woodruff Imberman, "Who Strikes—And Why?," in Alan M. Glassman et al., *Labor Relations: Reports from the Firing Line* (Business Publications Inc., 1988), p. 390.

8. Verma and Kochan, "The Growth and Nature of the Nonunion Sector," p. 108.

9. In an organization with seniority governing most personnel decisions, it can be argued that overall organizational efficiency may be compromised as workers see little payoffs for merit since the reward system is based mostly on seniority; however, it can also be argued that experience and productivity are linked ("learning by doing"). See Freeman and Medoff, *What Do Unions Do?*, p. 133.

10. Freeman and Medoff, *What Do Unions Do?*, p. 128.

11. This phenomenon is not new. Wholesale worker migration occurs periodically in the United States; the famous movement from the Dust Bowl of the 1930s to the West Coast, especially California, was immortalized in John Steinbeck's *The Grapes of Wrath*.

12. The NLRA and its amendments define supervisors and note that they are not considered employees as defined in Section 2 (3). Section 14 (a) discusses the employer's right to legally refuse to collectively bargain with supervisory people (Commerce Clearing House, *1989 Guidebook to Labor Relations,* 1989, pp. 49–51).

13. Freeman and Medoff, *What Do Unions Do?,* p. 134. "Minority" here means "protected" workers under the equal employment opportunity laws, including blacks, Hispanics, other minorities, and women.

14. Ibid., p. 135. The male difference averages about a year, but the female difference is reversed, with black women enjoying almost a year more seniority than white women.

15. *Wall Street Journal,* March 25, 1976, p. 4.

16. *Wall Street Journal,* April 16, 1985, p. 8.

17. Commerce Clearing House, *1989 Guidebook to Labor Relations,* p. 75.

18. Melvin W. Reder, *Labor in a Growing Economy* (Wiley, 1957), pp. 190–191.

19. Commerce Clearing House, *1989 Guidebook to Labor Relations,* p. 75.

20. *Wall Street Journal,* June 4, 1986, p. 1. In 1984, Eastern Airlines gave its workers four seats on its board of directors and 25 percent of the company for wage cuts and work rule changes (but in 1986, Eastern was bought by Texas Air, prompting a major labor–management confrontation that will be discussed in Chapter 13).

21. *Wall Street Journal,* June 4, 1986, p. 1.

22. Much of the discussion in this section is drawn from Reder's section in *Labor in a Growing Economy,* pp. 197–200, and Chapter 11 in Sumner H. Slichter et al., *The Impact of Collective Bargaining on Management* (Brookings Institution, 1960), pp. 317–341, and Slichter's piece, "Make Work Rules and Policies," in Joseph Shister, ed., *Readings in Labor Economics and Industrial Relations* (Lippincott, 1956), pp. 340–344. These last two pieces are classics in this field.

23. *Wall Street Journal,* June 4, 1986, p. 1, and Slichter, "Make Work Rules and Policies," p. 342.

24. The term *featherbedding,* however, is commonly used; see *Wall Street Journal,* November 23, 1987, p. 6.

25. *Wall Street Journal,* November 23, 1987, p. 6; and September 12, 1988, p. 8, where it was reported that Congress approved legislation to end a short strike and allow three-crew trains to be used by the CNW (Chicago & North Western) rail line, a move that should spread to most other railroads.

26. Slichter et al., *The Impact of Collective Bargaining,* p. 320.

27. Slichter et al., *The Impact of Collective Bargaining,* pp. 320–321.

28. Robert N. Mefford, "The Effect of Unions on Productivity in a Multinational Manufacturing Firm," *Industrial and Labor Relations Review* (October 1986): 106; *Wall Street Journal,* June 29, 1987, p. 6.

29. See, for example, *Wall Street Journal,* April 16, 1985, p. 6; June 4, 1986, p. 1; June 29, 1987, p. 6; and *Business Week,* October 26, 1987, p. 32.

30. *Wall Street Journal*, April 16, 1985, p. 6.

31. *Business Week*, January 15, 1990, p. 23.

32. *Wall Street Journal*, August 2, 1988, p. 24 (an editorial page article by Peter Drucker).

33. Ibid. (citing 125 classifications at a Ford plant in England and an average of 60 for American auto plants in the United States); *Wall Street Journal*, June 4, 1986, pp. 1 and 21 (citing *217 classifications* at a cable manufacturing plant) and April 16, 1985, p. 6 (citing *only* 120 classifications and noting that a typical auto parts plant had 75 or more classifications).

34. *Wall Street Journal*, August 2, 1988, p. 24.

35. *Wall Street Journal*, June 4, 1986, pp. 1 and 21.

36. Ibid.

37. *Wall Street Journal*, August 2, 1988, p. 24.

38. *Wall Street Journal*, August 12, 1987, p. 4. It was noted that "The advantage for Ford of course is they are able to buy those parts at world prices."

39. Slichter et al., *The Impact of Collective Bargaining*, p. 283. Much of the following discussion in this paragraph and the following one are based on the material in this chapter of the Slichter et al. book.

40. Slichter et al., *The Impact of Collective Bargaining*, p. 285.

41. *Wall Street Journal*, July 21, 1987, p. 6.

42. *Wall Street Journal*, April 28, 1988, p. 8.

43. Slichter et al., *The Impact of Collective Bargaining*, p. 292; indirect controls, since they were infrequent, are not discussed below.

44. *Wall Street Journal*, July 21, 1987, p. 6.

45. *Wall Street Journal*, September 18, 1987, p. 3 (Ford); October 9, 1987, p. 2 (GM); May 12, 1988 (Chrysler).

46. The Window-Glass Workers, a union of skilled glass makers, fought the introduction of new automatic machines that made window glass, and they disappeared in 1928 as a union. See Sumner H. Slichter, "Technological Change—The Policy of Control," in Joseph Shister, ed., *Readings in Labor Economics and Industrial Relations* (Lippincott, 1956), p. 347; Freeman and Medoff, *What Do Unions Do?*, p. 169.

47. Slichter et al., *The Impact of Collective Bargaining*, p. 344. The major drift of technological change now, automation, certainly fits this model, creating jobs for highly skilled workers while displacing less skilled ones. The bulk of these new jobs, however, requires professional training and education, and unions have had little success in organizing these types of workers, as was noted in Chapter 1.

48. Freeman and Medoff, *What Do Unions Do?* pp. 169–170, note that this was a John L. Lewis UMW policy in the 1950s and 1960s. Now several unions are pushing companies to modernize so that they can meet foreign competition and survive. This point was made by a National Academy of Science study which concluded that "rapid adoption of new industrial technology in the U.S. will

minimize unemployment rather than expand (it)," and the "painful and costly adjustments" to technological change should be alleviated through government actions (*Wall Street Journal*, June 18, 1987, p. 30).

49. The new jobs created require "high reading and math capabilities"; these are "high-skill occupations" primarily in the service sector (*Business Week*, September 19, 1988, p. 104).

50. Jerome A. Mark, "Technological Change and Employment: Some Results from BLS Research," *Monthly Labor Review* (April 1987): 27; computer-based technology has changed the jobs of 40 to 50 million people (*Business Week*, September 29, 1986, p. 71); Russell D. Lansbury, "Technological Change and Industrial Relations: An International Comparison," *Proceedings of the Thirty-Ninth Annual Meeting* (Industrial Relations Research Association, December 28–30, 1986), pp. 463–464.

51. Mark, "Technological Change and Employment," p. 26.

52. Freeman and Medoff, *What Do Unions Do?*, pp. 169–170.

53. The USW 13–week "sabbatical," granted every five years for workers with at least 15 years of seniority, was a prime example of this strategy. It was negotiated in the early 1970s.

54. *Wall Street Journal*, April 1, 1986, p. 1. *Inc.*, May 1988, p. 130, notes that job-sharing plans became more popular in the 1980s, with 16 percent of Great Lakes region companies and 13 percent of midwestern companies using them (but only 7 to 8 percent of eastern and western region companies utilizing these plans). See also Philip K. Way, "New Developments in Employment Flexibility," *Proceedings of the 1988 Spring Meeting* (Industrial Relations Research Association, March 23–25, 1988), p. 555, where "an upward trend in . . . working sharing . . . in the 1980s" is noted.

55. *Business Week*, September 29, 1986, p. 73; *Wall Street Journal*, August 8, 1986, p. 4; July 21, 1987, p. 6; August 12, 1987, p. 4; September 8, 1987, p. 7; September 18, 1987, p. 3; September 21, 1987, p. 2; October 9, 1987, p. 2.

56. Ibid., and *Wall Street Journal*, October 6, 1987, p. 20; October 13, 1987, p. 2; May 12, 1988, p. 26 (the Chrysler settlement).

57. *Wall Street Journal*, October, 5, 1988, p. A18, reported payments of $50,000 by a railroad under its "voluntary separation program"; *Business Week*, July 18, 1988, noted that CSX Transportation made a provision of $592 million for severance packages to be offered to 8,200 of its workers. The *Wall Street Journal*, September 26, 1988, p. 4, reported that Chrysler set up a $20 million fund to meet the needs of its 4,900 workers affected by the closing of its Kenosha, Wisconsin plant. A U.S. General Accounting Office study noted that 34 percent of companies offer severance pay to their displaced blue-collar workers, usually coupled with continued health insurance coverage (*Dislocated Workers: Extent of Business Closures, Layoffs, and the Public and Private Response*, GAO/HRD–86–11632, p. 19).

58. Steven Deutsch, "Successful Worker Training Programs Help Ease Impact of Technology," *Monthly Labor Review* (November 1987): 15–16.

59. *Business Week*, October 17, 1988, p. 78; *Wall Street Journal*, October 10, 1988, p. A3A.

60. *Wall Street Journal*, August 23, 1988, p. 1.

61. Deutsch, "Successful Worker Training Programs," pp. 14–20; Mark, "Technological Change and Employment," pp. 28–29. Outplacement was at one time a "termination" service for managerial personnel, but it has now been extended to cover surplused workers at almost all levels.

62. *Fortune*, October 9, 1989, p. 85.

63. U.S. General Accounting Office, *Plant Closings: Limited Advance Notice and Assistance Provided Dislocated Workers* (GAO/HRD–87–105, July 1987), pp. 34–35; see also *Wall Street Journal*, July 26, 1988, p. 1.

64. *Wall Street Journal*, August 4, 1988, p. 29; October 11, 1988, p. 1.

65. *Business Week*, September 12, 1988, p. 70; the Tavistock research in England in the early 1960s focused on "socio-technical systems" (see, e.g., Daniel Robey, *Designing Organizations* [Irwin, 1986], p. 158) as did the follow-on Aston studies in England in the late 1960s (see, e.g., Edwin A. Gerloff, *Organizational Theory and Design* [McGraw-Hill, 1985], pp. 84–92).

66. *Christian Science Monitor*, June 23, 1988, p. 5; *Business Week*, September 29, 1986, p. 73; and September 12, 1988, p. 73.

67. *Business Week*, September 29, 1986, pp. 70–75; September 12, 1988, p. 73; September 19, 1988, pp. 105–106; *Christian Science Monitor*, May 23, 1988, p. 16.

68. Unionization virtually means a grievance procedure, as 99 percent of existing labor contracts provide for one (William H. Holley and Kenneth M. Jennings, *The Labor Relations Process* [Dryden Press, 1988], p. 291). However, a growing number of nonunion companies have adopted grievance procedures strikingly similar to those in union companies (see Kochan et al., *The Transformation of American Industrial Relations*, p. 83).

69. In a nonunion setting and especially for managerial personnel, discharge has also been increasingly challenged in the absence of a grievance procedure through the courts (wrongful discharge suits) where a sympathetic judiciary and juries have been granting substantial awards to workers (*Business Week*, October 17, 1988, p. 122).

70. See, for example, Patrick L. McConnell, "Is Your Discipline Process the Victim of RED Tape?," in Fred Maidment, ed., *Human Resources 89/90* (Dushkin Publishing, 1989), pp. 226–227.

REFERENCES

BEMMELS, BRIAN. "How Unions Affect Productivity in Manufacturing Plants." *Industrial and Labor Relations Review* (January 1987): 241–253.

COMMERCE CLEARING HOUSE. *1989 Guidebook to Labor Relations.* 1989, Chs. 2, 3, and 4.

DEUTSCH, STEVEN. "Successful Worker Training Programs Help Ease Impact of Technology." *Monthly Labor Review* (November 1987): 14–20.

FREEMAN, RICHARD B., and JAMES L. MEDOFF. *What Do Unions Do?*. Basic Books, 1984, Chs. 8 and 11.

HAWKINS, MICHAEL W. "Employment at Will: A Survey." *Proceedings of the 1988 Spring Meeting.* Industrial Relations Research Association, March 23–25, 1988, pp. 525–527.

HOLLEY, WILLIAM H., and KENNETH M. JENNINGS. *The Labor Relations Process.* Dryden Press, 1988, Ch. 8.

HUNT, H. ALLAN. "Technological Change and Employment: Fears and Reality." *Proceedings of the Thirty-Ninth Annual Meeting.* Industrial Relations Research Association, December 28–30, 1986, pp. 447–454.

IMBERMAN, WOODRUFF. "Who Strikes—and Why?" In Alan M. Glassman, Naomi Berger Davidson, and Thomas G. Cummings, *Labor Relations: Reports from the Firing Line.* Business Publications, 1988, pp. 385–395.

KASSALOW, EVERETT M. "Employee Training and Development: A Joint Union–Management Response to Structural and Technological Change." *Proceedings of the Fortieth Annual Meeting.* Industrial Relations Research Association, December 28–30, 1987, pp. 107–117.

KOCHAN, THOMAS A., HARRY C. KATZ, and ROBERT B. McKERSIE. *The Transformation of American Industrial Relations.* Basic Books, 1986, Ch. 4.

LANSBURY, RUSSELL D. "Technological Change and Industrial Relations: An International Comparison." *Proceedings of the Thirty-Ninth Annual Meeting.* Industrial Relations Research Association, December 28–30, 1986, pp. 463–470.

LOVELL, MALCOLM R., JR. "The Task Force on Economic Adjustment and Worker Displacement—A Year Later." *Proceedings of the Fortieth Annual Meeting.* Industrial Relations Research Association, December 28–30, 1987, pp. 100–106.

MARK, JEROME A. "Technological Change and Employment: Some Results from BLS Research." *Monthly Labor Review* (April 1987): 26–29.

McCONNELL, PATRICK L. "Is Your Discipline Procedure the Victim of RED Tape?" In Fred Maidment, ed., *Human Resources 89/90.* Dushkin Publishing Group, 1989, pp. 226–229.

MEFFORD, ROBERT N. "The Effect of Unions on Productivity in a Multinational Manufacturing Firm." *Industrial and Labor Relations Review* (October 1986): 105–114.

MISHEL, LARRY, and MICHAEL PODGURSKY. "The Incidence of Displacement." *Proceedings of the Fortieth Annual Meeting.* Industrial Relations Research Association, December 28–30, 1987, pp. 118–124.

PIORE, MICHAEL J. "Perspectives on Labor Market Flexibility." *Industrial Relations* (Spring 1986): 146–166.

REDER, MELVIN W. *Labor in a Growing Economy.* John Wiley, 1957, Ch. 7.

SLICHTER, SUMNER H. "Make Work Rules and Policies." In Joseph Shister, *Readings in Labor Economics and Industrial Relations.* J. B. Lippincott, 1956, pp. 340–344.

———"Technological Change—The Policy of Control." In Shister, ed., *Readings in Labor Economics and Industrial Relations*, pp. 344–355.

———, JAMES J. HEALY, and E. ROBERT LIVERNASH. *The Impact of Collective Bargaining on Management.* Brookings Institution, 1960, Chs. 10, 11, and 12.

TARG, HARRY R., ROBERT PERRUCCI, CAROLYN PERRUCCI, and DENA TARG. "Worker Responses to Plant Closings." *Proceedings of the 1988 Spring Meeting.* Industrial Relations Research Association, March 23–25, 1988, pp. 562–566.

VERMA, ANIL, and THOMAS A. KOCHAN. "The Growth and Nature of the Nonunion Sector Within a Firm." In Thomas A. Kochan, ed., *Challenges and Choices Facing American Labor.* MIT Press, 1985, pp. 89–117.

WAY, PHILIP K. "New Developments in Employment Flexibility." *Proceedings of the 1988 Spring Meeting.* Industrial Relations Research Association, March 23–25, 1988, pp. 552–557.

WISE, E. E. "New Technology and Labor–Management Relations at Ford Motor Company." *Proceedings of the 1985 Spring Meeting.* Industrial Relations Research Association, April 18–19, 1985, pp. 574–575.

PART THREE

LABOR DISPUTES AND THEIR RESOLUTION

L abor–management relations, a two-party process at the least, will naturally include conflict. The traditional adversarial nature of this dynamic relationship places disputes in a central position and makes their resolution an ongoing process. The move toward cooperation will not do away with disputes, but it will give the process of resolution an even more important role in the relationship.

In Part Three, we discuss first the most common dispute resolution process, the grievance procedure with arbitration. Most of the daily problems at the workplace that cannot be solved informally will go through the grievance process. Next, we discuss alternative dispute resolution methods for handling both day-to-day problems and impasses in negotiations that may follow. Many of these alternative techniques are utilized primarily in nonunion settings. The last two chapters of Part Three, Chapters 13 and 14, deal with the forms of the disputes themselves, from the viewpoint of the exercise of union and management power. Impasses that are not resolved lead to open conflict. In the context of contract negotiations, this usually means a labor strike or management lockout; in Chapter 13 we discuss this type of open conflict. However, unresolved conflicts between labor and management can precipitate struggles in forms other than strikes or lockouts. We discuss these in Chapter 14. Many newer, innovative techniques being used by unions are the modern-day extension of Samuel Gompers' philosophy of working with the system to gain your ends.

CHAPTER 11

GRIEVANCE PROCEDURES AND ARBITRATION

The vast majority of disputes that occur between labor and management involve managerial decisions in the workplace that upset individual workers, groups of workers, or, in a unionized environment, the union. People who have a contract that was written to cover the rules of the workplace may feel that management is not abiding by its terms. In other words, labor disagrees with management about the interpretation and application of the myriad rules and regulations that make up a collective bargaining agreement, in terms of what it allows management to do and what rights it gives the workers or the union.* This should not be surprising, given the discussion in Chapter 9 on the various forms and typical ambiguity of contract clauses dealing with management rights. These disputes are adjudicated by the **grievance procedure,** a dispute resolution process that requires both sides to work things out and otherwise use a neutral party to come to a decision.

The grievance procedure is the cornerstone of **contract administration.**[1] It is the primary day-to-day job of the on-site union local. The union will file grievances for all workers it represents as exclusive bargaining agent if they wish to dispute any actions that management has taken. Indeed, the law requires the union to do

---

* In a nonunion environment, worker grievances would focus on company policies and regulations in the workplace, contained, for example, in a company personnel (employee) manual as well as job descriptions specific to a given worker. However, nonunion workplaces have much fewer job classifications, work rules, and the like. (See Thomas A. Kochan, et al., *The Transformation of American Industrial Relations*, Basic Books, 1986, p. 96.) The *Wall Street Journal*, March 16, 1988, p. 30, discusses the grievance procedure at Chrysler for its nonunion staff, a four-step procedure with arbitration.

just that. Workers can feel confident that any legitimate grievance they have can be resolved without risking their jobs and livelihood.

WHAT IS A GRIEVANCE? ========

A **grievance** is a complaint by a worker, or group of workers, or the union itself, regarding unfair treatment. As a complaint, the grievance must be presented to management by the union and processed until satisfactorily resolved by all parties involved. Grievances fall into two main categories: contract violations and shop problems.

Contract Violation Grievances

Contract violation grievances allege that the rights of workers and the union explicitly stated or implied in the collective bargaining contract have been violated. Supervisors who are not familiar with the contract can easily invoke a grievance, even over explicitly stated worker rights. These grievances are usually settled rapidly and informally. If the contract clause or section is not explicit in terms of the rights in protest, the grievance may go through to the bitter end if both sides feel that their interpretation is correct and the matter is important enough.

During 1989, the United Auto Workers' contract with General Motors prohibited plant shutdowns. However, in 1988 and 1989, GM "indefinitely idled" three U.S. assembly plants, with more idlings planned. The union saw the idlings as plant shutdowns, and it took the issue to arbitration contending GM was playing word games. Although GM was unlikely to reopen the plants even if the decision went the union's way, the company would have to pay out about $800 million in job security payments it avoided by idling the plants rather than closing them.[2] The decision went GM's way.

Shop Problem Grievances

Shop problem grievances are filed to emphasize a problem in the shop in an attempt to get management to address and correct it. In these cases, the worker(s) and union are not debating over the application or interpretation of the bargaining agreement, but are really stating that the agreement does not contain all the responsibilities management has with respect to the workers. Safety hazards such as faulty equipment (truck drivers refusing to drive vehicles with bad brakes may file grievances if ordered to drive) are an example of this type of problem. So are changes in past practices in the shop such as management attempting to cut out a ten-minute cleanup time at the end of a shift, when those practices are not covered in the agreement but are assumed by the workers to be a part of the rules of the workplace.

In some of these instances, grievances will be filed to lay the groundwork for covering these issues in the next round of negotiations. If this is the aim of the workers and union, a number of grievances will usually be filed over the same problem.

Other Reasons for Grievances

Naming the causes for disputes in the workplace would generate a list larger than this text itself. For example, a worker might file a grievance because he or she was not given overtime. In the absence of any rules governing overtime assignments, the worker might claim arbitrary managerial actions causing a loss of earnings![3] Or a grievance might be sparked by an incident between worker and supervisor that occurred outside the workplace, after working hours. Grievances can have many roots, some of which are important to the maintenance of good labor–management relations and others that are totally irrelevant.

Sometimes a grievance may have little or no merit, but the union might push it for political reasons. First, the union leadership may be under heavy internal pressure from a dissident group of workers. The leaders will vigorously pursue all member complaints, turning them into grievances, to garner rank-and-file support.

Second, the labor–management relations climate might be poor, which will lead to many grievances because the parties do not communicate except through the grievance procedure. Poor labor–management relations are usually accompanied by many grievances carried all the way through to the last steps of the grievance procedure, clogging the system and tying up many people in the processing of these disputes. Even the most flimsy grievances might be carried through the system, especially if more solid disputes are not available to clog up the works.[4]

Third, unions may actively push grievances to avoid "fair representation" suits. As was noted earlier, the union certified as exclusive bargaining agent for a defined bargaining unit must represent all workers in that unit equally, without regard to membership status. In the absence of a union shop arrangement, some workers in the unit may not be union members. If these nonmembers had a grievance, and the union leadership felt it was not strong enough to pursue through the system, the grievants might turn around and sue the union for not fairly representing them because they were not union members. The number of suits by both members and nonmembers for breach of a union's duty of fair representation has grown substantially in the last decade.[5]

The Grievance as Protected Protest

No matter what reason is behind the grievance, the ability of a worker(s) or union to complain by submitting a grievance to management is an important element in labor–management relations. It is one of the most important benefits secured by unions for their workers, giving the worker a "voice" at the workplace.[6]

Without a grievance mechanism, the individual worker who has a dispute with management will have little recourse to protest other than quitting. If the dispute involves several workers and/or the union, they might go out on strike. The grievance procedure allows protest on the job without risk of job loss or a major production stoppage.

THE GRIEVANCE PROCEDURE

Grievance processes are specified in almost all collective bargaining agreements.[7] They tend to be multistep processes, although the number of steps varies considerably.

The typical process in a manufacturing plant, involving an industrial union local, has four steps.[8] It is a hierarchical process, moving from the lowest level, the level at which the dispute originates, upward to top local (and possibly national) union officials and top plant and/or company management. At each step, a specified amount of time is given to resolve the grievance, and, if not resolved by then, it moves upward through the process.

The typical craft union procedure has only two steps: the business agent negotiates with the employer, and if they cannot reach a satisfactory solution in the time allotted, arbitration is generally used.[9]

The configuration discussed here will be the hierarchical model, utilized by most industrial unions. It covers many more workers than the simple two-step procedure.

The First Step: The Shop Floor

Grievances usually originate on the shop floor (or in the office), when a worker or workers feel their rights are being violated. At this first stage, the grievant(s) calls in the **shop steward** to deal with the foreperson or supervisor to "right the wrong."

Most shop stewards are very familiar with the collective bargaining contract, for it may well be as important to them as their actual jobs with the company. On the other hand, most shop supervisors are not nearly as well versed on this subject, because their jobs are much broader and involve many aspects that they must know well. At this first stage, then, the shop steward has the advantage of knowledge of the collective bargaining agreement to balance the supervisor's position as management. The steward also has something of a position of power, representing the union at this stage in the process.

In an environment characterized by good labor–management relations, and without any confounding political pressures, the majority of grievances can be settled informally and amicably at this stage. This is especially true if the grievant is personally involved at this point.[10]

The Second Step: Formalizing the Grievance

If the dispute is not resolved at the lowest level within a given time period, such as a week, it moves up a notch. Higher level management is now involved, as are more union officials. The department manager or even the plant industrial relations manager becomes involved. On the union side, the **plant grievance committee**, through its chairperson or even the entire committee, becomes involved.

The dispute becomes a *formal, written* grievance. At this stage, any solution will set a precedent; thus, the discussions are more deliberate and carefully framed by the involved parties. Settlement at this stage only affects the department.[11] Management has a substantial incentive to seek resolution at this level.

If the grievance, now a formal, written dispute, is not settled at the department level within a given time period, say ten working days, it moves up the ladder. It then becomes a plantwide or companywide issue.

The Third Step: The Top Level

A grievance at step three is companywide and will involve executive-level management and the highest local union grievance officials, and in some cases national union officials. The addition of higher level union and management people brings a new objectivity to the proceedings, because these people are far removed from the original grievance and the worker and supervisor involved. The company vice-president (or director) of industrial relations will be the responding management party in most cases.

The management response at this stage will set a companywide precedent. If the grievance involves a shop floor practice, granting it will set the "law" for the shop floor. For example, if workers have been stopping work 15 minutes before the end of the shift to clean up, and management has tried to put a stop to this practice by disciplining a worker, a grievance will be filed. At this stage, granting the grievance will mean workers throughout the company can, and will, stop work 15 minutes before the shift ends to clean up.

The only way management can change a precedent-setting decision is to address the issue specifically in the next collective bargaining negotiation and to get a prohibition of the practice written into the contract. If management doesn't grant the grievance, and the union feels the issue is important enough, it will go to arbitration, the fourth step of the grievance procedure.

The Fourth Step: Arbitration

A third-party neutral is called into the process at the fourth step to make a final and binding award. Resolution of the grievance at this step is taken out of the hands of the involved parties. The arbitrator, a neutral party, will resolve the dispute, upholding (granting) the grievance or denying it. A quasijudicial process, "rights" or grievance arbitration is the topic of the next section.

This process is shown schematically in Figure 11.1.

HOW ARBITRATION WORKS

Arbitration as the last step in the grievance procedure is common to almost all collective bargaining relationships.[12] Even in nonunion settings, approximately half of which have grievance procedures, arbitration is utilized in "a small but non-negligible proportion" of these procedures—about 25 percent.[13]

Rights arbitration, as grievance arbitration is commonly called, utilizes a third party linked to neither of the parties involved in the dispute. This third party resolves the dispute in an objective fashion as only a neutral, indeed, a professional neutral, can. Interest arbitration, a form of arbitration used extensively in resolving public sector contract disputes (impasses), will be discussed in the next chapter.

What Is Arbitration?

The arbitration of grievances is **voluntary, final,** and **binding.**[14] It is *voluntary,* for both parties to agree beforehand to submit all disputes they cannot resolve between themselves to arbitration. This is in exchange for a no-strike, no-lockout clause over grievances. These agreements are contained in the collective bargaining contract, a voluntarily negotiated document. It is *final,* for it is the last step in the grievance procedure, and only under very specific and narrow circumstances can an arbitration award be appealed to the courts. These circumstances involve either fraud or a breach

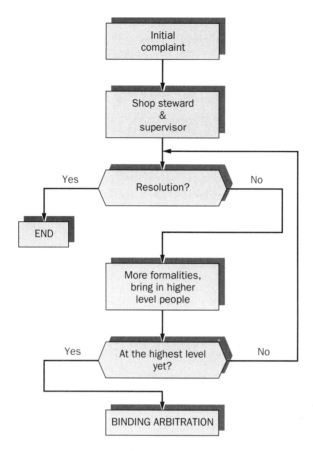

FIGURE 11.1 A typical grievance procedure.

of ethics on the part of the arbitrator or the granting of an arbitration award that goes beyond the scope of the arbitrator's charge or violates state or federal law. It is *binding* on both parties because they agree to abide by the arbitrator's decision. Furthermore, as noted above, only under rare circumstances will the judiciary entertain an appeal of the award.[15] However, such circumstances do occur, as in a recent case in which the arbitrator had a "sexual or intimate relationship" with the lawyer for one of the parties, causing the courts to intervene at the behest of the other party.[16]

What the Arbitrator Does

The role of the **arbitrator** in grievance arbitration is to interpret the situation, usually the collective bargaining agreement clause or clauses that are allegedly being violated by management, and decide if the relevant part of the agreement is indeed being violated. In many cases the arbitrator is dealing with inexact or ambiguous language and may have to base his or her decision on the intent of the parties.

Much of the time the interpretation of rights will hinge not on what is (rather ambiguously) written but rather on what has been past practice. If, for example, workers for years have been stopping work five minutes early to clean up, management cannot suddenly stop this practice. Specific contract language will be needed to halt this longtime practice, and an arbitrator, in the absence of such language, will uphold the workers' position. Consistency is important; if a worker has been disciplined in a given way (say, a one-week suspension) for a given violation, that discipline should have been used in the past with other workers committing the same or similar violations. Past practice plays an important role in arbitration, especially when contractual language is vague and ambiguous. It is akin to precedent.

Precedence—that is, the outcomes of prior arbitrations of similar cases, especially at that company—may be an important element in arbitration decisions. However, precedent is nonbinding in arbitration, unlike formal judicial proceedings. Remember, arbitration is a quasijudicial process. The arbitrator's award itself becomes a precedent that may be used in dealing with future problems that are similar in circumstance.

Finally, arbitrators will base awards on equity and fairness, especially when dealing with discipline (particularly termination) cases based on "just cause," a rather ambiguous term. When a worker's job is at stake, fairness is a particularly important basis for decision making.

In major league baseball, players with three or more years of experience can seek arbitration in salary disputes. The arbitrator chooses between the player's latest salary demand and his club's final offer and makes a decision based on what other players of comparable skill are being paid. Thus, the arbitrator bases his or her decision on both precedence and equity.[17]

The Arbitration Process

The process of arbitration starts with the selection of an arbitrator or **arbitration panel**. In most collective bargaining agreements, the use of a single arbitrator is specified. However, in some agreements, three arbitrators are used. The use of three is more expensive, but theoretically at least, the decision of a tribunal is better reasoned and more thoughtful than that of a single individual. It may be preferred if arbitration awards are felt to be important in terms of establishing the parameters of labor–management relations between a company and union.

Union and management usually share the expenses associated with arbitration. This arrangement is always explicitly stated in the collective bargaining agreement. If the expense is shared, the cost of one or of three arbitrators does not have to be borne by one party.[18]

Selecting the Arbitrator or Arbitration Panel

Most arbitrators are lawyers. They might also be academics, primarily those in the industrial relations field. Some arbitrators are trained and certified by organizations; in California, the University of California Institute of Industrial Relations set up an arbitrator training program about 15 years ago to meet the growing demand for arbitration, especially in the public sector (see Chapter 17). The American Arbitration Association (AAA) and the Federal Mediation and Conciliation Service (FMCS) certify arbitrators by virtue of adding them to the lists they maintain. These lists are divided into categories of expertise, such as discipline procedures or compensation issues. The selection of arbitrators is as varied as the variation in collective bargaining agreements themselves. However, two general approaches are used.

The first selection method is to specify, sometimes in the agreement itself, a permanent arbitrator. Large companies dealing with large union locals, in industries with rather complex operations, may utilize a permanent arbitrator for all their grievance arbitrations. This setup permits easier scheduling of grievance arbitration and reduces the time required for *ad hoc* arbitrators to familiarize themselves with the background facts that may well have many esoteric terms and phrases peculiar to the industry. It also saves time that outsiders to the relationship would need to familiarize themselves with the collective bargaining agreement. However, putting an arbitrator on retainer can be expensive. It can also encourage his or her more frequent use in the grievance settlement process, since the parties have prepaid much of the arbitration fee through the retainer and the arbitrator is "convenient." The utilization of permanent arbitrators is specified in about 6 percent of collective bargaining agreements.[19]

The vast majority of collective bargaining agreements specify the use of *ad hoc* arbitrators, chosen by the parties every time an arbitration is required. Companies and union may choose from lists of arbitrators maintained by local groups, such as the local bar association, or from lists maintained by state industrial relations agencies. Most agreements, especially those between larger companies and unions, choose (or actually agree on) an arbitrator from a list, or panel, supplied them by the AAA or the FMCS. When three arbitrators are used, each party picks one, either locally or from the AAA or FMCS. The two arbitrators then choose the third, who would be chairperson of the tribunal and who, as the truly impartial member of the group, would make most of the decisions and fashion the award.

Preparing for the Arbitration Hearing

Once the arbitrator(s) has been selected, the parties will prepare and submit a statement of their position on the matter at hand—the facts and the issue at question. In most cases, this statement will consist of a detailing of the contract clause (or clauses) at issue, and the party's interpretation of what it allows management to do. It will also include a rendering of the facts that prompted the grievance filing.

Each party can make the submission as a legal brief (a prehearing brief), or both parties can do it jointly showing agreement on the facts and the issue(s) involved and the remedy sought. If the submission is made jointly, it and the written grievance form the basis for the arbitration. If it is not joint, an arbitration agreement will have to present the issue(s) and remedy sought. The remedy sought by management is the denial of the grievance. Labor's remedy is the upholding of the grievance and some appropriate award if, for example, wages are lost. If the facts in the two briefs do not coincide, they will have to be ascertained at the hearing itself. Obviously, this approach increases the duration and cost of that hearing.

The Arbitration Hearing

As we noted earlier, arbitration is a quasijudicial process. The **arbitration hearing** may take under an hour or as long as two or three days. Rules of conduct and evidence are less formal than in a courtroom. Hearsay and "circumstantial" evidence, as well as surprise witnesses, are all acceptable in arbitration (if not advisable). The object is to seek an equitable solution and to arrive at this solution amicably so that both sides accept it with a minimum of resentment.

A parade of witnesses, exhibits, and long, drawn-out statements can make for a long hearing, especially if the facts of the case are under dispute. The substitution of emotional arguments for facts is a common error in arbitration hearings, as are the holding back of information and attempts to distort the truth (which is a nice way of saying *lying*).[20] All these tactics prolong the hearing and make the arbitrator's job more difficult. With legal representation, the hearing may become much more legalistic as well as longer.

The hearing usually involves four steps. First, the parties will make **opening statements** which invariably include the background of the case, the issue(s) involved, and why the party's position is right, given the background facts and contract and its interpretation of these facts. The union (labor) usually delivers its opening statement first, as it is typically the "plaintiff" who initially filed the grievance.

After the opening statements, both parties will present their witnesses to testify in support of their presentation of the facts and their position. This phase of the hearing will involve cross examination of the witnesses by each side as well as by the arbitrator.

In the third step, both union and management may present additional **evidence**, which is equivalent to exhibits in a courtroom trial. This evidence may include personnel files, pictures, and the like. The collective bargaining agreement and the written statement of the grievance can be included here, even though they are in the hands of both parties and the arbitrator prior to the hearing. In the absence of witnesses and other evidence/exhibits (other than the contract and written grievance), the hearing may proceed with rebuttals by each side to the other side's opening statements. This might occur in a situation where a smaller company and union are in arbitration.

The last step in the hearing will be the summaries and **closing statements** of each of the parties. In more complex and larger arbitration cases, the parties may supplement their closing presentations with written briefs. This occurs in about half of all arbitration cases.[21] Many times data or statistical evidence may be important in the case, and this type of evidence is difficult to get across in oral testimony, or the party or parties using it feel that the written evidence/exhibits did not do justice to the argument. The posthearing briefs may also be filed because of a lack of confidence in the presentation of the case during the hearing.

The Award

The last step in the arbitration process is the **award**. Awards are carefully written documents. In general, they include (1) a statement of the facts and issue(s) involved in the grievance, including the relevant provisions of the contract, (2) a summary of the union and management positions, (3) a discussion of the arbitrator's perceptions of the positions in terms of what the arbitrator viewed as the most important elements put forth and those that are most relevant to the issue(s)—in other words, the reasoning behind the award, and (4) the award including any back pay, benefits, or seniority asked for by the party whose position was upheld.

Problems with Arbitration

Although the judiciary has completely endorsed arbitration of labor disputes, there are several widespread criticisms of the process. Some of these criticisms have to do with the arbitrator as judge, a rather powerful position, but most have to do with problems inherent to the procedure itself. As was noted above, arbitration has become a more complicated and expensive procedure. One reason for the growing expense of arbitration is that it is being utilized in an increasing number of applications.

Playing to the Audience

Many critics contend that a major weakness of arbitration is the arbitrator and the arbitrator's position in the process. Unlike a judge, an arbitrator is selected by the parties in the dispute who also pay for the arbitration.

As the parties choose and pay the arbitrator, there is an incentive for the arbitrator to develop decisions and awards that insure being chosen for future arbitration cases. In a rational, analytical world, an award that is based purely on the facts and the contract provisions would be wholeheartedly accepted by both parties, and earn plaudits for the arbitrator. However, labor–management relations is an area in which emotions run high; therefore, rationality and careful analysis don't always carry the day.

Arbitrator Quality

Another problem with arbitration is the apparent lack of competence of some arbitrators as evidenced by their written awards.[22] The burgeoning demand for arbitrators, prompted by the growing use of arbitration for contract impasses, especially in the public sectors, and newer applications in industrial-commercial arbitration, has placed a great strain on the supply side. The supply of arbitrators has lagged behind the demand for them, causing the entry into the field of some unqualified people. Even some good arbitrators, in response to their busy schedules, may cut corners to accommodate to this schedule. Exacerbating this problem is the growing length of arbitration cases, tying up arbitrators for longer times on each case.

The Growing Length of the Arbitration Process

Problems are more commonly cited with the arbitration procedure than with the arbitrators themselves. These problems tend to focus on the ever-growing length and expense of arbitration. Some recent studies have shown that the average length of arbitration cases, from the filing of a request to arbitrate to the receipt of the award, has grown to about two-thirds of a year.[23] One case, between Synergy Gas Corporation, a New York propane-gas distributor, and a driver it discharged, represented by the Teamsters, recently gained notoriety as it entered its eighth year.[24]

Why are arbitration cases becoming so lengthy? There are several reasons. First, and linked to the preceding discussion of arbitrator ability, is the fact that many companies and unions will wait months to get an arbitrator they feel is experienced, competent, and fair, and will pass up newer arbitrators about whom they know nothing. Second, arbitration hearings are becoming more legalistic, with almost three-fourths of the cases involving attorneys representing one or both parties.[25] This also increases the cost of the proceedings.

The Award Format

Another factor contributing to the length of the process involves the award or decision format. Most arbitration awards, as noted above, contain the arbitrator's rationale or reasoning behind the award. The development of this part of the written decision can take substantial time. For a busy arbitrator, this time, which is preferably in a continuous block so that a coherent and well-reasoned document can be written, may not be readily available.

To cut down on the length of cases, it has been suggested that the reasoning behind the award not be included in the arbitrator's final writeup, which would just include the statement of the facts and issues, the summary of the union and management positions, and the decision-award. However, it has also been noted that the award rationale section of the arbitrator's decision is especially important to the losing party and helps them accept the adverse decision with less resentment. Trading this section off for time is a very controversial issue.[26]

The Value of Arbitration

The problems of competence, length, and expense are very real and very vexing. Numerous companies and unions are therefore experimenting with **expedited arbitration**. For example, the United Steel Workers and the can industry (the National Can Corporation and the American Can Company which is now Primerica, etc.) started using it in 1981.[27] Other approaches are being explored using relatively objective techniques. One example is to treat discharge cases as statistical problems (decision making under conditions of risk or uncertainty) and to apply decision tree analysis to them, as a rigorous approach to defining all major alternatives and outcomes.[28]

One thing is certain, however: arbitration of grievances is less costly and disruptive than work stoppages, and much less costly and lengthy than litigation. As a creation of labor and management through collective bargaining negotiations, it can be managed and changed by these parties through the same process.

DISCUSSION QUESTIONS

1. Define a grievance.
2. Name the specific kind of grievances a worker, a group of workers, and a union could have against management.

3. Outline a typical grievance procedure in an industrial union collective bargaining agreement and in a craft union collective bargaining agreement.

4. What is the role of an industrial union local shop steward in a grievance procedure? Of a first-line supervisor?

5. Why, at the second stage of the grievance procedure in an industrial union, does any solution set a precedent?

6. Why is rights, or grievance, arbitration referred to as voluntary, final, and binding?

7. If you were a plant manager for a small company in your city, dealing with a local independent union, what would you suggest to the union leaders when negotiating the section of the collective bargaining agreement that deals with choosing an arbitrator for grievances that go to arbitration? Explain your answer.

8. "Arbitrators are human, and respond to emotional arguments like all of us." Comment on this statement.

9. Devise a solution to one of the problems of arbitration listed in this chapter.

VOCABULARY LIST

grievance procedure	arbitrator
contract administration	precedence
grievance	arbitration panel
contract violation grievances	arbitration hearing
shop problem grievances	opening statement
shop steward	closing statement
plant grievance committee	award (decision)
rights arbitration	expedited arbitration
voluntary, final and binding	

FOOTNOTES

1. Chalmer E. Labig, Jr., and I. B. Helburn, "Union and Management Policy Influences on Grievance Initiation," *Journal of Labor Research* (Summer 1986): 269.

2. *Business Week*, November 6, 1989, p. 96.

3. William H. Holley and Kenneth M. Jennings, *The Labor Relations Process* (Dryden Press, 1988), pp. 288-289.

4. In an atmosphere of good labor–management relations, there may be a substantial number of grievances, but these are settled in the early, informal stages of the process. Thus, the rate of formal grievance filing is low, and the occurrence of grievance arbitration is rare (Labig and Helburn, "Union and Management Policy," p. 282).

5. See, for example, Robert J. Callaway, "Refurbishing the Grievance Procedure under Collective Bargaining," *Proceedings of the 1984 Spring Meeting* (Industrial Relations Research Association, May 2–4, 1984), pp. 485–489; Lewis Powell, "Liability of Union Which Violates Its Duty to Provide Fair Representation" (pp. 193–205) and no author, "Fair Representation Duty Not Broken by Failure to Warn of Strike Dangers," (pp. 206–208), both in Alan M. Glassman, et al., *Labor Relations, Reports from the Firing Line* (Business Publications, 1988), pp. 193–208.

6. One of the central points of Freeman and Medoff's landmark book is that unions provide the workers with a "voice" of some authority in the workplace, not the least part of which is through the grievance procedure. See Richard B. Freeman and James L. Medoff, *What Do Unions Do?* (Basic Books, 1984), pp. 7–11.

7. Freeman and Medoff, *What Do Unions Do?*, pp. 104–105; Casey Ichniowski and David Lewin, "Characteristics of Grievance Procedures: Evidence from Nonunion, Union, and Double-Breasted Businesses," *Proceedings of the Fortieth Annual Meeting* (Industrial Relations Research Association, December 28–30, 1987), pp. 415 and 417; Holley and Jennings, *The Labor Relations Process*, p. 291.

8. Holley and Jennings, *The Labor Relations Process*, p. 291; Freeman and Medoff, *What Do Unions Do?*, p. 104.

9. Balliet, Lee, *Survey of Labor Relations* (Bureau of National Affairs, 1987), p. 169.

10. Callaway, "Refurbishing the Grievance Procedure," p. 484.

11. Holley and Jennings, *The Labor Relations Process*, p. 292.

12. Ichniowski and Lewin, "Characteristics of Grievance Procedures," p. 415.

13. Ibid., p. 419. Chrysler's grievance procedure for nonunion white-collar staff includes third-party arbitration (*Wall Street Journal*, March 16, 1988, p. 30).

14. Arbitration in the public sector is usually advisory at the federal level (see Chapter 16); at the state, county, and municipal levels, interest arbitration is often involuntary, mandated by law (see Chapter 17).

15. Holley and Jennings, *The Labor Relations Process*, p. 318, discuss the Supreme Court decisions that defined the power of arbitrators to render final and binding decisions, limiting severely the roles of the courts to review these decisions; see also *Wall Street Journal*, December 2, 1987, p. 13; June 16, 1987, p. 4.

16. *Wall Street Journal*, February 14, 1990, p. A1. The arbitrator, a Mr. McIlwain, and lawyer, a Ms. Lasley, were seen leaving a hotel suite together.

17. *Business Week*, October 9, 1989, p. 96.

18. Balliet, *Survey of Labor Relations*, p. 167, where the splitting of arbitrators' fees is discussed. In many contracts, management bears the cost of witnesses from within the company (as the contract in the negotiating exercise at the end of this book notes, as does Balliet).

19. Holley and Jennings, *The Labor Relations Process*, p. 321.

20. Sterling H. Schoen and Raymond L. Hilgert, *Cases in Collective Bargaining and Labor Relations* (Richard D. Irwin, 1989), p. 230.

21. Holley and Jennings, *The Labor Relations Process*, p. 324.

22. Ibid., p. 340.

23. Ibid., p. 341.

24. *Wall Street Journal*, November 21, 1988, p. B3.

25. Richard N. Block and Jack Stieber, "The Impact of Attorneys and Arbitrators on Arbitration Awards," *Industrial and Labor Relations Review* (July 1987): 543.

26. Holley and Jennings, *The Labor Relations Process*, pp. 329–330.

27. Balliet, *Survey of Labor Relations*, p. 167; Elliot I. Beitner, "Justice and Dignity: A New Approach to Discipline," *Proceedings of the 1984 Spring Meeting* (Industrial Relations Research Association, May 2–4, 1984), pp. 501–504.

28. John E. Drotning and Bruce Fortado, "The Science of Discharge Arbitration," *Proceedings of the 1984 Spring Meeting* (Industrial Relations Research Association, May 2–4, 1984), pp. 505–511.

REFERENCES

BALLIET, LEE. *Survey of Labor Relations*. Bureau of National Affairs, 1987, Ch. 6.

BEITNER, ELLIOT I. "Justice and Dignity: A New Approach to Discipline." *Proceedings of the 1984 Spring Meeting*. Industrial Relations Research Association, May 2–4, 1984, pp. 500–505.

BLOCK, RICHARD N., and JACK STIEBER. "The Impact of Attorneys and Arbitrators on Arbitration Awards." *Industrial and Labor Relations Review* (July 1987): 543–555.

CALLAWAY, ROBERT J. "Refurbishing the Grievance Procedure under Collective Bargaining." *Proceedings of the 1984 Spring Meeting*. Industrial Relations Research Association, May 2–4, 1984, pp. 481–491.

CLARK, PAUL F., and DANIEL G. GALLAGHER. "Membership Perceptions of the Value and Effect of Grievance Procedures." *Proceedings of the Fortieth Annual Meeting*. Industrial Relations Research Association, December 28–30, 1987, pp. 406–414.

DROTNING, JOHN E., and BRUCE FORTADO. "The Science of Discharge Arbitration." *Proceedings of the 1984 Spring Meeting*. Industrial Relations Research Association, May 2–4, 1984, pp. 505–511.

FREEMAN, RICHARD B., and JAMES L. MEDOFF. *What Do Unions Do?*. Basic Books, 1984, Chs. 1 and 6.

GLASSMAN, ALAN M., NAOMI BERGER DAVIDSON, and THOMAS G. CUMMINGS. "Fair Representation Duty Not Broken by Failure to Warn of Strike Dangers." In Alan M. Glassman, Naomi Berger Davidson, and Thomas G. Cummings, *Labor Relations, Reports from the Firing Line*. Business Publications, Inc., 1988, pp. 206–208.

GORDON, MICHAEL E. "Grievance Systems and Workplace Justice: Tests of Behavioral Propositions about Procedural and Distributive Justice." *Proceedings of the Fortieth Annual Meeting*. Industrial Relations Research Association, December 28–30, 1987, pp. 390–397.

HAUCK, VERN E., and JOHN C. SOUTH. "Arbitrating Discrimination Grievances: An Empirical Model for Decision Standards." *Proceedings of the Thirty-Ninth Annual Meeting*. Industrial Relations Research Association, December 28–30, 1986, pp. 239–243.

HILL, MARVIN F., JR., and ANTHONY V. SINICROPI. *Evidence in Arbitration*. Bureau of National Affairs, 1987.

HOLLEY, WILLIAM H., and KENNETH M. JENNINGS. *The Labor Relations Process*. Dryden Press, 1988, Chs. 8 and 9.

ICHNIOWSKI, CASEY, and DAVID LEWIN. "Characteristics of Grievance Procedures: Evidence from Nonunion, Union, and Double-Breasted Businesses." *Proceedings of the Fortieth Annual Meeting*. Industrial Relations Research Association, December 28–30, 1987, pp. 415–424.

———. "Grievance Procedures and Firm Performance." In Morris M. Kleiner, Richard N. Block, Myron Roomkin, and Sidney W. Salsburg, eds., *Human Resources and the Performance of the Firm*. Industrial Relations Research Association, 1987, pp. 159–193.

KOCHAN, THOMAS A., HARRY C. KATZ, and ROBERT B. McKERSIE. *The Transformation of American Industrial Relations*. Basic Books, 1986, Ch. 4.

LABIG, CHALMER E., JR., and I. B. HELBURN. "Union and Management Policy Influences on Grievance Initiation." *Journal of Labor Research* (Summer 1986): 269–284.

McCABE, DOUGLAS M. "Grievance Processing in the Non-Union Setting—Peer Review Systems and Internal Corporate Tribunals: A Procedural Analysis." *Proceedings of the Spring 1988 Meeting*. Industrial Relations Research Association, March 23–25, 1988, pp. 496–502.

MEYER, DAVID, and WILLIAM COOKE. "Economic and Political Factors in Formal Grievance Resolution." *Industrial Relations* (Fall 1988): 318–335.

PETERSON, RICHARD B. "A Multiple-Measure Test of Grievance Procedure Effectiveness." *Proceedings of the Fortieth Annual Meeting*. Industrial Relations Research Association, December 28–30, 1987, pp. 398–405.

POWELL, LEWIS. "Liability of Union Which Violates Its Duty to Provide Fair Representation." In Alan M. Glassman, Naomi Berger Davidson, and Thomas G. Cummings, *Labor Relations, Reports from the Firing Line*. Business Publications, 1988, pp. 193–205.

SCHOEN, STERLING H., and RAYMOND L. HILGERT. *Cases in Collective Bargaining and Labor Relations*. Richard D. Irwin, 1989, Part Two, pp. 211–229.

SINICROPI, ANTHONY V. "Arbitrator Development: Programs and Models." *Arbitration Journal* (September 1982): 29.

A P P E N D I X *

ARBITRATION CASE #1**

Social Security Administration, Westminster Teleservice Center and American Federation of Government Employees, Local 3302

Issue   Was the Grievant entitled to emergency annual leave as she requested on February 16, 1988?

Background   The Grievant was employed as a Contact Representative by the Westminster, MD, Teleservice Center (TSC) on February 16, 1988. At the time, she and her seven year old son lived in Randallstown, which is some 30 miles from Westminster. They had been living in Randallstown for about five months. She had no relatives in the Randallstown/Baltimore area, but did have a sister in Washington, D.C., 52 miles away.

She made arrangements for child care as soon as she moved into the area. First, she got her primary caregiver, a Mrs. [A], from a list given her by the state Department of Social Services. (Mrs. [A] was also listed on the approved list maintained by the VIP program, which is a child care resource and referral service contracted for by the Agency). She used the VIP list to get a second person, a Mrs. [B], for times when Mrs. [A] might not be available. Before arranging for babysitting services, she visited each woman with her son to give them an opportunity to get acquainted with one another.

On February 16, Mrs. [A] called her at about 6 a.m. and told her she had had problems with her car over the weekend and would not be able to care for her son that day. (February 16 was a Tuesday, but Monday had been a holiday.) The Grievant then made a number of calls to Mrs. [B]. She was finally able to reach Mrs. [B] at about 8 a.m., but was told she could not care for her son because her husband had suffered a heart attack the night before and she had just come home from the hospital to change her clothes.

The Grievant called the office, a long distance call, at about 8:15 a.m. She asked the employee who answered, an Administrative Aide, to speak to [S1], her supervisor. [S1] was tied up on another call, and the Grievant was connected with another supervisor in the office, [S2]. The Grievant said that she could not get a babysitter and was requesting emergency annual leave. [S2] told her that this was a day after a holiday, the TSC was short-staffed and leave was restricted. She asked the Grievant to hold on while she checked to make sure of what the actual staffing situation was. The Grievant asked that she hurry because the call was long distance.

[S2] put her on hold and spoke briefly to [S1] and checked the office calendar. [S1] told her she was busy with her call and asked [S2] to handle the situation. She went back to the phone and told the Grievant that they were short-staffed,

---

* These cases are reproduced with permission from *Labor Arbitration Awards*, published and copyrighted by Commerce Clearing House, Inc., 4025 W. Peterson Ave., Chicago, Illinois, 60646.

** *Source:* Commerce Clearing House, *Labor Arbitration Awards*, 89–2 ARB Paragraph 8611.

that she would have to try to get a babysitter, and that she could not approve leave for the day. The Grievant then asked to speak to [S1]. When told that [S1] was still on the telephone, she asked that [S1] call her back. [S2] said [S1] would not do so because she, [S2], had taken care of the matter. At that point, the Grievant hung up. (At the hearing, the Grievant recalled [S2] asking her if she had any relatives in the area; [S2] did not remember asking.)

[S2] recounted the conversation to [S1] when the latter was no longer on the phone. Both assumed that the Grievant would try to get a babysitter. [S2] told [S1] that the Grievant had asked her to call her back, but [S1] decided not to do so because she felt that [S2] had acted within her authority and had handled the situation.

Shortly thereafter the Aide informed [S2] that the Grievant was again on the line and wanted to speak with her. She picked up the phone. The Grievant said "I just want to tell you one thing. I'm sick and tired of your bullshitting attitude. I'm not coming in. Put [S1] on the phone." However, at this point [S1] was again on the phone and [S2] told her that. The Grievant then screamed, "put it on notice, I'm not coming in" and she again hung up.

[S2] then discussed the situation with [S1]. She told her about the conversation, and that the Grievant had sounded nervous and upset. [S2] recommended the Grievant be carried as AWOL for the day because leave had not been approved and it did not appear that she would come in or make any further efforts to get a babysitter. [S1] tentatively agreed but decided to wait until the end of the shift before making a final decision.

[S2] stated at the hearing that she made that recommendation because of the workload situation and because she did not believe a true emergency existed. The Grievant ended the phone calls abruptly, before there was even a chance to discuss further options which might have been able to resolve her problem. The possible options were use of the VIP service which has an 800 number to provide referrals on an emergency basis, and also, the TSC has a child care coordinator who keeps lists of babysitters. She and others have been helped by the Coordinator in the past. [S2] stated that she wanted to be certain that all possible options had been explored before determining that an emergency existed. The Grievant hung up on her before this could be done.

With respect to workload, [S2] asserted that the months January through April are traditionally the TSC's busiest months. It was also the Tuesday after a holiday, making it, in effect, a Monday, which is the busiest day of the week. While the Grievant was not in her unit, she had the authority to approve or disapprove leave for her in the absence or unavailability of [S1].

When the Grievant came to work the next day, she explained her problem about getting a babysitter in detail to [S1]. She acknowledged that she had been irrational in her calls the day before, and that she should not have said some of the things she did to [S2]. [S1] asked if she had apologized to [S2] and she said she had not. [S1] said that [S2] had children of her own, that she understood these situations, and that she could have helped the Grievant if she had explained her problem to her.

The Grievant submitted a leave request that day. [S1] said that she would have to think about it and would get back to her. Later that day [S1] determined that she would not approve the request and would charge the absence to AWOL. However, she did not notify the Grievant at the time, and did not officially disapprove the request until February 25.

[S1] testified that, in order for her to have approved the leave request, the Grievant would have had to prove to her that there was an emergency and that she had exhausted all means to get a babysitter. In her view, there had been no emergency because the Grievant had not made additional attempts to secure a babysitter and also because, if the Grievant had explained what her problem was, the Agency could have helped her with the babysitting lists it maintains. There would have been an emergency only if the Agency had not been able to help. Further, the workload situation was such that she was needed at work. On February 16, of the 29 employees at the TSC, there were five employees out: three were on pre-approved leave and two had called in on sick leave.

The Grievant has 10 years of Federal work service and has never been disciplined. Prior to the event leading to the present grievance, she had never had a leave problem and had never before requested emergency annual leave because of a babysitting problem.

[S1] testified that the Grievant told her on February 17 that she was aware of the VIP 800 referral service. This was not disputed. However, it is the Union's claim that while the Grievant was aware that the service could be used to establishing a child-care relationship, and did in fact use it for that purpose, she was not aware that it could be used for emergency situations such as that facing her on February 16.

The basis for the Agency's view that the Grievant knew, or should have known, that the VIP service could provide an emergency referral is contained in a pamphlet "Child Care Strategies for Working Parents," given to employees, including the Grievant. The pertinent portion is contained on the first page:

> No matter how well the child care arrangements you have decided on seem to be working out, there may be days, even weeks, when your world will be set on end because of a child's illness or some temporary failure in your child care system. When these days come, your supervisor's guidance and support can make an important difference.
>
> Open communication with your management, important under any circumstances, can be critically important as you define your role as a working parent. If management understands your long-term goals and commitment, as well as any problems you may be experiencing in combining work and parenthood, it will be easier for your manager to help you.

Union Position   The Union offered into the record the definition of "emergency" from the Random House Dictionary of the English Language, Second Edition, Unabridged:

> 1. a sudden, urgent, usually unexpected occurrence or occasion requiring immediate action. 2. a state, esp. of need for help or relief, created by some unexpected event: a weather emergency; a financial emergency.

The Grievant's situation met the commonly understood meaning of "emergency." She had a child care emergency. It is not disputed that the two people she reasonably and legitimately depended upon for child care were suddenly and unexpectedly unavailable to her on February 16. Indeed, her circumstance exactly met the situation described in Article 20, Section 5, that is, there was an unexpected change in her child care arrangements.

Management Position The two cited sections of the agreement specify two criteria in connection with requests for emergency leave. They are, first, the existence of an emergency, and second, workload considerations. The Agency concedes there was no operational exigency on February 16. Both [S2] and [S1] considered the office short-staffed that day, and that the Grievant's presence was needed. While this was a factor in their thinking, it is clear that the primary consideration in the refusal of annual leave was the fact that they did not believe a true emergency existed.

PERTINENT CONTRACT PROVISIONS

Article 20. Child Care

Section 5. Leave The Employer agrees to grant emergency annual leave requests and to consider emergency requests for leave without pay brought about by unexpected changes in child care arrangements, contingent on the needs of the organization.

Article 31. Time and Leave

Section 2. Annual Leave B. Normally, leave requested in advance will be granted except where conflicts in scheduling or undue interference with the work of the Administration would preclude it. Leave may also be granted when it is not scheduled in advance and business permits. Leave for personal emergencies, ordinarily infrequent in number, will be granted unless there is an operational exigency which requires the employee's presence.

Question Was the Grievant's problem an emergency covered by the contract, or was she AWOL; what do you believe the arbitrator's award should be?

ARBITRATION CASE #2*

Burns International Security and UPGWA, Local No. 538

Issue Did the Company have just cause to discharge (A) on March 8, 1988, and, if not, what is the appropriate remedy?

Background The Grievant, Ms. (A), began her employment with the Company on or about October 21, 1986, as an unarmed guard. In January 1987 she was promoted

* *Source:* Commerce Clearing House, *Labor Arbitration Awards,* 90–1 ARB Paragraph 8005.

to armed guard after receiving training and passing the necessary tests. Later in 1987 she took the exam for sergeant on several occasions and was encouraged to continue her efforts to be promoted to sergeant by management, but she decided to pursue her union interests instead. There seems to be no question that she was knowledgeable and knew her job and her responsibilities.

Some of the responsibilities of the Post Order of the Switchgear Project Compensatory Post, which was the Post the Grievant was assigned to, are as follows:

1. Be continuously observant for any indication of perimeter intrusion or attempted intrusion.

2. Be continuously observant for any deficiencies or abnormal conditions along the fence lines.

3. Insure that no materials are handed through the fence line in either direction.

The Grievant, (A), was discharged for violation of a class one offense of the Burns Rules & Discipline Policy on March 4, 1988, to wit: Willful or gross neglect of duty (omission or act that could be citable by the Nuclear Regulatory Commission). At the time of her discharge Ms. (A) was an armed nuclear security guard.

The events leading to Ms. (A)'s discharge began on March 4, 1988 when the Company was testing its surveillance cameras. The person working the camera noticed Ms. (A) on her post in a guard shack sitting down with her head down, apparently reading. Ms. (A)'s activities were then videotaped and for between 5–6 minutes she was observed with her head down, reading something. The arbitrator was provided with a copy of the video which was admitted into evidence as Company Exhibit 2. A viewing of the video confirmed that Ms. (A) was sitting in a guard shack reading for more than 5 minutes with her head down. During this 5+ minute interval she did not look up to view the area that she was supposed to be guarding.

After the incident was reported to a supervisor, Ms. (A) was relieved of her duties and replaced by another guard. Upon relieving her a *National Enquirer* magazine was recovered from the guard shack and a page from that magazine was later surrendered by Ms. (A). At the time, Ms. (A) claimed to her supervisor that she was simply tearing a recipe from the magazine which she found in the guard shack. She was unaware that her activities had been videotaped. She was suspended from duty immediately, pending further investigation.

The following Monday, March 7, after a conversation with Chief of Security, (B), the Grievant was discharged.

Ms. (A) stated in her testimony that the magazine was behind a portable heater in the shack—but there was testimony and a report that indicates that a post cannot be accepted by a guard if it is not completely clean of debris and reading material except the Post Orders. The previous guard at the Post filed a report that he did not see any reading material on the post. Regardless of this fact, it was still a violation of the Post Order not to be continuously observant of the area she was guarding.

There was a great deal of emphasis about 2 previous incidents when reading material was discovered. In one instance a guard had a book on his person. And in another incident a guard was leafing through a paper back book to be sure there was nothing left in it before he loaned it to another employee. Neither case involved reading on post; neither case involved a compensatory post and in each case a suspension was given for the violation.

Union Position   The Union claims that there was not just cause for termination for a brief inattentiveness to duty; that there were previously similar violations by other employees that were treated with short suspensions and that the Grievant's discharge was motivated by the Company's antiunion attitude.

Management Position   The Company claims that the Grievant's conduct was in violation of the Company's policies, rules and regulations and the requirements of her job and assignment to a compensatory post. Further, that her termination was in no way related to her activities as an officer of the Union.

PERTINENT CONTRACT PROVISION

Article IV. Management Rights

This Agreement shall not be construed to infringe or impair any of the normal management rights of the Employer which are not inconsistent with the provisions of this Agreement. Included among management rights is the right to hire new employees and direct the working forces; the right to discipline, suspend, or discharge employees for just cause; the right to assign shifts; the right to transfer or lay-off employees because of lack of work; the right to require employees to observe Employer policies, rules, and regulations not inconsistent with this Agreement; the right to plan, direct, control, or discontinue operations; the right to determine the method and manner of operations and the number of employees necessary to perform operations; the right to establish the standards of work performance for employees; the right to introduce new or improved methods; the right to change existing business practices. This statement of management rights which remains unimpaired by this Agreement is not intended to exclude others which are not mentioned herein.

Question   Did the punishment (discharge) fit the crime, and if not, what punishment would; what should the arbitrator's award be?

ARBITRATION CASE #3*

Capitol Plastics of Ohio, Inc. and Amalgamated Clothing and Textile Workers Union, AFL–CIO/CLC and Local 1901

Issue   Whether Grievant's discharge was "unreasonable or not for just cause" and if so, what remedy is appropriate?

Background   Grievant was hired on December 16, 1985. His schedule required him to report on three consecutive days for twelve hour work shifts and then be off for three consecutive days.

---

* *Source:* Commerce Clearing House, *Labor Arbitration Awards*, 89–2 ARB Paragraph 8309.

On February 21, 1986 the Company gave written notice to "All Employees" that it was revising its Attendance Control Policy. The announcement said "It will also provide for specific progressive discipline when absences exceed a tolerable level." The new policy was based on "occurrences," defined as incidents of absence and tardy/leave early. Except for certain categories which are expressly excused, every absence and tardy/leave early incident is assigned a full or part occurrence. Correlated to the number of occurrences, the discipline systems involves four discipline stages, starting with a first warning, and then for a specified number of additional occurrences a "stage 2 warning."

Once a stage 2 warning has been received the employee needs to pay close attention to improving attendance at work. If any of the following occurs after a stage 2 warning, a three day disciplinary suspension will be imposed:...

2 occurrences in the succeeding 3 month period;

4 occurrences in the succeeding 6 month period....

In Stage 4, once suspended, an employee's job is in jeopardy if the attendance does not improve. If it does not, any of the following will lead to discharge:

2 occurrences in the succeeding 3 month period;

4 occurrences in the succeeding 6 month period...

During the six months of his employment Grievant attended satisfactorily. Then on August 15, 1987 he was issued a "1st warning" for three occurrences of Tardiness and Absenteeism. He improved in the third quarter but regressed somewhat in the fourth quarter although his occurrences were still within limits permitted by the Attendance Control Policy for the balance of the year.

In 1987 he was arrested for "Driving Under the Influence of Alcohol" and pled guilty. At that time he was given a three day sentence and the Judge warned that further violations would result in more severe punishment. He was allowed to serve his sentence without interfering with his work schedule.

In the first quarter of 1988, Grievant's occurrence "account" was slowly rising. The upward trend would ultimately merit a Stage 2 warning. Although Grievant continued to be a good worker, the Company's Personnel Director initiated communication with Grievant concerning suspected indulgence by Grievant in alcohol and possibly drugs, encouraging Grievant to use available assistance facilities. At that time Grievant denied drug and alcohol use and did not accept the Director's suggestions.

Grievant was again arrested in the first quarter of 1988 for Driving Under the Influence of Alcohol and for other charges. He decided to plead guilty and his attorney attempted to work out a plea bargain. While this process was under way Grievant came to the Company on several occasions to ask for consideration on his scheduling obligation so that he could serve whatever penalty was imposed by the Court without being considered absent without excuse. Grievant reported to Personnel Director [A] that his attorney thought the jail sentence might be for 10 to 15 days; he asked Mr. [A] for a leave of absence to serve the sentence. Mr.

[A] said he had to deny the leave request because he did not want to begin or establish a precedent of considering "incarceration" as a "justifiable cause" for leave under Section 13.2 of the Labor Agreement. However, Mr. [A] said he wanted to help Grievant so he suggested that Grievant ask to serve his sentence after the 1988 vacation season began on June 1, 1988. At that point Grievant had three days remaining from his 1987 vacation which was supposed to be used by May 31, 1988, and he would be eligible to use another 11 vacation days in the June 1, 1988 to May 31, 1989 vacation season.

On April 18, 1988 Grievant received an occurrence because he was tardy after appearing in Court. In Court he had pled guilty to various charges although he knew the Judge had said he would show Grievant "no mercy." The Court imposed a monetary fine, 30 day jail sentence, and the following conditions for three years:

No traffic offenses involving alcohol

No criminal offenses

Submit to alcohol test upon police demand

No drinking of alcohol

Complete evaluation/recommendation of Wood County Council on alcoholism

Suspension of driver's license

If any of the aforementioned conditions is violated in the three year period, Grievant is subject to resentencing.

The thirty day jail term would require Grievant to miss 14 work days, exactly the number of total vacation days to which Grievant was entitled. The Judge refused Grievant's request, suggested by Mr. [A], to serve the sentence in June when the Company would allow him to use vacation time rather than jeopardize his employment. The Court ordered Grievant to begin his sentence on April 25, 1988.

Grievant asked Mr. [A]'s permission to take the balance of his 1987 vacation and his 1988 beginning April 25, 1988. Mr. [A] refused on the ground that the Labor Agreement required the 1988 vacation season to begin June 1st.

Entering jail on April 25, Grievant was scheduled for release on May 24, 1988. During his absence, his father phoned in every one of the 14 days Grievant missed and reported that Grievant would be absent due to incarceration.

On May 24, the Company sent a certified letter to Grievant addressed to his home. The letter stated:

You have been absent from work for an extended period of time. Your last day at work was April 24, 1988. Your attendance record was not exemplary up until that time.

In view of your absences, you are terminated, effective immediately, and your seniority and benefits canceled accordingly.

May 24 was also the day Grievant was released from jail. The next morning he came to the Company ready to return to work. He was told about his discharge and given a copy of the letter which he had not yet received.

In the year since his incarceration, Grievant participated and completed a 20 week treatment program conducted by the Wood County Council on Alcoholism and Drug Abuse. He has not obtained a job other than part-time work at a dog shelter as part of a "work fare"/welfare program. To contribute to the support of his family, he has accepted sporadic work on lawn/yard maintenance, the only work he could find.

At arbitration Grievant admitted his prior abuse of alcohol and drugs, but testified that he does not and will not resume. He also asked for a "last chance" to live up to that commitment and fulfill his responsibilities as employee and parent.

On May 26, 1988, the Union filed the following case:

We feel the termination of [Grievant] was unfair and unjust. We are asking for his reinstatement and all back pay until this is settled.

The Company's written 3rd step disposition stated as follows:

The grievant's own actions caused his legal difficulties and subsequent absences. The discharge was correct and proper with no mitigating circumstances. Grievance denied.

There were several other supplemental third step meetings and answers but the Company maintained its position. Thereafter the Union appealed to arbitration. At the hearing the Parties stipulated that the Arbitrator has jurisdiction and that there are no procedural problems.

Union Position   The Company refused to grant the leave and discharged the grievant. The grievant was discharged by the employer when he was sentenced to 30 days in jail for driving while intoxicated. At the time of his sentencing the grievant requested a leave of absence from the Company pursuant to Article 13.2 of the Collective Bargaining Agreement.

It is the Union's position that in light of the grievant's past work record the Company should have granted the leave. Although the reason given in the request on its face may not seem justifiable, it is the Union's position in this case it was justifiable for the following reasons:

1. The grievant has a good work record.
2. The Company has granted vacation time in the past for similar occurrences for other employees.
3. The grievant has sought treatment for alcoholism.
4. Alcoholism is a disease and should be treated as a disability; therefore, a request for leave is justifiable.
5. Arbitrators have held that management's determination to grant or deny leaves for "personal business" must be reasonable and non-discriminatory.

Therefore, based on the above the Union's position is that the company's refusal to grant the leave was unreasonable and the grievant should be reinstated.

There was no just cause for discharge so the Company exceeded its rights under Article 3 and violated Grievant's seniority rights under Section 6.24 of the Labor Agreement.

Company Position   This matter is properly presented to the Arbitrator under the Bargaining Agreement in effect...

...The joint exhibits help to clarify the chronology and the logical progression of the circumstances of the grievance. The Union exhibits, while interesting, are not particularly significant to the specifics of this case. The Company has demonstrated in its exhibits that there has been consistent discipline, including discharge, for employees who have been absent from work. These exhibits illustrate that both the "Attendance Policy"...and just cause have been applied regularly in cases involving employees who have been absent. (See below.)

...[Grievant] specifically violated the attendance policy...his termination was not solely based on the attendance policy, but it was, in fact, for just cause as a result of his absences...[Grievant] had refused the direct Company suggestion of contacting various agencies, including the Wood County Council on Alcoholism (WCCA). ...the Company had attempted to offer various suggestions so that he might maintain his employment. His personal activities and the judicial system did not allow these suggestions to be accomplished.

...The Company also demonstrated a sense of fairness prior to [Grievant's] incarceration by the numerous contacts and various alternatives that were suggested by the Company. [Grievant's] own actions and his assistance caused his difficulty. The termination was proper.

...There is a preponderance of evidence, ...as to the Company's attempts at assistance offered, the consistency of attendance requirements expected of all employees, and consequences when satisfactory attendance is not maintained. The Company has acted fairly in this matter. We trust that the Arbitrator will find in favor of the Company.

Attendance Cases Submitted by the Company   To show that discharge is reasonable and just for Grievant's extended absences the Company submitted discharge notices given 14 employees in the period 2/11/87–2/1/89. Six of those discharges [B], [C], [D], [E], [F] and [G] are expressly stated to be "under the current Attendance Control Policy" which the Company does not purport to apply to Grievant's case. The other eight discharges were issued between 2/11/87 and 11/1/88 including five after Grievant's discharge.

> 2/11/87—Ms. H—was discharged because she left work 8½ hours early, was absent for 17 calendar days, worked six days but then was absent 17 more calendar days. In other words she was absent for two extended periods.

> 3/4/87—Mr. S—was discharged after supplying "altered medical documentation" for "an extended period" of absence.

> 4/25/88—Mr. R—was discharged because he failed "to supply adequate documentation for [extended] absences."

In four of the extended absence cases after Grievant's discharge, the cause was failure of the employee to maintain contact with the Company about his absence. In the last case the employee failed to supply documentation that continued absence was necessary.

PERTINENT CONTRACT PROVISIONS

Article III—Management Rights

3.1 Management Rights   The Parties that agree that subject only to the express provisions of this Agreement, the supervision, management, and control of the Company's business and and direction of the work force, operations and plants are exclusively the functions of the company.

3.2 Establishment of Work Rules   Without limiting the generality of the foregoing, the Company retains the sole right to promulgate and publish reasonable work rules and rules of conduct for employees while on the Company's property during their working hours and to fix and determine reasonable penalties for violations thereof. . . . All notices of violation of such rules shall be in writing and shall specify the offense and the penalty imposed and copies of such notices shall be given to the employee and the employee's steward. Any claims of wrongful or unreasonable discipline, suspension or discharge shall be subject to the grievance procedure provided herein.

6.24 Seniority Termination   Seniority and job rights shall be terminated for any of the following reasons: . . . (b) If he is discharged for just cause and his discharge is not reversed through the grievance procedure.

Article VII—Grievance and Arbitration Procedure

7.7 Arbitrator's Decision   The decision of the arbitrator shall be final and binding upon the Parties, and shall be complied with promptly.

7.9 Limits of Arbitrator   . . . The arbitrator shall decide the grievance, dispute or disagreement in writing and deliver a copy to each party as promptly as possible. Each party shall be bound by the decision of the arbitrator and shall comply therewith with all deliberate speed.

7.11 Grievance Time Limitation—Discharge or Suspension   If an employee desires to grieve his or her discharge or disciplinary suspension as being unreasonable or not for just cause, he or she must file a written grievance. . . .

Article XXX—Leaves of Absence

13.2 Leaves—Other Employees   Upon an employee's written request, supported by justifiable cause, the Company may grant an unpaid leave of absence without loss of seniority for up to thirty (30) days subject to reasonable extension. The written leave request shall state fully the reasons therefor and shall be presented also to the Union.

Question   Did the Company follow its published attendance policy; what award should the arbitrator make?

ARBITRATION CASE #4*

United Food and Commercial Workers Union, Local 775 and Levitz Furniture Company of the Pacific, Inc.

Issue   Did the Company violate the collective bargaining agreement when it refused to allow the Grievant to bump a retail sales associate for his weekly sales schedule?

Background   [A] (hereinafter called "Grievant") was hired by the Company in November 1972, and became a sales associate in October 1983, at the Company's San Francisco store. Sales associates are assigned to one of two crews. The A crew works Saturday through Tuesday and every other Wednesday. The B crew works Thursday through Sunday and every other Wednesday. These crews are usually equally staffed, with about 13 associates on each crew.

Before February 1988 the Grievant worked on the A crew. As a result of a personality conflict between two sales associates on the B crew, one of them, [B], was transferred by management to the A crew. This transfer caused an opening on the B crew. When no one volunteered to be transferred, the Branch Manager, [C], decided to transfer the Grievant to the B crew. The Grievant asked that [D], who became a sales associate in September 1987 and was thus junior to the Grievant, be moved instead of her.

The crux of the dispute is whether the Company acted properly when it transferred the Grievant instead of [D] to the B crew. There is contract language that must be interpreted, as well as past practice and bargaining history to consider.

Union Position   In its post-hearing brief, the Union contends that the Company has interpreted the term "seniority" to mean "volume." The real reason the Grievant was transferred is said to be that her sales volume was the same as [B]'s. Overemphasis by the Company on volume and equating volume with seniority is said to contradict the plain meaning of the term "seniority," which is continuous service with the Company.

The contract language in Article 8.5.2 is cited as requiring consideration of seniority in work scheduling, provided that adequate coverage and properly balanced shifts can be maintained. Branch Manager [C] and Vice President [E] are said to have not considered either the Grievant's seniority or her experience. Instead, their focus was strictly on the crew's relative sales volumes. The Union argues that this view renders seniority practically worthless. As a contractual right, seniority cannot be denied by the exercise of the management rights clause.

Past practice is said by the Union to support its position. Testimony of witnesses in arbitration is cited as examples of employees being bumped by more senior employees in the past. Also referenced is a meeting between Branch Manager [C] and all sales associates, at which [C] is supposed to have opened up all work

* *Source:* Commerce Clearing House, *Labor Arbitration Awards*, 89–1 ARB Paragraph 8187.

schedules for bidding by seniority. The Union argues that Article 24 of the agreement prevents a party from arguing a past practice as an implied contractual term, rather than precluding consideration of past practice to interpret an express term of the contract.

As to bargaining history during 1977 and the Company's understanding that shift selection by seniority was untenable, the Union contends that Mr. [E]'s understandings are not important in interpreting the language, because the Union negotiators did not concur with his views.

The remedy sought by the Union is restoration of the Grievant to her old schedule. This is said to be justified by her 15 more years of service and four more years of sales experience than that of [D].

Company Position   In its post-hearing brief, the Company argues that the collective bargaining agreement does not allow a right to sales associates to bump other sales associates for weekly schedules. In order for bumping to be allowed, it has to be clearly stated in the contract, which is not the case in the contract in question. Indeed, notes the Company, sales associates do not even have a right to select weekly schedules in the first place because that is for management to determine.

The Company points out its rationale in transferring the Grievant. She had a low volume of sales, much the same as [B], whereas [D]'s sales were twice as much. Because the word "ability" is used in the contract, sales volume is said to be significant in determining a sales associate's ability and thus is appropriately used in shift scheduling.

Past practice is argued to be irrelevant because no bumping is allowed by the contract. Even if past practice were relevant, the Company contends that it has not been adequately demonstrated. Cited in this regard are specific incidents of bumping testified by Union witnesses that allegedly took place in 1977, 1979, and 1982, the most recent over six years ago. Moreover, Article 24 of the contract indicates that the contract supersedes all prior agreement and practices.

Regarding the meeting at which Mr. [C] supposedly offered opportunities for crew changes based on seniority, the Company denies that such an offer was made. But even if it were made, argues the Company, it is not the same thing as one associate trying to bump another for shift schedule when there is no vacancy.

Further cited by the Company is bargaining history. In 1977 the Union proposed language that would have allowed work schedules to be determined by seniority. The fact that this language was not accepted by the Company indicates that there is no right to bump.

PERTINENT CONTRACT PROVISIONS

The following provisions of the negotiated agreement between the Parties are especially relevant:

Article 8—Hours and Overtime

8.5 Schedules

8.5.2 It is recognized that management has the right to establish such weekly work schedules as are necessary to meet the requirements of the business; however, requests for changes in weekly work schedules will be considered on a seniority basis and management will try to accommodate associates making such requests, provided that adequate coverage and properly balanced shifts (taking into account not only numbers but experience, ability, etc.) can be maintained. Whenever it is contemplated that a sales shift will be required to be scheduled for six (6) days in a work week while the other sales shift is intended to be scheduled for four (4) days in the same week the weekly schedule for both shifts shall be scheduled for five (5) days.

Article 21—Management Rights

The Union recognizes and agrees that, except as limited by the provisions of this Agreement as they may ultimately be interpreted and applied through the Grievance and Arbitration Procedures, the Company maintains the sole and exclusive right to manage its business in such manner as the Company shall determine to be in its best interest as long as in doing so it does not violate any of the terms of this Agreement. Subject to Article 19, the Company has the sole right to hire, classify, transfer, promote and discharge or discipline associates, and to maintain discipline and efficiency of associates, to maintain and enforce rules and regulations and further to assign work and overtime to associates. The above enumerated management rights shall not be deemed to exclude other management rights not herein specifically enumerated. The exercise or non-exercise of the rights retained by the Company shall not be deemed to waive any such rights or the discretion to exercise any such rights in some other way in the future.

Article 24—Entire Agreement

Unless otherwise provided for in writing between the parties, this Agreement constitutes the sole and entire existing Agreement between the parties and supersedes all prior Agreements, commitments, and practices, whether oral or written between the Company and the Union or the Company and any of the covered associates, except as incorporated herein in writing, and expresses all contractual obligations of and restrictions imposed on the Company and the Union. Section headings are descriptive only and shall not be used to add to, detract from or interpret in any manner the meaning of any provision of this Agreement.

Question   Did the contract allow a senior employee to bump a junior one to stay on her desired shift; is past practice clear in this matter; what should the arbitrator do?

ARBITRATION CASE #5*

Housing Authority of Louisville and Service Employees International Union, Local 557

Issue   Whether HAL (Housing Authority of Louisville) violated the agreement between the parties when it did not award a job promotion for maintenance mechanic at central maintenance garage to the grievant.

* *Source:* Commerce Clearing House, *Labor Arbitration Awards*, 89–1 ARB Paragraph 8277.

Background (Including Positions of the Parties)   In this grievance Mr. [A], an aide II maintenance employee, is claiming the position of maintenance mechanic at central maintenance garage, contending that it should have been awarded to him instead of to Mr. [B]. The position was first posted on November 20, 1987 for lateral bids. Because none of the individuals who applied was already classified in that position, the Authority could not fill it by lateral movement. HAL, therefore, posted the position for promotional bids on December 10, 1987. The second vacancy announcement read:

> Position: Mechanic Development, Central Maintenance; Salary: $7.70/hrly; Qualifications: High School graduate or its equivalent. Ability to read and write. Possession of a valid driver's license. Five (5) years experience in electrical work. An equivalent combination of experience and training may be substituted.

Six employees bid. Of those, one did not meet the minimum requirements and another withdrew his bid, leaving four employees to be considered for the promotion.

Mr. [C], deputy executive director of personnel services for five years, described HAL's promotion procedures beginning with his receipt of the bid sheets. His department prepares a job vacancy worksheet indicating the names and seniority dates of the bidders, reviews the personnel file to assure minimum qualifications are met, and arranges for the assistant director of maintenance, Mr. [D], to interview them. As identifying factors considered in the promotion decision, Mr. [C] pointed to: Article X, section 1 criteria; work records; work history prior to coming to HAL; most recent performance evaluation; attendance; disciplinary records; and the interview test results. After Mr. [D] conducts the interviews and submits his written recommendation, Mr. [C] reviews it. The two then meet. If Mr. [C] agrees that Mr. [D]'s recommendation is "proper," notification of the selection is sent to the bidders. In this case, Mr. [C] agreed with Mr. [D]'s February 1, 1988 recommendation that the maintenance mechanic position should be awarded to Mr. [B]. His seniority date is 12/13/83; Ms. [E]'s seniority date is 7/27/76; the grievant's seniority date is 10/11/82; and Mr. [F]'s seniority date is 11/17/86. In explaining the choice, it was agreed to confine the comparisons of relative qualifications to the selectee and the grievant.

Explaining the basis for selecting a junior employee, Mr. [D] testified that for two years he has been responsible for the overall supervision, planning, and directing of HAL's maintenance operations. As such, he conducts or participates in most of the interviews for maintenance employee promotions. HAL's promotion process, according to him, consists of evaluating objective criteria to determine "whether there is a basic equality in the bidders' qualifications and fitness to do the job." Where there is, the most senior employee is selected. He explained:

> ... Those criteria basically fall into the areas of job knowledge and job performance. Job knowledge being the experience and work history ... and also the ... interview process from the list of questions that are asked. And job performance being those factors relating to the performance evaluations and attendance and their disciplinary history.

Q.   ... [if] it appears that the more senior individual is slightly less qualified in terms of fitness, qualifications and ability; who would get the promotion, as you interpret the contract?

A.   I interpret that as being relatively equal...

Q.   ... what circumstances must exist before you would feel that you should promote a person who is not the most senior into a position?

A.   There should be a significant difference when you evaluate those criteria.

In this case, Mr. [D] concluded that an overall significant difference did exist in favor of the selectee between the grievant's job knowledge and performance and those of the selectee's.

The individual interviews were conducted by Mr. [D] on January 14, 1988 at which he read the same questions to each bidder; wrote down each answer "as close to the actual response as possible"; and ranked each answer on a scale of 0 to 5. Subjects covered by this method were: hot water heaters, furnaces, stoves (electronic spark pilot), frost-free refrigerators, floor tile, electrical, locks, and dry wall. Mr. [D] recalled that the selectee scored 86.7%, while the grievant scored 71.6%, and that the questions relating to dry wall and plaster made up the biggest difference in the overall score. Of the six questions asked in those two subject areas, to four of them the grievant responded, "don't know."

As for the performance evaluations, Mr. [D] stressed that although the grievant's score of 3.3 on a 4 point scale was above average, he felt there was a "significant difference" between it and the selectee's score of 3.8.

Regarding their work records, he found from their employment applications that the selectee's prior experience included four years as a production supervisor and truck driver for Bluegrass Pallet Company, and two years as a truckdriver for Horton's Fruit Company. The grievant's prior experience included one month as a cashier/checker for 7–11 Southland Industries, two months as a crowd patrolman for Metro Parks, and approximately two years as a utility clerk for Kroger Company. Their relative employment experience with HAL was considered "very different" by Mr. [D] because the selectee had been assigned for a longer period of time to the central maintenance garage, where, assigned to the emergency night crew, he was dispatched to various housing developments to address emergency problems which, said Mr. [D]:

> ... varied in nature significantly from heat-related problems to plumbing problems to electrical problems. And in that job, he's probably more subject to mechanical work.

On the other hand, the grievant's assignments with HAL had consisted of monitoring and maintaining heating systems at several housing sites. His assignment at the garage was primarily doing grounds work including tree removal, concrete work, and some fence repair.

Comparing their discipline records, Mr. [D] noted the lack of any for the selectee, and the one written warning in the grievant's file dated June 1987.

Looking at their attendance records for 1987 and 1988, Mr. [D] commented on the importance of being present on the job. He said the selectee only missed three days, while the grievant had used 17½ days sick leave, making the selectee's attendance record "much better."

Having reached the conclusion that "there was a significant difference overall," Mr. [D] met with Mr. [C] to review the recommendation to promote a junior employee. It was Mr. [D]'s further testimony that in making the decision, he did not consider the fact that the selectee's father was an employee of HAL because "to consider that would insinuate favoritism." Asked whether he made the recommendation to promote the selectee because the selectee was white and the grievant was black, Mr. [D] replied, "absolutely not."

Mr. [D] acknowledged that the qualifications specified in the December 10, 1987 posting were different from those in the November 20, 1987 posting. However, he added it was for the same job vacancy although the second posting emphasized five years experience in electrical work. Explaining that the emphasis on the electrical experience indicated the intention to make the initial assignment in that type of work, Mr. [D] pointed to the contractual job description of a maintenance mechanic. It reads:

MAINTENANCE MECHANIC

General Function

This is highly skilled work in one of the construction or building trades. Direction is exercised over other skilled and semi-skilled workers when assigned to the tasks involved by this employee. An employee in this classification may repair electrical apparatus, woodworking fabrication or auto repair and is called upon to perform highly skilled work at various locations as needed. Performs other work as assigned.

Examples of Work

. . .

Desirable Knowledge, Ability and Skill

Ability to direct the activities of skilled and semi-skilled workers assigned to assist in jobs.

May be skilled in one of the following trades:

Electrical—General maintenance and repair, console work, finish work, use and knowledge of hand and power tools.

Carpentry—General maintenance repair, cabinet work, finish work, use and knowledge of hand and power tools.

Plumbing—General maintenance and repair of plumbing and sewer lines.

Required Qualifications

High school graduation or its equivalent.

Five (5) years experience in the skill trade requested.

Possession of a valid driver's license.

Ability to read and write.

Must pass an employment medical examination (pertains to new employees).

An equivalent combination of education and experience may be substituted.

Questioned about his scoring system on the interview questions, Mr. [D] elaborated:

A.   Well, the scoring is based on the response that is received. And as far as the application of the score, there has to be a judgment made.
. . .

Q.   . . . in answer to what should the hot water be set at? The correct answer . . . is that it should be set between a 130 and a 135 but not over a 140. And you have down the [selectee's] response, a 120, and you've given that a grade of four.
. . . And to that same question . . . [the grievant's] answer was a 120 to 130, but he got a four, also. Wouldn't you say . . . that . . . answer was closer to the correct answer . . . ?

A.   . . . it calls for a judgment . . . both were close but not quite there, it's my opinion, so both were given fours. . . .

Q.   [In answer to the question "Where is the safety switch located?" on the furnace], . . . [the selectee] got a five for saying the inside bottom of the furnace; and . . . [the grievant] got a four for saying in the furnace. Why . . . ?

A.   . . . it was my opinion that he had an idea where to find that switch, but he didn't state specifically the correct answer so he was given credit based on that judgment. . . .

By memorandum dated February 5, 1988, Mr. [C] informed the grievant that he was not selected to fill the vacancy because he had "less qualifications than the successful bidder." A few days thereafter, the grievant filed the following grievance:

I do not feel that I received a fair chance in the selection of applicants for the maintenance mechanic position at Central Maintenance Garage.

Remedy Requested: for management to reconsider and award the maintenance mechanic position to me.

According to the grievant, for approximately one year he had been performing the job which was posted and, therefore, had demonstrated his qualifications. He said in the central garage there were three people in his crew: Mr. [G], maintenance lead person; Mr. [H], maintenance mechanic; and himself, the aide II. For six to eight months he was the grounds crew person until the maintenance mechanic got transferred and:

. . . I was more or less put . . . into his position, and I was operating all the heavy equipment.
. . .

> ...No one ever replaced Mr. [H].... I had done, you know, what normally would have been assigned to Mr. [H] or to our crew, it was a varied number of things....
>
> ...Mr. [I] placed me on the electrical truck... used me in all different types of position inside the shop. I mean, there wasn't anything that I never touched in that central garage....
>
> ...
>
> ...I feel I'm more than qualified.... The way I understood the job and the position that was supposed to be filled... provided by a gentleman leaving, the job that particular individual was doing, I had already been doing it.... I should have been awarded that job strictly because of that.
>
> ...

Referring to the written warning in his file, the grievant explained that an alleged altercation occurred between the maintenance mechanic and the lead person on his crew on June 9, 1987. Although present, he only witnessed the aftermath, he said, but the director of maintenance wrote in his report that:

> [A] refused to get involved and claimed he didn't know what happened. Later, though, he was quoted to say, "I did everything in my power to stop it." And that he wasn't going to cause anybody to lose his job.
>
> ...
>
> ...Mr. [A] should be given a stern warning for his lack of responsibility in giving testimony or false statements during the fact finding hearing. Mr. [A] should have more responsibility to his employer and the employees' safety than was exhibited.

For his "actions and lack of cooperation in the investigation," the grievant received a written warning. He did not grieve it because he considered it a warning, not a reprimand, and he felt he could offer his views on it when "the time came, and this warning letter did come up."

Asked about his interview with Mr. [D], the grievant replied that he didn't know whether Mr. [D] wrote down the answers he was giving; there were questions he did not understand; and although he "fell flat on his face" in dry wall, normally HAL has plasterers for those jobs, and when one is assigned to the garage, he does mechanic's work.

As for his contentions about race and favoritism having influenced the selection process, the grievant had this to say:

> ...The remark I made about the racial incident, as well as the familiar incident between Mr. [B] and his father, might have been a statement made out of anger.

The grievant and his union maintain that the selection process was flawed in several ways. First, it is argued that it was contractually impermissible to award the job to a junior employee because his qualifications were not even relatively equal to the grievant's, and therefore seniority must prevail. Next, it is contended that

HAL's actions were unfair, arbitrary, and capricious. To support this, it is asserted that the grievant demonstrated his qualifications by actually performing the work for a year and he had been with the Authority five years and two months; however, it is argued, there was no documented evidence that the selectee had the five years requisite experience in the skill trade requested and he had been with HAL only four years. It is stressed that Mr. [D]'s recommendation of February 1, 1988 was based in part on the selectee's evaluation, but the selectee's evaluation was not signed until March 1988. The union points to the interview, claiming its method of testing was unusual, its grading was unfair, and its score was a contractually improper basis upon which to award a promotion. It strenuously objects to penalizing the grievant for using his sick leave, asserting that HAL did so in order to create an advantage for the junior employee. And, it adds, changing the qualification requirements on the postings was another example of unfairness.

For its part, the Authority maintains that promoting the selectee was required by the contract. It points to the contractual factors of seniority, ability, qualifications and fitness, and stresses that seniority is to prevail only where qualifications and fitness are relatively equal, not when it is determined that all bidders meet the minimum qualifications. Here, says HAL, these factors were found not to be relatively equal based upon interview answers, evaluations, experience, attendance, and discipline records. In support of those contentions, the Authority states that the grievant was never assigned to a mechanic's position; he and the selectee were supervised and evaluated by the same supervisor; the grievant was not improperly penalized for taking sick leave because the established practice is to evaluate attendance on the basis of total absences; although the written warning was for a minor infraction, the selectee's record was unblemished; and . . . the selection was made in good faith, was reasonable, and was supported by concrete, tangible, objective and subjective proof.

Both parties cite numerous arbitration awards in support of their positions. The Arbitrator has carefully studied them and conducted additional research on her own.

PERTINENT CONTRACT PROVISIONS

Article VII is entitled Seniority and reads in part:

> Section 3—The Authority recognizes the principle of seniority and the Union recognizes the right of the Authority to direct the work force, assign work and determine qualification.
>
>   . . .
>   Length of service in the Authority and length of service in a position shall be included in determining qualifications.

Article X is titled Promotions and Lateral Transfers and provides in pertinent part:

> Section 1—When promoting, demoting, laying off, or recalling, the Authority shall consider seniority, ability, qualifications, and fitness to do a job. Where the last two (2) of the aforesaid factors are relatively equal, seniority shall prevail.
>   Qualifications for promotions must be achieved prior to any consideration for promotion.

Question   Did the grievant establish that his qualifications and fitness to do the job were relatively equal to those of the selectee, as the contract language states; what should the arbitrator do?

ARBITRATION CASE #6*

G.C.I.U., Local 261 and Harry Hoffman and Sons Printing

Issue   Did the Company violate the collective bargaining agreement in the manner in which it administered the apprenticeship of [A]?

Background   The facts leading to the instant matter are straightforward and not in dispute. On June 8, 1981 the Company promoted [A] to apprentice pressman. The apprenticeship period is four years. On July 19, 1983 [A] participated in a legal work stoppage with the result that he was permanently replaced. At the conclusion of the stoppage [A] was not recalled but, instead, was placed on a preferential hiring list. On February 12, 1987 [A] was recalled to work.

Between October 1983 and February 1987 [A] worked as a pressman for several employers. The Union maintains that he spent some 35 months as a 1st or 2nd journeyman pressman.

Upon his return to work [A] was placed in his former position as an apprentice and advised he would have to serve the two years of the apprenticeship that remained after he left work in July of 1983. On February 15, 1987 [A] presented the Company with a summary of his employment between 1983 and 1987. He asked that this outside employment be credited toward the completion of his apprenticeship. The company refused to accommodate him.

On April 10, 1987 the Union grieved the Company's decision. The Company denied the grievance on April 20. It is accordingly before the undersigned for binding arbitration.

Union Position   The Union argues that the Company has consistently credited employees' apprenticeships with time spent in the appropriate classification at other shops. Such crediting, says the Union, has, over time, become a binding past practice. The Union cites four examples of employees who have received such credit and five examples of employees who were promoted to journeyman prior to the completion of their apprenticeship.

The Union contends that arbitrators have consistently held that customs and practices, when established, become part of the parties' collective bargaining agreement. It cites cases in support of this position.

The Union further maintains that the practice here is of a duration exceeding 20 years and has been accepted by both parties. The Company, says the Union, does not dispute the practice but instead disagrees with its scope. Thus, says the Union, the Company claims that it has only credited outside service when hiring new employees. The Union believes outside service should be similarly applied when an employee's service is interrupted because the rationale for the crediting is the same in both instances.

* *Source:* Commerce Clearing House, *Labor Arbitration Awards*, 89–1 ARB Paragraph 8074.

The function of the apprenticeship, says the Union, is the provision of a "hands on" training period to allow employees to develop the skills and competency needed to become journeymen. The reason for crediting outside work experience, the Union contends, is that the Company recognizes that the requisite skills may be learned in similar occupations in other organizations. The Union maintains that because the Company has not questioned [A]'s ability to perform as a journeyman pressman and because it has seen no need to provide him with additional training since rehiring him, it must be concluded that he has learned what is necessary to become a journeyman.

To treat [A] as an apprentice, says the Union, violates the seniority provisions of the contract. These provisions, the Union notes, grant journeyman seniority rights as of the date the apprenticeship is completed rather than the date of hire. The result of the Company's decision, the Union emphasizes, is that employees hired after [A] would be treated as senior to him should a layoff occur.

The Union also argues that the apprenticeship agreement the Company signed with the Union requires that if advanced credit for prior experience is granted, it should be done uniformly. The Union notes that Company witness, [B], from the Department of Labor, agreed with this. Arbitrators, says the Union, have held that when a contract is arguably subject to two interpretations, the one which is invalid in law should not prevail.

The Union concludes that both practice and law favor its position. Accordingly it asks that the grievance be granted and that the Company be ordered to credit [A] with his pressman's experience with other employers and to grant him back pay and benefits.

Company Position   The Company argues that the Union has failed to prove that there was a contractual duty to credit [A]'s outside experience. Moreover, says the Company, the Union has proven neither that the contract is ambiguous nor that there is a well-established past practice regarding the granting of work credit toward an apprenticeship.

Article 3.2, says the Company, grants it all the powers which it has not specifically surrendered. The Company maintains that it has never surrendered the right to require apprentices to complete all of their apprenticeship time in the service of the Company.

Article 6.2, says the Company, clearly states that all modifications of the contract must be in writing and that limitations on management must be "expressly" set forth in the contract. The Company maintains that the Union has demonstrated no express agreement under which it must credit outside experience toward an apprenticeship. On the other hand, the Company notes, Article 20.8 requires it to credit such experience inside its plant. It concludes that the parties selected language which required that one and only one type of experience be credited.

The Company maintains that the apprenticeship agreement does not require the crediting of any outside experience. The Company does agree that the apprenticeship agreement requires it to be consistent in crediting experience gained before the start of the apprenticeship. Here, however, the Company contends that the experience in question was acquired during an interruption in the apprenticeship rather than prior to its commencement. The Company does not believe that [A]'s apprenticeship can sensibly be treated as the start of a new program.

The Company maintains that what the Union seeks is to credit work of uncertain character to its own apprentice program. This, says the Company, is not analogous to granting credit for prior experience because in the latter situation the Company is protected by the contractual probationary period. Moreover, says the Company, it is important for it to have flexibility in hiring so that it may respond to changes in the labor market and use the application of prior experience to induce qualified people to seek employment. Similarly, says the Company, it may shorten an apprenticeship period because it needs journeymen at certain points in time.

Because of the distinction described above the Company contends that there is no past practice regarding the granting of credit for outside work to an employee whose apprenticeship is interrupted. None of the examples cited by the Union, says the Company, involved an interrupted apprenticeship. The Company argues that because such a situation has never previously arisen, past practice is simply non-existent.

Moreover, says the Company, to establish a past practice, the Union must prove that the practice was mutually accepted. The Company does not believe this can be done with an issue that has arisen but once. Additionally, the Company maintains that a mere change in the way in which it exercises its discretion cannot constitute a mutually established practice. The Company cites cases to buttress its position.

The Company maintains that it made a reasoned determination that once an apprenticeship has begun, all time applied toward completion of the program should be worked while the apprentice is in its employ. It contends that neither the collective bargaining agreement nor the contract prohibits it from making this decision. Accordingly it asks that the grievance be denied.

PERTINENT CONTRACT PROVISIONS

Article 3, Function of Management

Section 3.1   The management of the business of the Company and the direction of its personnel, including the right to hire, promote, demote, transfer, assign to shifts, discharge and discipline for proper cause, and layoff for lack of work, subject to the terms of this contract, are the exclusive responsibility of the Company. The Company shall be the exclusive judge of all matters pertaining to continuance or discontinuance of its operation in whole or in part, subcontract of work, the products to be manufactured; the location of plants, the schedules of production and the methods, processes, means and materials to be used; the selection, training and direction of supervisory employees; and pertaining to safety, efficiency and discipline and to the protection of the Company's property and operations from injury by reason of sabotage, subversive activity or otherwise.

Section 3.2   All the functions, powers or authority which the Company has not specifically abridged, delegated or modified by this Agreement will be recognized by the Union as being retained by the Company.

Article 6, Term, Reopening and Scope of Agreement

Section 6.2   This contract sets forth the entire understanding and agreement of the parties and may not be modified in any respect except by writing subscribed to by both parties. Nothing in this contract shall be construed as requiring either party hereto to do or refrain from doing anything not explicitly and expressly set forth in this contract; nor shall either party be deemed to have agreed or promised to do or refrain from doing anything unless this contract explicitly and expressly sets forth such agreement or promise. Nothing in this Article shall be construed to limit the traditional rights and prerogatives of management, except as may be expressly limited by other provisions of this Agreement.

Article 11, Minimum Wage Scale

Section 11.2   It is further agreed by the Company that the minimum scale of wages to be paid to lithographic apprentices shall be not less than Three Dollars, Fifty Cents ($3.50) per hour. Every six (6) months thereafter, an increase in equal amounts shall be granted so that the last increase shall come at the end of the apprenticeship period and shall bring the rate of wages up to the minimum rate of wages specified for journeymen for that classification.

Article 18, Seniority

Section 18.1   In all cases of increase or decrease in the working forces, seniority shall govern and such seniority shall be determined by job classification and department.

Section 18.11   Indentured apprentices shall hold seniority in the job classification from which they were promoted until such time as they complete all of the requirements of their apprenticeship term and shall then take their seniority status as a journeyman in the job classification in which they were indentured as of the date their apprenticeship term is completed.

Article 20, Apprentices

Section 20.4   Apprentices shall not be allowed in any branch of the trade in which a journeyman is not employed. In the event of the working force being reduced in any branch of the trade, notwithstanding the ratio herein provided, all apprentices in the branch of the trade in which the work force is being reduced shall, without exception, be released prior to discharge or layoff of any journeyman in such branch.

Section 20.8   When an employee is promoted to an apprenticeable job classification, he shall be given credit for all time previously spent with the Company on such job classification on a temporary basis, if any, toward his wage progression to the journeyman wage rate.

Question   Did the employer improperly deny experience accumulated with another company to a former apprentice when he was rehired? What award should the arbitrator make?

ARBITRATION CASE #7*

Ohio Valley Coal Company and United Mine Workers of America, District No. 6, Local Union 1810

Issue   Did the Company violate the 1988 Wage Agreement on and after February 2, 1989, when it stopped providing drinking water in half-pint containers?

Background (Including Positions of the Parties)   On February 4, 1989, Local Union 1810 President and Mine Safety Committee Member [A] filed a grievance as follows:

> I feel management is violating my rights under the 1988 C.W.A.
>
> Management stopped the use of the small ½ pint containers of potable drinking water, that is required for all active working of the mine.
>
> Violating Art. III Sec. (i), Art. XXI Sec. (e) (11), Art. XXVI(b), a Local Union Agreement, and the Code of Federal Regulations 75.1718 and 75.1718-1.
>
> I am asking that management continue using the ½ pint containers of water.

The matter was duly processed by the parties but was not resolved.

Local Union President [A] explained that he filed the instant grievance as a result of a management decision on February 2, 1989 that drinking water would no longer be provided for the employees in half-pint sealed plastic bottles. Management stated that thereafter water would be provided in half-gallon plastic jug-type containers distributed by the same supplier that had provided the smaller bottles. The jug-type container was to be hung on a hook mounted from the ceiling above a picnic table at the "dinner hole," the area where the employees eat. The container has a spout which allows water to flow after a hole is punched to allow the entry of air.

[A] stated that he discussed the matter with members of management, including Safety Director [B], and was told that the reason for the change was that the employees littered the small bottles around the mine. [A] claimed that he offered the Union's cooperation to stop the littering. The Local Union President testified that management's final decision on the matter came on Saturday, February 4, and that he filed the instant grievance the same day.

On cross-examination, [A] conceded that on January 31, 1989, he acted as a "walk-around," accompanying a federal inspector who conducted an inspection of the mine. [A] stated that he questioned the inspector regarding the use of the half-gallon jugs, but denied that he registered a safety complaint. [A] claimed that the same day Safety Director [B] told him that he should "work out" any safety problems with him before "involving the inspector." The inspector looked at a jug which was not in use and did not have an air hole punched. The Local Union President stated that the inspector said that the use of such jugs "could be a safety violation," but he did not write out a violation.

It was the Local Union President's continued testimony that he discussed the present grievance with Personnel and Employee Relations Manager [C] and

---

* *Source:* Commerce Clearing House, *Labor Arbitration Awards*, 90–1 ARB Paragraph 8126.

O.V.C.O.A. President [D] approximately March 6, 1989. [A] did not recall management mentioning the federal inspector having a role in this matter. He did recall [D] stating that if the water jug hangs from the ceiling, vermin could not get at it. Finally, the Local Union President stated that management frequently asks for time to consider a given problem, and that it is understood that there could be a resultant delay in filing a grievance—under such circumstances management has not raised untimeliness as a defense.

[A] explained the Union's concern regarding the substitution of half-gallon jugs for half-pint bottles to provide potable water for the employees. [A] had been told that on prior occasions when jugs had been used, there were times when cups were not available and employees drank by putting their mouths to the spout. [A] also pointed out that there are no wash-up facilities in the mine so that when employees urinate or defecate, they cannot wash their hands and might touch the water spout with unwashed hands.

Moreover, the cups in use at the jug might be dirty and a dirty knife might be used to pierce the jug for the entry of air. Finally, the Local Union President stated that he had seen a jug in use, not hanging from the ceiling, but lying on the picnic table. He also saw the waxed paper cups provided for the employees lying around loose—i.e., the cups were not in a container or dispenser and could have become soiled.

International Safety and Health Representative [E] pointed out that he has worked full-time for the International Union on safety issues since 1975. [E] stated that he is familiar with Company obligations to provide potable water for mine employees and has encountered management's use of large jugs in said regard in at least two other mines. Both federal regulations and the collective bargaining agreement require that the Employer provide potable drinking water for employees working underground. The International Representative conceded that the size and type of container required for potable water are not set forth in the regulations or contract. [E] also agreed that the mines where jugs have been in use have been inspected, but that the use of jugs has neither been protested under the contract nor determined to be unhealthy.

The Safety and Health Representative, while conceding that water jugs were in use at the Windsor and Quarto No. 4 Mines, claimed that said manner of providing water for employees is rare in the industry. Among the reasons are that water dripping from the jug spout can attract the mice and rats that are frequently found in mines. [E] also supported [A] in pointing out that mines are dirty and in the absence of wash-up facilities, an employee can put his fingers on the spout after urinating. The small bottles not only obviate such problems, but are portable so that a miner can get a drink of water when he is away from the dinner hole.

On cross-examination, Safety and Health Representative [E] conceded that he was not present when the instant grievance was filed and had no firsthand knowledge that actual unsanitary conditions were encountered by the employees. [A] agreed that safety grievances are normally handled separately under the contract and that filing a grievance within twenty-four hours of knowledge of a safety dispute is required. On the other hand, [E] maintained that management might wait more than twenty-four hours before taking a position on an unsafe condition and that such delays occur frequently.

Mine Committee Chairman [F] pointed out that the presently contested Company action is the second time that management tried to switch to water jugs. In 1987 the Company began a "clean-up" program and stopped providing water in small bottles. At that time the parties discussed the issue, with the result that management conceded that the half-pint bottles did not really cause litter, and the small bottles were again provided. This actually was a continuation of the practice which began approximately December, 1980, in the wake of a Union complaint that the Company was not providing water as required by the contract. The company agreed "to try" the use of half-pint bottles and to continue such use "if there were no problem." Thereafter, except for the 1987 interruption and the present dispute, half-pint bottles of water have been provided by the Company.

Prior to submitting evidence on the merits of this case, the Company made a Motion for a Directed Verdict on the basis that even if all the Union evidence were accepted, the grievance would have to be dismissed. The Arbitrator declined to rule on the Motion at the hearing, but stated that the arguments raised would be considered in deciding the case.

Assistant Mine Manager [G], while not disputing that the company had provided half-pint bottles of water for the employees, denied that the Company ever agreed to do so indefinitely. [G] explained that prior to 1983 the Company was providing water in collapsible jugs which were filled on Company property. This was determined to be unsanitary and the Company went through several alternatives before going to the half-pint bottles.

[G] stated that he served as Superintendent at the Quarto Mine in 1986 and knew that the Company at said location provided water in jugs. [G] recalled being called by the No. 6 Mine management and asked about the Quarto practice. At the time [G] stated that there was nothing wrong with using jugs—nevertheless, the No. 6 Mine management continued the use of half-pint bottles.

[G] explained that No. 6 Mine management decided to switch to water jugs in January, 1989. On January 31, 1989, federal and state inspectors, accompanied by a Union representative, went through the mine and saw two jugs on the picnic table and one suspended from a bolt in the ceiling when they stopped at the dinner hole area. Paper cups kept in a dispenser were available and a garbage can was close by for disposal of the cups. No citation was written by the inspectors, although they normally act when regulations are violated.

Following the inspection, Local Union President [A] asked Assistant Mine Manager [G] whether the company was going back to the half-pint bottles and the answer was negative. [G] took the position that not only does providing water in jugs meet contractual requirements, but litter caused by small bottles is thereby prevented. The Assistant Mine Manager also conceded that using jugs is "more cost effective." [G] pointed out that the Grievant works on the surface in the Lampman classification and was not personally affected by the change to jugs. Moreover, [A] never suggested that he was unable to get good drinking water either at his work site or in the mine.

PERTINENT CONTRACT PROVISIONS

Article IA—Scope and Coverage

Section (d) Management of the Mines   The management of the mine, the direction of the working force and right to hire and discharge are vested exclusively in the Employer.

Article III—Health and Safety

Section (a) Right to a Safe Working Place   Every Employee covered by this Agreement is entitled to a safe and healthful place to work, and the parties jointly pledge their individual and joint efforts to attain and maintain this objective. Recognizing that the health and safety of the Employees covered by this Agreement are the highest priorities of the parties, the parties agree to comply fully with all lawful notices and orders issued pursuant to the Federal Mine Safety and Health Act of 1977, as amended, and pursuant to the various state mining laws.

Section (p) Settlement of Health and Safety Disputes   When a dispute arises at the mine involving health or safety, an immediate earnest and sincere effort shall be made to resolve the matter through the following steps:

1. By the aggrieved party and his immediate supervisor. Any grievance which is not filed by the aggrieved party within twenty-four (24) hours following the shift on which the grievant reasonably should have known of such grievance shall be considered invalid and not subject to further consideration under the grievance procedure. If the grievance is not settled at this step, the BCOA–UMWA Standard Health and Safety Grievance Form shall be completed and signed jointly by the parties.

2. If no agreement is reached at step 1, the grievance shall be taken up by the Mine Health and Safety Committee, and UMWA district health and safety representative and mine management within four days of the conclusion of step 1.

If the dispute involves an issue concerning compliance with federal or state mine safety laws or mandatory health or safety regulations, the appropriate federal or state inspection agency shall be called in immediately and the dispute shall be settled on the basis of the inspector's findings, with both parties reserving all statutory rights of appeal. If the dispute is not settled, a record shall be made of the position of the parties and the evidence at this step.

Article XXIII—Settlement of Disputes

Section (k) Prior Agreement   ... All decisions of the Arbitration Review Board rendered prior to the expiration of the National Bituminous Coal Wage Agreement of 1978 shall continue to have precedential effect under this agreement to the extent that the basis for such decisions have not been modified by subsequent changes in this agreement.

Article XXVI—District Agreements

Section (b) Prior Practice and Custom ...Except where abolished by mutual agreement of the parties, all prior practice and custom not in conflict with this Agreement shall be continued.

Question Did the Company violate the agreement by discontinuing past practice; what should the arbitrator do?

ARBITRATION CASE #8*

Shell Oil Company, Deer Park, Texas Complex and Oil, Chemical, and Atomic Workers International Union, Local 8–367

Issue Did the Company improperly refuse to permit a partially disabled employee to work, and did it improperly require him to retire; can the grievance procedure be used to remedy both these actions?

Background The Grievant, Mr. [A], is 59 years of age. He was employed by the Company on July 1, 1953 as a General Helper, and by November, 1963 he had advanced to the job of Pipefitter #1. On June 28, 1974 he was installing a 3 inch valve in a pipe rack, which required his working in a cramped position. According to his Compensation Claim his feet slipped, and he felt a sharp pain in his back.

The Grievant was treated by the Company's medical doctor, who prescribed medication and returned him to work with certain restrictions. They were:

1. No lifting, pushing, or pulling over thirty-five pounds.
2. Restrictions on climbing.
3. Restrictions on stooping.
4. No activities that will strain the back.
5. Limited driving.

The Grievant did not lose any work because of the back injury, and he continued to work as a Pipefitter #1, but at tasks which were within the medical restrictions. From the summer of 1974 up until December, 1986, he regularly reported for work, other than for some occasional absences which were not connected with his back. On November 1, 1974, he reported some tingling from his knee on down. Also, he stated that he wanted to have the complaint placed on his medical record. He had occasion to visit the Medical Department again, on August 26 and 27, 1985, when he was advised to put ice to his back for 20 minutes, because he complained that his legs were becoming numb.

Later in 1985 he visited the Medical Department because he had been off work with bronchitis and pharyngitis. On that visit he reported that he felt fine and was

---

* *Source:* Commerce Clearing House, *Labor Arbitration Awards*, 89–1 ARB Paragraph 8208.

able to do his job with his long-term restrictions. He was then released with the same long-term restrictions.

In May, 1986 he reported to the Medical Department because his back was giving him a moderate amount of pain. The Doctor's examination found forward bending of no more than 30 degrees, and there was a moderate amount of paravertebral muscle spasm. He was given medication and advised to start a Physical Therapy program to stretch his back muscles. After several visits that month, the Grievant was diagnosed as having a long history of chronic back trouble, and medical restrictions were renewed.

The Grievant was then absent from work in December, 1986 as the result of a moderate heart problem. Upon his return to work on January 26, 1987 he reported to the Medical Department, where the Company Doctor made note of the heart problem, but he also noted that there were no restrictions for that problem. He further noted that his chronic back pain was unchanged, and that the same long-term restrictions would remain.

Starting in June, 1986 a member of Management, Mr. [B], was transferred to second level Maintenance Supervisor for the Grievant's work area. According to his testimony he consulted with his predecessor and with the Grievant's first-line Supervisor. On the basis of these conversations he became aware of the limiting restrictions on Mr. [A]'s work assignments. By November-December, 1986 he came to the conclusion that

> We could no longer justify or rationalize carrying an additional pipefitter when they could not perform within the requirements of the pipefitter craft. . . .

Around February 5, 1987 Mr. [B] had a discussion with the Company's Medical Doctor, Dr. [C], regarding the Grievant's work restrictions. Although Dr. [C] advised that the lifting and pulling restriction could be modified and the restriction on driving could be removed, it was the Supervisor's conclusion that the remaining restrictions were so severe and restrictive that the Grievant could not be used productively on an ongoing basis. With the concurrence of other members of Management, the decision was made not to permit Mr. [A] to return to work.

The Grievant was placed on disability leave on February 5, 1987. For 13 weeks he received his full pay less $63 received from Workmens' Compensation. At the end of the 13 weeks, and for the next 39 weeks, he received one half of his regular pay plus the $63 compensation. On February 1, 1988 the disability pay ceased, and he only received the compensation payment of $63.

The Company did not return him to work, and the Grievant went to talk to a Mr. [D], who was in charge of pensions. The Grievant told the Manager that he did not want to retire, and that he would only sign the retirement papers with a written protest. That was not acceptable to Mr. [D]. Then, after talking to the Union's Secretary-Treasurer, Mr. [E], he returned to Mr. [D]'s where he stated he signed the papers, but with the understanding that there was a protest because he was not ready to retire. Because he was one year short of the full eligibility pension age of 60, he receives 95 percent of the full amount.

After the date was set for the arbitration hearing, Counsel for the Union notified the Company on April 26, 1988 that:

> The Union and Mr. [A] will ask the Arbitrator to reinstate Mr. [A] to active employment notwithstanding his subsequent retirement.

The Company's answer, given on May 17, 1988, stated that the Articles of Agreement remove from the Arbitrator the authority to grant the Union's request. It further stated that under Section 5.023 of the Agreement the Arbitrator would have no authority to address Mr. [A]'s termination in February, 1988.

The grievance, number 87–19, was filed February 15, 1988. It charges violation of Article 7, Section 7.01 and it states the following:

> Protest: Mr. [A] (Pipefitter) not being allowed to work with occupational restrictions.
>
> Remedy: The Union demands that the Company cease and desist from violating the Labor Agreement, that the incident(s) be rectified, that proper compensation, including benefits and overtime, at the applicable rate of pay, be paid for all losses; and further that those affected be made whole in every respect.

Union Position   The union view of the issue is whether the Company violated its obligations under Article 7, Section 7.01, and if so, what is the proper remedy.

It is the Union contention that from 1974 until the end of 1986 the Grievant worked as Pipefitter with medical restrictions on climbing, no lifting or pushing over thirty-five pounds, limited driving, minimal stooping, or any activity that would aggravate his low back condition. At all times the Company's Medical Department was fully aware of Mr. [A]'s medical limitations, and it continued to approve his active employment within those restrictions. During that twelve year period he accepted every job assignment given him, and at no time did any member of management ever complain to him or to the Union that he was unable to provide productive work because of his medical restrictions.

The Union stresses that even though he was limited in climbing ability, a substantial portion of the Pipefitter's work assignments are done at ground level. In support it calls attention to the estimates of Union witnesses that approximately 70% of the pipefitter work is at ground level. Even the Company estimate was that 50% was at ground level. Among his work assignments were the replacement of piping on ground level pipes, assistance to other crafts in the maintenance program, working as a materials gatherer, producing special gaskets on every maintenance turn around, fire watch duty, hole watch duty, drafting of pipe diagrams and housekeeping tasks in the crew's breakroom.

It was not until second-line Supervisor [B] came on the scene in the summer of 1986 that a question was raised about the efficient use of the Grievant as an effective employee. The conclusion was made that he was not an effective employee, even though nothing in the way of concrete evidence was offered to support that finding.

In December, 1986 the Grievant was absent from work due to a heart attack, which was treated with medication. When he returned to work on January 26, 1987, the Company Doctor found that no further restrictions were needed for the heart condition and only the old restrictions for his back condition would remain. In a follow-up examination the Doctor modified the restrictions for lifting and pulling and he removed the driving restrictions. However, second-line Supervisor [B] told the Grievant he had no work for him, and he was not permitted to return to work.

The Grievant was then placed on disability leave with a loss of income, and after one year, he was forced to take early retirement, because of financial hardship. The Union advised the Company that the retirement was taken under protest.

It is the contention of the Union that Section 7.01 is a negotiated protection for bargaining unit employees who are unable to perform their usual job duties because of on-the-job injury or illness. It is a protection that should not be narrowly interpreted, for a narrow interpretation would defeat the underlying protective mantle of the benefit. The provision does not require the Company to "create a job or make work," but it does obligate the Company to continue to provide such work as the Grievant is capable of performing.

The Union stresses the fact that the Company complied with Section 7.01 for 12 years, and no complaint was ever made about the Grievant's performance or the amount of work he performed. Since January, 1987, the same work performed by the Grievant is still being performed by other Pipefitters. It is clear, the Union contends, that the second-line Supervisor's desire to improve work place efficiency ran afoul of the Company's obligations to make a good faith effort to provide existing work that the Grievant was capable of doing, as required in Section 7.01. In support of its position the Union cited the arbitration decision of Arbitrator Robert F. Grabb, K.P. Manufacturing Co., 74 LA 1046 (1980). In that case there was similar protective language for an employee who sustained an occupational disability, and the Arbitrator upheld the grievance.

As a remedy for this case the Union requests that the Grievant be granted reinstatement as an active employee with full back pay less the disability leave payments plus the $63 per week compensation payments. It further argues that this Arbitrator has broad discretion in fashioning the appropriate remedy. Since the Company did not terminate or otherwise discharge Mr. [A], reinstatement to active employment will not run afoul of the Company's rights under Article 5, Section 5.023.

Company Position   The Company takes issue with the Union's view of what should be the remedy, should the finding be in favor of the Grievant. It calls attention to the correspondence, which was cited above, wherein the Company's position is that the Arbitrator lacks authority to fashion a remedy that would return to work an individual who was terminated by reason on retiring under the Company's Pension Plan.

It is the Company's position that the grievance was submitted a year before the retirement took place, and it protests the Grievant not being allowed to work with occupational restrictions. Thus, the issue before the Arbitrator is whether Mr. [A]'s retirement was for just cause.

Also, the Company contends that the language contained in Section 5.023 is clear and unambiguous, so that the Arbitrator must enforce its clear meaning, which is that Management has reserved the unreviewable discretion to pension employees who have reached a pensionable age. It is further Company position that the only issue is:

Did the Company violate Section 7.01 of the Articles of Agreement by placing Mr. [A] on occupational disability on February 5, 1987.

The Company agrees that for a period of over 12 years the Grievant had been performing various tasks, and that following his return to work after the absence due to a heart condition, Supervisor [B] did not allow him to do so. He informed the Grievant that after evaluating the current maintenance activity, management concluded there was not enough work available within his restrictions to keep him productively utilized. As a result, he was placed on disability leave until such time as his restrictions were moderated or the Company had a full time job he could perform within his restrictions. Following that leave Mr. [A] elected to retire February 1, 1988.

The Company stresses that, at the time involved, conditions in the oil refining industry were such that it was an absolute necessity for the Deer Park facility to improve the cost effectiveness of its maintenance activities. Among the actions taken was to reduce its dependency on contractors, with the result that Shell craftsmen had to do more of the heavy, physical work done by those contractors. Another was the agreement reached with the Union to relax craft jurisdictional lines and to authorize plant operations to perform certain maintenance tasks formerly performed exclusively by craftsmen. This resulted in improved productivity, so that the Company could operate with fewer employees performing a much broader range of activities, so that it was essential that each employee be fully productive.

As a part of this program in late 1985 and early 1986 Management initiated an evaluation of the productivity and utilization of employees with physical restrictions of a long-term or permanent nature. Out of this evaluation, by January, 1987, it became apparent that the Grievant's situation needed to be further evaluated. Through this process, it became apparent that Mr. [A]'s physical condition was such that he could never be expected to fulfill the job duties of a Pipefitter in a safe and efficient manner. While the Grievant was on disability leave he was never replaced.

Thus, it is the Company's position that the Grievant's physical condition was such that he was incapable of giving a fair day's work on an ongoing basis as a Pipefitter, and because his physical restrictions were permanent, there was no prospect things would change. The Company charges that because of the limited assignments that fell within his medical restrictions he had assumed responsibility for making coffee and keeping the break area clean as his primary responsibility. It also calls attention to the testimony of Supervisor [B], who stated that there were very few pipefitter tasks that he could perform adequately with his physical limitations.

Another position of the Company is that Management has the inherent right to refuse to allow an employee to return to work, who cannot give a fair day's work. In support of this position Management cited findings of several arbitrators, and contended that by not allowing the Grievant to return to work the action was in accordance with the vast weight of arbitral authority.

A third position of the Company is that the Company met its contractual obligations under Section 7.01, because that Section provides that the Company is not obligated to create a job or to make work. The Company agrees that there were some specific individual pipefitter tasks that the Grievant could have performed, but a job made up of those restricted activities did not exist and there were no jobs anywhere in the Complex that would meet his medical restrictions. In support of this position it cites Arbitrator William S. Rule, Data Transportation Co., 75 LA 1154 (1980). Also, it cites Arbitrator Pierce Davis in his decision, McGill Manufacturing Co., 58 LA 1120, who stated that "an employer is not required to risk payment of additional large sums of workman's compensation, which could result from the grievant's reinstatement, without strong and documented evidence of substantial improvement in her physical condition" (P1122).

The Company also contends that the Union is seeking to have the Arbitrator direct the Company to create a job and it calls attention to Union witnesses who agreed that there is not any pipefitter job which consists entirely of tasks that fall within the Grievant's restrictions.

Finally, the Company contends that its actions were not arbitrary, discriminatory or capricious. It contends that the record is void of any hint of disparate treatment, or evidence of arbitrary or discriminatory intent or behavior by the Company. No evidence was offered to show there are other employees with permanent medical restrictions of the type of what the Grievant had.

PERTINENT CONTRACT PROVISIONS

5.02 Discipline of Employees

5.023   Employees pensioned under the Company's Pension Plan shall not [be] considered discharged within the meaning of 5.02, and the right to terminate or to retain in its service employees who have reached a pensionable age rests solely with the company.

Article 7 is entitled Benefits, and Section 7.01 is entitled Disability of Employees. It states:

In case an employee becomes incapable of performing his regular work through occupational accident, or occupational disease, or occupational sickness, the Company will attempt to provide such work as the employee is capable of performing, provided, however, this does not obligate the Company to create a job or "make work" for this purpose. When the employee is able to return to his former duties, his seniority will not be affected.

Question   Did the Company have the right to deny the grievant, a partially disabled employee, work, and the right to retire him when he was of pensionable age? What should the arbitrator do?

CHAPTER 12

ALTERNATIVE DISPUTE RESOLUTION TECHNIQUES

Organizations spend a substantial amount of time and effort, and a significant amount of money, on resolving disputes that arise between workers and their employers. In the field of labor–management relations, these disputes are normally divided into two categories: a large category dealing with the day-to-day operations of the organization, primarily involving the rules of the workplace; and a smaller category dealing with collective bargaining negotiations.

Many innovative efforts have been made to design rules-of-the-workplace dispute resolution techniques. We first discussed this area in the preceding chapter and will extend our discussion here. Also covered will be negotiating or bargaining impasse resolution techniques short of the strike or lockout. The strike and lockout are the subject of Chapter 13, and impasse resolution in the public sector is discussed in Part Four.

NONUNION COMPLAINT RESOLUTION

The formal grievance procedure with third-party arbitration is the method utilized to resolve the daily disputes that arise between labor and management in a unionized organization. Management also uses this type of procedure to resolve disputes with nonunionized workers in some organizations.

Nonunion organizations more commonly make use of a variety of complaint resolution methods that are not modeled after the union-style grievance–arbitration procedure. These alternative dispute resolution techniques vary from appeals to higher management to resolution by tribunal.

All   ity and credibility.[1] *Formality* enables com-
plaini   he disposition of their problem in a timely
fashic   –in particular, complex written submissions
of co...,....   m utilizing the system. *Credibility* requires
both protection from supervisor reprisals and strict impartiality of the ultimate decision maker in the process. Accordingly, the person used at this ultimate step must be
far removed from the problem itself. Outsiders to the company, such as arbitrators,
certainly meet this requirement. Insiders must come from the higher management
levels, or must be nonmanagerial personnel.

Appeals to Management

Over 70 percent of companies have developed both formal complaint systems as
well as employee participation systems for their nonunion workers.[2] The larger the
company, the more likely such programs will be available. Thus, substantially more
than 70 percent of nonunion employees will have access to such systems. Employee
complaints take many forms, as we see in the following discussion.

Informational Complaints: Communications Programs

Many employee complaints are primarily informational. A worker may be unhappy, or
puzzled, as to why the company does some things one way and not another, or why a
particular benefit is not offered them. Since many employee complaints are not aimed
at specific unfair treatment but rather at general company practices, an **information
program** is an important component of any problem resolution effort.[3]

Because of the importance of maintaining communications with employees,
nonunion (and union) companies use a variety of methods both to disseminate information on company policies, procedures, and practices and to collect employee
information. The information from management to workers is contained in the employee handbook and in the various memos delivered to each employee at work or
home. Bulletin boards are also used, a device unions utilize extensively. Company
newsletters and newspapers are also vehicles for this information exchange.

The flow of information from employees to management is also multifaceted.
Many companies use questionnaires and attitude surveys to elicit employee sentiment about what the company is doing. Employee newsletters and newspapers are
another way to garner this information as well as direct information from management to workers. Some companies have even set up WATS lines for employees to
use from any place and at any time to answer employee questions.[4] Another device
used by many larger companies is the **exit interview,** in which employees are very
likely to be quite candid about what they see wrong with the organization they are
leaving.

Employee–Management Complaints: Open Door Policies

Other employee complaints, however, may center on perceptions of unfair treatment
at the hands of management. This type of complaint requires an appeals procedure
to higher levels than the one at which the individuals involved are situated.

A formal **open door policy** can be a useful procedure to resolve employee complaints, and it is typically used in conjunction with other techniques. An open door policy allows employees to start seeking a solution to their problem at a level beyond that of their immediate supervisor. In personnel problems, because the immediate supervisor's actions are being questioned, a natural antagonism exists between the employee and the supervisor.

Besides allowing the complaint to be aired at a higher level, many companies require a formal response by the manager within an allotted time period. This formalization of the process typically requires that the employee put the complaint in writing. This is sometimes done on a form specifically designed for this purpose. Sometimes it is just a submission of a page or less on plain paper, giving the details of who is involved and what the problem is perceived to be.

If management shows a strong commitment to the open door policy, and it is well (and continually) publicized, it can be an effective way of handling employee problems at a relatively informal level. It is particularly effective in small work units, where management is familiar with most, if not all, of the workers.

Most companies that utilize an open door procedure allow employees to appeal the first management decision. This is particularly true if the initial level of complaint is to the worker's direct supervisor. The use of appeals makes the open door procedure a step procedure.

Employee–Management Complaints: Step Procedures

Step procedures are commonly used to deal with complaints in all types of organizations. As noted above and in the preceding chapter, unionized organizations handle worker complaints through a step procedure, the union grievance procedure with arbitration. In nonunion environments, the steps usually involve appeals through the levels of management. Some appeals stop at the highest level in the worker's plant or office. However, this denial of appeal to the top is rare, and most appeals stop at the top management level in the company.[5] Yet another variation in the last stage of the appeal is to send unresolved disputes to peer review panels. This relatively new concept in human resources management will be discussed in the next section.

Step procedures to handle employee complaints are commonly merged with open door policies. They tend to be used more by production and clerical people than by professional and managerial personnel. The procedures allow the production or clerical worker who has a complaint to talk things out with management. Professional and lower level managerial personnel are in constant contact (and discussion) with their supervisors/managers and thus work out complaints during the normal course of the workday, while doing their jobs.[6]

Figure 12.1 illustrates a typical step procedure, which is similar in structure (if not participants) to a union grievance procedure.

Appeals to Peer Review Boards

In a growing (though still small) number of companies, step procedures are being designed with the last step entailing an appeal to an internal third party.[7] This appeals

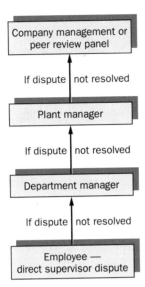

FIGURE 12.1 A typical step procedure.

board or tribunal is not directly involved with the dispute, and is expected to render an impartial decision. Working within the framework of an organization's employee relations handbook, these boards are usually empowered to hear, and decide, most discipline, work assignment, performance appraisal, and job promotion complaints.

Composition of Peer Review Boards

Peer review boards or **industrial tribunals** are generally made up of both the worker's peers and company management. Most peer review boards have more workers than managers; a commonly noted composition is three fellow employees and two managers.[8] Typically, the company's personnel department will have a management representative on the board whose primary function is to interpret for the other board members company personnel policies and procedures as they apply to the complaint under review.[9] Sometimes this manager from personnel is made chairperson of the board, voting only to break ties.

The choice of peers varies widely from system to system. In many cases, the employee selects them from a list of workers who have had some training in the company's peer review system. In some instances, they are chosen from a list of workers who have volunteered to serve but have had no training at all.

Function of Peer Review Boards

The decisions of most peer review boards or industrial tribunals are final. In some cases the employee may appeal the decision to top management, but this is not typically the case. The manager against whom the complaint is lodged can rarely appeal the decision.

The peer review boards or industrial tribunals in nonunion companies have been implemented in these organizations to bolster employee confidence in the complaint procedure, and so improve labor relations.[10] Bringing one's problem before an impartial board for resolution after trying to resolve the dispute with various managers tends to satisfy most people. If the complaining employee feels the board is really a neutral body, and management is truly committed to the system, it will work. Turnover will drop, and the company's employees will become less interested in union representation.

Appeals to Organizational Ombudspersons and Referees

The use of specialized personnel to manage and facilitate the resolution of complaints (grievances) in nonunion organizations is becoming increasingly popular.[11] To replace the union's grievance representatives (shop stewards, business agents, and grievance committees) and third parties, these organizations make available, to workers with complaints, employees usually called **ombudspersons** or referees. These people act as third parties in disputes, helping the complaining worker and his or her manager resolve their problem.

The Ombudsperson as Mediator

In most nonunion companies, the ombudsperson's function is to work with the two parties in the dispute, helping them resolve it themselves. As a facilitator in resolving the conflict, the ombudsperson acts primarily as a mediator. Mediation, which we will discuss in detail later in this chapter, is the intervention of a third party to assist in resolving labor disputes.[12]

As a mediator, the ombudsperson must first clarify the facts surrounding the dispute. The two parties involved rarely agree on the circumstances that caused the problem, but rather just the actions that gave rise to the complaint. Ferreting out the facts and getting both parties to accept them is a major task. Often, one or both parties may be totally blind to the realities of the situation. Investigation is very important.

Once all parties establish the facts of the situation and accept them, the ombudsperson can seek common ground for resolving the problem. Compromise is the key here. For example, if a supervisor suspended a worker for a week, the ombudsperson might first have to get the worker to accept the fact that he or she committed an act that warranted discipline. Then the ombudsperson might work with the parties to fashion a solution with a less severe penalty, say, a one- or two-day suspension, which shows that the supervisor was correct in disciplining the worker but that the discipline was too harsh. When the parties accept the compromise proposed by the mediating ombudsperson, the problem is resolved to the satisfaction of both parties.

The Ombudsperson as Decision Maker

Mediating employee complaints requires the development of solutions acceptable to both parties. If the facts surrounding the problem are established and accepted by both, compromises can be fashioned and a solution reached. In some cases, however, emotions override the issues, and a logical progression toward a solution is not possible. In these cases mediation will not work. A third party entering the dispute will have to have the authority to suggest and implement a solution to resolve the matter. In essence, the use of ombudspersons in this type of situation would combine, in one person, the roles of mediator and arbitrator.

The Hearing Officer as Decision Maker

Using the ombudsperson as fact finder, mediator, and arbitrator is not a common practice in industry and government.[13] The primary characteristic of the typical ombudsperson is skill in mediation. Fashioning solutions and then imposing them on the parties might lead one party to feel that the third party is not all that neutral. This could undercut the ombudsperson's effectiveness.

A more common setup in organizations that wish to use a dispute resolver with decision-making power is the hearing officer. The **hearing officer** is an employee of the company who has the power to resolve employee–employer disputes. He or she has a special staff and office set apart from the normal managerial hierarchy to ensure neutrality. The hearing officer is an intermediate step between peer review/ombudspersons and outside arbitrators.[14] Hearing officers are found only in large organizations with a large number of employee–employer disputes, which justifies their special staff whose only assignment is to handle such disputes.

METHODS OF CONTRACT IMPASSE RESOLUTION

A **contract impasse** occurs when the two parties negotiating a collective bargaining contract cannot reach agreement. No longer willing to make concessions to each other, the parties have four options. First, they can continue to work under the old contract and hope that something will happen to bring them back to the negotiating table.[15] A second option is to call a production disruption, which labor may do through a strike and management through a lockout (locking its workers out of the workplace). This second option will be discussed in the next chapter.

Two other options involve bringing in a third-party neutral in order to aid labor and management in overcoming the impasse. A conciliator or mediator may be called in, to keep the parties bargaining and act as a communications conduit for them (conciliation) or to suggest compromises to both parties (mediation). This option still leaves the fashioning of the final contract to the parties involved. The second use of a third-party neutral would be to set the terms of the contract (arbitration). An arbitrator does not suggest; rather he or she decides.

Actions of the Third-Party Neutral

Mediation and conciliation are commonly used techniques to help labor and management overcome bargaining impasses. The Taft–Hartley Act (LMRA) of 1947 established the **Federal Mediation and Conciliation Service (FMCS)**, recognizing the importance of these techniques in resolving labor–management impasses.[16] Forty-five states also have separate mediation and conciliation services, and four others have departments that will undertake these activities.[17] The LMRA requires that the FMCS be notified of any contract impasses 30 days before the beginning of a strike or lockout, allowing mediation and/or conciliation to be utilized before such a disruption.

Conciliation

Although mediation and conciliation are customarily used interchangeably, there is a technical difference between the two methods. **Conciliation** is aimed at keeping the parties talking to each other, by acting as a channel for communications. When the parties no longer can, or want to, interact face to face, the conciliator tells each what the other is saying. It is truly a neutral role.

The conciliator must be a good listener. He or she must faithfully transmit the parties' positions, acting purely as a go-between. Not charged with developing compromises for the parties to consider, the conciliator just keeps the two bargaining, hoping that they will start accommodating to each other. He or she may make suggestions that are appropriate in providing a basis for continued negotiations.[18] It is a very difficult job, requiring substantial patience and a sense of diplomacy. Working individually with each party and rephrasing messages to filter out the emotional content without changing the meaning represent major challenges for the conciliator.

Mediation

Mediation is a procedure that encompasses efforts to both keep parties bargaining with each other and to move them closer in position by proposing compromises for their consideration. Mediation usually requires substantial experience in labor–management relations as well as skills in interfacing with people who are somewhat hot under the collar. It is the epitome of conflict resolution.

The mediator fulfills many functions as a third-party neutral. Lacking the power to impose a solution, he or she must be very skillful at the job to get the parties in conflict to make the best use of the mediator's services and resolve the impasse.

The first function of the mediator may be to clearly define the issues underlying the impasse. The issues may have become distorted and even lost as communications and the flow of information have dwindled between the two parties. In particularly antagonistic contract negotiations, when both parties are using distributive bargaining tactics (as discussed in Chapter 6), the total divergence of interests may cause irrelevant issues to lead to the breakdown in negotiations.

Once both parties clearly see the basic issues, the mediator can concentrate on reestablishing communications between the parties. He or she can act as a conduit for both parties, or bring them together for face-to-face talks. Lack of clarity on the part of one or both sides can be overcome with the help of a mediator. Emotional content can be screened, so that the factual and persuasive elements of each side's position are clearly communicated.

With the actual issue out in the open and each side communicating with the other, the mediator can start to move the parties' positions closer, through compromise. Suggesting possible solutions to the issues is the major function that differentiates mediators from conciliators. Trying to fashion a workable agreement through a set of compromises is the basic aim of mediation. The mediator can serve as catalyst

Table 12.1 *Comparison of Three Roles for a Third-Party Neutral*

	Conciliation	Mediation	Med–Arb
Objective	Keep parties bargaining (communications)	Keep parties bargaining, suggest solutions	Keep parties bargaining, suggest solutions, finally mandate solutions
Primary skill	Listen	Listen, analyze, "sell"	Listen, analyze, "sell," impose (equitably)

because, as a neutral, his or her recommendations will be more acceptable to each side than recommendations of the opposing party. Furthermore, concessions made by either side in reaching an agreement can be blamed on the mediator, making the mediator the scapegoat rather than the negotiating team. In fact, a good mediator will help sell a compromise to the constituents being represented by the negotiators.

Med–Arb

Mediation–arbitration (med-arb) is a recent innovation in which the role of mediator and arbitrator is combined in one third-party neutral. It is an attempt to combine the best features of mediation and arbitration. In mediation, this feature is the development of a solution by the two parties involved who will have to live with that solution for the duration of the agreement. In arbitration, it is the assurance that a solution will be developed, albeit by the neutral party and not the parties involved.

In med–arb, the neutral first assumes the role of mediator. He or she tries to facilitate the parties' resolution of disputes that arise in their negotiations, suggesting avenues of compromise for the parties to consider. In med–arb, the parties will consider more carefully the suggestions of the third-party neutral as a mediator, because these suggestions may become the actual components of the agreement at a later date when the third party switches from mediator to arbitrator. Thus, the mediation effort is made more vital.

Once the neutral concludes that a true impasse has been reached, and any further mediation would be useless, he or she switches hats and becomes an arbitrator. The parties then present each of their proposals, or offers, to the arbitrator who will then fashion an agreement from them. The scope of the arbitrator to develop the terms of the agreement varies substantially, depending on the type of *interest arbitration* mandated for or agreed to by the parties involved (see section later in this chapter on interest arbitration).

Table 12.1 summarizes these three third-party neutral actions.

Governmental Actions under Emergency Provisions

The federal government has involved itself with bargaining impasses of interest to it for over 65 years. Under the Railway Labor Act (1926), the government can step in to prevent a strike in the railroad or airline industry by invoking mediation and/or fact finding. Under the Taft–Hartley Act (1947), the government can do the same for any dispute or strike that would endanger the health or safety of the public. Under both laws, government's authority does not allow the imposition of a solution. It only requires the two parties to continue to seek one themselves, with the help of a third party.

Intervention under the Railway Labor Act

The **Railway Labor Act (RLA)** provides an **emergency dispute resolution** mechanism for work stoppages in the railroad and airline industries. Because these are both critical transportation industries in which a strike or lockout could threaten the national health or safety, these emergency dispute provisions were written into the act in 1926. They allow the government to use its powers to prevent strikes of railroads (and airlines since 1936).[19]

The procedure requires the usual advance notice to terminate or change the collective bargaining agreement. Under the RLA, this is a 30-day advance notice. (Under the NLRA/LMRA, it is a 60-day requirement.) The **National Mediation Board (NMB)** oversees the negotiations for the new contract and mediates any disputes that arise during those negotiations. In some cases, mediation by the NMB has been exhaustive; in the 1988-1989 Eastern Airlines dispute it went on for 13 months.[20] If the NMB cannot successfully mediate the dispute, voluntary arbitration is recommended. If this is not acceptable to both parties, the NMB declares an impasse and removes itself from the dispute.

After the NMB removes itself, the terms of the present agreement are frozen for a 30-day period and the NMB notifies the president of the United States. If the president does not take action upon notification by the NMB, the parties are free to act as they see fit, which usually means a work stoppage.

If the president believes the dispute will threaten the national health or safety by significantly disrupting interstate commerce, he or she may delay the strike for 60 days and appoint an emergency board. This board will investigate the dispute, primarily as a fact-finding body, and make recommendations to resolve it within 30 days. During the remaining time, a 30-day period, the parties must work under the old contract.[21] If the board cannot get the parties to settle in the 60-day period, a work stoppage will occur. However, in most cases in which the parties have rejected the emergency board's terms, Congress has stepped in and mandated the settlement by legislation.[22]

When first enacted, the emergency dispute provisions of the RLA were used extensively. Most of the disputes centered on the use of firemen on diesel locomotives, and then the number of brakemen on a train. (See the discussion of input work rules in Chapter 10). After Congress legislated solutions to these problems, the emergency provisions were not used a great deal. In the 1989 Eastern Airlines strike, there was substantial pressure on President Bush to invoke the provisions, but he did not.[23]

Intervention under the Taft–Hartley Act

Emergency dispute provisions were added to the National Labor Relations Act by the 1947 **Taft–Hartley Act** (Labor-Management Relations Act, LMRA). They include a major role for the Federal Mediation and Conciliation Service, which was also created by the Taft–Hartley, and for fact finding.

The national emergency dispute procedure starts with the 60-day advance notification by one of the parties of an intent to modify the present agreement, a requirement for all unions and companies under the NLRA/LMRA. If within 30 days of the start of negotiations, the parties report an imminent impasse to the FMCS, they or a state mediation service will attempt to mediate the dispute.

If the mediator feels that a strike or lockout will occur, or if it does occur, the president can appoint a board of inquiry to fact find or investigate. This step would be taken if the president felt that the impending or actual work stoppage would endanger the national health or safety. The board expedites its investigations and reports its findings to the president quickly, typically in a day or two. At this point the president may ask the attorney general to secure an injunction to prevent or halt the work stoppage for 80 days.

During the 80-day cooling-off period, the FMCS continues its efforts to help the parties resolve their disputes and break the impasse. The board of inquiry is also reconvened to continue its fact-finding role. After 60 days of the cooling-off period have passed, the board reports the employer's final offer to the president. Over the final 20 days of the cooling-off period, the NLRB holds a secret ballot election to determine if the union members will accept the final offer. If not, the 80-day injunction dissolves, and the parties can act as they see fit. The procedure ends with a report by the president to Congress.[24]

Like the Railway Labor Act emergency dispute provisions, the provisions of the Taft–Hartley Act do not impose a settlement on the parties involved. They do not prevent work stoppages, but rather delay them, and, hopefully, through continued negotiations with third-party help, allow the participants to reach agreement without a work stoppage.

Criticism of Governmental Intervention

The Taft–Hartley provisions, like those of the Railway Labor Act, have been used very sparingly in the last 20 years or so: only 6 times.[25] They have been criticized for their many shortcomings as strike prevention tools. As Table 12.2 shows, government intervention during the first 25 years of the enactment of the emergency dispute provisions was not very successful in preventing strikes. The government invoked the provisions 34 times; in 29 of these cases a strike took place. Furthermore, in about one-third of the cases in which a strike occurred, the strike started or continued after the 80-day cooling-off period.

Major criticism has been leveled at the predictability of each step in the procedure: notifications, fact finding, reports, and election. A union that plans a strike can easily take into account the 80-day cooling-off period and undertake its strike at approximately the time it plans to do so.

Probably the most damning criticism concerns the board of inquiry's role and use of fact finding. Under the law, the board can only report on the facts of the situation as it finds them. It cannot recommend solutions and act, in essence, as a high-powered mediator. Consequently, the board cannot move the parties closer to agreement. To try to bring pressure on the parties and to break the impasse, the

Table 12.2 *Intervention under the Taft–Hartley National Emergency Dispute Provisions, 1948–1972*

Strikes and Settlements	Number of Disputes	Number of Workers[a] (thousands)
Total disputes	34	2,144.8
Strikes—total	29	1,800.0
Before 80-day injunction	18	1,384.1
After 80-day injunction	2[b]	73.0
Before and after 80-day injunction	7	259.7
No injunction issued	2[c]	83.2
Settlements—total	34	2,144.8
Settlements without strike	5[d]	344.8
Settlements after strike	29	1,800.0
Within 80-day injunction period	14	1,316.7
After 80-day injunction period	13	400.1
Without strike	4	67.4
After strike	9[b]	332.7
No injunction issued	2[c]	83.2

Source: Department of Labor, Bureau of Labor Statistics Summary Report, "National Emergency Disputes under the Labor–Management Relations (Taft–Hartley) Act, 1947–72," no date, Table 2 (page 2).

[a] The number of workers refers to those in the bargaining unit or those directly involved in the strike.

[b] One stoppage involved six maritime unions and the International Longshoremen's and Warehousemen's Union on the Atlantic, Gulf, and Pacific Coasts and the Great Lakes. Settlements were reached for the Atlantic and Gulf Coasts and the Great Lakes during or immediately after the injunction period. The ILWU and several maritime unions struck on the Pacific Coast after the injunction had expired.

[c] An injunction was not requested in the 1948 meatpacking dispute, and a request for an injunction in the 1971 Chicago grain elevator dispute was denied by the district court.

[d] Injunctions were not issued in three of the five cases.

president has used the fact finding of these boards in more of a political than an economic fashion.

Fact Finding

Fact finding is primarily the systematic collection of the facts surrounding a dispute. It also involves organizing and presenting the facts to the public, usually accompanied by recommended solutions. This act of publicizing the positions of the two disputing parties by a neutral party is meant to bring pressure on the parties to resolve their differences.[26]

Fact finding is rarely used in the private sector to help resolve impasses, except under the national emergency strike provisions, as was noted above. It is used extensively in public sector impasse procedures, a point that will be made in the section on state, county, and municipal government strike prevention techniques in Chapter 17. Because of the public airing of the dispute through fact finding, private sector labor and management shy away from it.

The use of fact finding in national emergency strikes and in public sector contract impasses puts the government squarely in the middle of labor–management relations in those cases. The politically charged environment colors the procedures, and fact finding commonly becomes a political tool. In national emergency strike situations it becomes the tool of the president, while in public sector impasses it is utilized as a political "club" by governors, county administrators, or mayors. It is difficult to look on fact finding as a purely neutral procedure, even though in many instances it is just that.

Contract Impasse Arbitration (Interest Arbitration)

Arbitration as discussed in the previous chapter and the beginning of this chapter is known as grievance or rights arbitration: the intervention of a third-party neutral to resolve disputes between labor and management over the rights each is accorded under a collective bargaining agreement or a personnel manual defining rules and regulations in the employment relationship or the commonly employed practices and procedures of the workplace. **Contract impasse arbitration,** or **interest arbitration,** involves the intervention of a third-party neutral to establish the terms of the agreement between the two parties when they cannot do so themselves through the negotiating process.

Without interest arbitration, the two parties at an impasse in negotiations would end those negotiations and take other action: a labor strike or a management lockout. When a work stoppage is felt to be intolerable, for whatever reason, interest arbitration will typically be used to resolve contract negotiation impasses.

Interest Arbitration in the Private Sector

Since the right of private parties to strike or utilize the lockout has never been seriously questioned, interest arbitration is rarely used in the private sector. Interest arbitration is an option (but not required) under the Railway Labor Act (see above). The National Mediation Board will recommend voluntary interest arbitration if it cannot successfully mediate an impasse between a railroad or an airline and its workers. Usually one or both parties decline this offer, and a work stoppage will occur. In some instances, however, the parties will agree to voluntary, binding arbitration, as both the Teamsters and the Transportation Workers Union, at impasse with Pan American World Airways, did recently.[27]

Perhaps the most well-known use in recent times of interest arbitration in the private sector was that contained in the Experimental Negotiating Agreement (ENA) between the United Steel Workers (USW) and the ten major steel producers in the 1970s. In exchange for COLA enhancements, various bonuses, and other considerations, the USW signed the ENA, a ten-year no-strike agreement. All unresolved issues in collective bargaining carried on every three years between the USW and the Coordinating Committee Steel Companies (the industrywide bargaining coalition of producers) were to be submitted to voluntary, binding arbitration. In 1980, the steel producers decided not to renew the ENA as the high rate of inflation of the 1970s caused the steel workers' pay to soar. Instead, the producers began seeking concessions from the USW.

Interest Arbitration in the Public Sector

The greatest use of interest arbitration is in the public sector. As noted earlier, as of 1988, 21 states had compulsory and binding interest arbitration laws.[28] For reasons that will be discussed later, strike prevention in the public sector, especially in protective services, is a major priority of state, county, and municipal governments.[29] Interest arbitration is a substitute for the strike, and thus it is mandatory in many states, counties, and municipalities in which collective bargaining occurs.

The Chilling Effect and Interest Arbitration

Mandating interest arbitration to replace a work stoppage alters the power balance in collective bargaining. Power in collective bargaining, as noted in Chapter 6, is defined in the context of a work stoppage. If labor can impose a greater cost on management than it—the union and its members—absorbs by striking, it holds the power balance in the relationship at that point in time. If the costs imposed on management by a strike are less than those of the union, management holds the power balance. Doing away with a work stoppage alters this balance.

If one party knows that the power of the other is greater, the weaker party has an incentive not to make concessions in bargaining and instead go to impasse. At that point, an arbitrator would be called in to set the terms of the contract. The weaker party, in other words, would rely on the arbitrator to give it a better deal than it could get in the give and take of good faith collective bargaining, since it is bargaining from a position of weakness. The reliance on arbitration to gain better contract terms then could be obtained through bargaining is called the **chilling effect**.[30]

As shown in Figure 12.2, under **conventional arbitration** where the arbitrator is free to fashion his or her own solution, the chilling effect occurs because the weaker party realizes that it would be "forced" to make much greater concessions than would the stronger party in a jointly bargained outcome (contract), and the contract would fall in the position shown above (theoretical power-balanced point). Thus, rather than bargain, it takes its chances on the outcome the arbitrator would choose, hoping he or she "splits the difference" between the two parties. This is as likely an outcome

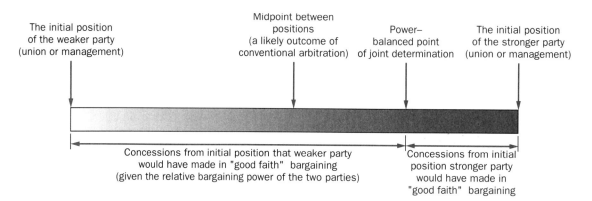

FIGURE 12.2 The chilling effect of conventional arbitration.

as one that would favor the more powerful party, for the arbitrator, an outsider, may not be able to assess the relative power of the two.

To overcome the chilling effect, several states, counties, and municipalities use **final offer arbitration.** Under this method, the arbitrator is not free to fashion the terms of the agreement, but must choose between the final offers of each party at the point of impasse. It is a winner-take-all situation, with no splitting the difference allowed. It thus promotes good faith bargaining as each party tries to make its final offer reasonable, given the situation, so that the arbitrator will choose it rather than the other party's final offer.

Since its introduction in 1966, final offer arbitration has been modified in several ways.[31] The most common adaptation has been to allow final offer arbitration issue by issue, so that it is not a winner-take-all situation as occurs when final offer arbitration is applied to the whole package. Going issue by issue, the arbitrator chooses one party's final offer over the other's. If ten issues were to be arbitrated, one party might have its final offer selected for five issues, while the other party's final offer would be selected for the other five. This gives the arbitrator some discretion in fashioning the terms of the agreement, but it still pushes the parties to bargain and make concessions to come up with reasonable offers on each issue.

The Narcotic Effect of Arbitration on Bargaining

Besides the chilling effect, interest arbitration has other adverse effects on bargaining. Without a deadline and a work stoppage hanging over them, both labor and management will behave differently in bargaining. This will be especially true in the final stage when they have developed a good feeling for each other's position and have settled some issues. When an impasse looms on a few issues, the urgency of a possible work stoppage will create a more compromising stance on the part of both labor and management. With interest arbitration replacing the work stoppage, that urgency is altered, and compromising is reduced. The arbitrator will decide. If the parties take this attitude, they may start to rely more and more on arbitration over time and less and less on bargaining to finalize their collective bargaining agreements. This third-party dependency is referred to as the **narcotic effect** of interest arbitration.[32]

Other adverse effects of interest arbitration focus on complaints that are similar to those made about rights arbitration (see Chapter 11). Arbitration costs, arbitrator competency (especially consistency), and the drawing out of the process are common criticisms. However, if strikes are to be prevented, some equitable dispute resolution technique is needed. Arbitration at this point is the most commonly utilized technique that will yield a solution. Without some form of arbitration, work stoppages will occur. These are the subject of the next chapter.

DISCUSSION QUESTIONS

1. Why is a sound communications program important in avoiding employee complaints in a nonunion organization?

2. What does an open door policy allow an aggrieved employee to do?

3. Who normally sits on peer review boards used to resolve employee complaints in a nonunion organization?

4. Differentiate between the roles of an ombudsperson as mediator and as decision maker.

5. Differentiate between conciliation and mediation.

6. Describe the emergency strike provisions in the Railway Labor Act; in the Taft–Hartley Act.

7. Discuss the different effect caused by using conventional interest arbitration and final offer interest arbitration.

8. What is meant by the narcotic effect of interest arbitration?

VOCABULARY LIST

information program

exit interview

open door policy

step procedure

peer review board/industrial tribunal

ombudsperson

hearing officer

contract impasse

Federal Mediation and Conciliation Service

conciliation

mediation

mediation–arbitration (med–arb)

emergency dispute resolution under the Railway Labor Act (RLA)

National Mediation Board (NMB)

emergency dispute provisions of the Taft–Hartley Act

fact finding

contract impasse arbitration/interest arbitration

chilling effect

conventional arbitration

final offer arbitration

narcotic effect

FOOTNOTES

1. Ronald Berenbeim, *Nonunion Complaint Systems: A Corporate Appraisal* (The Conference Board, 1980), pp. 8–9.

2. Thomas A. Kochan et al., *The Transformation of American Industrial Relations* (Basic Books, 1986), p. 100.

3. Cornelius Quinn et al., *Maintaining Nonunion Status* (CBI Publishing Co., 1982), p. 129.

4. Berenbeim, *Nonunion Complaint Systems*, p. 7.

5. Ibid., p. 15.

6. Ibid., p. 36.

7. Douglas M. McCabe, "Grievance Processing: Non-Union Setting—Peer Review Systems and Internal Corporate Tribunals: A Procedural Analysis," *Proceedings*

of the 1988 Spring Meeting (Industrial Relations Research Association, March 23–25, 1988), p. 496.

8. Ibid., p. 500; *Business Week*, September 15, 1986, p. 82.

9. McCabe, "Grievance Processing," p. 498.

10. *Business Week*, September 15, 1986, p. 82.

11. Kochan et al., *The Transformation of American Industrial Relations*, p. 95.

12. Nicholas Blain et al., "Mediation, Conciliation and Arbitration, An International Comparison of Australia, Great Britain, and the United States," *International Labor Review* (March–April 1987): 179.

13. Alan Balfour, "Five Types of Non-Union Grievance Systems," *Personnel* (March–April 1984): 70. As Balfour notes: "Commonly, the ombudsman doesn't have the right to arbitrate disputes."

14. Ibid., p. 74.

15. Under the Railway Labor Act, management may impose new terms after an impasse is reached (see below).

16. The FMCS replaced the U.S. Conciliation Service, a unit of the Department of Labor since 1913.

17. Blain et al., "Mediation, Conciliation and Arbitration," p. 183.

18. Ramsumair Singh, "Dispute Settlement and Mediation," *Industrial Relations* (Fall 1987): 315.

19. *Business Week*, March 20, 1989, p. 178.

20. Ibid.

21. William H. Holley and Kenneth M. Jennings, *The Labor Relations Process* (Dryden Press, 1988), p. 267.

22. *Business Week*, March 20, 1989, p. 178.

23. *New York Times*, February 21, 1989, p. C8; February 27, 1989, p. A12; March 8, 1989, p. A14; *Wall Street Journal*, February 27, 1989, p. A12; March 8, 1989, p. A1; *Business Week*, March 6, 1989, p. 26.

24. Holley and Jennings, *The Labor Relations Process*, pp. 267–270.

25. Charles M. Rehmus, "Emergency Strikes Revisited," *Industrial and Labor Relations Review* (January 1990): 177. The provision was not used at all in the 1980s, and the last time it was invoked, in 1978 by President Carter, the courts refused to grant an injunction to stop a 15-week coal strike.

26. Holley and Jennings, *The Labor Relations Process*, p. 248.

27. *Wall Street Journal*, January 14, 1988, p. 47; February 9, 1989, p. C6.

28. Susan Schwochau and Peter Feuille, "Interest Arbitrators and Their Decision Behavior," *Industrial Relations* (Winter 1988): 37.

29. Labor relations in state, county, and municipal government is the subject of Chapter 17.

30. Peter Feuille, "Final Offer Arbitration and the Chilling Effect," *Industrial Relations* (October 1975): 303–304.

31. Charles Feigenbaum, "Final Offer Arbitration: Better Theory Than Practice," *Industrial Relations* (October 1975): 311.

32. James R. Chelius and Marian M. Extejt, "The Narcotic Effect of Impasse–Resolution Procedures," *Industrial and Labor Relations Review* (July 1985): 629; Peter Feuille, "Selected Benefits and Costs of Compulsory Arbitration," *Industrial and Labor Relations Review* (October 1979): 73; Peter Feuille and John C. Anderson, "Public Sector Bargaining: Policy and Practice," *Industrial Relations* (Fall 1980): 318.

REFERENCES

BALFOUR, ALAN. "Five Types of Non-Union Grievance Systems." *Personnel* (March–April 1984): 67–76.

BERENBEIM, RONALD. *Nonunion Complaint Systems: A Corporate Appraisal.* The Conference Board, Report No. 770, 1980.

BLAIN, NICHOLAS, JOHN GOODMAN, and JOSEPH LOEWENBERG. "Mediation, Conciliation, and Arbitration, An International Comparison of Australia, Great Britain and the United States." *International Labor Review* (March–April 1987): 179–189.

CHELIUS, JAMES R., and MARIAN M. EXTEJT. "The Narcotic Effect of Impasse–Resolution Procedures." *Industrial and Labor Relations Review* (July 1985): 629–638.

FEIGENBAUM, CHARLES. "Final Offer Arbitration: Better Theory Than Practice." *Industrial Relations* (October 1975): 311–317.

FEUILLE, PETER. "Final Offer Arbitration and the Chilling Effect." *Industrial Relations* (October 1975): 302–310.

——. "Selected Benefits and Costs of Compulsory Arbitration." *Industrial and Labor Relations Review* (October 1979): 64–76.

—— and JOHN C. ANDERSON. "Public Sector Bargaining: Policy and Practice." *Industrial Relations* (Fall 1980): 309–324.

HOLLEY, WILLIAM H., and KENNETH M. JENNINGS. *The Labor Relations Process.* Dryden Press, 1988, Ch. 7.

KOCHAN, THOMAS A., HARRY C. KATZ, and ROBERT B. MCKERSIE. *The Transformation of American Industrial Relations.* Basic Books, 1986, Ch. 4.

MCCABE, DOUGLAS M. "Grievance Processing: Non-Union Setting—Peer Review Systems and Internal Corporate Tribunals: A Procedural Analysis." *Proceedings of the 1988 Spring Meeting.* Industrial Relations Research Association, March 23–25, 1988, pp. 496–502.

QUINN, CORNELIUS, THOMAS HILL, and JAMES L. NICHOLS. *Maintaining Nonunion Status.* CBI Publishing Co., 1982, Ch. 10.

REHMUS, CHARLES M. "Emergency Strikes Revisited." *Industrial and Labor Relations Review* (January 1990): 175–190.

SCHWOCHAU, SUSAN, and PETER FEUILLE. "Interest Arbitrators and Their Decision Behavior." *Industrial Relations* (Winter 1988): 37–55.

SINGH, RAMSUMAIR. "Dispute Settlement and Mediation." *Industrial Relations* (Fall 1987): 314–316.

TREBLE, JOHN G. "How New Is Final-Offer Arbitration." *Industrial Relations* (Winter 1986): 92–94.

WESTIN, ALAN F., and ALFRED G. FELIU. *Resolving Employment Disputes without Litigation*. Bureau of National Affairs, 1988.

CHAPTER 13

THE STRIKE

The strike has traditionally been labor's major weapon in any conflict with management. It was, and for the most part still is, the most important source of union power, causing an employer to think very seriously about not reaching agreement with its employees and the union representing them in collective bargaining. If agreement is not reached, the next step in the typical negotiating process is the economic strike, which is generally an integral part of that process. A variation on this theme would be the lockout, an employer's equivalent of the strike, when the workforce is locked out of the plant.

There are other types of strikes and lockouts besides the economic, but they are relatively rare. In fact, even major strikes and lockouts of all types, though highly publicized and thus quite visible, are rare. The Bureau of Labor Statistics, which has been keeping records of major work stoppages since 1947, reports that in no year did they cause more than 0.43 percent of lost production time, or just over 4 hours for every 1,000 hours worked.

Work stoppages have been declining for the last 15 years, as can be seen in Table 13.1. Less than 1 in 1,000 hours has been lost annually in major strikes and lockouts since 1979, declining to an all-time low of less than 0.02 percent (fewer than 2 in 10,000 hours), in 1987, 1988, and 1990. In those years, there were less than 50 work stoppages, about one-tenth of the peak number of these events (which occurred in 1952). This decline mirrors the general erosion of union power in the past dozen years or so. Work stoppages, most of which are strikes, are power struggles. As union power declines, the ability of unions to strike with a good chance of winning (settling on terms favorable to them) declines.

Table 13.1 *Major Work Stoppages, 1947–1990*

Year	Stoppages Beginning in Period		Days Idle	
	Number	Workers Involved (millions)	Number (thousands)	Percent of Estimated Working Time
1947	270	1.63	25.7	—
1948	245	1.44	26.1	0.22%
1949	262	2.54	43.4	0.38%
1950	424	1.70	30.4	0.26%
1951	415	1.46	15.1	0.12%
1952	470	2.75	48.8	0.38%
1953	437	1.62	18.1	0.14%
1954	265	1.08	16.6	0.13%
1955	363	2.06	21.2	0.16%
1956	287	1.37	26.8	0.20%
1957	279	0.89	10.3	0.07%
1958	332	1.59	17.9	0.13%
1959	245	1.38	60.9	0.43%
1960	222	0.90	13.3	0.09%
1961	195	1.03	10.1	0.07%
1962	211	0.79	11.8	0.08%
1963	181	0.51	10.0	0.07%
1964	246	1.18	16.2	0.11%
1965	268	1.00	15.1	0.10%
1966	321	1.30	16.0	0.10%
1967	381	2.19	31.3	0.18%
1968	392	1.86	35.4	0.20%
1969	412	1.58	29.4	0.16%
1970	381	2.47	52.8	0.29%

(continued)

ECONOMIC STRIKES AND LOCKOUTS

The **economic strike** is labor's ultimate weapon in the exercise of union power.[1] The right to strike nonviolently is guaranteed workers in sections 7 and 13 of the National Labor Relations Act (NLRA)/Labor–Management Relations Act (LMRA).[2]

Why Economic Strikes?

The economic strike is typically a tactical weapon in the trade union's arsenal. Its main purpose is to bring management "to its knees," begging the workers to return on the terms the union wants and had offered to management just prior to the walkout. Strikes have other purposes, however. The strike is a power struggle, and the union may call a strike to show its power. Sometimes strikes are called because the rank-and-file, independent of their leaders, want to strike for one reason or another. Finally, the union leaders might call a strike for other than tactical reasons relating to the collective bargaining relationship.

Table 13.1 *(Continued)*

| | Stoppages Beginning in Period | | Days Idle | |
Year	Number	Workers Involved (millions)	Number (thousands)	Percent of Estimated Working Time
1971	298	2.52	35.5	0.19%
1972	250	0.98	16.8	0.09%
1973	317	1.40	16.3	0.08%
1974	424	1.80	31.8	0.16%
1975	235	0.97	17.6	0.09%
1976	231	1.52	24.0	0.12%
1977	298	1.21	21.3	0.10%
1978	219	1.01	23.8	0.11%
1979	235	1.02	20.4	0.09%
1980	187	0.80	20.8	0.09%
1981	145	0.73	16.9	0.07%
1982	96	0.66	9.1	0.04%
1983	81	0.91	17.5	0.08%
1984	62	0.38	8.5	0.04%
1985	54	0.32	7.1	0.03%
1986	69	0.53	11.9	0.05%
1987	46	0.17	4.5	0.02%
1988	40	0.12	4.4	0.02%
1989	51	0.45	17.0	0.07%
1990	45	0.20	6.6	0.02%

Source: BLS, U.S. Department of Labor, "Major Work Stoppages: 1990," USDL New Release 91–38, February 5, 1991, Table 1.

The Strike as a Step in Collective Bargaining

The most common use of the strike is in the collective bargaining process. When labor and management reach an impasse in their negotiations for a new labor agreement, they can continue in several ways, summarized graphically in Figure 13.1. They can call in a third-party neutral to arbitrate (interest arbitration), but this alternative is almost unheard of in the private sector.

The two parties can call in a mediator who will hopefully break the impasse. In large companies dealing with large unions, mediation is a common first step in the process of attempting to break the stalemate. As was mentioned in Chapter 12, railways and airlines, which fall under the purview of the Railway Labor Act, must mediate impasses before taking any other action. Basic industries (steel, coal, etc.) whose labor relations fall under the NLRA/LMRA may also be asked to mediate, under the Taft–Hartley emergency dispute provisions, especially if a work stoppage would be industrywide.

When mediation fails, or if the parties do not utilize it at all, the impasse normally leads to a strike by the workers and their union or a lockout by management. The

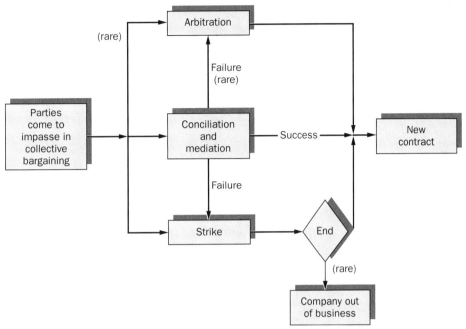

FIGURE 13.1   Impasse options.

primary purpose of the typical economic strike, as an integral part of collective bargaining, is to pressure management to agree to contract terms the union wants. These would be the terms the union has spelled out in negotiations just prior to the work stoppage. By stopping production, the workers and their union hope to force management to accept their demands and to agree to their terms in a new collective bargaining contract.

The management lockout, like the strike, is an exercise of power to pressure labor to agree to the contract terms management wants. However, unlike the strike, it is not management's ultimate weapon. Lockouts are less common than strikes, and, when utilized, they are short-lived. These weapons will be discussed separately later in this chapter.

Strikes and Bargaining Power: A Review of Costs and Power

How do the workers and their unions hope to force management to acquiesce to their demands? The work stoppage imposes several costs on management. These costs, discussed in detail in Chapter 6, are just summarized here.

The major cost of a strike to an employer is lost profit. The loss of profit is greatest when

1. The struck company cannot operate its plants because the production process is labor intensive (little automation) and/or because strike replacements are not readily available.

2. The product cannot be stockpiled, so that there is little or no inventory to meet some of the demand during a strike (e.g., nondurable or perishable goods and services).

3. The demand is great, as during boom times.

4. The strike is only against the company and not the entire industry, so competitors (especially if some are nonunion) continue to produce and sell, causing a loss of market share during the strike and into the future.

5. Workers and their union can cause government agencies to focus attention on the company and investigate its activities to see if they meet government standards. For instance, they may request FAA safety inspections of an airline trying to operate during a strike. This is referred to as whistleblowing (see also Chapter 14).

The longer the strike, the greater the profit loss, other things being equal. However, in imposing these costs on a company, the union and its members also bear some costs, notably:

1. Lost wages, less other income available—strike benefits, public assistance,[3] and alternative jobs (which are more likely to be available in boom times when labor markets are tight)—especially if the workers are in an illiquid position. (That is, they have little savings and lots of debt such as mortgages and credit payments on cars, furniture, and large appliances.)

2. Union divisiveness, especially if a fairly large, vocal faction opposes the strike.

3. Membership loss, especially if the strike is long and members find other permanent jobs in other industries, or the company goes out of business, and all the members are out of a job and will most likely leave the union.

Membership and job loss have become especially great risks in the last few years as management increasingly tries to operate with strike replacements.[4] Adding to the effect of this tougher management attitude have been two recent Supreme Court decisions. The one decision allows a member to quit the union and return to work without interference from the union (e.g., fines levied by the union),[5] and the other allows a struck employer to hire replacements on a permanent basis so that, at the end of a strike, returning workers with higher seniority may be denied reinstatement if their jobs are then held by strike replacements.[6]

The power balance in a strike will customarily be the major determinant in a union's decision to walk out. However, even if the balance favors management, a strike may occur. This may occur if the union leaders misjudge their power relative to that of the company. It may also occur because of rank-and-file militancy, forcing the leaders to strike even though they feel they might well lose. Lastly, a strike may be called for reasons other than the economic factors related to the collective bargaining round taking place.

The Strike as a Strategy for Future Union–Employer Relations

A strike might be called as part of the union's long-run strategy. A union that has never struck an employer may do so just to show it has the power to strike and disrupt production. This "show 'em" reason would benefit the union in future negotiations, lending credibility to the strike as a viable tactical weapon in collective bargaining. The membership would endorse this type of job action if the leaders explained its importance.

The Strike as Therapy for Internal Frustration

Another reason to strike might be related to the union membership's present state of mind. If the rank-and-file seems frustrated and angry at their inability (and the company's) to prosper and do well, a strike might be used as a therapeutic device. It could be one avenue for venting tension and anger. However, if the company is not doing well, a strike could do substantial economic harm and even push the company into bankruptcy. The Eastern Airlines strike of 1989 was partially the result of the frustration and anger of the International Association of Machinists (and Aerospace Workers) with Frank Lorenzo, chairman of Texas Air, Eastern's parent company. Within a week of the strike's onset, Eastern filed for bankruptcy. (The Eastern strike is discussed in detail below.)

Closely resembling a strike that stems from rank-and-file frustration and anger would be a strike utilized as a substitute for absenteeism, a sort of "vacation" for the workers. If a company has assigned a substantial amount of overtime, and/or absenteeism is running at a fairly high level, the union leadership, with strong support from the membership, might call a strike because they recognize their members need a respite. The strike would act as a therapeutic device.

In 1989, more than 57,000 members of the International Association of Machinists and Aerospace Workers walked off their jobs at Boeing Company, in large part because of their heavy workloads. When Boeing found itself unable to train enough workers to keep up with its backlog of orders, in order to maintain production schedules the company demanded that employees work 12-hour days and work for weeks without a day off. The workers complained that the situation was ruining their home lives and jeopardizing quality control.[7]

The Strike as a Strategy for Internal Union-Leadership Relations

Yet another reason why the leadership might call for a strike is to solidify union ranks in the face of a challenge to their position. An open conflict with management tends to bring the membership into line, backing their leaders in this conflict. This strategy might backfire, if the challenging faction can win over a substantial group (about one-fourth to one-half the membership) and convince them to go back to work and help initiate the overthrow of the present leadership that led them into this "ill-fated" strike. The challengers might even be successful in convincing the majority of the members to vote against going out on strike, delivering a blow to the leadership that could signal the beginning of the end for them.

An interesting variation on this theme of union divisiveness sparking a strike occurs when a dissident faction is more militant than the present leadership. The dissidents might start agitating the members to support a strike, and the leaders might have no choice but to invoke this option to show that they too are militant. Their actions would be aimed at defusing the issue embraced by the militant faction—a strike.

Finally, a strike might be called because of rank-and-file resentment, resentment that has been building since the 1980s in many industries. In these industries, unions and their members have granted many concessions to management, under the threat of plant closings and the like, in the face of steadily growing competitive pressures. In the latter part of the decade, many companies in these industries returned to profitability and in some cases even recorded record profits. However, in negotiating with unions, their claims are that the profitability may well be short-lived and that they must continue to contain costs. Tentative collective bargaining agreements hammered out by management and union leaders have featured modest pay increases and a slow phasing out of earlier concessions. Rank-and-file rejection of leader-endorsed collective bargaining agreements has increased substantially, as militant memberships are pushing to overturn concessions granted and make large gains. Some of these rejections have resulted in more bargaining and better contracts. The United Rubber Workers' rejection of the leader-negotiated pact with Goodyear, however, brought the union perilously close to a strike, averted just hours before the deadline by the company's concessions. *Business Week*, in assessing the situation, felt that "angry union members are venting frustration," a point noted above that might provoke a strike.[8]

As this discussion should make clear, not all strikes occur because impasses are reached in collective bargaining. Some are caused by a desire to exercise union power for long-run purposes, whereas others are caused by membership discontent or anger. Overall, however, many strikes are multipurpose, meeting needs related to both the present and future negotiations, and backed by the rank-and-file who have their own separate needs.

The Anatomy of a Dispute

The Eastern Airlines Strike

In 1986, Frank Lorenzo bought Eastern Airlines, adding it to Continental Airlines, held by Texas Air, his holding company. Continental, once a unionized airline, was put into bankruptcy in 1983; labor contracts were set aside, wages were halved, and it emerged in 1986 as a nonunion airline. Lorenzo sought major wage concessions from the unions representing Eastern's workers, and got them from the pilots (ALPA, Air Line Pilots Association) and flight attendants (TWU, Transport Workers Union) but not from the International Association of Machinists and Aerospace Workers (IAM) representing Eastern's mechanics and baggage handlers. During 1987 and 1988, Lorenzo sold Eastern's assets. Lorenzo had Eastern sign management contracts with Texas Air during this period, partially aimed at providing strike preparation planning. Eastern had been losing money when Texas Air bought it, and still was. Negotiations with the IAM, starting in October 1987, were not producing results. Eastern was steadily losing money.

November 1987   Mediation (by the Railway Labor Act's National Mediation Board, NMB) starts.

January 1988   The federal mediator announces that negotiations are reaching a critical phase. Eastern cancels a pilot replacement contract with a contract carrier as unions fight this type of strike preparation in court.

May 1988   The IAM raises the issue of safety problems at Eastern and presses the government to investigate these problems as well as the managerial and financial fitness of Eastern/Texas Air to operate the airline. The Department of Transportation looks into the matter, and finds Eastern and Texas Air management fit.

August 1988   Lorenzo loses a court case that would have allowed Eastern to continue to sell its assets and close down what were considered marginal operations, including the Eastern hub operation at Kansas City, accompanied by large layoffs. The appeals court in Washington, D.C., overturns this decision, allowing the shutdown.

September 1988   IAM members reject a contract offer from management with over 98 percent voting it down. The IAM does not call for a strike, and mediation continues. Eastern asks the NMB to declare an impasse, so that in 30 days it can impose contract terms on the IAM and the IAM will be free to strike (as required under the Railway Labor Act). The mediator refuses. Eastern sells ten planes to Federal Express.

November 1988   Eastern discontinues payments to Continental to train pilots in case of an IAM strike, assuming Eastern's pilots will not honor the IAM picket lines and stay out.

January 1989   The chairman of the NMB personally steps in to mediate the Eastern–IAM dispute. Mediation is suspended, but the NMB does not declare an impasse (which Eastern has been requesting for months).

February 1989   The NMB finally declares an impasse, after its offer of arbitration is rejected by management. This starts a 30-day countdown, after which the IAM can strike or Eastern can impose a new contract on the workers. The IAM says it will strike, causing work stoppages not only at Eastern and its sister airline, Continental, but also at United Airlines, USAir, TWA, and Northwest Airlines, as well as Northeast rail lines. It is felt that these threats from both the IAM leaders of Eastern's local union and IAM's national leaders are aimed at President Bush, to get him to appoint a Presidential Emergency Board to investigate the dispute, delaying any action by management or the IAM for another 60-day period. The AFL–CIO leadership also urges President Bush to take action, as does the NMB. Loss of business at Eastern accelerates, and the airline opposes presidential action so that it can impose the wage cuts it needs. Eastern accuses its mechanics of a slowdown and refusal of overtime, and seeks court approval to subcontract maintenance. The IAM petitions the FAA to investigate Eastern's maintenance operations.

Early March 1989   Eastern offers its pilots a new contract, in hopes that they will cross IAM picket lines during a strike; it is rejected. A new offer with lower wage cuts is made to the IAM the day before the end of the 30-day countdown to a strike; it, too, is rejected. Thirty-three senators ask President Bush to intervene; he does not. Eastern accelerates its hiring and training of nonunion mechanics. The IAM *strikes* Eastern Saturday, March 4. Pilots and flight attendants, in a rare show of labor solidarity, honor the picket lines.

Later in March   Eastern is essentially grounded. Federal courts issue temporary restraining orders enjoining secondary actions against railroads and other airlines (secondary actions are allowed under the Railway Labor Act), so the IAM does not picket these other carriers. A federal court, responding to an Eastern petition, refuses to order Eastern's pilots back to work. (Less than 100 of Eastern's 3,500 pilots were flying.) Picket lines are joined by laid-off nonstriking Eastern employees. Pressure mounts on President Bush to intervene; he refuses and says he will veto any legislation dictating intervention. Many hail the solid front presented by the labor movement as a step in arresting union decline in the United States, a warning to business that anti-union moves will be met by union power. Eastern files for bankruptcy on March 9, but with changes in the law Lorenzo cannot break Eastern's union contracts as he did with the Continental Airlines bankruptcy filing in September 1983. Furthermore, Texas Air and its other airline, Continental, are liable for Eastern's pensions under a 1987 law. An injunction against secondary action by railroad employees in support of the strike is issued. Eastern is flying only 100 flights a day, less than 12 percent of normal, with 200 nonstriking pilots; the majority of these are the Northeast shuttle. Eastern starts training new pilots (a two-month process) in case its petition in federal court to order the pilots back to work is refused. The FAA starts investigating union allegations that Eastern's maintenance operations involve supervisors signing off on work not done on aircraft.

April 1989   The sale of the Northeast shuttle to Trump is finalized, subject to bankruptcy court approval. New buyers for Eastern emerge. Texas Air agrees to sell Eastern (less the shuttle already sold to Trump) to Peter Ueberroth's group, as the three unions agree in principle to a five-year labor agreement with $210 million a year in concessions for a 30 percent ownership share. The deal falls through when Lorenzo refuses to accept a bankruptcy trustee to control getting Eastern back into business while the Ueberroth team takes over. The unions insist on this condition; they refuse to go back to work with Lorenzo in control. A federal judge rules that the sympathy strike of Eastern's pilots is legal, as their contract does not have a no-strike clause, and the strike is a true sympathy strike. As the strike continues in its second month, pilots are getting $2,400/month in strike benefits, mechanics and baggage handlers, $100/week, and flight attendants, nothing; the IAM is also distributing food from their union hall for mechanics, baggage handlers, and flight attendants. Some striking mechanics respond to a United advertisement. In the wake of the failure of the Ueberroth deal, Lorenzo announces that Texas Air will downsize Eastern and restructure it as a smaller nonunion airline, selling assets to raise $1.8 billion to pay off creditors and get Eastern back into the air. The plan must be approved by the bankruptcy court.

May 1989   Texas Air announces a first-quarter loss of $255.5 million, the largest in airline history (on top of the prior year's record loss of $718 million). Most of this loss was attributable to Eastern. Following investigations started in February (based on machinists' charges), the FAA finds maintenance violations at Eastern. Eastern loses its maintenance certificate at Kennedy International. The FAA announces an investigation of Eastern maintenance records at Miami (the airline's headquarters). Several bids for Eastern are in progress, as well as bids for parts of the airline (the shuttle, planes, and facilities). Texas Air claims that the airline is not for sale; rather, just $1.8 billion of its assets are on the market, so that it can emerge from bankruptcy as a smaller carrier. Meanwhile, the unions push for a complete sale. The court approves the sale of the Northeast shuttle to Trump, and it becomes Trump Airlines.

June 1989   All present bids for Eastern are ruled out. Eastern's management takes another pay cut (20 percent in addition to a previous 10 percent). Eastern presents its striking pilots with a new contract offer, with more pay cuts and the rehiring of only 950 of the 3,500 striking pilots. Eastern asks the bankruptcy court to abrogate its labor contract with the pilots. The company sells another 15 jets for $277.5 million. The FAA finds minor errors in recordkeeping at Eastern maintenance bases in Miami, Atlanta, and Boston but no fraud, allowing them to continue operating.

July 1989   Eastern is flying about 30 percent (226 flights per day) of its new, reduced flight schedule, filling over 70 percent of its seats as it offers steep price discounts. Plans are to fly 53 percent of its new schedule in August. Eastern withdraws its request to abrogate its labor contract with the pilots. The airline files its reorganization plan with the bankruptcy court. Texas Air announces a $109.3 million loss for the second quarter, down from the $255.9 million loss in 1988's second quarter. (Continental reported a small profit, while Eastern lost $129.3 million.)

August 1989   The pace of pilots returning to Eastern from their five-month strike picks up substantially. Eastern is flying about 50 percent (390 flights a day) of its new, reduced schedule, with a target of 75 percent (600) in September.

September 1989   Eastern's pilots replace the head of their union, as he advocates abandoning their walkout and returning to work, with a more militant leader. Eastern is flying about 75 percent (600 flights a day) of its schedule and is quietly raising its fares.

October 1989   Eastern's unions file suit against Texas Air, under the RICO Act, for "fraudulent empire building." Eastern's new reorganization plan calls for downsizing to 85 to 90 percent of its original size (versus two-thirds). The pilots' union wins a grievance (in arbitration) award of $60 to $100 million in back pay. (The grievance dated back to 1986.)

November 1989   Eastern increases the number of flights from 700 daily last month to 775 at the start of this month. Texas Air reports an increased third-quarter loss. The pilots and flight attendants halt their strike of 264 days after President Bush vetoes legislation setting up a special commission to investigate the Eastern dispute. Eastern meets with the two groups and notes that it will call back pilots and flight attendants as positions open. The IAM remains on strike, but, for all practical purposes, labor has lost the strike. However, Eastern's survival is still in question.

December 1989   Eastern now has 800 daily flights but is only filling about half the seats. It is targeting 909 flights for next year. Sale of the Latin American routes is concluded. In a cost-cutting move, the airline eliminated 600 jobs (mostly managerial) and imposed temporary pay cuts on half its 20,000 workers.

January 1990   Eastern is still having load factor problems, filling 55 to 60 percent of its seats.

February 1990   Texas Air reports a recordbreaking annual loss for 1989 ($885.6 million, with Eastern contributing $853.2 million of this total). But reorganization continues, and Eastern is still flying.

April 1990   The bankruptcy court replaces Lorenzo with a a trustee.

January 1991   Eastern Airlines ceases operations.

The Eastern Airlines dispute, which started as a show of solidarity for organized labor, ended in defeat for that group. Using a variety of tactics in addition to the strike (courts, whistleblowing), the unions still could not attain their goals.

Carrying Out a Strike

A strike, as the union's ultimate weapon, must be carefully planned and orchestrated. The full support of the membership as well as the rest of the union movement is important. The political aspects have to be utilized to the fullest extent possible. Moreover, financial support must be lined up as the strike becomes longer and longer. Finally, as the strike progresses, the workers' emotions and commitment need to be constantly recharged.

Strikes of Craft Versus Industrial Unions

There is a marked difference between the strikes of most craft and industrial unions. A craft union composed of skilled workers has some economic power, and it will normally utilize a strike to exercise and augment that power. Two primary reasons for craft union strikes are (1) to increase compensation and (2) to protect the craft's work from being done by "outsiders." These are economic reasons, and are governed by supply and demand considerations.

A strike for higher pay, the more common type undertaken by a craft union, is basically a waiting game. Because employers find it hard to get strike replacements for skilled workers, operations are usually disrupted. As costs mount on both sides, they are likely to sit down together and renew negotiations, seeking a compromise solution.

A strike to protect the craft's work from being done by outsiders is usually launched either to stop nonunion workers from doing the job normally done by the craft union, or to claim work by the craft union that might be awarded to another craft. An example of the second kind of conflict might involve the installation of prefabricated windows, work claimed by carpenters (the windows are framed in by wood) and glaziers (the windows are glass).[9] This is essentially a jurisdictional strike, and in most instances it is unlawful, a point that will be explained in detail later in this chapter.

The strikes of industrial unions are different. Strike replacements are relatively easy to find, and, if the operation is highly automated, management personnel can keep production going, though usually at a slower pace than at the pre-strike level. The remainder of this section will deal with the strikes of industrial unions.

Deciding to Strike

The decision to strike is normally preceded by three steps. First, the local leaders make the decision in the context of their negotiations with management. Second, and in most instances preceding the leaders' decision, the local's members decide to strike, indicated in a strike vote. Third, the local notifies the national or international union to have a sanctioned strike so that strike benefits are made available.

The strike vote of the workers is usually conducted in the early stage of the bargaining process. It signifies the workers' commitment to support a strike, and it lends credibility to the union's negotiators in their bargaining with management. The vote rarely sets a date and time for a strike; it just allows the leaders to call one if negotiations go to impasse. In some unions, the negotiating deadline is the present contract's expiration date. In many unions, negotiations will go on past the expiration of the present contract, with both sides allowing it to extend until either side stops negotiating.

Organizing Strike Activities

After the decision to strike has been made, and even before, the local has to organize and muster its resources—its people and its funds—to successfully carry out the work stoppage.

If union leaders and negotiators feel that a strike is more likely than not, they must garner the support of the rank-and-file. This involves intraorganizational bargaining (see Chapter 6) or aligning the membership behind an issue. Key people in this process are the shop stewards, who are in daily contact with the workers. They can rally support for a positive strike vote, and during the strike they can act as group leaders in the organization.

When the strike gets underway, a strike headquarters will be needed. This will usually be the local union hall; from here all strike activity is organized and all information flows. If the union hall is not near the struck plant, a "battlefield" headquarters will normally be established close to the action.

Many activities occur and must be taken care of during a strike. The most important is the establishing of picket lines (see Figure 13.2). Picketing is meant to shut the plant down, primarily by keeping strike replacements (and union members who don't want to strike) from entering. It also serves an informational purpose, hopefully garnering public support for the workers and their strike. If the plant can be effectively shut down, the spirit of the strikers will be very high. Mass picketing is unlawful under the Taft–Hartley Act, but typically the unions will engage in it until the authorities intervene.

Other activities must be organized during a strike. These involve the scheduling, care, and feeding of workers on the picket line, an activity usually centered around

FIGURE 13.2 Picketing during a strike.
Source: Baron Silverman / New York Times.

the battlefield headquarters near the plant. Transportation has to be arranged for the pickets and headquarters workers. Community support, especially material support, must be gathered. Publicity must be so arranged that the workers are seen as the underdogs in the dispute and the employer as the exploiter. A primary task of this activity is to ensure that no violence takes place on the picket line. In addition, in a long strike, the high emotional level of the workers must be maintained, a task usually undertaken by the shop stewards.

Last, but certainly not least, is the arrangement and distribution of strike benefits and any other material support available to the striking workers. If the strike is sanctioned by the national/international, which controls the funds of the union, strike benefits will be available. In addition, other unions may donate to the strike, and these donations must be distributed to the strikers. A possible third source of funds for striking workers is public assistance. As noted earlier, federal public assistance is denied striking workers, but some state programs allow it.

Trends in Work Stoppages

Traditionally, strikes have been most successful when called during economic expansion, for, as mentioned earlier, this enhances the cost to the employer (more to lose) and lowers the cost to the strikers (greater sources of alternative income). As Figure 13.3 shows, this has been the case in five postwar expansions (1945–1948, 1949–1953, 1954–1957, 1958–1960, and 1961–1969). There was first a drop and then an increase in strike activity in the 1970–1973 expansion; the increase continued in the first half of the 1973–1975 downturn before dropping drastically in 1975.

The increase in strikes in the first half of the 1973–1975 recession may have been due to the prevalence of **defensive strikes,** which are strikes against wage cuts, loss of job security, loss of works rules, and similar management demands.[10] These types of strikes tend to be correlated with the unemployment rate. **Offensive strikes** are work stoppages to gain improvements. However, the very high 9 percent unemployment rate in 1975 seemed to have damped strike activity of all sorts.

Strikes jumped again in the first half of the next expansion (1975–1980), but started declining in 1978 and dropped throughout the expansions of 1980–1981 and 1982–1990. The short recession in 1980 (six months) was relatively sharp and the following expansion was relatively weak, but this does not fully explain the variation of strike activity from its traditional pattern.

Two other aspects of the 1980s offer a better explanation of the slowing of strike activity in the United States. The first is the impact of foreign competition on American industry. In the expansions of 1980–1981 and 1982 to 1990 (first 36 months), the monthly rate of increase in imports was 1.28 percent and 1.58 percent, respectively.[11] These figures were greater than those for any other postwar expansion. Furthermore, the monthly rate of increase in exports was only 0.16 percent and 0.03 percent, lower by far than that for any other postwar expansion.[12]

The second factor that distinguished the 1980 expansions from earlier ones was the lowest level of the unemployment rate attained in those expansions. For 1980–1981, it was 7.2 percent, a rate that was higher than the peak unemployment rate in three postwar recessions (1953–1954, 1960–1961, and 1969–1970).[13] The unemployment

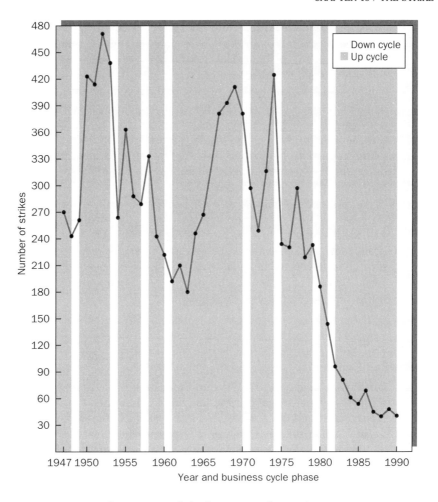

FIGURE 13.3 Strike activity and the business cycle, 1947–1990.
Sources: Table 13.1; and Kellner, Irwin, "The Manufacturers Hanover Economic Report," November 1985.

rate has dropped to about 5 percent for the 1982–1990 expansion, but during the first three years of this boom it was 7 percent or higher, and in 1990 was nearing 6 percent as recession loomed.

The picture that emerges from these figures shows substantial increases in foreign competition and a major concern for cost containment. The latter point, manifested in persistently high unemployment rates, implies cautious hiring and the use of overtime and/or temporary workers.[14] The hardened stance of management, swinging strongly to an anti-union position, and favored by the political climate of the 1980s, reinforces this picture. Moreover, the deregulation of several major industries has further spurred competition from primarily nonunion companies. These factors have sapped the power of American unions, and, whenever possible, they have shied away from a power struggle, the strike.

As seen in Table 13.1, however, a surge of strike activity took place in 1989. This seems to be a reaction of labor to the mounting management pressures to cut costs, primarily labor costs. This backlash was marked by major strikes at Eastern Airlines, Pittston Company, and several of the regional Bell operating companies.

As labor shifts from strikes, which are becoming harder to win, they are resorting to other tactics to assert their power in labor–management relations. An increasingly popular weapon is the **slowdown**.[15] By staying on the job, the union and its members can work from the inside to press their position. Work-to-rule, by slowing down production, can bring substantial pressure on management to accede to union demands. Furthermore, union members can file a massive number of grievances, further interfering with production.

An interesting aspect of work stoppages in the past decade has been management's increased willingness to operate plants during the strike using strike replacements.[16] In several cases, such as Eastern Airlines (1989) and Greyhound (1990), these replacements have become permanent workers, and many striking workers have lost their jobs. A recent Supreme Court decision upholds the right of an employer to retain strike replacements, after a strike, even though they have less seniority than the striking workers they have replaced.[17]

The Lockout

Like strikes, **lockouts** by management are work stoppages. However, the lockout as a response to an impasse or a strike is a very short-run tactic. It will jolt the workers and their union, and it may bring them back to the negotiating table with a more compromising attitude. But the longer a lockout lasts, the greater will be its costs to management and the greater will be its benefits to the workers in terms of alternative income, union solidarity, and ease of picketing.

If management closes down the plant, it still incurs the fixed or overhead costs associated with the plant and the company. Depreciation, management salaries, and various office expense must be covered. But no production and no revenue are available to cover these costs. Trying to operate the plant using management and/or strike replacements, and possibly some employees who chose not to strike, will generate some revenue to cover fixed costs during a strike, but not a lockout.

A management lockout in response to an impasse deprives the workers of their jobs. In some states, these workers can draw unemployment compensation which they would not be allowed to do if the union called a strike.[18] With this alternative income, workers can endure a longer work stoppage more comfortably. In addition, workers who would like to quit the strike (and the union) and return to work don't have that option during a lockout. In essence, aggressive management actions promote union solidarity.

If the plant is shut down, and all gates are locked, picketing becomes much easier for the workers. The pickets don't have to attempt to keep strike replacements out, because there will be none. With the gates sealed by management, no workers can enter.

OTHER TYPES OF STRIKES

Although the most common form of work stoppage is the economic strike which results from collective bargaining impasses, other types may be called. These work stoppages occur for many reasons, but for the most part they are sudden and usually short. Some of these different forms of strikes are unlawful under the NLRA/LMRA, whereas others are protected activities under the law. Some are economic in nature, whereas others are not. They all have one characteristic, however: they are work stoppages.

Strikes Protected by Law: Unfair Labor Practice Strikes

An **unfair labor practice strike** is a work stoppage initiated to protest an unfair labor practice. When a union goes out on strike, alleging an unfair labor practice on the part of management, the NLRB, through one of its regional offices, will investigate the charge.[19] If the charge is dismissed, the strike becomes an economic one (if the contract has expired and the action is sanctioned by the national union) or a wildcat one (if the contract is in force). If, however, the unfair labor practice is upheld, the strike becomes an unfair labor practice strike (subject to a formal finding by an NLRB administrative law judge, and, upon appeal, subject to a finding by the board itself; further appeal would be to a federal appeals court and then the U.S. Supreme Court).

An unfair labor practice strike is very different from an economic strike in one important dimension. Workers must be immediately reinstated at the conclusion of the strike. Permanent replacements cannot be hired as they can in an economic strike. Employees on an unfair labor practice strike also retain the right to vote in any decertification election, no matter how long they have been out on strike. Unlike any other type of strike, there is strong protection for unfair labor practice strikers.

Wildcat Strikes

A **wildcat strike** is a strike, typically by a local, that is not sanctioned by the national union. It normally occurs during the term of the collective bargaining agreement and so is in violation of the agreement's no-strike clause. A wildcat strike is a sign of poor labor–management relations between a local and management.

Wildcat strikes may occur for many reasons. The most common involve local economic conditions and workplace safety.[20] For example, if workers believe that dangerous conditions exist at work, and they are rebuffed by management in presenting their case to remedy these conditions immediately, they may walk off the job. This type of spontaneous action was very common in the coal industry; if the workers believed a mine was not safe, they would simply walk off the job until management did something about it.

Employers can deal with wildcat strikes in several ways. They can sue the local (but not the national, as it has not sanctioned the strike), but locals tend to have little money and damage suits for contract violation will yield little.[21] They can seek a court injunction to end the suit; a 1970 Supreme Court decision allows such actions when the labor agreement contains a no-strike clause and an arbitration agreement.[22]

Management can also formally request that the strikers return to work. It may ask the national union leaders to join them in this request, which they are obliged to do to show that the national did not sanction and does not support the walkout. If the wildcat strike persists, the company may fire the strikers.

The best way to prevent wildcat strikes is to maintain good relations with the union, the local, and the workers. If a particular local is especially militant, ongoing dialogue with its leaders and national union representatives is important to get at the root of problems before they lead to a walkout. However, the number of wildcat strikes, like that of pure economic strikes, fell substantially in the 1980s. The recent wildcat strikes by the mine workers that spread to ten states, strikes emanating from the unfair labor practice allegations against Pittston Company, was a notable exception; the UMW locals are known for their wildcat actions.[23]

Sympathy Strikes

A **sympathy strike** is a work stoppage by one union's workers in support of the economic strike of another union. A pure sympathy strike, in which workers as individuals refuse to cross the picket lines of another union that is on strike, is legal. Labor solidarity would be marked by this type of action. However, this kind of labor solidarity was not frequently seen in the American labor movement, especially in the 1980s, until the 1989 machinists' strike against Eastern Airlines.

Sympathy strikes are common in the construction industry. If one union, say the electricians, has a labor dispute with a contractor at a given work site, it will picket that site. Other union workers, say carpenters, plumbers, and bricklayers, will normally honor the electricians' picket lines. This would tend to shut the job down. If, however, the electricians explicitly sought the support of other unions to honor their picket lines, the resulting action of these other unions induced by the electricians would not be legal.[24] It would be a *secondary strike* (or strikes), which is prohibited by Section 8(b)(4) of the Taft–Hartley Act (LMRA).

Strikes Prohibited by Law

Besides an induced sympathy strike planned by a striking union with one or more other unions, several other strikes are unlawful under the NLRA/LMRA. Any strike whose purpose is unlawful (e.g., striking for a closed shop agreement—see Chapter 9) is itself unlawful. Most prohibited strikes are included under Section 8(b)(4) and are aimed at prohibiting a union from putting pressure on a neutral third party to further its dispute with an employer. A general prohibition on secondary actions, including boycotts (to be discussed in the next chapter) is contained in Section 8(b)(4). These provisions do not cover the railroads and airlines, which are under the Railway Labor Act. The RLA does allow secondary actions (see the above discussion of the Eastern Airlines strike).

Sitdown Strikes

The law prohibits **sitdown strikes.** A sitdown strike, as its name implies, is a strike in which the workers refuse not only to work but also to leave the plant, "sitting down" at their work stations. Sitdown strikes, employed at GM, Chrysler, and Goodyear in 1937, were used to form the United Auto Workers and the United Rubber Workers.

This type of strike is not a secondary action but is specifically prohibited under the law. However, workers can cause production disruptions by staying on the job and staging a slowdown. This action would be legal. If they went a step further, and started turning out bad parts or used some other forms of sabotage, they might well move over the legal line into illegal activities.

Jurisdictional Strikes

A **jurisdictional strike** is a strike by a union to have its members do work assigned by an employer to workers represented by another union or nonunion workers. It is unlawful unless the striking union's certification by the NLRB defines it as the bargaining agent for employees doing that type of work. This action, sometimes referred to as a **work assignment strike,** is an unfair labor practice. An injunction can be obtained to stop it.[25]

Jurisdictional (or work assignment) strikes are basically strikes involving NLRB certification. Work assigned to one union cannot be claimed by a second union unless that second union's NLRB certification gives its members the right to do that work. Even if the first union, assigned the work by management, is not explicitly certified to represent workers doing that type of job, the second union cannot force management to assign its members the work. This section of the law protects employers from union disputes over work assignments not explicitly reserved for members of any given union.

Recognitional Strikes

A **recognitional strike** is an action, usually dominated by picketing, by a union seeking to gain recognition and to bargain with an employer, when that employer recognizes and bargains with another union certified by the NLRB as exclusive bargaining agent for his or her workers. Another variation of this type of prohibited activity occurs when a union strikes an employer it bargains with to bring pressure on a second employer to recognize and bargain with that union. However, if the union has been certified as exclusive bargaining agent for the second employer's workers, this secondary action is legal.

Under Section 8(b)(7) of the law, any action (strikes, picketing), or threats of such action, by an uncertified union are unlawful. But an uncertified union can engage in informational picketing, as a practice of free speech, provided that union seeks to organize the employer's workers, who are not now organized, and intends to ask the NLRB to conduct a certification election.[26]

As the discussion above makes clear, and as was noted in Chapter 3, secondary-type actions regulated by Section (8)(b)(4) and recognitional/organizational actions regulated by Section 8(b)(7) involve very complex issues. Unlike economic strikes, these other types are severely restricted and, in most cases, prohibited.

STRIKE PREVENTION ═══════════

In an atmosphere of cooperation, marked by joint problem solving and decision making, work stoppages would be highly unlikely. However, as we have said, U.S. labor–management relations are not, in general, cooperative. Thus, work stoppages do, and will continue to, occur. Preventing strikes, therefore, has been a goal of management and labor (and the government) for many years. Strikes are costly for both sides as well as third parties that rely on products of the struck organization. In the public sector, the goal of strike prevention has a very high priority (as will be seen in Chapters 16 and 17).

In the private sector, strike prevention is attempted primarily by the application of the national emergency dispute provisions contained in both the Taft–Hartley Act and the Railway Labor Act. As discussed in Chapter 12, these provisions, when applied, are more successful in delaying work stoppages than in preventing them. For this reason, among others, the emergency dispute procedures have been infrequently utilized in the last two decades.

One sure way to prevent strikes is to make *all* strikes unlawful and to mandate arbitration to settle all bargaining impasses. This solution is used in some public sector labor–management jurisdictions. However, mandatory interest arbitration has several drawbacks, including lack of competent arbitrators, damage to the collective bargaining process, and intervention of government (see Chapter 12).

Prevention Through Government Seizure

Government seizure and operation of struck facilities to continue production is not new. Wartime seizure was especially prevalent in what would be classified as national emergency strikes, even after the passage of the Taft–Hartley Act with its national emergency dispute provisions.[27] A new approach to government seizure would be to have the government not only operate the plant, but also keep all profits and all union dues paid by the striking workers. The government-supplied workers (e.g., Army personnel) would be paid wages specified in the old contract.

This strike prevention scheme is aimed at increasing the cost of a strike to both parties. The company gets no profit, the union gets no dues, and the workers, as they are on strike, receive no pay. All these measures affect the costs imposed on both parties, but the effect may be unequal, altering the power balance unevenly. This could lead to a contract that does not reflect the realities of the economic situation and the company's market position.

Prevention Through Strike Fines

Fining a union, and possibly even its members, as well as the company during a strike might be another way to prevent strikes. As is true of the government seizure scheme, this alternative increases the cost of a work stoppage to both parties. This should make the strike a less attractive alternative than continued negotiations leading to a settlement.

Strike fines, like fines for polluting, bring up some interesting questions. A vexing one is, on what basis will fines be determined? Who will determine them—the

Department of Labor or Commerce, or some new agency? If fines are to be based on wages paid workers who opt to strike, and on profits of the company, what base period will be used to determine these amounts? Another interesting question is— can individual union members be fined?

The amount of the fines is critical, as they will alter the power balance in collective bargaining. An uneven imposition may alter the power balance in such a way that the resulting contract does not reflect the economic situation.

The Problems of Strike Prevention Plans

Trying to prevent strikes presents several major problems within the context of the American system of labor–management relations. The first of these problems involves imposing sanctions on the parties involved in a strike. If the imposition is unequal, resulting contracts will not reflect the actual economic position of the organization and the union with which it is at impasse.

A second, and probably more basic, problem is that production disruptions cannot be stopped or prevented without the agreement of labor and management. If the government were to intervene to stop work stoppages, workers could "strike on the job" through slowdowns, use work-to-rule tactics that would also slow things down, or go on "sickouts," tactics now used in place of outright strikes.[28] In a transit strike that took place in Washington, D.C., almost 25 years ago, bus drivers drove their buses but did not collect fares; they were "striking on the job." In the public sector, where strikes are not legal in most states and in federal government service, they do occur. With the exception of the PATCO strike of 1981, when the president, Ronald Reagan, fired all air traffic controllers who stayed on strike, governments have not punished public sector strikers who have staged unlawful strikes.

The stopping or preventing of strikes cannot be mandated; it must be a joint decision involving all parties—labor, management, and government.

DISCUSSION QUESTIONS

1. Do workers have the right to strike? Does your answer hold for all sectors of the economy?

2. Explain the place (in labor–management relations) and purpose of the typical economic strike.

3. What options are available to labor and management when they reach an impasse in their contract negotiations?

4. Why do you think Eastern Airlines sought an impasse in its negotiations with its unions, even though such a move could lead to a strike?

5. What spelled the defeat of the unions in their strike against Eastern Airlines?

6. What factors determine the amount of lost profits a company suffers during a strike?

7. What costs do a union and its members bear during a strike?

8. Under what conditions might a national union not support a strike by one of its locals?

9. Why might a union strike an employer even though the employer is ready to agree to the terms the union wants in a new contract?

10. What are the three steps that most local (plantwide) unions go through before actually going out on strike?

11. What is the most important activity undertaken by the union and its members during the course of a strike? Explain your answer.

12. Why has the frequency of strikes declined in the last decade or so?

13. The management lockout is usually quite short. Why?

14. From the viewpoint of the workers on strike, what is the major difference between an unfair labor practice strike and an economic strike?

15. What is a wildcat strike?

16. What is a sympathy strike, and what circumstances make it illegal?

17. Why might strike fines mandated by law prevent strikes?

VOCABULARY LIST

economic strike   wildcat strike

defensive strike   sympathy strike

offensive strike   sitdown strike

slowdown   jurisdictional strike

lockout   work assignment strike

unfair labor practice strike   recognitional strike

FOOTNOTES

1. *Wall Street Journal,* October 13, 1986, p. 6.

2. Commerce Clearing House, *1989 Guidebook to Labor Relations* (1989), p. 285.

3. The Supreme Court ruled that striking workers are ineligible for food stamps (*Wall Street Journal,* March 24, 1988, p. 14).

4. *New York Times,* May 2, 1989, p. A16. In the UAW strike against Colt Industries' firearms plant that began in January 1986, the company replaced the strikers. In September 1986, eight months into the strike, the union offered to end it, accepting management's terms, but required the firing of replacements so that workers could be reinstated. The company refused, and the strike continued for over four years.

5. *Wall Street Journal,* June 28, 1985, p. 10.

6. *Wall Street Journal,* March 1, 1989, p. A3; *Business Week,* March 13, 1989, p. 46.

7. *Newsweek,* October 16, 1989, p. 59.

8. *Business Week,* July 18, 1988, p. 103.

9. James P. Begin and Edwin F. Beal, *The Practice of Collective Bargaining* (Richard D. Irwin, 1985), p. 226.

10. Michele I. Naples, "An Analysis of Defensive Strikes," *Industrial Relations* (Winter 1987): 96.

11. Irwin Kellner, "The Manufacturers Hanover Economic Report," November 1985.

12. Ibid.

13. Ibid.

14. *Business Week*, March 13, 1989, pp. 40–41.

15. *Wall Street Journal*, May 22, 1987, p. 1.

16. *New York Times*, March 13, 1990, p. A11; Donald E. Cullen, "Recent Trends in Collective Bargaining in the United States." *International Labour Review* (May–June 1985): 311.

17. *Wall Street Journal*, March 1, 1989, p. A3; *Business Week*, March 13, 1989, p. 46.

18. Begin and Beal, *The Practice of Collective Bargaining*, p. 238.

19. *New York Times*, May 16, 1990, p. A10 (noting that the NLRB general counsel has authorized the filing of an unfair labor practice complaint against Greyhound Lines by one of the board's regional offices in the 11-week strike of the Amalgamated Transit Union against the company); *Wall Street Journal*, March 28, 1989, p. C19 (discussing the UMW strike and preliminary ruling of the regional NLRB office citing management for 20 violations of federal labor law at Pittston Company's coal operations); July 12, 1989, p. A5 (noting that an unfair labor practice complaint was issued by the NLRB, but had not yet been heard).

20. *Wall Street Journal*, October 17, 1988, p. C18.

21. Ibid.

22. Arthur A. Sloane and Fred Witney, *Labor Relations* (Prentice–Hall, 1985), p. 416.

23. *New York Times*, June 28, 1989, p. C21. A district court issued a restraining order, requested by the NLRB, against the United Mine Workers and the sympathy/wildcat strikers.

24. Commerce Clearing House, *1989 Guidebook*, p. 302. The special problem of construction site picketing and secondary action, referred to as common-situs picketing (p. 298), was addressed by Congress by the passage of a common-situs law to amend Section 8(b)(4), but the law was vetoed by President Ford in 1976. The problem still exists.

25. Ibid., pp. 311–314.

26. Ibid., pp. 314–321.

27. William H. Holley and Kenneth M. Jennings, *The Labor Relations Process* (Dryden Press, 1988), pp. 266–267.

28. *Wall Street Journal*, May 22, 1987, p. 1.

REFERENCES

BEGIN, JAMES P., and EDWIN F. BEAL. *The Practice of Collective Bargaining*. Richard D. Irwin, 1985, Ch. 8.

COMMERCE CLEARING HOUSE. *1989 Guidebook to Labor Relations*. 1989, Ch. 11.

CULLEN, DONALD E. "Recent Trends in Collective Bargaining in the United States." *International Labour Review* (May–June 1985): 299-322.

DILTS, DAVID A. "Strike Activity in the United States: An Analysis of the Stocks and Flows." *Journal of Labor Research* (Spring 1986): 187–199.

HOLLEY, WILLIAM H., and KENNETH M. JENNINGS. *The Labor Relations Process*. Dryden Press, 1988, Ch. 7.

NAPLES, MICHELE I. "An Analysis of Defensive Strikes." *Industrial Relations* (Winter 1987): 96–105.

REES, ALBERT. *The Economics of Trade Unions*. University of Chicago Press, 1977, Ch. II.

SLOANE, ARTHUR A., and FRED WITNEY. *Labor Relations*. Prentice–Hall, 1985, Ch. 9.

VROMAN, SUSAN B. "A Longitudinal Analysis of Strike Activity in U.S. Manufacturing: 1957–1984." *American Economic Review* (September 1989): 816–826.

CHAPTER 14

LABOR–MANAGEMENT DISPUTES: UNION BOYCOTTS AND CORPORATE CAMPAIGNS

Although the most common forms of labor–management disputes are grievances (on a day-to-day basis) and strikes (on a contract-to-contract basis), these disputes occasionally assume other forms. This is especially true of disputes arising out of collective bargaining negotiations. As the incidence of strikes decreases, other sources of union power are and will be utilized in disagreements with management.

UNION BOYCOTTS

One form that labor–management disputes can take is the boycott. Union boycotts can be powerful weapons. Though usually not as dramatic an action as the strike, the boycott both enhances a work stoppage and can be an effective weapon when a strike is not a feasible alternative. It has been applied as a bargaining and organizing tactic for over a century.[1]

Historically, the union boycott was quite popular and was often used both to supplement the strike and to gain union recognition from employers. Prior to the 1930s when labor legislation was passed to protect unions and unionizing, the boycott was employed frequently. Union boycotts were also used extensively in the 1930s, primarily as secondary actions, following the passage of the Norris–LaGuardia (Anti-Injunction) Act in 1932 and the Wagner (National Labor Relations) Act in 1935.[2] The Taft–Hartley (Labor–Management Relations) Act of 1947 sharply curtailed these secondary boycotts.* However, they were and still are allowed under the Railway Labor Act (governing railroads and airlines), but they are not used extensively in those industries because of the threat of political legislative or judicial actions to make them unlawful or stop them.[3] For the most part, boycotts were less effective in the United States than in Europe, owing mostly to the lack of working-class consciousness and labor solidarity in this country.

For about 20 years after the passage of the LMRA, the union boycott was rarely utilized. In the late 1960s and early 1970s, it reappeared as a major labor weapon in the United Farm Workers grape and lettuce boycotts. These were followed by the two-year Farah (1972–1974), the four-year J. P. Stevens (1976–1980), and the decade-long Coors boycotts (1977–1987). The special circumstances surrounding these labor–management disputes made these boycotts both major, necessary actions and successful ones.

Boycotts, as the above discussion implies, can be classified as primary (or consumer) or secondary. The discussion below will differentiate between these two types.

The Primary Boycott

The **primary,** or **consumer, boycott** is simply a call to the consuming public not to buy the product(s) of a company with which a labor organization is having a dispute. If the dispute involves a strike, the striking union's pickets will generally urge consumers not to do business with the struck company. However, if the pickets are set up at the company's manufacturing facility(s), their message will not reach consumers. To do this, picketing would have to be extended to the outlets that sell the company's product(s) to the general public.

The most important ingredient of a boycott is publicity, communicating the request not to do business with a company to the public. This involves such tactics as picketing the outlets that carry the company's products, using the media to get the message to consumers (a use that the AFL–CIO 1985 report, "The Changing Situation of Workers and Their Unions," urges be expanded), holding rallies, and, from the point of view of the union directly involved in the dispute, getting other labor organizations to support the boycott.

These activities require the mustering of union manpower and finances, as it takes substantial resources to establish and sustain a major national boycott. Consumers must be continually reminded to shun the target company's product(s). Picketing, leaflets, media spots, rallies with nationally known figures, and other means of getting the message across are needed to make for a successful boycott.

Over the last 30–35 years, the consumer boycott has been successfully employed under special circumstances. **Ethnic unionism** succeeding in a national environment of heightened antidiscrimination feelings is seen in the United Farm Workers (UFW) grape and lettuce boycotts and the Amalgamated Clothing Workers of America (ACW) boycott of Farah (an apparel manufacturer). The AFL–CIO (representing

---

* The secondary boycott, first discussed in Chapter 3 as an unfair labor practice under Section 8(b)(4) of the Taft–Hartley Act, is a boycott of a third party by a union to coerce that party into pressuring the company with which the union is having a dispute to settle on terms favorable to the union. Later in the chapter, secondary boycotts are discussed in detail.

a Federation local not affiliated with any national union) boycott of Coors and the Amalgamated Clothing and Textile Workers (ACTW) boycott of J. P. Stevens were examples of campaigns against well-known labor law violators and highly conservative company leaders, symbols of corporate injustice.[4]

Boycotts and Ethnic Unionism: Three Studies

The UFW and ACW actions of the late 1960s and early to mid-1970s were successful consumer boycotts.[5] But did they succeed through the mobilization of the U.S. labor movement, or because of public sympathy in that period for minority groups? There is no question that the labor movement brought the boycotts to the public's attention, and many unions were involved. The ultimate success, however—the consuming public's purchasing decisions—was to a great part a function of the sympathetic response of the public to the economic oppression of disadvantaged minority groups. Both boycotts were highly politicized and highly popularized.

The UFW and the Great Table Grape Boycott César Chavez and his United Farm Workers of America, a predominantly Mexican-American union, utilized the boycott as their main weapon against the California table grape growers. They could not win a strike, for the growers had access to a "virtually inexhaustible supply of relatively cheap replacement labor."[6] To win recognition and collective bargaining rights, the UFW (then known as the National Farm Workers Association, NFWA) launched the grape boycott in 1966 against wine grape growers in the Delano area of the San Joaquin Valley, as "La Causa" (the cause).[7] They received support from people and groups like the late Walter Reuther (United Auto Workers), the Migrant Ministry of the National Council of Churches, the Catholic Church in California, the AFL–CIO, the Ford Foundation's Center for Community Change, and numerous political activists.

Soon after the boycott started, the NFWA became the United Farm Workers Organizing Committee (UFWOC), with extensive support from the AFL–CIO. They won contracts in 1966 from the two major grape growers in Delano, Schenley (a large liquor conglomerate) and Di Giogio (a large agricultural conglomerate), both of which were particularly vulnerable to boycotts because of their national brand-name products. Pressure from unions in the form of refusals to handle these companies' grapes as well as threats of labor problems in their other, unionized, operations also made the boycotts effective. Other winery contracts were soon won (in 1967) throughout California, including one with Gallo and several in the Napa Valley.[8]

In 1967, the Great Table Grape Boycott was launched to force the growers to bargain with the union. Starting again with strikes, which the growers easily broke using the abundant supply of strike breakers available, the boycotts followed. In addition, as before, various religious groups, political activists, and students, as well as the labor movement, gave extensive support. The national scope of the boycott required this expansive support.

Yet the boycott faced a major problem—table grapes are identified only by labels on their shipping crates, not by brand names. Growers used a variety of labels on their crates, and it even became difficult to track "scab" shipments. The grapes were also distributed through a network that was very diffuse. Another aspect of the boycott, making it different from the prior year's wine grape boycott, was that this was a purely consumer boycott, as other unions did not deal with the table grape growers and could bring little pressure on them. Union threats to disrupt other operations were nonexistent, for the growers had no other unionized operations.[9]

The boycott was marked by several dramatic events designed to attract national attention. Chavez went on a 25-day fast in February 1968, an event that he also used to underscore the nonviolent nature of the UFW campaign. Senator Robert Kennedy, running for president, appeared with Chavez at a Mass ending the fast.

As the boycott picked up steam, sympathetic unionists in the transport and grocery industries (Teamsters, warehousemen, butchers, retail clerks) put pressure on brokers and stores to stop selling nonunion grapes, and instead switch to another fruit. The vast network of volunteers set up store pickets, and the primary boycotts became secondary boycotts, urging consumers to shop elsewhere.* This tactic was especially effective against large supermarket chains like A&P and Safeway.

Another tactic utilized was the "shop-in," which usually took one of two forms.[10] In one variation of this theme, a housewife, usually with children in tow, filled her shopping cart. In a final stop at the fruit counter, she would discover "scab" grapes, demand to see the manager, and loudly berate him for stocking them, given that many farm workers and their families were starving because the growers refused to pay them a living wage. She would then stride out of the store with her children, leaving the full shopping cart. The second variation, less embarrassing but more costly for the store, involved a boycott team filling shopping carts with grapes on the bottom, and frozen food and cans on top, smashing the grapes. The carts would be left in obscure nooks in the supermarket. A few hours later an anonymous phone call would be made to the store, noting the carts and their meaning—nonunion grape should not be stocked!

No matter what tactics were used in the boycott, stores had to be continually monitored. A manager might agree not to stock nonunion grapes one week but might renege on that agreement the next week. The need for continual surveillance, rallies, picketing, and other activities colored the strategy of choosing boycott targets. Large national chains in major metropolitan areas were more easily handled than the smaller chains and the myriad independents. They were also more vulnerable to the adverse publicity, for any one store affects the whole chain.

By 1969, the boycott was a big success in the major Eastern cities. California, especially the Los Angeles area, proved a more difficult hurdle. Nonetheless, on July 29, 1970, the last of the major table grape growers from the Delano area signed contracts with UFWOC.[11] The union's "Black Eagle" would appear on all shipping crates of California table grapes. The boycott was over.

The UFW and the Lettuce Boycott   Just as the table grape boycott was successfully completed, the lettuce boycott was poised to begin. Salinas Valley (California) lettuce growers refused to deal with the UFWOC and signed sweetheart contracts with the Teamsters. These contracts had terms very favorable to the growers and gained little for the field workers. Under pressure from the labor movement, the

---

* The secondary boycott, unlawful in most cases under the Taft–Hartley Act, can be carried on by farm workers who are not covered by national labor laws.

Teamsters withdrew from the contracts. Some strikes ensued, the boycott picked up steam, and UFWOC was given an AFL–CIO charter, becoming the United Farm Workers of America. The lettuce boycott never enjoyed the success of the Great Table Grape Boycott. Lettuce was a basic food staple, the labor movement did not rally behind the UFW as before, and the political climate (a Republican president and California governor) was unfavorable. Anti-farm labor legislation was introduced by Senator George Murphy, a California Republican, but it never got past the Democratic-controlled Congress. Similar legislation was attempted in California through the initiative process, but it never passed. In addition, in 1973 the Teamsters started negotiating contracts with the grape growers organized through the Great Table Grape Boycott. A new grape boycott was organized.

The more conservative climate of the 1970s, with a waning of public sympathy for disadvantaged minorities, had its effect on the lettuce and second grape boycotts. The lack of AFL–CIO support and of the labor movement in general added to the ineffectiveness of these boycotts.

In 1974, Jerry Brown, a liberal Democrat, a UFW supporter, and son of former Governor Pat Brown, was elected governor of California. During his administration the Agricultural Labor Relations Act was passed, and negotiated settlements within the scope of this law ended the strikes and boycotts. Chavez's UFW survives and has initiated other boycotts, but, in general, it has settled down into the mold of business unionism, with little political activism involved. Its recent loss of many contracts has put its continued survival in question.[12]

The ACW and the Farah Boycott   Like the UFW grape and lettuce boycotts, the Farah action started with a strike by the Amalgamated Clothing Workers of America at the company's El Paso pants plant. But replacements—strike breakers—were cheap and readily available: "Labor is cheap down there . . . and anyone would be willing to work."[13] Again, as was the case with the grape boycott, the primary supply of cheap labor were Mexicans (like the braceros in the California fields), who came across the border from neighboring Juarez, and some Mexican Americans in the El Paso area. One major difference between the two cases was that the ACW was an AFL–CIO union, and the clothing workers were covered by the national labor laws (which the farm workers were not).

The union had appealed to the NLRB, charging Farah Manufacturing with numerous unfair labor practices in the organization campaign and election. But management made full use of the many loopholes in NLRB procedures to draw these appeal procedures out: "a shrewd management team can draw out unfair labor practices until support for a union is so fractured and the atmosphere so poisoned that a free and fair election cannot be had."[14] A boycott was necessary.

From the start of the boycott against Farah clothing in 1972, labor movement support was forthcoming in unprecedented fashion. Full support and participation came from the AFL–CIO and its constituent unions, and then-independent unions such as the United Auto Workers, Teamsters, and United Mine Workers.

The active support of the religious community was a crucial element in the boycott's success. El Paso Bishop Sidney M. Metzger rallied behind the ACW action, and in October 1972 he asked his fellow Roman Catholic prelates throughout the United States to support the strike and boycott. Other religious groups endorsed the

FIGURE 14.1 Editorial cartoon supporting the United Farm Workers grape boycott.
Source: Shawn Turner, in *The Stockton Record*, Wednesday, August 24, 1989, p. A16.

ACW fight: the Texas Conference of Churches, the Episcopal dean of Washington, D.C., the United Methodist Church, the African Methodist Episcopal Church, the Progressive National Baptist Church, the United Board for Homeland Ministries, the National Council of Churches, the Union of American Hebrew Congregations, and the Central Conference of American Rabbis.[15]

In addition, political activists joined the fight, supporting a disadvantaged minority group struggling for its rights. Leaders of national civil rights groups rallied behind the ACW, participating in demonstrations and other public displays at stores carrying Farah goods. Many student groups, led by the National Student Association, supported the boycott and supplied numerous volunteers to picket and protest at stores selling Farah products. The National Organization of Women endorsed and supplied volunteers to participate in the boycott. Support was even forthcoming from professional athletes; most of the Minnesota Vikings starters participated in demonstrations to lend their support, and the National Football League Players Association endorsed the boycott.

The Farah boycott, at first a nationwide effort, was extended to Europe and the Far East with the cooperation and involvement of the International Textile and Garment Federation and European and Japanese unions. The scope of the boycott was immense, and in the 22-month period of the activity, sales of Farah pants dropped from $160 million annually to $100 million.[16] The company capitulated in 1974 and recognized the ACW. At that point, the firm was on the verge of collapse, and took a long time to recover.[17]

The Farah boycott, like the Great Table Grape Boycott, involved unions dominated by a disadvantaged minority group. As Sheinkman has noted, the nature of the Farah actions, "involving a minority group that had usually known only frustration, discrimination, and despair, . . . elicited broad support outside the labor movement."[18] Ethnic unionism, centered on groups fighting for their civil rights, was a major factor in the success of the Farah and table grape boycotts.

Boycotts and Corporate Injustice: Two Studies

The J. P. Stevens and Coors actions of the late 1970s and 1980s were also successful consumer boycotts. Unlike those discussed above, they did not center around ethnic unionism and disadvantaged minority groups, but rather around the nature of the companies and their executives. The boycotts were also longer than the Farah and table grape boycotts, as can be seen in Figure 14.2. Although both were successful, their success seems to lie as much with social issues as with labor solidarity. Furthermore, in the J. P. Stevens case, the boycott was one element in a long-drawn-out campaign that won recognition for the Clothing and Textile Workers.

The J. P. Stevens Boycott   In 1963, the union (then the ACW) won NLRB representation elections at J. P. Stevens' North Carolina facility.[19] The company's refusal to bargain with the union started a 17-year struggle, involving numerous unfair labor practice cases filed with the NLRB (with a significant portion of rulings against management, 22 by one count), a novel publicity campaign that grew into a corporate campaign (a union tactic discussed later in this chapter), and the national boycott.

The Stevens boycott started in 1976. It faced a set of difficulties that tend to make the boycott an ineffective tool. First, Stevens marketed goods that were **brand-insensitive.** Consumers usually purchase white goods (towels, sheet, etc.) with little thought of brand; in fact, many consumers are totally unaware of the brand names of white goods. Second, Stevens' goods were marketed under a variety of brand names. The company did not push a single brand name, but many.

Yet the boycott and parallel actions against the company were successful. A major reason for this success was the labor movement's ability to brand J. P. Stevens as the nation's number one labor-law violator. Unfair labor practices included the firing of

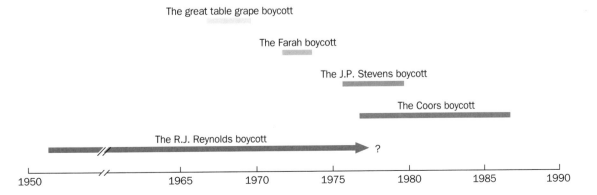

employees who supported the union and the refusal to bargain with the NLRB–certified union. The 1979 movie *Norma Rae* portrayed many of these actions. The boycott, which the union movement threatened to extend to other companies associated with Stevens, and the complementary corporate campaign, were organized around this theme of corporate injustice and violation of the law of the land.

In 1980, Stevens capitulated, and a collective bargaining contract was signed with the ACTWU. This 2 1/2-year contract covered the ten plants at which the union had won representation elections. It was also agreed that the contract would be extended to any of Stevens' other 70 or so plants if the union won elections at them. The contract provided for pay increases, including retroactive pay for many workers, and a checkoff. The union, in turn, agreed to stop its national boycott and corporate campaign.

The Coors Boycott   The boycott against Adolph Coors Company, the Colorado brewer, lasted *ten* years. It grew out of a strike initiated in 1977 by the AFL–CIO's directly affiliated Local Union 366 (a federal local that is not part of any national/international).[20] The strike was called because Coors refused to negotiate a new agreement with the local. Within a week of the start of the strike, which was not going well for the workers, the AFL–CIO geared up for a national boycott of Coors.

The boycott had all the ingredients of a successful campaign. First, the nature of the product was perfect for this type of action. The product was a brand-name one, Coors beer. Moreover, the product's consumers were traditionally blue-collar workers. Second, the boycott could be concentrated in the southern and western United States, as Coors' sales were in 15 states in those regions, particularly California (50 percent of sales).[21] Only in 1987, the last year of the boycott, did Coors begin to market its beer nationwide.

A third ingredient, and one crucial in terms of public support for the boycott, was the well-known stance of the Coors family. The family was outspokenly conservative and anti-union. Its public support of conservative causes earned it many ideological enemies on college campuses where Coors, and beer in general, is consumed in large amounts. The family's public expression of dislike for unions antagonized blue-collar union workers, another major group of consumers.

Coors' blatant anti-union activities also led to many NLRB hearings because the company had been accused of forcing several craft unions out of its Colorado brewery since 1960 and of firing workers without due cause. In addition, Coors used preemployment lie detector (polygraph) tests. As a corporation, Coors was easily portrayed by the boycott organizers as unjust, a violator of constitutional rights and the national labor laws. In many of its public statements relating to its personnel policies and support of conservative causes, Coors "shot itself in the foot."

The results of the strike were predictable. The strikers were fired, and a year later (1978) the union was decertified. The boycott, however, was a total success. After the first years, sales were down 11 to 12 percent. But the company "toughed it out." Nonetheless, the growing negative image portrayed by the boycott was having its effect on Coors. In 1985, the company began negotiating with the AFL–CIO on ending the dispute. In 1987, an agreement was reached. Over the course of the boycott, the AFL–CIO claimed the Coors' market share in California fell from 44 to

14 percent (Coors claimed the drop was from 39 to 16–18 percent), and in Colorado, from 47 to 22 percent (Coors claimed the drop was from 41 to 22 percent).

The agreement stipulated that the company would not interfere with union efforts to organize its employees and that any new construction undertaken by Coors would be by union contractors. For its part, the AFL–CIO agreed to call off the consumer boycott.

As an interesting postscript to the Coors boycott, the AFL–CIO had first given the task of organizing the Coors brewery to the International Association of Machinists (IAM) in 1987 when it reached agreement with the company. However, the Teamsters were also seeking to organize Coors. Upon reaffiliation (in October 1987) with the AFL–CIO, they were chosen to spearhead the organizing campaign as they represented more brewery workers than the IAM. In 1989, the employees at Coors rejected representation by the Teamsters by over 2 to 1, thus remaining nonunion.[22]

Consumer Boycotts Today

Labor boycotts have been successful when organized around major social as well as labor issues, such as minority rights and corporate injustice. Over the past 25 years, these issues have galvanized the efforts and gained the support of religious groups, political figures, and various social activists for boycotts.

Over that same 25-year period, the labor movement has undertaken several other less noted boycotts, buried in history as failures. The almost 40-year boycott of R. J. Reynolds Tobacco Company, started in 1951, never really got off the ground, but it is still going on. Present national boycotts, listed on the **AFL–CIO boycott list** (see Figure 14.3), have also met with little success, as they lack broad issues such as social injustice to rally the support of the consuming public. They have also not been backed with the large amount of dollar and human resources needed to carry on a national boycott. The same can be said about statewide boycotts, endorsed by state labor federations of the AFL–CIO. The present boycott list of the California Labor Federation, AFL–CIO, is shown in Figure 14.4.

Given the poor results of labor's consumer boycotts over the last several years, why are they still undertaken? There are several reasons. First, a former editor of the Federation's bimonthly *Label Letter,* which carries the national boycott list, has noted that the AFL–CIO "has an obligation to its member unions and, if they want a company on the list, then we'll keep it there."[23] Thus, many companies end up on the list and stay there, at the urging of a union that may not be pursuing the matter very vigorously.

This reason is related to a second one: many boycotts are started as additional actions during a strike. The Communications Workers of America (CWA) and the International Brotherhood of Electrical Workers (IBEW) asked, and received, the AFL–CIO's approval for a nationwide boycott of AT&T if they struck the company while negotiating a new contract in 1989.[24] They reached agreement, and so no strike and boycott occurred.

Some unions, however, do strike and run Federation-endorsed boycotts. The strikes may last years, and so do the boycotts, but as they lose steam they are not removed from the national boycott list. The Colt strike at the firearms maker's Hartford, Connecticut, plant, which lasted over four years, was supplemented by a

PLEASE POST

....

INTERNATIONAL PAPER COMPANY

Producer International and Hammermill bond, offset and writing paper and related products
United Paperworkers International Union

KAWASAKI ROLLING STOCK, U.S.A.

Motorcycles
Transport Workers Union of America

KRUEGER INTERNATIONAL, INCORPORATED

Brand name chairs: Matrix, Poly, Dorsal, Vertebra, Stax, Afka, Modular, Auditorium and University Seating (for airports and auditoriums)
International Association of Machinists & Aerospace Workers

LOUISIANA-PACIFIC CORP.

Brand name wood products: L-P Wolmanized, Cedartone, Waferwood, Fibrepine, Oro-Bond, Redex, Sidex, Ketchikan, Pabco, Xonolite
United Brotherhood of Carpenters & Joiners of America, and International Woodworkers of America

MOHAWK LIQUEUR CORPORATION

Mohawk labeled gin, rum, peppermint schnapps, and cordials
Distillery, Wine & Allied Workers International Union

R.J. REYNOLDS TOBACCO CO.

Cigarettes: Camel, Winston, Salem, Doral, Vantage, More, Now, Real, Bright, Century, Sterling, YSURitz; Smoking Tobaccos: Prince Albert, George Washington, Carter Hall, Apple, Madeira Mixture, Royal Comfort, Top, Our Advertiser; Little Cigars: Winchester
Bakery, Confectionery & Tobacco Workers International Union

ROME CABLE CORPORATION

Cables used in mining and construction industry
International Association of Machinists & Aerospace Workers

SHELL OIL COMPANY

Subsidiary of Royal Dutch Shell (parent company of Shell South Africa); gasoline, petroleum and natural gas products
AFL-CIO

SILO, INC.

National retailers of electronic equipment and appliances
International Brotherhood of Teamsters, Chauffeurs, Warehousemen & Helpers of America

UNITED STATES PLAYING CARD CO.

Brand names: Bee, Bicycle, Tally Ho, Aviator and Con
Retail, Wholesale & Department Store Union

ACE DRILL CORPORATION

Wire, jobber & letter drills, routers and steel bars
United Automobile, Aerospace & Agricultural Implement Workers of America International Union

BROWN CORPORATION

Motor mounts, brackets and dash assemblies
International Union of Electronic, Electrical Salaried, Machine & Furniture Workers

BROWN & SHARPE MFG. CO.

Measuring, cutting and machine tools and pumps
International Association of Machinists & Aerospace Workers

BRUCE CHURCH, INC.

Iceberg Lettuce: Red Coach, Friendly, Green Valley Farms, Lucky
United Farm Workers of America

CALIFORNIA TABLE GRAPES

Table grapes that do not bear the carton or crate
United Farm Workers of America

GARMENT CORPORATION OF AMERICA

Work clothes and uniforms
Amalgamated Clothing & Textile Workers Union

GREYHOUND LINES, INCORPORATED

Intercity bus and charter services
Amalgamated Transit Union

GUILD WINERIES & DISTILLERIES

Cook's Champagne
Distillery, Wine & Allied Workers International Union

HOLLY FARMS

Chickens and processed poultry products
International Brotherhood of Teamsters, Chauffeurs, Warehousemen & Helpers of America

At the request of the participating unions, the New York Daily News and Master Apparel have been removed from the boycott list.

Union Label and Service Trades Department, AFL-CIO July/August 1991

FIGURE 14.3 AFL–CIO national boycott list.
Source: "Label Letter," July/August 1991, p. 5 (AFL–CIO Union Label & Service Trades Department).

We Don't Patronize...

The following firms are currently on the "We Don't Patronize" list of the California Labor Federation, AFL–CIO. Firms are placed on the list in response to written requests from affiliates and only after approval by the Executive Council.

All trade unionists and friends of organized labor are urged not to patronize firms listed here.

Affiliates involved in any future contract settlements or other developments that would warrant the removal of any of these anti-union firms from the list.

Unfair firms are:

RESTAURANTS HOTELS, THEME PARKS

All Marriott Hotels in California with the specific exception of **the Marriott Hotel at Fisherman's Wharf in San Francisco**, which is a union house.

Contra Costa County

Days' Inn, Richmond.

Embassy Suites Hotel, Pleasant Hill.

Los Angeles Area

Hyatt Regency Downtown L.A.

Hyatt on Sunset Blvd.

Hyatt Wilshire.

The Pacifica Hotel, 6161 West Centinela Street in Culver City.

Park Plaza Hotel, LAX

Sheraton Los Angeles Airport, 6101 Century Blvd.

University Hilton Hotel, 3540 South Figueroa St.

Monterey Area

Asilomar Conference Center, Pacific Grove.

Casa Munras, Fremont and Munras, Monterey.

Doubletree Inn, 2 Portola Plaza, Monterey.

Days Inn, 1400 Del Monte Blvd., Seaside.

Sheraton Hotel, 350 Calle Principal, Monterey.

Napa

Napa Elks Lodge No. 832 bar and restaurant, 2480 Soscol Ave., Napa.

Oakland

Scott's Restaurant, 73 Jack London Square.

Ontario

Ontario Red Lion Inn.

Oxnard

Opus I Restaurant, in the Embassy Suites Hotel.

Oxnard Financial Plaza Hilton Hotel, 600 Esplanade Drive.

Sacramento Area

Auburn Joe's, 13480 Lincoln Way, Auburn.

The Club, 808 "O" St., Sacramento.

Continental Inn, 3343 Bradshaw, Rancho Cordova.

Courtyard, 10683 White Rock Rd., Rancho Cordova.

All Eppie's Restaurants.

Frank Fat's, 806 L St.

Frasinetti Winery & Restaurant, 7395 Frasinetti Rd., Florin.

Howard Johnson, 2300 Auburn Boulevard.

Hyatt Regency Hotel, L Street between 12th and 13th streets opposite Capitol Park.

Pennisi's Restaurant, 1030 J St.

Red Lion Inn, 2001 West Point Way, Sacramento.

Residence Inn, 1530 Howe Ave., Sacramento.

Sacramento Inn, Arden Way at Interstate 80, Sacramento.

Shanley's Bar & Grill, 5100 Folsom Blvd., Sacramento.

Sheraton Sunrise Hotel, Sunrise Blvd. at Highway 50.

Shot of Class, 1020 11th St.

Sierra Inn, 2600 Auburn Blvd.

The Nut Tree and Coffee Tree, Vacaville between Sacramento and San Francisco on Interstate 80.

Vagabond Inn, 909 3rd St.

San Diego Area

Anthony's Restaurants, 166 Solana Hills Dr., Solana Beach; 215 Bay Blvd., Chula Vista; 9530 Murray Dr., La Mesa; 1360 Harbor Dr., San Diego; 1355 Harbor Dr., San Diego; 11666 Avena Place, San Diego.

Bali Hai Restaurant, 2232 Shelter Island Dr., San Diego.

Hob Nob Restaurant, 2271 First Ave., San Diego.

San Diego Princess (formerly Vacation Village), 1404 W. Vacation Rd., San Diego.

Tom Ham's Light House, 2150 Harbor Island Dr., San Diego.

San Francisco

Alfred's, 886 Broadway.

Alioto's No. 8, Fisherman's Wharf.

Benihana of Tokyo, 1737 Post St.

Campton Place Hotel, 340 Sutter St.

Ernie's, 847 Montgomery St.

Fisherman's Grotto No. 9, Fisherman's Wharf.

Galleria Park Hotel, 191 Sutter St.

Jack In The Box, all locations.

Juliana Hotel, 590 Bush St.

The Mandarin, Ghirardelli Square.

Mandarin Oriental Hotel, 333 Sansome St.

McDonald's, all locations.

Miz Brown's, all locations.

Monticello Inn, 227 Ellis St.

Nikko Hotel, 222 Mason St.

North Beach Restaurant, 1512 Stockton St.

Parc Fifty-Five Hotel (Formerly Ramada Renaissance), 55 Cyril Magnin Place.

Park Hyatt, 333 Battery St.

Perry's, 1944 Union St.

Pompei's Grotto, Fisherman's Wharf.

Prescott Hotel, 545 Post St.

Richelieu Hotel, Van Ness Ave.

A. Sabella's, Fisherman's Wharf.

H. Salt Fish and Chips, all locations.

Col. Saunders Kentucky Fried Chicken, all locations.

Schroeder's, 240 Front St.

Tia Margarita, 19th Ave. and Clement St.

Trinity Suites, Eighth and Market Streets.

Vanessi's, 1177 California St.

Victorian Hotel, 54 Fourth St.

Villa Florence Hotel, 225 Powell St.

Vintage Court Hotel, 650 Bush St.

San Jose Area

Cindy's Restaurant, 17025 Condit Road, Morgan Hill.

DeAnza Hotel, 233 W. Santa Clara St., San Jose.

Giorgio's Pizza House, 1445 Foxworthy, San Jose.

House of Genji/Cathay Restaurant, 1335 N. First St., San Jose.

Holiday Inn—Palo Alto, 625 El Camino Real, Palo Alto.

Magic Pan Restaurant, 335 S. Winchester Blvd., San Jose.

Red Lion Inn at Gateway Place.

Travelodge, 940 Weddel Drive, Sunnyvale.

Vagabond Motor Hotel, 1488 North First, San Jose.

Santa Barbara Area

El Encanto Hotel and Garden Villas.

Santa Cruz Area

Seaside Co. properties including Santa Cruz Holiday Inn, and Boardwalk and Coconut Grove, Santa Cruz.

Stockton Area

Carmen's Mexican Restaurant, Lincoln Center.

Hilton Hotel, 2323 Grand Canal Blvd.

Ramada Inn, March Lane.

Stockton Inn Motel and Restaurants, 4219 Waterloo Road at Hwy. 99.

Vagabond Motor Hotel, 33 N. Center.

Las Vegas, Nevada

Landmark Hotel and Casino.

Sparks, Nevada

John Ascuaga's Nugget.

MANUFACTURING

Chir-Hit Displays, Santa Clara County.

Cook's Champagne.

Gaffers & Sattler products

Goehring Meat Co, Lodi.

Ito-Cariani Sausage Co., San Francisco: Cariani and Pocino brands.

Masonite Corp. plant, Cloverdale, Sonoma County.

New Life Bakery, Hayward, and its products including Phoenix, Pamela's, Bee Wise and Ultimate cookies; Fantastic Foods Natural Halvah; Gwetzell Brownies; Fruitsweet Macaroons and Cookies, and Nature's Warehouse foods including pastry poppers and cookies.

PRINTING

San Francisco Bay Guardian

Vallejo Times-Herald

New York Times, (Northwestern Edition).

THEATERS

Santa Cruz Area

Twin I & II Theaters, Aptos.

San Francisco

Alexandria, Balboa, Coronet, Coliseum, Metro, Stonestown Twin and **Vogue** (all United Artists) and **Cinema 21** and **Empire** (Syufy).

Sacramento Area

Capitol Theater; Century 21, 22, 23, 24 and **25 Theaters** (Syufy); **State Theater**; **Sacramento 6 Drive-In.**

Orange County

All United Artists Theaters in Orange County.

All Freedman Forum Theaters in Anaheim; **Cinemaland Theater**, Anaheim; **Brookhurst-Loge Theater**, Anaheim.

Valley View Twin Cinemas, Cypress; **Family Four Cinemas**, Fountain Valley; **Fox Fullerton**, Fullerton.

Syufy Cinedome, Stadium Drive-in and City Cinemas, all in Orange; **Villa Theater**, Orange; **Miramar Theater**, San Clemente; **Broadway Theater**, Santa Ana; **Stanton Theater**, Stanton.

OTHERS

Armstrong Painting & Waterproofing of San Francisco and its entities, including Armstrong Kitchens, Armstrong Construction, Armstrong Painting, and Armstrong Roofing.

Automotive, Sacramento area:

Walt Davis Chevrolet, Elk Grove.

Mel Rapton Honda.

All Paul Snider dealerships.

Swift Auto World.

Automotive, San Francisco area:

European Motors, 950 Van Ness Ave.

Ron Greenspan Volkswagen/ Subaru, Inc.

San Francisco Auto Center, 2300 16th St.

Van Ness Auto Plaza, 1000 Van Ness Ave.

Automotive, San Jose area:

Stevens Creek Acura.

Circuit City stores at 4080 Stevens Creek Blvd., San Jose; 1825 Hillsdale Ave., San Jose and 1250 Grant Road, Mountain View.

Costco Wholesale Warehouse grocery outlets at 1600 Coleman Ave., Santa Clara, and 1900 South 10th St., San Jose.

Dick's Rancho, Rancho Cordova.

Elk Grove General Store, Elk Grove.

Glass, Sacramento area:

Arrow Glass, Country Club Glass, Del Paso Glass, Fine Glass, Gaffney Glass, Golden West Glass, all locations; **Kinzel's Glass**, Carmichael; **Sam's Auto Glass, River City Glass, Victor Glass.**

Hertzka and Knowles, San Francisco, architects.

Keystone Company restaurant supply, San Jose.

Louisiana-Pacific Corporation products.

Montgomery Ward in Redding.

Mervyn's in Ventura.

Norbert Cronin & Co., insurance agents, San Francisco.

Non-Union Iceberg Lettuce.

Raley's Food Market, Oakhurst, Madera County.

Shoreline South Convalescent Hospital, Alameda.

Signs, Sacramento area: Dion Signs, Ellis Signage-Graphics, Fleming Silk Screen, House of Signs and River City Signs, all of Sacramento, and Young Electric Sign Co., West Sacramento.

State Farm Mutual Auto Insurance Co., Statewide.

Whole Foods Market, 200 Telegraph Ave., Berkeley.

Page 4

FIGURE 14.4 California Labor Federation, AFL–CIO boycott list.
Source: California AFL–CIO NEWS, June 14, 1991. (California Labor Federation, AFL–CIO).

boycott. International Paper, where a 16-month strike ended with the jobs of union members being held by replacement workers pending NLRB investigations (International Paper also locked workers out of one of its plants) is still on the AFL–CIO national boycott list (see Figure 14.3).[25]

Yet a third reason for the continued use of consumer boycotts is the part they play in corporate campaigns. As noted above, consumer boycotts were utilized rather successfully in the campaigns waged against J. P. Stevens, Farah, and Coors. (The Great Table Grape action *was* the campaign.) In addition, they were initiated in the Campbell Soup and SeaFirst (Seattle First National Bank) campaigns and played a major role in those campaigns, even if their effectiveness was questionable. They were also used in the Litton, Louisiana Pacific and BASF corporate campaigns, but as those companies primarily manufacture producer's goods not sold at the retail level, the actions were a combination of consumer and producer boycotts. (The Louisiana Pacific boycott is also still ongoing; see Figure 14.3.)[26] Corporate campaigns are discussed more fully later in this chapter.

The national consumer boycott remains a tool of unions. However, it is rarely the ultimate weapon; the strike usually fulfills this role. The boycott has become a tactic that is part of a larger action against management, such as the strike and the corporate campaign.

The Secondary Boycott

The second type of boycott that unions may use is the **secondary boycott,** in which the union boycotts a third, innocent employer to force that party to bring pressure on the primary employer with whom the union is having a dispute. For example, if the union is involved in a collective bargaining dispute with a company producing toys, it might boycott all retail toy stores (the third party) selling the company's products. The union has no dispute with the toy stores, but hopes that the stores, as customers of the toy producer, will bring pressure on the producer to settle its dispute with the union so that the boycott of their stores stops. The most obvious form of pressure would be to have the stores stop carrying the producer's toys, increasing the cost of the dispute to the company due to lost sales. An effective secondary boycott would involve pickets and a media campaign to stop shoppers from patronizing the "offending" (neutral) toy stores.

Secondary Boycotts under the Taft–Hartley Act

In the late 1930s, after the passage of the Wagner (National Labor Relations) Act, secondary boycotts flourished.[27] They were legal under both the Wagner Act and the Railway Labor Act. With the passage of the Taft–Hartley Act in 1947, secondary boycotts became, for the most part, unlawful actions or unfair labor practices. They were, and are still, lawful for railroad and airline unions that are covered by the Railway Labor Act.

Section 8(b)(4) of the Taft–Hartley regulates secondary boycotts, while Section 8(e) of the act prohibits hot-cargo clauses, a form of secondary boycott.[28] As noted in an earlier chapter, **hot-cargo agreements** between a union and an employer are contract clauses or contracts whereby the employer agrees to stop doing business with another company. These are expressly forbidden under the law as unfair labor practices except for subcontracting clauses aimed at preserving work for the members of the bargaining unit. In Section 8 (b) (4) (B), unions are prohibited from threatening or coercing, picketing, or inducing the picketing of, a neutral employer to force that neutral to stop doing business with the primary employer with whom the union has a dispute. The aim of this section is to protect neutral companies from being drawn into a labor dispute, and to keep the dispute confined to the union and employer directly involved. If, on the other hand, a secondary employer is not a neutral but is allied to the primary employer in one way or the other, it can be picketed. For example, if a company being struck contracts with another company to do work for it, the contracted firm becomes a party to the dispute. It can be picketed, as can commonly owned companies *if* they are not independently controlled.

The law, however, does allow several secondary actions. First, workers are allowed to refuse to cross the picket lines of a union having a dispute with its employer even if this action causes the employer of the workers honoring the picket lines to cease doing business with the picketed company. But these workers cannot be induced to honor the picket lines. A second, related instance, is peculiar to the construction industry. At a construction site, the picketing of a primary employer commonly results in the picketing of a secondary employer, because both are working at the same site. For example, if the electricians are involved in a dispute with their employer, an electrical subcontractor involved in the construction of a building, their pickets around the building site which are aimed at their employer also tend to interfere with other employers, such as the general contractor and other subcontractors. The picketing of the primary employer is not an unfair labor practice if it minimizes interference with the secondary employer(s) and its (their) employees. The NLRB has developed a set of rules to this effect. This type of action, referred to as **common-situs picketing,** has always been a major problem under the secondary actions section of the Taft–Hartley. Amendment of the law to allow any and all common-situs picketing in construction has been a goal of American labor for years, but it has not yet been attained.

A recent Supreme Court decision (April 1988) has broadened union use of secondary boycotts as free speech rights.[29] In that case, the Florida Gulf Coast Building and Construction Trades Council distributed leaflets at a Tampa shopping mall, urging customers not to shop at the mall because workers building a department store there were being paid substandard wages. The Court ruled that the leafletting was a First Amendment right; picketing would have been an unfair labor practice. Since that decision, many unions have used this tactic, especially at the local level.

Secondary Boycotts under the Railway Labor Act

Under the Railway Labor Act, secondary boycotts are still legal. Thus, as the Eastern Airlines strike got underway in March 1989, the International Association of Machinists could legitimately threaten to cause work stoppages not only at Eastern but also at other airlines and commuter railroads such as Amtrak. Reacting to this possibility, some railroads obtained temporary court injunctions against such secondary actions.[30]

Secondary boycotts in the rail and airline industries have been rare indeed. Though upheld by the Supreme Court in 1987, the secondary boycott has been used very sparingly by railroad unions in very short (a day or two) actions and has *never* been used by airline unions.[31] In fact, in response to the IAM threat to boycott other commuter lines at which they are bargaining unit representatives, President Bush threatened to ask Congress to amend the law to prohibit such actions.

This threat–counterthreat gets at the heart of the issue of secondary boycotts in the national transportation system. Systemwide disturbances would really upset the public. This would not, to say the least, enhance a union's image in a dispute with management. Moreover, a public outcry might well move Congress to act to prohibit such secondary boycotts under the Railway Labor Act. Thus, though now legal under that law, secondary boycotts are dangerous for rail and airline unions to utilize.

CORPORATE CAMPAIGNS

A more recent form that labor–management disputes have taken is the **corporate campaign.** In corporate campaigns, unions put pressure on groups that deal with an employer with which the union has a dispute. The objective is to get the employer to deal more favorably with the union under union-induced pressure of one sort or another from groups such as stockholders, financial institutions, customers, regulatory bodies, or legislatures.[32] The corporate campaign, first popularized by the J. P. Stevens campaign (which was aimed at organizing rather than collective bargaining), became a major union weapon in the 1980s and has been used many times in place of the strike.[33]

Unlike the strike or boycott, which results in fairly well-defined acts, the union corporate campaign presents management with an ill-defined set of activities. It does not really know what to expect. Most campaigns share one tactic, the strike, but beyond that, they seem to diverge substantially. Some encompass boycotts, or financial campaigns, or legal action through both the NLRB and/or the courts, or political action involving the executive and/or legislative branches of government, or protests aimed at corporate executives or at directors or at shareholders, or any combination of these tactics.

The Basic Elements of a Corporate Campaign

A union corporate campaign, like a corporate strategic plan, involves the determination of an organization's strengths and weaknesses, followed by action to take advantage of these characteristics. However, in a corporate campaign, the idea is to take advantage of the target organization's weaknesses, exploiting them to the utmost.

Once the target's vulnerability has been pinpointed, union actions to exploit it can take a variety of forms. However, no matter what tactics are used, certain elements seem to be common to most corporate campaigns undertaken in the last 10 to 15 years. These include (1) defining issues in the conflict such that labor is presented as the exploited, and the corporation as the exploiter and wrongdoer; (2) building coalitions within the labor movement and, beyond it, gaining as widespread a base of support as possible; (3) maintaining pressure on the corporation's points of vulnerability, be these political/legal, social, or economic; and (4) utilizing public relations to the fullest.

Defining the Issues

To mount a corporate campaign, a union needs widespread support. If the union is involved in a dispute with an employer over increased wages, fringe benefits, and other economic issues, it will not get much sympathy if it harps on those money issues. In general, union workers are not viewed as poorly paid; in fact, the general public feels that they are well paid. In a dispute with an employer, then, the union cannot garner support by calling that employer a "cheap skate" or "union buster."[34] For example, when the unions used the union buster charge as their rallying cry in their dispute with Eastern Airlines, they were unsuccessful.

The basic issues in a corporate campaign must go beyond the self-interests of the workers, and even those of the union movement. Several successful corporate campaigns (e.g., J. P. Stevens and Litton Industries) have painted the corporation and its executives as law breakers, out to rob workers of their legal rights. Numerous NLRB decisions against both J. P. Stevens and Litton were used to brand them as the nation's leading labor law violators. Some winning campaigns (e.g., Farah and Coors) have used a corporation's civil (and constitutional) rights violations (or alleged violations) to show the corporation in a bad light.

Defining the issues as going beyond the pay of workers or the strength of unions builds sympathy for those workers. Since community support is easier to garner, further coalition building is simpler.

Building Coalitions

Successful corporate campaigns are characterized by broad-based community support for the workers involved. First, support must be forthcoming from other trade unions. Hopefully, this support will be active (and even monetary). Just as important, however, or even more so, is support from outside the labor movement. Religious, political, and social activist groups have been instrumental in many successful corporate campaigns.

If the issues underlying the dispute between union and management are defined in relatively broad terms, encompassing concerns beyond those of the union and its members, coalitions can be built with a wide variety of groups. Civil rights issues in both the UFW (grape boycott) and Farah campaigns rallied religious groups and social activists to the union cause. Labor law violations brought support from many unions and social activists in the J. P. Stevens and Litton campaigns. Widespread support, based on building these coalitions, also helps the union maintain constant pressure on management in those areas in which they are most vulnerable.

Maintaining Pressure on the Corporation

The key to success in a corporate campaign, as in a national boycott, is to maintain pressure on the target corporation. This effort requires substantial resources; thus, a broad base of community support, both within and outside the labor movement, is important. Pressure maintained on the corporate points of vulnerability will normally get results, especially if union analysis has correctly identified those points.

A good example of assessing corporate vulnerability and making maximum use of those points is the Litton campaign.[35] By early 1980, Litton had "defeated" 18 different unions, and in that year the UE (United Electrical, Radio and Machine Workers, an independent union that left the CIO in 1950 because of alleged communist domination) won an NLRB election to represent workers at Litton's microwave oven plant in Sioux Falls, South Dakota. In early 1982, the UE, failing to negotiate a contract with Litton, embarked on a corporate campaign. Because of Litton's anti-union status and numerous labor law violations committed against several unions, the UE was able to gain the support of the AFL–CIO, through its Industrial Unions Department (IUD).

In mid-1982, the corporate campaign escalated. Up to this point, the J. P. Stevens corporate campaign was a model for this type of action. The main activities in that campaign were the attacks on the company's financial suppliers (banks mainly) and a consumer boycott, along with painting the company as the nation's leading labor law violator. But Litton Industries had billions in cash and produced few consumer products. It was a major labor law violator, however, having more NLRB decisions against it than J. P. Stevens.

Litton had a significant number of defense contracts, accounting for about a quarter of its revenues. This aspect of its business became a major point of pressure in the union's corporate campaign, along with the company's numerous labor law violations. The unions, led by the UE, lobbied for legislation that would bar NLRA violators from government contracts. This action upset numerous defense contractors, who, in turn, applied pressure on Litton to settle with its unions.

Litton's labor law violations were numerous, but they were spread throughout the conglomerate's divisions. The unions started to campaign to have the NLRB deal with conglomerates as single business units, so that sanctions from labor law violations would be applied companywide rather than only in the division in which the violation occurred. They succeeded in getting the NLRB to adopt this policy.

The "Number One Labor Law Violator" title applied to Litton (replacing J. P. Stevens) was used in another unique way. In general, Litton's board of directors was a rather conservative group, and its union sentiments were well known. However, several members were affiliated with universities (including Arjay Miller, then dean of Stanford's Graduate School of Business, and faculty members at George Washington University and the University of Southern California). The UE and its supporters held rallies at these three campuses, pushing the directors from academia into a position of nonsupport for Litton's lawbreaking labor policies.

Rallies were also held at stockholders' meetings in Los Angeles. With support from religious groups and college campuses, and the possibility of legislation that would bar Litton (and perhaps other major defense contractors) from holding government contracts, Litton capitulated. At the end of 1983 the company agreed to set up a committee to resolve the labor problems. The UE got its contract.

Utilizing Public Relations

Since mass media coverage is critical in making large corporations take notice, it is important to get the union message out, to build support for the campaign, and to keep up the pressure. There are many ways to bring the message of corporate malfeasance to the public. The mass media coverage was critical in the J. P. Stevens and Litton campaigns: coverage of rallies at the annual shareholders' meetings was significant in both campaigns.

In a campaign run by Ron Carver for the Boston local of the American Federation of Television and Radio Artists (AFTRA), newsletters, leaflets, and bumper stickers were utilized. A local (Boston) rock and roll FM station was purchased by Ardman Broadcasting of Palm Beach, Florida. Ardman, in negotiating a new contract with the local, demanded numerous changes, including elimination of the pension plan, cuts in health care coverage and severance pay, and expansion of the grounds for termination. The issue was job security, especially in light of the fact that "deejays" have fairly short-lived careers as it is.

A newsletter mailed in December 1988 to *all* 800 advertisers of WZOU described the company's attack on the employees' job security, and noted that the NLRB had issued a formal complaint against the station because of its "outrageous" behavior. It was pointed out that Ardman Broadcasting, a Florida-based concern, was "violating Boston community standards by attempting to eliminate pension and healthcare benefits and job security." This message was also repeated in the leaflets handed out around town (see Figure 14.5).

The bumper sticker utilized by AFTRA in its campaign was a unique public relations gimmick. Playing on the call letters of the station (referred to as The ZOU, a name that fits well with a rock and roll station), the bumper sticker accused The ZOU of becoming The Screw (see Figure 14.6). Leaflets and flyers are commonly utilized public relations instruments; the bumper sticker was quite an innovation.

The Eastern Airlines Dispute: A Case Study

The strike was the major weapon used in the dispute between Eastern Airlines and its unions (the IAM representing mechanics and baggage handlers, joined by the pilots and flight attendants—see Chapter 13). In addition, several other tactics were employed to get Eastern and Frank Lorenzo to back down from a position of pressing for major pay and work rule concessions from its employees. Analysis of Eastern and its parent, Texas Air, revealed several weaknesses: (1) the airline industry is still partially regulated by the Department of Transportation/Federal Aviation Administration; and (2) the Railway Labor Act gives unions substantial powers to intervene in many management decisions. Eastern was also losing money at a substantial rate.

Lawsuits

One set of actions the unions took in their campaign against Eastern involved use of the courts. First, the pilots' union sued to stop Eastern from training replacement pilots it would use in case of a strike. The machinists union and Eastern had been bargaining over a new contract for six months, and the airline had been contracting with and training replacement pilots in case the machinists went out on strike and the pilots honored their picket lines. The D.C. district court enjoined Eastern from these activities until a pilots' strike actually did occur.[36]

At about the same time (February), the machinists went to court to block the sale of Eastern's Northeast shuttle to another unit of Texas Air. The court upheld the

FIGURE 14.5 Leaflet from AFTRA campaign against Ardman Broadcasting.
Source: Ron Carver.

union position, ruling that that sale, as well as sales of other assets that Eastern was negotiating, would violate the status quo provisions in Eastern's collective bargaining agreement with the machinists. A federal appeals court reversed this decision in June, allowing Eastern to sell its Northeast shuttle.[37] However, the sale was being contested as part of a separate lawsuit filed by the pilots union, and Texas Air, rather unexpectedly, gave up its plans to transfer the shuttle from Eastern to another of its units.[38]

Texas Air and Eastern, in response to the spate of lawsuits by its unions, filed one itself, suing the machinists and pilots unions for $1.5 billion.[39] Management alleged

FIGURE 14.6 Bumper sticker from AFTRA campaign against Ardman Broadcasting. *Source:* Ron Carver.

that the unions were conspiring to destroy Eastern. By depressing the company's stock price, the unions were positioning themselves for a purchase of the company.

As an attempt to thwart an Eastern move to trim operations and lay off workers, the International Association of Machinists and the Air Line Pilots Association (ALPA) sued the airline in July 1988. The unions claimed that these adjustments had to be submitted to collective bargaining under the Railway Labor Act and could not be decided unilaterally by management. In August, the district court in Washington upheld the unions' position; however, in September, a three-judge panel of the appeals court in D.C. overturned this decision, allowing Eastern to close its Kansas City hub operation and lay off 4,000 employees. The full appeals court upheld the panel's decision in January 1989.[40]

By using the courts, the unions were able to disrupt management plans to prepare for a possible strike and to sell assets. In conjunction with their legislative campaign, to be discussed next, the unions succeeded in softening the company's stance at the bargaining table.

Legislative Initiatives

While fighting Eastern and Texas Air in the courts, the machinists and pilots unions also approached sympathetic friends in Congress to put further pressure on corporate management. Appealing to legislators sympathetic to their positions, the unions in March 1988 got 130 House members and five senators to co-sponsor resolutions asking the Department of Transportation (DOT) to investigate Texas Air's and Eastern's management, labor practices, and safety procedures.[41] The "unprecedented" DOT investigation of the airline and its parent concluded in May that management and the present safety procedures were acceptable but that employee relations posed a potential long-term safety hazard at Eastern. This situation could possibly lead to the revoking of Eastern's operating certificate (which it did not).[42] A committee of FAA and Eastern management and union people was formed to deal with safety problems in this context of sour labor–management relations.

The unions, especially ALPA, condemned the findings of the investigation, especially in the area of safety. ALPA requested that a new investigation of Eastern be undertaken, but the secretary of transportation turned the association down. He accused the union of "a transparent attempt to put pressure on Eastern by raising new safety concerns."[43]

Through legislative pressures, Eastern's unions were able to have the airline formally investigated and to bring the safety question out in public. Their success helped their position with the general public, for they were able to broaden the issue from that of wages and union-busting to include the safety of the flying public. They also set the stage for another tactic in their campaign against Eastern and Texas Air—whistleblowing.

Whistleblowing

The airline industry was deregulated over a decade ago, but airline safety is still regulated by the FAA. In February 1989, the FAA received allegations from members of Eastern's machinists union (the IAM) that a variety of safety violations were being committed by management. These included falsification of aircraft maintenance records.[44]

In May, two months into the Eastern strike, the FAA found that the airline had indeed violated prescribed maintenance procedures. Supervisors signed off on work without checking to see if the work was done. Some of the work was not done. Because of this falsification of maintenance records, Eastern's repair station certificate at Kennedy (New York) Airport was suspended.[45]

Whistleblowing is not a common union tactic, but it has been utilized more frequently in recent years. The United Food and Commercial Workers union (UFCW) used it very effectively in its campaign to organize IBP, Inc., the nation's largest meatpacker. In 1987 and 1988, the union brought unsafe work practices to the attention of the Occupational Safety and Health Administration (OSHA), resulting in $5.6 million in fines. The union also brought allegations of violations of the overtime requirement of the Fair Labor Standards Act, prompting an investigation by the Department of Labor, resulting in back pay claims of $40 million.[46] IBP voluntarily recognized the UFCW! The UFCW utilized the same methods in its dispute with John Morrell & Co., another meatpacker, with the same results—OSHA citations and fines, and back pay (overtime) claims by the Labor Department.[47] Federal laws protect whistleblowers in government.[48] It is hoped that new laws will protect them in the private sector, as the National Labor Relations Act protects the filers of unfair labors practices. Violations of laws and guidelines would not go undetected, as they do now in so many cases, if whistleblower protection were written into the law.

A Unique Union Response to Management Actions

Disputes with management take many forms, as this chapter and the two preceding chapters illustrate. Grievances and arbitration or some other appeals procedures are utilized to resolve day-to-day disputes on the job. Strikes, as power struggles, are usually "resolved" (really ended) when one side capitulates. Sometimes, however, the underlying issues in dispute are ironed out between the parties short of a strike with the help or direction of a neutral third party. Boycotts, like strikes, are power struggles, and end when one party surrenders. The corporate campaigns discussed above are also power struggles, like strikes and boycotts, mounted by unions to bring pressure on the party with which they are in dispute.

AN OPEN LETTER FROM
THE PILOTS OF NORTHWEST AIRLINES
TO THE BOARD OF DIRECTORS OF
AND THE BIDDERS FOR
NWA INC.

Ever since the deregulation of the airline industry in 1978, this country's major carriers have been divided into two groups: the "haves" and the "have-nots." All along, Northwest Airlines has been universally recognized as one of the strongest and most profitable of the "haves."

We are determined to keep it that way. As a labor union with an open contract, and as major stakeholders in the future success of Northwest Airlines, we will do whatever is necessary to protect our jobs as Northwest employees, and our careers as professional pilots.

For several months now, the arbs of Wall Street have toyed with this multi-billion-dollar corporation. The speculators and manipulators have pored through the books, looked over the assets, and dreamed about quick and easy profits.

These dreams are our nightmare, and that of every other concerned American who recognizes the danger and the recklessness inherent in what some of you may view as a "game." Transportation Secretary Skinner and the U.S. Senate have both expressed alarm over what you are considering. They are dead right. If certain money-changers on Wall Street are allowed their way, Northwest Airlines overnight will become a "have-not." What has always been one of the strongest major airlines in the United States will become a financially-crippled second-tier carrier, ill equipped to meet the challenges of business cycles, the economic and safety demands of fleet replacement, and the global competitive threat of government-subsidized foreign megacarriers.

For more than two years now, our ALPA negotiators have been meeting with management to try to work out the terms of a new contract to cover our 5,000 pilots. It has not been a pleasant or easy process. Half of our pilots are working under the terms of a contract signed with the management of the old Northwest Orient in 1983, an agreement which became amendable in the summer of 1986. The other half of our pilots—those who flew for Republic Airlines prior to the merger three years ago—have been working under a contract which was signed in 1984 and became amendable in 1987, and which contains many pay and work rule concessions granted to the management of Republic back when that airline was struggling to stay alive.

In recent years, Northwest Airlines has turned in record profits while keeping our wages frozen at outdated and, in the case of the former Republic pilots, concessionary and substandard levels. Our patience is nearly gone, and let there be no doubt as to our willingness to stand up and fight for what we believe in. Last fall, when negotiations reached an impasse, 96 percent of our pilots voted to strike rather than accept management's latest offer. A pilot walkout was averted at the 11th hour only when NWA management "blinked" and applied to the National Mediation Board for intervention, under whose auspices the talks have continued. As dictated by the Railway Labor Act, our pilots must keep flying while our negotiators keep talking, but this unfair situation cannot continue much longer. Major issues remain to be settled. Sooner or later, our contractual concerns must be resolved, or a pilot strike will be inevitable.

This letter is to serve notice that our concern for the long-term survival and success of Northwest Airlines must be the cornerstone of any new contract. As employees and professional pilots, we have as much—if not more—to lose than any other constituency if our airline becomes a debt-ridden carrier with an aging fleet that poses operational and safety problems. Just as lenders seek to protect their capital with financial covenants from the borrower, we intend to protect our "capital"—our careers—with enforceable safeguards against what we and outside objective observers would view as suicidal or self-interested corporate policies.

To us, the issue is very simple. Our collective future and our individual careers are on the line. Excessive debt incurred in connection with any transaction involving Northwest Airlines or NWA Inc. is something we simply will not accept. We will not willingly place our future in the hands of an unknown party whose highly-leveraged acquisition plans can only be financed by reliance on the breakup value of all or part of this corporation. We may have no choice except to take whatever action we can to ensure the continued growth and prosperity of Northwest Airlines into the 21st century. We have been preparing for this battle for a long time.

We know what we want, and we know what we need. We will not settle for anything less.

Sincerely yours,

H. T. Dodge, Chairman   Kirk A. Faupel, Chairman
Master Executive Council   Master Executive Council
Northwest Airlines   Republic Airlines
Air Line Pilots Association   Air Line Pilots Association

FIGURE 14.7 Open letter from ALPA local, Northwest Airlines.
Source: Courtesy ALPA, originally appeared in *Wall Street Journal.* Monday, June 12, 1989, p. B2.

A unique corporate campaign was employed by the pilots union (ALPA) local of Northwest Airlines. Its campaign was aimed at preventing a potential dispute with a potential new management. Northwest Airlines was rumored to be a takeover target; specifically (at that time), a $3.65 billion acquisition offer has been made by a Los Angeles investor.[49] To express its opposition to a highly leveraged buyout (LBO) that would saddle the airline with a huge debt, the Northwest ALPA local published an open letter in the *Wall Street Journal* on June 12, 1989 (see Figure 14.7). The strike threat contained in that letter has proven to be very effective, for a possible work stoppage would make it very difficult for any investor to borrow the money for the buyout. As one airline analyst has noted, "If there is a possibility the airline's operations will be disrupted the banks are going to get nervous."[50]

This novel approach is a good example of the unions' ability to adapt to changing circumstances. The Air Line Pilots Association, keeping abreast of the financial trends that might affect its members, especially LBOs, is being proactive rather than reactive. The growing popularity of corporate campaigns, as opposed to just strikes and boycotts, is another indication of an adaptive union movement. The expansion of the instruments of power that unions yield against management is a major plus for unions and their supporters. In many aspects, they are developing the strategic outlook that is so crucial to corporate survival in a changing world.

DISCUSSION QUESTIONS

1. What is the most important element in a consumer boycott, and why?

2. What did the Great Table Grape and Farah boycotts have in common that led to their success?

3. How did the fact that the Amalgamated Clothing Workers of America had to follow national labor laws cause the Farah boycott to differ from the Great Table Grape boycott?

4. What did the J. P. Stevens and Coors boycotts have in common that led to their success?

5. What characteristics of a company or company's products make the company susceptible to a boycott? In light of these characteristics, devise strategies for operating a company so that it would be relatively invulnerable to boycotts. Name two companies, one you think would be rather susceptible to a boycott and one that would be relatively invulnerable, and explain your reasoning.

6. Why are large national chains of stores in metropolitan areas more easily handled in boycotts than smaller chains and independent stores? What aspects of smaller chains and independents might be conducive to successful boycotts?

7. What are the major differences between a consumer (primary) boycott and a secondary boycott under the Railway Labor Act? Under the National Labor Relations Act and its amendments?

8. What tactics do unions use when they undertake a corporate campaign?

9. What is the first step a union should undertake when it plans a corporate campaign against a specific company?

10. What are the four basic elements of a corporate campaign?

11. What is whistleblowing, and why is it so effective in an industry like the airline industry?

12. How does the role of the media differ between a boycott and a corporate campaign?

VOCABULARY LIST ══════════

primary/consumer boycott	hot-cargo agreement
ethnic unionism	common-situs picketing
brand-insensitive	corporate campaign
AFL–CIO boycott list	whistleblowing
secondary boycott	

FOOTNOTES ══════════

1. *Wall Street Journal*, June 26, 1978, p. 1.

2. *New York Times*, March 6, 1989, p. A10.

3. Ibid.

4. The J. P. Stevens boycott was part of a corporate campaign that finally forced the company to recognize and bargain with the union 17 years (1953–1980) after its certification by the NLRB (*Wall Street Journal*, October 20, 1980, p. 1).

5. The phrase "ethnic unionism" and much of the details that follow are from two articles: Cletus Daniel, "The Boycott in the 70s: New Wine in an Old Bottle" and Jacob Sheinkman, "The Farah Boycott," *Industrial and Labor Relations Report* (New York State School of Industrial and Labor Relations, Fall 1974), pp. 6–10. See also *Wall Street Journal*, June 26, 1978, p. 1; and J. Craig Jenkins, *The Politics of Insurgency: The Farm Worker Movement in the 1960s* (Columbia University Press, 1985).

6. Daniel, "The Boycott in the 70s," p. 9; this was true in spite of the fact that the United States and Mexico had canceled the bracero program (the use of Mexican nationals as agricultural workers in California fields and orchards) in 1965 and were phasing it out.

7. Jenkins, *The Politics of Insurgency*, pp. 142–143. Many of the political activists were students from the Free Speech Movement (centered in Berkeley) and campus chapters of CORE (Congress of Racial Equality), SNCC (Student Nonviolent Coordinating Committee), and SDS (Students for a Democratic Society). Strikes were held in Delano in 1965, and although they got substantial support and publicity as "La Huelga" (the strike), they failed; boycotts succeeded.

8. Jenkins, *The Politics of Insurgency*, p. 162.

9. Ibid., pp. 163-164.

10. Ibid., pp. 168–169.

11. Ibid., p. 172.

12. Initiated in 1984, a present UFW table grape boycott, aimed at curtailing pesticide use on vines, has enjoyed little success (*New York Times*, June 30, 1989, p. A13; June 18, 1989, "Week in Review," p. 4; *Wall Street Journal*, November 1, 1988, p. A1) and is, some say, a sign of a union [the UFW] that is not powerful enough to mount a direct action against table grape growers. Non-UFW table grapes are still on the AFL–CIO national boycott list—see Figure 14.3.

13. Sheinkman, "The Farah Boycott," p. 6.

14. Ibid.

15. Ibid., p. 7.

16. Ibid., p. 8.

17. *Wall Street Journal*, June 26, 1978, p. 1.

18. Sheinkman, "The Farah Boycott," p. 7.

19. *Wall Street Journal*, October 20, 1980, p. 1. Many of the details in this section come from this article in the *Journal* ("How the Textile Union Finally Wins Contracts at J. P. Stevens Plant").

20. *Wall Street Journal*, August 20, 1987, p. 15, and *Business Week*, July 11, 1988, p. 61. Many of the details in this section come from these articles, especially the *Journal* ("Coors and Union to End Dispute on Organizing.").

21. *Wall Street Journal*, June 26, 1978, p. 18.

22. *Monthly Labor Review*, April 1989, p. 42.

23. *Wall Street Journal*, June 26, 1978, p. 18.

24. *Wall Street Journal*, May 3, 1989, p. A8.

25. *Wall Street Journal*, October 11, 1988, p. C14 (the IPC strike) and *New York Times*, May 2, 1989, p. A16 and March 23, 1990, p. B16 (the Colt strike).

26. Charles R. Perry, *Union Corporate Campaigns* (The Wharton School, University of Pennsylvania, 1987), pp. 76, 79.

27. *New York Times*, March 6, 1989, p. A10.

28. Commerce Clearing House, *1989 Guidebook to Labor Relations* (1989), pp. 291–293, 298–300.

29. *Wall Street Journal*, April 21, 1988, p. 6; *Business Week*, June 27, 1988, p. 82.

30. *New York Times*, March 6, 1989, p. A10. (Amtrak and 12 commuter railroads, governed by the Railway Labor Act, were listed as possible secondary boycott targets of the IAM.)

31. Ibid.

32. Perry, *Union Corporate Campaigns*, p. iii.

33. A recent Bay Area Labor Studies Seminar at the Institute of Industrial Relations, the University of California at Berkeley, by Ron Carver, union corporate campaign organizer for the UE and the Industrial Union Department, AFL–CIO, was entitled "When Strikes Won't Work: The Use of the Corporate Campaign..." (IIR, University of California, Berkeley, May 9, 1989).

34. Ibid.

35. Ibid., and Perry, *Union Corporate Campaigns*, pp. 155–169. Many of the details in this discussion are from these two sources.

36. *Wall Street Journal*, March 31, 1988, p. 4.

37. Ibid.; *Wall Street Journal*, May 20, 1988, p. 11; June 8, 1988, p. 2.

38. *Wall Street Journal*, July 5, 1988, p. 4.

39. *Wall Street Journal*, May 9, 1988, p. 4.

40. *Wall Street Journal*, July 29, 1988, p. 18; January 11, 1989, p. A16.

41. *Wall Street Journal*, March 31, 1988, p. 4.

42. *Wall Street Journal*, June 22, 1988, p. 26.

43. *Wall Street Journal*, December 20, 1988, p. A4.

44. *Wall Street Journal*, March 30, 1989, p. A4.

45. *Wall Street Journal*, May 5, 1989, p. A8.

46. *Business Week*, August 29, 1988, p. 82.

47. *Wall Street Journal*, October 25, 1988, p. A24.

48. *New York Times*, July 10, 1983, pp. A1, C3. The Federal False Claims Act of 1863, amended in 1986, covers companies under government contracts as well as government work itself.

49. *Wall Street Journal*, June 12, 1989, p. A3; June 30, 1989, p. A1; July 7, 1989, p. C10.

50. Ibid.

REFERENCES

CLETUS, DANIEL. "The Boycott in the 70s: New Wine in an Old Bottle." *Industrial and Labor Relations Report*. New York State School of Industrial and Labor Relations, Fall 1974, pp. 8–10.

COMMERCE CLEARING HOUSE. *1989 Guidebook to Labor Relations*. 1989, Ch. 11.

JENKINS, J. CRAIG. *The Politics of Insurgency: The Farm Worker Movement in the 1960s*. Columbia University Press, 1985, Ch. 6.

MULLINS, TERRY W., and PAUL LUEBKE. "Symbolic Victory and Political Reality in the Southern Textile Industry: The Meaning of the J. P. Stevens Settlement for Southern Labor Relations." *Journal of Labor Research* (Winter 1982): 81–88. Reprinted in Richard L. Rowan, *Readings in Labor Economics and Labor Relations* (Irwin, 1985), pp. 196–201.

PERRY, CHARLES R. *Union Corporate Campaigns*. Industrial Research Unit, The Wharton School, University of Pennsylvania, 1987.

SHEINKMAN, JACOB. "The Farah Boycott: Solidarity Forever." *Industrial and Labor Relations Report*. New York State School of Industrial and Labor Relations, Fall 1974, pp. 6–8.

PART FOUR

UNIONIZATION IN THE PUBLIC SECTOR

U nions in the U.S. public sector have been growing rapidly since the 1960s. Now, in a period of general union decline, the brightest spot in the American labor movement is in the public sector—federal, state, county, and municipal unions. With few exceptions, public sector labor organizations have maintained their memberships and coverage as growth in public sector employment in the 1980s has slowed. The next three chapters cover this sector and its labor organizations.

First, we examine the legal and political framework of public sector unionism, paralleling our treatment for the private sector in Chapter 3. Next, we discuss unionism in the federal government. Lastly, we cover the very broad and extremely diverse topic of public sector labor–management relations at the state, county, and municipal (local) levels. Every state has different laws covering unionism in its jurisdiction (and some have no laws at all covering this vital area). Thus, the discussion is couched in broad terms, and the state laws in California are used as an example. This chapter, like the preceding one, ends with a look at the question of the differences in public sector and private sector unionism.

CHAPTER 15

THE POLITICAL AND LEGAL FRAMEWORK IN THE PUBLIC SECTOR

T he legal and statutory framework of public sector labor relations has a relatively short history. Unlike the private sector, where collective bargaining laws are over 60 years old, executive orders and laws regulating labor–management relations in the public sector date back only 30 years. A surge of public employee unionization followed the late President John Kennedy's issuance of one of the first of these regulating instruments in the early 1960s and tapered off in the mid-1970s. Prior to that time, most collective bargaining efforts in government were stifled.

In order to understand the complexities of public sector labor relations, we must realize that the laws are not uniform from state to state and at the federal level. Each state, county, and municipality has a set of laws differing from every other governmental unit, and federal labor–management relations laws are very different from state, county, and municipal laws. The federal government does have a single law affecting many of its employees. However, Congress has also passed legislation for the specific benefit of some employees while ignoring other public sector workers. Thus, it is difficult to make any broad, sweeping generalizations regarding public sector labor relations laws.

It is difficult to generalize about public sector unions. We can state that some major differences exist between public sector and private sector unions. In the private sector, decisions are made on a centralized basis in the national headquarters, whereas in the public sector, the local union leaders determine policy and play a much more significant role than the national leaders.[1] Yet in the public sector, some unions are national in scope and others are small local organizations of workers, such as a fraternal order of the police. There are also primarily private sector unions, such as the Teamsters and Service Employees International, that organize public sector employees.

This chapter reviews the executive orders and laws governing labor–management relations in the federal government and then considers state issues. A section on strikes, a very controversial issue in the public sector, follows. Finally, we discuss general concepts and trends.

THE GROWTH OF PUBLIC SECTOR UNIONISM

Prior to 1960, there was very little union or employee organization activity in the public sector. Attempts had been made, but outside the U.S. Postal Service, unionization was slow moving.

From the 1960s through the mid-1970s, public sector unionization grew rapidly. Because of the changes in the federal legal framework, many of its civil employees could, and did, organize into collective bargaining units and negotiate some of the terms and conditions of their employment. However, major subjects of collective bargaining in the private sector such as wages, fringe benefits, and most work rules are not subjects in federal government labor negotiations and are restricted in many states. The scope of collective bargaining is much narrower in the public sector, especially at the federal level, than in the private sector.

Since the mid-1970s, the growth of public sector unions has slowed considerably. Some analysts assert that it is due to the passage of state and federal legislation protecting employees' rights.[2]. These protective measures would lessen the need for a union representative to bargain for some benefits provided by the laws. Others feel that the slowing of public sector unionization is a maturing process, as public sector union membership sits at about 37 percent of public sector employment, a rate over twice that in the private sector.[3]

FEDERAL EXECUTIVE ORDERS AND STATUTES

Both executive orders and statutes governing the collective bargaining of public employees have been issued and enacted over the last 30 years. In response to early attempts by public employees to unionize and seek improvements in working conditions, presidents of the United States effectively stopped the activity. However, persistent activity by federal employees, primarily those in the postal service unions which are the oldest in the federal government, led to the granting of public sector workers' rights to organize and bargain.

The Gag Rules

As early as 1883, the **Pendleton Act,** more commonly known as the **Civil Service Act,** was enacted. This law gave Congress the sole authority to regulate hours, wages, and other working conditions of the federal labor force. It also encouraged congressional lobbying activities by federal employees.

The postal workers, the earliest major unionized group of federal employees, were also one of the earliest groups to attempt to lobby Congress for improved benefits. In response to these efforts, President Theodore Roosevelt issued executive orders in 1906 prohibiting lobbying activities by federal employees. Federal employees, and associations acting on their behalf, were forbidden to lobby Congress for pay increases, subject to the penalty of job dismissal.

These **gag rules** were continued during President William Howard Taft's term. However, the postal workers ignored the ban, and in 1912 the **Lloyd–La Follette Act** was passed. The act, considered the Magna Carta for federal employees, permitted these employees and their employee organizations to lobby Congress for improvements in wages and working conditions.

The Kennedy Promise: Executive Order 10988

During the 1960 presidential campaign, the postal unions, along with other federal unions, obtained a promise from candidate John Kennedy to support a bill giving public sector employees bargaining rights. Section 2 of the 1935 National Labor Relations Act specifically excluded "employees of the United States or any state or political subdivision thereof," effectively denying them the right to collective bargain. Although President Kennedy did support legislation, none was passed by Congress.

Acting on the suggestion of a task force reviewing public sector employee rights, the president signed **Executive Order 10988** in January 1962.[4] Basically, it granted most public sector employees the right to organize for the purpose of collective bargaining. The specific governmental agency or department was charged with deciding if employees wanted a particular labor organization to represent them and if they were grouped in the appropriate bargaining unit. Unfair labor practices were heard and decided by the department head at the cabinet level. Arbitrators were also available to help an agency with labor relations problems.

Union Recognition under Executive Order 10988

One feature of the executive order was its provision for a variety of union recognition policies. A union could attain **exclusive recognition, formal recognition,** or **informal recognition** by the agency employer. The type of recognition was based on the percentage of employees supporting the union in the bargaining unit.

To attain exclusive recognition, a union had to show that it represented at least 10 percent of the employees in the respective unit and then had to be chosen, through election or the use of authorization cards, by a majority of the employees in the unit to be their representative. If so designated, the employer–agency had to meet and confer on personnel matters and working conditions. The union could negotiate for a written agreement or contract. This is the sole category of union recognition in the private sector.

To gain formal recognition status, a union had to show it represented 10 to 50 percent of the unit employees, usually by showing they belonged to the union. Under formal recognition, a union had to be consulted by the employer–agency on personnel matters.

Informal recognition status was granted if less than 10 percent of the unit employees were members of the union. The employer–agency had no duty or obligation to meet, consult, or negotiate with the union.

The Limited Scope of Collective Bargaining under Executive Order 10988

Executive Order 10988 had limited scope. During collective bargaining, the scope of the negotiable subjects was quite restrictive. One subject open to negotiation concerned the conditions of employment, especially grievance procedures. However, arbitration rights were excluded. No negotiations were allowed over work assignments, work rules, organizational structure, wages, or compulsory membership (including the agency shop). The contract, once hammered out, had to be approved by the agency–department head. Wages and fringe benefits were left to Congress to set. Strikes were not permitted.

The Civil Service Commission implemented the executive order. However, without the right to strike or binding arbitration rights, the Federal Mediation and Conciliation Service was used to help resolve disputes, although the order did not specifically provide for this intervention.

Correcting the Problems: Executive Order 11491

Almost everyone was unhappy with Executive Order 10988, especially the method developed for establishing representation and the administrative implementation. In 1969, President Richard Nixon issued **Executive Order 11491** to remedy some of these earlier problems.[5]

A New Administrative Structure

Executive Order 11491 revised the administrative structure. It vested the decision making in the three-member **Federal Labor Relations Council (FLRC)** which was modeled after the NLRB. The three members were the chairman of the Civil Service Commission, the Secretary of Labor, and a presidential appointee. Certain appeals could be brought before the FLRC.

The Assistant Secretary of Labor for Labor–Management Relations was given the responsibility to settle disputes over the composition of bargaining units and to hold and supervise representation elections. Unions could only gain exclusive recognition rather than one of the three forms of recognition under Executive Order 10988. To have exclusive recognition, a majority of the employees involved had to select the union by secret ballot. The Assistant Secretary for Labor–Management Relations could even prohibit unions from being recognized if it was shown that they were involved in corrupt activities. Any decisions of the assistant secretary could be appealed to the FLRC.

The act also created the **Federal Services Impasses Panel (FSIP)** which was to settle issues when they reached an impasse during contract negotiations. Arbitration of disputes was encouraged and, like all decisions, could be appealed to the FLRC. Arbitration was thus not final and binding.

The Postal Reorganization Act: "Privatizing" the Postal Service

Executive Order 11491 was still unsatisfactory for the postal workers. They struck for broader bargaining rights and representation practices similar to those in the private sector. As a result, the **Postal Reorganization Act** was enacted in 1970.[6] The act gave the U.S. Postal Service independent agency status under the control of the executive branch. It was to function more like a private enterprise. Under the act, the NLRB was given the power to determine bargaining units, oversee representation elections, and administer the law regarding unfair labor practices. Although the act did not give postal employees the right to strike, it did provide for binding arbitration if the parties could not settle their contract disputes. In essence, labor–management relations in the postal service were privatized.

The Civil Service Reform Act: Keeping Civil Service Workers Happy

The **Civil Service Reform Act of 1978 (CSRA)** provided a variety of reforms and benefits for civil employees.[7] It was the first time since 1912 that Congress passed a bill covering almost all federal employees. This statute, paralleling the Taft–Hartley Act, gave federal employees the right to refrain from and/or the right to form, join, or assist a labor organization without fear of reprisal. They were given the right to collectively bargain regarding conditions of employment. The law noted that these activities are in the public interest.

Labor–Management Relations under the CSRA

Conditions of employment were specifically defined in the statute as "personnel policies, practices, and matters whether established by rule, regulation or otherwise, affecting working conditions."[8] Wages were not made a bargaining issue under the definition. Blue-collar worker pay is set in the Coordinated Federal Wage System which gives these federal employees pay comparable to that in the private sector. The salaries of white-collar workers are set in the General Schedule (GS rating). The schedule is reviewed by the president who attempts to keep the federal and private sector pay levels for these employees in parity.

The CSRA allows for the filing of grievances for contract violations and other matters. For example, employees can file grievances for discriminatory practices by their employer, the government. Such grievances can be handled by a procedure established in the CSRA for binding arbitration, which itself can be appealed to a higher administrative authority, the Federal Labor Relations Authority. Such an appeal (exception) must be filed within 30 days of the arbitration award.

Similar to the Wagner and Taft–Hartley Acts, the CSRA establishes both employer and union unfair labor practices. There are eight of each (see Table 15.1). The first five employer unfair labor practices parallel those in the Wagner Act (see Chapter 3, Table 3.1). A government agency, for example, is prohibited from discriminating against an employee for union activity. The union or employee organization unfair labor practices are quite different from those in the Taft–Hartley Act (see Chapter 3, Table 3.2). One, for example, is calling or encouraging a strike or slowdown.

Table 15.1   *Unfair Labor Practices, Civil Service Reform Act*

Unfair Labor Practices of a Federal Agency

1. Interference with employees' rights to organize and bargain collectively
2. Domination of or interference in organizing or administering a labor organization
3. Discrimination in employment to discourage (or encourage) membership in a labor organization
4. Discrimination in employment because an employee files charges or gives testimony under the act
5. Failure to bargain collectively, in "good faith," with the representative of employees
6. Failure to cooperate on impasse procedures and decisions under the act
7. Failure to enforce any rule or regulation in conflict with a collective bargaining agreement
8. Failure to comply with all provisions in the act

Unfair Labor Practices of an Employee Organization

1. Interference with employees' rights to organize or choose not to have a bargaining representative
2. Causing or attempting to cause an employer to discriminate in employment because of labor organization membership
3. Disciplining of an employee for the purpose of interfering with his or her work
4. Membership discrimination on the basis of race, color, creed, national origin, sex, age, civil service status, political affiliation, marital status, or handicapped condition
5. Failure to bargain collectively, in "good faith," with representatives of the employer
6. Failure to cooperate on impasse procedures and decisions under the act
7. (A) Actions (strikes, inducing strikes, boycotts, slowdowns) that interfere with an agency's operations, or
   (B) Failure to take action to prevent or stop members from undertaking such activities as noted in A
8. Failure to comply with all provisions in the act

The Administrative Structure

To oversee the law, the CSRA established an administrative authority—the **Federal Labor Relations Authority** (**FLRA**), a three member board. It replaced the Federal Labor Relations Council and was made more independent of the administration than that board. Also established was an office of general counsel, appointed by the president for a five-year term, whose mandate was to investigate and prosecute unfair labor practice charges. The Federal Services Impasses Panel was retained for resolving disputes.

The FLRA members are appointed for five-year terms by the president. Members of the FLRA administer the CSRA. Like the National Labor Relations Board, the FLRA's major duties are to determine bargaining units, supervise representation elections, hold hearings, and resolve unfair labor practice disputes. The FLRA, also like the NLRB, may delegate its election responsibility to regional offices, and unfair labor practices disputes may be resolved by administrative law judges in these regional offices. The decisions made by these delegated authorities may be appealed to the FLRA. The FLRA's final opinions, except for unit determinations, may be appealed to the U.S. Court of Appeals. FLRA decisions are enforceable through the federal circuit courts.

If a body is found to engage in an unfair labor practice, a number of remedies are available. A cease and desist order may be issued, renegotiation with a retroactive effective date may be granted, or an employee can be awarded back pay. Even attorney's fees can be awarded in appropriate cases.[9]

PUBLIC EMPLOYEE RIGHTS AT THE STATE AND LOCAL LEVEL

It is not easy to make any broad statements regarding the laws affecting state, county, and municipal employee rights. Each has its own unique set of rules and regulations. The right to collectively bargain, however, is widespread. Two-thirds of the states have some form of collective bargaining statute(s). However, the variation in these laws is very great. Moreover, within states, some municipalities have their own laws. Again, the variation among them is substantial.

The Scope of Public Sector Laws: A Model

A good public sector labor relations law should have several features; seven are given here.

1. It should include or allow a wide scope of subjects for collective bargaining, as the NLRA's "wages, hours, and other terms and conditions of employment."
2. It should cover the use of union security arrangements, such as the union or agency shop.
3. It should include or allow for a grievance procedure, ideally ending in arbitration.
4. It should spell out impasse procedures, such as mediation, fact finding, and even interest arbitration.
5. It should cover the legal status of strikes.
6. It should list the unfair labor practices of employers and unions/employee organizations.
7. It should have some administrative apparatus, like a Public Employment Relations Board (PERB), akin to the NLRB, to oversee the law.

Procedures to Resolve Impasses

Negotiating impasses create special problems in the public sector, especially in the area of protective services where work stoppages normally cannot be tolerated. A variety of methods are used to resolve these types of disputes. However, particular to this sector are two methods: fact finding and interest arbitration, both conventional and final-offer arbitration. Since these methods were discussed in Chapter 12, they will only be briefly reviewed here.

Fact finding is a procedure in which a neutral party or board hears opposing testimony to ascertain the facts of the dispute. The fact finder(s) then makes a public report detailing these facts. In some cases, the neutral agent will also issue a recommendation to settle the dispute. Because of the public nature of fact finding, pressure is placed on the parties, especially the one that the facts seem to imply is in the wrong, to settle the dispute. Fact finding is supposed to be a neutral procedure, but it can be, and has been, used politically.

Interest arbitration, in contrast to rights arbitration, revolves around disputes concerning the terms of a contract. Again, a neutral party, an arbitrator, hears the evidence, but the arbitrator's decision, based on this evidence, is binding. Some states require such settlements whereas others do not. Interest arbitration is the most common dispute resolution mechanism utilized when strikes are illegal.

When first used, interest arbitration borrowed from the older use of arbitration in labor–management relations: rights (grievance) arbitration. Under **conventional arbitration,** an arbitrator fashions a solution. In the newer form of interest arbitration, **final offer arbitration,** the arbitrator chooses one of the final offers made by the parties. It is all or nothing for each party. A variation of this form allows the arbitrator to pick and choose parts of the different parties' offers on an issue-by-issue basis. The arbitrator can thereby make a new final offer composed of bits and pieces of each party's offer, rather than having to choose one whole final offer package.

California Laws—An Example

As mentioned earlier, each state has its own laws governing public sector labor relations. California, being the largest and one of the more progressive states, will serve as a good example of the legal framework for labor–management relations at the state and local level.

California has five major public sector bargaining laws that regulate public employee bargaining rights. These are known as the George Brown Act, the Meyers–Milias–Brown Act, the Rodda Act, the State Employer–Employee Relations Act (SEERA), and the Higher Education Employer–Employee Relations Act (HEERA). Table 15.2 summarizes the essence of these five statutes. These acts cover a variety of state and local employers and employees. There are also local laws, including ordinances in Los Angeles and San Francisco that will be noted below. The laws and applications are closely interrelated.

The George Brown Act

Coverage   The **George Brown Act,** enacted in 1961, is the oldest of the California public sector labor laws, and covers a wide variety of state workers.[10] These include employees in the Legislative Counsel Bureau, the Department of Personnel Administration, the Public Employment Relations Board (PERB), the State Personnel Board (nonclerical employees), and the State Conciliation Service of the Department of Industrial Relations (conciliators). Certain state employees are excluded from coverage, such as civil service employees, elected and appointed officials, employees of the state universities covered by the Higher Education Employer-Employee Relations Act (HEERA), and those covered by the State Employer–Employee Relations Act (SEERA).

Scope of Bargaining The George Brown Act governs labor relations between the state and many of its employees. The act defines and allows the formation of employee organizations or unions. An interesting and fairly unique feature of the act is that there is no exclusive representative, even if majority support for one union exists. Thus, many such organizations representing different groups can be found within an agency or department.

The act, like all the others that were enacted after it, requires the state as employer to **meet and confer** with employee organization representatives upon request. However, this act is not a traditional bargaining statute in that it does not require the parties to negotiate a collective bargaining agreement (usually referred to as a **memorandum of understanding** in public sector labor relations).[11] All the Brown Act says is that an employee may belong to a union that may negotiate on wages and employment conditions. The act does not require management to reach agreement. The representative of the employee organization may attend grievance and disciplinary hearings/interviews, notice of which the employer must give to the representative.

The Meyers–Milias–Brown Act

The **Meyers–Milias–Brown (MMB) Act** focuses on labor–management relations between local public employers and their employees. It covers most local districts (except schools) in negotiations over wages, hours, and other terms and conditions of employment. The MMB Act specifically calls for better communication between employers and workers.[12]

Coverage MMB applies to the public employees of any local public agency, including fire department employees. Under the act, the employees have the right to form, join, and/or participate in a labor organization. They may also choose to refrain from becoming involved and represent themselves individually in their employment relations.

Professional employees may join employee organizations that are separate from nonprofessional employees. For example, attorneys working for a local public agency, such as a county recorder's office, cannot join a nonprofessional employees organization. Even management and confidential employees may organize; a confidential employee is one who develops or presents management's position on labor issues and/or has access to confidential personnel information used in developing management policies. However, management and confidential employee organizations are prohibited from representing other employees. They must be in separate bargaining units and employee organizations.

If there are no local rules to resolve disputes on appropriate unit representation, the dispute may be submitted to the Division of Conciliation of the Department of Industrial Relations. The division is charged with resolving these bargaining unit disputes.

Scope of Bargaining Similar to the other California public sector bargaining laws, the "scope of representation" includes wages, hours, and other terms and conditions of employment. In 1981, MMB was amended to allow the negotiation of an agency shop security clause. The exclusive or majority bargaining agent represents

Table 15.2 *The Five Major California Public Sector Labor Laws*

	Coverage	Duty to Bargain
George Brown Act	State employees (excluding employees elected by popular vote, appointed by the governor, under civil service, covered by HEERA, and determined to be managerial or confidential under SEERA)	There is a duty to meet and confer in good faith; agreement (a memorandum of understanding) need not be reached
Meyers–Milias–Brown Act	Municipal and most local agency employees (excluding employees of school districts, of some transit districts, and elected or appointed by the governor); fire departments and fire services of counties, cities, and other areas are also covered by special "fire" legislation	There is a duty to meet and confer in good faith; any agreement must be finalized before the agency's budget is adopted; further, no agreement is finalized until approved by the agency head
Rodda Act	Educational employees through the community college level; covers certificated and classified employees (excluding employees elected or appointed by the governor, and determined to be managerial or confidential)	There is a duty to meet and confer in good faith with the exclusive representative; any agreement must be concluded before adoption of a final budget
SEERA (State Employer–Employee Relations Act)	All civil service employees of the state (excluding employees that are managerial, confidential, and work for PERB and other state industrial relations agencies)	There is a duty to meet and confer in good faith with the duly recognized employee organization; any agreement must be concluded before adoption of a budget (the George Brown Act applies until there is a duly recognized employee organization)
HEERA (Higher Education Employer–Employee Relations Act)	Employees of the University of California, Hastings College of Law, and the California State University and Colleges	There is a duty to meet and confer in good faith; any agreement, if reached, must be in the form of a written memo of understanding presented to the employer; if the agreement is not funded, the nonbudgetary issues are still effective; student representatives can attend meetings and present thoughts

Sources: Cal. Gov. Code §3525 *et seq.*, §3500 *et seq.*, §3540 *et seq.*, §3512 *et seq.*, and §3560 *et seq.*

Bargaining Subjects	Dispute Resolution
Wages, hours, and other terms and conditions of employment as in the NLRA/LMRA	None
Wages, hours, and other terms and conditions of employment as in the NLRA/LMRA	The parties can mutually agree to appoint a mediator if they fail to reach an agreement; costs are equally shared; no provision for fact finding or arbitration
Wages, hours, and other terms and conditions of employment including transfer and reassignment policies, class size, procedures to be used in the evaluation of employees, course content, and choice of textbooks	An impasse procedure provides for mediation and fact finding, with PERB paying the costs: if the mediator can't resolve the dispute, he/she then can call for fact finding
Wages, hours, and other terms and conditions of employment	An impasse procedure provides for mediation; no arbitration or fact finding is provided for
Wages, hours, and other terms and conditions of employment excluding procedures for appointment, promotion and tenure, and requirements for student admission and graduation	Mediation and fact-finding procedures available through PERB

all the employees in the bargaining unit. Since the agency shop provision was allowed, all unit employees lend some financial support to their exclusive bargaining agent. However, if an employee is a member of a religious group that has objections to union membership or union activities, the employee is required to pay fees equivalent to dues of the union to a charitable fund from among those listed in the memorandum of understanding.

The public agency and the employee organization have a mutual obligation to meet and confer in "good faith." Any agreement reached must be concluded before the agency adopts the final budget for the coming year. This agreement, or memorandum of understanding, becomes binding when the governing body, such as a city council, or its appointed representative, such as a city manager, approves it.

The public agency employer has a duty to notify all employee organizations, in writing, of any proposed local law that may have an impact on employee rights. This is done prior to any adoption of such a law in order to provide an opportunity for comments before its enactment. In emergency situations, the opportunity for notice and comments is provided for after enactment.

Impasse Resolution   In the event agreement cannot be reached, the parties can mutually consent to have a mediator come in and attempt to resolve the impasse. Costs are shared equally by the agency and the employee organization.

MMB fails to provide any impasse provisions or the right to strike. Before 1985, it was believed that the right to strike was prohibited. However, by court decision, employees were given this right.

The Educational Employment Relations Act (Rodda Act)

Coverage   The **Rodda Act** (**Educational Employment Relations Act**) provides public school employees at the elementary through community college levels with a comprehensive system for labor relations.[13] The act covers all certificated (i.e., those holding California state teaching certificates) and classified (e.g., secretaries, teachers' aides, bus drivers) employees.

Management, confidential employees, those appointed by the governor, and elected officials, as defined in the act, are excluded from coverage. According to the law, persons acting in managerial or confidential positions may, on personnel matters, represent themselves or be represented by a union composed only of similar individuals.

Scope of Bargaining   An employee organization's (union's) representative may request a meeting to discuss issues or negotiate. Once this request is made, the employer and the employee organization have a duty to meet and confer on matters delineated in the Rodda Act. If a matter is not specifically enumerated, the employer is not required to meet and negotiate. The employer, however, may choose to discuss matters outside the scope of the act.

The subject matter of collective bargaining encompasses the familiar areas of wages, hours, and other terms and conditions of employment, such as health and welfare benefits, leave, transfer, reassignment, and similar issues. Union security is another mandatory subject of negotiation. The Rodda Act stipulates that the employer and the employee organization must agree on a union security arrangement. This can be done by voluntary recognition or elections. The employer can require members of the organization to vote separately on the security provision in an agreement. If approved, after 12 months it can be rescinded if a majority of the members vote for rescission.

The exclusive representative of the certificated personnel also has the "right to consult on the definition of educational objectives," the content of courses, and selection of books.[14] Causes and procedures for disciplinary action, layoffs of certificated employees owing to lack of funds, and payment of additional compensation (not based on training or years of service) are subject to negotiations. However, if agreement is not reached, the appropriate sections of the educational code apply.

The Public Employment Relations Board   The Rodda Act provides for a **Public Employment Relations Board (PERB)**, a body that helps administer the application of the law. For example, if the parties execute an exclusive representative agreement, PERB Rule 32120 requires that a copy of the agreement be filed within 60 days with the board.

The Rodda Act includes both employer and employee unfair labor practices (See Table 15.3). PERB hears and rules on these practices.

Although PERB may rely on decisions made by the National Labor Relations Board (NLRB), the Rodda Act does not require that PERB follow such decisions. However, the California courts have relied on NLRB precedence in the interpretation of California statutory language which is the same or similar to that in the NLRA/LMRA.[15]

Table 15.3   *Unfair Labor Practices Under the Rodda Act*

Employer Unfair Labor Practices

1. Interference with the rights of employees to form, join, and/or participate in an employee organization for the purpose of collective action, or not to engage in these activities
2. Denial to employee organizations rights guaranteed to them under this law
3. Refusal to meet and negotiate in good faith with the exclusive representative of the employees
4. Domination or interference with the formation or administration of any employee organization or contribution of financial or other support to it
5. Refusal to participate in good faith in the impasse procedures under this law

Employee Organization Unfair Labor Practices

1. Causing an employer to commit an unfair labor practice
2. Interference with the rights of employees to form, join, and/or participate in an employee organization for the purpose of collective action, or not to engage in these activities
3. Refusal to meet and negotiate in good faith with the public school employer of the employees it represents
4. Refusal to participate in good faith in the impasse procedures under this law

Source: Rodda Act, Cal. Gov. Code §3543.5 and 3543.6.

The State Employer–Employee Relations Act (SEERA)

Coverage   The **State Employer–Employee Relations Act (SEERA)** applies to most California State civil service employees.[16] Supervisory personnel may organize, but they must comply with certain procedures. Excluded are managerial and confidential employees as well as PERB employees and certain other state personnel.

SEERA allows employees to form, join, and participate in a labor organization, or choose not to engage in these activities. An individual may elect to negotiate on his or her own behalf. SEERA, however, is unique in the sense that if there is no recognized employee organization, that is, if no organization wins a representation election, SEERA does not apply. The George Brown Act would be applicable in this situation. If, on the other hand, there is a recognized employee organization, SEERA comes into play.

A recognized employee organization is the exclusive representative in an appropriate bargaining unit, and only it can represent the unit. In order to become a recognized employee organization, certain steps adopted by PERB must be met.[17] When these conditions are met, PERB orders an election after issuing proper notice to the parties and the public. If another employee organization presents a representation claim, it must have at least 30 percent support in a unit. There are many other rules covering elections for recognition or certification as well as decertification.

Scope of Bargaining   The typical wages, hours, and other terms and conditions of employment are the subject matter for negotiations. Grievance procedures need not be bargained over, as they exist under state law. No specific provision allows employee organizations to participate in these procedures, but individuals may use the services of the employee organization to represent them, or they may represent themselves.

Other Matters   SEERA has a mediation provision in the event the parties cannot reach an agreement. However, it makes no provision for fact finding or arbitration.

SEERA requires that public meetings be held on all the initial "meet and confer" proposals. However, there are rules to protect sensitive materials and emergency situations where an open public hearing and record may not be desirable or possible. A deadline is set for bargaining: it must be completed before the state adopts the final budget for the next year. The collective bargaining agreement is then submitted in writing to the legislature for debate and approval. Negotiations can be resumed if the legislature fails to approve the proposal.

The Higher Education Employer–Employee Relations Act (HEERA)

Coverage   The **Higher Education Employer–Employee Relations Act (HEERA)** gave the employees at the University of California, the California state universities and colleges, and Hastings College of Law the opportunity to organize for the purpose of collective bargaining, or to refrain from such.[18] Confidential, managerial, and most student employees are exempt from coverage. Covered employees may choose employee organizations to represent them for the purpose of meeting and conferring on matters of employee relations, including wages, hours, and organizational (union) security. Appointment, evaluation for promotion, tenure and retention, and grievance procedures, all of which are provided for by state law, are excluded.

The act defines an employee organization as follows:

> "Employee organization" means any organization of any kind in which higher education employees participate and which exists for the purpose, in whole or in part, of dealing with higher education employers concerning...labor disputes, wages, hours, and other terms and conditions of employment of employees. Employee organization shall also include any person such an organization authorizes to act on its behalf. An academic senate, or other similar academic bodies, or divisions thereof, shall not be considered employee organizations for the purposes of this chapter.[19]

Certification   To become the exclusive representative, the employee organization files a written request with the employer stating that a majority of employees in a bargaining unit desire its representation. Proof of majority support must be filed with the Public Employment Relations Board. The organization can seek recognition from PERB by presenting proof of majority support without first petitioning the higher education employer.

The higher education employer may grant the request unless there is a competing claim by another organization which has filed a request within 15 days of the original recognition filing. There must be proof of at least 10 percent support for the competing organization before either a hearing or an election is held. PERB conducts secret ballot representation elections with the choice of "no representation" always included on the ballot.

Collective Bargaining   Employees, including supervisors, have the right to participate in employee organizations for the purpose of meeting and conferring with their employer. The employer is required to meet and confer in good faith at reasonable times with the exclusive representative. Budgetary issues can be discussed. When agreement is reached, it is written as a memorandum of understanding. If the agreement is not fully funded by the legislature, the nonbudgetary provisions are still binding.

If the parties cannot agree, either party can declare an impasse. Mediation and fact finding are available at that time. A mediator is given 15 days to settle an impasse. If unsuccessful, but the mediator believes fact finding to be of value, either party within five days of written notification from the mediator can request submission of their differences to a fact-finding panel. The panel then meets with the parties and collects and takes testimony. If after 30 days the issues are not resolved, or an extension is given, the panel must recommend a settlement which is only advisory. The recommendation may be made public after ten days of review by the parties.

A unique feature of HEERA is the fact that a student representative is designated to be present at all meet and confer sessions. The student, like all parties to the negotiations, must respect the confidential nature of the process.

Los Angeles County Ordinance No. 9646

Los Angeles County Ordinance No. 9646 covers labor relations with the county's employees.[20] Other laws also apply to some county employees, such as the Meyers–Milias–Brown Act and the Rodda Act for employees of school districts. Furthermore, employees of some transit districts may be governed by special legislation.

This ordinance permits employees to form, join, and/or participate in unions, or to refuse to engage in these activities. County workers or their representatives are permitted to meet and confer with employers on wages, hours, and other terms and conditions of employment.

The ordinance established the Employee Relations Commission which was given the responsibility to make unit determinations and to hear charges of violations of the ordinance's unfair labor practices. The list is similar to that in the Rodda Act (see Table 15.3). To settle impasses, mediation and arbitration are used. The parties involved share the costs equally.

Los Angeles City Ordinance No. 141,527

Los Angeles City Ordinance No. 141,527 governs the labor-management relations of the city's municipal employees. The purpose of the law is to "establish policies and procedures for the administration of employer–employee relations in City government, the formal recognition of employee organizations and the resolution of disputes regarding wages, hours and other terms and conditions of employment."[21] Employees can meet and confer with the city over the issues noted either individually or collectively through employee organizations.

The ordinance provides, among other things, the following: a procedure for mediation and fact finding when an impasse is reached, with costs shared equally by both parties; a list of unfair labor practices similar to that found in other statutes, such as the Rodda Act (see Table 15.3); and an Employee Relations Board to administer the ordinance—for example, to make unit determinations and hear unfair labor practice charges.

San Francisco City and County Employee Relations Ordinance 313–76

San Francisco City and County Employee Relations Ordinance 313–76 was enacted "to promote full communications between the city and county of San Francisco and its employees by providing a reasonable method of resolving disputes between the city and county and its employees and their employee organizations."[22] Similar to other California labor relations laws, the ordinance provides that employees may form and join labor organizations, or refuse to engage in such activities.

The ordinance spells out union and employer unfair labor practices. A City and County Municipal Employees Relations Panel has been established to administer it, and, for example, to help in bargaining unit determinations and to hear unfair labor practice charges.

A strike is treated as a union unfair labor practice, as it is in the federal government. To handle negotiating impasses, mediation and fact-finding procedures have been established. When utilized, both parties share the costs equally.

Fire Fighters

California is unique among the states in that it has so many laws that attempt to protect public sector employee rights. However, not only are some employees regulated by multiple laws, but also specialized laws are specifically enacted for them, such as those referring to fire fighters and fire services of the state, and its counties, cities, and other subdivisions.[23]

Under these specialized laws, fire fighters are permitted to form unions and participate in collective bargaining activities. They can even present grievances, but there is no right to arbitration. They cannot strike or recognize a picket line while in the line of duty.

THE RIGHT OF PUBLIC EMPLOYEES TO STRIKE

Traditionally, the common law required that the sovereign state grant authority to its employees before a strike since such activity could undermine the government, give employees excessive bargaining power, threaten the public health, safety, and welfare, and/or serve no legitimate interest.

Federal Employees: Without the Right to Strike

Clearly, the Kennedy and Nixon executive orders and the Civil Service Reform Act prohibited strikes and slowdowns by federal employees, but did not completely eliminate all work stoppages. Among such stoppages were postal workers' strikes, the last held in 1969, and early work slowdowns and stoppages by the Professional Air Traffic Controllers Organization (PATCO)—in six instances from 1968 to 1980.[24] The PATCO strike of 1981 did, however, halt any further consideration of such activity by federal employees.

In the PATCO case, the air traffic controllers, out on strike, refused to return to work after being given a 48-hour warning to do so or be fired. President Reagan fired 11,310 nonreturning controllers.[25] The union violated the law and lost its certification; the court upheld the decertification. It was a major shock for unionism, both in the public and the private sector. The PATCO dispute is discussed in detail in Chapter 16.

The State and Local Government Employees' Right to Strike

Although many state and local public sector employees are prohibited by law from striking, strikes are allowed in twelve states. In three states, court decisions rather than statutes have supported the right to strike. Montana, Idaho, and California each have different rationales supporting the right to strike.[26] In California, the court stated in part, "We must immediately caution, however, that the right of public employees to strike is by no means unlimited. Prudence and concern for the general public welfare require certain restrictions."[27] This case is summarized next.

The Workers Can Strike, and That's No Garbage

County Sanitation District No. 2 of Los Angeles County v. Los Angeles County Employees Association, Local 660
699 P. 2d 835 (CA 1985)

Facts   The defendant union was the certified bargaining representative of the blue collar employees of the Los Angeles Sanitation District. The plaintiff is one of Los Angeles's 27 sanitation districts. From 1973 until the time of this dispute, the parties had negotiated pursuant to the Meyers–Milias–Brown Act (MMBA). Approximately 75 percent of the District's employees went out on strike on July 5, 1976 after negotiations for a new collective bargaining agreement (memorandum of understanding) reached an impasse.

The District asked the court for an injunction and damages. The court granted a temporary restraining order. However, the strike continued for 11 more days, at which point the employees accepted a new memorandum of understanding, based on terms identical to those presented by the District prior to the strike.

The District then sought relief in court for money damages due to the illegal strike. The trial court awarded the District $246,904 in compensatory damages, $87,615.22 for pre-judgement interest and costs of $874.65. The union appealed to the Supreme Court of California.

Court Discussion   Common law decisions in other jurisdictions at one time held that no employee, whether public or private, had a right to strike in concert with fellow workers. In fact, such collective action was generally viewed as a conspiracy and held subject to both civil and criminal sanctions. Over the course of the 20th century, however, courts and legislatures gradually acted to change these laws as they applied to private sector employees; today, the right to strike is generally accepted as indispensable to the system of...labor–management relations in the private sector.

By contrast, American law continues to regard public sector strikes in a substantially different manner. A strike by employees of the United States government may still be treated as a crime, and strikes by state and local employees have been explicitly allowed by courts or statute in only 11 states...this court has repeatedly stated that the legality of strikes by public employees in California has remained an open question....

On its face, the MMBA neither denies nor grants local employees the right to strike. This omission is noteworthy since the Legislature has not hesitated to expressly prohibit strikes for certain classes of public employees...the absence of any such limitations on other public employees covered by the MMBA at the very least implies a lack of legislative intent to use the MMBA to enact a general strike prohibition....

As noted above, the Court of Appeals and various lower courts in this and other jurisdictions have repeatedly stated that, absent a specific statutory grant, all strikes by public employees are *per se* illegal....The various justifications for the common law prohibition can be summarized into four basic arguments. First—the traditional justification—that a strike by public employees is tantamount to a denial of governmental authority/sovereignty. Second, the terms of public employment are not subject to bilateral collective bargaining, as in the private sector, because they are set by the legislative body through unilateral lawmaking. Third, since legislative bodies are responsible for public employment decision making, granting public employees the right to strike would afford them excessive bargaining leverage, resulting in a distortion of the political process and an improper delegation of legislative authority. Finally, public employees provide essential public services which, if interrupted by strikes, would threaten the public welfare.

Our determination of the legality of strikes by public employees necessarily involves an analysis of the reasoning and current viability of each of these arguments....We conclude that the common law prohibition against public sector strikes should not be recognized in this state. Consequently, strikes by public sector employees in this state as such are neither illegal nor tortious under California common law. We must immediately caution, however, that the right of public employees to strike is by no means unlimited. Prudence and concern for the general public welfare require certain restrictions.

The Legislature has already prohibited strikes by fire fighters under any circumstance. It may conclude that other categories of public employees perform such essential services that a strike would invariably result in imminent danger to public health and safety, and must therefore be prohibited....Several statutes provide for injunctive relief against other types of striking public employees when the state clearly demonstrates that the continuation of such strikes will constitute an imminent threat or "clear and present danger" to public health and safety. Such an approach guarantees that essential public services will not be disrupted so as to genuinely threaten public health and safety, while also preserving the basic rights of public employees.

After consideration of the various alternatives before us, we believe the following standard may properly guide courts in the resolution of future disputes in this area: strikes by public employees are not unlawful at common law unless or until it is clearly demonstrated that such a strike creates a substantial and imminent threat to the health or safety of the public. This standard allows exceptions in certain essential areas of public employment (e.g., the prohibition against fire fighters and law enforcement personnel) and also requires the courts to determine on a case-by-case basis whether the public interest overrides the basic right to strike. [Further]... the close connection between striking and other constitutionally protected activity adds further weight to our rejection of the traditional common law rationales underlying the *per se* prohibition....

We conclude that it is not unlawful for public employees to engage in a concerted work stoppage for the purpose of improving their wages or conditions of employment, unless it has been determined that the work stoppage poses an imminent threat to public health or safety. Since the trial court's judgment for damage in this case was predicated upon an erroneous determination that defendants' strike was unlawful, the judgement for damages cannot be sustained.

The judgment is reversed.

This case allows strikes by public employees in California, providing such strikes would not endanger public health or safety, as a strike of police or fire fighters would.

EMERGING TRENDS

During the last few years the courts have altered their opinions regarding the rights of public sector employees. The area of privacy, primarily drug testing, has been particularly interesting, and significant decisions regarding wrongful discharge and free speech have been given. Many states have also passed laws regarding the rights of public sector employees.

Drug Testing

As mentioned in Chapter 3, the U.S. Supreme Court's recent decision, *Skinner v. Railway Labor Executives (1989)*, gave a boost to the federal government's campaign to promote a drug-free workplace.[28] The Supreme Court upheld federal regulations requiring drug and alcohol testing for railroad workers after the occurrence of accidents or major work-related incidents, such as shunting cars down the wrong track.

The Supreme Court also held, in *National Treasury Employees v. Von Raab (1989)*, that drug testing can be conducted on Customs Service employees in certain job categories.[29] The Court felt that use of controlled substances by Customs Service employees engaged in enforcement would seriously frustrate efforts to stop drug trafficking and the application of the drug laws.

On the state level, cases have established that government-imposed blood tests to check for drug and alcohol use are not undue intrusions on an individual's privacy. One example of such a case was *Schmerber v. California (1986)*.[30]

A number of other cases have reviewed the type of employees that can be subjected to this testing. For example, in *McDonell v. Hunter (1987)*, it was held that employees at a medium or maximum security prison may be subject to random testing.[31] The case further stated that reasonable suspicion standards must be adopted prior to performing any strip searches of correctional officers at prisons. In another case, *Kirkpatrick v. City of Los Angeles (1986)*, it was also held that prior to strip searches, in this case of police officers, a reasonable suspicion must exist that evidence will be found.[32]

In 1988, Nebraska, Kansas, and Tennessee passed testing laws for certain government officials. Thus, it appears that public employees who hold sensitive jobs, where the public safety may be at stake, may be losing some rights. They probably cannot collectively bargain over these issues, as the courts seem to be mandating these procedures that infringe on their privacy rights.

Wrongful Discharge

Wrongful discharge is another area in which employee rights seem to be undergoing major change. A variety of theories have been proposed to deal with employment termination, such an implied-in-fact (implied from the facts) or expressed contract theory (oral or written agreement), public policy theory (society's expectations), tort doctrines (civil wrongs), or the theory of breach of the covenant of good faith and fair dealings.

Courts have applied the **theory of breach of a covenant of good faith and fair dealings** to contested termination in the public sector.[33] In California decisions, the courts have held that the plaintiff, the discharged employee, is required to show a bad faith act by the employer aimed at depriving the employee of contractual rights. For example, if an employer terminates an employee to avoid paying a bonus or to avoid paying retirement benefits, then the court will find wrongful discharge. The plaintiff, the employee, bears the burden of proving the wrongful termination.

If the employer establishes that there is a reasonable basis for the termination, the employee must prove that it is a pretext for the real reason for dismissal. It is difficult for a discharged employee to win such a case in the state of California.

Many of the problems in California revolve around procedural issues. All public employees are required to exhaust their administrative remedies prior to suit.[34] To have an unfavorable administrative decision overturned, they must first file a *writ of mandamus*—a pleading filed with the court demanding that the public employer act or refrain from a particular act in question, or restore the employee's rights or privileges that have been illegally withdrawn. Only after the writ is acted on can a lawsuit be pursued in the courts.[35]

Free Speech

The Supreme Court has traditionally upheld the right of free speech, and it did so again in the case of *Rankin v. McPherson (1987)*.[36] Surprisingly, however, this was a 5 to 4 decision, thus barely upholding this basic constitutional right.

The case was based on the firing of a clerical employee in a county constable's office because of a statement she had made to her associates. She was not a commissioned police officer, did not wear a uniform or carry a gun, and did not have contact with the public as part of her job. While discussing the attempted assassination of President Reagan, she commented that if someone goes for him again, "I hope they get him."

She was fired for making the remark, and she sued. Although she did finally win the case, the four dissenters thought that her expression of violence was inappropriate for her position in a law enforcement agency. The majority felt that the speech was protected and did not affect the officer's ability to function. Clearly, the trend to limit public employees' rights is lurking just below the surface in the judiciary.

DISCUSSION QUESTIONS

1. Why do you think union membership in the public sector is more than twice that in the private sector? What characteristics of government employees make them likely to unionize?

2. Why do you think local union leaders play a larger role in public sector unions than in private sector unions?

3. How did Executive Order 11491 correct the perceived problems of Executive Order 10988?

4. Choose one public sector labor relations law from this chapter and describe which features correspond to the seven points of the public sector labor relations law model given in this chapter.

5. Why are fact finding and interest arbitration more common means of resolving disputes in the public sector than in the private sector? What characteristics of each method make it more useful in the public sector?

6. For each of the five California laws discussed in this chapter, give the specified legal duties of the employer and the employee organization.

7. What did the Supreme Court of California decide was the determining factor in deciding whether or not a strike by public employees was unlawful? On what grounds did the court cast down the common law notion that public sector strikes were per se illegal?

8. Do federal, state, and local employees have the legal right to strike? Discuss.

VOCABULARY LIST

Pendleton Act (Civil Service Act)

gag rules

Lloyd–La Follette Act

Executive Order 10988

exclusive recognition

formal recognition

informal recognition

Executive Order 11491

Federal Labor Relations Council (FLRC)

Federal Services Impasses Panel (FSIP)

Postal Reorganization Act

Civil Service Reform Act of 1978 (CSRA)

Federal Labor Relations Authority (FLRA)

fact finding

interest arbitration

conventional arbitration

final offer arbitration

George Brown Act

meet and confer

memorandum of understanding

Meyers-Milias-Brown (MMB) Act

Rodda Act (Educational Employment Relations Act)

Public Employment Relations Board (PERB)

State Employer–Employee Relations Act (SEERA)

Higher Education Employer–Employee Relations Act (HEERA)

theory of breach of covenant of good faith and fair dealings

FOOTNOTES

1. James L. Stern, "Unionism in the Public Sector," in Benjamin Aaron, Joyce M. Najita, and James L. Stern, *Public-Sector Bargaining*, Industrial Relations Research Association Series, Bureau of National Affairs (1988), p. 52.

2. Ron Carver, a union corporate campaign organizer for the United Electrical, Radio and Machine Workers and Industrial Union Department, AFL–CIO, at Bay Area Labor Studies Seminar, Institute of Industrial Relations, University of California, Berkeley (May 9, 1989).

3. U.S. Department of Labor, BLS *Bulletin 90–59*, February 7, 1990, Table 2.

4. Executive Order No. 10988, 5 U.S.C.A. §7101 at 4 (1962).

5. Executive Order No. 11491, 5 U.S.C.A. §7301 at 65 (1969).

6. 39 U.S.C. §1200 *et seq.* (1970).

7. Public Law No. 95–454, 5 U.S.C. §7101 *et seq.*

8. 5 U.S.C. §7103 (a)(14) (1978).

9. 5 U.S.C. §5596(b)(1)(A)(i) (1978).

10. Cal. Gov. Code §3525–3536.

11. Commerce Clearing House, *Public Employee Bargaining*, Vol. 1, California, Par. 405, p. 933.

12. Cal. Gov. Code §3500–3510.

13. Cal. Gov. Code §3540–3549.

14. Cal. Gov. Code §3542.

15. Commerce Clearing House, Par. 600, p. 1712.

16. Cal. Gov. Code §3512–3524.

17. Public Employment Relations Board, Rule 40310.

18. Cal. Gov. Code §3560 *et seq.*

19. Cal. Gov. Code §3562.

20. Los Angeles County Ordinance No. 9646.

21. Los Angeles Administrative Code, 4.800, Division 4, Chapt. 8 (2–2–71), Ordinance 4.800–4.890.

22. San Francisco Administrative Code Sections 16.200–16.222, Chapter 16, Article XI.A, enacted as Ordinance 313–76 (July 30, 1976).

23. Cal. Labor Code §1960–1963.

24. Herbert R. Northrup, "The Rise and Demise of PATCO," *Industrial and Labor Relations Review* (January 1984): 168–169.

25. Ibid., p. 178.

26. *Montana v. Public Employees Craft Council*, 529 P. 2d 785 (1974); *Fire Fighters Local 1494 v. City of Coeur D'Alene*, 100 LRRM 2079 (1978); *County Sanitation District No. 2 of Los Angeles County v. Local 660*, 38 Cal. 3rd 564, 699 P. 2d 835, 214 Cal. Rep. 424, Cert. denied, 106 S. Ct. 408 (1985).

27. Ibid.

28. *Skinner v. Railway Labor Executives' Association*, 109 S. Ct. 1402, 104 L.Ed. 2d 250 (1989).

29. *National Treasury Employees v. Von Raab*, 816 F. 2d 170 (5th Cir. 1987), *Cert. granted*, 483 U.S. 378, 107 S. Ct. 1384 (1989).

30. 384 U.S. 757 (1986).

31. 809 F.2d 1302 (8th Cir. 1987).

32. 803 F.2d 845 (9th Cir. 1986).

33. *Apte v. Regents of the University of California*, 198 Cal. App. 3d 1084 (1988); *Read v. City of Lynnwood*, 173 Cal. App. 3d 437 (1985); *Walter v. North San Diego City Hospital District*, 135 Cal. App. 3d 896 (1982).

34. *Knickerboker v. City of Stockton*, 199 Cal. App. 3d 235, 88 C.D.O.S. 1571 (1988).

35. *City of Fresno v. Superior Court*, 188 Cal. App. 3d 1484 (1987).

36. *Rankin v. McPherson*, 483 U.S. 378 (1987).

REFERENCES

BURTON, JOHN F., JR., and TERRY THOMASON. "The Extent of Collective Bargaining in the Public Sector." In Benjamin Aaron, Joyce M. Najita, and James L. Stern, *Public-Sector Bargaining*. Industrial Relations Research Association Series, Bureau of National Affairs, 1988, pp. 1–51.

COMMERCE CLEARING HOUSE. *Guidebook to Fair Employment Practices.* 1989.

———. *Guidebook to Labor Relations.* 1989, Ch. 16.

———. *Public Employee Bargaining.* Vol. 1 (California), 1983.

DERBER, MILTON. "Management Organization for Collective Bargaining in the Public Sector." In Aaron, Najita, and Stern, *Public-Sector Bargaining*, pp. 90–123.

LEIBIG, MICHAEL, and WENDY L. KAHN. *Public Employee Organizing and the Law.* Bureau of National Affairs, 1987.

NORTHRUP, HERBERT R. "The Rise and Demise of PATCO." *Industrial and Labor Relations Review* (January 1984): 167–184.

STERN, JAMES L. "Unionism in the Public Sector." In Aaron, Najita, and Stern, *Public-Sector Bargaining*, pp. 52–89.

CHAPTER 16

PUBLIC SECTOR UNIONISM: THE FEDERAL GOVERNMENT

A s discussed in Chapter 15, unionism in the federal government dates back to the turn of the century, when the major postal unions were organized. However, until the 1960s, no other unions of any size represented other federal employees in significant numbers. The development of unions and union representation in the period from 1960 to the mid-1970s was phenomenal. Within the constraints of laws and executive orders governing labor–management relations and collective bargaining in the federal government, the growth in that period was considered to be one of the most significant developments on the labor front in the preceding 25 years.[1]

The power of unions and employee organizations representing federal government workers is an important and complex issue. Under the rules and regulations that exist, unions in the federal sector face many constraints; however, the political climate has had a major effect on how these constraints have been applied. This concept was most vividly illustrated in the 1981 demise of the air traffic controllers' union for "pushing the wrong button at the wrong time."

Unionism in the federal government operates under a variety of constraints different from those of unionism in the private sector, and the nature of government goals and decision-making processes are different from those in the private sector. Thus, a question related to the power of federal government unionism is that of the difference between public and private sector unionism. We address all these points in this chapter and discuss the last one further in Chapter 17.

THE DEVELOPMENT OF FEDERAL GOVERNMENT UNIONISM

Until 1962, management was, if anything, rather anti-union. Since then, labor relations have gone through two distinct periods. The first, a period of high growth, has been followed by a second, stable period. Both periods have seen changes in the legal framework of federal labor relations, as well as in the political climate.

Labor Relations Prior to 1962: Lack of Activity

Before 1962, labor relations were primarily nonunion (except for the postal service), because of two dominant features of federal employment: (1) a legal framework that left little room in which unions could function, and (2) labor market conditions that were not conducive to union representation.

The Legal Framework

Chapter 15 discussed the legal framework of labor relations in the federal government. Here we will present a brief recap of that discussion and set the stage for the points developed in the rest of the chapter.

The Pendleton Act of 1883, the first step in setting up the **Civil Service Merit System**, gave Congress the sole authority to set wages, hours, and other terms and conditions of employment for federal employees. This encouraged employees to form organizations to lobby Congress to improve wages and working conditions. The newly formed postal unions were especially adept in this area and lobbied Congress quite openly. President Theodore Roosevelt's executive orders, or "gag rules," prohibited this lobbying. In 1912, Congress passed the Lloyd–La Follette Act, once again permitting employee organizations to address their concerns through lobbying.

The 1935 National Labor Relations Act, or Wagner Act, and its amendments, primarily the Taft–Hartley and Landrum–Griffin Acts, specifically exempted public employees from their coverage. So did the Railway Labor Act of 1926, which, because of its specific coverage, was designed for private employers and employees (the railroads and, later, the airlines). Public sector employers were not required to recognize unions or employee labor organizations, or to bargain with them. The scope of collective bargaining remained highly restrictive under the 1883 Pendleton Act. It was not until 1962 that this power was broadened, and the right of federal employees to form and join unions established.

The Labor Market Conditions

A dominant feature of federal employment is its stability, which has tended to give federal workers a sense of security.[2] Secure workers are not good targets for unionization. This characteristic, linked to (1) the legal requirement that wages, hours, and other terms and conditions of employment be set by Congress and not through collective bargaining and (2) the lack of any legal requirement that public employers recognize and bargain with unions or labor organizations, made unionization unlikely.

The makeup of the federal workforce also militated against unionization. Demographically, the composition has proportionately tilted toward women; occupationally, it is tilted toward white-collar workers.[3] It has traditionally been difficult for unions to organize these groups.

In 1959, the AFL–CIO executive council, in discussing the unionization of government workers, noted that "in terms of accepted collective bargaining procedures, government workers have no right beyond the authority to petition Congress—a right available to every citizen."[4]

Labor Relations, 1962 to the Mid-1970s: High Growth

The 1960s brought a major transformation in labor relations in the federal government. The favorable political climate was marked by a major change in the legal framework. The economic climate was marked by some unusual changes which sparked an almost breathtaking growth in public sector unionization. The proportion of nonpostal federal employees represented by unions climbed from 13 percent in 1961 to 60 percent in the mid-1970s.[5]

The Political Climate

The period of rapid growth in **public sector unionism** was highlighted at its start (1962) by President Kennedy's **Executive Order 10988**, giving federal employees the right to form and join unions/labor organizations through which they could negotiate on nonmonetary fringe benefits and nonwage issues.[6] This landmark issuance encouraged public sector union growth at all levels of government. It was the impetus for forming labor organizations for bargaining such as the now defunct Professional Air Traffic Controllers Organization (PATCO), as well as for the rapid growth of others, like the American Federation of Government Employees, AFL–CIO, whose membership rose from 68,000 in 1961 to 290,000 a decade later.[7] A list of the major unions/labor organizations representing federal employees is shown in Table 16.1.

As noted in Chapter 15, the Kennedy Executive Order 10988 was amended by Executive Order 11491, issued in 1969 by President Nixon. The new executive order remedied some problems that had become apparent over the seven years since 10988 was issued, and it led to further growth in federal government employee associations.

The Postal Reorganization Act of 1970 essentially moved labor–management relations in the Postal Service from the public to the private sector. For the most part, the National Labor Relations Act/Labor–Management Relations Act, administered by the NLRB, was to govern labor relations in the Postal Service. This expanded the scope of collective bargaining to wages, hours, and other terms and conditions of employment. However, strikes were still not allowed (interest arbitration was to be used over bargaining impasses), nor were compulsory union membership arrangements permissible. The Postal Reorganization Act had a major impact on the postal unions. It stimulated the formation of the largest postal union, the American Postal Workers Union, from the United Federation of Postal Clerks and four smaller unions (see Table 16.2).[8] It also entered into the ill-fated strategy of PATCO, the air traffic controllers employee organization from 1968 to 1981.

Table 16.1   *Unions/Organizations Representing Federal Employees, 1988*

Union/Employee Organization	Membership
American Federation of Government Employees (AFL–CIO)	180,000
National Treasury Employees Union (Ind.)	65,000
National Federation of Federal Employees (Ind.)	45,000
National Association of Government Employees, Service Employees International Union (AFL–CIO)	50,000
Metal Trades Council (AFL–CIO)	24,000[a]
International Association of Machinists and Aerospace Workers (AFL–CIO)	12,000[a]
National Air Traffic Controllers Association, Marine Engineers Beneficial Association (AFL–CIO)	12,800[b]

Sources: James L. Stern, "Unionism in the Public Sector," in Benjamin Aaron et al., eds., *Public-Sector Bargaining* (Industrial Relations Research Association Series, Bureau of National Affairs, 1988), p. 54, and Sar A. Levitan and Frank Gallo, "Can Employee Associations Negotiate New Growth?," *Monthly Labor Review* (July 1989): 10.

[a] 1985.

[b] 1987, when NATCA was certified (*Wall Street Journal*, June 12, 1987, p. 5).

The Civil Service Reform Act of 1978 (CSRA) did not seem to encourage further unionization of federal employees. It somewhat widened the scope of bargaining, but it retained the ban on compulsory membership (including the agency shop). In essence, the CSRA did not change the nature of labor–management relations in the federal government.

The Reagan administration did change labor–management relations in the federal government, however, and, by example, in the private sector too. As one author noted, "The election of Ronald Reagan in 1980 and his appointment in 1981 of Donald Devine as OPM [Office of Personnel Management] director . . . brought on more than four years of controversy and bitterness unprecedented in federal personnel annals."[9] The president was hostile to the Civil Service Reform Act and government unions, especially militant unions like PATCO. He was also determined to cut the nondefense part of the budget and to privatize many government functions. The deep recession of 1981–1982 exacerbated the Reagan administration's stance.

Table 16.2   *Postal Service Unions, 1983*

Union/Employee Organization	Membership
American Postal Workers Union (AFL–CIO)	226,000
National Association of Letter Carriers (AFL–CIO)	203,000
National Rural Letter Carriers Association (Ind.)	40,000
Post Office Mail Handlers, Laborers' International Union of North America (AFL–CIO)	40,000

Sources: See Table 16.1.

The Economic Conditions

According to Linda Edwards, "The most striking change that coincided with the high growth period in union membership [in the public sector] was the change in the economic environment."[10] In general, economic expansion in the 1960s and early 1970s was vigorous, and public sector growth was even more so. In the private sector, job growth, wage growth, and very low unemployment rates brought some interesting comparisons with a changing public sector.

One of the pre–1962 factors that served as a deterrent to union organizing was the relative stability of employment in the public sector. Between 1961 and 1965, very low levels of inflation and an unemployment rate that dipped below 4 percent made employment as stable in the private sector as in the public. Thus, the attitudes of public employees changed.

The rapid increase in public sector employment saw a growing portion of GNP devoted to the public sector. The expansion in employment attracted a greater proportion of younger and minority group workers, who tended to be more militant in their outlook on labor–management relations.[11] An orientation toward unionization grew.

As the early successes of public sector unions gained the headlines, such as the 1961 New York City teachers' strike, public sector workers drew the attention of private sector unions. Federal employee associations, in an effort to protect their "turf," moved toward collective bargaining and, in essence, became unions.[12] Public sector unions, like the American Federation of Government Employees which was formed in 1932 by the AFL, became more aggressive for the same reasons, even though, as an AFL–CIO union, they were protected by the Federation's "no-raiding" rule.

Labor Relations Since the Mid-1970s: Stability

Since the mid-1970s, federal employee union membership has dropped from a peak of over 40 percent (43.3 percent in 1972) of federal employment to about 37–38 percent.[13] However, over that period postal service unions show membership proportions of 85 to 90 percent. Thus, executive branch unions have a relatively small membership density.

The period of no growth was dominated by the labor relations policy of the Reagan administration. The tone of this policy was clearly set in 1981 when all striking air traffic controllers were fired and their union, PATCO, was decertified.

A relatively new policy of the federal government, the expanded use of temporary help, will further impact federal unions and employee associations. The Office of Personnel Management was immediately attacked by unions representing federal workers, such as the American Federation of Government Employees, for its central role in this policy decision.[14]

Even with the somewhat overt antagonism the administration showed toward federal employees and their unions during the 1980s, federal employment increased in this decade (see Table 16.3). At the same time, the federal government's share of total public employment dropped compared to that of state and local government.

Table 16.3   *Federal Government Employment, 1980–1990*

Year	Civil Employment (millions)	Employment as a Percentage of Total Government (federal, state, local)
1980	2.87	17.7%
1981	2.77	17.3%
1982	2.74	17.3%
1983	2.77	17.5%
1984	2.81	17.5%
1985	2.88	17.6%
1986	2.90	17.4%
1987	2.94	17.3%
1988	2.97	17.1%
1989	2.99	16.9%
1990	3.09	16.9%

Source: Monthly Labor Review (January 1990): Table 20, p. 101, (March 1990): 95, and (February 1991): 71.

THE POWER OF FEDERAL GOVERNMENT UNIONISM

Union power, as discussed in Chapters 6 and 13, is based on the relative costs imposed on union and management in the context of a work stoppage. Chapter 13 also stressed that the strike is the ultimate source of union power. However, strikes and work slowdowns are unlawful in federal labor relations. Federal employee unions and associations must build their power on a footing different from that of private sector unions. Public sector unions operate in two contexts: an economic one marked by collective bargaining and a political one marked by lobbying.

Bargaining Activities

Bargaining at the federal level is governed by Title VII of the **Civil Service Reform Act of 1978**, administered by the three-member **Federal Labor Relations Authority (FLRA)** and its General Counsel. This structure is similar to that of the NLRB in the private sector, but the similarities end there.

The Scope of Bargaining

Unions and employee associations in the federal government cannot bargain over a host of issues. Congress and independent presidential commissions set wages (or salaries) and economic fringe benefits, and the length of the workday (or workweek). However, agency managers do control, to a great extent, work schedules, hours, holiday and overtime pay, merit promotions, and personnel relations on the job.[15] These subjects can be brought to the bargaining table by innovative labor leaders, who can expand the limited scope of issues formally classified as bargainable.

One major area of collective bargaining that is closed to unions and employee associations is that of security clauses. Forms of compulsory membership such as the union shop are expressly prohibited. This prohibition includes the agency shop, a security clause that requires the financial support of the labor organization but not membership (see Chapter 9).

One important area of bargaining is the grievance procedure. Matters such as wages and fringe benefits set by Congress are excluded from the grievance procedure. Thus, grievances focus on nonmonetary issues, including discipline. Grievances not settled by the parties involved are submitted to arbitration. Unlike private sector rights arbitration which is voluntary, final, and binding, arbitration in the federal government is mandatory, and either party may ask the FLRA, as a final authority, to review, and overturn, an arbitration award.

Bargaining Impasses

Negotiating impasses are initially handled by the **Federal Mediation and Conciliation Service (FMCS)**. If the FMCS is not successful in mediating the impasse, it goes before the **Federal Services Impasses Panel (FSIP)**. The FSIP can use a wide variety of tactics to break a deadlock, including binding arbitration. The results of this interest (contract) arbitration, like the rights (grievance) arbitration discussed in the preceding paragraph, are subject to appeal to the FLRA.

Negotiating impasses cannot be settled by striking. Strikes are an unfair labor practice in the federal government (under both the Kennedy and Nixon executive orders and the Civil Service Reform Act). The penalty for a union that promotes, encourages, or engages in a strike, which includes a slowdown or similar concerted efforts to interrupt operations, is decertification. Strikes of federal government workers did, and do, occur. Strikes called by postal unions did not provoke government sanctions such as decertification, but they did play a part in the passage of the Postal Reorganization Act of 1970, which basically "privatized" labor–management relations in the U.S. Postal Service, placing it under the Wagner/Taft–Hartley Acts and the NLRB. Strikes are still forbidden in the Postal Service, but *binding* arbitration is utilized to overcome negotiation impasses.

Another federal government union that was involved in work stoppages was PATCO (the Professional Air Traffic Controllers Organization).[16] PATCO was involved in six work-related actions from 1968 to 1980 that would be classified as interruptions of operations and thus as unfair labor practices under federal regulations. These actions did not provoke the government, the Federal Aviation Administration in this case, into bringing the normal sanctions, decertification and dismissals, against PATCO and its membership. Several controllers were disciplined, and some were even dismissed but they were rehired upon appeal. PATCO itself was disqualified as bargaining agent for a short period (four months) but was reinstated fully. The 1981 strike, however, provoked a different response from the federal government. The Reagan administration fired 11,310 controllers who went out on strike, leaving about 5,100 nonstriking workers on the job. And PATCO was decertified! The setback to unionism in both the public and private sectors was substantial. A signal was sent to organized workers that management was going to be unyielding and that workers would therefore strike at their own risk. The climate for labor–management relations was set at the highest level, the U.S. presidency. A detailed account of PATCO's brief but turbulent history is presented in the case study below.

Federal Unionism Battered

The Rise and Fall of PATCO

The Professional Air Traffic Controllers Organization was founded in January 1968. Under its executive director, the lawyer F. Lee Bailey, it quickly showed a militancy unusual for federal government unions/employee organizations. This militant posture continued under its two presidents, John Leyden (1970–1980) and Robert Poli (1980–1981). Six times over the first twelve years of its existence, PATCO carried out successful strikes and slowdowns, in violation of federal regulations. The seventh job action, the 1981 strike in PATCO's thirteenth year, proved unlucky for the controllers, causing the decertification of the organization and the dismissal of 11,310 of its members.

July 1968   F. Lee Bailey institutes a month-long slowdown, seriously disrupting operations at several key airports. The federal government does *nothing*. PATCO's objectives are attained.

July 1969   PATCO undertakes a three-day slowdown. The FAA suspends 80 controllers (none for more than 15 days). No action is taken against PATCO. PATCO objectives are attained. The government convenes a committee to investigate the FAA–PATCO relationship, which is found to be "poor."

March 1970   PATCO institutes a 20-day sickout, with over 2,000 controllers at key airports participating, causing major air traffic disruptions. Both the Air Transport Association (ATA— the U.S. airlines trade association) and the FAA go to court to force the controllers back to work; ATA gets a permanent injunction against PATCO. The FAA discharges 67 controllers who are subsequently reinstated. The government disqualifies PATCO as a bargaining agent for 126 days. F. Lee Bailey is ousted by the union, and Leyden becomes president of the organization.

July and August 1976   PATCO initiates a series of five-day slowdowns at major airports. The short duration of these actions prevents ATA from going back to court for application of the 1970 permanent injunction, but they are totally effective in disrupting air traffic. The government does nothing. PATCO attains its objectives.

May and June 1978   PATCO calls for slowdowns at major airports. ATA presses the court to apply the 1970 permanent injunction, which is done. The government does nothing, even though the court publicly questions its inaction in the face of PATCO's illegal job actions.

August 1980   Under Poli, PATCO undertakes a slowdown at Chicago's O'Hare Airport for a day. The FAA goes to court for relief but does not find it. No sanctions at all are applied against the organization and its members.

August 1981   PATCO calls a nationwide strike. The Reagan administration, prepared for the union's move, puts its plans into action. Court and FLRA actions are initiated, and, almost immediately after the start of the strike, President Reagan gives the strikers 48 hours to return to work or be fired. After the deadline, 11,300 strikers are fired, and PATCO is decertified.

From the start, PATCO was trying to establish its right to negotiate over the complete range of collective bargaining subjects, including wages. After the 1970 Postal Reorganization Act, it was trying to "privatize" the FAA, as was done with the U.S. Postal Service, and even to go one step further—win the right to strike. Its gambles, in terms of job actions, worked for a dozen years, but an overly militant stance and a correspondingly hard position by management combined to destroy PATCO.

Source: Herbert R. Northrup, "The Rise and Demise of PATCO," *Industrial and Labor Relations Review* (January 1984): 167–184.

Political Activities

Although federal government unions cannot bargain over many subjects, such as wages and fringe benefits, they do have direct access to the "board of directors" (the U.S. Congress) that decides on these matters, as well as to the U.S. president who implements these decisions. **Lobbying** is a powerful tool in the hands of public sector unions.

Lobbying by the postal unions around the turn of the century was so pervasive that President Theodore Roosevelt attempted to stop it with his 1906 gag rule prohibiting the activity. In 1912, the Lloyd–La Follette Act once again allowed federal workers to directly petition Congress in search of higher wages and better working conditions. Lobbying picked up again, pressing individual members of Congress for increased appropriations to raise wages and other economic benefits and to support favorable legislation. The federal unions' strong lobbying in 1961, however, could not get a collective bargaining bill passed and led to President Kennedy's executive order in 1962.

Lobbying by federal unions had been referred to by postal union leaders as collective begging.[17] In the absence of any collective bargaining rights, labor organizations could only implore Congress to improve their members' wages, hours, and other terms and conditions of employment. Within the framework of collective bargaining, however, lobbying can be more focused by a well-organized union speaking for a large number of citizens (as well as workers). With most "other terms and conditions of employment" the subject matter for collective bargaining, federal sector unions can key their lobbying efforts to wages, as well as specific areas of concern such as union security (allowing the agency shop, for example).

IS FEDERAL GOVERNMENT UNIONISM DIFFERENT?

The industrial relations system in the federal government has many specific differences from its counterpart in the private sector: the legal and political framework; the economic environment; and the nature of the "business."[18] However, after taking into account all these important factors, we must still ask, is federal government unionism different from that in the private sector (or should it be)? We explore this question next.

The Legal and Political Framework

Federal sector unions operate under different laws than private sector unions. They also operate within a very different political context. These dissimilarities alone lead us to believe that unionism in the two sectors is very different.

Legal Frameworks Are Not Alike

Private sector unions operate under the National Labor Relations (Wagner) Act and its major amendments, primarily the Labor–Management Relations (Taft–Hartley) Act. Federal government unions, for the most part, are covered by the Civil Service Reform Act (CSRA). Postal unions operate under the NLRA, with one major area excepted: dispute resolution. The Postal Reorganization Act of 1970, which placed much of labor–management relations in the postal service under the NLRA, had very specific dispute resolution procedures since strikes are still forbidden.

Under the NLRA/LMRA, a board (the NLRB) was set up to administer the law, including holding representation elections and hearing unfair labor practice charges. Under the CSRA, a board (the Federal Labor Relations Authority, FLRA) does the same thing. However, under the CSRA, two of the unfair labor practices of unions are (1) carrying on a work stoppage, including a slowdown, and (2) requiring union membership of a worker.

Only under the Taft–Hartley national emergency dispute provisions can strikes in most of the private sector be postponed. This provision has not been used in the last decade, and rarely (only six times) was it employed in the decade prior to that. The Railway Labor Act provides for emergency boards to look into bargaining impasses, thus postponing strikes, but over the last two decades this provision has only been invoked once for airlines (and 41 times for railroads, about half of these being commuter railroads).[19] These provisions only postpone work stoppages, not prevent them.

Furthermore, compulsory unionism is allowed under the NLRA/LMRA. Only in the 21 right-to-work states is it prohibited, and this is due to state law which, by Section 14(b) of the Taft–Hartley, is allowed to preempt federal law. Compulsory unionism is prohibited in the federal government.

The Political Pressures Used by Public Sector Unions

Labor organizations in both the public and private sectors lobby lawmakers in quest of favorable legislation. However, in the federal sector, this lobbying is very highly focused—especially on wages; federal unions, except the postal ones, cannot bargain over wages and fringe benefits. Since Congress sets wages and benefits, lobbying is a necessary adjunct of collective bargaining in the federal government, which is not true in the private sector. Lobbying the employer by private sector unions is nonexistent.

Another difference in the political picture is the ability of public sector unions to make "end runs" around management and bring their case to the public or Congress in hopes of attaining their objectives.[20] Although more prevalent at the local government level, federal unions rally public opinion or legislative backing to put pressure on public managers. The ability to make these end runs is referred to as **multilateral bargaining**; unions bargain through the public and legislators as well as directly with managers.

By targeting key congressional districts, government employee unions can try to exert electoral pressure to persuade lawmakers to increase member wages or to improve member working conditions. They also attempt to induce senators and representatives, and even presidents, to intervene on the side of the unions in negotiations with department and agency management. The public that elects them is a powerful motivating force for these government officeholders. Private unions can only bring public pressure to bear on companies through consumer boycotts, which have not proven to be of great value over the past 50 years (see Chapter 14).

The Economic Environment

The economic environment of public sector unions is unlike that of their private sector counterparts. The dissimilarities include (1) the nature of the products, (2) the nature of competition, and (3) the revenue-generating mechanisms.

Public Versus Private Products

Most **"public goods"** are (1) unpriced, and provided by the government for the general public, and (2) services, not really goods. The first characteristic certainly differentiates these products from those in the private sector, while the second quality may be shared by products in both sectors.*

Economists have discussed the nature of public goods for a long time. The fact that many services provided by government would benefit nonpayers if bought privately ("externalities") makes them public goods. If you installed an ICBM as a deterrent in your yard, it would also serve to protect your neighbors. This would also be true, to a great extent, of a private police force. Because the buyer cannot singularly appropriate public goods, government has traditionally supplied them. No price can really be placed on peace, freedom, and safety, all outcomes of providing public goods.

The fact that most public goods are services is also important in discussing the dissimilarities between public and private sectors. The private sector also provides services, but the major differences are that a very high percentage of publicly provided services are (1) essential, and, related to this point, (2) rendered in a monopoly environment.

Because so many services provided by the government are essential, union interference in their delivery is strictly limited. Federal workers cannot disrupt service flow; strikes, including slowdowns, are prohibited by law. They cannot bargain over economic issues which, if allowed, could cause an unplanned increase in the budget for one type of service at the expense of others as they might have to take budget cuts, curtailing them. Moreover, government unions are prohibited from bargaining over the mission and objectives of any department or agency, because the elected

---

* Products are made up of goods and services.

representatives of the people establish what services are to be rendered. Finally, some federal government services are totally exempted from unionization because of their essential nature, coupled with the need for maximum flexibility. The armed forces are an example.

The Nature of Competition

The federal government is a monopolist in many of the markets in which it "sells" its services; no private firm can make this claim. In many areas, no private firm would want to compete, such as in national defense. In others, however, firms do wait to compete and do just that in the fringes of the market. The postal service is an example of this situation. Overnight and parcel delivery services are provided extensively by private firms as well as the U.S. Postal Service. In fact, since the Postal Reorganization Act of 1970, spinning off the service totally and truly "privatizing" it (placing it in competition with private sector firms) has been vigorously debated.[21]

Given their protected position as monopoly suppliers, most government agencies can accommodate to their unions. However, the discipline of the budget replaces market competition in reining in excessive demands of workers, and bargaining over economic issues is highly restricted in federal sector labor–management relations.

Revenue in the Public Sector

In the public sector, most revenue comes from taxes, with a small amount generated by user fees. In the private sector, most revenue comes from the sale of goods and services ("user fees") with a small amount generated by investments and the like. There is no direct, short-term connection between revenue and the demand for government services as there is in the private sector. In fact, there is no direct, short-term connection between revenue and the *supply* of government services. If revenue is based on taxes, a disruption or deterioration of services will not affect revenue.

Taxes, however, are ultimately controlled by the consumers of government outputs, through the electoral process.* The tax revolts of the 1960s and 1970s in several states, highlighted by the passage of California's Proposition 13, vividly illustrated this point. Thus, unions in both the private and public sectors are constrained by demand, the major difference being that this constraint acts more indirectly and in the longer run in the public sector.

The Nature of the Business

The kind of "business" conducted in the public and private sectors, respectively, is fundamentally different. Government and industry have different goals, different powers, and different structures. The legal and political and economic frameworks have already been discussed; these are all related to the differences in the "business" of business versus government.

---

* The consumers of government services are also the *owners* of government, for, as Abraham Lincoln said, our government is one "of the people, by the people, and for the people." This point is more prominent in the next chapter.

The Goals of Government and Business

The last two administrations have espoused a philosophy of deregulation and **privatization**, with an underlying assumption that private enterprise is efficient because of the requirements imposed by the market whereas government is not. The administrations have been measuring the efficiency of business and government against the primarily economic goal of minimizing cost (and thus being able to offer goods and services at the lowest possible price). Few would argue that this is the major goal of business, maximizing economic welfare which follows from maximizing individual unit welfare or profit. (Adam Smith's "invisible hand," the market, takes care of the connection.) But is this also the goal of government?

Political scientists and public administrators have been noting for years that the primary goal of government in the United States is not profit maximization, but the maximization of *democracy*.[22] Since elected officials are supposed to operate to accomplish this end, decision making is a slow, deliberative process. It is aimed at allowing as many people as feasible to participate, and it is carried out in full view of the public. Or is it?

If government is a democracy-maximizing institution, the intervention of unions and their collective power is certainly not optimal. However, this is also true of the intervention of business—both large corporations and industry trade associations that lobby government continually. In a rather imperfect world, the collective power of competing groups such as unions and industry probably is as much defensive as offensive. The internal positioning of public sector unions, however, might cause more problems for government in pursuing its goal than the lobbying of more "external" groups. This leads to the next point, the powers involved in goal maximizing.

Government Power and Business Power

In pursuing their goals, public and private sector organizations have very different powers. Business firms use financial/economic power; government uses **sovereign power**. An early argument against public sector unionism was that it "infringes on the sovereign power of the state in determining levels of service and rules for the behavior of public employees."[23] This was felt to be especially troublesome in the military and in the protective services (mainly at the state and local government level).

The question of public union power independent of the sovereign power of the elected government has several dimensions. One involves union power to expand expenditures (wages and fringe benefits) going to the activities of agencies for which their members work at the expense of other agencies and departments, given budget restrictions. In essence, then, unions would be determining government priorities. This point was touched on earlier in this chapter. At the federal level, the administrative setting of wage and fringes, removing them from the collective bargaining process, prevents this infringement on sovereign power.

Another dimension of this problem would involve one aspect of union power, the strike. Through strikes, public unions could disrupt the flow of essential services to the populace, endangering general health and safety as well as frustrating the will of the elected officials. Work stoppages at the federal level are forbidden, however, preventing this infringement on sovereign power.

A third dimension of union power is based on the unions' important function of allowing their members to question a whole range of management actions. They represent the members in grievances aimed at doing just this. Under federal laws, however, awards in grievance arbitration are subject to review by government officials, preventing most infringements on sovereign power by this route. However, the function of unions to allow their members to question almost all management discipline decisions is one major reason why unionization is forbidden in the military.

In sum, the differences between the legal, political, and economic environments of business and government, as well as the dissimilar nature of goals and power in the two sectors, make public sector unionism different from private sector unionism. Federal restrictions on the subject matter of collective bargaining and work stoppages highlight these differences.

DISCUSSION QUESTIONS

1. What major legal enactments spurred unionism in the federal government after 1960?

2. Discuss the economic conditions that helped promote federal sector unionism in the 1960s.

3. Discuss the status of strikes and similar job actions in federal labor–management relations.

4. Why do you think Congress sets wages and economic fringe benefits for federal workers but leaves other bargaining issues to agency managers?

5. Why might security clauses be prohibited in public sector unions? Are there hazards in compulsory membership that the government is seeking to avoid?

6. "Federal unions don't bargain over wages, but they certainly work hard to increase them." Discuss this assertion.

7. What might be the advantages of lobbying versus the traditional collective bargaining process?

8. Discuss the differences in the legal environment of federal government and private sector unions.

9. Do federal unions interfere with the government's exercise of its sovereign powers? Justify your answer.

10. What factors led the federal government to do little against PATCO for its six work-related actions from 1968 to 1981? What was different about the 1981 PATCO strike that made it "pushing the wrong button at the wrong time" and led President Reagan to take action at last? How do you think the current administration would react to a strike by air traffic controllers?

VOCABULARY LIST

Civil Service Merit System
public sector unionism

Federal Services Impasses Panel (FSIP)
lobbying

Executive Order 10988

Civil Service Reform Act of 1978

Federal Labor Relations Authority
(FLRA)

Federal Mediation and Conciliation
Service (FMCS)

multilateral bargaining

"public goods"

privatization

sovereign power

FOOTNOTES

1. James L. Stern, "Unionism in the Public Sector," in Benjamin Aaron et al., eds., *Public-Sector Bargaining* (Industrial Relations Research Association Series, Bureau of National Affairs, 1988), p. 52.

2. John F. Burton, Jr., and Terry Thomason, "The Extent of Collective Bargaining in the Public Sector," in Benjamin Aaron et al., eds., *Public-Sector Bargaining* (Industrial Relations Research Association Series, Bureau of National Affairs, 1988), p. 14.

3. Ibid.

4. Ibid., pp. 14–15.

5. Sar A. Levitan and Frank Gallo, "Can Employee Associations Negotiate New Growth?," *Monthly Labor Review* (July 1989): 10.

6. Linda N. Edwards, "The Future of Public Sector Unions: Stagnation or Growth?," *American Economics Association Papers and Proceedings* (May 1989): 161.

7. Stern, "Unionism in the Public Sector," p. 66.

8. Ibid., p. 57.

9. Milton Derber, "Management Organization for Collective Bargaining in the Public Sector," in Benjamin Aaron et al., eds., *Public-Sector Bargaining* (Industrial Relations Research Association Series, Bureau of National Affairs, 1988), p. 121.

10. Edwards, "The Future of Public Sector Unions," p. 162.

11. Burton and Thomason, "The Extent of Collective Bargaining in the Public Sector," p. 16.

12. Ibid.

13. Ibid., pp. 27–28.

14. *Insight*, November 14, 1988, p. 22; *Wall Street Journal*, October 21, 1988, p. 82.

15. Herbert R. Northrup, "The Rise and Demise of PATCO," *Industrial and Labor Relations Review* (January 1984): 167.

16. Ibid. Much of the details in this section are from Northrup's article.

17. Stern, "Unionism in the Public Sector," p. 55.

18. Richard B. Freeman, "Unionism Comes to the Public Sector," *Journal of Economic Literature* (March 1986): 49–53.

19. Charles M. Rehmus, "Emergency Strikes Revisited," *Industrial and Labor Relations Review* (January 1990): 177, 179.

20. Freeman, "Unionism Comes to the Public Sector," p. 53.

21. *Wall Street Journal*, March 31, 1988, p. 24, and May 12, 1989, p. A12.

22. The authors are and have been at Schools of Business and Public Administration, and have "lived with" poli sci and public administrators for years.

23. Freeman, "Unionism Comes to the Public Sector," p. 49.

REFERENCES

BURTON, JOHN F., JR., and TERRY THOMASON. "The Extent of Collective Bargaining in the Public Sector." In Benjamin Aaron, Joyce M. Najita, and James L. Stern, eds., *Public-Sector Bargaining*. Industrial Relations Research Association Series, Bureau of National Affairs, 1988, pp. 1–51.

DERBER, MILTON. "Management Organization for Collective Bargaining in the Public Sector." In Aaron et al., *Public-Sector Bargaining*, pp. 90–123.

EDWARDS, LINDA N. "The Future of Public Sector Unions: Stagnation or Growth?" *American Economics Association Papers and Proceedings* (May 1989): 161–165.

FOSSUM, JOHN A. *Labor Relations*. Business Publications, 1989, Ch. 15.

FREEMAN, RICHARD B. "Unionism Comes to the Public Sector." *Journal of Economic Literature* (March 1986): 41–86.

HOLLEY, WILLIAM H., and KENNETH M. JENNINGS. *The Labor Relations Process*. Dryden Press, 1988, Ch. 15.

KOCHAN, THOMAS A., and HARRY C. KATZ. *Collective Bargaining and Industrial Relations*. Irwin 1988, Ch. 14.

LEVITAN, SAR A., and FRANK GALLO. "Can Employee Associations Negotiate New Growth?" *Monthly Labor Review* (July 1989): 5–14.

NORTHRUP, HERBERT R. "The Rise and Demise of PATCO." *Industrial and Labor Relations Review* (January 1984): 167–184.

REHMUS, CHARLES M. "Emergency Strikes Revisited." *Industrial and Labor Relations Review* (January 1990): 175–190.

STERN, JAMES L. "Unionism in the Public Sector." In Aaron et al., *Public-Sector Bargaining*, pp. 52–89.

CHAPTER 17

PUBLIC SECTOR UNIONISM: STATE AND LOCAL GOVERNMENT

U nionism in state and local government is the brightest spot in the rather drab situation of American labor in the last third of the twentieth century. The American labor movement has seen its representation in the labor force fall to about 16 percent, but in the state and local government sector, representation is over two and a half times this figure. Growth in **public sector unionism** has virtually come to a halt in the last decade or so, but the sharp decline in private sector unionization over that period has not occurred in the public sector. As will be seen, decline is unlikely in the foreseeable future.

THE DEVELOPMENT OF STATE AND LOCAL GOVERNMENT UNIONS

The Explosion in Demand for Public Services

State and local government unions have been the fastest growing unions in the nation over the past 30 years. Much of the impetus for this growth can be traced to the acceleration in the demand for public services that started in the late 1950s, fueled by the postwar baby boom.[1]

The postwar baby boom started generating a rapid increase first in demand for education. The late 1950s saw that group invade the public schools, creating an increasing requirement for employees in that area. Escalating requirements spread

Table 17.1   *The Growth in State and Local Government Expenditures, 1950–1985*

Year	State and Local Government Expenditures ($ millions)	Average Annual Percentage Change	Expenditures as Percentage of GNP
1950	23	—	7.8%
1960	50	12%	9.7%
1970	134	17%	13.2%
1980	363	17%	13.3%
1985	516	8%	12.9%

Source: John F. Burton, Jr. and Terry Thomason, "The Extent of Collective Bargaining in the Public Sector," in Benjamin Aaron et al., eds., *Public-Sector Bargaining* (Industrial Relations Research Association Series, Bureau of National Affairs, 1988), p. 39.

from education to other public services and state and local government expenditures, and employment took off. As Table 17.1 shows, from 1960 to 1980, state and local government expenditures increased 17 percent a year. In Table 17.2, the same pattern can be seen for employment; from 1960 to 1980, the average annual increase was almost 7 percent.

State and local government became *the* growth industry of the period. In the private sector, growth industries attract needed workers by raising wage levels. However, in the public sector in the late 1950s and early 1960s, a growing number of workers were hired while wages were kept comparatively low by government bureaucracies. Private sector wages were not being matched, but the relative security and stability of government employment was an offsetting feature. The influx of government

Table 17.2   *State and Local Government Employment, 1960–1990 (in millions)*

Year	State	Local	Total
1960	—	—	5.65
1970	2.66	7.16	9.82
1980	3.61	9.77	13.38
1981	3.64	9.62	13.26
1982	3.64	9.46	13.10
1983	3.66	9.43	13.10
1984	3.73	9.48	13.22
1985	3.83	9.69	13.52
1986	3.89	9.90	13.79
1987	3.97	10.10	14.07
1988	4.08	10.34	14.42
1989	4.17	10.61	14.78
1990	4.28	10.93	15.21

Sources: Monthly Labor Review (January 1990), Table 20, p. 101, (March 1990), Table 20, p. 95, and (February 1991), Table 20, p. 71.

workers included a high proportion of younger people, who entered the government labor force with little experience and training. These young workers made up the basis of the takeoff of unionization in the public sector.

The Spurt in Public Sector Collective Bargaining Laws

A major contributor to the growth in public sector unionization was the rapid spread of legislation (and executive rulings), granting state and local government employees the right to organize and bargain collectively. As employment in state and local government grew, the number of younger, more militant workers in this workforce mounted. And as the economy took off in a sustained boom in the 1960s, the relatively low wages of public employees and the ineffective merit systems of state and local government came under increasing attack. Pressure mounted to pass laws enabling collective bargaining. In 1959, Wisconsin enacted the first public sector bargaining law. Within ten years, 33 states had such laws.[2]

Most of the state (and local) labor relations laws are quite comprehensive. They cover the major areas discussed earlier in Chapter 15:

1. The scope of bargaining (subjects of negotiation).
2. The use of union security arrangements.
3. Grievance procedures, including arbitration.
4. Impasse procedures, such as mediation, fact finding, and even interest arbitration.
5. The legal status of strikes.
6. Unfair labor practices.
7. The administrative apparatus to oversee the law.

As of this writing, 40 states and the District of Columbia guarantee their employees the right to organize and bargain collectively.[3] Furthermore, in the ten states that have no such laws, the right to belong to a union or employee association was established by the *AFSCME, AFL–CIO v. Woodward* case in 1969.[4]

The Slowing of Public Sector Unionization

In the late 1970s, the spectacular growth in state and local government unionization started to slow down. The baby boomers were out of the age group requiring public education, and as they entered the family formation age group, small families became the vogue. The "Yuppie" generation focused on small families, in many cases with no children.

In conjunction with this decline in demand and as a natural consequence of the success of public sector unions in the 1960s and 1970s, state **tax revolts** in the late 1970s and early 1980s cut government revenues.* The most widely publicized of

---

* The advances in relative wages that state and local government employees made in the 1960s and 1970s increased the cost of public services. This was part of the reason for the tax revolts of the late 1970s and 1980s. See Thomas A. Kochan and Harry C. Katz, *Collective Bargaining and Industrial Relations* (Richard D. Irwin, 1988), p. 426.

these revolts was California's Proposition 13, passed by the voters in 1979, limiting taxes and tax increases. The voters followed up by passing the "Gann Initiative," which limited annual increases in government spending.

These tax revolts had a major effect on government expenditures and employment. The 17 percent average annual growth in state and local government expenditures from 1960 to 1980 dropped by more than half in the 1980–1985 period (see Table 17.1). And the 8 percent annual employment growth from 1960 to 1980 dropped by almost a factor of 10, to 10 percent for the *entire decade* of the 1980s.

The Public Sector Unions

Unions and employee associations in state and local government vary substantially. The largest are in education, as you might have guessed from the discussion so far. But there are also public employee unions and associations in the protective services (police and fire), health care, and transportation as well as general unions of public employees not tied to a given profession. Many unions made up of predominantly private sector employees have fairly large public employee memberships. Table 17.3 lists the major national unions and employee associations in the state and local government sector.

Table 17.3   *Major National Unions in State and Local Government*

Single-Profession Unions/Employee Associations

National Education Association (Indep.)
American Federation of Teachers (AFL–CIO)
American Association of University Professors (Indep.)
International Association of Fire Fighters (AFL–CIO)
Fraternal Order of Police (Indep.)
Police Benevolent Association (Indep.)
American Nurses Association (Indep.)
Amalgamated Transit Union (AFL–CIO)
Transport Workers Union (AFL–CIO)

General Unions Predominantly for Public Sector Workers

American Federation of State, County, and Municipal Employees (AFL–CIO)
Assembly of Governmental Employees (Disbanded)

Private Sector Unions with Significant Number of Public Sector Members

Service Employees International Union (AFL–CIO)
International Brotherhood of Teamsters, Chauffeurs, Warehousemen and Helpers of America (AFL–CIO)
Laborers' International Union of North America (AFL–CIO)
Communications Workers of America (AFL–CIO)
United Automobile, Aerospace and Agricultural Implement Workers of America (AFL–CIO)

Source: James L. Stern, "Unionism in the Public Sector," in Benjamin Aaron, et al. eds., *Public-Sector Bargaining* (Industrial Relations Research Association Series, Bureau of National Affairs, 1988).

Teacher Unions

The largest teachers' union is the **National Education Association** (**NEA**), which calls itself an employee association, not a union. With nearly 2 million members, it is the largest collective bargaining organization in the country. Founded in 1857, the NEA at first was concerned primarily with doing educational research (when government did little in this area) and increasing educational budgets.[5] It moved into collective bargaining in the 1960s, spurred by the loss of New York City teachers to the American Federation of Teachers (AFT), AFL–CIO, in a 1961 representation election. The spread of public sector labor relations laws also contributed to the move to collective bargaining. When the AFT's New York local (the United Federation of Teachers) won an impressive strike in 1962, the NEA's widespread dominance among public school teachers was threatened. At its 1962 convention, the association resolved to use strikes ("professional sanctions") if appropriate, and in 1968 it explicitly endorsed collective bargaining and the right of teachers to strike.[6]

The **American Federation of Teachers** (**AFT**) is the NEA's major rival. Founded in 1916, the AFT immediately affiliated with the AFL. A militant group, advocating basic union bread-and-butter issues, the AFT provided a stark contrast to the conservative NEA. The New York City local's president, Albert Shanker, who became national president in 1974, spent 15 days in jail for leading the UFT (AFT's New York chapter) strikes in the early 1960s.[7] The AFT tends to be strong in major cities. Besides New York, it holds bargaining rights in Chicago, Philadelphia, Detroit, Boston, Pittsburgh, Cleveland, Minneapolis, Denver, and Baltimore.[8]

The spectacular growth in AFT membership since the early 1960s and the NEA membership growth burst that started about ten years later are shown in Table 17.4. The AFT is soliciting growth in many ways and has started "associate groups" (in Texas, the Texas Federation of Teachers—Professional Educators Group, for example) to introduce teachers to unionization without requiring them to join the union; associate members can avail themselves of many benefits and services offered through the union.[9]

A third education/teachers' union is the **American Association of University Professors** (**AAUP**). The AAUP, founded in 1915 as a professional association whose prime concerns were academic freedom, individual rights (including tenure), faculty governance, and the promotion of higher education, abandoned its opposition to collective bargaining in 1972.[10] Up to that time, AAUP leaders felt that collective bargaining and faculty governance were in direct conflict. They changed this opinion as NEA and AFT locals won representation rights for faculty groups at the City University of New York and state laws permitting faculty collective bargaining were passed (in 19 states during the 1970s).[11] Though not a major collective bargaining organization, the AAUP has been involved in joint campus organizational drives with both the NEA and AFT as well as other local employee associations. It has been asked to join with these organizations because of its established reputation on university campuses and its familiarity with faculty governance systems.

Protective Services Unions

The protective services are usually defined as police and fire. Among firefighters, the **International Association of Fire Fighters** (**IAFF**), AFL–CIO, has little competition. Almost all unionized firefighters belong to this AFL–CIO union.

Table 17.4 *Teacher Participation in Employee Organizations, 1955–1988*

Year	Total Number of Elementary and Secondary Teachers	Percent in NEA	Percent in AFT
1955	1,141,000	54%	4%
1960	1,408,000	51%	4%
1965	1,710,000	55%	6%
1970	2,055,000	53%	10%
1975	2,196,000	77%	21%
1980	2,184,000	77%	25%
1985	2,207,000	76%	27%
1988	2,276,000	80%	29%

Source: Sar A. Levitan and Frank Gallo, "Can Employee Associations Negotiate New Growth?" *Monthly Labor Review* (July 1989): 7.

The situation is very different for police. The largest of the labor organizations representing police is the **Fraternal Order of Police (FOP)**, an independent employee association with an estimated 150,000 to 170,000 members. This represents about one-fourth of all police officers, about half of whom belong to unions.[12] The remaining one-half of unionized police officers belong to the **Police Benevolent Association** or independent local organizations. On the West Coast and in New England, the **Service Employees International Union (SEIU)** has organized some police officers.[13]

Local Transit Employee Unions

Three major unions represent employees of local transit districts. The **Amalgamated Transit Union (ATU)** and the **Transport Workers Union (TWU)** have about an equal number of members. The third union, the local transit division of the **United Transportation Union (UTU)**, represents a much smaller number of these employees. The ATU, in general, represents workers in a greater cross section of transit districts, while the TWU (and UTU) have fewer but larger locals in major cities.[14]

Labor relations in many transit districts are different from those for state and local government employees. In many states separate collective bargaining legislation has been enacted for transit districts as in California (see Chapter 15). The cities have also passed special purpose legislation. In many of these states, public transit labor relations are now being integrated into public sector labor relations for the state in general. As a result, the bargaining policies and procedures of the transit unions will more closely approximate those of other public sector unions.

General State and Local Government Employee Unions

The **American Federation of State, County, and Municipal Employees (AFSCME)**, AFL–CIO, is the most dominant of the state and local government employee unions outside of education. AFSCME was the largest affiliate of the AFL–CIO until the Teamsters rejoined in 1987, and it is the fastest growing union in the Federation. Over the last dozen years, while membership has dropped by over 30 percent in traditional industrial union giants like the Steel Workers and Auto Workers, AFSCME membership has grown by about two-thirds.[15]

This growth was partially the result of the affiliation of many state civil service employee organizations with the AFSCME. The largest of these organizations, the New York State Civil Service Employee Association (CSEA), joined the union in 1978. Another large organization, the Ohio State Classified Employee Association, joined in 1983. In addition, AFSCME is expanding organization efforts into areas in which it has traditionally not been represented; for example, it is establishing a separate department to represent nurses.[16] This move represents a direct challenge to the **American Nurses Association,** a professional organization that, like the NEA, adopted collective bargaining as a major function and bargains for nurses in both the private and public sector.

Another major component in the growth of AFSCME was the continued growth in the public sector (see Tables 17.1 and 17.2). This growth, coupled with the spread of public sector bargaining laws from state to state, was a great stimulus to AFSCME's expansion.

A second organization of state and local government employees deserving some note would be the **Assembly of Government Employees (AGE),** but it was never a union per se. Rather, it was an umbrella organization for the independent state **civil service employee associations (CSEAs).** In the period prior to the blossoming of public sector collective bargaining, AGE was a major lobbying organization for the state CSEAs. However, since the spread of bargaining by state employee organizations, the defections from AGE have mounted. The New York State CSEA, its largest affiliate, shifted to AFSCME in 1978. The California CSEA, its second largest, joined the Service Employees International Union in 1983.[17] Because of these mergers, AGE disbanded, and recent estimates place the nationwide membership of CSEAs not in education at under 200,000.[18]

Predominantly Private Sector Unions with Public Sector Members

Several large unions in the AFL–CIO whose memberships consist predominantly of private sector workers have organized extensively in the public sector. The Service Employees International Union (SEIU), AFL–CIO, has the largest public sector component of this group. Its absorption of the National Association of Government Employees in 1982 and of the California Civil Service Employee Association in 1983 was a major step in its upsurge as a public employee bargaining agent.

The Teamsters (IBT), AFL–CIO, has a public sector component that is second only to the SEIU's. Their coverage, as in the private sector, is very diverse, ranging from blue-collar workers to workers in blue (police) to nurses.

Other unions that have a fairly large component of public sector workers include the Laborers' International Union, the Communications Workers, and the Auto Workers (see Table 17.3).

MAJOR ISSUES IN STATE AND LOCAL GOVERNMENT LABOR RELATIONS

State and local government employees have used collective bargaining on a widespread basis for only 30 years or so. Arguments against it revolve around four interrelated issues:

1. Sovereign power and public accountability.
2. Fiscal responsibility and public budgeting.
3. Public goods and monopoly.
4. The right to strike.

Infringing on the Sovereign Power of the State

One of the early objections to public sector unionism was the argument that these unions would directly affect the **sovereign power** of the state to determine service levels for various programs and rules and regulations for public employee behavior.[19] It was felt that unions, as private interest groups, would be able to wield enough power to unduly influence public decisions.

Affecting Government Priorities

One of the primary aims of the union, as the representative of its members, is to increase the pay and benefits of these members. When government decision makers, the officials elected by the populace, develop a budget, it reflects their priorities. However, if a union obtains raises that "break" program budgets, monies will be reallocated from one program (or set of programs) to another to meet the new pay requirements.

Recent studies have shown that, indeed, this reallocation seems to be the case. One study indicated that unionized local government departments have higher employment levels than nonunion departments, while at the same time having higher compensation levels.[20] A second study found that unionized municipal departments have higher expenditures (budgets) than nonunionized ones.[21]

Thus, unions seem to be able to exert influence on public decisions as a strong special interest group. However, there are many special interest groups that petition government to further their own ends. Are unions of public sector employees different from these groups? We would have to answer *yes* to this question, as unions are internal groups in the governmental process. Unions can exert direct pressure on government managers by strikes, or threats of strikes, accompanied by vigorous public relations programs that would cause public pressure on government officials to restore or prevent interruption of services. We discuss this point in greater detail later in this chapter in the section on the right to strike.

Unions Are Not Accountable to the Public

Public officials are accountable to the electorate, the populace that elects them. The decisions they make are open to the scrutiny of that electorate. If those decisions are not popular, the public officials will be out of office, through the recall process or at the next election.

Private interest groups, like public sector unions, are not accountable to the public. Thus, there are problems if they are major players in the public decision-making process. If unions unduly influence public decisions, especially expenditure decisions, the electorate cannot vote them out of office when it disagrees with those decisions. The public's only recourse is to replace the government officials who caved in to the unions with others that hopefully will not.

Another breach of **public accountability** occurs when labor–management impasses are solved by arbitration, as, for example, in states where strikes are illegal or for protective services that cannot legally strike in almost all states and localities. When the public managers and public union negotiators reach a deadlock, mandatory interest (contract) arbitration entails an arbitrator coming in, making a decision, and then "riding off into the sunset." The union, its members, city management, and the populace will live with that decision, but the arbitrator will not.

Fiscal Responsibility

One of the major concerns of public officials is the **fiscal responsibility** that holding office places on them. Public budgets are constraints, for the ability to pay operates in the public sector as well as in the private.

In the heyday of public sector unions, the 1960s and 1970s, the ability to pay did not seem to be an operative constraint for state and local (and the federal) governments. Expenditures grew and grew, as did the taxes to fund them. Union demands were regularly being met, inflating state, county, and municipal budgets, and raising tax rates, especially property taxes, the major component of local government revenues that these governments control.

The end of the 1970s saw the beginning of the tax revolt. New York City's financial crisis in the 1970s was the most notable example of exploding public budgets that stiffened taxpayer resistance to growing public expenditures and taxes. Nine states adopted tax and/or spending limits, the most well known being Proposition 13, an initiative put on the ballot and passed by the voters in California in 1979.[22] Public budgeting moved from the realm of chaotic uncertainty to the objective world of fiscal constraint. Elected officials, operating with fixed budgets and small reserves, could no longer grant union monetary demands without cutting employment and/or reallocating funds; both approaches would lower levels of service.

As fiscal constraint took hold in the late 1970s, the growth of public sector unionism slowed. The public budget and the fiscal responsibility of public officials do operate to protect the public interest, albeit sometimes with direct prodding from that public.

The Government as a Monopoly Supplier

Much of the output of government (public goods) is supplied to the populace by government only. Police and fire protection are the best examples of the government as a monopolist.* In other areas, the government is a "near-monopolist": in elementary and secondary education, public schools are overwhelmingly more numerous than private schools.

In addition to its **monopoly power,** another factor about the government as a supplier of public goods stands out. Most of these goods are *services,* which cannot be inventoried and thus make their supplier susceptible to union pressure. A work stoppage would completely interrupt the flow of these services to customers (or users). This characteristic gives the union more bargaining power vis-à-vis the employer. Moreover, many of these services such as police and fire protection are *essential,* and not having them endangers public health and safety. This fact further enhances public sector union power. However, since a union's bargaining power relates to its ability to curtail employer revenue during a work stoppage, the union's power is not that great: during a work stoppage, most government revenue (taxes) continues. Only a small share, from user fees, would be lost.

In the not very long run, states, counties, and municipalities are not monopolist. Citizens, including businesses, can move from one locality to another if they are not happy with the level of government services provided and/or the taxes charged to support that level. The dilemma of New York City is an example of this flight. Corporations moved (and continue to move) their operations from the city, and even from the state, to other jurisdictions, as New York's financial crisis caused the curtailment of government-supplied services. This flight cuts the tax base, requiring further reductions in the level of services supplied by government.

The Right to Strike

The issue of **public sector strikes** is a contentious one. In 12 states, strikes are legal for some government workers: these states are listed in Table 17.5. In 24 states and the District of Columbia, strikes are either not covered by public sector labor relations laws or are prohibited, but no sanctions or penalties are specified for

---

* However, government can privatize services, even police protection, as illustrated fictionally in the 1988 movie *Robocop.*

Table 17.5   *States That Allow Public Sector Strikes*

Alaska	Montana[a]
California[a]	Ohio
Hawaii	Oregon
Idaho[a]	Pennsylvania
Illinois	Vermont
Minnesota	Wisconsin

Sources: Richard B. Freeman, "Unionism Comes to the Public Sector," *Journal of Economic Literature* (March 1986): 68; and Craig A. Olson, "Dispute Resolution in the Public Sector," in Benjamin Aaron et al., eds., *Public-Sector Bargaining* (Industrial Relations Research Association Series, Bureau of National Affairs, 1988), p. 163.

[a] Allowed by court decision (see Chapter 15).

FIGURE 17.1 Parents picket in a public-sector (teacher) strike.
Source: Rich Turner, The Stockton Record, January 8, 1990, p. B1.

carrying them out. Fifteen states specify severe penalties for striking workers and their employee association or union.[23]

The aversion to strikes in the public sector is related to the issue of the government as monopolist and supplier of essential services. It is argued that strikes may endanger the health and safety of the population. This would certainly be true of police or firefighter, and even sanitation worker, strikes.

What about teacher strikes, however, or transit worker strikes? The costs of these work stoppages, like those of police, firefighters, or sanitation workers, are borne primarily by the customer. In the private sector, the two disputing parties, the employees and the employer, carry the cost burden. The customers may be somewhat inconvenienced, having to shop at a different store than they would normally patronize, or buy a different brand than normal, but these are minor costs. In the public sector, the costs fall primarily on the users of the service. However, these users are really the *employers,* and they are expected to bear a large portion of the costs of a work stoppage. In fact, in many public sector strikes, the costs to elected officials are political costs, for public pressure to settle the strike may lead to the removal of those officials if the stoppage is prolonged. Teacher pickets during strikes are often joined by parents, as shown in Figure 17.1, urging the local Board of Education to settle.

The issue of the public sector workers' right to strike leads into the next discussion of impasse procedures.

IMPASSE PROCEDURES AS ALTERNATIVES TO THE STRIKE

When labor and management are negotiating a collective bargaining contract, they may reach a point at which neither party is willing to make any further concessions to narrow (or close) the gap between their respective positions. This impasse can lead to

1. Mediation and conciliation.
2. Fact finding.
3. Arbitration.
4. A work stoppage.

The first three **impasse procedures,** discussed in Chapter 12, are reviewed here; the fourth option, the subject of Chapter 13, is not discussed again.

Mediation and Conciliation

Mediation and **conciliation,** the most informal of the third-party intervention techniques, are widely used in both the private and public sector as a first step in overcoming bargaining impasses. Under the Railway Labor Act, mediation is mandatory and can go on for extended periods; in the Eastern Airlines dispute, for example, mediation began in November 1987 and ended in January 1989. Virtually all states have departments offering mediation and conciliation services, as does the federal government (the Federal Mediation and Conciliation Service and the National Mediation Board which was involved in the Eastern dispute).[24]

Mediators and conciliators function as facilitators. In their role as neutrals, they maintain communications between the two parties. In some instances they act to reestablish face-to-face talks. In addition, mediation involves proposing solutions to the impasse. However, adoption of such proposals by labor and management is purely voluntary.

Fact Finding

Fact finding is a frequently used impasse resolution technique in the public sector. It is a more formal third-party intervention in the collective bargaining process than mediation and conciliation. However, like mediation, it leads to recommendations to solve the impasse, not decisions.

The fact finder, or fact-finding panel, is called in (1) to study the situation, systematically collecting all the facts surrounding a dispute, and (2) to organize and present the facts to both parties and the public, usually with a recommended solution to the dispute. Making public the positions of the two disputing parties is designed to bring pressure on them to reach a settlement.

Research has shown rather conclusively that fact finding in the public sector has not been effective in overcoming bargaining impasses.[25] In most cases the attempts at publicizing the dispute are not successful, for the public interest seems to be aroused only when the hardships of a strike are felt. A much more effective impasse

Table 17.6   *States That Use Compulsory Arbitration to Resolve Public Sector Bargaining Impasses* [a]

Alaska[b]	New Jersey
Connecticut	New York
Hawaii[b]	Ohio[b]
Illinois[b]	Oregon[b]
Iowa	Pennsylvania[b]
Maine	Rhode Island
Michigan	Vermont[b]
Minnesota[b]	Washington
Montana[b]	Wisconsin[b]
Nebraska	Wyoming
Nevada	

Source: Susan Schwochau and Peter Feuille, "Interest Arbitrators and Their Decision Behavior," *Industrial Relations* (Winter 1988): 37.

[a] Massachusetts required arbitration until 1981; South Dakota and Utah utilized it in the 1970s.

[b] Strikes are legal for some public employees (see Table 17.5).

procedure is arbitration, in which the third-party neutral imposes a solution (i.e., makes a decision rather than a recommendation).

Arbitration

Arbitration of bargaining impasses, referred to as **contract** or **interest arbitration,** is widely used in the public sector to avoid strikes by replacing them. Over half of the 40 states with public sector labor laws make use of arbitration to settle impasses (see Table 17.6). The groups most frequently mandated to use these procedures are police and firefighters, because they are the groups almost always prohibited from striking.

Conventional Versus Final Offer Arbitration

Two forms of arbitration are utilized under state **mandatory arbitration** statutes: conventional and final offer arbitration. Under **conventional arbitration,** the third-party neutral is free to fashion any award deemed appropriate. Under **final offer arbitration,** the arbitrator must choose either the employer or union proposal. A further distinction in final offer arbitration is to choose either side's entire *package* or the final proposal of either side *issue-by-issue.*

Effects of Arbitration

The use of final offer arbitration is supposed to overcome the **chilling effect** that conventional arbitration produces. The chilling effect is the curtailment in contract negotiations, especially on the part of the weaker of the two parties, when interest arbitration is mandated. The nonbargaining party is throwing itself on the mercy of the arbitrator in the hopes of obtaining a better result than it could through bargaining. The weaker side is banking on the arbitrator coming in and "splitting the difference." Under final offer arbitration this is not possible (see Chapter 12).

This type of third-party intervention has other side effects besides the damping of bargaining (the chilling effect). One is the **narcotic effect,** which, as its name suggests, is the growing reliance of both parties on arbitration at the expense of bargaining and negotiating. An addiction to arbitration to solve problems that the two parties should be bargaining on, face to face, leaves them with less work but with imposed solutions. In addition, without the urgency imposed by an imminent strike or a lockout, the necessity of compromise is diluted.

Another effect of mandatory arbitration is the imposition of a contract that may alter the allocation of a local government's financial resources. The arbitrator, however, will not be affected by this action, as he or she comes in, makes a binding decision, and then leaves.

If strikes are to be averted, however, some mechanism to resolve contract disputes is needed. Binding arbitration is, at this point, the only such technique available.

IS STATE AND LOCAL GOVERNMENT UNIONISM DIFFERENT?

In the previous chapter, the question of whether federal government unionism was different from private sector unionism was answered in the affirmative. The differences in the legal framework (in terms of bargaining subjects and the right to strike) and the political framework (in terms of the use of political pressure) were obvious. Differences in the economic environment were not as telling, even though the federal government is a monopolist in supplying many of the services it produces. Differences in the nature of the "business" itself showed great dissimilarities.

The Legal and Political Framework

The Legal Framework Does Not Create Differences

Public sector labor laws vary from state to state. In some states, collective bargaining laws are not that different from the National Labor Relations Act/Labor–Management Relations Act. In other states they do differ, and, in fact, ten states have no statutes governing collective bargaining for their public employees. In reviewing the public sector legal framework, it was seen that

1. Forty states (plus the District of Columbia) have public sector labor laws, and most of these are fairly comprehensive.
2. All these states allow financial as well as nonmonetary subjects in bargaining.
3. Twelve states allow strikes of some public employees, and 25 others have no sanctions or penalties specified for striking workers.

But even in states that have no public sector labor law (e.g., West Virginia) or that prohibit strikes and impose penalties for this action (e.g., Oklahoma), unions/employee associations thrive and do strike. In West Virginia, a statewide teachers' strike was held from March 7 to March 19, 1990; the 16,000-member state NEA chapter and the 3,000-member AFT chapter (out of 22,000 teachers in the state) struck over the average teacher pay; West Virginia's pay ranked forty-eighth among the states.[26] In Oklahoma, the 30,000-member state NEA chapter (representing 80 percent of the state's public school teachers) called a five-day walkout in April 1990 to bolster pay.[27] The Oklahoma teachers' average salary, as reported by the NEA, is just over $23,000 per year, $8,200 below the national average and forty-fifth among the states.[28]

We can conclude that the legal environment of state and local government unionism, though technically different from that of the private sector, does not make unions operate very differently in the two sectors.

The Political Frameworks Are Not Alike

The political frameworks of public and private sector unions are quite dissimilar. Unlike private sector unions, public sector unions use substantial political pressure, especially at the local level.

The public sector strike is basically a political tool, and the relevant costs are primarily political.[29] In the private sector, the strike is basically an economic weapon. The public sector strike involves the garnering of public support behind employees and their union to pressure public officials to make concessions to end the strike. As Figure 17.1 illustrates, for education unions, the successful public sector strike includes acts like getting the *owners* (for that, in essence, are what the parents are) to *picket* their own *management* group (the board of education and school superintendent).

In public sector negotiations, before the strike, the union can use public relations ploys to gather public support for their demands. When negotiating with a management team, which, in education, for example, is appointed by the local superintendent of schools, the union negotiators can try to approach the elected officials, the local board of education, to enlist their aid. This action, referred to as **multilateral bargaining,** is rare in the private sector. A private sector union, in negotiating with corporate management, will seldom take its case to the corporation's board of directors, or its owners. However, striking private sector unions will often try to rally local support for their strikes, in hopes that local government officials might try to pressure management to end a strike. But these public officials have no power over private corporations.

The Economic Environment

The economic environment of public sector unions at the state and local government level is not unlike that of private sector unions. The issues and comparisons, in economic terms, include the nature of the products and the competition as well as the revenue-generating mechanisms.

The Nature of the Products: Public Versus Private Goods

State and local output consists primarily of services. Many of these are essential services, in contrast to the private sector where a greater balance between goods and services exists. However, beyond police and fire protection, many public services are either in competition with those of the private sector or are sometimes subcontracted to private organizations.

In education, at all levels, private schools are in competition with public schools. Recreation services are also supplied competitively by public and private organizations, even parks (KOA, for camping). Privatizing public services through subcontracting is quite common in the public sector at the local level (e.g., garbage collection). Very few areas have municipal utility districts, because privately owned corporate public utilities supply most of the nation's power.

The Nature of Competition: Qualifying the Monopoly Issue

State and local governments are not monopolies in the same sense as the federal government is. In the short run, states, counties, and cities and their special districts (such as educational school districts) are monopoly (or near-monopoly) suppliers of certain services. However, businesses and individuals, being mobile, can move from one locality (state or county or city) to another quite easily and do so in the short and intermediate run. Most political jurisdictions have special departments or agencies whose major function is to lure business to that jurisdiction, in order to increase the tax base and area employment. These states, counties, and cities vigorously compete with each other for these businesses for economic development. The level of competition is as great as that between companies and industries in the private sector. But the local governments are selling location (government services, etc.) rather than goods and services.

Generating Revenue: Taxes Versus the Market

In the public sector, most revenue is generated by taxes, whereas in the private sector most revenue comes from sales to customers. These are, on the face of it, very different ways of making money. But, given the tax revolts of the last 10 to 12 years and the general opposition of many citizens to increases in taxes, especially at the local level, the dissimilarity may not be that great. The limits imposed on revenue and hence spending by public sector and private sector organizations are user- or customer-based: the tax-weary users of government (the citizens) and the price-wary users of private goods and services (the customers in the market).

State and local governments cannot spend more than they take in without going to the money market, a constraint that also holds for private sector organizations. This constraint, however, does not hold for the federal government which has the power to print money. The passage of the Gramm–Rudman bill has not changed its position. Gramm–Rudman requires, *ex ante*, a balanced budget, but, *ex post*, deficits are the rule as the law has no enforcement mechanism.

In general, then, great dissimilarities in the revenue side between the public and private sectors show up when comparisons include the federal government. When we compare state and local government with private companies, the differences are much less.

The Nature of the Business

The chief concern of government is to govern democratically, whereas business seeks to allocate scarce resources to best meet competing needs. The success of business is measured mainly by profitability; the success of government is much more difficult to measure (or even define).

What effect does this difference have on an evaluation of unionism in government versus business? This is mainly a question of power. To maximize profits, firms apply economic power, which is primarily the power unions in America use. To maximize democratic governing, governments apply sovereign power (see Chapter 16). Earlier discussions of the political framework of public and private sector unionism noted that public sector unions have a much greater ability to apply political pressures on their employers. In this dimension there are major differences in public and private sector unionism. These differences and the lesser ones in the legal framework and economic environment lead to the conclusion that unionism in state and local government is different from unionism in the private sector (but the dissimilarities are not as substantial as those that become apparent when we compare federal government and private sector unionism).

DISCUSSION QUESTIONS

1. Compare the growth and aims of the National Education Association (NEA) and the American Federation of Teachers (AFT), AFL–CIO.

2. Discuss the development and phenomenal growth of the American Federation of State, County, and Municipal Employees (AFSCME) in the 1970s and 1980s.

3. Do you think public sector unions infringe on the sovereign powers of local governments? Explain your answer.

4. Do public sector unions make government officials fiscally irresponsible? Explain your answer.

5. Should local government unions have the right to strike? Explain your answer.

6. "In the public sector the costs (of strikes) fall primarily on the users of the service. However, these users are really the employers (of the workers)." Discuss this assertion.

7. If public sector unions are not given the right to strike, how would you recommend that bargaining and negotiating impasses be resolved? Why?

8. How could you make a public sector arbitrator more responsible for the fiscal aspects of the solutions he or she develops?

9. Why is multilateral bargaining generally more effective in the public sector than in the private sector?

10. What seems to be the major factors that make state and local government unionism different from private sector unionism?

VOCABULARY LIST

public sector unionism   sovereign power

tax revolts   public accountability

National Education Association (NEA)   fiscal responsibility

American Federation of Teachers (AFT)

American Association of University Professors (AAUP)

International Association of Fire Fighters (IAFF)

Fraternal Order of Police (FOP)

Police Benevolent Association

Service Employees International Union (SEIU)

Amalgamated Transit Union (ATU)

Transport Workers Union (TWU)

United Transportation Union (UTU)

American Federation of State, County, and Municipal Employees (AFSCME)

American Nurses Association

Assembly of Government Employees (AGE)

civil service employee association (CSEA)

monopoly power

public sector strikes

impasse procedure

mediation

conciliation

fact finding

mandatory arbitration

contract or interest arbitration

conventional arbitration

final offer arbitration

chilling effect

narcotic effect

multilateral bargaining

FOOTNOTES

1. William H. Holley and Kenneth M. Jennings, *The Labor Relations Process* (Dryden Press, 1988), p. 545.

2. Linda N. Edwards, "The Future of Public Sector Unions: Stagnation or Growth?," *American Economic Association Papers and Proceedings* (May 1989): 161.

3. Ibid., p. 163, updated by the January 1988–1990 *Monthly Labor Review* articles on state labor legislation enacted in the prior year.

4. 406 F. 2d 137 (1969).

5. Sar A. Levitan and Frank Gallo, "Can Employee Associations Negotiate New Growth?," *Monthly Labor Review* (July 1989): 6.

6. Ibid., p. 7.

7. *Wall Street Journal*, November 24, 1987, p. 58.

8. James L. Stern, "Unionism in the Public Sector," in Benjamin Aaron et al., eds., *Public-Sector Bargaining* (Industrial Relations Research Association Series, Bureau of National Affairs, 1988), p. 76.

9. *Business Week*, October 13, 1986, p. 126.

10. Stern, "Unionism in the Public Sector," p. 79.

11. Levitan and Gallo, "Can Employee Associations Negotiate New Growth?," p. 8.

12. Stern, "Unionism in the Public Sector," pp. 82–83.

13. Ibid. The SEIU absorbed the National Association of Government Employees (NAGE) and thus became bargaining representative for several New England police organizations that belonged to NAGE.

14. Stern, "Unionism in the Public Sector," p. 84.

15. Holley and Jennings, *The Labor Relations Process,* p. 531.

16. *Wall Street Journal,* March 13, 1990, p. A1.

17. Stern, "Unionism in the Public Sector," p. 83.

18. Levitan and Gallo, "Can Employee Associations Negotiate New Growth?," p. 120.

19. Richard B. Freeman, "Unionism Comes to the Public Sector," *Journal of Economic Literature* (March 1986): 49.

20. Jeffrey S. Zax, "Employment and Local Public Sector Unions," *Industrial Relations* (Winter 1989): 30.

21. Robert G. Valletta, "The Impact of Unionism on Municipal Expenditures and Revenues," *Industrial and Labor Relations Review* (April 1989): 439.

22. Thomas A. Kochan and Harry C. Katz, *Collective Bargaining and Industrial Relations* (Richard D. Irwin, 1988), p. 429.

23. Freeman, "Unionism Comes to the Public Sector," pp. 68–69; and Craig A. Olson, "Dispute Resolution in the Public Sector," in Benjamin Aaron et al., eds., *Public-Sector Bargaining* (Industrial Relations Research Association Series, Bureau of National Affairs, 1988), p. 163.

24. Nicholas Blain et al., "Mediation, Conciliation, and Arbitration, An International Comparison of Australia, Great Britain, and the United States," *International Labour Review* (March–April 1987): 179.

25. Kochan and Katz, *Collective Bargaining,* p. 281.

26. *New York Times,* March 20, 1990, p. A8.

27. *New York Times,* April 17, 1990, p. A8.

28. *New York Times,* May 2, 1990, p. B6.

29. Olson, "Dispute Resolution in the Public Sector," p. 161.

REFERENCES

BLAIN, NICHOLAS, JOHN GOODMAN, and JOSEPH LOEWENBERG. "Mediation, Conciliation, and Arbitration, An International Comparison of Australia, Great Britain and the United States." *International Labour Review* (March–April 1987): 179–189.

CHELIUS, JAMES R., and MARIAN M. EXTEJT. "The Narcotic Effect of Impasse-Resolution Procedures." *Industrial and Labor Relations Review* (July 1985): 629–638.

EDWARDS, LINDA N. "The Future of Public Sector Unions: Stagnation or Growth?" *American Economic Association Papers and Proceedings* (May 1989): 161–165.

FREEMAN, RICHARD B. "Unionism Comes to the Public Sector." *Journal of Economic Literature* (March 1986): 41–86.

HOLLEY, WILLIAM H., and KENNETH M. JENNINGS. *The Labor Relations Process.* Dryden Press, 1988, Ch. 14.

HUNT, JANET C., JOSEPH V. TERZA, RUDOLPH A. WHITE, and THOMAS A. MOORE. "Wages, Union Membership, and Public Sector Bargaining Legislation: Simultaneous Equations with an Ordinal Qualitative Variable." *Journal of Labor Research* (Summer 1986): 255–267.

KOCHAN, THOMAS A., and HARRY C. KATZ. *Collective Bargaining and Industrial Relations*. Richard D. Irwin, 1988, Ch. 14.

LEVITAN, SAR A., and FRANK GALLO. "Can Employee Associations Negotiate New Growth?" *Monthly Labor Review* (July 1989): 5–14.

OLSON, CRAIG A. "Dispute Resolution in the Public Sector." In Benjamin Aaron, Joyce M. Najita, and James L. Stern, eds., *Public-Sector Bargaining*. Industrial Relations Research Association Series, Bureau of National Affairs, 1988, pp. 160–188.

SCHWOCHAU, SUSAN, and PETER FEUILLE. "Interest Arbitrators and Their Decision Behavior." *Industrial Relations* (Winter 1988): 37–55.

STERN, JAMES L. "Unionism in the Public Sector." In Aaron, et al., *Public-Sector Bargaining*, pp. 52–89.

TREBLE, JOHN G. "How New Is Final-Offer Arbitration?" *Industrial Relations* (Winter 1986): 92–94.

VALLETTA, ROBERT G. "The Impact of Unionism on Municipal Expenditures and Revenues." *Industrial and Labor Relations Review* (April 1989): 430–442.

ZAX, JEFFREY S. "Employment and Local Public Sector Unions." *Industrial Relations* (Winter 1989): 21–31.

PART FIVE

THE FUTURE OF LABOR–MANAGEMENT RELATIONS

In the concluding part of this book, we explore some issues of special current interest in labor–management relations, and we reach some conclusions about the future form of American labor–management relations. In the next chapter we examine three issues: inflation and its link to wages and unions; labor–management cooperation, especially in the United States but also in other industrialized countries; and comparable worth, equal pay for "comparable" (not equal) work.

In the final chapter we both summarize the state of the unions and the labor movement in America and make some projections about its future. However, as the changes in the last year or two in Eastern Europe and the Soviet Union have shown us, predicting the future in a dynamic world is a hazardous business. We know you will keep this in mind as you read this book in the early to mid-1990s.

CHAPTER 18

CURRENT ISSUES, FUTURE CONCERNS

As the 1980s ended and the 1990s dawned, many important issues were pressing American labor and the labor–management relations system in the United States. The decade of the 1980s was a period of union decline in America; this decline was caused by an economy that was moving further from its long-established manufacturing base to a greater service orientation, as it was being battered by foreign competition in those base industries. The economy grew throughout the 1980s, but it is faltering as we move into the 1990s.

A concern of American unions in the 1980s was management's newly invigorated anti-union attitude. This hardened resistance to unions and even to unionization took form early in the decade, in 1981, with the president's busting of the air traffic controllers union. The growing antagonism between labor and management, so deeply rooted in the American labor–management relations system, has been blunted in some areas by cooperation. In part this came as a *quid pro quo* for union concessions in collective bargaining, but also in part it reflected a genuine coordinated response to economic adversity from, for example, foreign competition.

Yet another concern for American unions in the 1980s, and for the three decades preceding that, was and is the changing composition of the workforce. The typical American worker is no longer, and has not been for some time, the white adult male. This worker is now as likely to be a female and/or a minority, and further, to be a part-timer. This worker has tended to fill different jobs (primarily in the service industry) than the older, male workers of the industrial labor force of the prewar period (to the 1930s). The disparity in pay between typical "female" jobs and "male" jobs is, and will continue to be, a major issue.

In this chapter we discuss these issues and concerns as special present and future factors in American labor–management relations.

UNIONS AND INFLATION ═══════

The decade of the 1980s was marked by the longest peacetime economic expansion in the history of the United States. By the end of the decade, inflationary pressures started to mount, but the weakening of the economy in 1990 assuaged these pressures somewhat.[1] The increase in labor costs in the late 1980s was a major factor in the concern over inflation.

Wages and Prices: Cost-Push Inflation

Inflation, the rise in the overall or average price of all goods and services, can be caused by many factors, one of which is the cost of labor. **Cost-push inflation** is considered inflation that results from the sellers of productive inputs, especially labor, "persistently and unilaterally" raising the price of their inputs, for example, wages.[2]

The Wage–Price Connection

Wages are related to prices in a rather complex fashion. For an increase in wages to result in an increase in prices, several other conditions must hold. First, the wage increase must exceed the increase in labor productivity, causing unit labor costs to increase. **Labor productivity** is the output a worker can produce in an hour, an output–input ratio. If wages go up 5 percent and productivity also increases 5 percent, there will be no change in unit labor costs. However, if wages go up 5 percent and productivity goes up 2 percent, unit labor costs will increase by 3 percent.

The next phase in the relationship between wages and prices involves the incidence of the labor cost increase—or, who will pay the extra labor costs? If the firms pass on the costs to the consumer through higher prices, inflation occurs. The higher costs may instead be borne by other groups. One of these is the owners, who may absorb the higher costs by making lower profits. Another group may be other factors of production; for example, capital suppliers may experience lower interest rates or material suppliers lower prices. If the wage increase is a union one pushing up union labor costs, another factor of production can bear this burden: nonunion labor, through wage increases lower than their productivity increases, or, more drastically, through wage cuts.

Another aspect important to the wage–price connection involves the question, how much of a factor in costs is labor? If labor cost is a small percentage (say 5 to 10 percent) of total cost, a 5 percent increase (in labor cost, not wages) will raise total cost only 0.25 to 0.5 percent. If, however, labor cost is 50 percent of total cost, that 5 percent increase will raise a firm's cost by 2.5 percent, which represents a significant amount. Thus, labor's share of total cost is important in assessing the impact of labor cost increases.

These relationships between wages, productivity, unit labor costs, and prices (or profits or returns to other factors of production) are illustrated in Figure 18.1.

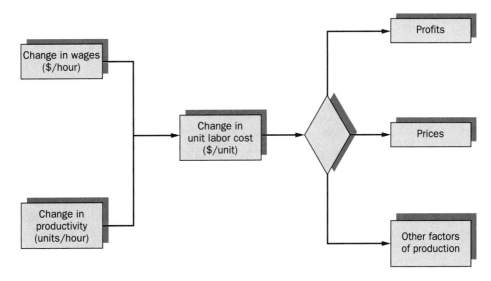

FIGURE 18.1 The connection between wages and prices.

The Union Wage Connection to Prices

Now that we see how wage increases can lead to price increases and inflation, let's focus on *union* wage (and fringe benefit) increases. Will increases in the union wage level have the same effect on prices or profits as discussed in the preceding section? They will, if they are widespread enough and if they are a large enough factor in total costs. However, recall that unions represent only 16 percent or so of the labor force. Will a union wage increase cause widespread labor cost increases? Or, as economists put it, is there an effective **wage-gain transmission** or **spillover** to the nonunion sector?[3]

Research over the years has shown that union wage gains are, to varying degrees, effectively transmitted to nonunion workers. The intrafirm transmission mechanism is very effective. A company that gives its unionized workers a 5 percent wage increase and a given package of fringe benefit changes is most likely to extend this pay hike to its nonunion (e.g., clerical) workers, for reasons of equity and to keep the nonunion workers from unionizing. The equity argument is rather straightforward. Keeping nonunion workers from unionizing by paying them the union wage has been discussed before (see Chapter 7 and the discussion of the relative wage effect of unionism) and is called the **threat effect**.

In assessing union wage-gain spillover, the threat effect is important. Within a firm, in a limited geographic area, and, to lesser extent, in an industry, union gains would be transmitted to nonunion workers to forestall unionization.[4] In addition, within a product market, firms (as well as union officials) are aware of the decisions each makes, and there are "strong economic incentives to coordinate these decisions."[5] Thus, union wage gains in a company are often imitated in other unionized companies; in turn these gains are transmitted to nonunion workers in the imitating firms. This concept of "patterns" in collective bargaining, discussed in Chapter 7 as an aspect of union wage policy, provides an effective transmission of union wage gains within and even across industry lines.

The Current Picture

The effort to offset current increases in labor costs has taken several routes, for these increases have several sources. They can be classified into two categories: increases in fringe benefit costs, and increases in white-collar (nonunion) employee wages and benefits.[6]

First, the labor cost statistics clearly indicate an increase. The Labor Department's Employment Cost Index (ECI), a measure of the cost of wages and benefits, showed an acceleration of these costs from mid-1987 to mid-1990, with a 3.8 percent increase the first year, 4.6 percent the second year, and 5.2 percent the last year. During this period, the Labor Department's statistics showed an annual productivity gain of about 1 percent. Thus, unit labor costs increased by 2.8 to 4.2 percent per year. A further breakdown of these employment cost statistics shows that fringe benefit costs, not wages, are the big gainers. For example, from September 1987 to September 1988, benefit expenses grew by 6.7 percent, whereas wages and salaries were up just 3.7 percent.[7] Two items in the benefit package whose cost has really jumped stand out: health insurance (premiums) and Social Security (taxes). Firms have concentrated on reducing health care costs, using approaches such as HMOs (Health Maintenance Organizations), outpatient clinics, and physician networks. (These approaches were discussed in Chapter 8.) Little can be done about the increasing Social Security costs.

Statistics also show that the average annual white-collar pay gain for 1988–1989 was 5.1 percent versus 4.2 percent for blue-collar workers. Thus, the inflationary pressures generated by rising labor costs seem to come from the nonunion rather than the unionized sector. This was the conclusion reached in Chapter 7 (see Table 7.5), which showed an average annual wage and salary increase for union workers of 4.8 percent and nonunion, 5.3 percent, for the 1980s. Firms' reactions to the growth in white-collar costs have been to start laying off white-collar workers, especially highly paid professionals. To meet some of their needs, these firms are increasingly using temporary help services that specialize in these types of workers, services like Accountemps which specializes in accounting and finance professionals. The early 1990s are expected to see heavy layoffs of white-collar workers, as witnessed by such layoffs at corporate giants like Caterpillar, Chrysler, H. J. Heinz, IBM, and Lockheed.

Many companies, particularly those facing stiff international competition, have not resorted to price increases when faced with unit labor cost increases of 3 to 4 percent. Fearing loss of market share, these companies are using profits to pay for higher labor costs. The Department of Labor's index of unit profits dropped from 128.8 in 1988 to 112.5 in 1989, almost 13 percent. Sometimes increased unit labor costs are borne not by consumers in the form of inflation, but by owners in the form of lower profits.

Escalator (COLA) Clauses and Inflation

One argument that is made to support the thesis that unions are one of the underlying causes of inflation in the United States is their negotiated **cost-of-living** adjustment (**COLA**) clauses. It is argued that COLAs sustain or magnify inflation in a kind of **wage–price spiral** (see Chapter 7). As prices (the general price level) increase, COLAs automatically kick in to increase costs, which puts more pressures on prices so that they increase, an increase that again causes a COLA wage increase, and so on. An inflation psychology can result from this spiraling escalation of wages and price.

The unions counter that COLAs are a *reaction* to inflation, not a cause of it. Prices go up—inflation—and the COLA kicks in. COLAs have historically not given a 100 percent restoration of purchasing power, that is, a 1 percent wage increase for a 1 percent jump in prices, a jump usually measured by the CPI (Consumer Price Index).[8] Moreover, an increasing number of COLAs have *caps*, keeping their periodic wage adjustments to stipulated upper limits. Overall, it has been argued that wage indexing through COLAs is not a major cause or stimulation of inflation.[9]

Wages, Prices, and Employment: The Phillips Curve

Discussions of labor, wages, and prices often link these subjects, through the mechanism of the labor market, to the level of employment (or unemployment). The first of these linkages was the **Phillips curve,** and it is still a core concept in the wage/price–unemployment relationship.[10] The original Phillips curve related the rate of change in wages to the unemployment rate. Most modifications of it replace the wage change variable with price change, based on the assumption that prices are determined by costs (**markup pricing**), and labor costs changes thus become price changes.

The Phillips curve, pictured in Figure 18.2, is an important concept in economic policy. It shows a tradeoff between price stability and full employment. The theory behind the tradeoff is, that at low unemployment rates (a tight labor market), wage growth quickens and productivity growth slows. This occurs because, in a tight labor market, alternative employment for most workers mitigates the threat of job loss, and worker motivation (and efficiency) drops. In addition, to attract workers in a tight labor market, wages must increase to lure them from other jobs, as the unemployment pool is small and made up of the poorest workers.

The details of the Phillips curve have been debated vigorously over the last three decades. The specific numbers and shape differ from one economy to another and change over time as economic structures change. The natural rate of unemployment, supposedly where the curve becomes asymptotic to the vertical axis (the price or wage change axis), is a function of the geographic size of an economy and other factors affecting worker mobility. Every economy, if operating correctly, should have some unemployment as workers shift to better jobs opening up to them, and so on. The "zero-inflation" rate of unemployment, where the curve crosses the horizontal axis, is a point whose very existence and the desirability of ever reaching it have been questioned. In fact, some of the underlying assumptions of the Phillips curve, like the widespread use of markup pricing and motivating force of the threat of job loss, have been questioned.[11] However, the construct is still important in policy, and it links government labor market policies with monetary and fiscal policies aimed at stable prices and high levels of employment.

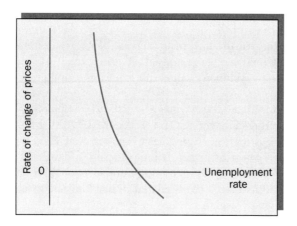

FIGURE 18.2 A typical Phillips curve.

LABOR–MANAGEMENT COOPERATION

As the 1980s unfolded, few people in the United States felt that labor–management cooperation, more commonly referred to as **worker participation** or **employee involvement (EI)**, was of any value. As the 1990s begin, EI is a widespread movement with a large following that believe it has had and will have a major role in improving worker commitment and productivity and product quality.[12] The spread of EI in the 1980s can be illustrated by the fact that every one of General Motors' facilities in the United States (151 in all) had an EI program by 1985.[13]

The International Experience

In many other labor relations systems, worker participation or employee involvement is highly developed. The best example of this involvement is the German system of co-determination, with three levels of labor participation. As you recall (from Chapter 5), under this system workers share an equal role with management at the shop floor level through works councils. A labor director represents them and their interests at the top operating level, on the management or executive committee. At the policymaking level on the board of supervisors (the German name for the board of directors), labor will control one-third to one-half the seats. The German co-determination system involves joint labor–management *problem solving* (in the works councils primarily) and *decision making* (in management or executive committees and on boards of supervisors). This requires a total sharing of information between unions/workers and management.

Another labor relations system known for its high degree of worker participation is the Japanese system. As we learned in Chapter 5, the cooperative nature of labor relations in Japan may be traced to the workers' view that their interests coincide with those of their company. The enterprise unions in Japanese companies function as vehicles for participative management as well as collective bargaining. However, most of the participation and employee involvement occurs at the shop level, and is primarily joint *problem solving*, requiring less information sharing than joint decision making.

The American Experience

The American experience with cooperation over the last decade or so has been very volatile. Worker participation has ranged from all kinds of shop level arrangements to seats on company boards of directors. Much of this involvement has come as a response to competitive pressures and can be characterized as either "closing ranks" or a *quid pro quo* for concessions granted in collective bargaining. Thus, rather than cooperative efforts, these would be better characterized as compromises.

A Model of Labor–Management Cooperation in a Union Setting

The most comprehensive model of labor–management cooperation and change in a union environment is the **Kochan–Dyer three-stage model**.[14] The model has two basic assumptions:

1. Individual employees, the employer, and the union each have different but interdependent sets of interests and goals, and although these are typically incompatible, they are accepted as legitimate by all three parties.
2. Union and management share power, as required by law, but management accepts the union as having a legitimate role in deciding the organization's response to change, even though their interests and goals are in conflict.

These assumptions underlie the model's increase in cooperation as pressure builds for change.

The first of the model's three stages, as shown in Figure 18.3, is the *stimulus for change* that must arise to move the players to act jointly and cooperatively. The stimulus can be internal but is most likely to be external, as it was in the 1980s. Economic difficulty, stemming from strong competition, is a prime example of a stimulus for change. It usually invokes a call to increase productivity and cut costs. To gain union and worker support, however, these ends cannot be achieved primarily by cutting wages and/or employment.

The second stage is the initial program stage. It involves the commitment of labor and management to *implement* a specific change (cooperation) program. To move from the decision to cooperate to program implementation, the parties must agree on the goals to be met, the programs that will meet these goals, and then which of the most likely programs is the best to use.

The final stage involves *institutionalizing the program*. If goals are initially met and it is expected that they will continue to be met by the program that has been implemented, and the stimulus that started the process is still there, the parties will think of continuing the program. Management usually is more likely to suggest

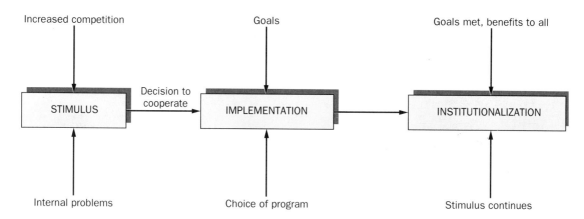

FIGURE 18.3 The Kochan–Dyer three-stage model of labor–management cooperation and change.

thinking about change programs (stage 1) and supporting their implementation (stage 2), and so, at this stage, it is important that the union (1) sees that some of the initial benefits of the program go to it and its members, and (2) will get some of the credit for implementing the program and attaining initial goals. If these conditions are met, the union (and management) will keep supporting the program.

A final important point in the change/cooperation model is that the efforts in all stages must be kept apart from collective bargaining. The very nature of collective bargaining is adversarial. An adversarial process cannot lead to cooperative programs.

The Recent Record of Labor–Management Cooperation

In the United States, a flurry of cooperative programs marked the 1980s and continued into the 1990s. Two trends seem to stand out: (1) the early programs were problem-solving programs and, where successful or where change pressures intensified, these spawned higher level participation programs; and (2) problem-solving groups in which active union involvement was lacking did not survive and so tended not to lead to further worker participation programs.[15] Table 18.1 provides a listing and definition of popular programs.

A typical program progression in a company is that of the Automotive Products Company of the A. O. Smith Corporation.[16] At the start of the 1980s, labor relations at the company, which supplies car and truck frames to the major auto makers, were very poor. In 1981, at the urging of their major customers, the Big 3 auto makers (GM, Chrysler, and Ford) who themselves were under substantial pressure from Japanese imports, the company started a **quality-circle program**. The suggestions of the workers from the quality-circle program helped a bit, but the lack of union involvement doomed the program. In 1984, it was replaced by joint **union–management (problem-solving) committees** for the shop floor, and joint advisory committees for operational planning at the plantwide and companywide levels. Again, quality improved somewhat, but the pressure of Japanese imports on the Big

Table 18.1   *Worker Participation/Employee Involvement Programs and Practices*

Practice	Definition
Suggestion System	Program that elicits individual employee suggestions on improving work or the work environment
Survey Feedback	Use of employee attitude surveys, as part of a larger problem-solving process in which survey data are used to encourage, structure, and measure the effectiveness of employee participation
Quality Circle	Group of employees that meet voluntarily in a structured environment to identify and suggest work-related improvements; the group's only power is to suggest changes
Quality of Work-Life Committee or Union–Management Committee	Committee of employees representing the union and management, usually prohibited from addressing contractual issues; it usually focuses on issues to improve organizational performance and employee work-life
Job Redesign	Redesign of work to increase employee performance; for example, job enlargement to increase use of employee skills, broaden the variety of work performed, and provide the individual with greater autonomy
Self-Managing Team or Work Team	Group of employees given responsibility for a product or service and empowered to make decisions about assignment tasks and work methods; the team may also be responsible for its own support services and perform certain personnel functions
Employee Participation Group	Group of employees, such as a team or work council, that does not fall within the definition of quality circle or a self-managing team

Source: U.S. General Accounting Office, *Employee Involvement, Issues for Agencies to Consider in Designing and Implementing Programs*, GAO/GGD–88–82, May 1988, p. 6.

3 filtered down to A. O. Smith, in the form of price cuts, requiring further action by the company and its unions (primarily the Steel Workers). In 1987, **work teams** replaced the normal assembly line operations. These teams of five to seven workers do innumerable jobs and control most of the production aspects previously handled by management, such as scheduling, including overtime, ordering maintenance work, and quality control. Productivity growth doubled in the first year of the program (1988), and a profit-sharing plan paid each worker a bonus.

In general, the many comparable programs that have been studied have shown substantial gains from cooperation and, in particular, the use of work teams. Work teams are being used successfully by many companies, including (in addition to A. O. Smith) Boeing, Caterpillar, Cummins Engine (since 1973), D.E.C., General Mills, Ford, GE, GM, Monsanto, Procter & Gamble (since 1962), and Tektronix.[17] Work teams are also showing up in the office for clerical workers; they are being used by AT&T at both Bell Labs and AT&T Credit Corporation, by insurance companies (Shenandoah Life, Aid Association for Lutherans), and by many others.[18]

All is not rosy, however. The United Auto Workers and the Big 3 have a history of cooperative efforts in the 1980s. As late as mid-1989, the UAW leadership gave these programs and the policy of cooperation a vote of confidence.[19] However, GM's "indefinite idling" of four of its plants (in Pontiac, Michigan, Kansas City, Framingham, Massachusetts, and Atlanta) between 1988 and 1990 brought a blistering response from the UAW.[20] Their 1987 collective bargaining contract prohibited plant closings. The UAW, led by the new head of its GM department, Stephen Yokich, filed a grievance against the plant closings. They lost the dispute in arbitration, for the arbitrator ruled that the contract allowed layoffs when sales slump. The "indefinite idlings" were ruled to be layoffs, not plant closings. The union response was to attempt to alleviate long-term layoffs in new job security provisions in the September 1990 contract. The new strained relations between the UAW and GM do not bode well for the cooperative labor–management relationship they nurtured through the 1980s.

The legal status of worker participation efforts such as quality circles is now being openly questioned by some unions who do not want to be involved in them with management. The chemical workers union at DuPont filed unfair labor practice charges against the company for "domination of a labor organization," a violation of Section 8(a)(2) of the National Labor Relations Act.[21] The charge was upheld by an NLRB administrative law judge. More unfair labor practice charges are pending on this issue against DuPont and other organizations, for example, the U.S. Postal Service, which is being charged by the American Postal Workers Union. It seems that worker participation must have the support of the union if (1) it is to succeed and (2) it is not to be legally challenged.

ESOPs: The Ultimate in Labor Participation

Most labor–management cooperation occurs at the lower levels of companies—at the shop floor or in the office. Quality circles, work teams, and other employee involvement arrangements are primarily joint problem-solving ones. In a few cases, however, labor/worker participation occurs at the highest level.

In several companies, labor participation is at the highest level of decision making: the board of directors. As we will recall from Chapter 9, union representatives hold board of directors seats at Chrysler (United Auto Workers), Pan Am (Flight Engineers, as well as a representative of nonunion employees), Wheeling-Pittsburgh Steel, CF & I Steel and Kaiser Aluminum (United Steel Workers), and PIE Nationwide and Transcon (Teamsters, as well as a nonunion employee representative on Transcon's Board).[22]

The ultimate form of employee involvement is ownership, especially through an **employee stock ownership plan (ESOP)**. Because of their effect on productivity, favorable tax treatment, and usefulness in deterring takeovers, ESOPs have become widespread; many involve substantial money (see Table 18.2). By 1988, about 700 to 800 new ESOPs were being created each year, and about 9,000 American companies—most of them small and private—had ESOPs.[23]

Table 18.2   *Major ESOPs*

Company	ESOP ($ Millions)
Avis	1,750
Healthtrust	1,700
Procter & Gamble	1,000
Epic Healthcare	856
J. C. Penney	700
Parsons	560
Anheuser–Busch	500
Lockheed	500
Ralston Purina	500
Texaco	500
U.S. West	500
Whitman	500
Polaroid	300
Avondale	282

Sources: Business Week, March 20, 1989, p. 144; April 24, 1989, p. 124; May 15, 1989, p. 116; and *Forbes*, October 6, 1988, p. 72.

The ESOP is a trust set up to hold company stock for the employees. The company creates the trust, and annually it contributes stock and/or cash to it. Any cash contributions are used to buy stock from the existing shareholders to add to the company stock contributions to the trust. Stock in an ESOP trust is credited to accounts set up for each employee, and over a period of years, up to seven, are vested, just as a pension would be.[24] This process is illustrated in Figure 18.4. If the ESOP is leveraged (like the very popular leveraged buyouts in the 1980s), the process works as just described except the trust borrows the money to buy the company's stock. Then annual company contributions *and* stock dividends are used to pay off the loan. As it is paid off, the stock it was used to buy is credited to the employees' accounts.

Another benefit to company and employees is the ESOP's replacement of retirement benefits. If a company's profitability increases as its employees become its owners, the value of the stock jumps. This can provide for pension benefits that are rich and growing. As the ultimate form of worker participation, ESOPs can have great payoffs for company, management, and workers.

One success story is that of BCM Engineers, Inc. In 1977, BCM employees bought their $6.5 million business from Betz Laboratories, Inc.; a newly organized ESOP paid $3.8 million of that sum. In 1988, BCM earned about $50 million in revenues. A share of stock worth $2.40 in 1977 paid $21.25 at the end of 1987, and the ESOP owned more than 85 percent of the shares. BCM typically contributes 4 to 6 percent of compensation per year to employee ESOP accounts. Employees also get annual dividend checks on their shares, and they can vote in shareholder elections after as little as six months of service.[25]

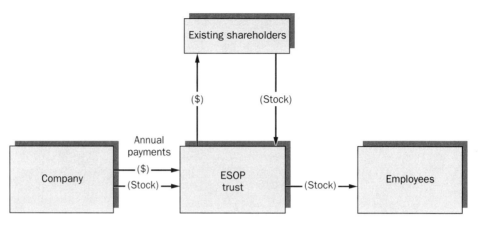

FIGURE 18.4 How ESOPs work.

The AFL–CIO has set up a fund to help its affiliated unions to finance leveraged ESOPs, because lenders usually want cash immediately for equity purchases before putting up the debt financing for the buyout.[26] The **Employee Partnership Fund (EPF)**, however, has another, more pressing goal in providing funding: to prevent plant closings and layoffs by buying these ailing facilities. But it would still give the company tu its workers (and union), to turn it around through increased productivity and other efficiency and effectiveness measures.

COMPARABLE WORTH: EQUAL MONEY FOR EQUAL VALUE

Discrimination in the labor market based on sex, race, color, religion, or national origin is prohibited under Title VII of the 1964 Civil Rights Act (as amended by the 1972 Equal Employment Opportunity Act). Furthermore, the 1963 Equal Pay Act prohibits paying a woman less than a man purely on the basis of sex, when they are doing the same work. Nonetheless, it is common knowledge that women, on the average, earn about 70 percent of what men do, as full-time, year-round employees.[27] Under the law, they are not making less for equal work but less for "comparable" work. The issue is not one of pay equality, but of **pay equity** or **comparable worth**.

The Earnings Gap

The **earnings gap** between men and women is the basis for the comparable worth controversy. That women make less than men is an indisputable, long-standing fact. Why? Three explanations are commonly proposed, based on

1. Differences in the characteristics, as workers, of men and women.
2. Differences in the occupations or jobs that men and women tend to take.
3. Discrimination in the labor market.[28]

The first factor involves productive capacity characteristics such as age, education, and work (labor market) experience. Studies indicate that sex differences in this set of characteristics explain a relatively small portion of the gap. Similarly, discrimination studies, when controlling for the work characteristics of individuals and occupational patterns, explain a relatively small portion of the gap. However, "the introduction of occupational controls simply changes the question from one of earnings differences between men and women to the puzzle of differences in occupational employment patterns by sex."[29]

With regard to the second factor, differences in jobs taken leading to differences in pay, studies have shown that employment patterns explain much of the earnings gap. A major question then emerges: why are women in low-paying occupations? Labor market discrimination (unequal access to high-paying occupations) provides part of the answer. This factor is changing, however; evidence of women entering high-paying professional jobs is mounting.[30] But a second factor in **occupational segregation** is individual choice. Jobs with work schedules that are flexible or that don't require nights and holidays draw women because they don't interfere with family (home) responsibilities.[31] Changes in the allocation of family duties may alter this factor somewhat, but how much remains to be seen.

The Goal of Comparable Worth

From the evidence accumulated over the past two decades, the comparable worth problem seems to involve job/occupation patterns; there are female-dominated jobs, and they pay less than "comparable" male-dominated jobs. The natural forces of the market are not likely to alter these pay differences. It has also been observed that as women move into previously male-dominated occupations, making them female-dominated, relative pay levels fall. This occurred for cigar-makers (later 1800s), stenographers (turn of the century), bank tellers (postwar), typesetters (1970s), and insurance adjusters (1980s).[32] It seems that society puts less value on women's work, as expressed by the economic forces of the market.

Thus, the goal of comparable worth is to close this earnings or pay gap by having organizations set wages for different jobs to reflect differences in the value of the job. This value would be measured by the job's basic characteristics, primarily skill, effort, responsibility, and working conditions. The measuring instrument would be a **job evaluation system** (see Chapter 7) that assigns point values to the basic characteristics of a job and sums these up to get a score for the job. Table 18.3 illustrates a typical evaluation. Jobs with equivalent scores would rate equivalent pay. An important, and as yet unanswered, question is whether a widespread job evaluation/comparable worth system can produce a pay structure that will not only correct the inequities, but will also efficiently allocate resources which a market mechanism supposedly does.

Comparable Worth in Place

Comparable worth systems have been implemented in several states, counties, and cities for public sector workers. The Minnesota and Washington state efforts have been most widely publicized and will be discussed here. The provincial system in Ontario, Canada, which covers the private as well as public sector, will also be discussed. Finally, we will touch on some of the emerging issues.

Table 18.3 *Job Evaluations in a Comparable Worth System*

Criteria	Receptionist	Warehouseman
Education	106	80
Experience	79	86
Complexity	81	76
Supervisory responsibilities	0	0
Independence of action	55	55
Consequence of errors	46	51
Confidentiality	14	0
Contacts	48	33
Physical skill and effort	44	76
Working conditions	19	38
TOTAL[a]	492 points	495 points

Source: New York Times, July 27, 1989, p. A1.

  [a] Jobs evaluated within 3 points of each other are considered equivalent.

Washington's Comparable Worth Program

The Washington comparable worth program was born out of a 1981 pay discrimination lawsuit filed by nine female employees, who were joined by the American Federation of State, County, and Municipal Employees (AFSCME). In 1983, a federal district court found the state guilty under the Civil Rights Act, but this verdict was overturned in 1985 by the Ninth U.S. Circuit Court of Appeals. Since AFSCME and the state had already negotiated a settlement to remedy the pay discrimination, no appeal of the overturning was attempted. The negotiated settlement set aside $41.6 million in 1985, $46.5 million in 1986, and $10 million annually in the next six years. Pay adjustments started in 1986 for the state's 62,000 employees.[33]

After the first four years of the program, as the 1990s began, Washington's system seemed to be accomplishing what it set out to do: to eliminate (or practically eliminate) the pay gap between men and women doing equivalent or comparable work. However, occupational segregation has not changed for the most part. And market forces have caused some unforeseen problems. The major one is the difficulty the state is having in hiring (and retaining) men in jobs in which relative pay fell behind that in the private sector. (In some of these jobs, relative pay fell over 30 percent). To remedy some of the unintended consequences of the comparable worth program, pay in some jobs has had to be raised above the program-dictated level to recruit and hold workers, such as psychiatrists and pharmacists.[34]

Another interesting (and unintended) outcome of the new pay structure is the refusal of some workers to accept promotions. For example, a clerk-typist, comprising the largest group of workers in the state, would normally seek promotion to fiscal technician (mostly bookkeeping), which could then lead to accountant. However, the pay changes discourage clerk-typists from moving to fiscal technicians and taking a *pay cut*. This shuts them out of promotion to accountant. This dilemma is illustrated in Figure 18.5. These problems are causing a lot of rethinking of the program.

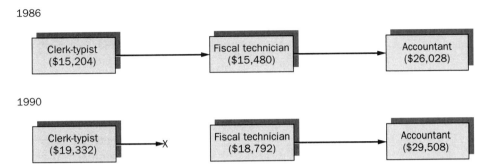

FIGURE 18.5 Comparable worth and promotion paths.

Minnesota's Comparable Worth Program

In the mid-1970s, Minnesota's Council on the Economic Status of Women analyzed the state payroll and found that female-dominated jobs were underpaid; the council felt that legislation was needed to remedy this inequity.[35] The legislation was passed and the four-year program started in 1983, with strong support from the unions, the largest of which was the AFSCME.

The state's program went so smoothly that the legislature extended it to all cities, counties, and school districts. At these levels, troubles started to appear, for the cost of the program caused some major financial hardships on cities.[36] However, the widely supported program is not having many problems at the statewide level.

Ontario's Comparable Worth Program

The Ontario comparable worth program, adopted in 1987, is one of the broadest ever attempted.[37] Like Minnesota's, it was passed by the legislature voluntarily, but unlike that plan, it covers private as well as public workers.[38] It requires public sector comparable worth adjustments to start in mid-1989 with a 1994 target for full pay equivalency. In the private sector, it requires all companies with over 500 workers to post the details of their programs (primarily wage adjustments) at the start of 1990 and to begin the wage adjustments a year later, with a three-year implementation period. Smaller firms start later, with a six-year horizon for their programs.

The Ontario program is the most expansive of any to date. Many interested parties throughout the world are watching it very closely.

Comparable Worth in the Future

With 22 states in the United States in the midst of comparable worth programs for their public sectors as well as Ontario's program for public and private sectors, much information is being gathered on the effects of implementing comparable worth. Added to the information generated from Washington's program, started in 1986, a picture is beginning to emerge.

The male–female pay or earnings gap narrowed or is narrowing: the main goal of the programs was attained or is being attained. However, certain unintended consequences have also been incurred. Many of these, such as the shortage of job applicants in positions where relative pay has dropped (e.g., psychiatrists and pharmacists in Washington), could have been predicted by the straightforward use of economic theory.[39]

An across-the-board increase for a set of job categories should lower employment in those occupations: in Washington State it did.[40] With relatively higher pay, however, these same female-dominated jobs will attract a greater labor supply, especially women who have traditionally filled these jobs. This will slow down occupational desegregation, as it seems to have done in Washington.[41]

Some interesting quirks that pop up in comparable worth programs have cast shadows over them. For example, in the Ontario program, the *Toronto Sun* found that twelve male groups (jobs categories) made *less* than comparable female groups. Because the law requires comparable worth adjustments for women only, the men are stuck.[42]

The emerging picture shows a rocky future for comparable worth because of the market distortions it causes. The issue in the 1990s will not be comparable worth programs per se, but how to reach the goal of comparable worth systems without overly distorting the relatively efficient resource allocation mechanism of the market.

DISCUSSION QUESTIONS

1. Explain how wage changes could cause price changes, that is, the linkage between wage and price changes.

2. Why might *inflationary* union wage increases in a company not be reflected in higher prices?

3. Develop two arguments (or models, if you like): one to *support* and one to *refute* the contention that unions are an important cause of inflation in the United States.

4. Explain why, in the Phillips curve, the rate of change of prices is small when unemployment is high.

5. Discuss the differences in worker participation in Germany and Japan.

6. Discuss the Kochan–Dyer three-stage model of cooperation and change in a union setting.

7. Compare a *work team* with a *quality circle*.

8. What is an ESOP? Why are they so popular with managers and employees (and unions)?

9. What are the three most likely reasons why women's earnings, on the average, are about two-thirds those of men?

10. What is "occupational segregation" and why is it such a problem in the United States?

11. What is the goal of comparable worth?

12. What might be some of the unforeseen or unintended consequences of a comparable worth program like that in the state of Washington?

VOCABULARY LIST

cost-push inflation

labor productivity

wage-gain transmission or spillover

threat effect

cost-of-living adjustment (COLA)

wage–price spiral

Phillips curve

markup pricing

worker participation/employee involvement (EI)

Kochan–Dyer three-stage model

quality-circle program

union–management (problem-solving) committee

work team

employee stock ownership plan (ESOP)

Employee Partnership Fund (EPF)

pay equity

comparable worth

earnings gap

occupational segregation

job evaluation system

FOOTNOTES

1. *Wall Street Journal*, July 24, 1989, p. A2; *New York Times*, June 4, 1990, p. C2; *Business Week*, June 11, 1990, p. 15.

2. Dallas S. Batten, "Inflation: The Cost-Push Myth," *Federal Reserve Bank of St. Louis Review* (June–July 1981): 20.

3. Albert Rees, *The Economics of Trade Unions* (University of Chicago Press, 1977), p. 97; Daniel J. B. Mitchell, *Unions, Wages, and Inflation* (Brookings Institution, 1980), p. 173.

4. Rees, *The Economics of Trade Unions*, p. 98; Mitchell, *Union, Wages, and Inflation*, p. 179.

5. Ibid.

6. *New York Times*, June 4, 1990, p. C2; the statistics cited are from this piece.

7. *Business Week*, November 7, 1988, p. 30.

8. Rees, *The Economics of Trade Unions*, p. 108; Wayne Vroman, "Cost-of-Living Escalators and Price–Wage Linkages in the U.S. Economy, 1968–1980," *Industrial and Labor Relations Review* (January 1985): 229.

9. Ibid., p. 235.

10. A. W. Phillips, "The Relation between Unemployment and the Rate of Change of Money Wages in the United Kingdom, 1861–1957," *Economica* (November 1958): 283–299.

11. See, for example, Robert J. Gordon, "The Role of Wages in the Inflation Process" (pp. 276, 281–282) and James B. Rebitzer, "Unemployment, Labor Relations, and Unit Labor Costs" (pp. 389, 393–394), both in *American Economic Association Papers and Proceedings* (May 1988).

12. *Business Week*, April 30, 1990, p. 57.

13. Charlotte Gold, *Labor–Management Committees: Confrontation, Cooptation, or Cooperation?* (Cornell University, ILR Press, 1986), p. 7.

14. Michael Schuster, "Models of Cooperation and Change in Union Settings," *Industrial Relations* (Fall 1985): 383. Much of this section comes from this article.

15. Robert Drago, "Quality Circle Survival: An Exploratory Analysis," *Industrial Relations* (Fall 1988): 349.

16. *Business Week*, May 29, 1989, p. 66.

17. *Business Week*, July 10, 1989, p. 58, and August 21, 1989, p. 67.

18. *Business Week*, November 28, 1988, p. 64, and July 10, 1989, p. 59.

19. *Wall Street Journal*, June 21, 1989, p. A2.

20. *Business Week*, November 6, 1989, p. 96, and April 16, 1990, p. 28.

21. *Wall Street Journal*, March 28, 1990, p. B1.

22. *Business Week*, December 14, 1987, p. 128.

23. *Inc.* (June 1988): 94.

24. Ibid., p. 95.

25. Ibid., pp. 94–95.

26. *New York Times*, February 20, 1990, p. C6.

27. *New York Times*, May 31, 1990, p. A1.

28. Janice Shack-Marquez, "Earnings Differences between Men and Women: An Introductory Note," *Monthly Labor Review* (June 1984): 15.

29. Ibid., p. 16.

30. *Business Week*, February 29, 1988, p. 48.

31. Ibid., p. 52; June O'Neill et al., "Effects of Comparable Worth Policy: Evidence from Washington State," *American Economic Association Papers and Proceedings* (May 1989): 305.

32. Carolyn Shaw Bell, "Comparable Worth: How Do We Know It Will Work?," *Monthly Labor Review* (December 1985): 6; *Business Week*, February 29, 1988, p. 49.

33. *Monthly Labor Review* (March 1986): 43.

34. *New York Times*, May 31, 1990, p. A1.

35. Kathleen Sylvester, "'Comparable Worth' Revisited: Whatever Happened after Washington State?," *Governing* (June 1988): 42–43.

36. Ibid., p. 44.

37. *Wall Street Journal*, June 17, 1987, p. 28.

38. *Wall Street Journal*, March 9, 1990, p. B1.

39. Sandra E. Gleason, "Comparable Worth: Some Questions Still Unanswered," *Monthly Labor Review* (December 1985): 17.

40. O'Neill et al., "Effects of Comparable Worth Policy," p. 309.

41. *New York Times,* May 31, 1990, p. A1.

42. *Wall Street Journal,* March 9, 1990, p. B1.

REFERENCES

AARON, HENRY J., and CAMERAN M. LOUGY. *The Comparable Worth Controversy.* The Brookings Institution, 1986.

ALDRICH, MARK, and ROBERT BUCHELE. *The Economics of Comparable Worth.* Ballinger Publishing, 1986.

BATTEN, DALLAS S. "Inflation: The Cost-Push Myth." *Federal Reserve Bank of St. Louis Review* (June–July 1981): 20–26.

BELL, CAROLYN SHAW. "Comparable Worth: How Do We Know It Will Work?" *Monthly Labor Review* (December 1985): 5–12.

BLANCHARD, OLIVER J. "The Wage Price Spiral." *Quarterly Journal of Economics* (August 1986): 543–565.

BUCHELE, ROBERT, and MARK ALDRICH. "How Much Difference Would Comparable Worth Make?" *Industrial Relations* (Spring 1985): 222–233.

CANTOR, RICHARD, and JOHN WENNINGER. "Current Labor Market Trends and Inflation." *Federal Reserve Bank of New York Quarterly Review* (Autumn 1987): 36–48.

CARLSON, KEITH M. "How Much Lower Can the Unemployment Rate Go?" *Federal Reserve Bank of St. Louis Review* (July–August 1988): 44–57.

DRAGO, ROBERT. "Quality Circle Survival: An Exploratory Analysis." *Industrial Relations* (Fall 1988): 336–351.

EATON, ADRIENNE E., and PAULA B. VOOS. "The Ability of Unions to Adapt to Innovative Workplace Arrangements." *American Economic Association Papers and Proceedings* (May 1989): 172–176.

GLEASON, SANDRA E. "Comparable Worth: Some Questions Still Unanswered." *Monthly Labor Review* (December 1985): 17–18.

GOLD, CHARLOTTE. *Labor–Management Committees: Confrontation, Cooptation, or Cooperation?* Cornell University, ILR Press, Key Issues No. 29, 1986.

GORDON, ROBERT J. "The Role of Wages in the Inflation Process." *American Economic Association Papers and Proceedings* (May 1988): 276–283.

KAHN, LAWRENCE M. "Union Strength and Wage Inflation." *Industrial Relations* (Spring 1979): 144–155.

KILLINGSWORTH, MARK R. "Comparable Worth in the Job Market: Estimating Its Effects." *Monthly Labor Review* (July 1985): 39–41.

KOZIARA, KAREN SHALLCROSS. "Comparable Worth: Organizational Dilemmas." *Monthly Labor Review* (December 1985): 13–16.

LEWIN, DAVID. "The Future of Employee Involvement/Participation in the United States." *Proceedings of the 1989 Spring Meeting.* Industrial Relations Research Association, April 5–7, 1989, pp. 470–475.

LIGHT, AUDREY, and MANUELITA URETA. "Gender Differences in Wages and Job Turnover Among Continuously Employed Workers." *American Economic Association Papers and Proceedings* (May 1990): 293–297.

MITCHELL, DANIEL J. B. *Unions, Wages, and Inflation.* The Brookings Institution, 1980.

NORWOOD, JANET L. "Perspectives on Comparable Worth: An Introduction to the Numbers." *Monthly Labor Review* (December 1985): 3–4.

O'NEILL, JUNE, MICHAEL BRIEN, and JAMES CUNNINGHAM. "Effects of Comparable Worth Policy: Evidence from Washington State." *American Economic Association Papers and Proceedings* (May 1989): 305–309.

PHILLIPS, A. W. "The Relation between Unemployment and the Rate of Change of Money Wages in the United Kingdom, 1861–1957." *Economica* (November 1958): 283–299.

REBITZER, JAMES B. "Unemployment, Labor Relations, and Unit Labor Costs." *American Economic Association Papers and Proceedings* (May 1988): 389–394.

REES, ALBERT. *The Economics of Trade Unions.* University of Chicago Press, 1977, Ch. V.

ROSOW, JEROME M., ed. *Teamwork: Joint Labor–Management Programs in America.* Pergamon Press, 1986.

SCHUSTER, MICHAEL. "Models of Cooperation and Change in Union Settings." *Industrial Relations* (Fall 1985): 382–394.

———. *Union–Management Cooperation.* W. E. Upjohn Institute for Employment Research, 1984.

SHACK-MARQUEZ, JANICE. "Earnings Differences between Men and Women: An Introductory Note." *Monthly Labor Review* (June 1984): 15–16.

SIEGEL, IRVING H., and EDGAR WEINBERG. *Labor–Management Cooperation: The American Experience.* W. E. Upjohn Institute for Employment Research, 1982.

SIELING, MARK S. "Staffing Patterns Prominent in Female–Male Earnings Gap." *Monthly Labor Review* (June 1984): 29–33.

SMITH, ROBERT S. "Comparable Worth: Limited Coverage and the Exacerbation of Inequality." *Industrial and Labor Relations Review* (January 1988): 227–239.

SORENSEN, ELAINE. "Effect of Comparable Worth Policies on Earnings." *Industrial Relations* (Fall 1987): 227–239.

———. "Implementing Comparable Worth: A Survey of Recent Job Evaluation Studies." *American Economic Association Papers and Proceedings* (May 1986): 364–367.

SYLVESTER, KATHLEEN. "'Comparable Worth' Revisited: Whatever Happened after Washington State?" *Governing* (June 1988): 41–45.

VERMA, ANIL, and ROBERT B. MCKERSIE. "Employment Involvement: The Implication of Noninvolvement by Unions." *Industrial and Labor Relations Review* (July 1987): 556–568.

Voos, Paula B. "The Practices Consonant with Cooperative Labor Relations." *Proceedings of the 1989 Spring Meeting.* Industrial Relations Research Association, April 5–7, 1989, pp. 483–490.

Vroman, Wayne. "Cost-of-Living Escalators and Price–Wage Linkages in the U.S. Economy, 1968–1980." *Industrial and Labor Relations Review* (January 1985): 225–235.

CHAPTER 19

THE FUTURE SHAPE OF LABOR–MANAGEMENT RELATIONS

L abor–management relations in the 1990s and into the twenty-first century will be different from what they are today, just as labor–management relations today and in the 1980s were different from what they were in the 1970s. Yet some of the basic characteristics that emerged at the end of the nineteenth century are still pretty much intact today. Recently, John Dunlop highlighted the following six fundamental features of the system:

1. *Exclusive representation,* or one union for a given group of workers, selected by a majority vote.

2. *Collective bargaining agreements* with a sharp distinction between *negotiating the agreement* (with the negotiating period being the only legitimate strike time) and *interpreting it* (by private, third-party neutrals, over a term that is fixed and during which there are no strikes or lockouts).

3. *Decentralized collective bargaining* by many unions and, in many cases, by many locals of these unions.

4. *National union organizations* with *relatively high dues and large staffs* to negotiate and administer, or help negotiate and administer, the countless private, decentralized agreements (as there is no significant intervention by government).

5. *Intense employer opposition to unions and unionization,* only slightly modified by legislation enacted over 50 years ago to protect labor.

6. A relatively *passive role for government* in most aspects of labor–management relations, but a highly legalistic and drawn-out role, administratively and judicially, in the details of labor–employment law and regulation (of health and safety, pensions, and equal employment opportunity).[1]

Because of the drastic drop in union membership in the 1980s, stemming from changing economic, demographic, and legal-political conditions, the question of radical change in the system has come to the fore. Questions range from the rather drastic one of whether unions will disappear by the end of this century (less than a decade from now) to how the function of unions will change.

THE END OF AMERICAN UNIONS?

As concession bargaining and declining membership accelerated in the 1980s, people started to ask if unions could survive. A sampling of some of the titles in the literature of the period reveals this questioning attitude:

Peter Pestillo's "Can Unions Meet the Needs of a 'New' Work Force?" in the *Monthly Labor Review,* as early as 1979.

"The De-Unionization of America" in the British *Economist* (October 23, 1983).

Joseph Garbarino's "Unionism without Unions: The New Industrial Relations?" in *Industrial Relations,* Winter 1984.

"Beyond Unions," the *Business Week* cover story in the July 8, 1985, issue.

The conclusion in these and similar articles was that unions might be shaky and under great pressures, but they were highly likely to survive on the American scene.

An interesting quote points to the vitality of the American labor movement. In the 1920s, the AFL had lost 40 percent of its membership. The American Plan and welfare capitalism had unions reeling (sound familiar?). In his presidential address to the American Economic Association in December 1932, George E. Barnett noted:

The past ten years have seen changes of amazing magnitude in the organization of American economic society. It is one of these fundamental alterations that I wish to speak of this evening. . . . The change to which I refer is the lessening importance of trade unionism in American economic organization.[2]

This assessment came on the eve of "the largest explosion in union growth in this country's history."[3]

American unions probably will not see an "explosion of growth" as occurred in the tumultuous years of the Great Depression and World War II, but the potential for growth is there. The American labor force has many unorganized workers, but not in the core industries as in the 1930s. They are spread far and wide, many in small service-oriented businesses. However, before getting into optimistic outlooks for the American labor movement, let's look at what a continuation of the status quo would mean.

WHAT DOES "MORE OF THE SAME" MEAN? ═══════

If American unions continue to do what they are doing now, what is the likely shape of things to come? Will their decline abate and even be reversed? Are we going through a transitional stage of intense competition, accompanied by heightened management opposition to trade unions?

First, the political climate is changing. The anti-union posture of the Reagan administration has been replaced by the more moderate stand of the Bush administration. But America is not moving in a liberal direction at breakneck speed; there is no danger that the liberal politics of Roosevelt's New Deal, Kennedy's New Frontier, and Johnson's Great Society will be upon us in the near future.

The economic picture, however, is not changing, at least in terms of the trends. We can expect a greater **globalization** of economic activity, with more competition on an international scale. The market integration in Europe, the growing manufacturing muscle of the newly industrialized economies and Third World countries on top of that of the new Eastern bloc all foretell greater international competition. Most of this competition will be in manufacturing. As a result, the service sector in the United States will continue to be the growth sector. The decline of mass production presents a challenge to the standing of unions in American society.[4]

The American labor force and the demographics that shape it seem to indicate more change and in similar directions as recent changes. First, although the labor force is shrinking, and will continue to do so in the 2000s, increases in productivity (especially in the service sector) are predicted to offset much of this decline.[5] Second, the steady increase of female participation in the labor force that started in the postwar period seems to have ended, or at least hit a plateau. Nonetheless, women will continue to make up an increasing percentage of workers as more men than women will be retiring in the next decade or so.[6] Furthermore, recent studies have indicated that women are more likely than men to want to join a union.[7] Third, the proportion of minorities, blacks and Hispanics in the labor force will continue to increase. The growing number of young Hispanics will account for almost 30 percent of the new workers in this decade, while blacks will account for just over 15 percent.[8] Adding a new twist to the labor force picture in the 1990s and beyond is the rapid growth of the **contingent workforce,** workers that lack full-time jobs and/or long-term ties to a company, many by choice. They include part-timers, "temps" (workers supplied by temporary-help firms), outside contractors' employees, and self-employed professionals doing mainly free-lance work. This group now makes up at least one-fourth of the workforce.[9] Members of this group are attractive to employers because they allow for flexibility in the size and makeup of a company's workforce, a useful feature in a competitive environment. Further, in many cases these workers don't receive any of the benefits that full-timers receive.

If American unions continue to do what they are, in general, doing now, their prospects for the future are dim. Under the status quo, most predictions for American unions are that by the end of the century they will represent only about 5 percent of the workforce.[10] (Usually this projection is for unionization of the private sector workforce as public sector unions are not expected to decline much in the next ten years.)

What unions are doing now is not very different from what they have always done: business unionism is concerned with wages, hours, and other terms and conditions of employment for union members. On the *wage* front, 1990 figures show that unionized workers made 20.4 percent more than nonunionized workers; this figure was up from 14.6 percent 15 years earlier.[11] This earnings gap, however, was built in the 1970s; nonunion wages grew faster than union wages through most of the 1980s. A new National Bureau of Economic Research (NBER) study has concluded that the unions' success in raising wages has actually been a major contributing factor in their decline. Higher wages gained in the intense economic conditions of the 1970s and early 1980s led to greater management opposition to unions and unionization, manifested in tactics such as the use of permanent strike replacements and the movement of operations from union to nonunion areas.[12]

As union strength and coverage decline, workers (and unions) will increasingly turn to the courts and legislation to gain protection from employers. The 1988 plant closing law provides just such an example, as does the major effort of workers' groups in trying to get a national parental leave bill (the vetoed and sidelined Family and Medical Leave Act) through Congress, starting back in 1988. The child care legislative campaign is another good example of resorting to legislation rather than bargaining. The growing litigation over wrongful discharge illustrates the pursuit of employee rights through the courts rather than at the bargaining table.

TURNING IT AROUND

Can American unions turn their situation around? Can they effectively represent their present members, protecting them from job loss and maintaining and enhancing their real incomes by keeping wages and fringe benefits ahead of price changes? Most importantly, can they extend the scope of unionism to a greater portion of the American labor force? We believe they can.

Effectively Representing Current Members

Unions can more effectively represent their current membership by changing their attitudes and tactics in dealing with management. This would primarily entail meeting mangement's hard line with their own, exerting a militancy and fervor that got results before and will get them results again. The cooperative emphasis between many unions and employers must be tempered by an emphasis, first and foremost, on the interests of the workers.

Unions accepted cooperative programs in the 1980s under the stimulus of adverse economic conditions. Through these programs, labor and management improved product (quality) and productivity. In many of these programs, however, the payoffs for labor were minimal as accommodating unions soft-pedaled demands. In the late 1980s when economic conditions (and the unemployment rate) improved, unions expected to see a greater payoff for their members. But many did not see these benefits. The example of GM plant "idlings" in the face of the numerous cooperative efforts between the company and the United Auto Workers cried for union action. Union action finally did come forth, strongly supported by the new UAW head of the GM division (now UAW president) over the hesitation of other national UAW leaders. If labor cooperation is sought, rewards for the union and its membership must be concrete and visible. As the economy comes out of the 1990–1991 recession, unions will again expect payoffs for years of cooperation.

In bargaining, unions must seek rewards commensurate with a company's financial position. If management is not willing to share information in this area, unions have to hold tight. If everyone makes sacrifices to keep a company afloat, as happened at Chrysler in the late 1970s, then labor can expect to make sacrifices. But when other participants in the company are getting rewards, labor should also.

Strikes may not be the most effective means to combat management intransigence given the widespread use of replacements. However, in the Greyhound strike (1990), in which the company could not hire enough replacement drivers, the company was forced into bankruptcy. Other methods to move management can be used; the **corporate campaigns** discussed in Chapter 14 can be effective instruments of pressure. At one university, maintenance workers and their union knew a strike would not be effective in their bargaining impasse; it would very quickly cost them their jobs and not accomplish anything. So they set up demonstrations and pickets at regional recruiting meetings that the school organized. The university's point of vulnerability was linked to its prospective students (and their parents). In a corporate campaign where coalitions are so important, union coalition building and public relations afford an opportunity to expand membership.

Recruiting New Members

To maintain a major presence in both society and the economy, American unions must reverse their decline and expand to represent a significantly greater portion of the labor force than they do now. Their position as labor's voice in social, political, and economic terms can be regained as they win back public support. This objective can be accomplished in several complementary ways. Using both new techniques and old techniques employed in new ways, unions can organize and represent an increasing portion of American workers, especially those in the rapidly growing service sector of the economy. Organized labor can show the public they are the protectors of the rights of workers in the United States.

First, the American labor movement must build (or rebuild) *coalitions* with other groups in the country by

1. Widening their concerns from the relatively narrow focus of their members to the working class in general, which they can show in their picketing, through the media, and so on.
2. Taking the lead in seeking change that is important to others, for example, women's and minority groups, thus broadening their potential impact.[13]

Building bridges to these other groups, such as women and minorities, is critical in expanding union coverage, because these are the fastest growing groups in the labor force. Unions have political clout and have been successful in leading the fight for legislation such as the plant closing law, polygraph protection law, and trade bills.[14] They can now bring this power to bear on important women's issues like child care and parental leave, general workers' issues like health care, and minority issues like the strengthening of equal employment opportunity and affirmative action laws. Some of these issues endanger some union programs. Seniority is often in conflict with affirmative action, as we explained in Chapter 10. Moreover, legislation protecting basic employee rights may "rob" unions of some of the functions they now fulfill. European unions have seen increasing government intervention in this area for the last two decades, and, though suspicious of the trend at first, they have found that new rights mandated by government have turned out to be an effective tool for organizing and *extending* their representation.[15] Thus, in some areas, such as affirmative action with its effect on seniority systems, compromise by the labor movement is necessary to retain its position in America. In other areas, government intervention may well help the labor movement regain its position without requiring sacrifices of it.

Second, American unions must utilize strategic planning approaches in their quest to "turn it around." One of the key concepts in strategic planning is to identify *strengths* and utilize them to the maximum. The AFL–CIO's February 1985 report, *The Changing Situation of Workers and Their Unions,* was a good start in this direction. The report analyzed the environment of the labor movement and made a series of recommendations, but mostly to overcome or improve American unionism's *weaknesses.* What are some of the major strengths of the American labor movement, and what is the best way to utilize them in the environment in which the movement operates? One major match of strength and environment comes immediately to mind: public sector unions, and the largest and fastest growing (and least organized) sector of the labor force, the service sector. Why not let the AFL–CIO's public sector unions that have been so successful in organizing white-collar workers in government, like the American Federation of Government Employees (AFGE) and the American Federation of State, County, and Municipal Employees (AFSCME), try their hand in the private sector? This is not a new suggestion but one that requires overcoming some jurisdictional problems that tend to hold up much potential union activity.[16]

A third technique that unions can use (and some are already using it) is to extend their membership reach through *new forms of membership.* This recommendation came from the AFL-CIO's *The Changing Situation of Workers and Their Unions* (Recommendation 1.2). As mentioned in Chapter 17, the American Federation of Teachers (AFT) implemented an **associate membership program,** starting in Texas as early as 1985. Other unions have also adopted this type of program.[17] For example, the Amalgamated Clothing and Textile Workers Union (ACTWU) uses it in the South in order to keep union supporters of failed organization drives in nonunion plants in contact with the ACTWU and to gain a foothold in plants as a tentative step toward an organization drive. This type of association has also been used by the International Brotherhood of Electrical Workers (IBEW) to build bridges to nonunion electricians to tout the union. By providing services such as inexpensive insurance and similar benefits, or job training and career counseling, unions may be able to gain standing with potential members by first recruiting them as "associates" who pay a nominal fee and need expend no participation efforts. Recruiting associate members draws little, if any, reaction from management and does not require anything under the NLRA/LMRA. The nonunion pool is huge and growing; efforts to bridge the gap to it are very important to the American labor movement.

The future of American unions is uncertain. The fervor that unions displayed in the 1930s and 1940s has been lacking for three or four decades, but new life can be breathed into the movement. In a democratic society, some form of worker participation is necessary. As we see in both Europe and Pacific Asia, the trade union movement is important in providing this participation. In the United States, this has also been true and, we believe, will continue to be. The shape of labor–management relations will be somewhat different in the future than it is today. We believe the differences will involve a core relationship between union and employer that is similar to what exists today, but with a stronger union mission to protect members' rights and, indeed, the rights of all workers, and peripheral relationships between unions and nonmembers with benefits for both. A stronger and more dedicated labor movement in the future is a necessary component of America's economy and society.

DISCUSSION QUESTIONS

1. Briefly describe the six fundamental features of the American labor–management relations system that John Dunlop highlighted.
2. If you had to choose one feature of Dunlop's American labor–management relations system that you think will change in the twenty-first century, which would you pick, and why?
3. What does the future of the American labor movement look like if the status quo holds?
4. What must unions do to better represent their members, especially those involved in cooperative labor–management programs?
5. The hard line of labor in bargaining has traditionally been backed by the strike or the threat of a strike; why might this not be true now, and what tools might unions put to better use to back up their demands?
6. What might be some of the problems of building coalitions with women's and minority groups?
7. What do you see as some of the strengths of the American labor movement today?
8. What are some of the benefits of new forms of membership to unions? To workers as "associates" (rather than regular members)?

VOCABULARY LIST

globalization
contingent workforce

corporate campaign
associate membership program

FOOTNOTES ══════

1. John T. Dunlop, "Have the 1980's Changed U.S. Industrial Relations?" *Monthly Labor Review* (May 1988): 31.

2. Michael Goldfield, *The Decline of Organized Labor in the United States* (University of Chicago Press, 1987), p. 245.

3. Ibid.

4. Michael Piore, "The Decline of Mass Production and the Challenge to Union Survival," *Industrial Relations Journal* (Autumn 1986): 207.

5. *Wall Street Journal*, May 8, 1989, p. A1, and May 16, 1989, p. A1; *Business Week*, January 9, 1989, p. 39, April 3, 1989, p. 82, and September 25, 1989, p. 154.

6. *Wall Street Journal*, March 7, 1989, p. B1.

7. *Executive Female* (March–April 1989): 6.

8. *Wall Street Journal*, March 7, 1989, p. B1.

9. Richard S. Belous, *The Contingent Economy: The Growth of the Temporary, Part-time and Subcontracted Workforce* (National Planning Association, 1989); *Washington Post*, July 12, 1989, p. A22.

10. *Wall Street Journal*, April 17, 1990, p. A1.

11. Ibid.

12. *Wall Street Journal*, June 13, 1990, p. A14.

13. Charles Heckscher, "Crisis and Opportunity for Labor," *Proceedings of the 1987 Spring Meeting* (Industrial Relations Research Association, April 29–May 1, 1987), p. 469.

14. *Fortune*, October 24, 1988, p. 8.

15. Heckscher, "Crisis and Opportunity for Labor," p. 470.

16. *Wall Street Journal*, June 13, 1990, p. A14.

17. *Business Week*, October 13, 1986, p. 126.

REFERENCES ══════

AFL–CIO Committee on the Evolution of Work. *The Changing Situation of Workers and Their Unions.* AFL–CIO, February 1985.

BELOUS, RICHARD S. *The Contingent Economy: The Growth of the Temporary, Part-time and Subcontracted Workforce.* National Planning Association, 1989.

DUNLOP, JOHN T. "Have the 1980's Changed U.S. Industrial Relations?" *Monthly Labor Review* (May 1988): 29–34.

FREEDMAN, AUDREY. "How the 1980's Have Changed U.S. Industrial Relations." *Monthly Labor Review* (May 1988): 35–38.

GARBARINO, JOSEPH W. "Unionism without Unions: The New Industrial Relations?" *Industrial Relations* (Winter 1984): 40–51.

GOLDFIELD, MICHAEL. *The Decline of Organized Labor in the United States*. University of Chicago Press, 1987, Ch. 11.

HECKSCHER, CHARLES. "Crisis and Opportunity for Labor." *Proceedings of the 1987 Spring Meeting*. Industrial Relations Research Association, April 29–May 1, 1987, pp. 465–470.

KOCHAN, THOMAS A., ed. *Challenges and Choices Facing American Labor*. MIT Press, 1985, "Epilogue: Is a New Industrial Relations System Emerging?," pp. 339–345.

KRISLOV, JOSEPH. "Unions in the Next Century: An Exploratory Essay." *Journal of Labor Research* (Spring 1986): 165–173.

MITCHELL, DANIEL J. B. "Will Collective Bargaining Outcomes in the 1990s Look Like Those of the 1980s?" *Proceedings of the 1989 Spring Meeting*. Industrial Relations Research Association, April 5–7, 1989, pp. 490–496.

PESTILLO, PETER J. "Can Unions Meet the Needs of a 'New' Work Force?" *Monthly Labor Review* (February 1979): 33–34.

PIORE, MICHAEL. "The Decline of Mass Production and the Challenge to Union Survival." *Industrial Relations Journal* (Autumn 1986): 207–213.

STEPINA, LEE P., and JACK FIORITO. "Toward a Comprehensive Theory of Union Growth and Decline." *Industrial Relations* (Fall 1986): 248–264.

THE NEGOTIATING EXERCISE

This negotiating exercise is a simulation. You, the students, will be taking the roles of union and management team members in collective bargaining for a new contract. You will be able to apply some of the theoretical material you have learned so far in studying labor–management relations to a realistic union–management interaction. The degree of realism reflected by this exercise depends on you, as the participants, and on your instructor, as the administrator.

The discussion of the exercise is divided into six parts. First, we discuss the process of developing bargaining objectives and strategies. Then we outline the background of the company and the union and examine their relationship. Third, we suggest a format for the negotiations, including roles for the participants as members of the union and the management bargaining teams; we also include some guidelines for the conduct of the exercise. Next, we detail the current collective bargaining contract. In the fifth section we give statistical information relevant to the negotiations.* A short final section contains some notes on the computer program that can be used in the exercise to cost out proposals.

BARGAINING OBJECTIVES AND STRATEGIES

Define Areas

In actual labor–management negotiations, both parties do a substantial amount of preparation before bargaining. Of course, much data must be gathered; the tables

---

* All names—of the company, union, and individuals—are fictitious.

in this exercise provide most of these data. The parties determine overall objectives. For example, the union may want a given level of job security and an increase of 5 to 6 percent in the economic package (wage rates and fringes), while management may aim for a given level of flexibility (through relaxation of work rules) which they estimate may increase productivity by about 3 percent and an economic package increase of no more than 3 to 5 percent. These objectives are then broken down to cover specific parts of the contract which they want to change and which they *think* the other side may bring up for change. Change not only includes altering a given item (like wage rates or health insurance coverage), but also deleting or adding new items. Additions have tended to come in fringe benefits, but now new job security measures are becoming popular as are flexibility measures.

Develop Ranges

Once specific areas are defined, they can be quantified to meet each side's overall objectives. A range has to be placed on items like wage rate changes, giving the level of the first offer, the expected level that will be agreed on, and the minimally acceptable level. For management, minimally acceptable levels are usually maximums (e.g., the maximum wage increase they will grant), while initial offers are usually very low (e.g., no wage increase, or a 1 percent wage increase which, using an overall average, would be about $.082 per hour in this exercise). Cost out these "proposals," especially at the "probably agreed upon" level. Then place yourself in the shoes of the other side, to get a feel for their reactions. Trying to apply this ranging of initial offer to minimally acceptable offer to what you think the other side will be asking for is quite a challenge!

Assign Priorities

After breaking down items and developing ranges for the quantifiable items, priorities must be assigned. The items must be ranked, and this ranking should be in line with the overall objectives of each party. It may be useful to assign your priorities as a team before developing the ranges for quantifiable elements. It is very difficult to guess at the other side's priorities, and it is usually more productive just to try to rank the items you think they will bargain over into two categories: more important and less important. Your highest priority items will be those over which you bargain hardest; the same should be true for the other side, so your guesses as to what you think the other side will be stressing better prepares you for the sessions ahead.

If your instructor supplies it to you, cost out your proposals with the computer program. Know what you are asking for, in dollar terms. And try to gauge the reaction of the other side, even if you can't cost out the proposals you expect from them.

As you get into the exercise, try to imagine that it is your job, prestige, and pay that is on the line. Be firm, analytical, and objective, but remember that you have to work with the union (if you're management) or the management (if you're union) for many years. And, of course, you have to "live" with the other members of your team for those years. Work together as a team. In collective bargaining, there is a need for sharp, analytical people, but interpersonal skills are of equal importance.

FIGURE A.1   Your bargaining objectives.

Item	Priority	Initial offer and cost (if relevant)	Expected level agreed upon (and cost if relevant)	Minimally acceptable level

Figures A.1 and A.2 are included for your use in preparing for the negotiations. Figure A.3 is a form you can use for selected items your team may want to cost out at several different levels.

THE BACKGROUND

This section lays the groundwork for the simulation and should give you guidance in developing and arranging your bargaining objectives and strategies.

The Company

American Computer Products (ACP) is a small, privately owned corporation that has been in business since 1975, over 15 years. The Ballow brothers started assembling and selling personal computer keyboards in a garage in Stockville, California, about 75 miles east of the San Francisco Bay Area's "Silicon Valley." They supplied these keyboards to a new personal computer company located in the Bay Area that had been started by two college classmates of the Ballows. After about two years, they hired three workers, for business started to pick up owing to the success of their one customer, Orange Personal Computers. By the end of 1983, ACP had 45 production workers, 3 supervisors, and 5 engineers, and business was increasing about 25 percent per year. They now had a network of customers. They incorporated and moved into

FIGURE A.2   The other side's bargaining objectives.

Item	Importance (more/less)	Expected initial offer	Expected level agreed upon[a]	Minimally acceptable level

[a] If item is the same as yours, the expected level agreed upon should be the same as in Figure A.1.

their present plant the following year, and by the end of that year the 45 production workers were unionized, becoming Local 15 of the Allied Assemblers of America (AAA). Now ACP had 126 production workers, 11 engineers, 6 salespersons, and an office staff of 16. Besides the two Ballow brothers, they had 6 other managers, and 13 supervisors (see Figure A.4). For the fiscal year ending September 30, 1990, company sales were $10,300,000, and net earnings (after taxes) were over $737,000 (see Figure A.5).

ACP signed its first contract with the AAA, Local 15, on November 1, 1984. During the organizing campaign, the company treated the union very fairly and did not oppose the unionizing of the 45 production workers. This amicable relationship deteriorated somewhat in 1985 and 1986, the strain being related mainly to the slowdown in business as the computer industry's growth rate slowed substantially. By 1987, the growth rate of the industry picked up again, and ACP's expansion paralleled, and even exceeded, the industry's. Over these past four years, company sales almost doubled, and employment much more than doubled. But debt also increased substantially, most of it long term used for expanding capacity (Figure A.6).

Industry sales, which had expanded by over 10 percent for the past four years, are predicted to expand by 8 to 10 percent this year, but the remainder of the 1990s

FIGURE A.3   Costs of an item at various offer levels.

Item: _____

	Proposal/counterproposal	Cost

1. Initial: _____

2. Next expected
    proposal: _____

3. Next expected
    proposal: _____

ETC.

n. Minimally acceptable
    level: _____

should be a questionable era for the microcomputer sector of the computer industry. Market saturation is rapidly approaching, and the industry leader is not expected to hurt its present product line, introduced three to four years ago, by coming out with a new line of machines. It is concentrating more on super minicomputers and larger mainframes, where its market share has been severely eroded. Over 80 percent of ACP's business is in the microcomputer part of the industry, and they don't expect to see their growth rate, substantially above industry average, continue to be that high. In fact, they expect growth in company sales to drop to the industry average this year and next, and then fall below that predicted rate for the next several years. The industry leader kept its basic product line for six to seven years over the last cycle. Expectations are that it will keep its new line, now three to four

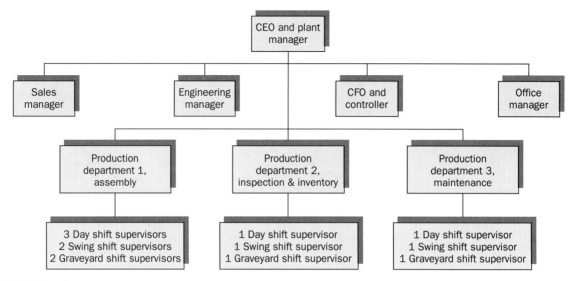

FIGURE A.4 American Computer Products, Inc. organization chart.

years old, for at least another four years, which means major innovation is unlikely until 1994 at the earliest. Thus, ACP is estimating 10 to 15 percent growth this year (1990), dropping to below 10 percent the following year, and averaging no more than 5 percent for the next three years.

The Union

The Allied Assemblers of America is a relatively new industrial union. Formed in 1975 as a local in the Santa Clara ("Silicon") Valley, AAA organized eight major computer companies in its first three years. In the next six-year period, it added nine more, spreading out from the Bay Area to Santa Cruz and the Central Valley. One of these nine was ACP in Stockville. Over the last six years four more companies have been organized by the Allied Assemblers, which still remains an unaffiliated union with 21 local units, all in northern California.

Headquartered in Palo Alto, the union staff, small but very active, has helped all its locals in collective bargaining negotiations, arbitrations, and other related matters. The staff also continually seeks to organize nonunion companies involved in the production of computers and related equipment. A last major function of the Palo Alto group is to maintain a close liaison with the AFL–CIO and unions operating in related areas, especially the Electronic Workers of America which has four very large locals in the Bay Area.

Local 15, AAA, is a medium-sized local. With 126 members, it has a mix of mostly semiskilled workers such as assemblers, inspectors, and production clerks/expediters (See Table A.1e). The maintenance technicians are skilled workers and make up only 12 percent of the bargaining unit.

FIGURE A.5a   *American Computer Products, Inc. Income Statement (Year Ending September 30, 1990)*

Sales (net)		$10,300,000
Expenses:		
Cost of goods sold	$5,644,360	
Salary expenses	825,120	
R & D	624,200	
Depreciation	848,250	
Selling & Administrative Expenses	655,000	
Interest Expenses	604,000	9,200,930
Earnings Before Taxes		$1,099,070
Income Taxes		361,934
Net Earnings (After Taxes)		$ 737,136

The president of Local 15, Karen Hopie, has been in that position for just over two years, so she was not on the team that negotiated the present contract. The chairperson of the local's Plant Grievance Committee, Myra Carty, has held that position for over four years and so was on the team that got this contract. The other members of the Plant Grievance Committee, the local's secretary (Dave Edwards) and treasurer (Jan Herich), had, like Ms. Hopie, held those offices in the local for the past two years or so. The three officers were elected primarily because of some unhappiness with the last contract, which many felt had insufficient wage increases and lacked fringe benefits (e.g., a pension plan) that should have been obtained.

Labor–Management Relations at ACP

After the first contract was signed in November 1984, a contract that seemed fair to all concerned, the downturn in the computer industry in 1985–1986 caused ACP to bring hiring to a virtual halt. Although nobody was laid off, the workforce was somewhat demoralized. Wage cuts granted in 1986 but made up the following year were hard to swallow.

FIGURE A.5b   *American Computer Products, Inc. Condensed Income Statements, 1987–1989*

	1987	1988	1989
Net Sales	$5,600,000	$6,750,000	$8,500,000
COGS	3,472,450	3,982,520	4,945,730
Other Expenses	1,796,320	2,188,650	2,781,380
E.B.T.	$ 331,230	$ 578,830	$ 772,890
Taxes	109,306	191,013	255,049
E.A.T.	$ 221,924	$ 387,817	$ 517,841

FIGURE A.6   *American Computer Products, Inc. Balance Sheet, September 30, 1990*

Assets	
Current Assets:	
Cash	$ 885,000
Marketable Securities	550,000
Accounts Receivable	1,245,000
Inventories	1,430,000
Total	$4,110,000
Fixed Assets	
Plant & Equipment (Net of Accumulated Depreciation)	$5,835,000
Total Assets	$9,945,000

Liabilities & Stockholders' Equity	
Current Liabilities:	
Accounts Payable	$1,820,000
Short-Term Loans	800,000
Accrued Expenses	199,000
Total	$2,819,000
Long-Term Debt	4,600,000
Total Liabilities	$7,419,000
Stockholders' Equity:	
Capital Stock	1,200,000
Retained Earnings	1,326,000
Total Stockholders' Equity	$2,526,000
Total Liabilities & Stockholders' Equity	$9,945,000

In 1987, 15 workers were hired as the computer industry, now "mature" after its first major slump, recovered, especially the microcomputer sector. A new contract was negotiated that year. The bargaining was not as pleasant as it had been in 1984, because management had the 1985–1986 downturn fresh in their minds. Wage increases were held to 2 percent for the first year and 3 percent for each of the next two years, and a COLA was established. The COLA clause called for a $.02 per hour raise for each percentage point jump in the Bay Area (San Francisco–Oakland–San Jose) CPI (see Table A.5), rounded off to the nearest cent. Adjustments were to be made quarterly, starting with January 31, 1988. Although pay is traditionally lower in the Central Valley than in the Bay Area because of the differences in the cost of living, the Bay Area CPI was chosen because it was used in contracts that the Allied Assemblers had with other electronic and computer companies, and changes in the cost of living were not that different in the two areas. Because of the differences in the cost-of-living levels, however, ACP jobs paid wages that were about 20 percent lower than comparable jobs in the Bay Area, except at the skilled level, where the difference was closer to 25 percent (See Table A.6).

Labor and Pay Issues

As bargaining for the 1990 contract approached, the workers were keyed up about pay. After receiving only an 8 percent raise over the three-year period of the last contract, and in the face of the rapid growth in company sales over that same period, the workers expected to get at least three to four times as much as they got in the last contract. Older workers wanted additional pay for seniority; they argued that loyalty to the company should be rewarded with seniority step raises. Another pay issue dealt with the wage rate of the maintenance technicians, the only skilled workers in the bargaining unit. When the first contract was signed near the end of 1984, their basic wage was almost 50 percent greater than that of the assemblers. Three years ago, just before the present contract was signed, the differential was under 43 percent, and now it was 35 percent. Their demands were for a return to a 45 to 50 percent wage differential; if these demands were not met, they just might invoke their rights under federal labor law and leave the bargaining unit, to affiliate with the Electronic Workers of America, or form their own independent local union. A last pay issue involved updating the COLA formula, to better represent present pay levels, not 1987 levels.

Labor and Benefits

The rank-and-file also wanted an improvement in fringe benefits. A major portion wanted dental benefits and better health care coverage for themselves as well as dependents, with the company paying most or all of the premiums. This majority also wanted greater benefits under the sickness and accident insurance and life insurance plans, as well as a better vacation schedule, allowing longer vacations at lower seniority levels. The older workers in the unit wanted a pension plan; although they made up only 20 percent of the membership, they had a substantial impact on union policy.

Management and Pay Issues

Management was somewhat sympathetic to the pressures the union negotiating team was under, given the relatively small increases granted in 1987. However, management wanted to keep labor costs (wages and fringe benefits) at around 25 percent of sales, the present ratio. The industry labor cost (wages and fringe benefits) to sales ratio ranged from 25 to 35 percent; ACP was at the low end of the range now. However, wages are higher in the Silicon Valley, which tends to push the industry average up. ACP felt that its labor cost to sales ratio should be at the low end of the range. ACP's management knew it would have to grant an appreciably greater increase in wage rates than it did three years ago, update the COLA formula figure, and push the differential up for the skilled maintenance techs.

Management and Benefits

Management did, however, hope to hold the line on expansion of fringe benefits, both the variety and dollar amount. The managerial negotiating team felt that it could not expand both medical care benefits, to include higher amounts and new plans like dental, and extend coverage to dependents. Moreover, it did not want to alter the present employee contribution to premium payments by much, if any. Management was also very concerned about the adoption of a pension plan, not only because of the cost but also because of the impact of government regulations. It wanted to hold the line on expanding benefits for sickness and accident insurance and life insurance plans. Because management felt that near-term growth might equal levels of several years ago, perhaps about 8 to 10 percent per annum, it was strongly opposed to expanding vacations or holidays, as this might well require hiring of new workers in the very near future. It hoped to stabilize the workforce, especially since it had just hired 36 more workers this past year.

ROLES AND RULES

The negotiation exercise is a role-playing simulation, and so roles should be defined. The roles for the union and management bargaining team are similar to actual membership on such teams in smaller unions dealing with smaller companies. They have been expanded some to allow for larger negotiating teams in the simulation exercise, but some roles need not be filled if smaller teams are used. Like all exercises, some ground rules are given and should be followed to enhance the realism of the exercise and its value as a learning tool.

The Union Negotiating Team

The union has a five-person negotiating team. It is headed by the local president, and it also includes the local's Plant Grievance Committee chairperson as well as the secretary and treasurer and the representative of the Allied Assemblers from the Palo Alto headquarters staff.

Karen Hopie, Local 15 President: she has been president since May 1988, so she was not part of the team that negotiated the 1987 contract, negotiations that were somewhat acrimonious. Ms. Hopie is an assembler with over six years of seniority, so she was around when the plant was unionized and the first contract was signed in 1984. As a married woman with two teenaged children, one now in college, she feels strongly about expanding benefits to dependents and increasing the benefit amounts. She also feels that the maintenance technicians have a legitimate gripe. As this is her first negotiation, she is somewhat apprehensive but wants to do a good job.

Myra Carty, Chairperson, Local 15 Plant Grievance Committee: she has been chairing the grievance committee for over four years and is the only member of the negotiating team that was party to the 1987 negotiations. As a result, Ms. Carty is the most militant of the 1990 bargaining team. As an assembler, she thinks the wage rate of her job classification and the other three unskilled/semiskilled classifications (which is about $7.90) should be increased to over $12 an hour, and maintenance technicians certainly deserve $4 to $5 more. With almost eight years of seniority, she also feels ACP can do more for its higher seniority workers. Ms. Carty is single, so her natural tendency with respect to fringe benefits is to tilt the increases more toward the coverage of the workers than their families, but, of course, she knows that over one-half the employees in the bargaining unit are married.

Dave Edwards, Local 15 Secretary: he is one of the three new local officers, with just over two years in office. Mr. Edwards is also a member of the local's Plant Grievance Committee, along with Myra Carty and Jan Herich. He is a maintenance technician, a position he has held for only three years, but that job classification has had substantial turnover. He is a strong proponent of a return to a 50 percent pay differential of the maintenance tech wage rate over that of assembler. As a relatively low-seniority, young (24) worker, Mr. Edwards is more concerned about higher wages than higher fringe benefits. As the only skilled worker on the negotiating team, he feels that he must protect the interests of his work group and get wages back to a respectable level for all.

Jan Herich, Local 15 Treasurer: she has been treasurer since May 1988 and feels that she can singlehandedly put management at bay in the upcoming negotiations. Ms. Herich thinks the union can get at least a 30 percent wage increase over the term of the next contract, and probably an extra 20 to 30 percent in addition to that for the maintenance technicians. She also feels that the union can get a major increase in fringe benefits, at least doubling the benefit for hospitalization and life insurance, and obtain a dental and pension plan. She is also a strong proponent of dependent coverage in the hospitalization plan. Ms. Herich, though at ACP for only four years, is very ambitious. She feels that if she leads the way others will follow in pressing management for major wage and benefit increases.

Caroline Garcia, Allied Assemblers HQ Staff: she is the main liaison with the locals. Working out of the Palo Alto office, Ms. Garcia spends almost a third of her time in the field, visiting locals, helping them with sticky grievances, arbitration, and collective bargaining negotiations. She seems to be inexhaustible. Her major function on the negotiating team is to make sure that a local contract doesn't get too far out of line with union (AAA) policy. During the 1987 negotiations, she encouraged Local 15 to press harder, and now she feels she may have to restrain them. The union feels that the 20 to 25 percent pay differential between Central Valley and Bay Area jobs is not out of line, given the differences in cost of living, especially housing.

The Management Negotiating Team

ACP has a five-person negotiating team. It is headed by the CEO and plant manager, Carter Ballow, an engineer, and the CFO and controller Andrew Ballow, an accountant. The two brothers are joined by their three production department heads, Valerie Hines, Ray August, and Bill Perry. All three have been with the company over eight years. Hines and August were on the 1984 negotiating team; all three were on the 1987 team.

Carter Ballow, CEO/Plant Manager: he was the engineer who created the innovative products that launched the company. As CEO, he tends to be more of a plant manager than an executive, leaving much of the executive function to be filled by his brother Andrew. Mr. Ballow is very sympathetic to the workers' complaints and is amenable to a 30 percent pay and benefit raise. He is the negotiating team's "safety"; his only objection to negotiations is the presence of the AAA headquarter's staffer.

Andrew Ballow, CFO/Controller: he keeps a tight hold on the finances of the company and does a lot of the PR work that his brother shuns. Mr. Ballow led the negotiating team in 1987, and he, more than any of the others, kept the wage and fringe benefit increases down. He figured that the upcoming negotiations would be very tough and that the union would get a 25 to 30 percent raise in pay over the next contract, plus COLA increases. He also realized that fringe benefits would have to increase, but he hoped to give only one of the three new fringes sought: pensions or dental or hospitalization for dependents. He was the one who established the guideline that the maximum labor cost to sales ratio shouldn't exceed 25 percent.

Valerie Hines, Assembly Department Manager: she heads the largest production department at ACP. After four years as an assembler, she was promoted to department manager, and in that position she helped negotiate the first ACP–AAA contract. In 1987, she supported Andrew Ballow's tough stance. She feels that the company may have been a little hard on the workers then and thus will have to give in to them on many issues this time around. She would rather see fringes than pay increases expanded, but knows that the union will go for healthy increases in both.

Ray August, Inspection/Inventory Department Manager: he was the first expediter-receiving/shipping clerk at ACP and has headed the department since 1982. In the 1987 negotiations, he supported a higher raise for the workers. He now feels that wages at ACP have gotten out of step with the rest of the industry's wages, and believes the workers may start their pay demands with a 17 to 20 percent raise per year. He thinks the company may have to give about a 12 to 14 percent annual increase. Fringe benefit increase demands will probably include increased benefits, coverage, and company premium payments for hospitalization, a dental and pension plan, increased sickness/accident and life insurance benefits, as well as more holidays, sick days, and vacation days. He looks to Andrew Ballow to sort out these demands and come up with feasible counterproposals for the negotiating team.

Bill Perry, Maintenance Department Manager: he is the least senior member of the negotiating team and of the management team overall. Mr. Perry knows that his workers will have to be given a big bump in pay. He is very sympathetic to their demands. He would like to see pay raises held down somewhat for all other workers, in the 10 percent a year range, with maintenance technicians getting about twice that. He feels the company can do this by liberalizing fringe benefits. He is an articulate spokesman for both his workers and his position on negotiations for 1990.

Some Basic Ground Rules

The format and timetable for this collective bargaining simulation will be set by your instructor. *Adhere to these.* If you do, the objectives of the exercise can be met. And be prepared: read and be familiar with all the material given, in the text and any supplementary material given to you by your instructor. Most of the information you will need is contained in the exercise: the background material, the present contract, and the data in the various tables (which usually take union and management months to accumulate). The issues are presented rather clearly; again study these materials (which usually take months in actual labor–management relationships to feel out and define). You will probably be asked to supply an agenda for the meeting at which your team first presents its position. A format for an agenda is given in Figure A.7.

You will be in teams, and each team should have a chief spokesperson. But everyone must contribute if the teams are to be effective. Meet as teams before each session, to develop proposals and counterproposals. Each of these should be costed out. You should also try to predict the other team's demands or proposals.

Teams should *not* interact outside the bargaining sessions. Members of one team should not consult with members of the other as individuals at any time. In bargaining sessions, the only interaction of individuals on opposing teams should be as spokespersons for their teams.

It is expected that both sides will bring to bear considerable creativity in their analysis and in developing their proposal and counterproposals. But these must be based on material given in the exercise. Know and use the background, contract, and data given. But don't "stretch" the facts; the other team has the same material and will catch you at this!

As the exercise has a finite life, it will end with either agreement and a new contract or no agreement. With no agreement, one of three things can happen: (1) a strike takes place, (2) the two sides write up their final offers on issues they have not yet agreed to and submit these (with any supporting material, written and/or oral, they feel is appropriate) to an arbitrator for (final offer) arbitration, or (3) the contract deadline is extended. Your instructor will let you know which of these three events will occur. But you may not find out until the original deadline is upon you!

THE PRESENT CONTRACT

Below, the present contract, signed November 1, 1987, and expiring on October 31 in 1990, is given in its entirety. It is your basic point of departure for the collective bargaining negotiations.

CONTRACT BETWEEN AMERICAN COMPUTER PRODUCTS, INC. AND LOCAL 15, ALLIED ASSEMBLERS OF AMERICA

AGREEMENT

This Agreement, dated November 1, 1987, is jointly entered into by American Computer Products, Inc., of Stockville, California (hereinafter referred to as the "Company" or the "Employer"), and Local 15 of the Allied Assemblers of America (hereinafter referred to as the "Union").

Article I, Purpose

It is the purpose of the parties to this Agreement to establish industrial and economic harmony through sound relations between the Company and its employees for the mutual benefit of both, assuring orderly and expeditious adjustment of any and all differences pertaining to

Figure A.7   *Agenda Format*

Item	Amount/Level Proposed	Present Amount/Level, or if Already Discussed, Latest Proposed Amount/Level

wages, hours of work, and other terms and conditions of employment that may arise under this Agreement. This Agreement is intended to set forth all the rights, duties, and responsibilities of the Union and the employees it represents under this Contract with the Company.

Article II, Recognition

Section 1   The Company recognizes the Union as the exclusive bargaining agent, for all assemblers, maintenance technicians, production inspectors, production clerks/expediters, receiving/shipping clerks, and any other production workers, excluding supervisors, in all matters pertaining to wages, hours of work, and other terms and conditions of employment.

Section 2   The Union agrees that all production and maintenance employees will work for the Company as provided for in this Agreement, and both parties further agree that all of these employees will become and remain members in good standing of the Union not later than the sixtieth day following the beginning of their employment or of the execution date of this Agreement, whichever is the latter.

Section 3   The Company agrees, upon receipt of written voluntary authorization of the employee, to deduct from his/her first paycheck each month initiation fees, dues, and other payments to the Union as permitted by law.

Article III, Management

Section 1   Management of the Company retains all of its rights, duties, and responsibilities, to direct the operations of the Company effectively and efficiently, except as explicitly modified by this Agreement.

Section 2   The Company will develop, maintain, and distribute, to the Union and employees, a written manual of reasonable rules to govern the conduct and conditions of the workplace.

Article IV. Representation

Section 1   The investigation or processing of any and all worker complaints or grievances shall be conducted at a mutually agreed upon time by both the Union and the Company; the Union's rightfully chosen shop stewards, whose names shall be submitted to the Company before they assume their duties, must first obtain permission from the supervisor, or in his/her absence, the department manager, before leaving their job to assist in processing worker complaints or grievances.

Section 2   The Union representative shall have the right to meet privately with employees in the investigation or processing of complaints or grievances, provided that such meetings are reasonable in terms of time and personnel involved, and after notification is given to the office of the plant manager.

Section 3   Grievances and arbitration shall be processed and conducted with no lost time to employees; three employees chosen by the Union, whose names shall be submitted to the office of the plant manager before they assume their duties, shall constitute the Plant Grievance Committee.

Section 4   Contract negotiations shall take place at a time and location mutually agreed upon by both the Union and the Company. The Contract Committee may include any employee and as many as two nonemployees from the national union with which the Union is affiliated.

Article V, Work Stoppages

Section 1   During the life of this Agreement, the Union agrees that there shall be no picketing, strikes, slowdowns, or other forms of work stoppages for any cause whatsoever, and the Company agrees that there shall be no lockouts for any cause whatsoever.

Section 2   Both parties agree that the occurrence of any actions mentioned in Section 1 above is a violation of this Agreement, and the Union agrees to immediately undertake in good faith all reasonable means to induce any and all employees engaged in such work stoppages to cease these actions. It is also agreed that if these actions occur, under no circumstances will disputes or grievances be discussed or conducted until these actions cease.

Article VI, Seniority

Section 1   Seniority, defined as length of continuous service with the Company in a specified job classification, shall be granted to all production workers in those job classifications established by the Company in consultation with the Union; as of the effective date of this Agreement those classifications include Assembler, Maintenance Technician, Production Inspector, Production Clerk/Expediter, and Receiving/Shipping Clerk.

Section 2   Employees eligible to move from one job classification to another may request, in writing, that the Company transfer their seniority to their new job classification; the Company must notify the Union of this request within one (1) working day of receipt of such, and must render an answer, in writing, within five working days of receipt of such. Employees promoted to supervisory positions will have their seniority frozen and will regain it at the frozen level if transferred back to the bargaining unit within 24 months of the effective date of the promotion.

Section 3   In all reductions in workforce and recall from layoff, seniority shall govern.

Section 4   Superseniority, defined as seniority greater than any earned seniority (earned by continuous length of service with the Company) in a job classification, shall be awarded to the following Union officials:

1. The President
2. The Secretary
3. The Treasurer
4. The Chairperson of the Plant Grievance Committee
5. All Shop Stewards as defined in Article IV, Section 1.

Article VII, Hours of Work

Section 1   The regular workweek shall consist of five (5) consecutive days; a workday shall begin at the normal starting time of an employee's shift, and will last for 8 hours and 30 minutes.

Section 2   The normal shift schedules shall be:

First (day) shift: 8 A.M.–4:30 P.M.

Second (swing) shift: 4 P.M.–12:30 A.M.

Third (graveyard) shift: 12 midnight–8:30 A.M.

Section 3   The Company agrees to give each employee a paid 15-minute rest period during the first half of each shift and a paid 15-minute rest period during the second half of each shift.

Section 4   The Company agrees to give each employee a 1-hour lunch period, 30 minutes of which shall be paid as work time and 30 minutes of which shall be without pay, to be scheduled for the middle of the shift.

Section 5   Time and one-half shall be paid for all hours worked at the request of the Company in excess of eight (8) in any one workday and forty (40) in any one workweek; double time shall be paid for work done at the request of the Company on any holiday specified in this Agreement. This overtime work will be made available to employees on the basis of seniority.

Section 6   Shift assignments shall be governed by seniority; requests for shift change shall be made in writing to the Company.

Article VIII, Wages

Section 1   Wages shall be paid each Friday for the work performed the previous week, except when that day falls on a holiday specified in this Agreement in which case wages shall be paid the day immediately prior.

Section 2   The following wage schedule of base wage rates shall be in effect upon the effective date of this Agreement:

Assembler:	$6.65 per hour
Maintenance Technician:	9.42 per hour
Production Inspector:	6.75 per hour
Production Clerk/Expediter:	6.81 per hour
Receiving/Shipping Clerk:	6.36 per hour

Section 3   At the end of the first year of this Agreement, each employee shall receive a $.21 per hour increase in base wage rate; at the end of the second year of this Agreement, each employee shall receive a further $.21 per hour increase in base wage rate.

Section 4   At the end of the first quarter of this Agreement, and every quarter following this until the termination of this Agreement, every employee shall receive a Cost of Living Adjustment in base wage rate. This adjustment shall be calculated as $.02 per hour for every percentage point increase in the Consumer Price Index for All Urban Consumers in the San Francisco–Oakland–San Jose region (published by the Bureau of Labor Statistics, U.S. Department of Labor), rounded off to the nearest $.01. These twelve (12) adjustments will be calculated at the end of the month following the end of each quarter, but will apply retroactively to that month. The base CPI figure to be used will be that for the month of October 1987.

Section 5   All employees assigned to the second (swing) shift shall receive a wage premium of $.15 per hour; all employees assigned to the third (graveyard) shift shall receive a wage premium of $.21 per hour.

Article IX, Holidays

Section 1   Each eligible employee shall receive pay, for eight (8) hours at his or her base wage rate at that time, for ten (10) holidays each year:

New Year's Day	Thanksgiving Day
Martin Luther King's Birthday	Friday after Thanksgiving
Memorial Day	Christmas Eve Day
Fourth of July	Christmas Day
Labor Day	New Year's Eve Day

Section 2   An employee is eligible for holiday pay provided he or she: (a) has been employed for not less than sixty (60) days, (b) worked the last scheduled day following the holiday, and the first scheduled day after the holiday, unless the Company has given him or her written permission to miss either of or both those days, (c) was not on disciplinary suspension on the day of the holiday, and (d) has not refused to work on the holiday if requested to do so by the Company.

Section 3   Holidays falling on a Saturday will be observed on the Friday preceding them; holidays falling on a Sunday will be observed on the Monday following them.

Section 4   If an eligible employee's vacation includes a holiday, he or she shall receive an extra vacation day, so that the total of vacation days and holidays are equal to what the employee is eligible to receive that year.

Article X, Vacations

Section 1   Employees shall be eligible for vacations with pay based upon the following schedule:

After one (1) year of service, 1 workweek

After three (3) years of service, 2 workweeks

After ten (10) years of service, 3 workweeks

After twenty (20) years of service, 4 workweeks

Section 2   The pay for each vacation day shall be calculated based upon eight (8) hours of work at the employee's base wage rate at that time. Payment for scheduled vacation time shall be made on the payday immediately preceding the beginning of the vacation.

Section 3   Vacation days are not cumulative from one year to the next; vacation time not taken within the defined service year of the employee is forfeited.

Article XI, Sick Leave

Section 1   Each employee is allowed six (6) sick days per calendar year. Sick leave pay shall be calculated for an eight (8) hour day at the employee's base wage rate at that time.

Section 2   Employees may not take sick leave the day before a scheduled holiday or their vacation, nor the day following either of those events.

Section 3   Sick leave is not cumulative from one calendar year to the next; sick leave not taken within a year is forfeited.

Article XII, Sickness and Accident Insurance

Section 1   Each eligible employee shall be provided with a sickness and accident insurance policy payable in cases leading to inability to work, which shall pay the employee $100 per week, after the first week of inability to work, and for as many as 13 consecutive weeks in any calendar year.

Section 2   An employee is eligible for sickness and accident insurance provided he or she has been employed by the Company for at least sixty (60) days.

Article XIII, Life Insurance

Section 1   Each eligible employee shall be provided with a life insurance policy in the amount of $10,000, payable to the beneficiary of his or her choice.

Section 2   An employee is eligible for life insurance provided he or she has been employed by the Company for at least sixty (60) days.

Article XIV, Hospital, Medical, and Surgical Insurance

Section 1   Each eligible employee shall be covered by a group hospital, medical, and surgical insurance plan if he or she wishes to participate; 75 percent of the cost of this insurance shall be paid by the Company, and 25 percent of the cost shall be paid by the employee.

Section 2   The coverage shall include a benefit amount of $25,000 per calendar year, for hospital, medical (doctors both in the office and at the hospital) and surgical (both hospital and doctors) costs; there shall be no deductible. All claims will be handled by the plan administrator, which shall be chosen by the Company who will provide all information on the plan to employees within one (1) week of the effective date of this Agreement, and thereinafter as the administrator updates the plan.

Section 3   Dependents of eligible employees shall be allowed to purchase the same hospital, medical, and surgical insurance as the employees; the cost of this coverage (monthly premium) will be paid entirely by the employee.

Section 4   An employee is eligible for hospital, medical, and surgical benefits provided he or she has been employed by the Company for at least sixty (60) days. An eligible employee will continue to be covered by these benefits with the company paying 75 percent of the cost for the employee, for ninety (90) days after he or she is laid off; after this period the laid-off employee may continue coverage at his or her own expense.

Article XV, Grievances

Section 1   The procedure set forth herein shall provide the sole recourse for any claim/grievance by an employee with respect to the application or interpretation of this Agreement, or on any matter concerning wages, hours of work, or other terms and conditions of employment.

Section 2   These claims/grievances shall first be discussed between the aggrieved employee, who may ask the Union shop steward to represent his or her position, and the employee's immediate supervisor.

Section 3   If a claim/grievance is not satisfactorily resolved by the parties noted in Section 2, the claim/grievance shall be put in writing and submitted to the department manager within ten (10) working days of the placing of the claim/grievance with the immediate supervisor. The employee, with the Union shop steward and the chairperson of the Union Grievance Committee, shall discuss the written grievance with the department manager.

Section 4   If the written grievance is not satisfactorily resolved by the parties noted in Section 3, within ten (10) working days of such submission, it must be pursued with the plant manager. The employee, represented by the Union Plant Grievance Committee, shall present the issue to the plant manager. If within ten (10) working days there is no satisfactory resolution of the grievance, the matter shall be referred to arbitration.

Section 5   All meeting of parties in Sections 2 through 4 shall be governed by the provisions of Article IV, Section 3.

Article XVI, Arbitration

Section 1   All grievances not satisfactorily resolved through the procedure defined in Article XV shall be submitted to arbitration for a final and binding decision.

Section 2   A written grievance not resolved by the plant manager and the Union's Plant Grievance Committee within the allowable ten (10) days noted in Article XV, Section 4 shall be submitted, accompanied by a request for arbitration (in written form), to the Company within ten (10) working days. The Company shall then meet with the Union, within five (5) working days of this request for arbitration, to jointly select an arbitrator. If an arbitrator cannot jointly be selected within (10) working days by the parties, the parties shall ask the Federal Mediation and Conciliation Service to submit a list of arbitrators from which a selection shall be made by the parties within five (5) working days of receipt of such list. If such a selection is not made, the parties shall request the Director of the Federal Mediation and Conciliation Service to appoint an arbitrator.

Section 3   The arbitrator shall make all possible effort to schedule the arbitration hearing within twenty (20) working days of appointment, and shall submit his or her decision, in writing, to the parties within one (1) calendar month of the conclusion of the hearing.

Section 4   The cost of the Arbitration shall be borne by the Company, and no cost shall be borne by employees as noted in Article IV, Section 3.

Article XVII, Miscellaneous Matters

Section 1   The Company shall provide the Union with a bulletin board, in the plant, for posting information regarding the business and operations of the Union. Copies of all posting shall be submitted to the office of the plant manager.

Section 2   The Company shall, at the request of the Union, entertain a written request for leaves of absence from any employee. However, the Company shall make the final decision on such requests.

Section 3   The Company shall allow any employee to take two (2) sick days a year for personal reasons, such as attendance at a family funeral, pursuant to the restriction noted in Article XI, Section 2. The employee shall request such personnel days off in writing three (3) working days prior to the requested time off.

Section 4   Any employee who is called for jury duty will be excused from work for the length of that service. He or she will receive payment from the Company equal to eight (8) hours at his or her base wage rate at that time less payment for jury duty for each day of that service. If the employee is assigned to the swing or graveyard shift, the Company may reassign another employee to that shift to maintain its staffing while the absent employee fulfills his or her jury service.

Article XVIII, Legal Status, Amendments, and Termination

Section 1   During the duration of this Agreement, if any provision(s) contained herein is unlawful or unenforceable under Federal or State law, the remainder of this Agreement shall be binding and not affected by any failing provision.

Section 2   This Agreement may be amended in writing at any time during its duration by mutual consent of the parties to it. Any such amendments shall become a part of said Agreement, and shall terminate at the same time as said Agreement.

Section 3   This Agreement shall continue in full force and effect for a period of three (3) years, from the first day of November, 1987 until the thirty-first day of October, 1990. If not terminated on the thirty-first day of October, this Agreement shall automatically renew, ad infinitum, for another one (1) year period. If either party wishes to terminate this Agreement as of the thirty-first day of October, 1990, they must submit such an intention, in writing, to the other party no later than sixty (60) days prior to said date, or any subsequent expiration date of said Agreement.

IN WITNESS HEREOF, the parties execute this agreement on the first day of November in the year 1987.

Allied Assemblers of America	American Computer Products
by _____ President, Local 15	by _____ Chief Executive Officer, Plant Manager
_____ Staff Organizer	_____ Chief Financial Officer, Controller

STATISTICAL INFORMATION

In the six tables in this section, we provide, in conjunction with the background and present contract already covered, most of the data you will need for this negotiating exercise. Table A.1, which is actually six tables (parts a through f), gives a profile of the bargaining unit. Tables A.2 and A.3 deal with wages, both the present level and the cost of a 1 percent increase. Table A.4 provides information on coverage levels and costs of fringe benefits.

Table A.1   *Bargaining Unit Profile*

a. Employee Seniority (present)

10 years and over	=	18
7 to 10 years	=	21
5 to 7 years	=	6
3 to 5 years	=	18
1 to 3 years	=	27
Less than 1 year	=	36
		126

(Average seniority = 4 years)

b. Four-Year Seniority Tabulation (current employees)

	10/31/90	10/31/91	10/31/92	10/31/93
Less than 1 year	36	0	0	0
1 year	15	36	0	0
2 years	12	15	36	0
3 years	15	12	15	36
4 years	3	15	12	15
5 years	0	3	15	12
6 years	6	0	3	15
7 years	12	6	0	3
8 years	9	12	6	0
9 years	0	9	12	6
10 years	3	0	9	12
11 years	6	3	0	9
12 years	6	6	3	0
13 years	3	6	6	3
14 years	0	3	6	6
15 years	0	0	3	6
16 years	0	0	0	3
	126	126	126	126

c. Age Categories of Employees

Category	Number
Over 50	6
40 to 50	18
30 to 40	63
20 to 30	36
Under 20	3
	126

(Average age = 35)

(continued)

Table A.1   (*Continued*)

d. Employees' Family Status

Marital Status	Number
Married	68
Single	58
	126

Average number of dependents = 1.15

e. Current Number of Employees and Base Wage Rate
   by Job Classification

Job Classification	Number	Hourly Wage Rate
Assembler	93	$ 7.89
Maintenance Technician	15	10.66
Production Inspector	10	7.99
Production Clerk/Expediter	5	8.05
Receiving/Shipping Clerk	3	7.60

f. Shift Assignments by Job Classification

Job Classification	Number on First Shift	Number on Second Shift	Number on Third Shift	Total Number
Assembler	45	26	22	93
Maintenance Technician	9	3	3	15
Production Inspector	6	2	2	10
Production Clerk/Expediter	3	1	1	5
Receiving/Shipping Clerk	3	0	0	3

Table A.2   *Current Wage Costs*

Job Classification	Number	Base Wage Rate	Total Daily Wage Cost[a]	Total Annual Wage Cost[b]
Assembler	93	$ 7.89	$5,938.32	$1,543,963.20
Maintenance Technician	15	10.66	1,287.84	334,838.40
Production Inspector	10	7.99	644.96	167,689.60
Production Clerk/Expediter	5	8.05	324.88	84,468.80
Receiving/Shipping Clerk	3	7.60	182.40	47,424.00
Total	126	[$8.227] average	$8,378.40	$2,178,384.00

[a] Includes base rate and shift differentials.

[b] Based on a 52-week year, 5-day week (260 work days per year or 2080 hours).

Table A.3   *Annual Cost of $0.082[a] Increase in Basic Wage Rates and $0.01 in Shift Differentials*

Job Classification	Number	Annual Cost of Base Wage Rate Increase	Annual Cost of Shift Differential Increase	Total Annual Cost
Assemblers	93	$15,862.08	$998.40	$16,860.48
Maintenance Technicians	15	2,558.40	124.80	2,683.20
Production Inspectors	10	1,705.60	83.20	1,788.80
Production Clerk/Expediters	5	852.80	41.60	894.40
Receiving/Shipping Clerks	3	511.68		511.68
Total	126	$21,490.56	$1,248.00	$22,738.56

[a]This is 1 percent of the current average wage rate of $8.227.

Table A.4   *Fringe Benefit Coverages and Costs*

Fringe Benefit	Current Benefit	Current Cost	Benefit and Cost Increases
Hospital/Medical/ Surgical Insurance (2/3 of employees participate)	$25,000 coverage, employee only	$75/month/participant 3/4 paid by employer (company cost, about $.325/hour/ participating employee)	1) To $50,000 coverage an added $.06/hour/ participant (company cost, at 75% of increase, would be $.045/hour/participant) 2) To $75,000 coverage, an added $.10/hour/participant (company cost, at 75% of increase, would be $.075/ hour/participant)
Hospital/Medical/ Surgical Insurance, dependents	None	None	For the average employee with dependents, $40/month, if participating in the plan for employees
Sickness/Accident Insurance	13 weeks, $100/ week (after first week)	$9.36/month/employee, paid by company	Increments of $10/week would cost an added $1.04/month/ employee
Life Insurance	$10,000 benefit	$3.90/month/employee, paid by ompany	1) To $15,000, an added $2.60/month/employee 2) Increments of $5000 (above $15,000) would cost an added $1.733/month/employee
Dental Plan	None	None	Standard Cal-Dental Plan would cost approximately $.23/hour/ employee ($39.87/month/ employee)
Pension Plan	None	None	The Allied Assemblers of America can join the plan sponsored by the Electronic Workers of America and the Santa Clara Valley Employers Association; the cost would be $.28/hour/employee

The last two tables in this section (A.5 and A.6) will allow you to make time and geographical comparisons. The first of these, Table A.5, gives the CPI for the 34 months leading up to the present negotiations. In working with the COLA clause, this should be a useful table. Table A.6 gives comparable wages in the Bay Area. You may want to use these in developing bargaining objectives (Figure A.1), especially those for the Maintenance Technicians.

Table A.5 *CPI, All Urban Consumers, 1988–September 1990 (1965 = 100)*

Month	CPI, U.S. City Average	CPI, San Franciso Oakland-San Jose
January 1988	326.6	335.2
February	327.4	336.4
March	328.4	337.5
April	327.5	340.1
May	326.0	339.5
June	325.3	339.8
July	326.3	340.4
August	327.9	342.0
September	328.0	342.5
October	328.6	343.5
November	330.2	344.0
December	330.5	344.3
January 1989	330.8	344.5
February	331.1	344.6
March	333.1	345.8
April	334.4	348.8
May	335.9	349.6
June	337.7	353.0
July	338.7	353.5
August	340.1	353.6
September	340.8	356.0
October	342.7	356.9
November	344.4	358.5
December	345.3	359.9
January 1990	345.8	360.5
February	345.7	360.9
March	346.7	362.9
April	347.4	362.3
May	349.0	363.1
June	350.8	364.8
July	352.0	367.9
August	353.5	369.1
September	355.2	370.9
October[a]	357.0	372.9

[a] Estimated.

Table A.6 *Comparable Job Classification Wages and Salaries, Electrical/Electronic Industry, San Francisco/Oakland Bay Area, 1989*

Occupation	Straight-Time Weekly Earnings
Assembly Worker	$382
Production Inspector	390
Production Expediter	393
Production Planning Clerk	388
Inventory Clerk	371
Shipping Clerk	361
Maintenance Worker	560

THE COMPUTER PROGRAM

A diskette is available for this exercise; if your instructor wants you to use it he or she will supply you with a copy. It is designed to run on any IBM PC (including the PS/2 models) or compatible microcomputer. The program costs out your collective bargaining proposals.

To run the program, put the diskette in the A drive (after the machine is on, that is, has been "booted"). Then, making sure you are addressing the A drive (the A > prompt should be on the screen), enter *NEGEX*. The program is self-prompting. If you should want to stop at any point in the program before completing it (if you made an error, for example), hit *control-c* (the *control* key and *c* key together). This will bring you back to the A prompt, or, on some machines, it will flash the question "Terminate batch job (Y/N)?" which you would answer with Y, bringing you back to the A prompt. You then enter NEGEX again, and start from the beginning. Do *not* do this (interrupt the program with control-c) the first time you use the program; if you make an error during your first use, go through the costing and run it, and just start a new run after.

First-time users will be asked to enter their name, and remember exactly how they entered it. To use the program again you will have to reenter your name *exactly* as it was entered the first time. If you capitalized letters the first time, you must always enter cap's. Or if you entered your first and last name with no spaces between them, or two spaces, you must enter it that way again. After entering your name correctly, you will be asked to enter a title for your costing run. Doing this will bring you into the program module that asks for the parameters of your proposal and the underlying assumptions you are using for the three-year period (1991–1993). The input prompts, sample responses, and a sample output based on these are given in Figure A.8. The wage rates for 1991–1993 given in the output *include* COLA increases.

In the input section, two elements that may be confusing should be noted; both of them deal with the seniority table (Table A.1b, which is also reproduced twice in the program and thus shown in Figure A.8). First, in selecting the seniority step raises, you should realize that the year inputted for each level is the last year for the step raise given for workers with seniority in that level. Thus, if you wanted to give three step raises, the first after five years (say $.25), the second after 10 years (say $.35), and the third after 15 years (say $.50), you would enter *4* for the number of seniority levels, then (1) *5* for the year level 1 changes and *0* for the step raise, (2) *10* for the year level 2 changes and *$.25* for the step raise, (3) *15* for the year level 3 changes and *$.35* for the step raise, and (4) *16* or *17* or even *20* for the year level 4 changes (any year over 15 is treated as "15 +" by the program) and *$.50* for the step raise. You can only use *one* (1) year over 15 in the program (so, if you use *16* and *21*, the program will not work). Choosing vacation levels works in a similar fashion; if you want no vacation for workers with under one year of seniority, that must be counted as a level.

As Figure A.8 shows, the program is self-prompting and quite easy to use. We're sure you'll have no trouble with it. Oh, one other matter: if your printer is not connected to the parallel port of the computer, you won't be able to print your output. If it is a serial connection (the printer is connected to the computer's serial port), then, instead of inputting:

COPY NEGO.OUT TO LPT1

Input:

COPY NEGO.OUT TO COM1

and you will be able to get your output. Check with your instructor on this matter if you are not sure about it. And, of course, after sending your output to the printer, you have to delete the NEGO.OUT file by inputting:

DEL NEGO.OUT

so you can run the program again. Enjoy your negotiating exercise!

FIGURE A.8 *A Sample Run of the Computer Program for Costing Proposals.*

```
A:\>NEGEX

This program is a supplement to Ballot, Kail,
Lichter-Heath & Wang, LABOR-MANAGEMENT RELATIONS
IN A CHANGING ENVIRONMENT, and is only authorized
for use with that text.  Any other use is illegal.

Enter your name exactly as you have done before:KAREN

Enter title you wish to use for report.
TEST

Enter parameters as prompted on screen.  All
percentages are entered as 6.2 for 6.2%
```

(*continued*)

FIGURE A.8 *(Continued)*

Enter revenue increase between 0 and 50% per year: 8

Enter inflation between −10% and 30% per year: 5

Enter base pay hike between $0 and $9.
This is total amount for 3 year contract period,
not per year amount: 4.50

Enter maintenance pay hike between $0 and $6.
This is total amount for 3 year contract period,
not per year amount: 2.00

How much per hour should wages increase for each
one percentage point of the inflation rate (CPI)? .03

The company currently pays 75% of the cost for
hospitalization. Do you wish to change this? Y
Enter employer contribution percentage: 100

Two thirds of the employees now participate in the
hospitalization plan. Do you wish to change this? Y
Enter the participation percentage: 100

There is a $25,000 maximum benefit under the
current policy. This may be increased to $50,000 or $75,000.
Enter 25, 50 or 75 to indicate maximum benefit: 50

The company currently does not pay for dependent
coverage. Should this policy be changed? Y
What percentage of participating employees have dependent
coverage? 45

What percentage of dependent coverage should the employer
pay for? 50

The company now provides for ten paid holidays.
Should this be changed? Y
How many paid holidays should employees receive? 12

Sick leave is now 6 days per year. Do you wish
to change this? Y
How many sick days per year shall be given? 8

Sickness and accident insurance entitles each employee
to $100 per week for 13 weeks. Do you wish to change
this amount? Y
Enter the amount to be added to the $100 in $10
increments [e.g., 5 would mean an added $50]:8

(continued)

FIGURE A.8 (*Continued*)

Currently there is no pension plan. Do you
wish to add a pension plan to the benefit package? Y

There are no dental benefits under the current
contract. Should these benefits be added? Y

Life insurance is at $10,000 per employee. Should
this amount be increased? Y
Enter in $5,000 increments the total amount of life
insurance desired above the $10,000 base [e.g.,
2 would mean an added $10,000]:2

The shift differential for second shift is now
$0.15 per hour. Do you want to change this amount? Y
How much should the second shift differential
be per hour? .19

The shift differential for third shift is now
$0.21 per hour. Do you want to change this amount? Y
How much should the third shift differential
be per hour? .25

CATEGORY	SENIORITY	1990	1991	1992	1993
1	TO 1 YR	36	0	0	0
2	1 TO 2	15	36	0	0
3	2 TO 3	12	15	36	0
4	3 TO 4	15	12	15	36
5	4 TO 5	3	15	12	15
6	5 TO 6	0	3	15	12
7	6 TO 7	6	0	3	15
8	7 TO 8	12	6	0	3
9	8 TO 9	9	12	6	0
10	9 TO 10	0	9	12	6
11	10 TO 11	3	0	9	12
12	11 TO 12	6	3	0	9
13	12 TO 13	6	6	3	0
14	13 TO 14	3	6	6	3
15	14 TO 15	0	3	6	6
16	OVER 15	0	0	3	9

There can be up to eight seniority levels with a step raise for each
level. Using the above chart as a guide, decide how many seniority
levels you wish to use. You will be prompted to enter the level breaks
and the step raises. If you do not want the seniority wages, enter
zero; if you do, you must have at least two breaks. Enter the number of seniority levels you have decided to use: 6

(*continued*)

FIGURE A.8 (*Continued*)

For each seniority level, first enter the year to indicate the year at which the seniority changes and then the dollar and cents per hour pay differential for that level.

Enter year at which seniority level 1 changes: 2
Enter step raise for that level: 0
Enter year at which seniority level 2 changes: 5
Enter step raise for that level: .10
Enter year at which seniority level 3 changes: 8
Enter step raise for that level: .15
Enter year at which seniority level 4 changes: 11
Enter step raise for that level: .20
Enter year at which seniority level 5 changes: 14
Enter step raise for that level: .25
Enter year at which seniority level 6 changes: 17
Enter step raise for that level: .30

CATEGORY	SENIORITY	1990	1991	1992	1993
1	TO 1 YR	36	0	0	0
2	1 TO 2	15	36	0	0
3	2 TO 3	12	15	36	0
4	3 TO 4	15	12	15	36
5	4 TO 5	3	15	12	15
6	5 TO 6	0	3	15	12
7	6 TO 7	6	0	3	15
8	7 TO 8	12	6	0	3
9	8 TO 9	9	12	6	0
10	9 TO 10	0	9	12	6
11	10 TO 11	3	0	9	12
12	11 TO 12	6	3	0	9
13	12 TO 13	6	6	3	0
14	13 TO 14	3	6	6	3
15	14 TO 15	0	3	6	6
16	OVER 15	0	0	3	9

There can be up to five vacation levels. Using the above chart, decide where the vacation levels will change. How many levels will you be using? 5

For each vacation level, using the year number to indicate the last year for that level, enter the level break and the number of weeks vacation earned for that level.
Enter the year for vacation level 1 break: 1
Enter number weeks vacation: 1
Enter the year for vacation level 2 break: 5
Enter number weeks vacation: 2

(*continued*)

FIGURE A.8 (*Continued*)

Enter the year for vacation level 3 break: 9
Enter number weeks vacation: 3
Enter the year for vacation level 4 break: 13
Enter number weeks vacation: 4
Enter the year for vacation level 5 break: 17
Enter number weeks vacation: 5

Your output has been saved to an external file.
To print it, enter the following:

    COPY NEGO.OUT LPT1

After you get your printout, you must delete the
file before running the program again or you will
get an error and won't be able to run it again.

To delete the file, enter:

    DEL NEGO.OUT

<u>PROGRAM OUTPUT</u>

TEST   KAREN

REVENUE INCREASE PER YEAR (%/YR)	8.00		
INFLATION FACTOR (%/YR)	5.00		
BASE PAY HIKE ($)	4.50		
MAINTENANCE PAY HIKE ($)	2.00		
COLA ($ PER % POINT)	.03		
% EMPLOYER SHARE OF HOSPITAL INS.	100.00		
% EMPLOYEE PARTICIPATION	100.00		
MAXIMUM BENEFIT/HOSPITALIZATION	50000.		
% OF EMPLOYEES COVERING DEPENDENTS	45.00		
% EMPLOYER SHARE OF DEPENDENT COST	50.00		
NUMBER OF ANNUAL PAID HOLIDAYS	12.		
NUMBER OF PAID SICK DAYS	8.		
SICKNESS AND ACCIDENT WKLY BENEFIT	180.		
LIFE INSURANCE COVERAGE	20000.		
SECOND SHIFT PAY DIFFERENTIAL	.19		
THIRD SHIFT PAY DIFFERENTIAL	.25		
COMPANY HAS DENTAL BENEFITS			
COMPANY HAS EMPLOYEE PENSION PLAN			

YEAR	1990.	1991.	1992.	1993.
SALES	10300000.	11680200.	13245350.	15020220.

(*continued*)

FIGURE A.8 (*Continued*)

INDIVIDUAL WAGES

ASSEMBLER WAGES	7.89	9.54	11.19	12.84
MAINTENANCE TECH. WAGES	10.66	12.98	15.29	17.61
PRODUCTION INSPECTOR WAGES	7.99	9.64	11.29	12.94
PROD. CLERK/EXPEDITER WAGES	8.05	9.70	11.35	13.00
REC/SHIP CLERK WAGES	7.60	9.25	10.90	12.55
AVERAGE WAGE	8.23	9.96	11.69	13.42
AVG. WAGE W/SHIFT DIFF.	8.31	10.06	11.79	13.52
AVG. WAGE W/SH. DIFF. & SEN.	8.31	10.17	11.97	13.75

SENIORITY

SENIORITY LEVEL	PAY DIFFERENTIAL
0. - 2.	.00
2. - 5.	.10
5. - 8.	.15
8. - 11.	.20
11. - 14.	.25
14. - 15+	.30

FRINGE BENEFITS

SICKNESS & ACCIDENT INSURANCE	14152.	15410.	15410.	15410.
DENTAL PLAN COVERAGE	0.	60278.	60278.	60278.
HOSPITAL/MEDICAL/SURGICAL INS	56704.	129127.	129127.	129127.
DEPENDENT INSURANCE COST	0.	13608.	13608.	13608.
LIFE INSURANCE	5897.	7208.	7208.	7208.
PENSION - COST PER YEAR	0.	73382.	73382.	73382.
TOTAL FRINGE BENEFITS	76753.	299014.	299014.	299014.

LABOR COST

TOTAL YEARLY WAGES	2178384.	2666560.	3138200.	3603600.
FICA (7.51%)	163597.	200259.	235679.	270630.
F/SUTA ($441)	441.	441.	441.	441.
TOTAL FRINGE BENEFITS	76753.	299014.	299014.	299014.
TOTAL LABOR COST	2419175.	3166274.	3673334.	4173685.
TOTAL AS % OF SALES	.23	.27	.28	.28

VACATION SCHEDULE

VACATION STEP	WEEKS EARNED
0. - 1.	1.
1. - 5.	2.
5. - 9.	3.
9. - 13.	4.
13. - 15+	5.

(*continued*)

FIGURE A.8 (*Continued*)

LABOR COST - INCLUDING VACATION/HOLIDAYS/SICK DAYS

TOTAL YEARLY WAGES	2178384.	2666560.	3138200.	3603600.
FICA (7.51%)	163597.	200259.	235679.	270630.
F/SUTA ($441)	441.	441.	441.	441.
TOTAL FRINGE BENEFITS	76753.	299014.	299014.	299014.
TOTAL VACATION COST	22737.	136747.	176739.	214500.
TOTAL HOLIDAY COST	83784.	123072.	144840.	166320.
SICK LEAVE COST	50270.	82048.	96560.	110880.
TOTAL LABOR COST	2575966.	3508141.	4091473.	4665385.
TOTAL AS % OF SALES:	.25	.30	.31	.31

INDEX

Ability to pay, 174, 204, 206, 208–209, 211, 223, 475

Adaira v. United States, 61

Affirmative action, 80, 84, 219, 281, 511, 515. *See also* Discrimination in the labor market

AFSCME, AFL–CIO v. Woodward, 469

Age Discrimination in Employment Act, 79, 83, 91

Agency shop, 74, 265, 267, 268, 269, 274, 430, 433, 435, 438, 454, 457, 459. *See also* Compulsory union membership (clause)

Air Line Pilots Association, 382–385, 415–418, 419, 420

All-China Federation of Trade Unions, 149, 150

Amalgamated Clothing and Textile Workers Union, 107, 329, 401, 405–406, 515

Amalgamated Clothing Workers, 40, 267, 400, 401, 403–404, 405

Amalgamated Meat Cutters and Butcher Workmen of North America, *see* United Food and Commercial Workers

Amalgamated Transit Union, 397, 470, 472

American Arbitration Association, 315–316

American Association of University Professors, 470, 471

American Federation of Government Employees, 324, 453, 454, 455, 515

American Federation of Labor–Congress of Industrial Organizations, 9, 27, 28–29, 31, 36–37, 39, 40, 41, 42, 43, 45, 58, 59, 88, 106, 107, 108–112, 115, 116, 117, 120, 123, 128, 129, 135, 148, 155, 157, 209, 212, 235, 238, 240, 285, 383,

400, 401, 403, 406–407, 408, 409, 414, 422, 453, 455, 471, 473, 500, 511, 515

American Federation of State, County, and Municipal Employees, 45, 470, 472–473, 502, 503, 515

American Federation of Teachers, 45, 470, 471, 472, 481, 515

American Federation of Television and Radio Artists, 415, 416, 417

American Nurses Association, 128, 470, 473

American Plan, 37, 39, 47, 511

American Postal Workers Union, 453, 454, 498

American Railway Union, 30

Americans with Disabilities Act, 79, 84

Annual wage increment (improvement factor), 212, 213–214, 216, 230, 299

Anti-injunction Act, *see*
Norris–LaGuardia Act
Apprentice/apprenticeship, 19,
107, 207, 209, 217, 234, 235,
347
*Apte v. Regents of the University
of California*, 449
Arbitration (arbitrator), 61, 74,
217, 359, 363, 429
interest, 62, 63, 69, 134, 313,
318, 321, 363, 365, 366,
369–371, 378, 379, 383,
394, 430, 431, 433, 434,
437, 440, 442, 453, 457,
469, 475, 478, 479–480.
rights, 44, 63, 117, 118, 136,
139, 270, 289, 307, 309,
310, 312, 313–319, 320,
324–357, 358, 360, 369,
371, 385, 391, 418, 431,
433, 434, 443, 457, 464,
469, 498
See also Final offer
arbitration
Assembly of Government
Employees, 470, 473
Associate member(ship), unions,
116, 471, 515
Attitudinal structuring, 179–180
Australian Council of Trade
Unions, 157
Authorization card, 73, 168, 169,
429
Automation, 144, 182, 291–293,
301, 379, 386
Auto workers (union), *see* United
Automobile Workers

Barbers, Beauticians, and Allied
Industries International, *see*
United Food and Commercial
Workers
Bargaining power, 127, 180–186,
188, 370, 379–380, 394, 395,
443, 456, 463, 476
Bargaining structure:
centralized, 113, 114, 129,
137, 141, 157, 158, 187,
205, 280
coalition, 188–189

coordinated, 189
decentralized or fragmented,
114, 142, 143, 152, 205,
510
multi-employer, 136, 183, 188,
192
multi-tier, 186–187
multi-union, 136, 188–189
Bargaining unit, 63, 70, 73, 126,
167, 169–170, 171, 185, 189,
218, 225, 264, 267, 268, 269,
280-281, 282, 287, 288, 289,
311, 368, 430, 431, 432, 435,
438, 440, 441, 442
Beck, Dave, 42
*Bedford Cut Stone Co. v. Jour-
neymen Stone Cutters'
Association of North
America*, 39, 61, 99–101
Bituminous Coal Operators
Association, 188
Blacklisting, 25, 37, 40, 61
Blue-collar worker, *see* Worker,
blue-collar
Boycott, 25, 30, 31, 33, 39, 58,
59, 61, 399–400, 412,
418, 432
primary, 400–410, 413, 414,
421, 422, 461
secondary, 60, 67, 68, 69, 70,
108, 392, 400, 402,
410–412, 422. *See also*
Secondary action
Brass-knuckles unionism,
41
Bread-and-butter unionism, 27,
29, 45, 121, 403, 471, 513.
See also Pure and simple
unionism
Brody, David, 38, 51, 52
Brotherhood of Sleeping Car
Porters, 42
Bumping, 277, 278
Bureau of Labor Statistics, 11,
15, 175, 194–197, 230, 247,
252, 253, 376
Business agent, 119, 121, 264,
269, 312, 362
Business unionism, *see* Bread-
and-butter unionism

Cafeteria plan, *see* Flexible bene-
fit plan
Carpenters (union), *see* United
Brotherhood of Carpenters
and Joiners of America
Centralized bargaining, *see* Bar-
gaining structure, centralized
Central Organization of Profes-
sional Employees (Sweden),
142
Central Organization of Salaried
Employees (Sweden), 142
Certification, 68, 73, 74, 167–171,
192, 393, 421, 440, 441, 443,
454
Certified bargaining
agent/representative, *see* Ex-
clusive bargaining agent
Chamberlain, Neil, 180, 191, 193
Chavez, Cesar, 401–403
Checkoff, 134, 225, 269, 406
Chicago Bridge v. OSHRC, 96
Child care, 251, 252–253, 327,
513, 515
Child labor laws, 29, 35, 75
Chilling effect, 370–371, 479. *See
also* Final offer arbitration
Chinese Federation of Labor
(Taiwan), 156
Churitsuroren, *see* Federation of
Independent Unions of Japan
City and County Municipal
Employees Relations Panel
(San Francisco), 442
City federation(s) of labor, 22–23
City of Fresno v. Superior Court,
449
Civil Rights Act of 1866, 81
Civil Rights Act of 1964, 75,
79–82, 84, 91, 281, 500, 502
Civil Service Act (and Merit
System), 428, 452
Civil Service Commission, 430
Civil service employee associa-
tion, 473
Civil Service Reform Act,
431–433, 443, 454, 456, 457,
460
Clayton (Antitrust) Act, 34, 39,
55, 58, 59–61, 93, 94

Closed shop, 21, 37, 43, 60, 137, 265, 266, 269, 392. *See also* Compulsory union membership (clause)

Clothing and textile workers (union), *see* Amalgamated Clothing and Textile Workers Union

Clothing workers (union), *see* Amalgamated Clothing Workers

Coalition bargaining, *see* Bargaining structure, coalition

Co-determination, 138–140, 144, 271, 494

Committee for Industrial Organization, 41

Committee on Political Education, 43, 110, 116. *See also* Political action committee

Common law, 55, 56–58, 137, 443, 444, 445

Common-situs picketing, *see* Picket (line) and picketing, common-situs

Commonwealth v. Hunt, 22, 57–58, 93

Commonwealth v. Pullis (Philadelphia Cordwainers), 57

Communication Workers of America, 252, 407, 470, 473

Company union, 37, 38, 40

Comparable worth, 83, 221, 487, 500–504

Compulsory union membership (clause), 43, 69, 74, 109, 126, 138, 171, 187, 191, 201, 203, 224, 225, 263–269, 430, 433, 438–439, 440–441, 453, 454, 457, 459, 460, 469. *See also* Agency shop; Closed shop Preferential shop; Union shop

Concession bargaining (concessions, bargaining), 13, 114, 115, 117, 172, 173, 175, 177, 187–188, 191, 198, 199, 201, 208, 209, 211, 213, 214, 215, 217, 218, 226, 237, 245, 247, 248, 264, 271, 272, 283, 289,

369, 382, 384, 415, 489, 495, 511

Conciliation/conciliator, 139, 363, 364, 365, 379, 434, 478

Confederation of Mexican Workers, 135

Congress of Industrial Organizations, *see* American Federation of Labor-Congress of Industrial Organizations

Consent election, 73–74, 170

Consolidated Rail v. Railway Labor Executives Assn., 94

Conspiracy Cases, 21–22, 57

Consumer boycott, *see* Boycott, primary

Consumer Price Index, 173, 175, 176, 214, 215, 216, 493

Contingent worker (workforce), 242, 389, 455, 492, 512. *See also* Worker, part-time

Contract arbitration, *see* Arbitration, interest

Contract impasse, *see* Impasse, collective bargaining

Contract ratification, *see* Ratification of contracts

Coordinated bargaining, *see* Bargaining structure, coordinated

Coronado Coal Company v. United Mine Workers of America, 59

Corporate campaign, 405, 406, 410, 412–420, 421, 422, 448, 514

Corruption, union, 45, 106, 111, 123–124, 135, 154, 240–241

Cost-of-living adjustment (clause), 44, 173, 210, 212, 214–215, 216, 230, 237, 299, 369, 492–493

Cost-push inflation, 490–493

Council of Trade Unions (USSR), 146

County Sanitation District No. 2 of Los Angeles County v. Los Angeles County Employees Assoc., Local 660, 444–445, 449

Craftspeople, 18, 19, 20, 27, 290

Craft union, 22, 26, 27, 29, 30, 37, 39, 42, 107–108, 110, 115, 117, 118, 121, 136, 157, 188, 189, 217, 234, 235, 266, 312, 386, 406

Crew size, *see* Manning requirements

Crowding effect, 225

DGB, *see* Federation of German Unions

Danbury Hatters, see Loewe v. Lawlor

Davis-Bacon Act, 76, 91, 95

Day care, *see* Child care

Debs, Eugene V., 26, 30

Decentralized (fragmented) bargaining, *see* Bargaining structure, decentralized

Decertification, 43, 46, 73, 126, 186, 192, 264, 391, 406, 440, 443, 453, 457, 458

Defensive strike, *see* Strike, defensive

DeLeon, Daniel, 30

Demand curve for labor, *see* Labor demand (curve)

Democracy, union, 106, 120, 123, 125–127, 135, 172, 264

Democratic Republican Independent Voter Education committee, 110, 116. *See also* Political action committee

Demonstration effect, 224

Deregulation, 5, 11, 46, 114, 173, 188, 211, 389, 418, 463

Derived demand, 201

Diaz v. Pan American World Airways, Inc., 82

Directed election, 170

Disability insurance, 243, 252

Discrimination in the labor market, 75, 79–84, 95, 110, 217, 221, 223, 281, 432, 500, 501, 502. *See also* Affirmative action

harassment, 80, 81, 82

Dismissal without just cause, *see* Wrongful discharge

Distributive bargaining, 179, 364

Domei, *see* Japanese Confederation of Labor

Drug testing, 62, 88–89, 445, 446

Dual-earner (dual-worker) family, 185, 249, 251, 252, 254

Dubinsky, David, 40, 41

Dunlop, John, 108, 201, 203, 229, 232, 257, 262, 510, 517

Duplex Printing Press Co. v. Deering, 39, 60

Duty of fair representation, 191, 219, 264, 311

Elasticity of demand, 201, 202, 203, 209, 210

Elder care plan/program, 243, 250, 251

Electrical workers (union), *see* International Brotherhood of Electrical Workers

Emergency dispute (provisions), *see* National emergency dispute (provisions)

Employee involvement, 137, 484–500. *See also* Co-determination; Labor-management relations, nature of, cooperation; Participative management

Employee Partnership Fund, 500

Employee Polygraph Protection Act, 89, 110, 514. *See also* Polygraph testing

Employee Relations Commission and Board (Los Angeles), 442

Employee representation plan, *see* Company union

Employee Retirement Income Security Act, 8, 75, 86, 87, 91, 109, 238, 239, 240, 257, 258

Employee stock ownership (plan), 38, 191, 498–500

Employment-at-will, 4, 8, 56, 91, 291

Employment Cost Index, 227, 492

Employment effect, 200, 201, 203, 206, 207. *See also* Labor demand (curve)

Employment level program, 294–295
    Guaranteed Employment Number (Ford), 295
    Secured Employment Level (GM), 295

Enterprise union/unionism, 143, 145, 146, 154, 156, 494

Equal employment opportunity, *see* Affirmative action

Equal Employment Opportunity Act, 79, 91, 110, 500

Equal Employment Opportunity Commission, 79–80, 83, 84

Equal Pay Act, 76, 79, 83, 91, 500

Escalator clause, *see* Cost-of-living adjustment (clause)

Ethnic unionism, 400, 401–405, 421

Ettor, Joseph, 32, 50

European Trade Union Confederation, 136

Exclusive bargaining agent/representative, 73, 125–126, 167, 170, 171, 263, 264, 265, 268, 270, 282, 311, 393, 406, 412, 429, 430, 435, 436, 438, 439, 440, 441, 444, 458, 510

Executive Order 10988, 429–430, 443, 453

Executive Order 11491, 429–430, 443, 453

Experimental Negotiating Agreement, 193, 369

Fact finding, 363, 366, 367, 368–369, 433, 434, 437, 440, 441, 442, 469, 478

Factory system, 20–21, 23, 24, 26, 32, 35

Fair Labor Standards Act, 75–76, 91, 183, 217–218, 247, 418

Family (medical) leave, *see* Parental leave

Featherbedding, 283, 286, 300

Federal Insurance Contributions Act, 77

Federal Labor Relations Authority, 6, 431, 432–433, 456, 457, 458, 460

Federal Labor Relations Council, 430, 432

Federal Mediation and Conciliation Service, 6, 68, 74, 315–316, 363–364, 367, 373, 430, 457, 478

Federal Services Impasses Panel, 430, 432, 457

Federal Trade Commission (Act), 34, 55, 58, 59–61, 93

Federal Unemployment Tax Act, 79, 91, 95

Federation of German Unions, 139

Federation of Independent Unions of Japan, 143

Federation of Korean Trade Unions, 154

Federation of Organized Trade and Labor Unions, 29

Fetal protection policy, 80, 81, 82

Final offer arbitration, 371, 434, 479, 480

Fire Fighters Local 1494 v. City of Coeur d'Alene, 449

Five Dollar Day Plan, 35–36

Flexible benefit plan, 249, 254–255

Flexible work schedule, 251, 253–254, 501

Flexibility, organizational, 10, 44, 142, 165, 224, 248, 271, 276, 282, 285, 287, 462, 512

Flight attendants (union), *see* Transport Workers Union

Fragmented bargaining, *see* Bargaining structure, decentralized

Fraternal Order of Police, 428, 470, 472

Freight Haulers Association, 188

Gain sharing, 147

General Council of Trade Unions of Japan, 143, 144

General strike, *see* Strike, general

Geographic wage differential, 221, 222

George Meany Center for Labor Studies, 111

Gompers, Samuel, 29, 33, 34, 37, 39, 53, 106, 107, 108, 111, 120, 193, 209, 307

Gompers v. Bucks Stove and Range Co., 59

Green, William, 37, 39, 42

Grievance, 10, 38, 44, 117, 118, 150, 153, 171, 269, 270, 274, 309–319, 320, 362, 385, 389, 399, 418, 431, 443, 457, 464, 498

Grievance arbitration, *see* Arbitration, rights

Grievance committee, plant, 117, 119, 264, 282, 312, 362

Grievance procedure, 9, 10, 11, 44, 45, 117, 118, 125, 126, 174, 187, 203, 265, 276, 281, 282, 289, 297, 303, 307, 309–319, 334, 358, 360, 430, 433, 435, 440, 441, 457, 469

Griggs v. Duke Power Co., 80

Guaranteed Employment Number (Ford), *see* Employment level program, Guaranteed Employment Number

Guaranteed Income Stream, 244, 245–246, 260, 289, 295, 296

Haywood, William (Big Bill), 31–32

Health and safety regulation/ code, 5, 25, 35, 75, 153, 156, 283, 351, 511. *See also* Occupational Safety and Health Act/Administration

Health care (insurance) plan, 43, 44, 86, 89, 90, 144, 178, 184, 227, 235, 236, 237, 241–243, 247, 249, 250, 251, 252, 253, 254, 258, 259, 295, 415, 438, 492, 515

Hearing officer (alternative dispute resolution), 363

Hierarchy of needs, *see* Maslow's hierarchy of needs

Hill, Joe, 31

Hillman, Sidney, 40, 41

Hiring hall, 266, 274

Hodgsen v. Robert Hall Clothes, Inc., 83

Hoffa, James (Jimmy), 42, 120, 121, 124

Holiday, 139, 153, 178, 235, 237, 248–249, 294, 456, 501

Homestead strike of 1892, 26

Hong Kong and Kowloon Trade Union Council, 153

Hong Kong Federation of Trade Unions, 153

Hospital (insurance) plan (hospitalization), *see* Health care (insurance) plan

Hot cargo clause, 67, 68, 70, 410

Hotel and restaurant workers (union), *see* International Union of Hotel and Restaurant Employees and Bartenders

Howard, Charles, 41

Human resources policies and administration/management, 13, 35, 38, 115, 145, 221, 231, 250, 297, 360, 361, 431

Impasse, collective bargaining, 6, 62, 63, 69, 157, 178, 307, 313, 358, 363–371, 378, 379, 382, 383, 386, 390, 394, 395, 430, 432, 433, 437, 438, 439, 441, 442, 444, 453, 457, 460, 469, 475, 478–480, 514

Indentured servant, 18

Industrial tribunal (alternative dispute resolution), *see* Peer review board, Industrial tribunal (Australia), 157

Industrial union, 27, 30, 31, 36, 39, 42, 107–108, 110, 113–114, 117, 118, 121, 128, 189, 213, 218, 222, 223, 234, 235, 290, 311–312, 386

Industrial Union Department, AFL–CIO, 414, 422, 448

Industrial wage differential, 221, 222–223

Industrial Workers of the World, 27, 30–32, 33, 34

Inelastic demand, *see* Elasticity of demand

Initiation fee, union, 67, 68, 265, 267, 269, 274

Injunction, labor/anti-union, 26, 30, 37, 39, 60, 63, 64, 68, 367, 368, 373, 384, 391, 392, 411, 415, 444, 445, 458

Input work rules/standards, *see* Production standards (work rules), input

Insurance Workers Union, *see* United Food and Commercial Workers

Integrative bargaining, 179

Interest arbitration, *see* Arbitration, interest

Interindustry wage differential, *see* Industrial wage differential

International Association of Fire Fighters, 470, 471

International Association of Machinists, 23, 42, 107, 110, 184, 381, 382–385, 392, 407, 411–412, 415–418, 422, 454

International Brotherhood of Electrical Workers, 42, 107, 189, 252, 407, 515

International Brotherhood of Teamsters, 42, 88, 110, 111, 120, 121, 122, 123, 124, 128, 129, 130, 172, 173, 191, 192, 213, 214, 240, 273, 318, 369, 402, 403, 407, 428, 470, 473, 498

International Confederation of Free Trade Unions, 112

International Labor Organization, 112

International Ladies' Garment Workers Union, 36–37, 40, 240, 267

International Longshoremen's and Warehousemen's Union, 43, 111, 368

International Longshoremen's Association, 88, 111, 123, 124

International Typographical Union, 22, 284

International Union of Hotel and Restaurant Employees and Bartenders, 124

Intraorganizational bargaining, 179, 180, 387

Japanese Confederation of Labor, 143, 144

Job bank program, 245, 246, 289, 294–295, 296

Job classification (rules), 44, 217, 218, 219, 282, 285, 286–288, 301, 309

Job enrichment and enlargement, 47, 154, 497

Job evaluation, 139, 212, 220–221, 231, 501, 502

Job placement (services), *see* Reemployment

Job property rights, 235, 236, 277, 279, 280

Job security, 4, 5, 8, 9, 174, 198, 215, 217, 223, 225, 227, 276, 277, 278, 279, 283, 289, 294, 295, 296, 310, 388, 415, 452, 468, 498

Job sharing, *see* Work sharing

Joint problem solving and decision making, *see* Participative management

Journeyman, 18, 19, 21, 57, 217, 234

Jurisdictional strike, *see* Strike, jurisdictional

Key bargain, *see* Pattern bargaining

Kirkpatrick v. City of Los Angeles, 446

Knickboker v. City of Stockton, 449

Knights of Labor, 26, 27–28, 29, 50, 128

Kochan–Dyer three-stage model of labor-management cooperation and change, 495–496

LO, *see* Swedish Confederation of Trade Unions

Labor demand (curve), 199–200, 201, 202, 203, 207, 225, 386. *See also* Employment effect

Laborers' International Union of North America, 454, 470, 473

Labor involvement, *see* Employee involvement

Labor-management relations, nature of:
  adversarial, 6, 17, 24, 47, 136, 155, 179, 271, 283, 289, 307, 496
  compromise, 6–7, 271
  confrontation, 5, 6–7, 271
  cooperation, 5, 7, 135, 175, 271, 289, 307, 394, 487, 489, 494–500, 513, 514. *See also* Employee involvement; Participative management
  mutual dependency, 6–7

Labor–Management Relations Act, 6, 42–43, 65, 66–69, 70, 71, 74, 91, 94, 108, 115, 128, 177, 191, 264, 265, 266, 267, 268, 283, 285, 363, 366–368, 377, 378, 387, 391, 392, 394, 399, 400, 402, 410–411, 431, 437, 439, 452, 453, 457, 460, 480, 516

Labor–Management Reporting and Disclosure Act, 6, 45, 65, 68, 70, 71, 91, 94, 120, 126, 130, 137, 266, 267, 452

Labor participation, *see* Participative management

Labor supply (curve), 29, 107, 152, 199–200, 207, 209, 224, 225, 386, 504

Landrum–Griffin Act, *see* Labor–Management Reporting and Disclosure Act

Lauf v. E. G. Shinner & Co., 64

Layoff, 4, 42, 87, 139, 156, 169, 201, 202, 206, 209, 244, 245, 277, 278, 281, 282, 289, 294, 296, 299, 383, 417, 439, 498, 500

Leave bank, 249

Legal services plan, 250

Lewis, John L., 39, 40, 41, 51, 301

Lie detector testing, *see* Polygraph testing

Life insurance plan, 178, 235, 236, 237, 250, 295

Lifetime employment (Japan), 143, 144, 145, 146

Limits of acceptance, 176, 178

Lloyd-LaFollette Act, 429, 452, 459

Lockout, 68, 74, 153, 178, 307, 358, 363, 364, 366, 367, 369, 376, 378, 379, 390, 480, 510

Loewe v. Lawlor (Danbury Hatters), 58, 59, 97–99

Lump-sum payments, 212, 213, 247, 295

Machinists (union), *see* International Association of Machinists

Maintenance of membership clause, 265, 268, 269

Management rights, 42, 157, 165, 187, 269–273, 289, 309, 329, 334, 337

Mandatory bargaining subjects, 73

Manning requirements, 283–284, 286

Marginal productivity theory, 207–208, 211

Marine Engineers Beneficial Association, *see* National Air Traffic Controllers Association

Markup pricing, 493

Marshall v. Barlow's, Inc., 96

Marshall v. Brunner, 95

Martin v. Wilkes, 80

Maslow's hierarchy of needs, 7–9

Massachusetts Bonding and Insurance Co. v. U. S., 93

Maternity leave, *see* Family leave

McClellan Committee, 70, 120, 123, 124

McDonell v. Hunter, 446

McMonagle v. Northeast Women's Center, Inc., 96

Meany, George, 42
Mechanic society, 20
Mechanization, 24, 25, 31, 36, 291, 292–293, 294
Med–arb (mediation–arbitration), 365
Mediation/mediator, 4, 61, 62, 63, 64, 178, 362, 363, 364–365, 366, 367, 369, 378, 379, 382–383, 433, 437, 438, 440, 441, 442, 457, 469, 478
Medical (insurance) plan, *see* Health care (insurance) plan
Medicare, 78, 241, 243
Memorandum of understanding, 435, 436, 438, 441, 444
Merchant capitalist, 20–21, 23, 24
Mergers, union, 106, 110, 117
Meritor Savings Bank v. Vinson, 82
Metal Trades Council, 454
Mine workers (union), *see* United Mine Workers
Minimum wage, 36, 75–76, 95, 153, 155
Mobility, labor (or factor), 207, 209, 239–240, 279–281, 493
Montana v. Public Employees Craft Council, 449
Multi-employer bargaining, *see* Bargaining structure, multi-employer
Multilateral bargaining, 461, 481
Multi-tier bargaining, *see* Bargaining structuring, multi-tier
Multi-union bargaining, *see* Bargaining structure, multi-union

Narcotic effect, 371, 480
National Air Traffic Controllers Association, 454
National Association of Government Employees, 454, 473, 484
National Association of Letter Carriers, 454
National Association of Manufacturers, 33
National Brotherhood of Packing-house and Industrial Workers,

see United Food and Commercial Workers
National Civic Federation, 33–34
National Education Association, 128, 470, 471, 472, 481
National emergency dispute (provisions), 67–69, 74, 365–368, 369, 373, 378, 394, 460
National Federation of Federal Employees, 454
National Federation of Industrial Organizations (Japan), 143
National Industrial Recovery Act, 39–40, 55, 64–65, 94
National Institute of Occupational Safety and Health, 85
National Labor Board, 40, 64, 65
National Labor Relations Act, 6, 40–41, 42, 55, 65–66, 67, 70, 71, 72, 73, 90, 94, 109, 134, 167, 169, 177, 191, 263, 264, 300, 366, 367, 377, 378, 391, 392, 399, 410, 414, 418, 429, 431, 433, 437, 439, 452, 453, 457, 460, 480, 498, 516
National Labor Relations Board, 6, 9, 40, 43, 47, 65–66, 67, 70–74, 115, 116, 167–171, 192, 282, 367, 391, 393, 397, 403, 405, 406, 410, 411, 412, 413, 414, 415, 421, 430, 431, 432, 433, 439, 453, 456, 457, 460, 498
NLRB v. Fainblatt, 71
NLRB v. Jones and Laughlin Steel Corp., 65
NLRB v. Reliance Fuel Oil Corp., 71, 102–104
National Labor Union, 26–27, 29
National Master Freight Agreement, 121
National Mediation Board, 6, 62, 63, 69, 366, 369, 382–383, 478
National Railway Adjustment Board, 62, 63
National Recovery Administration, 40, 64
National Rural Letter Carriers Association, 454
National Trades' Union, 23

National Trade Union Conference (Singapore), 152
National Treasury Employees Union, 454
National Treasury Employees Union v. Von Raab, 88, 89, 446, 449
National Typographical Union, *see* International Typographical Union
National Union of Hospital and Health Care Employees, *see* Service Employees International Union
Negotiating impasse, *see* Impasse, collective bargaining
New Negro Alliance v. Sanitary Grocery Co., Inc., 64
Nonproduction bonus, 247
No-raiding pact (rule), 43, 110, 455
Norris–LaGuardia Act, 55, 63–64, 90, 94, 399
Nursing home care plan/program, 241, 243, 250, 251

OPZZ, *see* Polish Trade Union Alliance
Occupational Safety and Health Act/Administration, 8, 75, 85–86, 91, 109, 183, 418
Occupational Safety and Health Review Commission, 85, 86
Occupational segregation and desegregation, 501, 502, 504
Occupational wage differential, *see* Skill differential
Office of Personnel Management, 454, 455
Oil, Chemical, and Atomic Workers International Union, 130, 352
Ombudsperson, 362–363, 373
Open door policy, 359–360
Open shop, 37, 60, 74, 268. *See also* Right-to-work laws (and states)
Orbits of coercive comparison, 203–204, 205

Organizational strike, *see* Strike, recognitional

Organizing and organization campaign, union, 9, 30, 37, 39, 40, 41, 45, 46, 47, 111, 115–116, 167–171, 202, 291, 403, 407, 412, 418, 453, 514, 515

Outplacement (services), *see* Reemployment

Output work rules/standards, *see* Production standards (work rules), output

Outsourcing, *see* Subcontract(ing)

Overtime, 32, 75, 76, 139, 182, 217–218, 247, 277, 279, 294, 311, 381, 383, 389, 418, 456, 497

Package approach, 235, 236

Parental leave, 82, 83, 241, 252, 253, 513, 515

Participative management, 7, 47, 126, 135, 136, 143, 144, 154, 179, 271–273, 494–500, 516. *See also* Co-determination; Employee involvement;Labor-management relations, nature of, cooperation

Part-time worker, *see* Worker, part-time

Paternity leave, *see* Parental leave

Pattern bargaining, 187–188, 204–205, 211, 491

Patterson v. McLean Credit Union, 81

Pay equity, *see* Comparable worth

Peer review board/panel, 360–362

Pendleton Act, *see* Civil Service Act

Pension, 5, 25, 44, 73, 75, 77, 84, 86, 87, 155, 199, 235, 236, 237–241, 247, 257, 258, 279, 295, 384, 415, 499, 511
vesting, 86, 238, 239, 240, 257, 258, 499

Pension Benefit Guaranty Corporation, 86, 258

People v. Melvin, 57

Permanent (strike) replacements, *see* Strike replacements

Personal days (time) off, 248, 249

Personnel policies and administration, *see* Human resources policies and administration

Philadelphia Cordwainers, *see* *Commonwealth v. Pullis*

Phillips curve, 493–494

Physical fitness plan/program, 241, 243, 250. *See also* Health care (insurance) plan

Picket (line) and picketing, 39, 64, 67, 68, 70, 383, 387, 388, 390, 392, 393, 400, 402, 404, 410, 411, 443, 477, 481, 514
common-situs, 108, 397, 411

Pilots (union), *see* Air Line Pilots Association

Pittsburgh and Lake Erie Railway v. Railway Labor Executives Assn., 94

Plant closing, 5, 46, 66, 87, 114, 122, 187, 206, 209, 244, 245, 288, 289, 294, 310, 382, 498, 500
advance notice, 5, 87, 109, 296. *See also* Worker Adjustment and Retraining Notification Act

Plumbers (union), *see* United Association of Journeymen and Apprentices of the Plumbing and Pipefitting Industry of the U. S. and Canada

Police Benevolent Association, 470, 472

Polish Trade Union Alliance, 147–148

Political action committee, 110, 116, 188. *See also* Committee on Political Education; Democratic Republican Independent Voter Education committee

Polygraph testing, 88, 89–90, 406. *See also* Employee Polygraph Protection Act

Portal to Portal Act, 76

Postal Reorganization Act, 71, 431, 453, 457, 459, 460, 462

Post Office Mail Handlers, *see* Laborers' International Union of North America

Powderly, Terence, 27–28

Power center, union, 27–28, 106

Preferential shop, 265, 266–267, 269. *See also* Compulsory union membership (clause)

Pregnancy Discrimination Act, 79, 82, 91, 95

Prepaid legal services plan, *see* Legal services plan

Price Waterhouse v. Hopkins, 81, 104–105

Primary boycott, *see* Boycott, primary

Privatization, 135, 431, 454, 457, 459, 462, 463, 476, 482

Probationary period, employee, 207, 224, 267

Problem-solving committee, *see* Quality of work(ing) life committee/program

Producer cooperative, 23, 27

Production disruption, *see* Work stoppage

Production standards (work rules), 283–286, 288. *See also* Work rules
input, 283–285, 286, 366
output, 283, 285–286
technique or method, 283, 286

Productivity, 4, 5, 7, 11, 32, 35, 38, 44, 46, 150, 152, 165, 174, 206, 207, 210, 213, 223, 229, 248, 250, 251, 271, 272, 276, 278–279, 282, 285, 287, 288, 289, 295, 299, 490, 491, 492, 493, 494, 495, 497, 498, 500, 513

Professional Air Traffic Controllers Organization, 395, 443, 453, 454, 455, 457, 458–459

Profit sharing, 36, 73, 191, 208, 209, 235, 247, 248, 497

Progressive Movement, Progressives, 34–35, 51, 128

Property rights of the job, *see* Job property rights

Public Employment Relations Board, 433, 434, 437, 439, 440, 441, 449

Pullman strike of 1894, 26, 30, 34, 50, 61

Pure and simple unionism, 24, 29. *See also* Bread-and-butter unionism

Quality circle, 496, 497, 498

Quality of work(ing) life committee/program, 272, 496, 497

Racketeering Influenced and Corrupt Organizations Act, 88, 123, 385

Railway Labor Act and Board, 6, 55, 61–63, 69, 72, 90, 94, 365–366, 367, 369, 373, 378, 382–383, 392, 394, 400, 410, 411–412, 415, 417, 452, 460, 478

Randolph, A. Phillip, 42

Rankin v. McPherson, 447, 449

Ratification of contracts, 119, 172, 191, 264

Read v. City of Lynnwood, 449

Recognitional strike, *see* Strike, recognitional

Reemployment, 5, 295–296, 303

Regents of the University of California v. Bakke, 81

Reserved rights doctrine, *see* Residual theory of management rights

Residual theory of management rights, 270

Retail Clerks International Union, *see* United Food and Commercial Workers

Retail Workers Union, *see* United Food and Commercial Workers

Retirement benefits, *see* Pension

Retroactive seniority, 281

Reuther, Victor, 42

Reuther, Walter, 42, 44, 120, 401

Reverse discrimination, 80, 81

Rex v. Journeymen Tailors of Cambridge, 57

Richmond v. Cronson, 80

Rights arbitration, *see* Arbitration, rights

Right-to-work laws (and states), 46, 69, 74, 109, 265, 268, 460

Ross, Arthur, 203, 229, 233

Rubber workers (union), *see* United Rubber Workers

Rules of the workplace, 4, 10, 44, 276, 309, 310, 358. *See also* Work rules

Runyon v. McCrary, 81

SACO/SR, *see* Central Organization of Professional Employees (Sweden)

Scab, *see* Strike replacements

Schecter Poultry Corp. v. United States, 65

Schmerber v. California, 446

Secondary action/strike, 67, 68, 108, 383–384, 392, 393, 397, 399, 411. *See also* Boycott, secondary

Secondary boycott, *see* Boycott, secondary

Secured Employment Level (GM), *see* Employment level program, Secured Employment Level

Self-Employment Contributions Act, 79, 95

Self-managing work team, *see* Work team

Senate Committee on Improper Activities in the Labor Field, *see* McClellan Committee

Senate Select Committee on Organized Crime, *see* McClellan Committee

Seniority, 9, 44, 80, 83, 144, 145, 165, 187, 203, 206, 217, 218, 219, 221, 223, 226, 235, 236, 244, 245, 246, 248, 276–282, 294, 295, 299, 300, 302, 318, 334, 343, 347, 380, 389, 515

Senn v. Tile Layers Protective Union, 64, 101–102

Service Employees International Union, 117, 337, 428, 454, 470, 472, 473, 484

Severance pay, 5, 153, 156, 237, 244, 295, 296, 302, 415

Sexual harassment, *see* Discrimination in the labor market, harassment

Shanker, Albert, 471

Shared problem solving and decision making, *see* Participative management

Sheet Metal Workers International Association, 189, 240

Sherman (Antitrust) Act, 30, 55, 58–59, 61

Shift differential, 217, 247

Shinsanbetsu, *see* National Federation of Industrial Organizations (Japan)

Shop steward, 111, 118, 119, 122, 138, 174, 264, 269, 282, 312, 314, 362, 387, 388

Shunto, *see* Spring Labor Offensive (Japan)

Sick leave, 199, 235, 237, 243, 249

Sickout, 395, 458

Siemans Mailing Service (NLRB case), 71, 94

Single-parent family, 251

Sitdown strike, *see* Strike, sitdown

Skill differential, 218, 221, 222, 223

Skinner v. Railway Labor Executives Assn., 88, 446, 449

Slowdown, 19, 24, 44, 137, 154, 156, 383, 389, 393, 395, 431, 432, 443, 456, 457, 458, 460, 461

Social Security, 43, 75, 77–79, 91, 95, 154, 199, 238, 239, 244, 247, 257, 295, 492

Sociotechnical systems, 296–297, 303

Sohyo, *see* General Council of Trade Unions of Japan

Sole bargaining agent/representative, *see* Exclusive bargaining agent

Solidarity (Poland), 147–148
Southeastern Community College v. Davis, 84
Spillover, wage gains, 491–492
Spring Labor Offensive (Japan), 144–145
Standard Oil Company v. United States, 59, 93
State authoritarianism, 135
Steel workers (union), *see* United Steel Workers
Steel Workers Organizing Committee, 41
Stephens, Uriah, 27
Strasser, Adolph, 28
Strike, 4, 10, 19, 21, 22, 24, 25, 26, 28, 29, 31, 32, 34, 37, 38, 39, 40, 41, 42, 43, 44, 45, 47, 61, 63, 64, 68, 74, 112, 135, 137, 142, 146, 147, 148, 151, 153, 154, 155, 156, 178, 192, 206, 216, 267, 286, 287, 307, 311, 358, 363, 364, 365, 366, 367, 368, 369, 370, 376–395, 396–397, 399, 400, 401, 403, 406, 407, 410, 412, 415, 417, 418, 420, 421, 430, 431, 432, 433, 438, 442, 443–445, 453, 456, 457, 458–459, 460, 461, 463, 469, 471, 474, 475, 476–480, 481, 510, 514. *See also* Work stoppage
    defensive, 388
    general, 28, 40, 42
    jurisdictional, 386, 393
    recognitional, 393
    sitdown, 41, 42, 51, 147, 392–393
    sympathy, 60, 384, 392, 397
    wildcat, 44, 46, 136, 137, 155, 391–392, 397
Strikebreakers, *see* Strike replacements
Strike funds or benefits, 112, 184, 186, 380, 384, 386
Strike replacements, 26, 30, 47, 70, 181, 183, 186, 192, 379, 380, 382, 386, 387, 388, 389, 391, 396, 401, 402, 403, 410, 415, 513, 514

Structure of the economy, 3, 11, 46, 115, 142, 245, 292, 493
Structure of the labor force/workforce, 4, 11, 46, 115, 142, 245, 489
Subcontract(ing), 10, 288–290, 294, 383, 411, 482
Sunrise-to-sunset system, 22, 23
Superseniority, 276, 277, 282
Supplemental Security Income, 78
Supplemental Unemployment Benefits, 44, 237, 244–245, 246, 260, 289, 295, 296
Supply curve for labor, *see* Labor supply (curve)
Swedish Confederation of Trade Unions, 141
Sweetheart contract, 123, 130, 402
Sylvis, William, 27
Sympathy strike, *see* Strike, sympathy
Syndicalism, 27, 30

TCO, *see* Central Organization of Salaried Employees (Sweden)
Taft–Hartley Act, *see* Labor–Management Relations Act
Tax revolt, 462, 469–470, 475, 482
Teamsters, *see* International Brotherhood of Teamsters
Teamsters for a Democratic Union, 172, 173
Technique or method work rules/standards, *see* Production standards (work rules), technique or method
Technological change, 283, 286, 287, 288, 290–297, 301, 302. *See also* Automation; Mechanization
Temporary worker, *see* Contingent worker
Threat effect, 11, 224, 491
Title VII, *see* Civil Rights Act of 1964
Trade Union Congress (Britain), 138
Transmission, wage gains, *see* Spillover, wage gains

Transport Workers Union, 369, 382–385, 415, 470, 472
Tudor Industrial Code, 19
Two-income family, *see* Dual-earner family
Two-tier wage plan, 173, 199, 217, 218–220

UE, *see* United Electrical, Radio, and Machine Workers
Unemployment compensation (benefits), 25, 44, 75, 78–79, 243, 244, 246, 247, 257, 294, 390
Unfair labor practice, 40, 65, 66, 67, 68, 70, 71, 72, 115, 283, 393, 400, 405, 410, 411, 429, 431, 432, 433, 439, 442, 457, 460, 469
    allegation or charge or dispute, 9, 13, 115, 129, 391, 392, 397, 403, 405, 418, 432, 442, 498
    procedure, 72
    strike, 391
Union–management committee, *see* Quality of work(ing) life committee/program
Union power, *see* Bargaining power
Union security (clause), *see* Compulsory union membership (clause)
Union shop, 9, 64, 68, 74, 137, 191, 201, 265, 267, 268, 269, 311, 433, 457. *See also* Compulsory union membership (clause)
United Association of Journeymen and Apprentices of the Plumbing and Pipefitting Industry of the U. S. and Canada, 107
United Automobile Workers, 5, 41, 42, 44, 107, 113, 117, 120, 121, 122, 133, 169, 187, 189, 204, 208, 214, 223, 229, 244, 245, 260, 273, 289, 290, 294, 295, 296, 310, 393, 396, 401, 403, 470, 473, 498, 513–514

United Automobile Workers,
U. A. W. v. Johnson Controls,
Inc., 81
United Brotherhood of
Carpenters and Joiners of
America, 42, 107
United Electrical, Radio and
Machine Workers, 43, 111,
128, 189, 414, 422, 448
United Farm Workers of
America, 400, 401–403,
404, 413, 422
United Federation of Postal
Clerks, *see* American Postal
Workers Union
United Federation of Teachers,
see American Federation of
Teachers
United Food and Commercial
Workers, 117, 118, 121, 130,
183, 213, 214, 219, 335, 402,
418
United Mine Workers, 4, 10, 29,
34, 36, 39, 40, 44, 107, 128,
130, 286, 294, 301, 348, 392,
397, 403
United Rubber Workers, 41, 213,
214, 244, 382
United Steel Workers, 107, 113,
114, 191, 192, 202, 206, 211,
215, 244, 248, 272, 273, 290,
294, 302, 319, 369, 473, 498
United Transport Union,
472
Unit labor cost, 213, 230, 490,
491, 492
Universal Camera Corp. v.
NLRB, 72
Unjust dismissal, *see* Wrongful
discharge
Unlawful discharge, *see* Wrongful
discharge

Vacation, 235, 236, 237, 248–249,
277, 279, 294, 381

Vesting of pensions, *see* Pension,
vesting
Vocational Rehabilitation Act, 79,
84, 91
Voluntarism, 29, 108

Wage and seniority system
(Japan), 144–145, 146
Wage bill, 207
Wage drift, 158
Wage-price spiral, 213,
214, 493
Wage reopener, 212, 216
Wages and Hours Act, *see* Fair
Labor Standards Act
Wagner Act, *see* National Labor
Relations Act
Walsh–Healy Act, 76, 91, 95
Walter v. North San Diego City
Hospital District, 449
Wards Cove v. Atonio, 80
Welfare capitalism, 38–39,
511
Wellness plan/program, *see*
Physical fitness plan/
program
Western Federation of Miners,
121, 130
Whipsawing, 183, 187, 188
Whistleblowing, 183, 184, 380,
385, 418
White-collar worker, *see* Worker,
white-collar
Wildcat strike, *see* Strike,
wildcat
Wobblies, *see* Industrial Workers
of the World
Work assignment (rules), 285,
286, 287, 361, 430
Work assignment strike, *see*
Strike, jurisdictional
Worker:
blue-collar, 4, 13, 45, 46, 141,
143, 144, 292, 302, 406,
431, 444, 473, 492

part-time, 12, 13, 115, 173,
242, 253, 254, 489, 512
white-collar, 4, 9, 11, 13, 45,
46, 142, 143, 144, 291, 292,
293, 431, 453, 492, 515
Worker Adjustment and Retraining Notification Act, 8, 14, 87,
91, 96, 109, 296, 513, 514
Worker involvement, *see*
Employee involvement
Worker participation, *see*
Participative management
Workers (workmens)
compensation, 35, 154,
243, 247, 257, 259
Work jurisdiction (rules), *see*
Work assignment (rules)
Work rules, 10, 44, 115, 138, 141,
165, 187, 203, 224, 271, 272,
276, 282–296, 300, 309, 388,
415, 428, 430. *See also* Production standards; Rules of
the workplace
Works council, 138, 139, 140,
160, 494, 497
Work sharing, 253, 294,
296, 302
Work stoppage, 7, 34, 40, 62,
147, 178, 180–186, 188, 319,
366, 367, 369, 370, 371, 376,
377–378, 379, 383, 388, 391,
394, 395, 399, 411, 433, 456,
464, 476. *See also* Lockout;
Strike
Work team, 47, 497, 498
Work-to-rule, 137, 287, 389, 395
Work transfer, *see*
Subcontract(ing)
World Federation of Trade
Unions, 112
Wrongful discharge, 4, 8, 9, 19,
281, 297, 303, 445, 446–447,
513

Yellow-dog contract, 37, 39, 63